HTML WEB PUBLISHER'S CONSTRUCTION KIT

WAITE GROUP PRESS™
Corte Madera, CA

DAVID FOX
TROY DOWNING

Publisher • **Mitchell Waite**
Editor-in-Chief • **Charles Drucker**
Editorial Director • **John Crudo**
Managing Editor • **Dan Scherf**
Copy Editor • **Hilary Powers**
Technical Editor • **Miko Matsumura**
Production Director • **Julianne Ososke**
Production Manager • **Cecile Kaufman**
Production Coordinator • **Ingrid Owen**
Cover Design • **Sestina Quarequio**
Designer • **Karen Johnston**
Illustrations • **Kristin Peterson**
Production • **Michele Cuneo**

Published by Waite Group Press™, 200 Tamal Plaza, Corte Madera, CA 94925.

Waite Group Press is distributed to bookstores and book wholesalers by Publishers Group West, Box 8843, Emeryville, CA 94662, 1-800-788-3123 (in California 1-510-658-3453).

Printed in the United States of America
95 96 97 98 • 10 9 8 7 6 5 4 3 2 1

Fox, David
HTML Web publisher's construction kit / David Fox, Troy Downing
p. cm.
Includes index.
ISBN: 1-57169-018-2
1. Hypertext systems. 2. HTML (Document markup language)
I . Downing, Troy. II. Title.
QA76.76.H94F69 1995
005.75--dc20
95-19286
CIP

DEDICATION

To Amy. Yup, I said Amy.
— *David Fox*

I would like to dedicate this to my wife Laura for putting up with my late nights at work, and to my daughter Morgan—may this help pay your college tuition.
—*Troy Downing*

Message from the **Publisher**

Welcome to Our Nervous System

Some people say that the World Wide Web is a graphical extension of the information superhighway, just a network of humans and machines sending each other long lists of the equivalent of digital junk mail.

I think it is much more than that. To me the Web is nothing less than the nervous system of the entire planet—not just a collection of computer brains connected together, but more like a billion silicon neurons entangled and recirculating electro-chemical signals of information and data, each contributing to the birth of another CPU and another Web site.

Think of each person's hard disk connected at once to every other hard disk on earth, driven by human navigators searching like Columbus for the New World. Seen this way the Web is more of a super entity, a growing, living thing, controlled by the universal human will to expand, to be more. Yet unlike a purposeful business plan with rigid rules, the Web expands in a nonlinear, unpredictable, creative way that echoes natural evolution.

We created our Web site not just to extend the reach of our computer book products but to be part of this synaptic neural network, to experience, like a nerve in the body, the flow of ideas and then to pass those ideas up the food chain of the mind. Your mind. Even more, we wanted to pump some of our own creative juices into this rich wine of technology.

Taste our Digital Wine

And so we ask you to taste our wine by visiting the body of our business. Begin by understanding the metaphor we have created for our Web site—a universal learning center, situated in outer space in the form of a space station. A place where you can journey to study any topic from the convenience of your own screen. Right now we are focusing on computer topics, but the stars are the limit on the Web.

If you are interested in discussing this Web site, or finding out more about the Waite Group, please send me email with your comments and I will be happy to respond. Being a programmer myself, I love to talk about technology and find out what our readers are looking for.

Sincerely,

Mitchell Waite

Mitchell Waite, C.E.O. and Publisher

200 Tamal Plaza
Corte Madera CA 94925
415 924 2575
415 924 2576 fax

Internet email:
mwaite@waite.com

CompuServe email:
75146,3515

Website:
http://www.waite.com/waite

Creating the Highest Quality Computer Books in the Industry

Waite Group Press
Waite Group New Media

Come Visit

WAITE.COM

Waite Group Press World Wide Web Site

Now find all the latest information on Waite Group books at our new Web site, **http://www.waite.com/waite.** You'll find an online catalog where you can examine and order any title, review upcoming books, and send email to our authors and editors. Our ftp site has all you need to update your book: the latest program listings, errata sheets, most recent versions of Fractint, POV Ray, Polyray, DMorph, and all the programs featured in our books. So download, talk to us, ask questions, on **http://www.waite.com/waite.**

The New Arrivals Room has all our new books listed by month. Just click for a description, Index, Table of Contents, and links to authors.

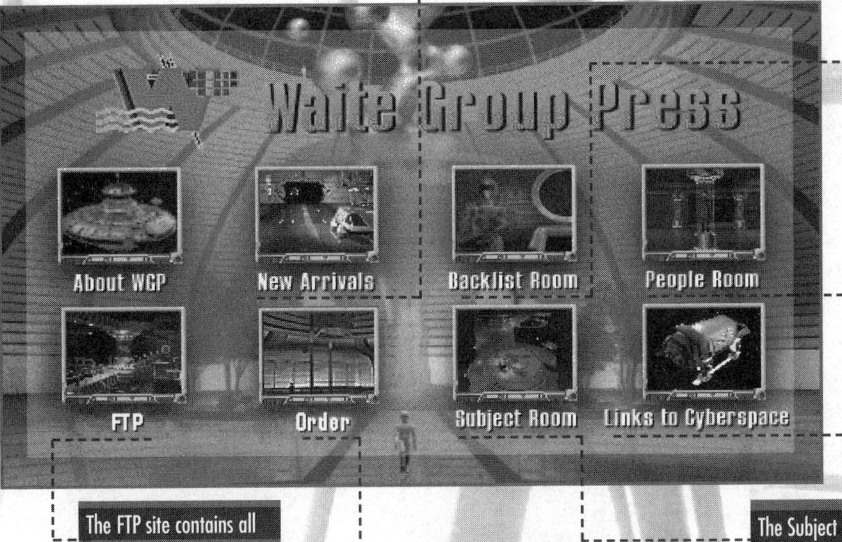

The Backlist Room has all our books listed alphabetically.

The People Room is where you'll interact with Waite Group employees

Links to Cyberspace get you in touch with other computer book publishers and other interesting Web sites.

The FTP site contains all program listings, errata sheets, etc.

The Order Room is where you can order any of our books online.

The Subject Room contains typical book pages which show description, Index, Table of Contents, and links to authors.

World Wide Web:

COME SURF OUR TURF—THE WAITE GROUP WEB

http://www.waite.com/waite
Gopher: gopher.waite.com
FTP: ftp.waite.com

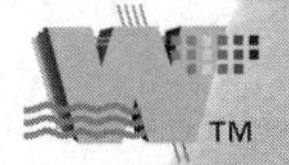

ABOUT THE AUTHORS

David Fox lives in New York City, where he writes novels, screenplays, articles, and technical stuff, depending on how broke he is. Currently he's keeping pretty darn busy programming for a major multimedia company. He's the author of several books, including The Waite Group's *Love Bytes: The Online Dating Handbook*. Reach him at http://found.cs.nyu.edu/dfox.

Troy Downing is a Research Scientist, Programmer, System Administrator, and Web Administrator at New York University's Media Research Lab. Troy is a primary force in WWW development at the Lab and has helped set up WWW services for NYU's Computer Science Department and the Center for Advanced Technology, as well as the Media Research Lab. When not sitting in front of a computer terminal, you will find Troy playing with his daughter, racing mountain bikes, or perfecting his latest batch of homebrew.

Troy can be found at: http://found.cs.nyu.edu/downing.

CONTENTS

TABLE OF CONTENTS

ACKNOWLEDGMENTS

First the technical stuff... Thanks to Tim Berners-Lee and CERN, the fore-folks of the Web. Thanks to NCSA for tiling cyberspace with their Mosaic. Thanks much to the brilliant authors of the software on the CD; the Web'd be empty without ya. Thanks to New York University, the Media Research Lab, and the Center for Advanced Technology for their excellent resources. Thanks also to Ken Perlin, Gus Estrella, and Robert Denny.

Now the personal stuff... Thanks to the friends whose nights about town I've forsaken while writing this. Thanks to Mom, Pop, and Jay (who loves to see his name in print). Thanks to Bob Dylan for the soundtrack. Thanks to Dan Scherf, who, as usual, saw this project through nearly hitchless and had a bit of fun besides (I hope!). Thanks to Jill Pisoni and Mitch Waite, who helped develop this book into the powerhouse it is. Heck—let's be fair—thanks to all the Waite Group Press for the tremendous job they did.

INTRODUCTION

Ah, the beauty, the sheer beauty of this string of weird words:

```
http://found.cs.nyu.edu/graphics.b./student/dsf4185/html/
```

The address of my World Wide Web home page.

It took several months, from start to finish, to get the page looking the way I wanted. It started one way and ended completely different. But in the end, I loved the result. It had writing samples, artwork, descriptions of my current projects, lists of my specialties, and an easy way of letting folks visit my favorite sites around the Web. Getting my Web pages working was equal to the thrill of publishing my first book. Here was all the information I could hope to share—free, open, and offered to an audience of nearly 30 million people.

I wasn't publicizing my home page, so only a dozen or so users a day would actually stumble there. But still, that's a dozen people who know my name, who know what I'm about, who know where and how and why to reach me. And, more importantly, a dozen more people to whom I've given the gift of information or entertainment.

WHO THIS BOOK IS FOR

This is actually three books in one, as evidenced by the three sections:

HTML A book for people who want to learn about what the Web is, how to access it, and how to navigate around using a number of popular tools. Maybe you've never heard of the Web before, or maybe you're a seasoned ol' net-dog hoping to learn some new tricks. Either way, the first section of this book, Connecting to the Web, has what you need. Popular software such as Winsock, The Internet Adapter, Lynx, SlipKnot, NCSA Mosaic, and Netscape are covered in full.

HTML A toolbox and guide for artists, advertisers, marketers, programmers, or professional "webspinners" who want to develop really cool stuff to put on the Web. Most likely, you think creating a Web page looks way too complicated. This book shows you that that's the furthest thing from the truth. Perhaps you've already fooled a bit with Web production and creation, but have no idea how to achieve that professional look you've seen elsewhere. Or perhaps you just want a handy reference bible in your tool belt. This section has it all, from the simplest detail to the latest hypertext specs.

HTML A tutorial on starting your own Web site, whether you're a home hobbyist or an international conglomerate. Maybe you want to start a commercial Web, renting your computer space to other Web developers. Or maybe you just want to learn about how the guts of the World Wide Web really work.

WHY THIS BOOK IS DIFFERENT

Although the Web has only recently become popular, there are many books clamoring for your attention. Some books discuss the theory and history of the Web. There are books showing you exactly how to use the NCSA Mosaic Web browser. Many act as travel-guides, indexing popular places on the Web. A few may talk about the language used to create Web pages: The Hypertext Markup Language.

This book does all of the above and more. The *Web Publisher's Construction Kit* takes you way beyond the basics. *Every* popular World Wide Web browser is covered fully, including Lynx, SlipKnot, Mosaic, and Netscape. You will learn the ins and outs of text, hypertext, artwork, fonts, images, movies, sounds, interactive forms, custom programs. This book doesn't stop at technical commands and how-tos, but it looks beneath the hood at creative issues. When you put down this book, your head should be overflowing with tons of cool ideas, along with the knowledge to implement them quickly and easily.

Further, this book delves into the mysteries of creating a Web site of your very own. This involves knowing more than what software to install and which commands to type. It also requires a lot of keen skill, savvy, and creativity.

Most importantly, all the Web browsers, Web servers, development tools, hypertext editors, scripts, clip art, sounds, movies, or other media you need to accomplish these goals are bundled with the book on one jam-packed CD-ROM.

All in all, this book doesn't just teach you to use the Web, put together a Web page, and create a Web site of your own; it teaches you how to do it professionally, slickly, and in complete detail. In the end, your efforts will clearly stand out in a Web which is already overpopulated with lots of boring or lackluster corners.

WHAT THIS BOOK ASSUMES YOU KNOW

This book assumes you're vaguely familiar with the online world, the Internet, and Microsoft Windows. If you've never messed with a modem, or you think Unix are the people who guard harems (sorry, a very old joke), then you should check out a good, basic Internet book, such as The Waite Group's *Internet How-To.*

Other than that, chapters in this book each have a number of lessons. Easy concepts are covered first, more difficult and obscure things come later. You can read enough to become proficient, or you can skip the easy parts and jump right into expert design, implementation, and production issues.

However you use this book, I look forward to seeing you around the Web...

THE CHAMELEON SAMPLER

The NetManage Internet Chameleon is one of the most versatile and easy-to-use set of Internet tools in the world. Chameleon helps you sign up with an Internet provider, connect cleanly to the Internet, and access a variety of resources—including a pretty cool Web browser. The Chameleon package includes

- HTML *Custom,* for connecting to the Internet
- HTML *WebSurfer,* a full-featured World Wide Web browser
- HTML *Gopher,* which lets you access any gopher menu worldwide
- HTML *NEWTNews,* a Usenet newsreader
- HTML *Mail,* a convenient way to send and receive e-mail
- HTML *Archie,* which lets you search for a file over the Internet
- HTML *Telnet,* for connecting to a remote computer
- HTML *FTP,* for transferring files over the Internet
- HTML *FTP Server,* which lets you allow others to download or upload files to your PC
- HTML *Mail Utilities,* programs that help you compact or organize your mailbox files to save space
- HTML *Ping,* to test if you're connected to a remote computer
- HTML *Finger,* to check if a friend is connected to the Internet
- HTML *Whois,* to get information about people registered in the NIC (Network Information Center) database

You can sample the Chameleon tools for 30 days at no charge. If you like what you see, you can register everything for 50 bucks.

INSTALLING THE CHAMELEON

NOTE: In the installation directions here, we assume that your hard disk is the C: drive and your CD-ROM is the D: drive. If this doesn't match your computer, substitute C: or D: with the correct drive designation.

To copy the sampler software onto your hard disk, run the Setup program. While under Windows, select File, Run in the Program Manager. In the Run dialog box, type

```
d:\windows\browsers\ntmanage\disk_1\setup.exe
```

and then press the OK button.

The Setup program will ask you where to install the NetManage program. The default suggested is fine for most people. If you want it installed elsewhere, type in the drive and directory of your choosing and select Continue.

After a few moments, the Setup program will ask you to type in the path of the second batch of files. Select the *1* in *DISK_1* and change it to 2, and select Continue.

After another few moments, the Setup program will ask you to type in the path of the third batch of files. Select the 2 in *DISK_2* and change it to 3, and select Continue.

Click OK when Setup tells you that installation is complete. You are now ready to setup your Internet account!

SIGNING UP FOR AN INTERNET PROVIDER ACCOUNT

If you don't already have one, the Chameleon package makes it easy to sign up with one of several popular Internet providers. Read Chapter 1 for more information about what services are offered by Internet providers.

If you'd like to sign up using the Chameleon software, run the Automatic Internet-Click to Start icon.

To learn about a particular Internet provider, click one of the tabs (other than NetManage) in the Select Internet Provider window. Most providers give you several hours (or even a month) of free trial time. To read about the

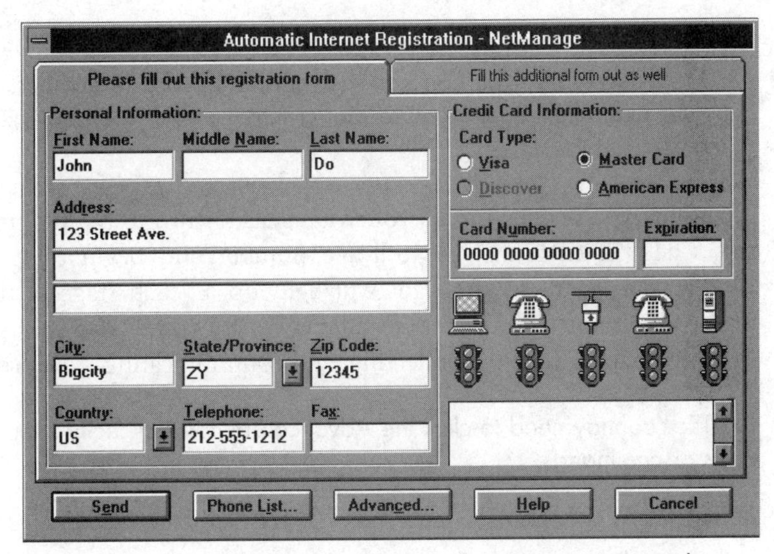

Figure I-1 The easiest way to sign up for an Internet provider

locations an Internet provider can cover, the monthly price, and other important information, click the More Info button at the bottom of the screen. If you have specific questions, contact the provider directly.

When you're ready to begin the sign-up procedure, click the Signup button. You'll see a registration screen similar to the one in Figure I-1. Fill in your name (as it appears on your credit card), address, phone number, and credit card information.

NOTE: You will not actually be charged any provider fees until you officially register with the service. You can cancel the registration transaction at any time during the sign-on process. If you do decide to register, your credit card number will be sent over a secure phone line.

As you work through the sign-up process, there may be other tabs asking for additional information. If so, click these tabs and fill in the forms.

Select the Phone List button at the bottom of the screen. The Phone List dialog appears, listing possible phone numbers you can use to register. If one of the numbers is in your area code, select it. Otherwise, select the toll-free 800 number.

NOTE: If necessary, you can edit the registration phone number. Some systems, for example, require you to dial a 9 to reach an outside line. Just type in this 9.

When you've typed in all your vital stats, return to the first registration tab. Click Send to dial the toll-free number and begin the registration process. The icons to the right will light up as each stage of the dialing process is completed. The set of traffic lights tell you if each stage—initializing the modem, dialing, connecting, and communicating—has worked.

NOTE: You may need to click the Advanced button to specify special modem ports or commands.

Follow the instructions that appear as the registration proceeds. You will be given the option to select from various service and pricing plans. Your account information (username, e-mail address, password, dial-up number, and IP address) will automatically be configured into the Chameleon package. An interface will be created for the Custom program, which quickly and flawlessly connects you to the Internet.

That's it! You can now reboot your system to kick-start everything.

REGISTERING THE CHAMELEON SOFTWARE

If you already have an Internet account, you can set up the Internet Chameleon software (shown in Figure I-2) and start using it within minutes. Run the Automatic Internet-Click to Start program.

Make sure the NetManage tab is selected, and then click the Signup button. You can now activate the software for a free 30-day demonstration period. After this period, the Chameleon software will no longer work. If you decide to register the Chameleon package (for $50), your credit card will be charged and your software will be activated permanently.

Fill in all the information on both forms, as shown in Figure I-1, including your credit card number (it won't be charged unless you complete the registration). You may need to contact your Internet provider for the Internet information on the second form.

Select the Phone button, and choose a local or toll-free phone number. Then click the Send button to dial in to NetManage and get your software activated.

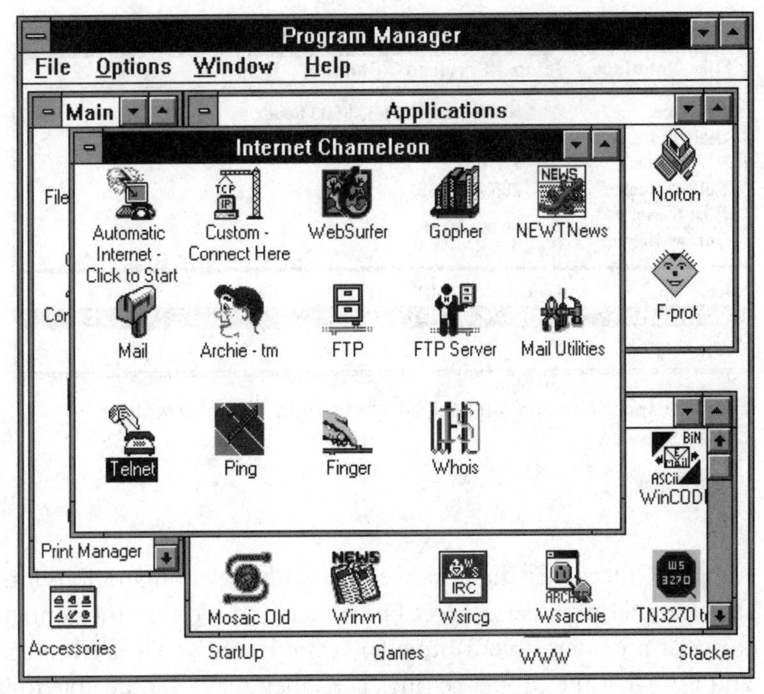

Figure I-2 The full Chameleon package in the Internet Chameleon program group

Once you connect, you are given the following choices:

- Activate your software for a free 30-day demonstration.
- Purchase your software to activate it permanently.
- Configure your connection (if your Chameleon software has already been activated).

CONNECTING TO THE INTERNET

Now that you have selected a provider and registered your software, you can actually get hooked in to the Internet. To do this, you need to run the Custom program (Figure I-3) from Windows File Manager.

If you used the Chameleon package to sign up with your Internet provider, an automatic configuration file should have already been written

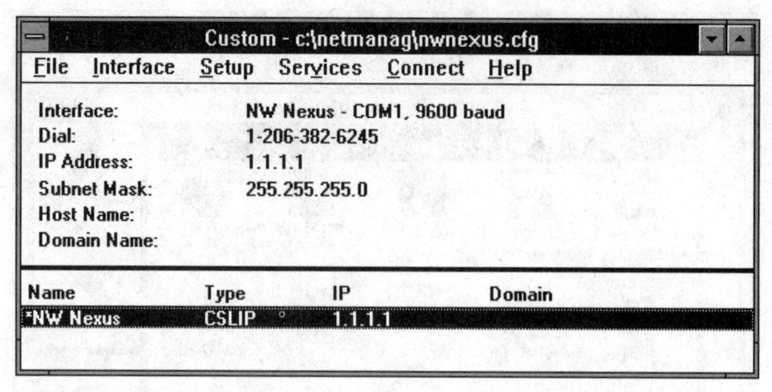

Figure I-3 Your customized on-ramp onto the Information Superhighway

for you. Otherwise, Chameleon comes with the configurations for most popular Internet providers. Select File, Open and look for the configuration file for your provider. If your provider is not listed, you'll need to contact them and ask what the proper settings are. They may even be able to send you a prewritten Chameleon configuration file.

If you do need to enter the connection settings yourself, use the appropriate values you have obtained from your Internet provider. You can verify or edit the following information under the Setup menu:

- IP Address
- Subnet Mask
- Host Name
- Domain Name
- Port
- Modem
- Dial
- Login
- Interface Name

- BOOTP

You may also need to fill in the following under the Services menu:

- Default Gateway
- Domain Servers

Read Chapter 1 for more information about these terms.

Logging In

Once your configuration settings are in place, simply click the Connect menu to dial up your Internet provider and get connected. If all goes well, you should hear a small beep, and a program known as Newt will run. This program lets Windows communicate with the Internet. You can then minimize the Custom program and run the Internet application of your choice.

Logging Out

When you're done using the Internet, call up the Custom program and click the Disconnect menu.

WEB BROWSING WITH WEBSURFER

WebSurfer is a full-featured World Wide Web browser similar to Mosaic. You can read all about browsers in Chapter 2 and about Mosaic in Chapter 5. To start exploring the Web, first use the Chameleon Custom program to connect to the Internet. Then run the WebSurfer program.

Like Mosaic, WebSurfer has a toolbar (see the top of Figure I-4) that acts as a shortcut for most commands. The toolbar contains

- Show Connection Status: Shows you which links are currently being loaded.
- Go to URL: Opens a specific Web URL (defined in Chapter 1).
- Get URL: Reloads the current document.
- Hotlist: Shows the list of your favorite Web pages for you to choose from. To go to a page, just double-click on it. You can also delete pages from the list by selecting the page and clicking Remove.

- Make Hot: Adds the current Web page to your hotlist.
- Back: Revisits the Web page you just came from.
- Forward: Goes to the next Web page in the series, if applicable.
- Home: Returns to the Web page you started from.
- Cancel All: Stops the loading of the current Web page.

Loading a Web Page From the Internet

Like Mosaic, WebSurfer combines text and graphics on the same page. Any text in blue or graphics with a blue border are hypertext links to other Web pages, multimedia files, or Internet areas. To load a link, just click on it.

You can also load up a document directly. Just select Retrieve, Go To URL and type in the document's exact URL. Alternatively, you can type a document's URL in the Dialog bar's URL box and press ENTER to load it.

If the document is a Web page, it will be displayed. If the document is a graphic, sound, or movie, the WebSurfer program will attempt to call up a viewer program to display/play it. If the document is any other type of multimedia file, WebSurfer allows you to save the document directly to your hard disk.

To find out more about the current Web document, select Retrieve, Properties.

Loading a Web Page From Your Hard Disk

If you have any Web pages on your hard disk (perhaps ones that you've created yourself), you can easily use WebSurfer to view them. Select Retrieve, Open Local File. Choose the file you want to view and click OK.

You can even edit the current Web document—a very handy capability for Web developers. Select Retrieve, Edit HTML. Then access the Retrieve, Refresh From Disk menu item to reload the page in a flash and see what your edits look like.

OTHER INTERNET TOOLS

The Chameleon package contains software for every Internet resource you could possibly want. To use FTP, e-mail, telnet, gopher, or any other Internet program, first connect to the Internet using the Custom application. Then

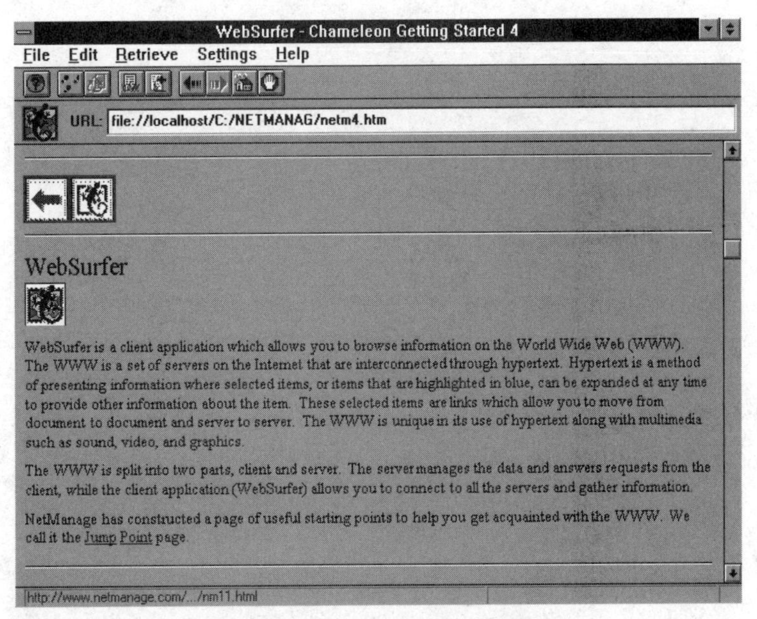

Figure I-4 The WebSurfer browser in all its glory

you can communicate with friends across the world using Mail, read or post messages to thousands of newsgroups using NEWTNews, browse menus of data using gopher, download tons of cool software using FTP, and much more.

1

CATCHING THE INTERNET IN A WEB

1

Some call it W3 for short, or just WWW. Most folks refer to it as "the Web." Techies may go so far as to call it a global-network hypermedia retrieval tool. In other words, it can shoot graphics, sounds, databases, software, movies, and formatted text across the world, combining everything on one *Web page*—that is, one screen.

In theory, the World Wide Web consists of the entire 20-million-person Internet. It includes every gopher menu site, FTP file library, telnet public-access computer, Usenet newsgroup, and WAIS database. And when any other hot Internet resources come along, it'll probably include them, too. All in all, the Web is the largest body of computerized data in the world.

The Web is called the Web, however, because it links together these pages and resources in a way that lets you reach any point on it from any other. Imagine strands of silk, stretching from every spot to dozens or hundreds of other spots. With tens of thousands of potential sites, that's a lot of virtual silk. If you tried to draw what all this would look like, you'd probably come up with—that's right—an enormous psychedelic web. That sounds like a tangled mess, but you can navigate it through an easy point-and-click interface known as *hypertext*. We'll talk more about hypertext later in this chapter.

But the true magic of the Web isn't its size or its multimedia snazziness. It isn't the fact that individual Web pages can be seen by people worldwide, no matter what computer or operating system they use. The true magic of the Web is that anybody can do it. Anybody can weave Web pages—complete with hypertext and everything else—and spin them onto the Web for the world to see. And doing it is easier than you might think.

HOW THE WEB WAS WOVEN

The *Internet*—the interconnected network of networks—came into being during the chilliest part of the cold war. The Defense Department linked together computers around the world to form something known as Arpanet. Slowly this network melted into the civilian sector. Looking to expand its communication power, a university or major corporation would tie into Arpanet, and students and employees were soon linked to the minds and data of other students and employees. The Net spread like a virus. By 1993, the Internet had nearly 15 million users in almost 70 countries.

The Internet rapidly turned into a global city, complete with virtual public libraries, storefronts, business offices, art galleries, museums, and even bars. There were some private sites, locked up tight, but most were open to anyone who knew where to look. Libraries offered card catalogs. Universities offered all sorts of academic papers. Software companies offered support files. There were places to post messages and places to chat. This was great stuff. It added up to a *lot* of text.

All this text was hard to sort through, and, frankly, it had a tendency to get boring. If you wanted a particular article, first you had to find what and where it was, then you had to figure out a way to get at it. You might have to use a newsreader program to grab it. Or maybe you'd need to log in to someone else's computer by typing something like *telnet somewhere.com*. Or maybe you would have to use the file transfer protocol (FTP) to download the file.

Utilities like gopher came into being. By selecting from a jungle of menus, you could retrieve files and articles, or log in to remote sites. There were a few images and sounds online, but you needed specialized hardware and software to take advantage of them. Gopher was a step better than the barrage of Internet commands, but still far from perfect. Different documents were hard to sift through. It didn't feel like a newspaper or magazine or even a TV show, it felt like a blizzard of text and photos and files swirling around you.

CERN: The Concept

In 1989, a bunch of High Energy Physics dudes at the Conseil Europeen pour la Recherche Nucleaire (CERN)—led by an ambitious Tim Berners-Lee—developed a way to share all sorts of information over the Internet. CERN was an international organization, and members across the world wanted a way to communicate quickly and consistently. The World Wide Web was born. Using the Web, a team of scientists in Geneva using Sun computers and a Unix operating system could read about particle propulsion tests stored on a PC in Dallas, Texas. Everything could be hassle-free.

NCSA: The Tool

But it wasn't quite hassle-free until a few years later, when the National Center for Supercomputing Applications (NCSA) developed an attractive way to look at this universe of information. One lovely summer day in 1993, NCSA officially released *Mosaic* to the public. The Mosaic software could consistently and elegantly display Web graphics, text styles, hypertext, and other files on the same page like a sort of, yup, mosaic. The Mosaic Web browser was released as noncommercial software, for the benefit and use of the entire Internet community. Versions were created for all major platforms—Windows, Macintosh, Unix, Sun, and Silicon Graphics workstations. Before Mosaic, the Web was like a bunch of TV signals without the TV.

The New Fabric

Much like the Internet itself, the Web caught fire without really trying. New Web users put their own pages of information over the Web. This new variety of information attracted more Web readers, who in turn put more information on the Web, which in turn . . . you get the idea. Before 1993, the Web had about 100 official sites. After Mosaic came out, Web traffic steadily increased. A year later, the Web had nearly 10,000 sites.

As fast PCs and modems became less expensive, the everyday computer user could transfer large files such as graphics, movies, and sound. Soon these media found their way onto the Web. The old fascinating but frustrating Internet suddenly became streamlined, organized, and really, really neat to look at.

And this isn't ancient history. The most exciting aspect of all this is that it *just* happened. The Web is in its infancy right now, and it's growing fast. It seems likely that it will serve as the backbone for tomorrow's video teleconferencing, interactive television, and shared virtual reality. You can be a cyberspace pioneer by weaving your own little Web corner today.

THE WEB'S EVOLUTIONARY EDGE

The World Wide Web isn't the first tool for fishing data out of the Internet, but it's the best so far—and it will keep on evolving. Here are the features that make the Web the global superhighway hypermedia information retrieval system of choice:

- HTML The Web is simple. Once you're online with a program like Mosaic, all you need to access a world of data is a pair of eyes, a mouse, and a healthy curiosity.
- HTML Documents look great. Instead of plowing through endless text files, you'll find a mix of fonts, styles, and layouts. You'll even get graphics and text together on the same screen, presented seamlessly.
- HTML The Web keeps growing. It can deal with gopher, FTP, telnet, and other Internet tools now, and built-in features will let it adapt as new standards, protocols, data types, and languages develop.
- HTML The Web can be accessed anytime, anywhere, any which way. You can surf the Web from most any type of computer or operating system, and from any country and any part of the Internet.
- HTML The Web lets you go anywhere even when you don't know where you're going! With hypermedia links, each Web page points to lots of others; you can skip around the Internet randomly, pursuing any topic that interests you from site to site.
- HTML The Web has no owner. With the right equipment and software, anybody can read the Web or distribute data on it—even you.

All this sounds great, but how is it possible? Read on . . .

WORLD WIDE WEB LAYOUT

Most any type of network consists of computers known as *clients* and *servers*. The server is a powerful computer that does all the grunt work, holding most of the files, memory, data, and resources. Individual PCs usually act as clients. Though weaker and dumber, clients exploit the mighty server.

The Web can be thought of as a vast network of data. As such, it has its own servers and clients, as illustrated in Figure 1–1. The servers hold all the Web data and dish it out, much like publishers or TV stations. The clients can access the Web data itself. Client programs like Mosaic are called *Web browsers*, since you use them to browse through the Web.

To access the Web, you need to install a browser on your computer, turning it into a Web client. Your browser then uses the Internet to connect to another computer running the Web server software. The server serves up whichever Web page your client asks for. Your client then slaps the Web document onto your screen. The Web is nothing more than a tangle of these client-server interactions, all happening thousands of times a second.

Figure 1–1 Web servers distribute Web pages; Web clients bring them to users' computer screens

The Server

A Web server can be much smaller and simpler than you may expect. Most major Internet providers have their own Web servers. If you have a permanent Internet connection, you can even install a server on your own machine.

You can learn how to install and configure a Web server in Chapter 21, Starting Your Own Web Site. Chapter 20, Where To Place Your HTML Documents, discusses existing Web servers who can publish your Web pages for you.

The Client Browser

Since the advent of Mosaic, dozens of browsers have hit the market. Some are commercial, others are perfectly free. Each browser has its own perks, bells, and whistles. The next chapter discusses browsers in general. Chapter 5, NCSA Mosaic, is a hands-on tutorial of the Mosaic software. Other chapters discuss the popular Netscape browser, the Lynx text-only browser, and the revolutionary SlipKnot browser.

NAVIGATING WEB PAGES

A Web page can be anything you imagine it to be: a hypertext document, graphics, sound, animation, tabular data, software files, a discussion group, a search index, a specialized program, and more. Most every Web site has a standard, default page known as the *home page.* This page acts as a sort of front door. Anybody who accesses a site usually starts off at that site's home page.

Many people create personal home pages for themselves, including things like their photograph, current projects, addresses, hobbies, even complete resumes. These *author pages* stick a human face onto the Web.

Most browsers use uniform fonts and styles. This means every Web page will have a similar layout and look. Web pages can contain everything from academic articles to shopping catalogs to art galleries to travel guides. Chapter 8, What Can I Do?, is a photo-essay tour of some of the world's most popular Web pages. Some pages will haunt you, others will teach you, most will entertain you. In general, though, there are only two ways you can interact with a Web page:

- HTML Click on a *hypermedia link* to access another page, program, or Internet service
- HTML Search for a keyword within a *search index* or fill in input fields in a form

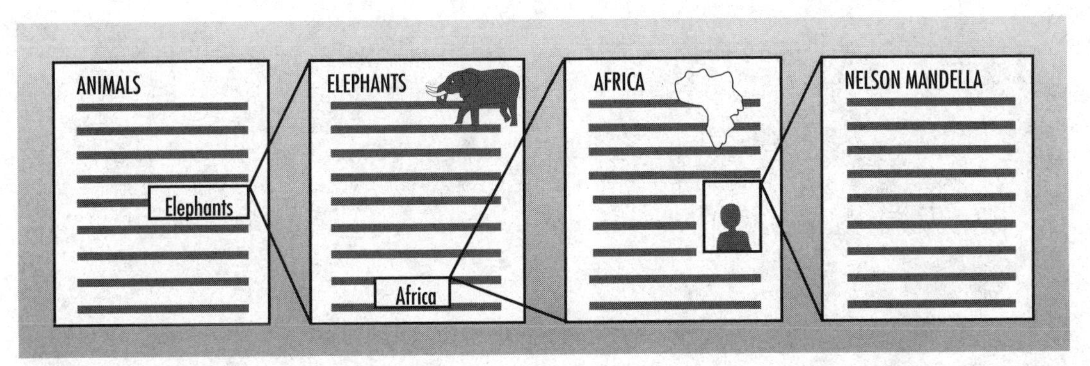

Figure 1–2 Hyper about hypermedia: a word or image on one page acts as the gateway to a different topic's page

Hypermedia Links

You're cozy in your favorite armchair reading a really good book about the Civil War when you come across a footnote that has something to do with the death of General Lee. You turn to the back of the book and find out that there's another complete book about General Lee's last days. You rush out to the bookstore and buy that book. It cites still other books. References like these let you keep on learning forever.

Hypertext is the same idea, computerized and made instant. You're sitting at your computer, reading about the Civil War, and you notice that the words "General Lee's death," are printed in blue. You click on the blue words with your mouse and an entire article about General Lee's last stand pops onto your screen. Hypertext combines documents by topics, not by sequence. That means you can jump from Tickling to Feathers to Birds to Penguins to The Arctic to Snow to Frosty-the-Snowman. Hypertext works the same way your mind does—by association. Using hypertext you can access an infinite range of data, make sense of it faster than you ever have before, and have a lot more fun doing it.

The World Wide Web uses hypertext to link all its pages together. And since a page can be a movie, a graphic, a song, a database, an Internet resource, or a computer file, hypertext melds with multimedia to form *hypermedia*. See Figure 1–2 for an illustration of hypermedia.

A Web page may have no *hyperlinks* or hundreds of them. Sometimes a Web page is nothing more than a huge list of links, all geared toward one subject. There are two types of hyperlinks:

HTML Text links

HTML Graphic links

HYPERMEDIA
The photo adjacent to this paragraph is surrounded by a blue border. This means it is a hyperimage. If you click on it you will be transported to another Web page, image, sound, movie, Internet resource, or another program.
Text itself can have hypertext links. As a dumb example, the word "hypertext" in the previous sentence has been made into a hypertext link.

Figure 1–3 A typical Web page with various hyperlinks

A Web browser generally highlights any text link. For example, links in Mosaic and Netscape are generally underlined and colored blue, as shown in Figure 1–3. Cello surrounds the text with a perforated box. Lynx displays all links in bold print.

Graphic links may be small icons, buttons, logos, or any other photo, illustration, or design. A graphic link is usually surrounded by a blue border, also shown in Figure 1–3. To follow a graphic link, just click anywhere on the image. Some graphic links are *imagemaps*—clicking on different parts of the image transports you to different places. See the section on imagemaps in Chapter 12, Graphics, for more details.

You never know exactly where a hyperlink will take you, or exactly what will happen. Be brave, be whimsical, follow your gut. Most every browser has a Previous Page button or Back command. If you jump somewhere you don't really want to be, you can return to the previous page with the press of a key. Most browsers also have a *history list* that shows you all the pages you've visited and lets you return to any of them with ease.

Search Indexes

Hypertext makes it easy to get lost. That's part of the appeal. You can start out reading about Sperm Whales and end up reading about the Prince of Wales. But what if you want to find pages dealing with a specific topic?

Luckily, the Web is full of indexes. An index is a special Web page that allows you to type in a search term or keyword. The index then spits out a list of Web pages matching your search. You can then click on any page that

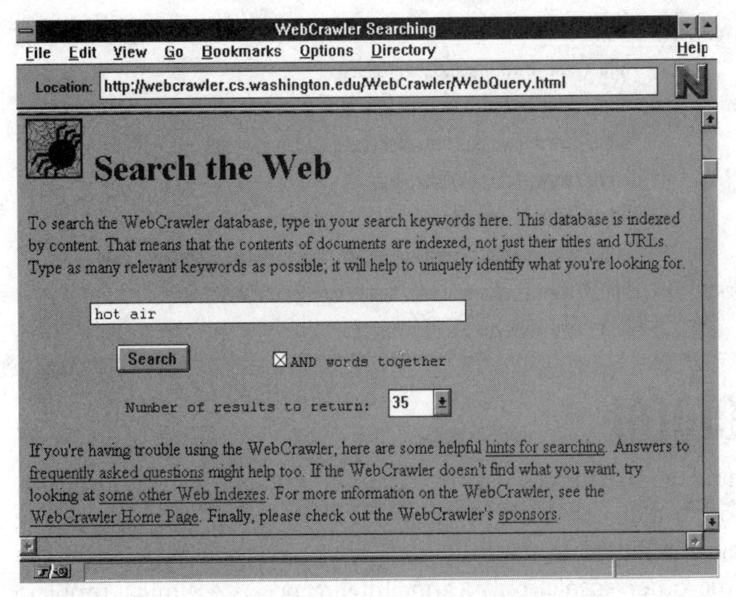

Figure 1–4 Searching for a Web starting point

catches your interest and transfer there automatically. Some indexes are manual: A person keeps track of all the Web pages he or she comes across. Others are created using *search robots*—small programs that crawl through the Web, following every hyperlink, keeping a list of every new place or topic they come across. Figure 1–4 shows a typical index search screen.

Many indexes allow you to search the full contents of thousands of Web pages. Other indexes let you search for titles, keywords, or geographical locations. Some indexes have a series of forms or menu items you can customize, allowing you to find exactly what you want. In most cases, you fill in a search term or phrase in a box and then click the Submit or Search button.

Some of the most popular indexes, and their URLs, are listed in Table 1–1. If you don't know what a URL is, check out URLs, URLs, URLs section, later in this chapter.

Table 1–1 Places to go Web hunting for that topic, file, or resource of interest

Search Index	URL
ALIWeb Archie Search	http://web.nexor.co.uk/aliweb/doc/aliweb.html
ArchiePlex Form File Search	http://www.lerc.nasa.gov/Doc/archieplex-httpd.html
CUI Index of Search Engines	http://cui_www.unige.ch/meta-index.html

Continued on next page

Continued from previous page

Search Index	URL
CUI Web Catalog	http://cui_www.unige.ch/w3catalog
CUSI Index of Search Engines	http://Web.nexor.co.uk/susi/cusi.html
Home Pages Broker	http://www.town.hall.org/brokers/www-home-pages/query.html
JumpStation Search Page	http://www.stir.ac.uk/jsbin/js
Lycos Search Engine	http://lycos.cs.cmu.edu
WebCrawler	http://webcrawler.cs.washington.edu/WebCrawler/WebQuery.html
WWWW: World Wide Web Worm	http://www.cs.colorado.edu/home/mcbryan/WWWW.html
Zorbamatic Title Search	http://www.rns.com/cgi-bin/nomad

THE HTTP PROTOCOL

When communication fails it's usually because of intelligence. Maybe the speaker is more intelligent than the listener, or vice versa. Or, more likely, two people are intelligent in very different ways—say, one is an expert in Swahili and the other speaks only Latin. Intelligence is a similar problem over the Internet. You can design a great way to ship data—fast, accurate, with lots of options. But unless other net surfers conform to your standard, they won't see your data.

The Web works so well because, at its heart, it's so stupid and trusting. The Web doesn't care what type of data you pump out, or what program you use to view the data. It treats everything the same. This means everybody can use their own browsers and their own data formats, and it'll all be friendly. You don't need to use different programs to access different types of data—the Web handles it all without complaining. All Web clients should be able to communicate with all Web servers.

The secret behind this is a simple, no-frills data protocol known as the *Hypertext Transfer Protocol* or *HTTP.* HTTP has the capacity to deal with most any Internet tool, file format, or resource. A Web browser client and the HTTP server communicate, coordinating things, before a Web page gets sent. If you could hear them talk, they'd sound something like this:

BROWSER: Hey, here's the page I want, here's how I want it.

HTTP SERVER: Uhh... sure. Can you handle JPEG graphics?

BROWSER: Yup. I sure can.

HTTP SERVER: Ah, good. Here you go, then. Here's your page, hot off the press.

NOTE: Web servers are usually called *httpd,* which stands for HTTP Daemon. A daemon is a program that hides in the computer's memory and is always active. To learn all about servers, including how to set one up, flip to Chapter 21, Starting Your Own Web Site.

URLS, URLS, URLS

A *URL* (or *Universal Resource Locator*) is the address of a document, file, or other Internet resource. If you're familiar with the Internet, you know that each person has his or her own e-mail address. Each resource also has its own address. The World Wide Web gives every article, newsgroup, database, computer, file, or other Internet fragment its very own URL. A URL can consist of these elements:

- The scheme, protocol, or type of Internet *service* the resource is using
- The name of the *host* computer on which the resource is stored
- The *port* number of the service
- The directory where the resource is stored
- The name of the resource itself
- A term to search for in an index

Some of these attributes are optional, depending upon the type of resource. The port attribute, for example, is almost never used.

A URL will typically look like the phrase shown in Figure 1–5. In general, you don't need to be an expert at crafting or even decoding URLs. A browser always shows you the current document's URL, usually at the top of the page. Whenever you use your Web browser to move anywhere or retrieve any file, its URL is shown. It's a good idea, then, to brief yourself about the basic types of URLs so when you come across them, you'll know what to expect.

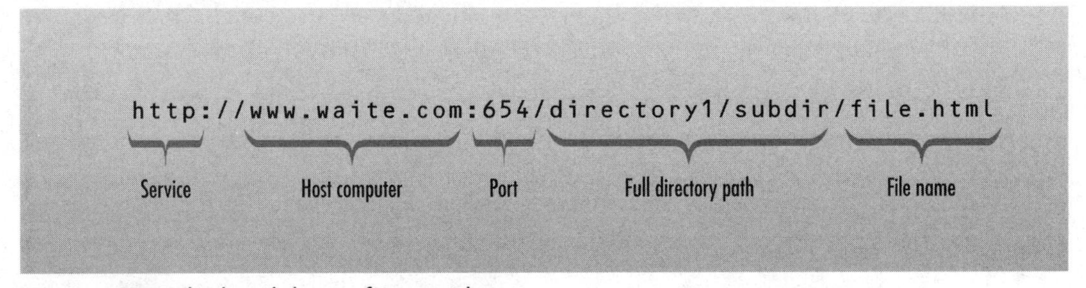

Figure 1–5 The breakdown of a typical URL

If you're reading a magazine, newspaper, or book and come across a URL that sounds pretty groovy, you can usually just type it into your Web browser. Your browser will then retrieve, display, or save the appropriate information on your hard disk.

NOTE: Since a URL usually accesses a Unix file system, upper and lower case are important. Be careful. Most URLs are expressed in lower case. Also, unlike DOS, Unix file and directory names can be any length. Don't be surprised when you come across a 20 letter filename. Another difference is directories: Unix doesn't use backslashes and drive-letter colons. The DOS file **C:\DIR1\DIR2\DIR3\FILE.HTM**, for example, is expressed in a URL as file:**///C|/dir1/dir2/dir3/file.htm**.

The Composition of a URL

The first part of the URL is always the name of a given service (see the next section for a list of services) followed by a colon. The second part of most URLs is the full Internet address of the machine where the resource is located. A host address always begins with a double slash: //. Most addresses are located at default ports, but in some cases you need to specify a specific port by following the address with a colon and then typing the port number. To specify the default port, simply leave out the colon.

After the host computer address, you need to specify the exact directory where the given resource is located. Type a slash between each level in the directory. Finally you can end the URL with the filename of the resource. This filename can be a hypertext document, a database, an index, a text file, a sound file, a graphic, or pretty much any other computerized resource in the world.

In some cases, the filename is followed by the hash mark (#) to specify a particular section within the file. A filename may also include a question mark (?) if it is an index or fill-in form, designating a term to be searched for. Search terms following a question mark are usually separated by the plus sign (+) and may use the equals sign (=). You may also come across a percent sign followed by two letters or numbers (%d1), which represents various extended ASCII characters.

Services

A URL always begins with the name of a service. You can use URLs to access the following services:

- http
- ftp
- file
- gopher
- mailto
- news
- telnet
- tn3270
- rlogin
- wais

New services are always being implemented as new Internet tools, protocols, and resources are created. If you come across a URL not listed here, try it out and see what happens.

Most of the time, you use URLs to call another hypertext Web page using the http service. You can also link documents to ftp file libraries, gopher menus, telnet machines, e-mail addresses, WAIS databases, or any other Internet resources. Chapter 16 discusses these resources in more detail.

Whenever you click on a hyperlink, you're actually requesting a specific URL. The Web server searches far and wide until it finds the URL, which it then delivers to your screen.

HTTP

The http service quickly and consistently calls up any Web page, text, graphic, or other supported item. Most Web pages are written using the *Hypertext Markup Language* (*HTML*), which is covered in Chapter 10. HTML files generally have the .html extension, such as *index.html*.

To reference the file *index.html* in the */web/smith/* directory of a computer at address *www.smartpants.edu*, for example, you'd use the following URL:

```
http://www.smartpants.edu/web/smith/index.html
```

Most Web servers automatically search for a default file named *index.html* or *home.html*, depending on the brand of server and its current settings. If this is the case, you don't need to specify a filename to get an index. Just enter

```
http://www.smartpants.edu/web/smith/
```

Here are some sample valid—but fictional—URLs, ranging from the most basic to the most complicated:

- http://www.moolah.com/
- http://www.moolah.com/money/moremoney/
- http://www.moolah.com/money/moremoney/money.html
- http://www.testlabs.edu/Experiments-In-Science/Monkeys.html
- http://www.testlabs.edu/Experiments%2FIn%2FScience/Crocodiles
- http://strange.org:1234/strangness/hmm.html
- http://strange.org/strangness/hmm.html#novelty
- http://bigindex.edu.ca/reference/dictionary?cumquat
- http://abc.123.com:1234/abcdefg/hijk/lm/n/o/p/q/r/s/t/u/v/search?h*%20this%20now

FTP, File

A URL using the ftp or file service retrieves a file. To log into the FTP archive at Netcom, for example, you would use the URL:

```
ftp://ftp.netcom.com/
```

Most browsers then show you an index of files. Each file type may even be preceded by a special icon, letting you know whether it's a directory, a text file, an image, or whatnot. You can then click on various directories until you come across a file you're interested in. Just click on that file to download it onto your hard disk or display it on your screen.

NOTE: The Web server automatically logs you in as an anonymous user. Most public FTP sites happily accept anonymous visitors. You can, however, specify a specific username and password if you've got them; this may get you wider access to the site. See the FTP section in Chapter 16, Other Web Resources, for more information.

You can also use a URL to access a particular directory directly. For example, the URL

```
ftp://ftp.netcom.com/pub/pc/win3/games/
```

would automatically place you in the */pub/pc/win3/games/* directory, as long as such a directory exists.

You can even use a URL to immediately download a specific file. For example, if you wanted the file *pacboy.zip* in the */pub/pc/win3/games/* directory, you would use the following URL:

```
ftp://ftp.netcom.com/pub/pc/win3/games/pacboy.zip
```

The file service is almost identical to the ftp service, but is a quicker way of retrieving local files. You can use file URLs to load and display sound, image, or text files, as follows:

```
file://www.smartpants.edu/soundoff.au
```

Gopher

To connect to a gopher menu, simply use the gopher URL followed by the appropriate gopher code:

```
gopher://gopher.uchicago.edu/
```

Most browsers print the gopher menu on your screen, complete with different icons for different types of services.

You can use the gopher service to access everything available through ordinary gopher menus: phone books, search indexes like Veronica, images, sounds, or files. For example, to retrieve a specific phone-book index, your URL would look something like

```
gopher://mainman.herenorthere.edu:1234/phones.txt
```

Mailto

This is a relatively new URL that lets you send e-mail to a specific user. For example:

```
mailto:dsf4185@graphics.cs.nyu
```

Browsers which support the mailto URL automatically enter a text editor, allowing you to fill in a subject line, return address, and message. Your browser can then send your letter across the Web, quickly and easily.

News, NNTP

Some browsers use the news service to access your news server, retrieving an entire newsgroup, a specific message, or accessing anything using

Usenet's NNTP (*Network News Transfer Protocol*). To access a particular newsgroup, you'd use a URL similar to

```
news:alt.cream.cheese
```

You can even access a specific list of groups by using search marks like the wildcard asterisk or the question mark. For example, to see every group that starts with *alt.p,* you could use the URL:

```
news:alt.p*
```

Telnet, rlogin, tn3270

You can use the telnet, rlogin, or tn3270 services to log into a remote computer. Once you access one of these URLs your browser automatically dials up the remote system. You can use this to enter Internet-based bulletin boards, mainframes, MUD games, or other distant resources.

The telnet, rlogin, and tn3270 services are essentially the same. In general, you use telnet for most connections and tn3270 to telnet to 3270-type mainframes. A typical telnet URL would look like:

```
telnet://bbs.neato.com:1234
```

WAIS

The wais service links the Web to a *Wide Area Information Service* (*WAIS*) database or document. You can include specific search terms, databases, or other WAIS items.

ACCESSING THE WEB

You now know more about the history and theory of the Web than you really need, but you probably can't picture how everything fits together. The only way to grasp this unique medium is to experience it. Depending on where you live, the type of computer you have, and your technical expertise, connecting to the Web can range from a few minutes' work to a day or two of detailed software installation and setups. Don't sweat it too much, though. This book guides you through the steps. In fact, you may already be connected to the Web without knowing it.

What Computer Do I Need?

Most any computer worth its weight in salt can access the Web. That's part of the Web's appeal. However, this book focuses on PCs running Windows. If you have a choice, get a 386 or better PC with at least 4 MB of memory, a hard disk with lots of free room, and Windows 3.1 or Windows for Workgroups. To take full advantage of this book, you need a CD-ROM drive as well.

You also want a Super VGA monitor, so Web graphics look their best. It's also a great plus if your PC has a sound card and speakers, allowing you to hear speech, music, or sound effects, all at CD quality.

What About the Modem?

If your computer is already connected to the Internet through a Local Area Network (LAN) or some other direct connection, then you won't need a modem. However, in most cases you need to call up a commercial Internet provider. A modem lets your computer communicate over the phone lines.

If you want graphics, sounds, and other huge files delivered to you in less than an eternity, you need a high-speed modem. Get one of these:

- V.32 9600 baud
- V.32bis 14,400 baud
- V.34 28,800 baud

The V.32, V.32bis and V.34 specifications are very important. These are standard protocols used by most Internet providers, so you want your modem to use them too. Modems using other protocols will usually transfer data just fine, but not at their advertised best speeds.

If you're just buying a modem, the V.32bis 14,400 is probably the most cost-effective choice, providing a good mix of speed and economy. You should also stick to a brand name; they don't cost much more than no-name brands, and they're less likely to have bugs or other errors to slow them down.

NOTE: If you want to use a 2400-baud or slower modem to access the Web, you should use a text-only browser like Lynx. This browser doesn't require a direct SLIP Internet connection: any Internet account will do.

What Type of Internet Account Do I Need?

You have several choices. The most convenient way of accessing the Web is to become part of a network. If you belong to a large corporation, organization, military group, or university, your institution probably already has Internet access. If your machine is connected to a Local Area Network (LAN), then all you may need is some software allowing your PC to communicate via the Internet. Ask your system administrator if your personal PC has Internet connectivity. The system administrator can also help you set everything up.

If you're using a home computer, however, you need to use your modem to connect to the Internet. In most cases, the easiest way to do this is to call up a commercial Internet provider and use its computing power.

You may already be connected to the Internet through a standard *Unix shell* account. This means you dial up a service using a terminal emulator and can type commands like *telnet, ftp, gopher,* and *mail.* In most cases, this standard shell account is not powerful enough to connect efficiently to the Web. Instead, you need to make your home computer an actual part of the vast network. This requires network-level access, which is known as SLIP or PPP. However, there are several options available to the standard Internet user.

The next few sections cover these methods of hooking up to the Web:

- SLIP and PPP accounts
- Standard Internet Unix shell accounts running a text-only browser
- Standard Internet accounts running the SlipKnot browser, a full graphical browser that runs hand-in-hand with Lynx
- Standard Internet accounts running The Internet Adapter, a complete SLIP emulator for the Unix shell

SLIP ACCOUNTS

SLIP has nothing to do with banana peels. Rather, it stands for *Serial Line Internet Protocol. CSLIP* is compressed SLIP, a variation typically used over the telephone. *PPP* is the *Point to Point Protocol.* All three protocols do the same thing for you: they let your computer connect directly to the Internet through phone lines instead of through network wires.

If you have a regular old Unix shell, your computer acts only as a window for another large computer, somewhere up in some office building, which is attached to the Internet. A SLIP account skips the middleman—your personal machine actually becomes another corner of the Internet (see Figure 1–6). This means you can easily and conveniently use any PC Internet client, including Mosaic, Netscape, or any other Web browser that comes along. You can also use a SLIP account with cool graphical Windows Internet programs like WinGopher, the Trumpet Winsock newsreader, or

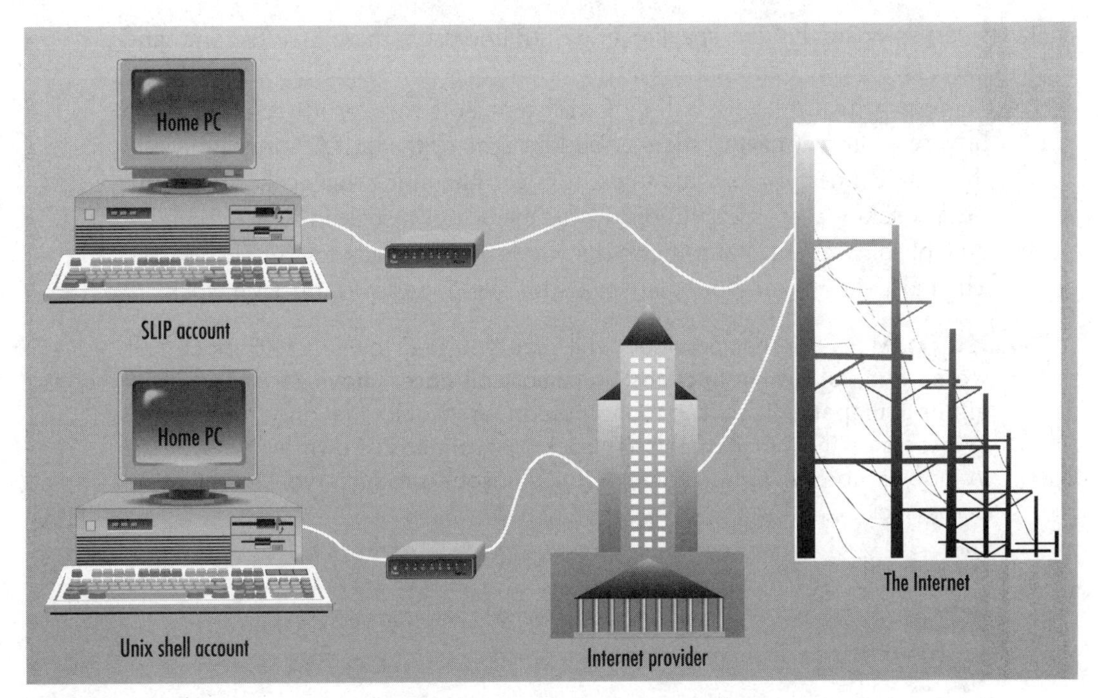

Figure 1–6 A SLIP account compared to a standard Unix shell account

Eudora e-mail. These shareware products are discussed in Appendix B. SLIP access is also generally faster than a Unix shell.

Most every major Internet provider is beginning to offer SLIP or PPP accounts. Some of the most popular are listed in Appendix A, Internet Providers. SLIP often costs a few dollars more than a standard Unix shell account, though prices are steadily decreasing. You should be able to find an unlimited SLIP account for about $10 to $20 per month.

TCP/IP

SLIP itself just connects your machine to the rest of the Internet. But just as a telephone line is worthless without a telephone, a SLIP account is worthless if it can't carry data back and forth. To do anything useful with SLIP, you need to speak the same language as the rest of the Internet: the *TCP/IP, Transmission Control Protocol/Internet Protocol.*

The Internet is comprised of millions of machines worldwide. TCP/IP is the standard they all use to talk to each other. Every Internet client or Web browser speaks using TCP/IP *packets*—small bundles of computerese. Before you can do anything with your account, you'll need some pretty smart software that can speak over a SLIP line using these TCP/IP command packets.

We're dealing with a lot of different software products: The Web browser, Internet clients such as Eudora e-mail, the TCP/IP translator, and the SLIP connection. All this software is combined in what's called a TCP/IP *stack*. Luckily, there's a solution to this mess: put a sock in it. Yes, there's a type of software that coordinates the whole TCP/IP stack for you: the *Socket*. The most versatile and popular socket for Windows is Trumpet Winsock.

NOTE: Many Internet providers will give you their own TCP/IP stack software, with its own instructions. In almost all cases, however, this will be either Trumpet Winsock or Chameleon Winsock, the only Shareware Winsocks on the market. Each Winsock program has its own *WINSOCK.DLL* Windows library. Other commercial Winsock products you might come across include:

- Spry
- Novell
- FTP
- NetManage
- PC/NFS

Installing and Configuring Trumpet Winsock

Trumpet Winsock can be found at the site listed in Appendix D. To install everything, just unzip and copy the entire directory to your hard disk. You may want to create a directory similar to

```
C:\WINSOCK
```

You now have a choice. If you're familiar with DOS, you can add this directory to your path by changing your AUTOEXEC.BAT file. For example, if your current path is

```
PATH C:\WINDOWS;C:\DOS;C:\UTIL
```

then you add your Winsock directory to the end of the line, after a semicolon:

```
PATH C:\WINDOWS;C:\DOS;C:\UTIL;C:\WINSOCK
```

You should now reboot your computer to make the new path take effect.

If you prefer, you can just move the *WINSOCK.DLL* file to your C:\WINDOWS directory—or any other directory in your path.

You should also set up an icon for WinSock's *TCPMAN.EXE* file in your Windows Program Manager, since it's a program you'll be accessing quite often.

NOTE: Trumpet Winsock is not freeware. If you use Winsock regularly, you should register your version for $20. Read the registration information in the included INSTALL document.

You now need to set up Winsock so it knows how to communicate. At this point, you should already have a SLIP account at an Internet provider. Your provider should give you the following information:

- Phone. The telephone number of your Internet provider's SLIP computers. This should ideally be a local call.
- Username. The name you'll use to log in to the system; it may be your last name, a combination of your initials, or a meaningless ID number.
- Password. The code you'll use to assure the system that you're the one using your account. It can be any series of letters or numbers. Keep track of upper and lower-case letters—if your password is Froggie, "froggie" may not get you into the system.
- IP Address. Your provider's Internet Protocol address, in the IP number form 1.2.3.4. The value for this may be the word *bootp* (in lower case) or the value 0.0.0.0.
- Name Server. The IP number of the machine you'll be calling to look up Internet domain names.
- Gateway. The address of the Internet gateway or router being used.
- Time Server. The IP number of the Time server machine. Usually unused or the same as the Name server.
- Domain Suffix. The address of your Internet provider, in the form *name.com.* You may need several of these.

The first time you run Winsock, the Network Configuration window appears, as in Figure 1–7. To return to this window in the future, select File, Setup.

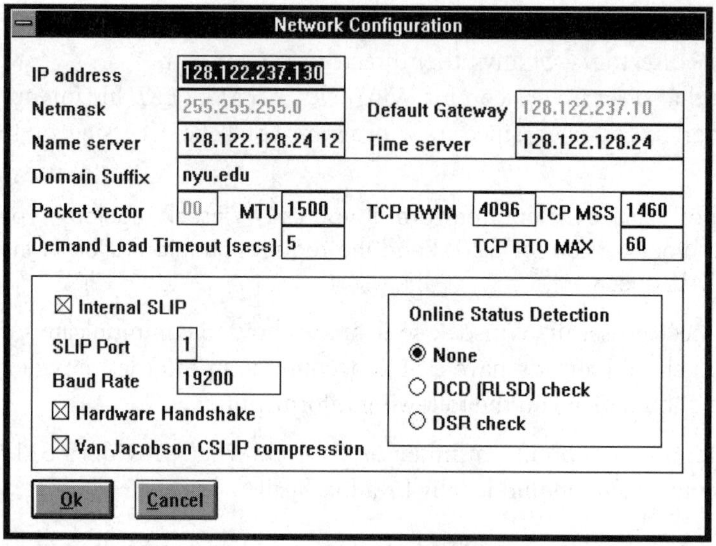

Network Configuration

IP address 128.122.237.130
Netmask 255.255.255.0
Default Gateway 128.122.237.10
Name server 128.122.128.24 12
Time server 128.122.128.24
Domain Suffix nyu.edu
Packet vector 00
MTU 1500
TCP RWIN 4096
TCP MSS 1460
Demand Load Timeout (secs) 5
TCP RTO MAX 60

☒ Internal SLIP
SLIP Port 1
Baud Rate 19200
☒ Hardware Handshake
☒ Van Jacobson CSLIP compression

Online Status Detection
◉ None
○ DCD (RLSD) check
○ DSR check

Ok Cancel

Figure 1-7 Configuring Trumpet Winsock

Check the Internal SLIP check box. Type the COM port your modem is connected to in the SLIP Port box. This should be a number from 1 to 4. For example, if your modem is wired to COM2, type 2. Fill in your modem's maximum baud rate. Do not use commas as part of the number. If you're running 14,400 baud you should fill in the maximum data rate:

```
19200
```

Select the Hardware Handshake checkbox unless your Internet provider tells you not to. Typically, you need to check the Van Jacobson CSLIP Compression box too. This means you'll be using CSLIP instead of SLIP, which is a common way of sending SLIP over telephone lines. If you know your modem can handle DCD (RLSD) or DSR Online Status Detection, you can click one of these values. Otherwise, click None.

You can now fill in the IP Address, Name Server, and other values. If you're supposed to use several Domain Suffixes, separate each by a space. You now need to fill in some specific data speed values. The values for these depend on whether you're using SLIP or CSLIP compression. If your Internet provider doesn't give you exact values, try the defaults:

- HTML MTU. This is the Maximum Transmission Unit, which depends on the Maximum Segment Size (MSS). Winsock recommends you use the MSS value plus 40.

HTML TCP RWIN. The TCP Receive Window. Winsock recommends you use your MSS number times 3 or 4.

HTML TCP MSS. The TCP Maximum Segment Size. This number should be around 512 for SLIP or around 255 or less for CSLIP.

You should leave all other values at their defaults, unless your Internet provider tells you otherwise. When everything is filled in, click OK. A message appears, letting you know that you must restart Trumpet Winsock before any of your settings will take effect. Exit Winsock by selecting File, Exit and then reload it.

NOTE: If your machine is connected directly to the Internet through a Local Area Network, you need to install a TCP/IP packet driver such as WINPKT. You can then use SlipKnot to handle the stack. Internal SLIP should be unchecked. Ask your system administrator for the value of your institution's IP Address, NetMask, Default Gateway, and all other values.

Manual Login

You now need to call your Internet service provider to be sure everything works. At first, make the call manually. Eventually, you want to create a script file that can automatically dial the Internet provider, log in using all appropriate names and passwords, and start up your SLIP connection using the proper commands.

To use the manual login, select Dialler, Manual Login. The following message should appear:

```
Manually dialing.
AFTER LOGGING IN, PRESS THE <ESC> KEY TO RETURN TO NORMAL SLIP
PROCESSING
SLIP DISABLED
```

You now need to use your modem's built-in dialing commands to call up your Internet provider. The dial command is ATDT followed by a valid phone number. For example, if your Internet provider is located at 555-1234, you would type

```
ATDT 555-1234
```

The Winsock program then becomes a generic terminal-type communications program. What you type next depends on your Internet provider. The provider should give you full instructions. In some cases, you may need to type the word *SLIP*, or just press ENTER. In any case, you should eventually see a login prompt similar to

```
login:
```

Type your username and press ENTER. You should now be asked for your

```
Password:
```

Type in the password. In most cases, you need to start the SLIP protocol by typing the word

```
slip
```

A message similar to the following should now appear:

```
Switching to SLIP.
Annex address is 123.456.789.10. Your address is 123.456.7.8.
```

What you do next depends on whether you have a *static* SLIP account or a *dynamic* one. If your Internet provider assigned you your own personal IP number then you have a static account and everything should be set up fine. You should now run the *bootp* protocol, to get specific addresses, ports, and other information from your network. In most cases, you need only type:

```
BOOTP
```

Press ESC to stop the manual login process. The following message should appear:

```
SLIP ENABLED
```

However, many Internet providers use dynamic accounts instead of static ones. These providers have several valid IP numbers, and assign them on a per-call basis. When you dial in on a dynamic account, you get one of the IP numbers no one else happens to be using at the moment. To finish the login process, you need to select File, Setup and type your assigned IP number in the IP Address box. Click OK. A message appears, telling you that you need to close Winsock before any change can take effect. Press the ESC key, exit Winsock (by selecting File, Exit), and then restart Winsock.

You can now run Mosaic, Netscape, Eudora, FTP, or any other whizbang Internet software. If things don't seem to be working, check out the Shooting Down Troubles section later in this chapter. Otherwise, you're ready to set up an automatic script.

Login Scripting

If your manual login seemed to work just fine, it should be easy to create an autopilot that dials you up, logs you in, and sets everything running. Many Internet providers can give you a customized Winsock script file if you ask. The file should be called *login.cmd*. Copy the file to your Winsock directory. To log in now, just select Dialler, Login.

NOTE: You can have Winsock automatically call your Internet provider every time you run it. Select Dialler, Options. Click the Automatic Login On Startup Only radio button and select OK.

There are several useful script commands you need to know:

- *input <timeout> <message>*. Waits <timeout> seconds for the <message> to appear.
- *output <message>*. Sends the <message> over the modem.
- *password <prompt>*. Open a dialog box asking the user for the password.
- *username <prompt>*. Open a dialog box asking the user for a username.
- *BOOTP*. Run the bootp protocol.
- *#*. A comment.
- *\13*. Send a carriage return; the same as pressing the ENTER key.
- *\i*. Send the specified IP address.
- *\p*. Send the password that was obtained in the Password dialog box.
- *\u*. Send the username that was obtained in the Username dialog box.

The idea is to write a small program that mimics the exact steps you performed during the manual login. Every script begins with the ATDT dialing command. You should then wait for a specific prompt. For example, if the first thing your Internet provider requires you to do is type *login* at the *Welcome>>* prompt, the beginning of your script would look like:

```
#Call up your Internet provider
output atdt555-1234\13
#Wait for the CONNECT message
input 30 CONNECT
#Send <ENTER> to kick the system into action
output \13
#Wait for the Welcome>> prompt; you only need to specify the last
#few letters.
input 30 come>>
#Type the login command
output login\13
```

The best way to begin writing a script is to edit Winsock's sample login script and fill in the proper phone number or connect values. Select Dialler, Edit Scripts. The File Open dialog box appears. Select the *login.cmd* program and choose OK. A sample script follows. You should replace the sections in boldface print with valid values.

```
# Dial-in script to a typical SLIP Internet provider
#
#                       Initialize modem:
output at\13
#              Wait for 'OK' from modem
input 10 OK\n
#              Dial the Internet provider's phone number
output atdt555-1234\13
#              Wait for the CONNECT message
input 30 CONNECT
#              Wait for Username: prompt
input 10 name:
#              Prompt user for username using a dialog box
username Username
#              Type out that username
output \u\13
#              Wait for Password: prompt
input 10 word:
#              Prompt user for password using a dialog box
password Password
#              Type out that password
output \p\13
#              Invoke the SLIP protocol by typing the word "slip"
#                     You may have to move this line prior to the
#                     logging-in step.
output slip\13
#              Wait for IP address string
input 30 Your address is
#              Parse address (for dynamic SLIP accounts)
#                     If you have a static slip account you can
#                     delete the next line
address 30
input 30 \n
display \n
display Connection Attempt Complete!
display \n
#              Get network information using BOOTP protocol
BOOTP
```

Logging Out

To hang up manually, select Dialler, Manual Login. Type three plusses:

```
+++
```

and then type the modem hang-up command:

```
ATH
```

You can also log out using the standard logout script. Select Dialler, Bye.

UNIX SHELL WEB BROWSERS

A Unix shell is the traditional way of accessing the Internet from a home computer. You dial up an Internet provider's modem and, using a terminal program, you control the provider's computer and talk through it to the Internet.

This gives you command of the Internet, but it has many limitations. Since you're using somebody else's computer, you are limited to a simple form of communication. In most cases, you can only view or type text. Anything like graphics gets far too complicated.

A SLIP account actually makes your home computer a part of the Internet. But sometimes even SLIP isn't the answer. For instance:

- Your modem may be too slow; less than 9600 baud
- SLIP may be too expensive in your area
- There may be no local SLIP provider
- Your computer may not have the resources to run SLIP
- You're already connected to the Internet using a great Unix shell and don't want to give this up

Just because you're limited to a Unix shell account doesn't mean the situation is hopeless. Far from it. There are several surefire ways to access the Web from your Unix shell. The easiest way is to use a Unix-shell-compatible Web browser, such as the text-only Lynx or WWW or a graphical browser such as SlipKnot.

Text: Lynx or WWW

The simplest solution is to get a text-only browser like Lynx or WWW. These browsers run on your Internet provider's Unix machines, not on your home PC. Most Unix servers, however, should already have a working copy ready for you to use. Lynx and WWW allow you full access to the Web with one catch: You won't be able to see any graphics, hear any sounds, or be wowed by any other multimedia perks. The Lynx browser is covered fully in Chapter 3. If you can't run a local version of Lynx or WWW, you can telnet to it. See the Telneting To A Public Browser section in the next chapter.

To access Lynx or WWW, you can usually just go to your Unix prompt and type

```
lynx
```

or

```
www
```

Graphics: SlipKnot

MicroMind's SlipKnot is a terribly clever graphical Windows Web browser that works using dial-up Unix shell accounts. You need no SLIP, PPP, or TCP/IP software of any kind. SlipKnot loads up Web pages much more sluggishly than a SLIP Web browser, but if your modem is fast enough it's a very viable option. SlipKnot also has a number of other nice features. For instance, once you load up a Web page, you can load it again instantaneously. You can also view several Web pages at once.

SlipKnot is covered fully in Chapter 4.

THE INTERNET ADAPTER

If you can't access a SLIP account, the best solution is to emulate SLIP over your Unix shell. For $25, The Internet Adapter (TIA) software by Cyberspace Development, Inc., does this task most excellently. If Winsock is the socket, TIA is the three-pronged adapter that plugs the Internet into your home computer. Once TIA is installed, you can use Mosaic, Netscape, or any other multimedia Internet tools, the exact same way you would over a true SLIP line. A Unix Internet account equipped with TIA usually runs just as fast as any other SLIP.

Since TIA rides atop your standard Unix shell, it's a good idea to be fairly familiar with basic Unix and Internet commands before you try installing it. You might want to check out a command-line Internet book such as the Waite Group's *Internet How-To.*

NOTE: If a SLIP account costs much more per month than a standard Unix shell account, The Internet Adapter often pays for itself quickly.

Determining Your Unix Platform

The Internet Adapter does not run on your home PC—it is Unix software and is stored and accessed on your Internet provider's hard disk. Before you install TIA, be sure you have enough space. If not, you may have to request or buy additional space from your Internet service provider. Also beware: Some Internet providers do not allow you to use TIA because it interferes with their regular SLIP service.

All Unixes are not built the same. There are many platforms, or flavors, of the Unix operating system. Likewise, there are many different versions of TIA depending on which Unix shell you are using. TIA supports the following hardware/operating system configurations:

- Sun Sparc: Solaris 2.x or SunOS 4.1.x
- 386/486: BSDI 1.x, SCO, or LINUX
- DEC Alpha: OSF/1 2.0
- DEC: ULTRIX 4.3
- IBM RS/6000: AIX 3.2
- SGI: IRIX 4.0
- HP 9000: HPUX 9.0

If you're not sure what system you're using, you can ask your Internet provider. Alternatively, you can run a special script program to help you guess your brand of Unix. This script is not PC software. You'll need to use your Unix shell account to download the script directly via FTP. To log in to the FTP archive, type

```
ftp marketplace.com
```

When asked for a login name, type

```
anonymous
```

When asked for your password, type your e-mail address. Now type the following sequence of commands at the *FTP>* prompt to grab the file:

```
cd tia
ascii
get config.guess
bye
```

To make the script executable (able to be run), type

```
chmod u+x config.guess
```

And then type the following to run the script:

```
./config.guess
```

If worst comes to worst, you can download each version of TIA and try them out until you find one that seems to work.

Getting Your License Code

Since there are several different versions of TIA, you need to download TIA directly from its creators. Cyberspace Development issues free evaluation copies of TIA that you can try for 14 days. After that point, the software is automatically disabled.

To get a copy of the evaluation software, you need to order it, along with your own personal license code. To snag the order form, send a blank e-mail letter to: *tia-single@marketplace.com*. With most Unix accounts, you would type:

```
mail tia-single@marketplace.com
```

You could then press ENTER when asked for a subject and press CTRL-D to send the blank letter.

Cyberspace Development mails a user form to you immediately. When you get the form, load it up using any text editor and fill it in. You should fill in an answer to each question between the dotted lines and after the colon. For example, when it says:

```
-------------------------------------------|
# FIRST NAME:
-------------------------------------------|
```

you would put the cursor after the colon and type

```
-------------------------------------------|
# FIRST NAME: David
-------------------------------------------|
```

assuming, of course, your first name actually was David. Be sure to put an *X* next to the Evaluation order type when asked, unless you'd like to use your credit card and order a registered copy of the software right away.

```
-------------------------------------------|
# ORDER TYPE: Evaluation (X) Purchase ( )
-------------------------------------------|
```

When you're done, mail back the completed form to *tia-single@marketplace.com*. If you have any questions or problems with this process, you can send mail to:

```
tia-order-desk@marketplace.com
```

NOTE: After evaluating TIA for 14 days you may decide to buy a registered license code. You can resubmit the same form, this time including your credit card or other payment details. You can also order TIA by phone using a credit card by calling SoftAware at 310-314-1466.

Shortly, you get two messages back: your License Code and Installation Instructions.

Getting the Software

Once you receive your TIA Evaluation License Code, save the e-mail message in a file in your *home directory* called *.tia*. You can do this using the extract command of your Unix mail program. Read the e-mail message that contains your TIACODE and then type:

```
s .tia
```

Alternatively, you can create the .tia file in your current directory using your favorite Unix text editor. Print or write down your TIACODE, Login Name, and Domain Name. You can then create a *.tia* file that looks similar to the following:

```
TIACODE:abcd22ggdg2h3g4yutfgfj2h3j4h3jh3jh2j3h3
Login Name: <jsmith>
Domain Name: <smartpants.edu>
```

NOTE: If you purchase a registered TIACODE, the process is the same. Be sure to put the latest code in your *.tia* file. You should also keep a copy of the code in a separate file or on your home PC so that if your Unix provider's hard disk crashes, you can easily reinstall TIA.

You're now ready to download the TIA program itself. You'll need to know what Unix platform you're working on. To access the FTP archives, type the following command at your Unix prompt:

```
ftp marketplace.com
```

When asked for your login name, type

```
anonymous
```

When prompted for a password, type your complete e-mail address. You can now access the TIA file by changing to the proper directory. Change to the *tia* directory by typing

```
cd tia
```

NOTE: Some versions of the software may be available in the *tiabeta* directory.

To see the available versions, type

```
dir
```

You can now retrieve the proper version of TIA by using the *get* command. For example, if you need the *sparc.solaris.tia* version, you would type the following series of commands:

```
binary
get sparc.solaris.tia
bye
```

Installing The Internet Adapter

You should now have a working copy of TIA in your Unix machine's home directory. You can rename the file you just retrieved to *tia* using the *mv* command. For example:

```
mv sparc.solaris.tia tia
```

You now need to make the TIA software executable by using the *chmod* command:

```
chmod u+x tia
```

You can verify that The Internet Adapter is working by typing:

```
./tia
```

The following message should appear:

```
The Internet Adapter (tm) 1.0 for BSDI Unix
Copyright (c) 1994 Cyberspace Development, Inc.
Single License
Ready to start your SLIP software.
```

WARNING: An evaluation copy of TIA only works for 14 days from date of issue, so it needs to get the current date from your Unix machine. The evaluation version will not run at all if it can't read the date. Unfortunately, some Internet providers do not allow public access to the time utilities. If you hit on this problem, you can still try TIA if you can persuade your Internet provider to allow time-server access, or if you go ahead and buy a registered copy of TIA.

Configuring Winsock for The Internet Adapter

Once The Internet Adapter is successfully installed on your Unix system, you can run the Trumpet Winsock program as usual. Instead of dialing a SLIP account, you dial up your Unix shell account and run The Internet Adapter. Before you make the call, however, you should fine-tune some of Winsock's settings so that it works in tandem with TIA.

The Setup

To set up Winsock, run it and select File, Setup. Be sure the Internal SLIP box is checked. You now need to fill in a number of values. Since TIA only emulates a SLIP account, there is no actual IP address. Instead, you should use the dummy IP address of 192.0.2.1. Your Netmask should be 255.255.255.0.

The TIA program itself can figure out what value you need to put in the Name Server box. Dial up your Unix account and type:

```
./tia -address
```

TIA tells you the IP address for the Gateway and the Name server. If your machine has several Name servers, separate each with a space. If this command doesn't work, you can try Unix's own Name server command:

```
whois -h internic.net domain.xxx
```

If neither of the above two commands seems to work, you'll need to ask your Internet provider for the IP number of the Name server.

You can leave the Time Server and Domain Suffix boxes blank. You now need to set the data flow values. Use the following values:

- MTU: 1500
- TCP RWIN: 4096
- TCP MSS: 1460
- TCP RTO MAX: 60
- Demand Load Timeout: 5

You should now fill in your Winsock communications settings, as described earlier in this chapter. Fill in the correct SLIP Port, Baud Rate, and Hardware Handshake values. Be sure the Van Jacobson CSLIP Compression attribute is *not* checked.

Trumpet Winsock should now be a perfect match with The Internet Adapter. Click OK, exit Trumpet, and restart it.

Dialing Manually

You can now use Trumpet Winsock to dial your Unix system manually, as described earlier in this chapter. Select Dialler, Manual Login. Dial up your system and log in the way your normally would. Instead of typing *slip*, however, you should type:

```
./tia
```

You should now see the message:

```
Ready to start your SLIP software
```

Press the ESC key to end the manual login sequence. Hearty congratulations to you! You now have full SLIP access to the Internet.

NOTE: If your Unix Internet account uses a series of menus, you need to find some way of getting to the Unix command prompt. Ask your Internet provider if a standard shell account is available. If not, you'll need to create a Winsock script to navigate the proper menu choices.

Dialing with a Script

Alternatively, you can create a Winsock script that logs into your Unix shell account and runs the TIA program. This script should look like the one earlier in this chapter, with the additional line:

```
output ./tia\13
```

Exiting TIA

To quit TIA manually, select the Manual Login item from Winsock's Dialler menu. Slowly type CTRL-C five times to exit the TIA program. You'll return to the Unix prompt, where you can use Unix Internet commands as usual. You can rerun TIA at any time.

SHOOTING DOWN TROUBLES

Stacks can often tumble. The complex combinations of TCP/IP software, socket software, SLIP software, Internet client software, Web browsers, your Internet provider's Unix system, your machine, and Windows itself can cause lots of headaches.

Whenever you have a problem, be sure to check each component individually. If you're using The Internet Adapter, run it and be sure it doesn't give you any error messages. If it does, you may need a different version of the software. If you're running a Winsock script that doesn't seem to work, first try logging in manually to see if the problem is with your script or with Winsock itself. Make sure your modem is connected when you think it should be: just pick up the phone and listen; if you hear a low-pitched grumbling noise, you're online.

That said, here are a few common errors and easy ways to squash them:

Your Modem Won't Respond

If you try dialing using Winsock but nothing seems to be happening, this could indicate one of several problems:

- Your modem isn't attached to your computer. Check to be sure the cables are inserted tightly.
- Your modem isn't attached to your phone line. Plug a phone into the line to be sure you're getting a dial tone.
- Your modem isn't turned on.
- Your modem hasn't been properly reset or initialized. Check your modem owner's manual for guidelines. If possible, contact your modem's manufacturer.
- Your port isn't configured properly in Windows. Run the Windows Control Panel and select the Port icon. Select the port your modem is connected to and click the Settings button. Be sure the settings correspond to your modem's baud rate. Note that a 14,400 baud modem's port should be set to 19,200. The port should also be set for 8 data bits, no parity, 1 stop bit, and the Flow Control type should be Hardware.

If your modem works fine one moment but then suddenly stops responding, the modem might just be a little tipsy. Turn off the modem and turn it back on or reboot your computer.

The "DNS Lookup Failed" Message

This is probably the most common error message you're likely to run across. It means your Web browser is having trouble accessing remote URLs.

Most likely, there's a wrong value in your Winsock setup window. Double-check the IP numbers of your Domain server and your Name server. Contact your Internet provider to be sure they gave you the right information in the first place. All these numbers can get confusing; you may have copied something down wrong. Using the wrong IP number is as useless as dialing the wrong phone number.

The "Unable to Resolve Host Name" Message

If everything seems to run, but your Internet tools have problems connecting to specific hosts, your Domain Name Server (DNS) information is probably wrong. Check SlipKnot's setup and double-check the Name server entry.

WHAT NOW?

You're now connected to the Internet, either using SLIP or The Internet Adapter. Your next step is to install, configure, and learn to use a Web browser so you can start flipping through those tens of thousands of multimedia Web pages. Chapter 2 introduces you to the wild world of the Web browser. Later chapters deal with particular brands of browsers:

- Chapter 3 is a hands-on guide to using the text-only Lynx browser.
- Chapter 4 covers the SlipKnot graphical Unix shell browser.
- Chapter 5 shows you everything you need to know about the acclaimed NCSA Mosaic browser.
- Chapter 6 guides you through the sleek Netscape browser.
- Chapter 7 takes a brief look at other Web browsers available for the Windows PC.

2

WEB BROWSERS

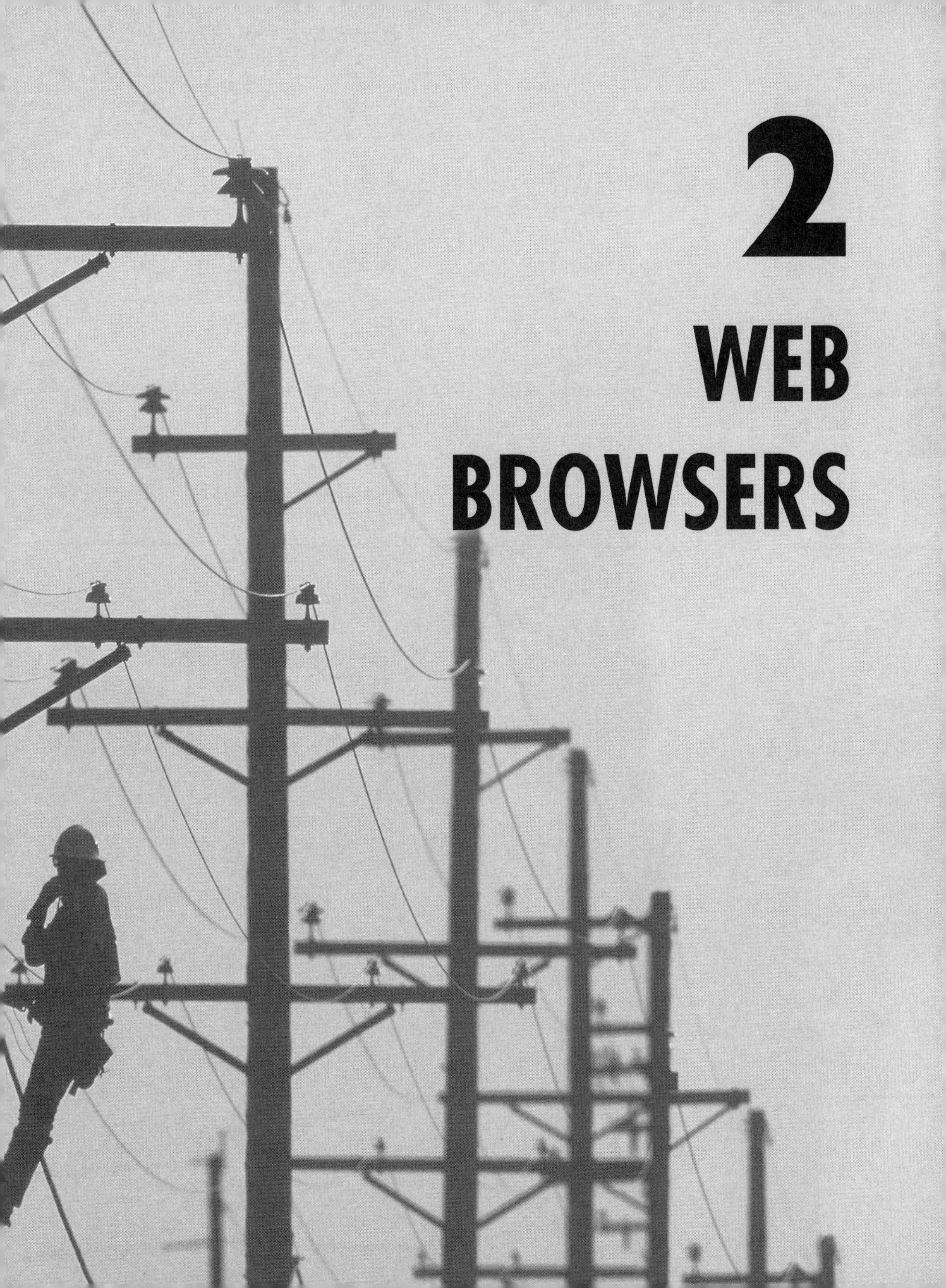

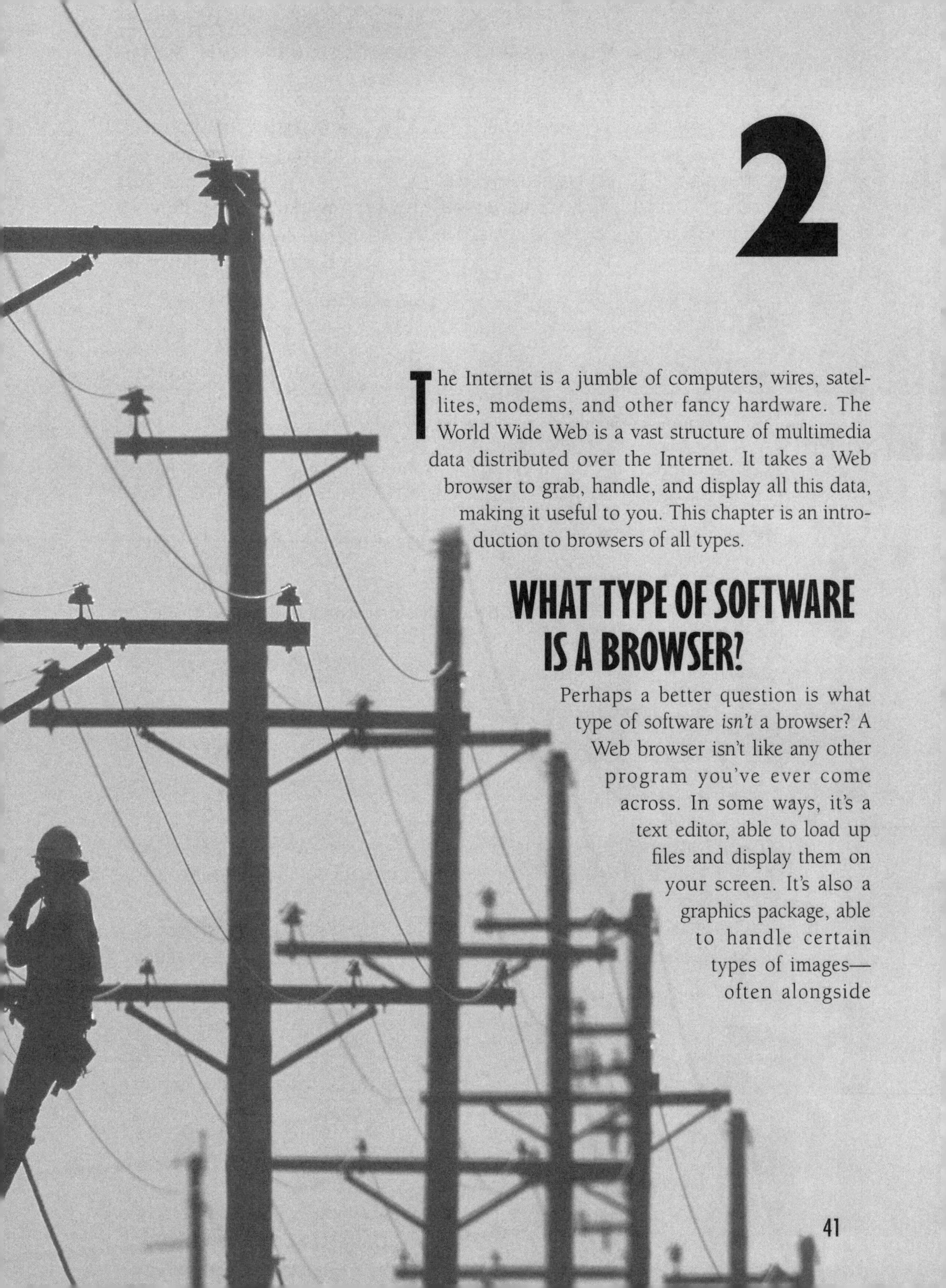

2

The Internet is a jumble of computers, wires, satellites, modems, and other fancy hardware. The World Wide Web is a vast structure of multimedia data distributed over the Internet. It takes a Web browser to grab, handle, and display all this data, making it useful to you. This chapter is an introduction to browsers of all types.

WHAT TYPE OF SOFTWARE IS A BROWSER?

Perhaps a better question is what type of software *isn't* a browser? A Web browser isn't like any other program you've ever come across. In some ways, it's a text editor, able to load up files and display them on your screen. It's also a graphics package, able to handle certain types of images—often alongside the text. On the other side of the coin, a Web browser is a full-featured online navigation tool, often combining common Internet artifacts such as e-mail, news, FTP file transfers, and telnet.

You'll find literally hundreds of browsers available for different computers and operating systems. The PC alone has nearly 40 different browsers for you to choose from. Most browsers share the following features:

- Hypertext document viewing.
- Text formatting. That is, you see text broken into paragraphs, lists, headings, or other elements; with each element having its own unique appearance.
- Internet service access. Usually including gopher, telnet, news NNTP, FTP, or WAIS.
- *History list* maintenance. So you can get back to previously-visited Web pages or other URLs.
- *Bookmark list* (also called *hot list*) maintenance. To keep track of your favorite Web pages or other URLs.
- Interactive forms. Fill-in forms complete with blank fields, check-boxes, radio buttons, and menus.
- Usenet news reading and posting.
- E-mail sending.
- Authentication. This lets users keep certain pages secure by requiring passwords or special signatures for access.

Browsers that run on a windowing operating system (such as Unix X-Windows, Macintosh, or Microsoft Windows) have these additional qualities:

- Mouse-driven commands.
- Ability to process full hypermedia documents.
- Ability to work with embedded graphics, tables, and complex mathematical equations.
- Wide range of fonts, font sizes, special characters, and font styles.

WHICH BROWSER SHOULD I USE?

In theory, all browsers should be similar. Browsers are supposed to be uniform, handling a common Web language. However, the latest browsers each come out with their own fancy features and commands, hoping to become the standard. This means some Web pages look great using one browser, and pretty shoddy using another. This, in a way, undermines the whole global idea of the Web. On the other hand, many of these new features eventually make their way into the mainstream, creating an ever more useful and beautiful Web.

So what was supposed to be uniform has become competitive. There are currently tons of Web browsers out on the market, with new products announced each month. Luckily, there are only four or five browsers that seem to have withstood the rigor of the real-world Web.

If there is a standard, NCSA Mosaic is probably it. This doesn't mean it works the fastest (it doesn't), is the easiest to use (nope), or has the most features (uh-uh). This *does* mean that tons of people use Mosaic, and thus most Web pages will look pretty good on it. NCSA also provides Mosaic absolutely free to the Internet community. Chapter 5 discusses the Mosaic browser.

The best Web browser is clearly Netscape. The Netscape software works the fastest, has the most bells and whistles, and is the easiest to use and the least prone to errors. All told, it has a pretty darn slick look to it. Netscape's latest release, unfortunately, is not free to all users. Chapter 6 covers Netscape for you.

As far as the thirty or so other available Web browsers are concerned, most are basically Mosaic clones. Although you'll find some excellent products, these third-party browsers are used by a tiny percentage of Webbers. One of these browsers may, however, have that one particular feature you've been dying for. You'll find a brief survey of Cello, WinWeb, Spry AIR Mosaic, and other Windows browsers in Chapter 7.

If you're not using a SLIP account or The Internet Adapter (both discussed in the previous chapter), and if you don't have a networked connection to the Internet, then you only have two choices when it comes to browsing:

HTML You can use a text-based browser such as Lynx or WWW. These browsers are usually lightning-fast and come complete with all popular features. The big drawback is that there are, of course, no graphics, font sizes, styles, lines, or other special characters. This drastically lowers the aesthetic value of a Web page. Chapter 3 covers the Lynx browser.

HTML The SlipKnot browser is your second option. It can display all basic multimedia Web pages, complete with text styles, fonts, and graphics. SlipKnot is not free, however, and it takes quite a long time for each Web page to load. Chapter 4 gives you a hands-on guide to the SlipKnot browser.

HELPFUL HANDS

In many ways, a Web browser acts like its own operating system. It knows how to handle most every type of data or resource stored over the Internet. If it can't display or otherwise use the data, it is smart enough to pass the data on to a program that can. These secondary programs are known as *viewers* because they're typically used to view fancy graphics or photos.

A browser can also perform many actions. It can, of course, hop around the Web using hypertext links. It can also usually send or retrieve a file from an FTP archive, send e-mail, or even act as a full Usenet newsreader. However, there are some things even a Web browser can't do itself yet, like telnet to remote computers. If you ask a browser to perform an action it can't handle, it'll usually run a more suitable program for you. These programs are known as *external applications.*

Viewers

Most Web browsers can't actually play sounds or run movies. However, a browser can retrieve the sound or movie file and automatically hand this file over to a viewer. In this way, viewers piggyback on the browsers, greatly extending their powers.

For example, most Windows browsers display any movies or animations using the Windows MPEG viewer. If the browser can't recognize the file, it'll generally read it in as plain text. Most browsers allow you to configure your favorite brand of viewer for each type of file.

External Applications

If you're using a Unix browser, most external applications should be a basic part of your Internet provider's service. If you're using your home PC with a SLIP line, however, there are some resources you might eventually want:

- A *telnet client* to log you in to remote computers.
- A *newsreader* to read or post Usenet news.
- An *FTP client* to send or receive files over the Internet.
- A *talk client* to let you hold a split-screen live chat with anybody else on the Internet.
- An *IRC client* to get you into Internet Relay Chat (IRC), where thousands of users chat about thousands of topics.
- A *finger client* to tell you about people who are currently logged onto the Internet.
- An *archie client* to search for particular files over the Internet.
- A *gopher client* to run the gopher menuing system.

Many Web browsers already have these programs built in. In some cases, however, you may want to use a separate client because it is faster, easier to use, or offers more commands. Most browsers allow you to designate any external applications you want for any given function.

More information about obtaining and using this Internet client software can be found in Appendix B, Other Software Sources.

The Talking MIME

The Web combines graphics, video, sound, text, hypertext, and more. Keeping track of what's what and how to use it can get confusing. After all, every file is stored in its own unique way—and there are a *lot* of possibilities.

Web servers use a coding scheme called the *Multipurpose Internet Mail Extension* (*MIME*) to differentiate different types of data. Whenever your browser asks for a particular file, the server lets the browser know what MIME type it'll be dealing with. Web browsers have the ability to recognize most popular types of files. Some files can be displayed on the fly. Others need to be sent to external viewers.

In most cases, the browser recognizes a file by its extension. Most every file on your computer has a specialized extension. For example, Microsoft Word files usually end in .DOC while plain text files end in .TXT. When you open a document using your favorite word processor, for example, your software often guesses what format the file is in based on its extension. Web browsers use filename extensions similarly.

NOTE: Most Web documents are stored on Unix operating systems, not on DOS. Unix extensions are not limited in length. For example, *the.history.of.the.world* is the name of a valid Unix file. Also unlike DOS, Unix is case sensitive. This means that the file called *HELLO* is a different file from the one called *hello*. On Unix systems, Web hypermedia files generally end with the lowercase extension *.html*.

Since a Web document can have links not only to other Web documents but to graphics, sounds, text, Internet resources, and so on, it's important for both you and your Web browser to know what type of file is currently being dealt with. Table 2–1 lists some standard extensions and file formats.

Table 2–1 Standard extensions for file formats found on the Web

File Extension	File Format
Text	
.txt	Plain text file (extension is sometimes .text on non-DOS systems)
.rtf	Rich text format
Graphics	
.gif	CompuServe Graphics Interchange Format for any type of image
.tif	Targa Image File Format (extension is *.tiff* on non-DOS systems)
.jpg	Joint Photographic Experts Group (extension is *.jpeg* on non-DOS systems)
.bmp	Windows or OS/2 bitmap
.tga	Truevision Targa
.pcx	Windows Paint pixelmap
.rle	Run Length Encoded image
.xbm	A black and white bitmap from the X operating system
.xpm	A color pixelmap from the X operating system
.ps	PostScript printer-output file
Video / Animation	
.mpg	A Motion Picture Experts Group video or animated movie file (extension is *.mpeg* on non-DOS systems)
.mov	QuickTime movie (extension is *.moov* on non-DOS systems)
.avi	Audio/Video Interleave Windows multimedia movie
.fli	Autodesk Animator flick
.gl	Grasprt animation
Audio	
.au or .snd	Sun or NeXT audio
.aif	Audio Image File Format (extension is *.aiff* on non-DOS systems)

File Extension	File Format
.iff	IFF
.voc	Soundblaster Creative Voice
.wav	Windows Waveform
.sf	IRCAM
.mod or .nst	Amiga Mod
.snd or .fssd	Miscellaneous Amiga, PC, or Mac
.ul	US telephony
Compression	
.Z	A file compressed using compress (Unix)
.zip	A file compressed using pkzip
.gz	A file compressed using gzip (Unix)
.uue	An uuencoded binary file (Unix)

TELNETING TO A PUBLIC BROWSER

Maybe you're not sold yet. I mean, maybe the Web sounds kinda interesting, kinda fun, but you just aren't sure what it is that makes the Web so talked-about, so hyped. Before you buy a SLIP account or The Internet Adapter, you want a test drive.

NOTE: Telneting to a public browser is also useful if you want to access a page's text very quickly.

If you already have an Internet account, you should run the Lynx or WWW browser, described in the next chapter. At your Unix prompt, try typing:

```
lynx
```

or

```
www
```

If nothing happens with either of these commands, you can grab a very basic tour of the Web by using telnet to jump to a public Web browser. Almost every Unix account in the world offers the *telnet* command. Public WWW sites are listed in Table 2–2. Type *telnet* followed by the name of the site. For example, to log into the Funet site, which contains a public Lynx browser, you would type:

```
telnet info.funet.fi
```

When asked to

```
Login:
```

type

```
www
```

When you telnet to a remote site, you may be asked to

```
Select interface?
```

in which case you can try typing

```
lynx
```

to access the Lynx text-based browser.

A special beginner's page usually appears, as shown in Figure 2–1. There are no mouse or cursor controls. To access a hypertext link, type in the number or word that appears in brackets. You can also type the word *back* to go to a previous page, or *quit* to exit.

Be warned: The generic WWW browser is the most ill-mannered, simple-minded browser you could find, but it should give you some idea of how the Web works. Lynx is a little more functional, but is still limited to simple text only.

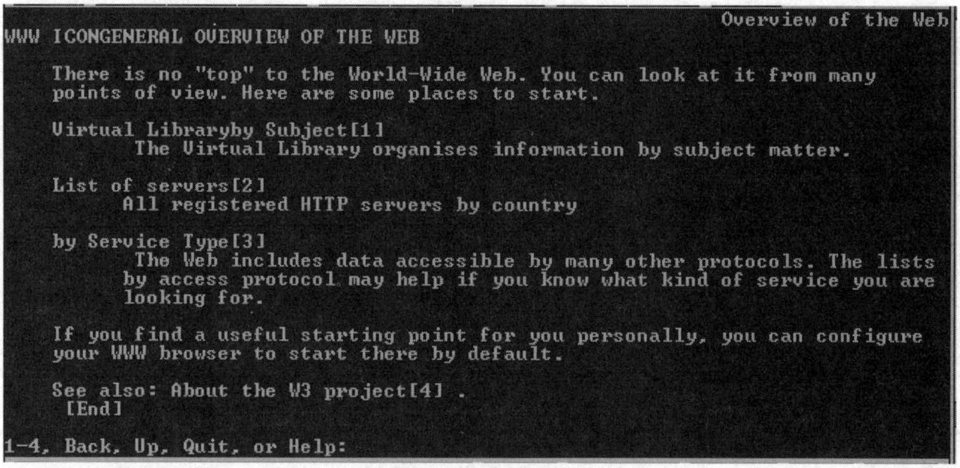

```
                                                                Overview of the Web
WWW ICONGENERAL OVERVIEW OF THE WEB

    There is no "top" to the World-Wide Web. You can look at it from many
    points of view. Here are some places to start.

    Virtual Libraryby Subject[1]
          The Virtual Library organises information by subject matter.

    List of servers[2]
         All registered HTTP servers by country

    by Service Type[3]
          The Web includes data accessible by many other protocols. The lists
         by access protocol may help if you know what kind of service you are
         looking for.

    If you find a useful starting point for you personally, you can configure
    your WWW browser to start there by default.

    See also: About the W3 project[4] .
     [End]
1-4, Back, Up, Quit, or Help:
```

Figure 2–1 The simplest Web browser in the world

Table 2–2 Publicly accessible Web browsers

Browser	Public Site
WWW	fatty.law.cornell.edu
WWW	www.edu.tw
WWW	fserv.kfki.hu
WWW	telnet.w3.org
WWW	www.njit.edu
Lynx	info.funet.fi
Lynx	www.cc.ukans.edu
Generic	www.huji.ac.il
Generic	sun.uakom.cs

You can now flip through this book, especially Chapter 8, What Can I Do? If you see a page that looks interesting, note its URL. Telnet to a public browser, press G, and then type in that exact URL. The page is loaded up for you. These simple browsers may require you to type *go URL*. For instance, to jump to http://www.smartpants.edu/ you could type:

```
go http://www.smartpants.edu/
```

WWW VIA E-MAIL

If you're *really* in a hurry, or if the telnet command doesn't work for you, you can have the contents of a Web page mailed to you. You'll need to know the exact URL of the document you want. There are two addresses you can try. To send mail, type the following at your Unix prompt:

```
mail server@mail.w3.org
```

or

```
mail listserv@info.cern.ch
```

You should leave the subject blank. As the body of your message, type

```
send [URL]
```

and replace [URL] with the actual URL of the page you want to see. The CERN site automatically processes the request, loads up the page, and sends the text directly to your mailbox.

Each hypertext link in the document will be followed by a bracketed number, such as [3]. At the bottom of the mail message, there'll be a listing of each number and its corresponding URL. If you want to follow one of the URLs, just send off another message.

BROWSING WITHOUT THE INTERNET ALTOGETHER

Maybe you haven't subscribed to your SLIP Internet account yet and want to browse through some *.html* files on your hard disk. Or maybe you're designing HTML Web pages on your local PC and want to check them out. Since most browsers (Cello, Netscape, and so forth) communicate via TCP/IP stacks, you'll need to make them think that your machine is actually connected to a network.

Some companies are also investigating ways of creating small, private Webs. A *Local Area Web* is not distributed via the Internet, but over the company's own LAN. Such companies may want to use their own networking software. However, they could also set it up so employees could use Mosaic, Netscape, or any other browser to distribute confidential company information in a sleek hypermedia format.

Stand-Alone Browsers

The latest versions of Mosaic and SlipKnot are *stand-alone* browsers. When you run them, they load up just fine even if you're not using socket or TCP/IP software. You can then use the File, Open command to bring up any document or file stored on your hard disk. Giving browsers a stand-alone mode seems to be the trend, since many people use their browsers to look at local Web pages.

Minimizing Winsock

Many other browsers, however, give you a strange error message if you try to run them with no other Internet software installed:

```
Application Error
Call To Undefined Dynalink
```

However, you don't actually have to be connected to your Internet provider to use a browser. Just run the Winsock program in the background by selecting the control box in the upper left corner of the window and choosing the Minimize item. Most browsers should run just fine.

Nullsock

If you don't have a modem or network connection at all, you can still play with Web browser programs if you install a fake socket library. This fake library, known as *nullsock,* works in lieu of Winsock's true *WINSOCK.DLL.*

The nullsock file is available at the site listed in Appendix D. Download and copy the WINSOCK.DLL file to your Windows system directory:

```
C:\WINDOWS\SYSTEM
```

Be sure to erase Winsock's real WINSOCK.DLL. You can now run Winsock along with your favorite browser or other Internet software. Winsock, of course, is crippled; it can't do much more than initialize.

WHAT NOW?

You're now ready to install and use a browser on your own machine. The next five chapters cover the most popular types of browser programs. Chapter 3 begins with an overview of Lynx, a Unix browser.

3

LYNX

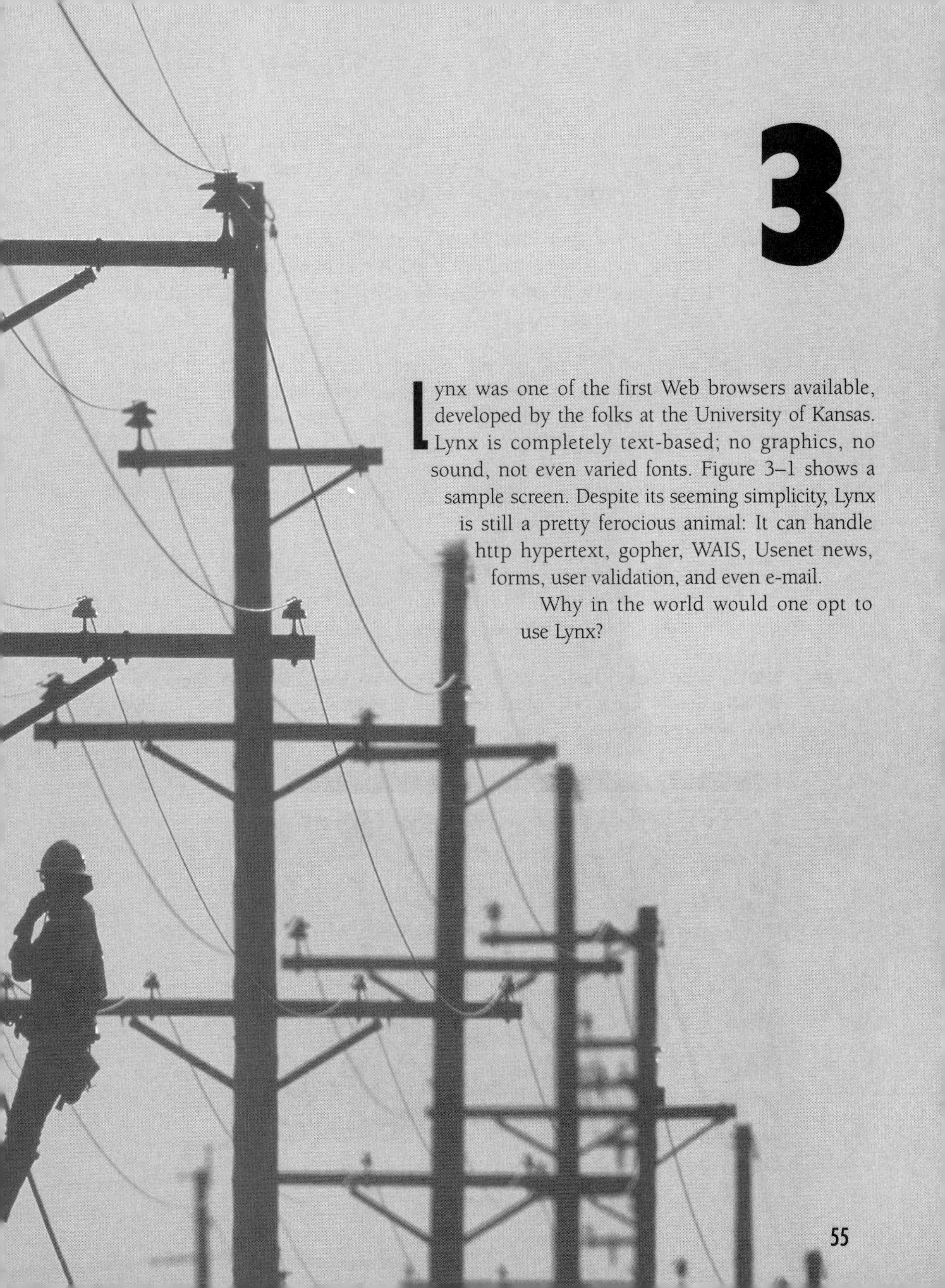

3

Lynx was one of the first Web browsers available, developed by the folks at the University of Kansas. Lynx is completely text-based; no graphics, no sound, not even varied fonts. Figure 3–1 shows a sample screen. Despite its seeming simplicity, Lynx is still a pretty ferocious animal: It can handle http hypertext, gopher, WAIS, Usenet news, forms, user validation, and even e-mail.

Why in the world would one opt to use Lynx?

- Speed: Lynx doesn't care about fancy fonts, gloppy graphics, or any other large bits of design, so hypertext zooms in about ten times as fast as your typical graphical browser.

- Portability: If you don't have a SLIP/PPP account, or if your computer or modem isn't fast enough to run a graphical browser, Lynx is a great alternative. Almost any Internet-connected Unix system has it installed.

- Convenience: Suppose you're logged on to your Internet Unix account, browsing through your e-mail, transferring files, fun stuff like that, and suddenly you come across a URL you want to check out. It's often a pain to log off, dial up your separate SLIP account, and run Netscape. Lynx can snag that URL for you, then and there. You can then decide, after a cursory view, if it's worth bothering to use a fancier Web browser.

- Unix Development: If, for whatever reason, you'd like to develop your Web pages directly on a Unix system, Lynx is the easiest way to test your hypertext.

NOTE: Lynx doesn't run on Windows, it runs on Unix and VMS (there's a DOS version in the works). Most any Internet service you call will probably have Lynx installed—if not, ask them, beg them, get on your knees and cry

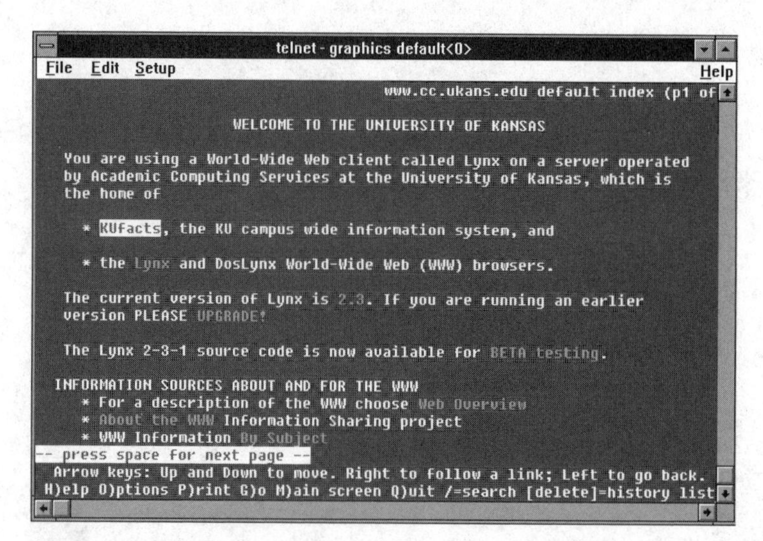

Figure 3–1 A quick look at Lynx

for them. It's a free program. You can even go so far as to download Lynx yourself from *ftp://ftp2.cc.ukans.edu/pub/lynx*. You can then give this file to your Internet provider and ask them to install it.

LESSON #1: THE LYNX'S MEOW

To use Lynx, you need a VT-100 or ANSI terminal emulator. Most dial-in Unix accounts are set up for VT-100 by default. Depending on the type of Unix computer you're calling, the command for setting the terminal varies. If Lynx doesn't seem to work, ask your Internet provider how to configure VT-100. Be sure your own communications program is set up to emulate VT-100, as well.

To run Lynx, just type

```
lynx
```

Lynx defaults to its own home page, at the University of Kansas. If your Internet site has a Web page of its own, you'll probably get that instead.

You can also use Lynx to open up a hypertext or even plain ASCII text file in the current directory: Most hypertext files are written using the Hypertext Markup Language (HTML) and end with the *.html* extension. To load a local HTML file, type:

```
lynx sample.html
```

To load a file that is located in a different directory, include the file's full pathname:

```
lynx /private/webstuff/sample.html
```

Typically, though, you want to use Lynx to load up a URL directly:

```
lynx http://www.ncsa.uiuc.edu/
```

When Lynx first runs, it loads up the file you specified, as shown in Figure 3–1. All commands are listed along the bottom, making it easy to remember what does what. Also notice that some text appears in bold print. These are hyperlinks. The first hyperlink is usually highlighted in reverse video, which indicates that it's currently selected. Depending on the display you're using, selected hyperlinks may also appear in a different color or in italics.

A multimedia browser would usually display graphics alongside the text. Lynx generally uses the word

```
[Image]
```

when confronted with inline graphics.

LESSON #2: NAVIGATING

Lynx makes moving around the Web incredibly fast and easy. You can execute most navigation commands with the arrow keys. Once your fingers get fast enough, you can flip through a dozen Web pages in the same time it would take a graphical Web browser to load up just one page. Table 3–1 lists the Lynx navigation commands.

If the Web page is more than one screen long, you can flip to the next screen by pressing the plus key + or the space bar. If you try this when you get to the bottom of a page, Lynx displays the message:

```
You're already at the end of this document.
```

To scroll back to the previous screen, press the minus key - or B.

Table 3–1 Lynx navigation commands

Key	Function
+, SPACE	Scroll down to the next screen
-, B	Scroll up to the previous screen
↓	Select the next hyperlink
↑	Select the previous hyperlink
→, ENTER	Follow a hyperlink topic
←	Flip back to the previous Web page
=	View information about the current page and its hyperlinks
G	Go to a distant URL
Z	Cancel the current transfer
BACKSPACE	View the history list
D	Download the current link
M	Return to the main home screen
Q	Quit
SHIFT-Q, CTRL-D	Quick quit
\	View the Web page's HTML source
C	Comment (e-mail) to whoever wrote the current Web page
E	Edit the currently displayed text file
O	Configure your options
P	Print the page to disk, e-mail, or a printer
I	Show an index of documents
/	Search for a word or phrase in the current Web page
N	Find the next occurrence of the search term
S	Search for a word or phrase in a separate index
!	Run the Unix shell

Key	Function
CTRL-R	Reload the current Web page
CTRL-W	Refresh the screen
CTRL-U	Erase whatever you just typed on the input line
CTRL-G	Cancel an input or a transfer
?, H	Help

Following Lynx Links

Most pages have their own hyperlinks, printed in bold. One of these hyperlinks is always selected, usually printed in reverse video. To select the next hyperlink, just press ↓. The ↑ key, naturally, selects a previous hyperlink. Even if two links are on the same line, these arrow keys cycle between them. When you reach a page's last hyperlink, ↓ flips you to the next page. If a screen has no hyperlinks, press ↓ to keep flipping pages until you find one.

To follow a link that sounds interesting, just press → or ENTER. The new Web page or Internet resource appears.

Link Info

If you want to know where a link will take you before you follow it, press the equals key =. An information screen appears, as in Figure 3–2. This screen lets you know:

- HTML The current document's URL
- HTML The number of lines in the document
- HTML The document's title
- HTML The document's owner (the person who wrote the Web page)
- HTML The selected link's URL
- HTML The document type of the selected link

Loading a Specific URL

To jump to a specific URL—whether it be another hypertext Web page, an Internet resource, an e-mail letter you want to send, a newsgroup, or a file—just press G. Type in the full URL. Lynx loads it up, quick as it's able.

If the URL is not valid, you bounce back to the current Web page.

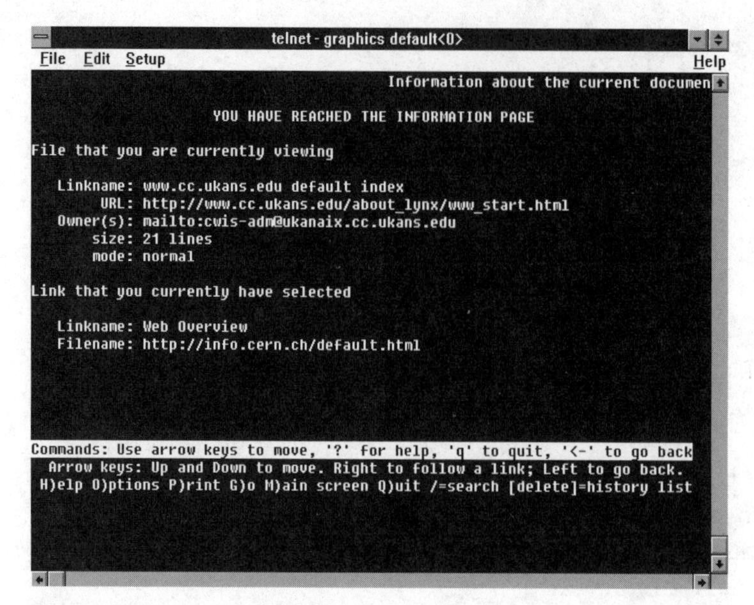

Figure 3–2 A screenful of information about the current Web page and the currently selected link

HALTING a Load

Often, you access a Web page at the same time as dozens of other people. Lynx may want several minutes while it tries to get through to a Web server. If you get fed up and want to cancel a page as it is being loaded, press Z.

If Lynx managed to grab any text or data prior to the moment you interrupted a load, it will display whatever it got.

Exiting Lynx

When you are done rolling around the Web, press Q. You are asked if you really want to quit. Press Y if you're sure, press N if you're not so sure (to which Lynx will reply, "Excellent!").

If you want to quit immediately, without any second-guessing, press SHIFT-Q or CTRL-D.

LESSON #3: THE HISTORY LIST

Every time you visit a Web page, Lynx keeps track of it. If, at any point, you want to experience some deja vu, press BACKSPACE to view your history list. A series of hyperlinks appears, as in Figure 3–3. The history list shows the

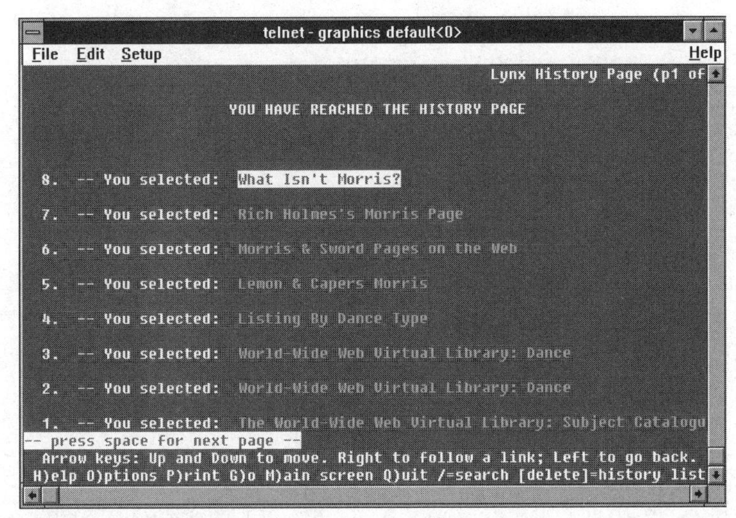

Figure 3–3 The Lynx history list lets you quickly revisit an old Web page

title of each page you've visited—in the order you visited it, from latest to oldest. Select the page you want and press ENTER.

If you want to return to the home page—the document you first loaded when you ran Lynx, press M. Just keep in mind that this clears out your history list, allowing you to begin a fresh session. This is very useful if that's what you wanted to do but a tad frustrating if it wasn't.

LESSON #4: SCREEN-WASHING

Sometimes data gets lost or added as it roams the millions of miles of Internet cables. If a page pops onto your screen but doesn't look the way it should, you can easily reload it by pressing CTRL-R.

Other times, your screen might fill up with things it shouldn't. Things like incoming e-mail, static-filled phone lines, or other Unix messages may appear in the middle of your Web page. To wipe the screen clean, press CTRL-W. The current page is redrawn, but not reloaded.

LESSON #5: PRINTING A PAGE

Once you read a Web page, you may be so impressed that you'd like to keep a copy of it. Lynx allows you to easily print out a page to the screen, save it to your disk, or mail it to yourself.

To print out the current document, press P. A menu of Print Options appears, letting you know how long the document is:

```
There are 21 lines, or approximately 1 page, to print.
You have the following print choices.
Please select one:
Save to a local file
Mail the file to yourself
Print to the screen
```

NOTE: If you use telnet to reach Lynx then you will not be able to save the page to a local file. Other options, such as printing to a laser printer, may also be available.

Using the arrow keys, select one of the print options and press ENTER.

Saving

If you select the Save To A Local File option, the system asks for a filename. Type in any name you wish. Lynx then writes the entire text of the current web page to your Unix account's disk.

A saved document can then be mailed to someone, edited using any Unix text editor, uploaded to someone else's machine, or downloaded to your home PC.

Mailing

Many people find working with e-mail easier than working with files. If you're one of these folks, you can mail the current Web page to yourself. Lynx asks you for your e-mail address and then zooms the text off to you.

Once you receive the mail, you can forward it, extract it, or keep it saved in your mailbox for later reference.

Printing

If you print to the screen, a text version of the current document quickly scrolls by. This is useful if your communications program lets you backtrack using a screen buffer. You can move up to the part of the document you're interested in, copy or cut it, and then paste it in your favorite word processor or text editor.

You could not easily grab sections of an ordinary Lynx Web document because only one page at a time is shown. If the section you want appears on two separate pages, there would be a bunch of commands, status messages, and other garbage text stuck in the middle.

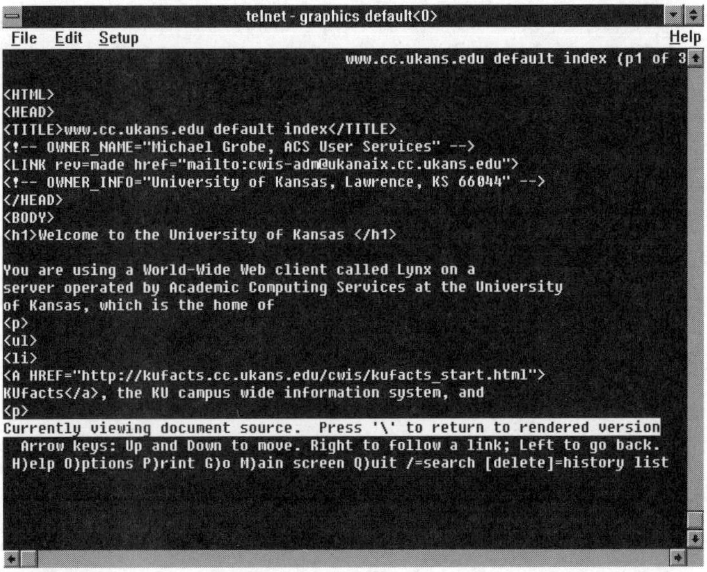

```
telnet - graphics default<0>
File  Edit  Setup                                                          Help
                                     www.cc.ukans.edu default index (p1 of 3

<HTML>
<HEAD>
<TITLE>www.cc.ukans.edu default index</TITLE>
<!-- OWNER_NAME="Michael Grobe, ACS User Services" -->
<LINK rev=made href="mailto:cwis-adm@ukanaix.cc.ukans.edu">
<!-- OWNER_INFO="University of Kansas, Lawrence, KS 66044" -->
</HEAD>
<BODY>
<h1>Welcome to the University of Kansas </h1>

You are using a World-Wide Web client called Lynx on a
server operated by Academic Computing Services at the University
of Kansas, which is the home of
<p>
<ul>
<li>
<A HREF="http://kufacts.cc.ukans.edu/cwis/kufacts_start.html">
KUFacts</a>, the KU campus wide information system, and
<p>
Currently viewing document source.  Press '\' to return to rendered version
  Arrow keys: Up and Down to move. Right to follow a link; Left to go back.
 H)elp O)ptions P)rint G)o M)ain screen Q)uit /=search [delete]=history list
```

Figure 3–4 A Web page skeleton: the source markup

LESSON #6: GETTING TO THE SOURCE

As you begin to create your own Web pages, you'll find it very valuable to study how other pages you admire were made. Lynx allows you to view a document's full HTML source simply by pressing \ (the backslash key).

The actual Web page is replaced by the commands that tell Lynx what to do and how to do it, as shown in Figure 3–4. You can then print this source markup to your disk, screen, or mailbox, as discussed in the previous section. Once you retrieve a Web page's source file, you can base your own documents on its structure. Part II of this book goes into detail on how HTML works.

Saving the Source

If you save a copy of the source to your disk you can have Lynx automatically open the file at any time. Be sure you use a filename with the *.html* extension.

For example, suppose you come across a great index of rock music Web sites. You happen to know that this index is very popular, and thus difficult to access; you've tried accessing the index many times and been turned down. You can solve the problem by creating your own local copy. Press \

to view the source and then press P to make a printout. Select the Save to a local file option. When asked for a filename, type something similar to:

```
rockindex.html
```

The next time you want to start rockin', just type:

```
lynx rockindex.html
```

Returning to the Regular View

When you're done working with a Web page's source, just press \ again to switch to the actual Web page. This quick-switching between a rendered page and its markup commands can come in handy any time you want to quickly take a peek at how a certain Web effect was achieved.

LESSON #7: EDITING A PAGE

Lynx has the ability to call up a text editor on-the-fly. This allows you to edit text documents, Web pages, or Web HTML source listings.

NOTE: To do any editing, you must have an editor defined in the Options Menu. See the Lynx Options section, later in this chapter.

To edit whatever is currently on the screen, press E to call the editor you specified in the Options Menu. You can add text, delete lines, or move paragraphs around. You can then save the current file to disk. When you're done playing around with the editor, exit. You automatically return to Lynx. The file you were editing is reloaded with all changes intact. This allows you to immediately see the results of your hard work.

Editing an HTML source file in this way is a great tool for Web page developers. You can make small changes, instantly see how they look, and then continue editing.

LESSON #8: BOOKMARKS

Since the Web is so huge and ungainly, it can often be impossible to find a page you accessed just a day earlier. It's like getting lost in a forest where all the trees look pretty much alike. Whenever you come across a Web page you really like, stick a bookmark in it. Lynx provides a special *bookmark file* to help you keep track of your favorite pages, so you can call them up at any time.

The bookmark file is usually stored in a file named:

```
lynx_bookmarks.html
```

However, you can give the bookmark file any name you wish by setting the Lynx Option Menu, which is discussed later in this chapter.

Table 3–2 covers the various bookmark commands.

Table 3–2 Lynx bookmark commands

Key	Function
A	Add the current link or Web page to your bookmark file
V	View your bookmark file
R	Remove an entry from your bookmark file

Adding a Bookmark

If you want to stick a bookmark in the current document or the currently selected hyperlink, just press A. Lynx asks:

```
Save D)ocument or L)ink to bookmark file or C)ancel (d,l,c) ?
```

If you press D then the URL of the current Web page itself is added to your bookmark file. If you press L then the currently highlighted hyperlink's URL is added.

NOTE: You may want to follow a link before you add it to your bookmark file to be sure it contains what you want.

Viewing Bookmarks

If you want to flip back to a bookmarked page, you can start Lynx with the bookmark file as its home:

```
lynx lynx_bookmarks.html
```

If you're already running Lynx, just press V to view your bookmark list, as in Figure 3–5. A listing of each Web page's title appears. Use the cursor keys to select the title you want and then press ENTER.

To delete a bookmark from your list, just select it using the arrow keys and then press R to remove it. Lynx yanks the selected Web page from your bookmark list.

LESSON #9: THE INDEX

Lynx has a neat one-key command that loads up a vast search index. Press I and the default index page loads up, as shown in Figure 3–6. In most cases, this is the CERN meta-index with links to subjects, geographical locations, and other indexes. Your system administrator can configure Lynx to

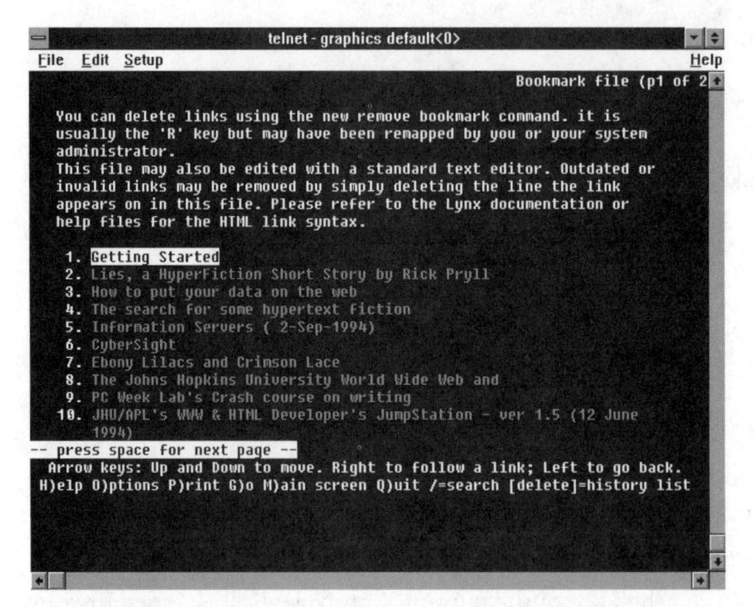

Figure 3–5 The bookmark file is a handy list of all your favorite Web pages

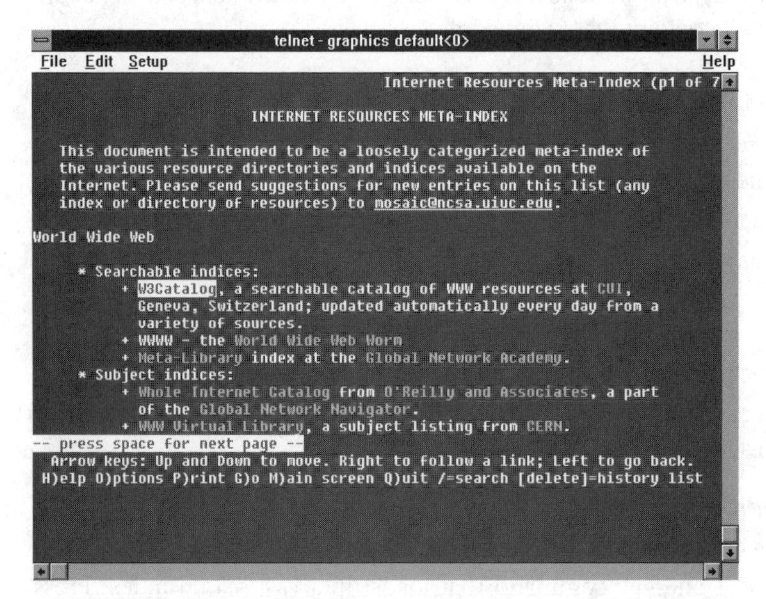

Figure 3–6 It's easy to find a given document with Lynx using the quick index command

call up any given Web index. If your prefer a different index, just add your favorite index to your bookmark list.

LESSON #10: SEARCHING

Often, a Web page is way too long to flip through. Instead, you'd rather search for a particular phrase or key topic. You may even be using a specialized search index, one that keeps most of its data behind the scenes and expects you to ask for what you want. Lynx makes searching of all sorts as easy as a keypress.

Page Searching

While viewing a Web page, just press the slash key /. Lynx asks you to type in a word or phrase. Depending on how your Options Menu is set (see the Options section, later in this chapter), the search can be case sensitive or case insensitive. You are warped to the first occurrence of your search term.

To search for the same word again, press N. Lynx finds the next occurrence of your search term and highlights it for you.

Index Documents

Many Web search utilities, encyclopedias, and dictionaries are a special type of Web page known as a search index. When you load up an index, Lynx tells you so at the bottom of your screen:

```
This is an index document.
```

To search an index document, press S. You can then type in a search term, phrase, or keyword. Lynx searches the index document and displays the results on your screen.

LESSON #11: SAVING A MULTIMEDIA FILE

Not every hyperlink leads to another Web page. Some may lead to an image, a movie, a sound, or a piece of software. A multimedia browser may be able to display the images, roll the movies, play the sounds, or access the software; Lynx cannot do any of these things. However, you don't have to miss out: you can download a multimedia file and use it later.

Whenever Lynx comes across a *binary* (nontext) file, you are asked if you want to download it. If you want to grab a copy, press D. Lynx retrieves a temporary copy of the file. If the file is long, the status of the download is displayed at the bottom of the screen. A list of options now appears. Most versions of Lynx only have one option:

```
Save the file to disk
```

There may also be alternate download methods such as Xmodem, Ymodem, Kermit, FTP, or Zmodem, which you can use to download the file directly to your home PC's hard disk.

Select the option you want. If you choose Save The File To Disk, then the file appears in your current directory. You can now exit Lynx and copy the file, edit it, or download it to your home PC.

NOTE: To download a file you can typically use Unix's *sz* (send Zmodem) command. For example, to send the file named *image.gif* you would type:

```
sz image.gif
```

You can now start your communications program's download command using the Zmodem protocol.

For example, an online art gallery probably won't look too interesting with Lynx. But if you come across the name of a painting you really, really want to see, you can select its hyperlink anyway. Press D to download the file and then save the image to your disk. Exit Unix and download the image using Zmodem. Voila! The image is now on your home PC's hard disk, and you can use your favorite image viewing software to check it out.

LESSON #12: FILLING OUT FORMS

Though Lynx is a simple text-only browser, it offers a very useful and recent feature: forms. A Web page with fill-out forms allows you to interact with the page, selecting options, filling in fields, checking check boxes, tapping radio buttons, or browsing pop-up menus.

The Form of a Form

If a form appears, you should be able to tell immediately, as in Figure 3–7. Fields you can fill in are followed by a blank row of underline characters:

```
What is your E-mail address?________________________________
```

To fill in a field, just use the cursor keys to select it. The message

```
(Text entry field) Enter text.
```

appears at the bottom of your screen. Type in any text you desire. When done, you can exit the field by using the up and down cursor keys or by pressing TAB.

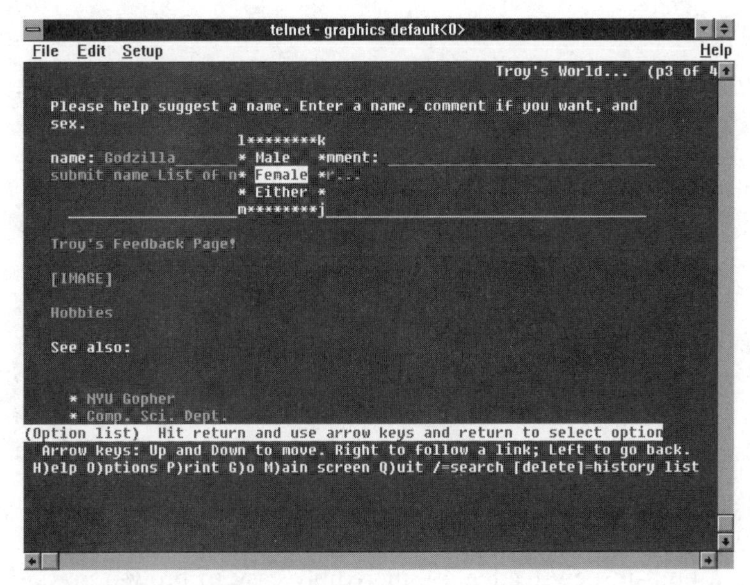

Figure 3–7 Full-featured fill-in forms in Lynx

Checkboxes and radio buttons look like empty parentheses:

```
( ) Check here if you want us to mail you more information.
```

When you select a check box, this message appears at the bottom of your Lynx screen:

```
(Checkbox field)
```

To check or uncheck the box, press → or ENTER. To exit the checkbox, press ←.

Pop-up menus look like boxes:

```
                                              +=============+
What type of computer do you have?            |   IBM 486   |
                                              +=============+
```

When you select a pop-up menu, Lynx displays the following message at the bottom of the screen:

```
(Option List)
```

Press ENTER to open up the menu. A list of items appears. Select the item you want using the up and down arrows and then press ENTER again.

When you're done filling in a form, there's usually a

```
[Submit]
```

button. Select this to send the form away.

User Validation

Lynx also supports the recent user validation feature. A Web page may have user validation if it is a commercial service, a private company's classified information, or an online service with subscribers like Hotwired.

If you follow a hyperlink that leads to a Web server requiring access authorization, a message appears at the bottom of the Lynx screen asking you for your username. Type it and press ENTER. Lynx then asks you for your password. Type it and press ENTER. If you provide valid information, the Web page loads up for you to see.

If you access another Web page on the same server that also needs a username and password, Lynx is smart enough to fill in these values for you automatically.

LESSON #13: USENET NEWS POSTING

Lynx also has a built-in newsreader. It's incredibly easy to browse newsgroups, read articles, and post messages of your own using Lynx. To kick off the newsreading features, you may select a *news* URL hyperlink that leads to a newsgroup. You can also open a *news* URL of your own. For example, if you want to check out the *alt.abortion* newsgroup, just press G to open a URL and then type:

```
news:alt.abortion
```

Selecting a Group

If you use a URL asking for all newsgroups—that is, you type in

```
news:*
```

you get a list of all applicable newsgroups, along with a short description of each. You can browse through the list with ↑ and ↓ or search with /. When you find the newsgroup you want, just select it and press ENTER.

Browsing Articles

Once you enter a particular newsgroup, a list of recent articles appears as in Figure 3–8. To view earlier articles, select the first hyperlink:

```
Earlier Articles
```

The title of each article is shown alongside the author's name. Select the article you want and press ENTER. If you want to post a message, scroll down to the very bottom of the Web page. The last hyperlink should be:

```
Post an article to this newsgroup.
```

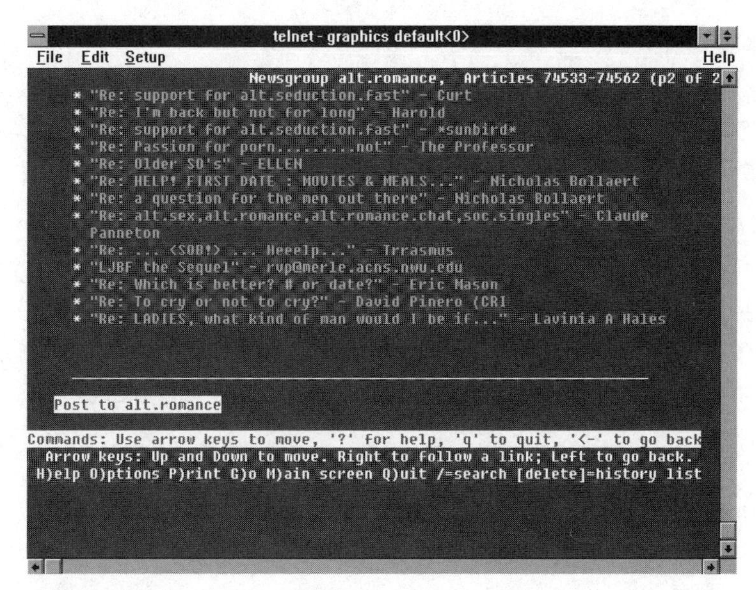

Figure 3–8 Lynx can act as a simple newsreader

Reading an Article

Any article you select is shown on your screen, like any other Web page. Scroll through it using ↑ and ↓. To go back to the list of articles, press ←.

NOTE: Lynx has a neat feature that highlights any e-mail address or URL within an article. To send a comment to the e-mail address or to access the URL, just select it as usual and press ENTER.

At the top of each article there are two response hyperlinks:

```
Reply to name
Reply to newsgroup(s)
```

To send a private message to the author of the current article, select the Reply To *Name* link, where *name* is replaced by the author's actual name. You can then send e-mail to the author's given address, as detailed in the next section. You are also usually asked if you'd like to include the current article as part of your reply. If you opt to do this, the current article appears in full, quoted before the rest of your e-mail message.

If you want to reply publicly, select Reply To Newsgroup(s). You can now post an article to the current newsgroup, as well as any other newsgroups the current article appeared in. You are also asked if you'd like to include the original message in your reply.

Posting an Article

If you decide to post a message, a special post screen appears. Type in your e-mail address when the system asks for it, and, if your posting is new, a subject. If you set up a specific Unix text editor in the Options Menu, then this comes up so you can create your article.

Otherwise, Lynx has a simple built-in editor. Type your message, pressing ENTER at the end of each line. When you finish your message, type period . on its own line and press ENTER. You are then asked:

```
Send this post? (y/n)
```

Press Y to post your message to the newsgroup. Otherwise, cancel the posting by pressing N.

LESSON #14: SENDING E-MAIL

The new *mailto* URL allows people to create hyperlinks that send off e-mail. If you access one of these hyperlinks, Lynx can act as its own e-mailer. You can also send mail to anyone by opening your own *mailto* URL. For example, to send mail to george@smartpants.edu, type G to open a URL and then type:

```
mailto:george@smartpants.edu
```

A special mailing screen appears, as shown in Figure 3–9. The address of the person to receive your comment appears at the top of the screen. Fill in a subject, your real name, and your e-mail address when the system asks for them.

NOTE: You can tell Lynx your e-mail address in the Options Menu, which is described later in this chapter. If Lynx knows your address, it fills it in automatically.

As before, if you set up a specific Unix text editor in the Options Menu, it comes up so you can type in your e-mail. If not, Lynx uses its built-in editor. Type your comments, being sure to press ENTER at the end of each line. You can cancel a comment as you write it by pressing CTRL-C. When you're done typing, type a period . by itself and then press ENTER. If you're using a separate text editor, exit it. Lynx then asks you:

```
Send this comment? (y/n)
```

Press Y to mail the comment away. If you change your mind, press N, and your comment goes into the trash.

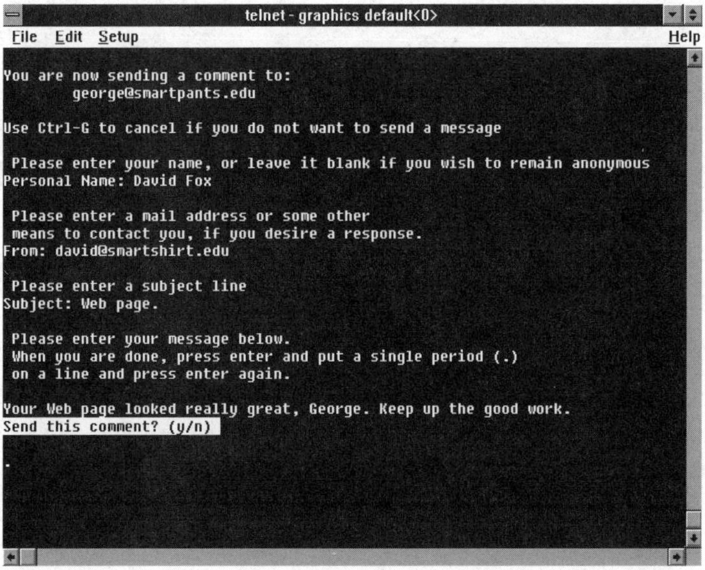

```
telnet - graphics default<0>
File  Edit  Setup                                                    Help

You are now sending a comment to:
        george@smartpants.edu

Use Ctrl-G to cancel if you do not want to send a message

 Please enter your name, or leave it blank if you wish to remain anonymous
Personal Name: David Fox

 Please enter a mail address or some other
 means to contact you, if you desire a response.
From: david@smartshirt.edu

 Please enter a subject line
Subject: Web page.

 Please enter your message below.
 When you are done, press enter and put a single period (.)
 on a line and press enter again.

Your Web page looked really great, George. Keep up the good work.
Send this comment? (y/n)
```

Figure 3–9 Using Lynx to send off a quick e-mail comment

If you're reading a Web page and want to make an urgent comment about it, you can also press c to send e-mail to whoever is in charge of the current page. However, if the creator or owner of the current page hasn't been specified you will get the message:

```
No owner is supplied for this page
```

And no mail is sent.

LESSON #15: THE LYNX OPTIONS MENU

You can customize a bunch of options by accessing Lynx's Options Menu. Simply press the o key, and the menu appears as in Figure 3–10.

The Options Menu has the following options:

- E)ditor
- D)isplay variable
- B)ookmark file
- P)ersonal mail address
- S)earching type

- C)haracter set
- V)I keys
- e(M)acs keys
- K)eypad as arrows or Numbered links
- U)ser mode
- L)ocal execution links

The following subsections discuss each option, but here are some general procedures, first. To select an option, type in the letter that's flagged with a parenthesis. For example, to change the Emacs keys, press M. This highlights the space next to the option, and you can now type any valid value in the highlighted field. To erase the current value, press CTRL-U. When you're done typing, press ENTER.

Some options allow you to choose from a list of values. To toggle between the values, press any key at all except ENTER. When you've selected the value you want, then press ENTER.

When you're done setting options, press → to save everything so it can be used in the future. To return to Lynx, press R.

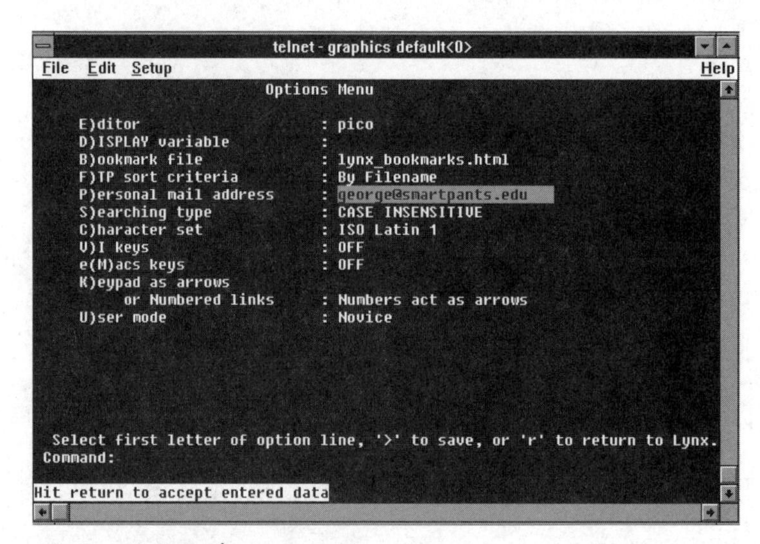

Figure 3–10 The Lynx Options Menu

Editor

Unix has many flavors of text editors, such as *vi, emacs,* or *pico.* You probably have your own favorite. Lynx calls up an editor to change HTML code, to send e-mail messages, or to post news articles. To make Lynx use your favorite editor, type its name in the slot. If you know the full pathname of your editor, type it in:

```
/local/usr/bin/pico
```

Bookmark File

You can give your Lynx bookmark file any name you wish—just type in a valid Unix filename. The file automatically ends with the *.html* extension. If you want to save your bookmark file in a different directory, type that directory's full path prior to the filename.

Personal Mail Address

Whenever you send e-mail or post a Usenet article, Lynx asks you to type in your e-mail address. To save this step, you can enter your personal e-mail address here. Type your full Internet address, the way someone from a remote system would if they wanted to send mail to you.

Searching Type

The Searching Type option only has two values:

- HTML Case Insensitive (default)
- HTML Case Sensitive

Whenever you use the slash key / to search a Web page, this option comes into play. If you select Case Insensitive, then the word you're searching for is displayed whether it appears in upper or lower case. If you choose case sensitive, then your search term must find an exact match. For example, the word "Cat" would not find "Concatenate."

VI Keys

This option only has two values: ON or OFF. If you set this to ON, the lowercase H, J, K, and L keys emulate the cursor arrows, becoming ←, ↓, ↑, and →, respectively. This is useful for devotees of the *vi* text editor who are used to using these keys to navigate.

Emacs Keys

Likewise, if you're a big fan of the Emacs editor, you can set this option to ON. You can now use the CTRL-P, CTRL-N, CTRL-F, and CTRL-B keys to move up, down, right, and left, respectively.

Keypad As Arrows or Numbered Links

If you don't like using the arrow keys to select hyperlinks, you can change this setting to Numbered Links. A number appears next to each hyperlink. For example, the first link on a page is followed by [1] and the second link is followed by [2]. To follow a link, you need to type its number and press ENTER. The WWW Web browser uses a similar process.

User Mode

Lynx normally displays two lines of help at the bottom of each screen, showing you which keys correspond to most popular commands. If you're just starting out, this is really helpful. If you're already used to Lynx, however, these lines can get annoying. You can use this option to tell Lynx how much help you need. You have three choices:

- Novice (default)
- Intermediate
- Advanced

The Novice mode shows you the help lines. Intermediate mode simply turns off the two lines of help and keeps the bottom of your page blank. The Advanced mode makes Lynx act much like Mosaic or Netscape: The URL of any link you select is shown at the bottom of the screen. This can help you predict where a hyperlink will take you before you make the jump.

Local Execution Scripts or Links

This advanced setting allows you to affect how local programs are accessed via Lynx. If you ask Lynx to run a separate script program, these options determine whether Lynx will actually run it. Some hyperlinks are also used to run a local script file.

NOTE: Your system administrator may have disabled this option altogether.

If the Local Execution Scripts option appears, you have three choices:

- HTML Always Off: Lynx cannot run local scripts. This is good if you're worried about security.
- HTML For Local Files Only: Lynx can only run script files that are located on the current machine.
- HTML Always On: All local scripts can be run.

You can read more about scripts in Chapter 15. If a script cannot be run, Lynx tells you so when the time comes.

WHAT NOW?

After using Lynx for a while, you may yearn for a multimedia Web browser. Try out SlipKnot to get a feel for the power of included graphics. The SlipKnot graphical browser can run on your Unix shell, as is, as long as you have Lynx installed. Read up about SlipKnot in Chapter 4.

Maybe you want to try to the real thing: A full-speed, full-powered multimedia browser. If you don't have a SLIP/PPP account or The Internet Adapter yet, you can read about these in Chapter 1. You can then install a graphical browser such as Mosaic or Netscape, covered in Chapters 5 and 6.

If you'd like to begin developing your own Web pages, jump to Part II, Creating Web Pages, which starts with Chapter 8.

4

SLIPKNOT

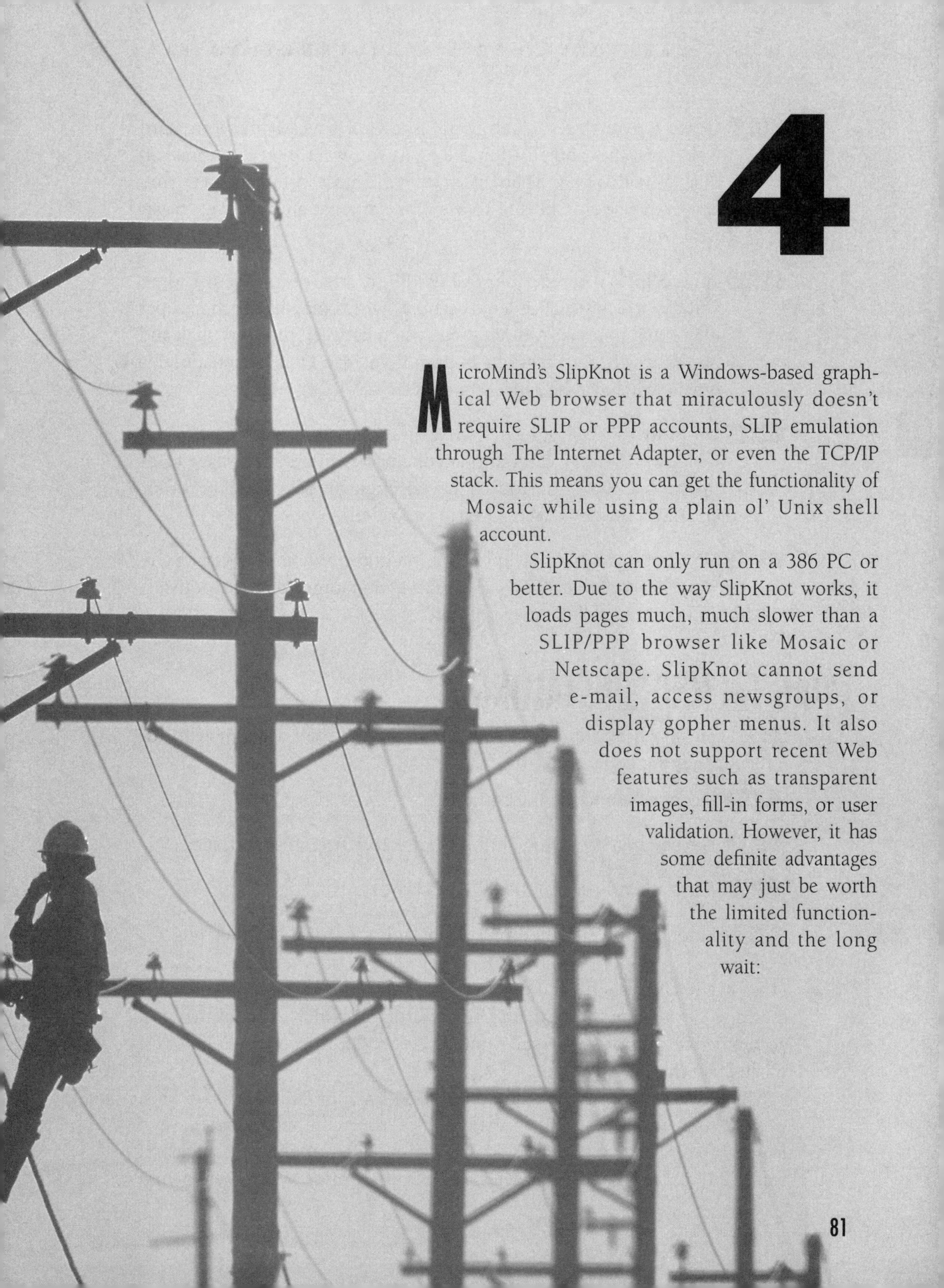

4

MicroMind's SlipKnot is a Windows-based graphical Web browser that miraculously doesn't require SLIP or PPP accounts, SLIP emulation through The Internet Adapter, or even the TCP/IP stack. This means you can get the functionality of Mosaic while using a plain ol' Unix shell account.

SlipKnot can only run on a 386 PC or better. Due to the way SlipKnot works, it loads pages much, much slower than a SLIP/PPP browser like Mosaic or Netscape. SlipKnot cannot send e-mail, access newsgroups, or display gopher menus. It also does not support recent Web features such as transparent images, fill-in forms, or user validation. However, it has some definite advantages that may just be worth the limited functionality and the long wait:

- Once you retrieve a Web page, SlipKnot saves it on your hard disk—graphics and all—for as long as you want to keep it. You can then view this page again, at any time, almost instantaneously. You can even use this feature to view or demonstrate real Web pages while offline.
- Since SlipKnot doesn't need SLIP/PPP in any way, shape, or form, you can use any dial-in Unix account, which may be much cheaper than other options. You can even switch between the Unix shell and SlipKnot with the press of a button. If you're a Unix aficionado, this quick-switch can be a great time saver.
- Up to five Web pages can be displayed simultaneously in different windows. You can scroll through one page while another page loads in the background. You can even click on several hyperlinks, creating a queue of Web pages to be loaded.
- SlipKnot has a built-in upgrading program. When new versions of SlipKnot come out, you can use this upgrading routine to quickly and easily install the new features.

TYING THE KNOT: INSTALLING

Before you install SlipKnot you must have a Unix shell account with the following requirements:

- A connection to the Internet
- The ability to write to your home directory from the Unix shell
- The standard Lynx or WWW Web browser
- Xmodem or Ymodem protocols for uploading and downloading

Most every Unix shell account meets these requirements. If something seems to be missing, check with your Internet provider to see if they can accommodate you. If you're still hunting, Appendix A gives you a good list of alternate Internet providers.

SlipKnot itself does not write to or reside on your Unix machine. Most of the action takes place on your home PC. Your computer must have at least 4 MB of memory, though 8 MB is recommended. You must also have at least 2 MB of free hard disk space. Since SlipKnot saves Web pages to your disk, it can often take up a lot of room. You should also have a 14,400 baud modem or better.

NOTE: SlipKnot is shareware. You have three months to evaluate it. If you decide to keep using SlipKnot after this period, you must register it for $29.95.

To install SlipKnot, run the SETUP.EXE program from the \WINDOWS\BROWSERS\SLIPKNOT\ directory of the enclosed CD-ROM. When asked, tell the setup program which directory you'd like to store SlipKnot in. The Setup program automatically copies all necessary files and creates a special Windows Program Manager group.

HOW SLIPKNOT SLIPS

SlipKnot was designed from the ground up for home PC users with modems. The SlipKnot package is actually comprised of two separate programs:

- SlipKnot Terminal
- SlipKnot Web

The Terminal calls up your Unix shell and gets everything started correctly. The Web program is the browser itself; it loads the Web pages, stores pages to disk, and displays pages. When you access a Web page, SlipKnot Web accesses SlipKnot Terminal. It calls a Unix Web browser such as Lynx or WWW to load up the page for it, and then downloads the page to your home PC. The SlipKnot Web then assembles the page, renders it, and shows you the completed results. If there are any graphics on the page, these get downloaded in the same way.

To get everything working correctly, then, you need to set up the Terminal and the Web separately.

SETTING UP THE TERMINAL

The first time you run SlipKnot, the setup routine guides you through several menus. In most cases, you need to set up the Terminal only once.

Setting Up the Host

The most important options are for the *host*. The host is the Unix machine you'll be using to access Lynx, WWW, the Web, and the Internet. The Host Settings window in Figure 4–1 may appear automatically. If not, you can access it by selecting Setup, Host.

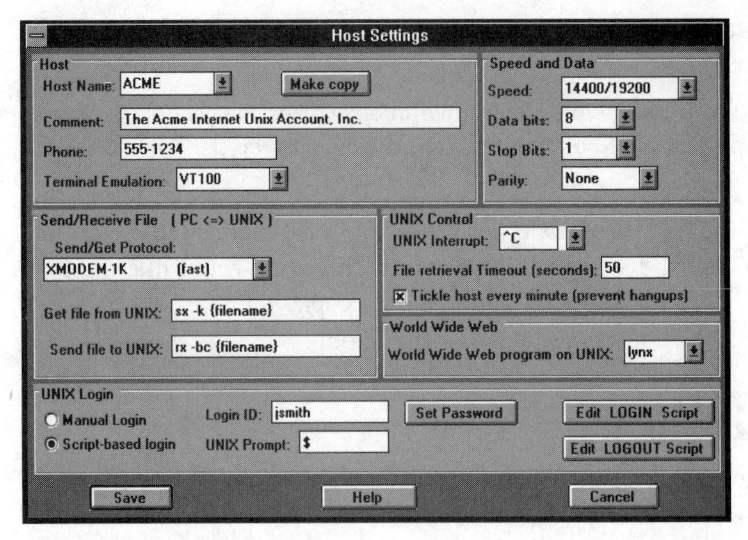

Figure 4–1 Everything SlipKnot needs to know about your host machine and isn't afraid to ask

SlipKnot shows you a sample host setup. Make a copy of this sample setup by pressing the Make Copy button. SlipKnot asks you for the name of your setup. Type in up to eight characters; you may want to use the name of your Internet provider, such as Netcom or Cyber. You can now begin filling in boxes or changing values. You can generally keep most values the way they are.

Host Options

Type in the full name of your Internet provider host or any other important info in the Comment slot. Type the host's full phone number in the phone slot. If you need to add a 9 to reach an outside line or a 1 to call a different area code, be sure to put that in. Select a Terminal Emulation type from the pull-down menu. Most providers expect VT-100 or ANSI.

Speed and Data Options

The Speed and Data options correspond to the type of modem you have. Select your modem's baud rate for the Speed entry. Unless your Internet provider tells you otherwise, you should generally use 8 Data bits, 1 Stop bit, and None for Parity.

Send/Receive File Options

You now need to select the type of protocol your Unix account will use to speak with your home PC. If you're not sure what protocols your host supports, try one of the two fastest protocols:

- Xmodem-1K
- Ymodem-Batch

If this doesn't seem to work, try the much slower protocols Xmodem Checksum or Xmodem CRC. The Get File From Unix and Send File To Unix commands should be updated automatically depending on the protocol you choose. Do not change these unless your Internet provider tells you to. If you still have problems retrieving files, contact your Internet provider and ask for the uploading and downloading command sequence.

NOTE: If you fill in your own Get File From Unix command, be sure to follow the command with the word *{filename}* in curly brackets. SlipKnot fills in the actual filename automatically.

Unix Control Options

You can generally keep the Unix control commands set to their default values. The Unix Interrupt is the keystroke that is pressed to stop a current command. In some rare cases, this may be DEL but it is almost always CTRL-C. File Timeout is the number of seconds SlipKnot will wait for a file to start transferring. This number should not be less than 50 seconds. Keep the Tickle Host Every Minute box checked if you want to make sure your Internet provider doesn't hang up on you while you're waiting for a file or a Web page.

World Wide Web Options

The most important host option is the World Wide Web program on Unix. You must have either Lynx or the WWW program installed. If you have both, select Lynx—it's faster. You can learn more about Lynx in Chapter 3. To check if these programs are available, call up your Internet host, get to the Unix prompt, and type

```
lynx
```

If you don't get a Lynx home page in response, check for the WWW browser by typing

```
www
```

If that command doesn't work either, consult your Internet provider. You will need one of these programs up and running before you can use SlipKnot.

Unix Login Option

You can now tell SlipKnot exactly how to log in to your Internet provider. Select Manual Login if you prefer to type things like your username and password yourself. You should select this the first time you try to run SlipKnot to be sure everything is working. When you log in manually, be sure to notice the exact process. Write down everything the computer tells you and everything you type. You can then easily duplicate this process using a script. If you decide to log in manually, your Host setup is done. Click the Save button.

If you want SlipKnot to log in automatically for you, select Script-Based Login. SlipKnot comes with a sample script that works for most every Internet provider. You can now fill in some common variables for the script to use when it tries to log in. Type your username in the Login ID box. Click the Set Password button and enter your password, twice. Fill in the type of Unix Prompt you like to work with. The prompt is usually a piece of punctuation that appears before you type any commands. Some possible Unix prompts are:

```
$
(graphics)%
WELCOME>
```

To figure out your Unix prompt, just log in to your Internet provider as usual. Notice what's written on each line before you type a command. The single letter or symbol that immediately precedes your typed command is the prompt.

You can now edit the login script using SlipKnot's built-in script language. Click the Edit LOGIN Script button. In many cases, you won't need to make any changes. Anything preceded by the pound sign (#) is a comment. Other commands you may need to use are:

- HTML send "*string*": Types out the given *string*. If you want to type a carriage-return after the string use the ^*M* symbol. For example: *send "shark^M"* is the same is typing the word shark and pressing ENTER.

- HTML waitfor "*string*" *seconds:* Waits a given number of *seconds* for your computer to write the word *string*.

HTML wait for prompt *seconds*: Waits a given number of seconds for your Unix prompt to appear.

Here's a copy of the sample script included with SlipKnot:

```
# ===================================
# Sample login script follows
# ===================================
#       Call up the Internet provider
dial
#       Wait 30 seconds for a connection
waitfor connect 30
#       Wait three seconds for the host to start working
delay 3
#       Wait for the word "ogin" as part of a Login prompt
send "^M" waitfor "ogin" 3 retry 5
#Send the specified user's login ID followed by a carriage-return
send loginid
send "^M"
#       Wait for the word "ssword" as part of a Password prompt
waitfor "ssword" 20
#       Send the specified password followed by a carriage-return
send password
send "^M"
```

If you wish, you can also change the logout script by clicking the Edit LOGOUT Script button. The default logout script works with 99 percent of Unix systems, so you generally do not need to worry too much about this.

When you're done configuring the login script to work with your Internet provider and all your other options look OK, click the Save button.

Setting Up Communications

The communications options let SlipKnot know exactly what type of modem you're using. The Communication window may appear automatically. If not, you can access it by selecting Setup, Communication.

The only commands you generally need to worry about are the Port and the Dialing Type. Set the Port to the communications port your modem is connected to (COM1 through COM4). The Dialing Type is set to Tone by default. If your phone lines don't support touch tones, select Pulse.

Setting Up the Terminal

Although you won't be using the SlipKnot Terminal to actually browse the Web, your screen might as well look as good as it possibly can while the Terminal dials your Internet provider and takes care of other loose ends. To change the current font, select Setup, Terminal Font. You can now pick the Font, Font Style, and Size of your choice.

If you select too large a font size, words may scroll off your screen. Too small a font size may be hard to read. You should use a monospaced font such as Courier, FixedSys, or Terminal to ensure that everything looks the way it should.

LESSON #1: CONNECTING

You're now ready to connect to your Unix account and give SlipKnot a spin. The SlipKnot Terminal is a full-featured communications program in itself. If you've used communications software before, this step should be easy.

Logging In

To log in, select File, Connect To Host or click the Connect button at the bottom of the screen. If you opted to log in manually, you must now type your username, password, and whatever else you usually type. If you're using a script to log in, SlipKnot runs through each command, one at a time. The current command is shown at the bottom of the screen. If something goes awry, it's easy to tell which command caused the problem.

NOTE: You can not make Setup changes while you are connected. If you need to alter a host option or change your login script, you must first disconnect.

If all goes well, your Unix shell prompt should appear. You can now type any Unix or Internet commands the way you normally would. To fire up the SlipKnot Web browser, select File, To World Wide Web, or press the World Wide Web button.

The first time you run the browser, SlipKnot sends several short script files to your Unix account. This takes a few seconds. If there's a problem, press the Help button. The SlipKnot program is pretty smart, and in most cases can tell you what options you need to change.

Logging Out

To quit your Unix connection, select File, Disconnect or click the Disconnect! button at the bottom of the screen.

LESSON #2: NAVIGATING

The SlipKnot Web browser itself now appears, as shown in Figure 4–2. It asks if you want to keep Web pages that were retrieved during previous sessions. If you have plenty of room on your hard disk, or if you think you'll want to access old pages again, select Yes. Otherwise select No to erase everything and clear up some disk space.

NOTE: You can pick and choose which Web pages you want to keep by fiddling with the history list, which is described later in this chapter.

The SlipKnot home page is now automatically loaded. The home page is stored on your hard disk, so it makes no difference whether you're currently connected to the Internet or not.

NOTE: If you don't want to waste time loading the SlipKnot page each time you start a session, select Configure, Paint Home Page On Startup? and uncheck it.

Along the top of the screen, you should notice five colorful shortcut buttons:

- Home: This house-shaped button displays SlipKnot's home page. This page provides general information about the SlipKnot program, the Web itself, and the Internet. You can jump from here to the What's New Page to find out about SlipKnot's latest features or upgrades.

- History List: The circular arrow button shows you a listing of every Web page you've ever retrieved. These documents are stored on your hard disk and can thus be loaded almost immediately. Select the title of the page you're interested in and it appears within a window on the SlipKnot surface.

- Bookmark: The folder button lets you retrieve a previously saved Web page.

- Next: The arrow button takes you to the next document window. You can show up to five Web pages at once, each in a different window. The arrow switches between them.

- Retrieve: The arrow pointing into the Web button lets you open and retrieve any URL.

Figure 4–2 The desktop for the SlipKnot Web program can hold up to five open pages at once

Up to five different Web pages can appear on your SlipKnot desktop. When you try opening a sixth, SlipKnot beeps at you, asking you to close one of the existing pages. When you're done browsing through a Web page, you can close it by double-clicking its control box in the upper left corner.

You can also minimize a Web page by clicking the minimize arrow at the top right of the window; the page then appears as a numbered icon at the top of the screen. To open up the page again, just click on its number. To browse a Web page, click anywhere in its window. You can now scroll through it with the scroll bar.

Following a Link

SlipKnot colors all hyperlinks blue. Hyperimages have blue borders. To follow a link, just click on it with the mouse. The Retrieve window appears, as in Figure 4–4, complete with the full URL of the destination Web page. Click the Retrieve From The Internet button to load up the new page.

When a page loads, you'll see a brightly colored status bar across your screen, as shown in Figure 4–3. This bar is the beginning of an *evolving window*—a window that will eventually become the Web page itself. At first, the bar says "Downloading" as it grabs the Web page itself. It then says "Analyzing" as it figures out how many images the page needs. The "Embedded Images" message lets you know that SlipKnot is retrieving the page's graphics. Finally, the word "Plotting" tells you that SlipKnot is creating the Web page itself.

Figure 4–3 This special evolving window tracks the status of a loading Web page

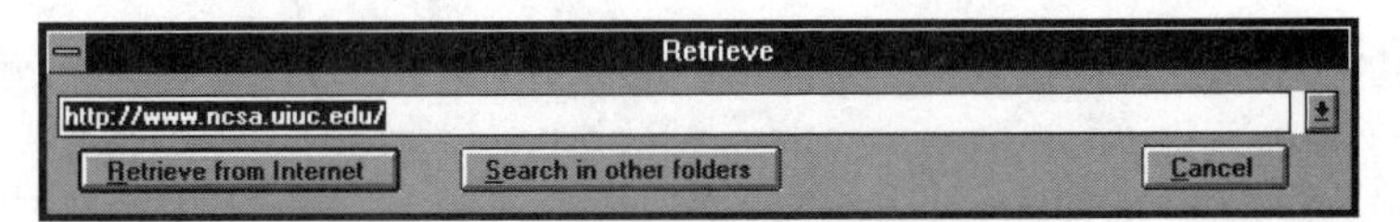

Figure 4–4 The Retrieve window lets you load up any URL on the Internet

This loading routine can take quite a while, especially if the Web page has lots of graphics. In the meantime, however, you can browse through other open pages. You can even click on other hyperlinks. SlipKnot keeps a queue of requested Web pages, and loads one page at a time. To see this list of jobs, select the See Jobs! menu. You can even select a waiting job from this list and click the Delete One Job button to get rid of it.

Snagging a Particular URL

If you want to load up a particular URL, simply click the Retrieve shortcut button or select Navigate, Get Document From The Internet. The Retrieve window appears, as in Figure 4–4. You can either type in a full URL or click the arrow to the right, in which case a full list of recently visited URLs appears.

Stopping a Load

At times, you may start loading an image but then decide you don't want it after all. Rather than waste time and energy, you can tell SlipKnot to cancel the current load. Just click on SlipKnot's icon (the large rainbow-like Web at the top of the screen). This halts the load. If any data was already retrieved, SlipKnot will try to analyze and display it.

You can also close a window as it evolves by double-clicking the control box in its upper left corner.

Loading a Local File

One of the nicest features about SlipKnot Web is that it works just fine without being connected to the Internet at all. This makes it a useful tool for Web developers. You can run the SlipKnot Web and test your own HTML Web pages. You can also easily load up any other Web page HTML source that you might have saved.

To load a local page, select Navigate, Display Local HTML File. Specify the Drive, Directory, and File and then click OK.

Retrieve Again!

The Retrieve Again! option at the top of each Web page's window comes in useful for a number of reasons:

- Reloading the same page with graphics retrieval turned on, if it previously was off.
- Loading up a page that, for whatever reason, arrived garbled.
- Reviewing a Web page you are designing. You can edit your Web page using an HTML editor, save it, and then switch over to SlipKnot. Load up your Web page by selecting Navigate, Display Local HTML File. You can now switch back to your HTML editor, change some things around, and then switch back to SlipKnot. All you need to do is click Retrieve Again! and the fruits of your efforts automatically appear.

LESSON #3: TURNING OFF IMAGES

To drastically speed up SlipKnot, you can request that images not be loaded. Uncheck the Retrieve Embedded Graphics item under the Configure pull-down menu. Whenever you load a new Web page, its images are replaced by the message:

```
Picture not retrieved.
```

If you want to see a page's images, just select the Configure, Retrieve Embedded Graphics item again. Click the Retrieve Again! menu at the top of the Web page's window. The same page is reloaded, this time complete with graphics.

LESSON #4: RETRIEVING MULTIMEDIA FILES

SlipKnot lets you retrieve not only Web pages but sounds, graphics, movies, or any other file or piece of software. If you click on a hyperlink that is meant to retrieve anything other than a Web page, SlipKnot displays the Viewer box as in Figure 4–5.

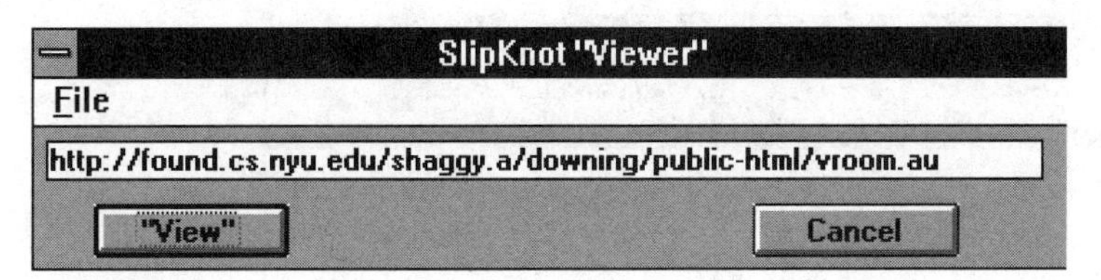

Figure 4–5 SlipKnot gives the option of "Viewing" or saving any multimedia file

Viewing

If you've previously configured a viewer that can handle the type of multimedia file being loaded (see the Configuring Viewers section, later in this chapter), then click the "View" button on the Viewer dialog box. SlipKnot loads your viewer, which promptly displays your image, plays your sound, or runs your movie.

Saving

If SlipKnot doesn't recognize the file type, or if you want to keep a copy of the file, you can select File, Save As from the Viewer dialog box. The file is now stored on your hard disk. You are now able to view, edit, or otherwise use the file at your leisure, at any time.

FTP Files

You can also use SlipKnot to retrieve anonymous FTP files. Whenever you ask for a specific file—directly or through a hyperlink—SlipKnot loads it up in the background. Once the file comes in, SlipKnot asks you what Drive, Directory and Filename to use when it stores the file.

LESSON #5: YOU'RE HISTORY

Whenever you retrieve a Web page, SlipKnot automatically saves it on your hard disk. You can quickly and easily "reload" the page at any time by using the history list. To sneak a peek at your history list, click the History List shortcut icon, or select Document, History. The This Session's Documents window appears, as in Figure 4–6.

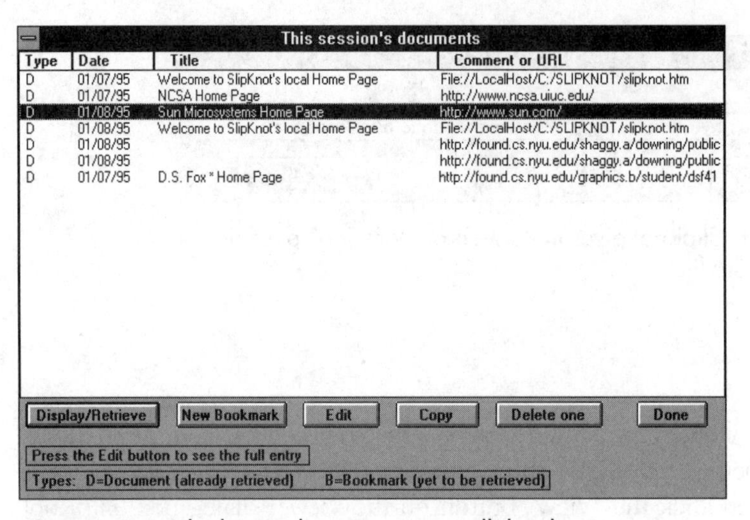

Figure 4–6 The history list can contain all the documents you've recently viewed, as well as Web pages from previous sessions

The history list shows you the Type (D for document, B for bookmark), Date, Title, and URL of all recently viewed Web Pages. To take another look at any Web page, select it and click the Display/Retrieve button. The page appears almost instantaneously.

Cleaning Up

Often, the same Web page appears numerous times on your history list. To delete duplicate pages or pages you're no longer interested in, select the page and click the Delete One button. SlipKnot asks you if you're sure. If so, click Yes. Your history list is now one item shorter.

Cleaning Up for Good

Every time you start a new SlipKnot session, you're asked if you want to erase your history list and start from scratch. Since history lists can tend to get long, tangled, and confusing, it's a good idea to do this every so often. Each Web page on a history list also takes up lots of disk space. It's silly to waste space with Web pages you'll never look at again in your life.

Instead, you should move pages you really like to their own folders. The next section discusses how to save cool documents.

LESSON #6: THE PERMANENT SAVE

As one becomes a seasoned Webber, one tends to gather a collection of favorite pages, pages returned to time and time again. Most Web browsers, including SlipKnot, allow you to keep a list of bookmarks to these favorite pages. SlipKnot, however, goes one step further, allowing you to save the actual pages themselves. This lets you retrieve your hippest pages at the snap of your fingers (or, at least, the click of your mouse).

Local Keepers: Saving a Complete Web Page

When SlipKnot saves a Web page, it collects all the relevant text and graphics files and stores this packet of information on your disk. It then creates a master file that coordinates this information and knows how to quickly load it up again. The history list is a temporary collection of these master files.

To permanently save a Web page, however, you need to create a special *save folder* for it. Folders act like directories, except they can have long names. To create or access a folder, select Documents, Folders or click the Folders shortcut icon. The folders dialog in Figure 4–7 appears.

NOTE: The (This Session's Documents) folder is the same thing as the history list.

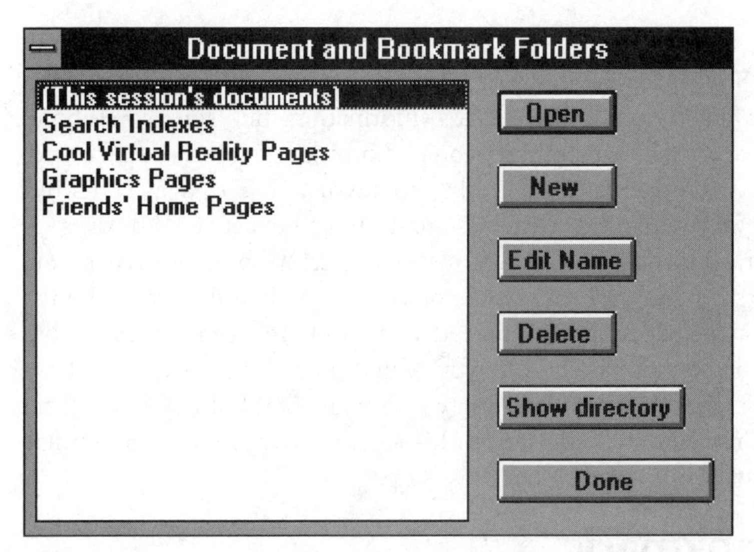

Figure 4–7 Organizing your favorite Web pages in folders for easy retrieval

To create a new folder, simply press New and type in a descriptive name. You can also use the Edit Name or Delete buttons to rename or erase any of your folders. To access one of your existing folders, just double-click on it or select the folder and then click on Open. A list of Web pages appears, identical to the history list in Figure 4–6.

Just as with the history list, you can Display/Retrieve a Web page or Delete one by selecting the page and clicking the appropriate button.

Saving a Page

To save a Web page in one of your folders, you have two choices:

- While browsing the Web page, select File, Save Document In Folder from the menu at the top of the window. A list of folders appears. Select the folder you want and click the Copy To button. You can now type in a Comment to help you remember what the page contains. Click Done and your page is now stored for easy access at any time in the future.

- Browse through your history list, as described in the previous section. If you want to save one of the Web pages to a more permanent folder, select that page and click Copy. Choose the folder you want and click the Copy To button.

Remote Keepers: Bookmarks

Maybe you want to save a Web page's information, but don't care about saving the page itself. Or perhaps you're running out of disk space and simply don't have room to save all your favorite Web pages. Luckily, SlipKnot allows you to create easy bookmarks in lieu of actual Web pages.

Bookmarks are stored in folders, just like other Web pages. When you view a folder's contents, a bookmark is preceded by a B in the Type column, whereas an actual document is preceded by a D. You can retrieve, edit, delete, or copy bookmarks the way you would other items in your folders. The only difference is, when you retrieve a bookmark, SlipKnot goes out to the Internet instead of to your hard disk—so you'll have to wait the normal amount of time while the Web page loads up.

Placing a Bookmark

While browsing a page, you can easily add it to your bookmark list. Simply select File, Save As Bookmark from the menu at the top of the Web page's window. A list of your folders appears. Select an applicable folder and click the Copy To button. You can now type in a descriptive Comment. Then click Done.

LESSON #7: CHECKING OUT THE SOURCE

Viewing how a Web document is put together can give you some great ideas when it comes to developing your own Web pages. SlipKnot makes it easy to save a Web page's HTML source.

While viewing a page, select File, Save As HTML File from the menu at the top of the Web page's window. You can now specify the Drive, Directory, and Filename where the source should be stored.

NOTE: Most HTML source files end with the *.HTM* extension when stored on a DOS PC.

When you save the HTML markup of a file, that's all you get—no images or other peripheral files. To view or edit the source markup, open up the .HTM file using your favorite text editor or HTML editor. You can then play around with the source markup, study it, or copy sections of it.

LESSON #8: CONFIGURING VIEWERS

If SlipKnot comes across a graphics, sound, or movie file it doesn't know how to display, it sends this file to an outside viewer program. To set up viewers, select Configure, "Viewers". The Viewers dialog box appears, listing any previously installed viewers, the type of files they can handle, and a short comment.

You can get rid of a viewer you no longer need by selecting it and clicking the Delete button.

Editing LView or WPLANY

SlipKnot comes configured to work with the LView graphic viewer and the WPLANY sound viewer. You should install these two viewers (see Chapters 12 and 13 for instructions). To set up the specifics, select one of the viewers and click Edit.

The Edit Viewer dialog box appears, as in Figure 4–8. You now need to tell SlipKnot exactly where your WPLANY or LVIEW31 program is stored. Click the Browse For Program Name button. You can now specify the Drive, Directory, and Filename of the relevant viewer. When you find the program you want, click OK. To finalize the viewer setup, click the Save button.

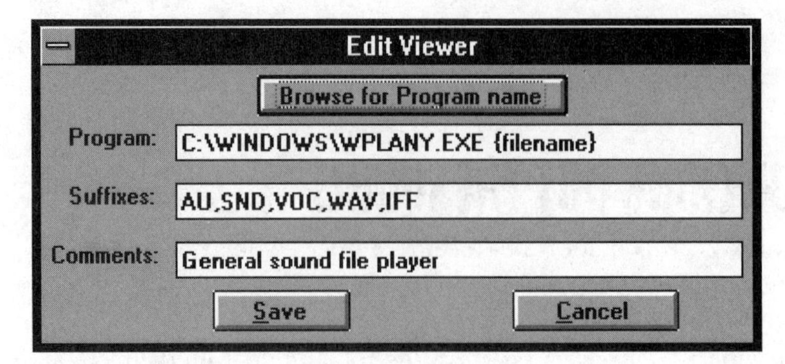

Figure 4–8 Setting your viewers up so that they can actually view

Adding a New Viewer

To configure a new viewer, such as MPEGplay, select the New button while in the Viewers dialog box. The New Viewer dialog appears, similarly to the Edit Viewer dialog in Figure 4–8.

First, you need to specify the exact filename of your viewer in the Program box. Click the Browse For Program Name button, select the appropriate Drive, Directory, and Filename, and then click OK. The full pathname of the file should appear, followed by the word *{filename}*. Be sure that *{filename}* always follows the name of your viewer, since this indicates that SlipKnot should tell the viewer what file to view.

NOTE: If the Viewer program is in your path (for example, stored in the C:\WINDOWS directory), then you need only enter the name of the viewer by itself, followed by the *{filename}* tag.

You can now fill in the Suffixes. These are the typical extensions of the files your viewer is able to access. For example, if you installed MPEGplay, the suffix would be MPG. Separate each suffix with a comma. A good list of valid suffixes can be found in Table 2–1.

Finally, you can type in any Comments you wish. This can help you remember what the viewer's full name is, what limitations it has, etc. When done, click Save. The next time SlipKnot comes across a file with the suffix you indicated, it will call up the viewer you just configured.

LESSON #9: MAKING IT LOOK PRETTY

Now that you're an expert at navigating SlipKnot, you can play around with some of the cosmetic features. This way, each Web page can have the look you want to give it.

Setting Colors

Select Configure, Colors to turn your Web pages the hue you think they should be. You now have two choices:

- HTML Background Color: To set the background of your Web pages. The default is gray. Be sure to pick a color that makes overlaid text easy to read.
- HTML Link Color: To set hyperlinks and borders around hyperimages. The default is blue. Pick something that stands out.

In either case, a Color dialog pops up. You can choose from 48 basic colors or you can define 16 of your own custom colors. Click on the color you want and then choose OK.

Customizing Fonts

Most Web browsers decide what each heading, text style, or other emphasized text within your Web pages should look like. SlipKnot allows you to customize these fonts to appear however you desire.

When a Web page is loaded, SlipKnot reads through the HTML code creating different elements such as headings, lists, or block quotes. You can use the custom fonts feature to decide how SlipKnot renders each separate element.

NOTE: You cannot change fonts with a Web page on the screen. Close all Web pages before you begin.

To define your own fonts, select Configure, Screen Fonts. You now have the following choices:

- HTML Title: The Web page's title
- HTML Header1: The first, main heading
- HTML Header2: The second subheading
- HTML Header3: The third subheading
- HTML Header4: The fourth subheading
- HTML Header5: The fifth subheading
- HTML Header6: The sixth subheading
- HTML Monospaced: An item meant to be drawn in typewriter-like print

HTML Address: A person's address

HTML List Item: An item in a numbered or bulleted list

HTML Block Quote: A separate chunk of quoted text

Once you select one of the above elements, the Font dialog box appears. Select the Font (from the fonts you have installed on your system), Font Style (Regular, Italic, Bold, or Bold Italic), Size (generally ranging from 8 to 72), Effects (Strikeout or Underline), and Color (select from 16 basic colors). You can see how the font will look by checking out the Sample box.

Printer Fonts

SlipKnot can print out any Web page's text if you select File, Print. Using the exact same procedure as with screen fonts, you can customize these printer fonts. Select Configure, Printer Fonts to define each separate element.

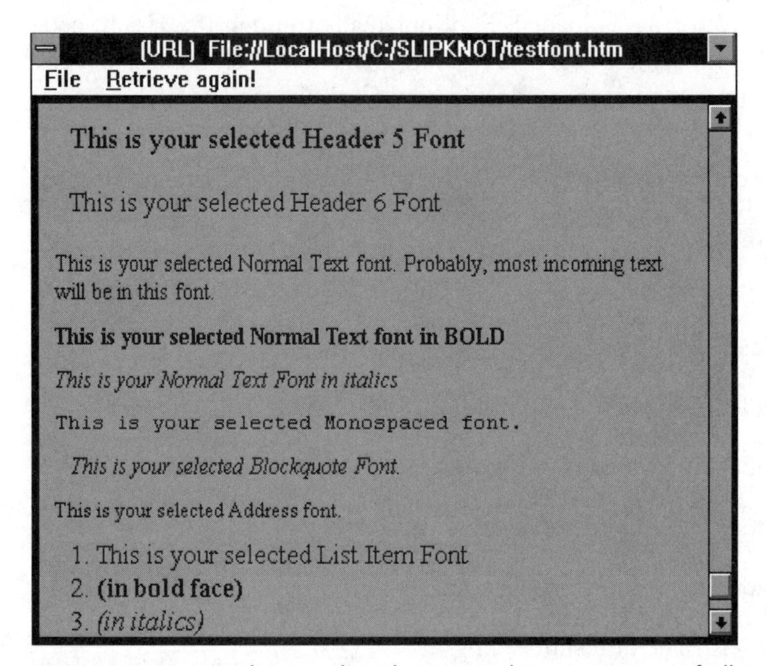

Figure 4–9 A Web page that shows you the appearance of all relevant screen fonts

Viewing the Results

SlipKnot has a special font-test Web page, as shown in Figure 4–9. To load this up, access the SlipKnot home page and click the To Test Your Screen Fonts *(Click Here)* hyperlink.

If you don't like the way something looks, you can now close this font-test page and reconfigure your screen fonts. To quickly reload the font-test page, select it from the history list.

Background

SlipKnot puts each Web page in its own window, so the main navigation controls are limited to the top of the screen. Since you're in a window, you can choose to run SlipKnot with an invisible background. This makes it easy to access other Windows programs, such as your word processor, HTML editor, or communication programs.

Select Options, Black Background? to turn off the default background and make the screen look something like Figure 4–10. If your screen appears too cluttered, you can turn the background back on by reselecting the Black Background? item.

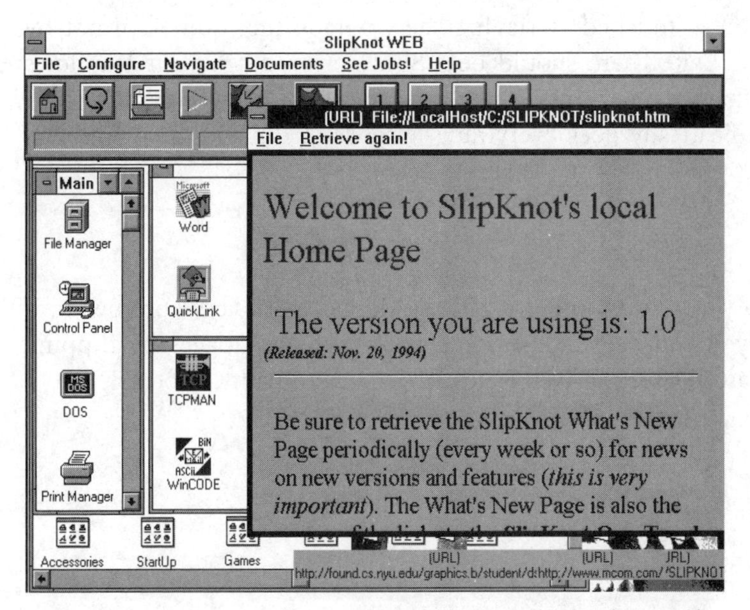

Figure 4–10 Using SlipKnot with a transparent background

LESSON #10: SWITCHING TO THE TERMINAL

SlipKnot makes it easy to switch back to the SlipKnot Terminal program and regain control of your Unix account. To close out the SlipKnot Web program, select File, Temporarily Return To SlipKnot Terminal.

You can now use your Unix account to manipulate files, run gopher, check a WAIS database, finger somebody, talk to a friend, or whatever. To go back to the Web, simply click on the World Wide Web button. You can now access your history list and reload any pages you lost.

LESSON #11: UPGRADING

SlipKnot comes with a unique one-touch upgrade feature. Whenever a new version of SlipKnot comes out, you can easily download the necessarily files and reconfigure SlipKnot to use the latest set of features.

To get the latest version of SlipKnot, view the SlipKnot Local Home Page. This page usually loads automatically. If not, you can access it by hitting the Home shortcut icon. Click on any hyperlink to the SlipKnot What's New Page. If there's a new version announced, you can usually click on a hyperlink that automatically retrieves the Upgrade file for you.

When you've finished retrieving the Upgrade file, quit SlipKnot by selecting File, Exit. There should be a SlipKnot group in your Windows Program Manager. Open this group and select the New Upgrade icon. SlipKnot automatically does everything it needs to do. The next time you run SlipKnot, you'll be using the latest version.

WHAT NOW?

In Chapter 5 you'll look closely at NC SA Mosaic, a classic Web browser. If you prefer, you can begin developing your own Web pages by flipping forward to Part II: Creating Web Pages, which begins with Chapter 8.

5

NCSA MOSAIC

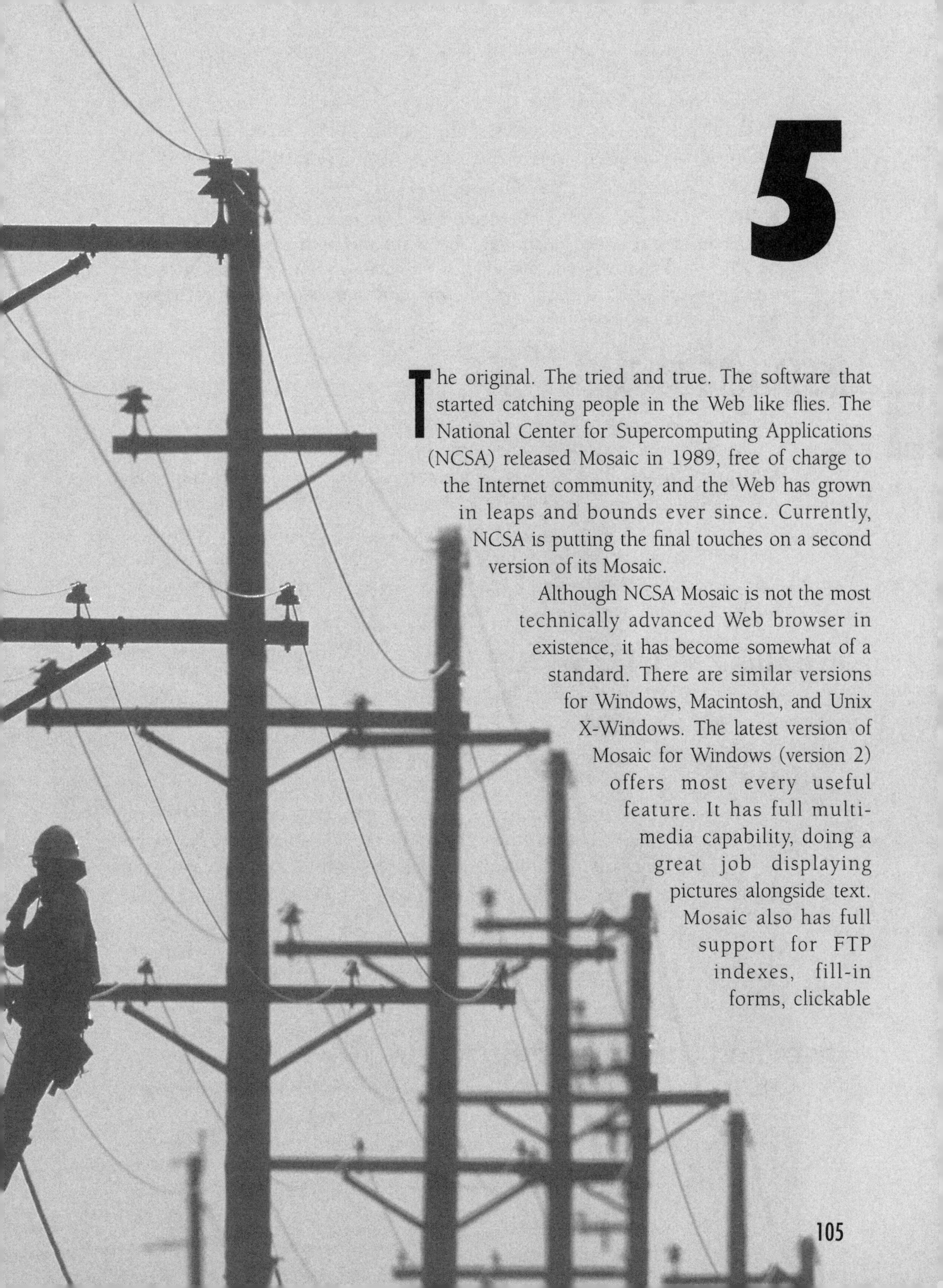

5

The original. The tried and true. The software that started catching people in the Web like flies. The National Center for Supercomputing Applications (NCSA) released Mosaic in 1989, free of charge to the Internet community, and the Web has grown in leaps and bounds ever since. Currently, NCSA is putting the final touches on a second version of its Mosaic.

Although NCSA Mosaic is not the most technically advanced Web browser in existence, it has become somewhat of a standard. There are similar versions for Windows, Macintosh, and Unix X-Windows. The latest version of Mosaic for Windows (version 2) offers most every useful feature. It has full multimedia capability, doing a great job displaying pictures alongside text. Mosaic also has full support for FTP indexes, fill-in forms, clickable image maps, transparent graphics, and most types of styles. Mosaic has even sprung ahead of the crowd as one of the first Web browsers to allow custom tables.

NOTE: The second version of Mosaic is in beta release. This means certain commands are disabled, there tend to be strange bugs, and other features may not work the way you intended. If the latest version of Mosaic doesn't seem to work at all on your system, you can retrieve an older version at ftp://ftp.ncsa.uiuc.edu/Mosaic/.

INSTALLING MOSAIC

The latest version of Windows Mosaic was built to run under Windows NT or Windows 95, both 32-bit operating systems. This is all well and good, but poor old Microsoft Windows 3.1 and Windows for Workgroups are only 16-bit operating systems. To run Mosaic, you'll need to turbocharge Windows so that it can run 32-bit applications. Fortunately, Microsoft distributes a free 32-bit emulator called WIN32S-OLE. Once you have the Win32S files installed in your Windows directory, they are automatically loaded each time you start Windows.

Installing WIN32S-OLE

You can find WIN32S-OLE (1.20) at one of the following sites (the filename is usually WIN32S.ZIP):

```
ftp://ftp.microsoft.com/developer/DEVTOOLS/WIN32DK
ftp://ftp.ncsa.uiuc.edu/Mosaic/Windows
```

To install everything, unzip the WIN32S file in a temporary directory and then run the SETUP.EXE file. The setup program automatically copies all the necessary files to the C:\WINDOWS\SYSTEM\WIN32 directory and configures the Windows drivers. Then it exits Windows and restarts it, to kick the Win32S software into effect.

To be sure Win32S installed properly, try running the enclosed solitaire game. If this game doesn't seem to work, repeat the installation. Be sure you specify a legal drive and directory, and be sure to agree to restart Windows.

Installing the Mosaic Browser

NCSA Mosaic itself can be downloaded from NCSA. Check out the Mosaic homepage at:

```
http://www.ncsa.uiuc.edu/SDG/Software/Mosaic
```

You can FTP any version of Mosaic by switching to the Unix, Mac, or PC directory under:

```
ftp://ftp.ncsa.uiuc.edu/Mosaic
```

Mosaic usually comes as an executable file named something like WMOS20A9.EXE. Unzip or execute this file into a temporary directory. Again, run the SETUP.EXE program using the Windows Program Manager. The installation program creates a directory (usually C:\MOSAIC) and creates all the necessary files. The MOSAIC.INI file, which handles most Mosaic settings, is copied to your Windows directory.

To run Mosaic, just double-click on its icon.

NOTE: Be sure to check NCSA's Mosaic home page every so often for latest release information.

LESSON #1: NAVIGATING USING THE VIEW WINDOW

When you first run Mosaic, its distinctive View Window appears. At the top of the screen are two fields, one holding the current Web page's Document Title and one telling you the Document URL. Below these indicators you get a *toolbar* with useful buttons.

NOTE: If you want to display more of the current Web page, you can get rid of the toolbar, the Document Title, the Document URL, or the status bar. Just deselect Show Current URL/Title, Show Status Bar, or Show Toolbar from the Options pull-down menu.

You can access most useful Mosaic commands with one click of the toolbar. The toolbar includes the following buttons:

- Open: Allows you to enter a new URL or select a Web page from your hotlist.
- Save: Saves the current Web page to disk.
- Back: Loads up the last Web page you visited.
- Forward: Loads up the next Web page in your history list.
- Reload: Loads the current Web page again.
- Home: Returns you to your default Web page.
- Copy: Copies the currently selected text from your Web page to the clipboard.

- Paste: Pastes copied text.
- Find: Searches the current Web page for a given search term.
- Print: Prints out the current Web page.
- About: Learn about NCSA Mosaic.

Following Hyperlinks

When you first run NCSA Mosaic, it loads up the Mosaic Home Page by default. You can tell Mosaic to start at a more suitable home page. See the Configuring Mosaic section, later in this chapter.

Figure 5–1 shows a sample Web page. You can scroll through the page by using the scroll bar or by pressing PGUP or PGDOWN. Underlined blue text generally indicates a hyperlink, as does a blue border on an image. When you move your cursor over a hyperlink, the arrow changes into a pointing finger. The URL that the hyperlink will load is then displayed at the bottom of the screen, in the status bar.

To follow a hypertext or hyperimage link, just click on it. The link will load up a new Web page, a graphic, a movie, an audio file, or it will send you around the Internet to a telnet, FTP, or gopher site.

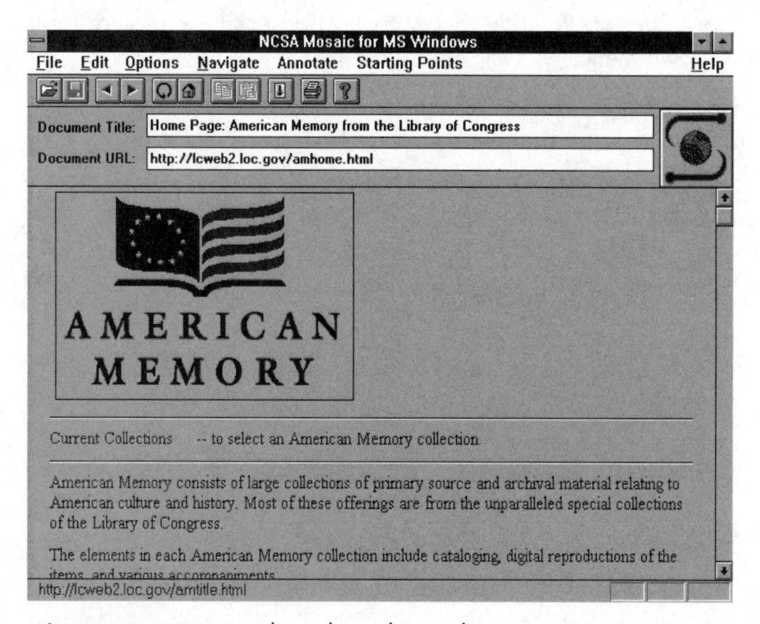

Figure 5–1 A sample multimedia Web page in NCSA Mosaic

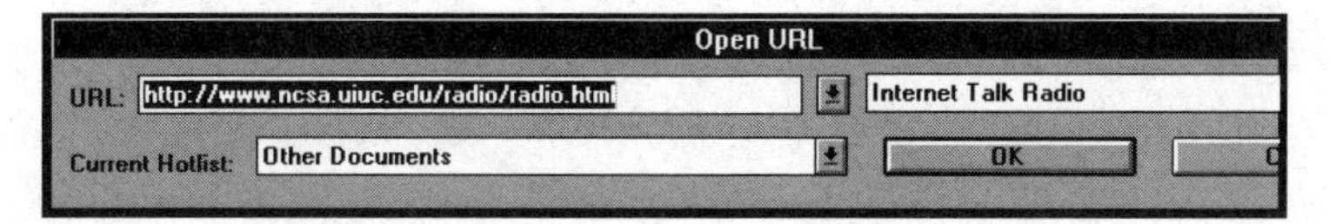

Figure 5–2 The full-featured Open URL dialog box

If you follow a link and don't really like what you see, you can return to the previous page by clicking the Previous button in the toolbar.

Moving to a Specific URL

To load a specific Web page, just type a valid URL in the Document URL field at the top of the screen and press ENTER. You can also select File, Open URL and then type in the desired URL. The Open URL dialog box, shown in Figure 5–2, also includes a built-in menu of hotlists that allows you to easily jump to your favorite pages. See the section called The Hotlist, later in this chapter.

The Right Mouse Button

The latest version of Mosaic allows you to perform lots of complicated commands simply by clicking the right mouse button. Many of these commands are useful for the Web publisher, letting you know things about a given entity such as its URL, size, or type.

If your cursor is pointing to some ordinary text (not an image, hyperlink, or hyperimage), then the following choices appear in a pop-up menu:

- Save to Disk: Allows you to save the current Web page to disk.
- Create an Internet Shortcut: Saves the current page's URL to a file on your hard disk.
- Spawn Mosaic From Anchor: A new window opens up containing the current Web page. This allows you to view several Web pages at once.

Clicking on an Image

If you click on an image, a slightly different menu appears:

- Save Image: Allows you to save the current image to your disk, as either a Windows BMP bitmap or the Remote Site Format, usually a GIF.

HTML Image Information: A box appears with fields describing the image—URL, Size, Last Modified (date), MIME Type, Server Type, and MIME version number.

Clicking on a Hyperimage

If the image you right-click is a hyperimage, a menu appears with Save Image and Image Information options. You also have several more choices:

HTML Load Anchor to disk: The resource the current link leads to will be saved to your disk, whether it's a Web page, another image, or some other sort of multimedia file.

HTML Anchor Information: A box appears with fields describing the link's destination anchor—URL, Size, Last Modified (date), MIME Type, Server Type, and MIME version number.

HTML Create Internet Shortcut: The anchor's URL is saved to your disk in a URL file.

HTML Spawn Mosaic From Anchor: The anchor is opened into a new window, letting you view the current page and the destination Web page side by side.

Clicking on Hypertext

The right mouse button is perhaps most useful when you click it while pointing to a hypertext link. Along with Anchor Information, Create Internet Shortcut, and Spawn Mosaic From Anchor, you also have the option to Load Anchor To Disk, which saves the destination URL to your hard disk.

Halting: the Secret button

When a Web page loads, you'll probably notice the neat NCSA logo in the top right corner: The globe spins and the "S" seems to transmit yellow sparks. At the bottom of the screen, you're told whether Mosaic has connected to the remote URL, what percentage of the HTML document has loaded, and how many GIF images or other resources have arrived.

This logo is actually a useful button. If a Web page is taking way too long to load, you can abort the load by clicking on the logo. If any text or graphics were already loaded into memory, these will be displayed.

LESSON #2: IGNORING IMAGES

The most lengthy part of Webbing is the loading of graphics. Text can zoom, and hyperlinks are never a problem, but inlined images can make your Web pages load sluggishly. Slow modems, slow computers, or busy Internet connections all magnify this problem.

Mosaic allows you to switch off graphics, vastly increasing your system's performance. Simply select Options, Display Inline Images to remove the check mark next to it.

The next time you load a Web page, all images are replaced by a tiny Mosaic logo and the word *Image,* as shown in Figure 5–3. You still get the blue borders surrounding any hyperimages; just click on the logo to follow the link. If you come across a page that seems to contain images to die for, select Option, Display Inline Images again and then click the Reload toolbar button, or select Navigate, Reload.

NOTE: Reloading is also useful if the current Web page happens to appear skewed or with garbage instead of text. This can sometimes happen if Mosaic comes across a bad connection.

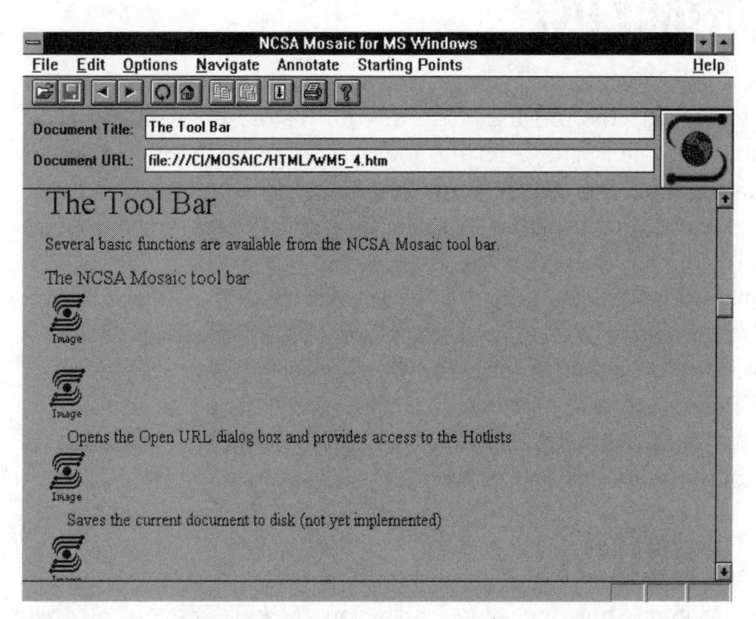

Figure 5–3 When graphics aren't included, loading a Web page can happen dozens of times more quickly

An even nicer feature allows you to load just the images you want to see. Move your mouse arrow to the image icon and click the *right* mouse button. The selected inline image loads up, but all the other icons stay put.

LESSON #3: MULTIMEDIA FILES

NCSA Mosaic can handle any hypertext HTML document or GIF graphics. Most other formats, however, must be passed on to a viewer. See the Configuring Viewers section, later in this chapter, for information on setting up these external applications.

If you try to load a document and Mosaic doesn't know what to do with it, it asks if you want to save the resource to disk. Select Yes. The Save As box appears. Specify a Drive, Directory, and Filename and then click OK.

NOTE: Many Web pages or other documents may have long or complicated Unix filenames. Any file you download is automatically converted to fit within the DOS filename standard (eight-letter filename, three-letter extension). If a Unix filename has more than one segment separated by a period, the last segment becomes the file extension. As an example, the file *History.Of.The.World.txt* becomes *HISTORY.TXT.*

LESSON #4: HISTORY LIST

Any time you load a Web page during a Web session, Mosaic stores it in the history list. To move to the previous item in your history list, you can click the Back button (the left arrow) on the toolbar. To go to the next item in your list, if applicable, you can click on the Forward (right arrow) button. You can also move through the list by selecting Navigate, Back or Navigate, Forward.

Many times, however, you don't just want to check out an adjacent Web page; you want to review a screen you saw 10 or 15 Web pages ago. To view your entire history list, as shown in Figure 5–4, select Navigate, History.

The screen lists the URLs of every page you've visited this session, in the order you visited them. To reload a page, select it and click on Load. If you decide not to use the history list after all, click Dismiss.

LESSON #5: THE HOTLIST

History lists are great, but once you finish your Mosaic session, all that information disappears. A *hotlist* allows you to keep track of your favorite Web pages, files, or other Internet resources. You can organize these lists

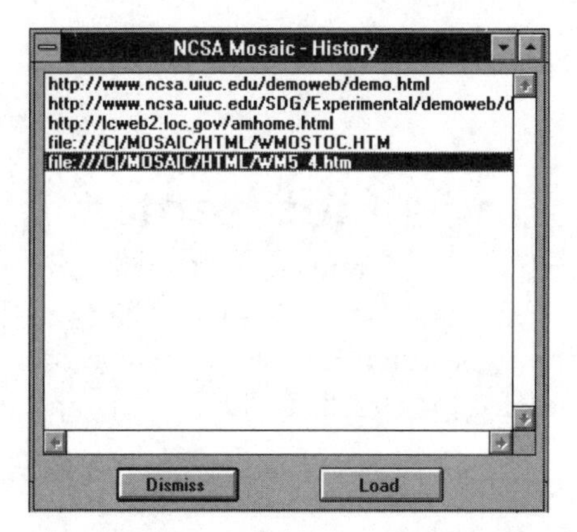

Figure 5-4 The history list reminds you where you've been, and lets you quickly reexperience a blast from the past

and make them available as an item in your Mosaic pull-down menu. In other words, once you add a Web page to your hotlist, getting to it just takes a few clicks. This is similar to placing a bookmark at an important page in a very thick book.

NCSA comes with several built-in hotlists. Select the Starting Points menu to check some of these out. There are Internet starting points, demo documents, NCSA information, other Web resources, famous home pages, famous gopher sites, and even useful search tools such as Finger, Whois, and Archie. Some items in the menu are followed by a small black arrow. This means that the current item is the heading of yet another menu of items. When you find the page you want, just select it. The page is loaded up ASAP.

You can also access an item from your hotlist by selecting File, Open URL, or pressing CTRL-O, or selecting the Open button from the toolbar. The Open URL dialog box appears. Select the Hotlist pop-up menu and select the category of hotlist you're interested in. You can now select one of the two upper pop-up menus: the list of URLs on the left or the corresponding list of Web page titles on the right. Once you decide on a page, select it and click OK.

Mosaic includes two basic types of hotlists:

HTML The Quicklist: The hottest of your hot pages. Pages in your quicklist are ones you're likely to access all the time.

HTML User-configurable menus: Organized categories for different hotlists.

Getting Hot: Quickly Creating a Hot Item

Whenever you come across a page you think you'll want to visit again, add it to the hotlist by selecting Navigate, Add Current To Hotlist. The Web page is tacked onto the end of the currently selected hotlist. To change the current hotlist, open the Open URL dialog box (select File, Open) and choose a hotlist from the pop-up menu.

NCSA comes configured with many categories of hotlists. If you want, however, you can create your own categories. This way you can keep lists of your favorite music pages, or your favorite educational pages, or the most useful search indexes.

Customizing Your Mosaic Menu

To add, edit, or delete an item from your menu of hotlists, select Navigate, Menu Editor. The Personal Menus window appears, as in Figure 5–5.

All your current user-configurable menus (including the Quicklist) appear in the Menus box. The main menu is Starting Points. Typical submenus–which are indented in the list–include World Wide Web Info, Home Pages, Gopher Services, and Other Documents. To work with one of these menus, select it. A list of all that menu's items appears to the right, in

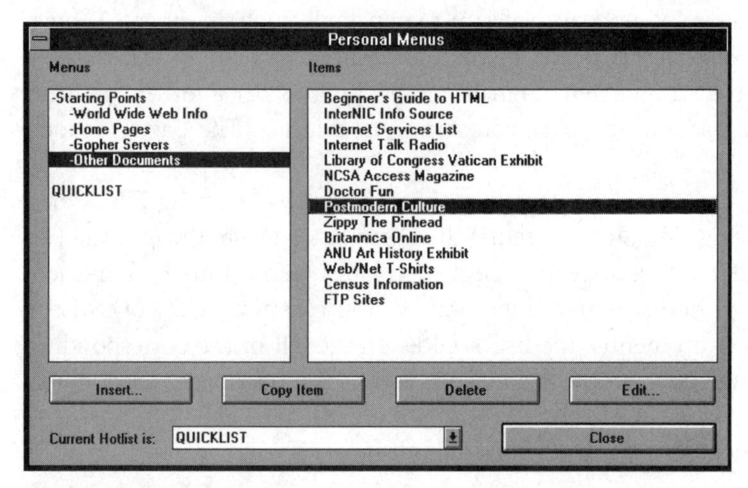

Figure 5–5 Customizing your menus puts your favorite Web pages at your fingertip, literally

the Items box. Some items are preceded by an arrow (>). This indicates that the menu item is actually another menu.

Working with Items

To work with an item, just select it and click Edit. The Title and URL of the item appear in the Edit Item dialog box. If you wish, you can change the item's title or URL address. To delete an item from your hotlist, select it and click Delete. You are asked if you're sure. If you are, click OK.

You can also add an item to the currently selected menu—just click Insert. The Add Item dialog box appears. If you have a Web page currently loaded, then that page's Title and URL appear in the dialog box. You can also type in a Title and URL of your own. When everything is filled in properly, click OK.

NOTE: Each menu can have up to 40 entries.

When you add an item, it appears at the end of the currently selected menu. If you wish to insert it someplace else, select the location you want from the Items list before you click Insert. Your new hot item will appear directly before the currently selected item.

If you want to copy a current hotlist item and move it to a different menu, select it and click the Copy Item button. You can now delete the item from the old list by clicking Delete. Move to the menu where you want to place your new item and select Insert. When the Add Item dialog box appears, the URL and Title boxes will automatically include the hotlist item you just copied. Simply click OK.

Creating Menus

One of Mosaic's premiere features is the ability to create customized menus and submenus. To create a top-level menu, select the blank space in the Menus list between the list of user-configurable menus and the QUICKLIST line. To create a menu within an existing menu, just select that menu's name from the Menus list.

Now click the Insert button. The Add Item dialog box appears. Click the Menu radio button and then type in a descriptive Title for your menu. When you're done, click OK. Your new menu now appears, indented where it belongs, in the Menus list. You can now begin adding or copying items to your new menu.

You can easily delete a menu by selecting it and clicking the Delete button. A dialog box appears, double-checking. If you're sure you want to delete the menu, click OK. The menu, all its items, and all its submenus are then erased. You cannot delete the quicklist.

The Separator

With all these menus within menus, your hotlists can get hard to manage. Separator lines help you divvy up a menu into subcategories of its own. Click on an item in the Items list and then select Insert. Select the Separator radio button and then click OK. A separator line appears directly over the currently selected item.

When you open up your Mosaic menu, each of your separator lines runs entirely across the menu, giving it the appearance of being two or more separate boxes.

The Quicklist

The quicklist does not appear as a menu. You can only load a quicklist item by selecting File, Open URL, or clicking the Open toolbar button and selecting QUICKLIST as the Current Hotlist. The quicklist can contain an unlimited number of items.

Sharing Hotlists

If you're researching anything, you can probably find lots of relevant information on the Web. You'll probably want to keep a separate hotlist with all the research-related resources you find. Exporting hotlists allows you to share this list of sources with a colleague, friend, or student.

NOTE: Mosaic can hold up to 20 hotlists (not including the quicklist).

Mosaic has no specific import or export commands. However, all hotlist menus are stored in your MOSAIC.INI file, which is usually located in your Windows directory. To share a hotlist, use a text editor to load up your MOSAIC.INI file. Find the titles and URLs of the pages you want to share. You can then give this text file to your friend. She can then copy and paste any items she's interested in to her own hotlist.

LESSON #6: KEEPING THE PAGE

If you come across a really good Web page, you may want to snag it so you can use it for reference at any time. Mosaic includes two easy commands that allow you to either save a Web page to disk or print it out.

Save It

To save a Web page to your hard disk, just select File, Save As. A dialog box pops up asking you to specify a Drive, Directory, and Filename. You can save the Web page in one of three formats:

- ASCII: Saves the document as plain text. This is useful if you want to load the information up using a word processor or text editor.
- HTML: Saves the document in hypertext format. This is useful if the Web page has lots of hyperlinks. You can then open up this file with Mosaic (select File, Open Local) and view it at any time, offline. This is also useful if you want to edit or borrow parts of the current Web page's source markup to create your own HTML Web pages.
- Binary: Saves the current file as a piece of software. This feature is not yet implemented on the current version of Windows Mosaic.

If you save your file as text or HTML, you do not get copies of the inlined graphics.

Load It to Disk

What if you want to keep a great Web page on your home computer, artwork, fonts, images and all? Mosaic has a great feature allowing you to save a complete Web page to disk. Open the Options pull-down menu and be sure a checkmark appears next to the Load To Disk item. The next time you click on a hyperlink, the entire document goes onto your hard disk instead of appearing on your screen. The Save As menu appears allowing you to specify a Drive, Directory, and Filename.

Alternatively, you can load a page to disk by holding down the SHIFT key *before* clicking on the hyperlink.

Loading to disk is a great way to retrieve images, sounds, or other software files that you know you don't want to display or listen to right away. Mosaic will not load up a viewer when the Load to Disk option is selected.

Print It

If you have a printer attached to your PC, you can easily create a hard copy of any Web page. Simply select File, Print. A dialog box appears. If you need to, adjust the options. Click OK when you're ready to print.

If you want to try before you buy, you can see what your printout will look like by selecting File, Print Preview. To change your printer or alter other print options, select File, Print Setup.

LESSON #7: SEARCHING

If the current Web page is long, unwieldy, or confusing, you can easily search for a particular word or phrase. Select Edit, Find. The Find dialog box appears. You can now type a word, a part of a word, or an entire phrase in the blank box. Click Find Next. The first occurrence of your search term is brought up and highlighted.

If you're searching for a proper noun, a heading in all capital letters, or any other case-sensitive search term, be sure to select the Match Case checkbox. If you search for the word "Fig," then words like "configuration" and "figure" will be skipped.

If you want to find the next occurrence of the search term, click the Find Next button again. When Mosaic reaches the end of the Web page, the "Failed to find string!" box appears.

LESSON #8: THE SOURCE OF IT ALL

Once you start creating your own Web pages, you'll find out that the best way to learn the intricacies of HTML is to study other people's pages. NCSA Mosaic allows you to view the current page's HTML source markup by selecting File, Document Source.

NOTE: If the current Web page is a plain text document, "Document Source" gives you the ASCII text.

A Source window appears, as in Figure 5–6. This window has its own menus: File and Edit. You can now scroll through the markup until you find the section or element you're interested in. To copy a piece of the markup to your Windows clipboard, select the text using your mouse and then select Edit, Copy. If you want to save the entire HTML file to your hard disk, select File, Save.

LESSON #9: FORMS

Mosaic fully supports forms, so a Web page can request information as well as offer it. You can use forms to order things, to send in specific comments or feedback, to request specific items from a database, to complete a survey

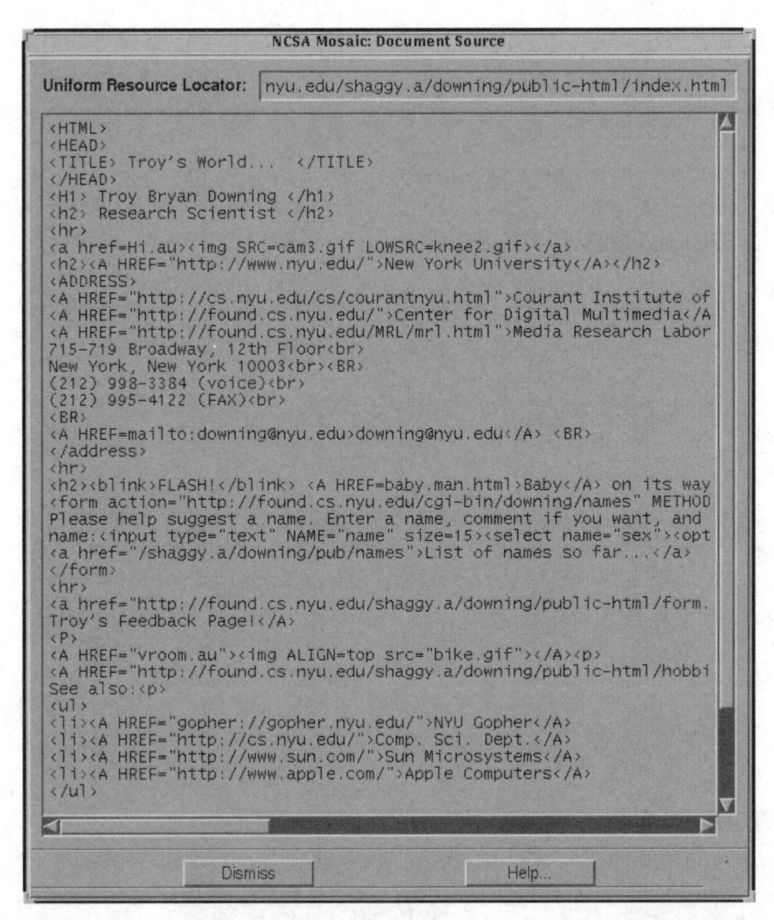

NCSA Mosaic: Document Source

Uniform Resource Locator: nyu.edu/shaggy.a/downing/public-html/index.html

```
<HTML>
<HEAD>
<TITLE> Troy's World...  </TITLE>
</HEAD>
<H1> Troy Bryan Downing </h1>
<h2> Research Scientist </h2>
<hr>
<a href=Hi.au><img SRC=cam3.gif LOWSRC=knee2.gif></a>
<h2><A HREF="http://www.nyu.edu/">New York University</A></h2>
<ADDRESS>
<A HREF="http://cs.nyu.edu/cs/courantnyu.html">Courant Institute of
<A HREF="http://found.cs.nyu.edu/">Center for Digital Multimedia</A
<A HREF="http://found.cs.nyu.edu/MRL/mrl.html">Media Research Labor
715-719 Broadway, 12th Floor<br>
New York, New York 10003<br><BR>
(212) 998-3384 (voice)<br>
(212) 995-4122 (FAX)<br>
<BR>
<A HREF=mailto:downing@nyu.edu>downing@nyu.edu</A> <BR>
</address>
<hr>
<h2><blink>FLASH!</blink> <A HREF=baby.man.html>Baby</A> on its way
<form action="http://found.cs.nyu.edu/cgi-bin/downing/names" METHOD
Please help suggest a name. Enter a name, comment if you want, and
name:<input type="text" NAME="name" size=15><select name="sex"><opt
<a href="/shaggy.a/downing/pub/names">List of names so far...</a>
</form>
<hr>
<a href="http://found.cs.nyu.edu/shaggy.a/downing/public-html/form.
Troy's Feedback Page!</A>
<P>
<A HREF="vroom.au"><img ALIGN=top src="bike.gif"></A><p>
<A HREF="http://found.cs.nyu.edu/shaggy.a/downing/public-html/hobbi
See also:<p>
<ul>
<li><A HREF="gopher://gopher.nyu.edu/">NYU Gopher</A>
<li><A HREF="http://cs.nyu.edu/">Comp. Sci. Dept.</A>
<li><A HREF="http://www.sun.com/">Sun Microsystems</A>
<li><A HREF="http://www.apple.com/">Apple Computers</A>
</ul>
```

Dismiss　Help...

Figure 5–6 Peeking behind the scenes to see the source HTML markup of the current Web page

or poll, or even to exchange comments with others as a sort of slow-motion chat. Figure 5–7 illustrates a sample form.

You are likely to come across five types of form items:

HTML Blank fields: A blank box allowing you to enter as much text as you wish. Just click on the field and begin editing or typing. Some boxes may be one line long; others may be as large as the entire screen. A field may have a default value already written in. Some fields only accept numbers, passwords, or dates. You can also move from field to field by pressing TAB, if you wish.

- HTML Radio buttons: Circular buttons preceding a list of several competing items. You can click on one, and only one, radio button in each list. If a radio button is selected, it appears filled in.
- HTML Check boxes: Square boxes preceding a list of one or more noncompeting items. Check as many of these boxes as you like. A selected box is filled with an *X*.
- HTML Pop-up menus: Click on the small arrow to open up a larger menu of choices. The menu closes after you select the item you want.
- HTML Selection menus: A list of several items. You can often select more than one item by holding down CTRL and clicking the items you want.

Most forms also have a Send or Submit button. When you're done filling in a form, click on Submit to send the data to the distant Web server. A form may also have a Clear or Default button that allows you to erase any filled-in data and start from scratch.

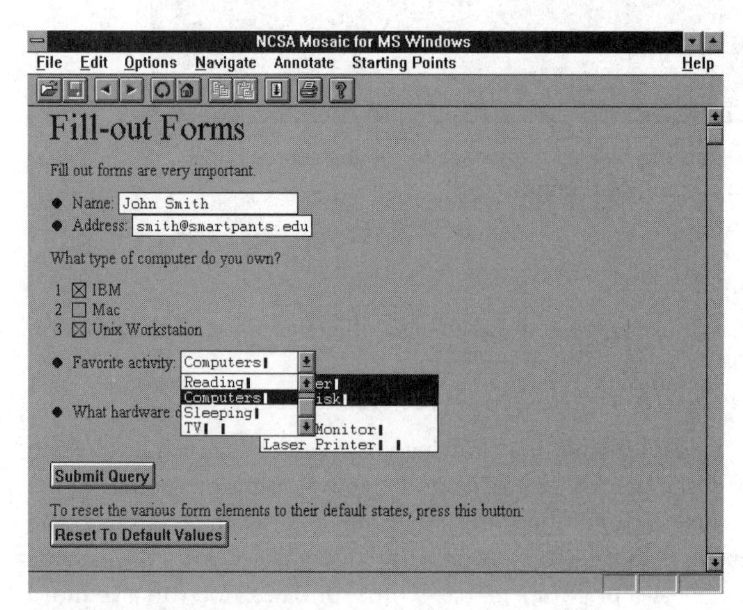

Figure 5–7 Filling in forms with Mosaic

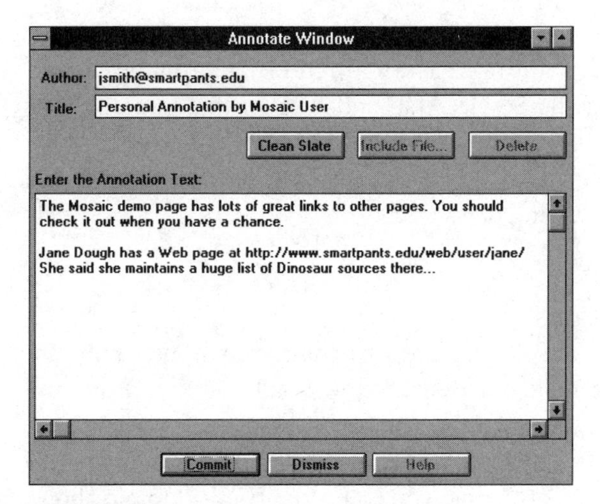

Figure 5-8 Annotating a Web page

LESSON #10: ANNOTATING

As you browse the Web, you'll probably come across tons of great quotes, ideas, or important e-mail or URL addresses. Mosaic has a unique Annotations feature that allows you to quickly jot down notes, the way you might in the margin of a book.

To create an annotation, select Annotate, Annotate. The Annotate Window appears, as in Figure 5-8. Type your comments in the box. Whenever you access this Web page in the future, a note appears at the bottom of the page letting you know that there's an attached annotation.

NOTE: If you don't want annotations to be shown, deselect the Options, Show Group Annotations item.

You can edit an annotation attached to the page you're looking at by selecting Annotate, Edit This Annotation. The Annotate Window appears. You can now edit, delete, or add on to the existing annotation.

To get rid of an attached annotation, select Annotate, Delete This Annotation. Anytime you come to this page in the future, the annotation will be gone.

LESSON #11: GOOD NEWS AND BAD NEWS

The latest version of Mosaic allows you to easily read articles from Usenet newsgroups. Before you can do this, however, you need to specify a news server. This is a machine that handles all your newsgroups. If you're not sure of your NNTP server's address, ask your Internet provider. Select Option, Preferences. Select the Services tab and type in the name of your NNTP Server in the box.

You can now browse, read, or post Usenet articles. See Chapter 16 for more information about accessing news URLs.

LESSON #12: FTP

When you retrieve a piece of software over the Internet, you generally use the FTP protocol. Mosaic makes it easy to download software from any anonymous FTP site across the world.

But what if you want to browse an FTP archive? Sometimes you're not sure of the name or directory of the file you want to retrieve. Mosaic allows you to view any FTP index, as shown in Figure 5–9. The small icons help you get oriented: Directories have a yellow directory folder, files have a blank sheet of paper, and HTML pages have a scrawled-on piece of paper. You can click on any directory to access it. Clicking on a file allows you to retrieve or view it.

NOTE: An FTP Web page usually includes an icon before each filename, file sizes, and other extended information. If you want to display only the names

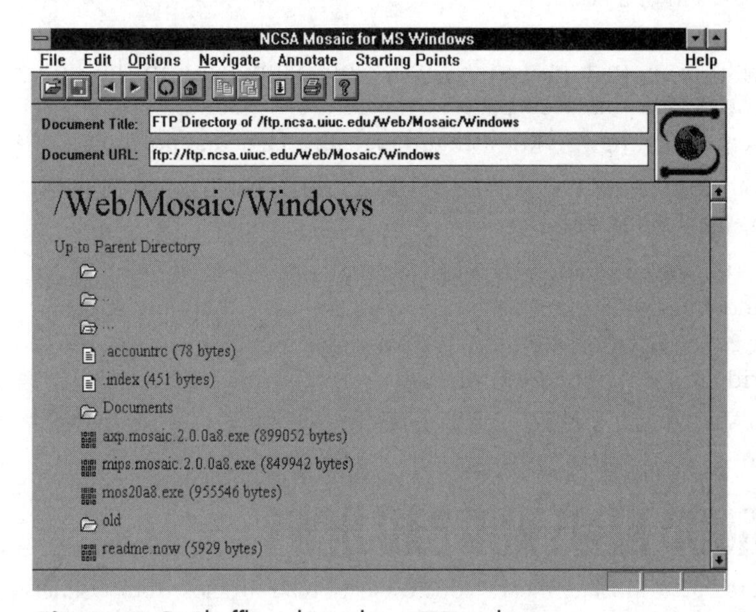

Figure 5–9 Shuffling through an FTP archive

of FTP files or directories, deselect the Options, Extended FTP Directory Parsing item.

LESSON #13: E-MAIL

Mosaic allows you to send simple e-mail. Before you can do this, however, you need to specify a mail server. Select Option, Preferences and click the Services tab. Type in the name of your SMTP Server in the box. This is usually your e-mail address, minus your name. For example, if your address is jsmith@smartpants.edu, then your mail server is usually smartpants.edu. If you're not sure, contact your system administrator or Internet provider.

Sending Mail

From now on, whenever you access a *mailto* URL, a simple mail dialog box appears. You can now type in a subject and your message.

You could send mail to jsmith@smartpants.edu, for example, by opening the following URL:

```
mailto:jsmith@smartpants.edu
```

Mail to Developers

Mosaic is still in development, so they're happy to receive any ideas, tips, bugs, or compliments. To send some basic e-mail to the Mosaic crew, select Help, Mail To Developers.... Perhaps your contribution will help make the next version of Mosaic even more powerful.

LESSON #14: PRESENTATION MODE

The latest version of Mosaic has a nifty presentation mode that lets you view Web page's full screen–that is, with all toolbars, menu commands, and status bars stripped away. This mode is great for demos, tours of the Web, showing off your pages to friends, etc.

To access presentation mode, press ALT-P. You can switch off just the Status bar by pressing ALT-S; press ALT-S again to turn the bar back on. Turn the toolbar off or on by hitting ALT-T. Finally, you can toggle the URL bar by pressing ALT-U.

To return to the normal viewing mode, just press ALT-P again, or the ESC key.

NOTE: Whenever you call a viewer such as LView to display a graphic or MPEGPlay to play a movie, the viewer appears atop your Web page.

LESSON #15: VIEWERS AND OTHER HELPERS

Since Mosaic version 2 is still not officially released, some important options are a little difficult to describe. One of any browser's most important tasks is to send multimedia files to external viewer programs. This way, sound can be heard, video can be seen, and images can be viewed as you browse through the Web.

With the latest version of Mosaic, you can specify and configure all your viewers by selecting Options, Viewers. The Viewers dialog box appears, comprised of two subsections. The first section tells Mosaic what types of files it should send to which viewers. The second section tells Mosaic exactly where to find these viewers.

Older versions of Mosaic require you to edit the MOSAIC.INI file, which is usually located in the Windows directory. In any case, each type of viewable file appears in a list. One item might look like:

```
image/jpeg=.jpeg,.jpe,.jpg
```

The first item of each line is the MIME file type. The remaining items are the standard extensions for that type of file. You can specify as many extensions as you wish for each MIME type, just separate each with a comma. The last extension on a line is the most important one: This is the suffix Mosaic will use if it writes the file to your hard disk or sends the file to a viewer.

For example, the line

```
image/jpeg=.jpeg,.jpe,.jpg
```

will tell Mosaic that any file ending with .jpeg, .jpe, or .jpg is a JPEG graphic. When Mosaic sends such a file to a viewer, it uses the .jpg extension.

You can then fill in the viewer application for each type of file in the Application box. Use the Browse button to specify a Drive, Directory, and Filename. For example, for your image/jpeg files, you would probably use the LView viewer. If your LView was in the C:\LVIEW directory, you would type something similar to:

```
C:\LVIEW\LVIEWP1A.EXE
```

Besides viewers, Mosaic may sometimes need to call other special programs to access various parts of the Web. For example, if you want to telnet to another site, you'll need to tell Mosaic which telnet program it can use.

Specify the full pathname for helper applications at the end of the [Viewers] section in the MOSAIC.INI file. For example:

```
TELNET="C:\TRUMPET\TELW.EXE"
```

LESSON #16: OTHER MOSAIC OPTIONS

The way your screen looks is almost as important as the data that's on it. You might as well tweak Mosaic so that fonts and colors look pretty as can be.

The Fonts You Want

You've probably noticed that every Web page you load has a similar look to it. Headings, emphasized text, and other styles are uniform. Mosaic allows you to customize common screen fonts so Web pages look the way you want them to.

Select Options, Choose Font. A list of the following paragraph types appears:

- Normal: The standard text on a Web page.
- Header 1 through Header 7: Header 1 is the main heading, header 2 is the first subheading, and so on.
- Menu: A list of menued items.
- Directory: A thin column-like list of many items.
- Address: An indented style for postal or e-mail addresses.
- Block Quote: An indented paragraph quoted from another source.
- Example: Short examples of text to be typed.
- Preformatted: A fixed-width typewriter style font where all text is spaced evenly.
- Listing: Longer examples of program listings.

Select one of these types. The Font dialog box appears. Specify a new Font, Style, and Size. From now on, any time a Web page contains this style of text, it appears in the exact font you specified.

Colors

Colors can be configured by editing the [Settings] section of the MOSAIC.INI file. This file should be in your Windows directory. If not, use File Manager and select File, Search to search for it. Once you find MOSAIC.INI, open it up using the Windows notepad–you can do this automatically by double-clicking on it while in the Windows File Manager.

Scroll down through your MOSAIC.INI file until you find a section titled:

```
[Settings]
```

Search for the following line and change the color to be whatever you wish:

```
Anchor Color=0,0,255
```

This color is expressed in the RGB triplet: Red, Green, Blue. Each value can range from 0 to 255. Experiment with different numbers until you find one you like.

If you want, you can have Mosaic work with a default background, by disabling the Grey Background option. Search for the "Grey Background=" line in MOSAIC.INI and change it from "yes" to "no."

Home Sweet Home

Your MOSAIC.INI file includes other options you can change. For example, you can change your e-mail address, the location of the default home page, whether the home page should automatically be loaded, and so on. You can edit the following lines:

```
[Main]
E-mail="jsmith@smartpants.edu"
Autoload Home Page=yes
Home Page=http://www.ncsa.uiuc.edu/SDG/Software/Mosaic/
```

WHAT NOW?

Now that you're a pro at one of the world's premiere browsers, you can easily start exploring the Web. If you're not sure where to begin, check out some of Mosaic's built-in hotlists. Try to get the feel for different parts of the Web and the Internet. Play around with Web pages, download a few sounds or movies, flip through some newsgroups, share the wealth from a couple of FTP sites. You can also explore the sites that are reviewed in Chapter 8, What Can I Do?

If you think you're ready to start creating your own Web pages, flip to Part II, Creating Web Pages, which begins with Chapter 8. In the next chapter, you'll learn about another browser, Netscape Network Navigator.

6

THE NETSCAPE NAVIGATOR

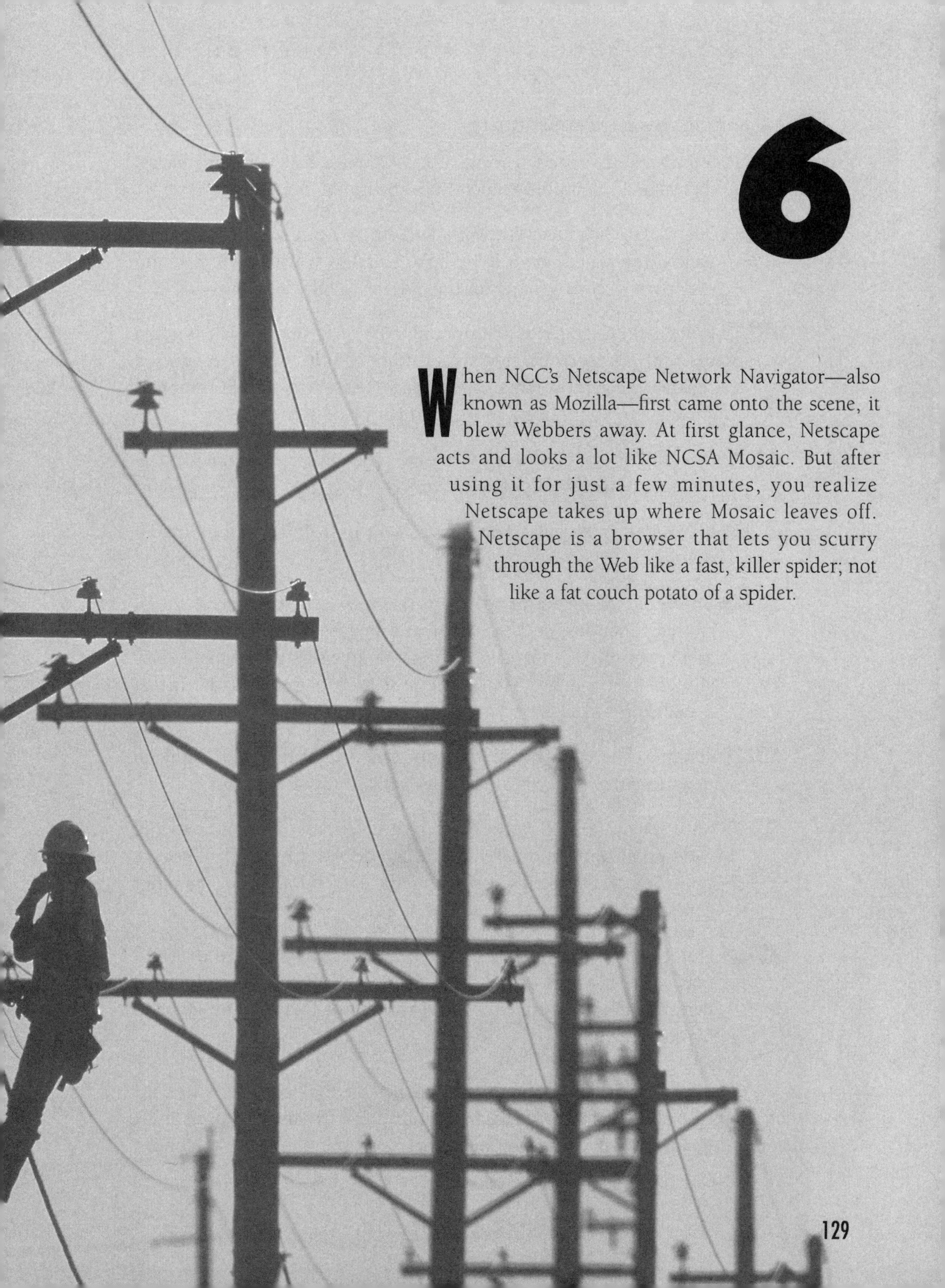

6

When NCC's Netscape Network Navigator—also known as Mozilla—first came onto the scene, it blew Webbers away. At first glance, Netscape acts and looks a lot like NCSA Mosaic. But after using it for just a few minutes, you realize Netscape takes up where Mosaic leaves off. Netscape is a browser that lets you scurry through the Web like a fast, killer spider; not like a fat couch potato of a spider.

Netscape has these major features:

- HTML Simultaneous image loading: If a Web page has a dozen images, they all fade in at pretty much the same time.
- HTML *Interruptable* loading: As images fade in, you can scroll through the page or even click on a hyperlink. This lets you move to a brand new page without waiting for the old one to fully load.
- HTML Inlined JPEG graphics: The popular JPEG format, which is often used for photographs, fine art, or other colorful images, requires a separate viewer if you're using Mosaic. Netscape puts JPEG graphics smack onto your screen, in their proper place in the text.
- HTML Standard operating system: Netscape runs great on Windows 3.1—no fancy 32-bit Windows required.
- HTML Menu dialog box: Netscape gives you pull-down menus for all options.
- HTML Broad HTML+ command support: Netscape supports a lot of special functions, such as automatic image sizing, text-wrapping around an image, font sizing, horizontal line sizing, and more. This allows for a much greater variety of Web pages, and the nicest overall appearance in cyberspace.
- HTML Complete network news: Netscape has a fully functional built-in newsreader, which lets you post as well as browse.
- HTML Security options: If you connect the Netscape Navigator to the Netscape Commerce Server, you can access a number of secure options for transferring money, credit card information, or other confidential data.
- HTML Home-style modem support: Netscape designers realize that you may not have high-speed network access to the Internet, so its performance is fine-tuned to work with home PCs and 14,400 baud modems.

Pricewise, Netscape is a little hazy. Officially, the software is free for academic or nonprofit individuals or organizations. Commercial users must register it, for $39. If you're not sure where you stand, be sure to contact NCC.

INSTALLING NETSCAPE

Netscape can be downloaded quite easily. Access

```
ftp://ftp.netscape.com/
```

to get the latest files. You can read about the latest Netscape releases by checking out:

```
http://home.netscape.com/
```

Once you get the NETSCAPE.EXE file, unzip or execute this file into a temporary directory. Run the SETUP.EXE program. The Netscape Setup program will install Netscape in a directory of your choice (default C:\NETSCAPE), add a Netscape section to your WIN.INI file, set up a NETSCAPE.INI file, and create a Program Manager group and item.

To run Netscape, you need to run the Trumpet Winsock TCP/IP stack. Dial in to your SLIP or TIA account by selecting Dialler, Login. You can then minimize the Winsock program by clicking the minimize box in the upper right corner of the window. Winsock is now working.

You're now ready to run Netscape. Just double-click its icon.

LESSON #1: SCAPING THE NET

When you first run Netscape, a screen with many buttons and status bars appears as in Figure 6–1. Netscape loads your *home page*. A toolbar of common buttons appears at the top of the screen. These *toolbar* buttons include:

- Back: Revisit the previous Web page. Using this button, you can continue moving back through your history list.
- Forward: Move to the next Web page in a series. If you used the Back button to load up a previous page, you can use this button to move forward again.
- Home: Load up the home page.
- Reload: Load the current page again. This is useful if a load is interrupted or a page appears somehow garbled. You can also reload an HTML page you are currently developing to see its continuing progress.
- Images: Load the current page again, this time showing all the images. (See Lesson #2 in this chapter to find out how to skip the images in the first place.)

- Open: Jump directly to a specific URL.
- Find: Search for a word or phrase in the current Web page.
- Stop: Halt the loading of a Web page.

Directly beneath the toolbar lurks a set of directory buttons. These buttons make it quick and easy to access different parts of the Internet. You can also access any of these directory pages by selecting them from the Directory menu. The possible directory pages include:

- Welcome: Access NCC's Netscape Welcome page.
- What's New!: Read about Netscape's latest features.
- What's Cool!: A bunch of links to Web pages that NCC thinks are worth your while.
- Questions: Answers to frequently asked questions.
- Net Search: Search the Internet for a topic or item.
- Net Directory: See a list of Internet tools, resources, and other servers.

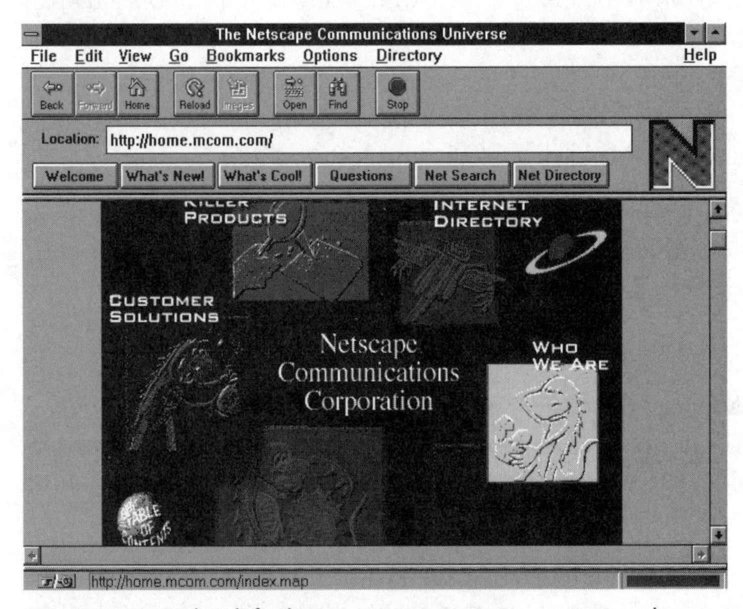

Figure 6–1 The default Netscape navigation screen, with tons of buttons, status indicators, and other gizmos

Finally, below the directory buttons, Netscape shows you the Location of the current Web page. You can also edit this field, or type in your own URL to bring up a specific page or Internet service.

NOTE: Netscape allows you to customize the entire look of the screen. You can have the toolbar and directory buttons displayed as pictures, text, both, or neither. You can decide whether or not you want the current Location to be shown. You can even designate the home page to be any Web page you wish. You can control most of these settings from the Options menu. Select Options and click on Show Toolbar, Show Location, or Show Directory Buttons to select or deselect each option. Also see the Customizing Your Netscape Experience section, later in this chapter, for more details.

Following Hyperlinks

Hyperlinks are generally underlined and colored blue. Images, icons, or any other pieces of art with blue borders are usually also hyperlinks. To follow any link, just move the mouse cursor on it. The mouse arrow becomes a pointing hand. The URL of the selected hyperlink appears at the bottom of the screen. If you want to follow the link, just click on it.

NOTE: Netscape allows you to customize the look of these links. Underlining is optional and you can make a link any color you wish. See the Customizing Your Netscape Experience section, later in this chapter.

Once you've followed a hyperlink, Netscape changes that link's color—usually to purple. The subtlety of links can often make things confusing, so this handy *followed-link* feature helps you remember where you've been and prevents you from exploring the same path more than once.

NOTE: Netscape allows you to open several Web pages at once, each appearing in a different window. Select File, New Window. This allows you to keep several different connections open at the same time. Switch between simultaneous Web page windows the way you would with any other Windows program—by pressing SHIFT-TAB or by selecting the page from a Task List.

Moving to a Specific URL

There are two ways to move to a URL of your choice:

- Click the Location field at the top of the screen. The word *Location* changes to *Go To*. Type the new URL, in full, in the field and press ENTER.
- Click the Open button, select File, Open Location, or press CTRL-L. The Open Location window appears. Type in your URL and select Open.

Loading Indicators

Whenever you access a Web page, the red *progress bar* at the bottom of the screen acts as a meter, showing you what percentage of the page has been loaded. The bottom line of the Netscape screen also acts a status bar. It lets you know what's happening as it searches for the Web page's host, contacts the host, and retrieves the data.

As a Web page loads, the status bars tell you how many kilobytes of text, images, or other files have been loaded. As Netscape is working, you may also notice how the Netscape "N" logo appears to pop out of and sink into the screen.

NOTE: Clicking on the logo loads up Netscape's home page.

Stop It!

If a page seems to take forever to load, you may decide to just give up on it. To halt a load in progress, click the Stop button in the toolbar, press the ESC key, or select Go, Stop Loading.

The Web Page Appears

Netscape doesn't necessarily load an entire page at once. At first, the page's text appears. Images appear as empty boxes. You can often scroll down through a Web page as it is being loaded.

Images then fade in, all at the same time. Depending on its type, an image may appear one row at a time, like the dropping of a curtain. Other images load in several spaced-out rows at a time, like venetian blinds. Some images appear blurred at first and then become sharper and sharper as more information comes in.

You can browse up and down through each Web page using the vertical scroll bar. Some pages use special extended fonts and may require the horizontal scroll bar as well. You can select text on the page with the mouse, copy it (Edit, Copy), and paste it to your favorite word processor or text editor.

Safe and Secure

If you're interested in sending secure or confidential information over the Internet, Netscape has come up with a way. Using special Netscape servers, you can have the Netscape Navigator send and receive credit card numbers, money, or company secrets.

You can know how secure a given page is by looking at the bottom of your screen. If the Web page is secure, a gold key appears in the lower left corner. If the document is not secure, the key appears broken in two. Secure documents also display a blue bar of color along the top of the window.

If you're not dealing with secure information, you might as well hide the security colorbar. Select Option, Show Security Colorbar to unselect this option.

LESSON #2: GRAPHICLESS: NO AUTO LOADING

The most time-consuming part of Web crawling is the loading of large files such as graphics, sounds, and movies. In particular, most Web pages have tons of inlined images scattered through the text. Netscape Navigator supports three major graphic formats of inlined images: GIF, JPEG, and XBM. If you want to give Netscape a super boost, you can go graphicless by turning off the auto loading of these inlined graphics.

To toggle auto loading, select Options, Auto Load Images. A checkmark appears next to the menu item if auto loading is on. Netscape automatically

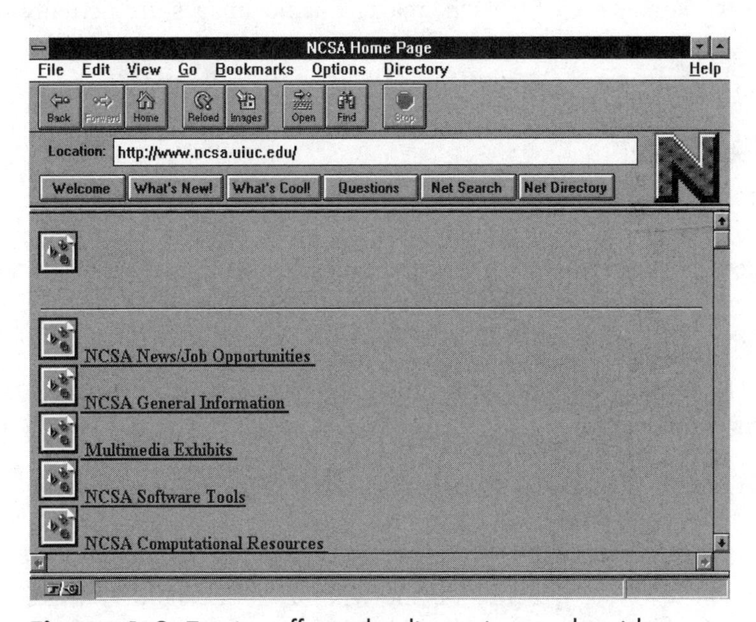

Figure 6–2 Turning off auto loading to ignore sluggish images

remembers your auto load settings from your previous session. When auto loading is off, Netscape loads up each page in a fraction of the time, displaying a small cube-like icon wherever an image would usually be, as in Figure 6-2. If the image is a hyperlink, then this cube is surrounded by a blue border.

The only problem with turning off images is you tend to miss out on a lot. Many pages have beautiful or helpful supporting images. Some pages are *all* graphical—having no text at all to speak of. If a page looks really interesting, you can grab the graphics by clicking the Images toolbar button, pressing CTRL-I, or selecting View, Load Images.

Loading Later

If you're the type of person who doesn't like waiting, but who doesn't want to sacrifice the quality of a page, you can tell Netscape to show images only after they're entirely loaded. Select Options, Preferences. From the Preferences window, select the Network, Images, and Security preferences by clicking the pop-up menu at the very top. Finally, click the After Loading radio button in the Display Images area.

Netscape loads up each Web page, displaying the text as soon as it is available. Space is allocated for each image, but no images are actually shown. You can now read through the page or even follow hyperlinks. If you wait long enough, however, all the images will eventually appear.

Hither and Dither

Many images actually have more colors than your monitor, or Netscape itself, is able to display. The Netscape Navigator is smart enough to make some educated guesses when it comes it complicated images—it draws the available colors closest to the image's actual colors. This process is known as *dithering*. You can display image color using two options:

- HTML Dither to Color Cube: Netscape dithers image to fit with the available system colors.

- HTML Use Closest Color in Color Cube: Netscape picks the closest available color.

The decision to dither depends on the type of monitor and graphics card you use. Try both selections and see which one makes images seem sharper.

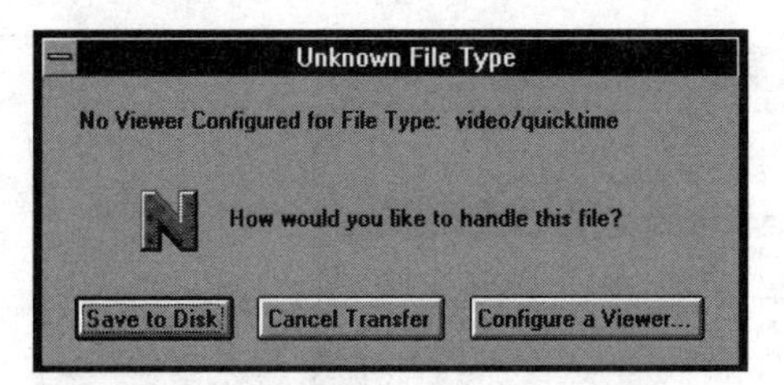

Figure 6–3 If Netscape can't show you a multimedia file, it's nice enough to let you save it

LESSON #3: RETRIEVING MULTIMEDIA FILES

When you load up an image file, Netscape displays what it can—anything in the GIF, JPEG, or XBM graphic formats. If it can't display an image, sound, movie, animation, or other file type, Netscape tries to send it to a viewer or *helper application.*

If Netscape doesn't know how to display the file you want to retrieve, it tells you so. The Unknown File Type dialog box in Figure 6–3 appears. To store the file on your hard disk, click the Save To Disk option and specify a Drive, Directory, and Filename. Click OK. Netscape then retrieves the file and saves it on your disk.

From the Unknown File Type window you can also click the Configure A Viewer button. You can now type in the filename of the software that can view the given file type. See the Configuring Viewers section, later in this chapter, for details.

If an image, text file, or even binary file appears on your Netscape screen, you can easily save it by selecting File, Save As. You can then specify a Drive, Directory, and Filename.

LESSON #4: ANCIENT HISTORY

Often, you're reading an important Web page but are then distracted by a cool hyperlink. You follow the link, read a bit, follow another link, and pretty soon you're lost in cyberspace. Luckily, it's easy to return from where you came by using Netscape's history list.

Netscape automatically keeps track of every page you visit. To see the last bunch of pages you've been to, simply open the Go menu at the top of

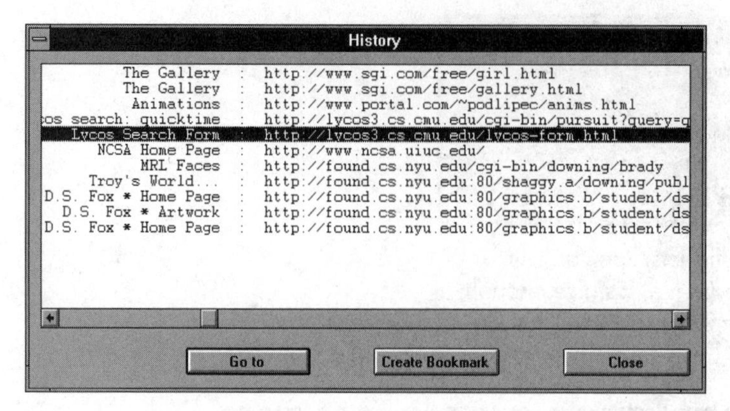

Figure 6–4 Time traveling through the Web using the history list

the screen. At the bottom of the menu is an impromptu history list with the title of each page. To revisit one of these pages, just click on its name.

If the page you want isn't in the Go menu, the menu probably just isn't long enough to display it. To see the actual history list, select Go, View History or press CTRL-H. The History window in Figure 6–4 appears. The full title and URL of each page is shown. The page you most recently visited is at the top of the list, your home page should be at the bottom. To open a page, double-click on it or select it and choose Go To.

NOTE: Whenever you retrieve a Web page, images are stored in memory. If you return to a page you've already seen, images load much faster due to this *memory cache.*

If you think you'll visit often, you may want to add it to your permanent bookmark list. Select the page and click the Create Bookmark item.

Netscape keeps track of the pages you visit and the order you visit them in. Whenever you backtrack through pages, nonconsecutive pages are removed from the history list. For example, if you move from page A to page B to page C and then move back to A, link B disappears.

LESSON #5: BOOKMARKS

In your journeys around the Web, you're bound to come across a page or two that you absolutely adore. Whenever you find a page you're likely to use again, Netscape makes it easy to place a bookmark. Simply select Bookmarks, Add Bookmark or press CTRL-A.

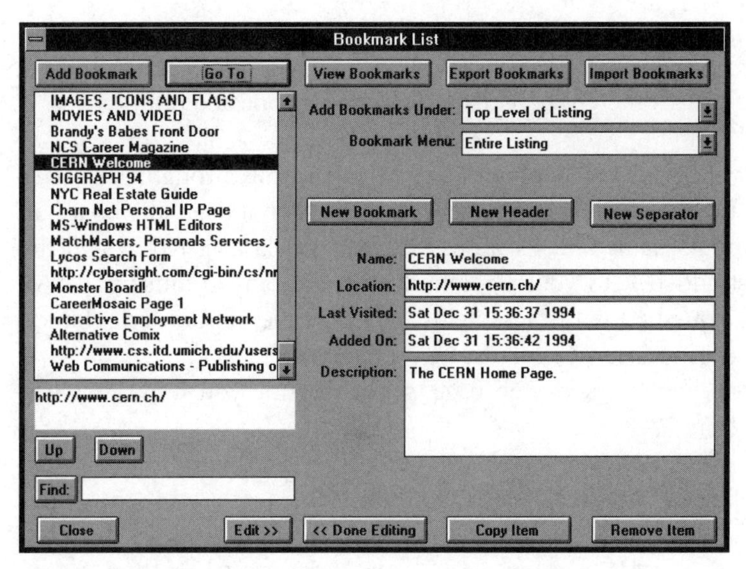

Figure 6–5 The full Bookmark List window lets you organize, search, import, export, or move to any bookmark of your choosing

Your first few dozen bookmarks are stored under the Bookmarks pull-down menu. Every time you bookmark a page, the title of that page becomes a permanent item in the Bookmark list. To move to a given page, just select its title. Once you create a bookmark, it is stored forever. This helps you personalize your copy of Netscape so you can use it to quickly get to your favorite corners of the Internet.

Dealing with Bookmarks

After a while, you may accumulate so many bookmarks that your Bookmark menu stretches way off the screen. You can use the full Bookmark List (Figure 6-5) to access, organize, or search your bookmarks. To access the full list, select Bookmarks, View Bookmarks or press CTRL-B.

NOTE: To see the entire Bookmark List window, you may need to press the Edit>> button in the bottom right corner.

You now have access to many advanced bookmark options:

- Go to the bookmarked page.
- Search for a particular bookmark.
- Edit your current bookmarks.

- Organize your bookmarks into separate groups.
- Keep many different bookmark files and use one at a time.

When you're viewing bookmarks, you can scroll through the list of page titles using the scroll bar. Whenever you click on a page, the boxes on the right show its name and location, the date you last visited it, and the date you first added it to your Bookmark List, and any comments you've entered. You can edit any of these fields. For example, if you don't think a page's title is descriptive enough, just type a new one.

To access a bookmarked Web page, select the title you want and click the Go To button.

Adding or Deleting Bookmarks

If you have a URL you'd like to add as a new bookmark, select the New Bookmark button. This creates an item called "? New Item"—which you replace with the actual Name and Location. You can move the item to a different order within the bookmark list by clicking the Up and Down buttons.

After a while, a bookmarked Web page may no longer exist. If you no longer need a bookmark, select it and click the Remove Item button.

Searching Your Bookmarks

Soon you may have more bookmarks than you know how to deal with. Luckily, Netscape makes it easy to search your bookmark list for a particular word or phrase.

Type the search term in the Find box and then click the Find button. Any bookmark containing the search term is automatically selected. To find the next suitable bookmark, click Find again.

Describing a Bookmark

Some Web pages have lousy titles. Other Web pages have similar titles. Netscape allows you to enter comments for each bookmark. Simply select the title of the page from the Bookmark List and then click inside the Description box. You can now type helpful notes, annotations, or ideas.

For example, if you've created bookmarks for ten Web pages, all entitled "Dancing," you can add a note to one page saying, "This one has great pictures of famous dancers," and a note to another saying, "This page is a comprehensive site-list of dance competitions."

The next time you get lost or confused, your own comments can help show you the way.

Organizing Bookmarks

Perhaps the best way of dealing with billions of bookmarks is to separate them into categories. For example, you can keep a group of search indexes in one category, you can stick entertainment-related Web pages in another group, and put your job search pages in a third group.

Groups

To place a bookmark in a new group, click anywhere in your bookmark list and then select the New Header button. A bookmark called "New Header" appears. Rename the bookmark by typing an appropriate name in the Name box. For example, you may want to call it "Search Indexes." Your new header appears in your bookmark list with a little dot next to it.

Now select the item beneath the header you just created and click the Up key. The item becomes indented. This means it is part of the group. To add any other bookmarks to the group, just move them directly below the header. If a bookmark is *above* the header, select it and continue pressing Down until it is indented below the header. If the bookmark you want is *below* the header, click Up until you've moved it into the group. A final organized list might look like Figure 6–6.

From now on, when you click on the Bookmarks menu, a list of your groups appears. Whenever you select a group, a side menu of other subgroups or bookmarks pops up. You can select a Web page's title to jump to it. If you select a subgroup, a third side menu pops up with yet more choices.

You can go on like this, creating subgroups within existing groups. For example, you can have one group called Music, with subgroups Rock and Roll, Jazz, and Classical. Remember—the easier your Bookmark List is to read, the faster you can access it to grab a useful page.

NOTE: If you move a header or subheader using the Up or Down buttons, the entire group moves with it.

Collapsing and Expanding

You can make your bookmark list even easier to sift through by *collapsing* a group. Simply double-click on the header name. A plus (+) appears next to the header, and all items and subgroups within the group seem to disappear.

To *expand* a group, just double-click on the header name again. All items immediately reappear.

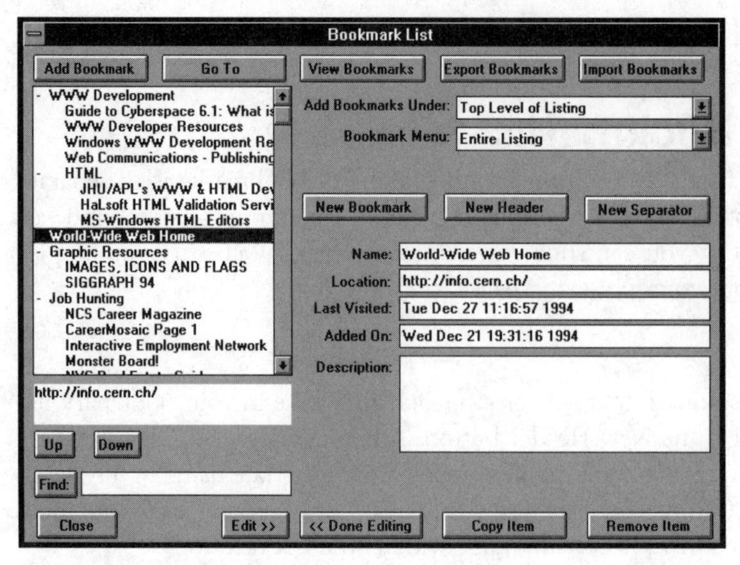

Figure 6–6 A bookmark list made manageable by organizing items into various groups

The Separator

A nice Netscape bookmark feature allows you to place separator bars between any bookmark items, groups, or subgroups. Simply click anywhere in your bookmark list and select the New Separator button. An item is created below the current selection that looks similar to:

```
------------------------
```

The next time you use the Bookmarks menu, a line will be drawn between items above the separator and items below the separator. This can help you create eye-pleasing groupings of bookmarks.

Customizing the Menu

If you want all new bookmarks to be placed in a particular group by default, select the Add Bookmarks Under pull-down menu. You can now select the heading under which all new bookmarks should be stored.

You can also customize the look of your Netscape Bookmark pull-down menu. By default, all main groups and nongrouped items are shown. If you want to display only one particular group, select the Bookmark Menu pull-down list and select the group's header. To display all groups, select the Entire Listing item.

For example, if you happen to be working on stock prices, you may want to have a listing of your favorite financial Web pages at your fingertips. If you had a group called "Finance," you could select this as the Bookmark Menu default. The next time you check out the bookmark menu, only pages having something to do with finance will appear.

The Bookmark Files

Bookmarks are so darn useful you may find yourself trading them or creating special groups of them. Bookmark files help you make your Bookmark List portable for easy access to large lists of data.

Creating a Web of Hyperlinks

If you like, you can use your Bookmark List to create a Web page containing links to all your favorite places. You can then give this page to other people, or even post it on the Web for the world to use.

To see what your bookmark list would look like as a Web page, select the View Bookmarks button. You can now close the Bookmark List and browse through the list using Netscape's usual browsing commands. If you like the way the page looks, you can save it as HTML source code by selecting File, Save As and typing in a Drive, Directory, and Filename. Click OK.

You can reload this Web page of bookmarks at any time by selecting File, Open File (or pressing CTRL-O) and specifying the name of your custom bookmark file.

Importing and Exporting

You can also save your bookmark list directly by clicking the Export Bookmarks button from your Bookmark List. Again, you need to Designate a Drive, Directory, and Filename and then click OK. Your bookmark file should have the .HTM extension. Your bookmarks are then saved in a special format that Netscape can easily read back in.

To open a previously saved bookmark file, select the Import Bookmarks button. Find the proper .HTM file and then click OK. All the new bookmarks are added on to your existing bookmark list. If the new bookmarks aren't already grouped, you'll probably want to create a subgroup to put them under.

For example, suppose you have a hundred bookmarks leading to animation-related Web pages. You can save this list in a file called ANIMATE.HTM. You can also give the ANIMATE.HTM file to a friend. All she would have to do to see your bookmarks is select the Import Bookmarks button. All your animation bookmarks would then be inserted into her existing bookmark file.

LESSON #6: KEEPING A WEB PAGE

Keeping bookmarks to pages is fine and dandy, but often you'll want to keep the text of a page itself. For example:

- You're an HTML developer and want to study how the current page was put together.
- You want to use parts of the document in a paper you're writing.
- You want to save or print out the document and read it at your own leisure.

Netscape has a number of commands that allow you to snag the information from a Web page and save it to your disk, print it out, or even e-mail it across the world.

Saving to Disk

Netscape makes it easy to save a given Web page to your hard disk for later retrieval. You can even save a page to disk in lieu of viewing it.

To save the currently displayed Web page, select File, Save As or press CTRL-S, then specify a Drive, Directory, and Filename. Most Web pages are stored as HTML source files, and should end with the .HTM extension. When done, click OK.

NOTE: When you save a Web page, only the text is stored on your drive. The inlined graphics are not included.

If you come across a hyperlink you know you want to save to disk, hold down the SHIFT key before clicking on the link. Again, you can save the incoming text directly to your hard disk. You can use this feature to pull in non-hypertext pages such as lists of numbers, text files, or other data very quickly.

Loading

To load any HTML Web page you've saved, simply select File, Open File or press CTRL-O. You can now specify the Drive, Directory, and Filename of the file you wish to open. Click OK. The Web page is then instantly drawn on your screen. As long as you're connected to the Internet, any hyperlinks should work just fine.

Printing

If you have a printer attached to your computer, you can easily generate a hard copy of the current Web page. In most cases, all text and graphics go to the printer, so your Web page looks the same on paper as it did on the screen.

Before you actually waste the ink, you may want to see exactly what your printed page will look like. Select File, Print Preview. Netscape formats the pages and shows you a graphical representation of what the final printout will be. Click on a part of the page to zoom in on it. To zoom out, just click again. You can view two facing pages at once with the Two Page button. To flip to the next page, if there *is* a next page, click the Next Page button.

A page is generally printed at the same width as the Web page on the screen. If text goes beyond the confines of the screen, horizontally or vertically, this text is printed on a separate page. If your print preview makes the pages seem too wide, you can narrow your Netscape window. You may also want to try printing your page as a landscape instead of as a portrait. You can set these options by clicking the Setup button in the Print dialog box.

NOTE: To zoom a Netscape window to its default size, select the Zoom box arrow in the upper right corner of the window.

To print, select File, Print or press CTRL-P. The Print dialog box appears. The default printer is shown at the top of the box. If you want to use a different printer, or if you want to fine-tune your page setup, select the Setup button.

If the Web "page" is longer than one printed page, you can specify the range of pages you want printed by clicking the Pages button and filling in the first page in the From box and the last page in the To box.

Mail Document

Netscape has a neat feature that allows you to mail part of the current Web page to yourself or to anyone else in the world with an Internet account.

Select File, Mail Document or press CTRL-M. The Mail Document window appears. Fill in the Internet address of the person you want to send mail to in the To box. To quote from the current Web page, click the Include Document Text button. The first 30,000 characters of the Web page appear in the editing window. Each line of the Web page starts with a greater-than sign (>), to indicate that the text is quoted from another source.

You can now add your own message, erase sections, or cut and paste. When your message looks the way you want it to, click the Send Mail button. See the E-Mailing section, later in this chapter, for more details.

LESSON #7: SEARCHING A PAGE

Web pages can be really long. To search a page for a particular heading, phrase, or key word, you can use Netscape's find command. Simply click the Find button in the toolbar, select Edit, Find, or press CTRL-F. The Find dialog box appears as in Figure 6–7.

Type a search term or two in the Find What box. If you want Netscape to differentiate between uppercase and lowercase, check the Match Case checkbox. If you're at the top of the Web page, you generally want to search downward. Be sure the Down Direction is checked. If your downward search doesn't yield any results, try searching upward by selecting Up.

To begin the search, click the Find Next button. If your search term appears anywhere in the Web page, it is moved to and highlighted. For example, if you search for "man" then the words "manual" and "woman" will be found. If the Match Case checkbox isn't selected then words like "MANDATORY" and "Mandible" will also be found.

The Find dialog box stays on the screen once a word is found. If you want to search for the next occurrence of the word, click the Find Next button again. If you've found what you were looking for, click Cancel to close the Find box.

If Netscape reaches the beginning or end of the Web page without finding anything, a dialog box tells you so. You are then given the option to try the search in the opposite direction.

LESSON #8: GETTING TO THE SOURCE

The HTML source of Web pages is the Web developer's greatest tool. By studying the commands that make a Web page do its stuff, you can learn to emulate and surpass that page.

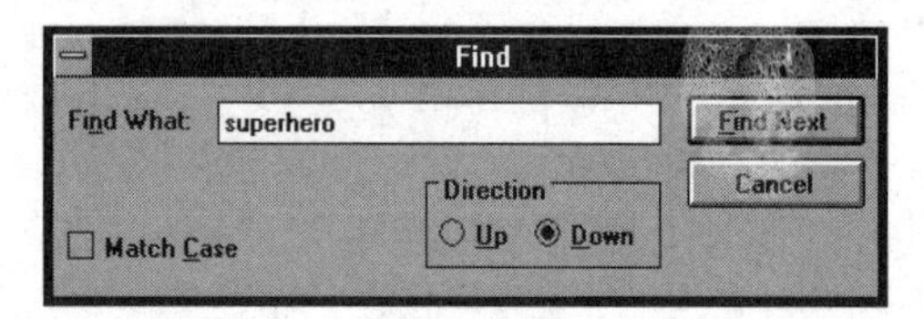

Figure 6–7 Finding text in a Web page

To immediately view a Web page's HTML markup, select View, Source. A window appears showing you source code for the current page. You can scroll through the source using the scroll bars. When you're done peeking, click OK. Some View Source windows also have a Save button, allowing you to save the source code to disk.

NOTE: If you need a refresher on saving a Web page's HTML markup, turn back to the Keeping a Web Page section earlier in this chapter.

If you like, you can have Netscape use a more advanced text editor—such as Windows Notepad—to view a page's source. Select Options, Preferences and choose the Directory, Applications, and News options from the pop-up menu at the top of the window. Click the Browse button next to the empty View Source box. You can now specify the Drive, Directory, and Filename of your text editor. The NOTEPAD.EXE program, for example, is usually located in the C:\WINDOWS directory. Click OK. From now on, Netscape will call this application to help view your Web pages.

NOTE: Some versions of Netscape have a bug that doesn't allow you to use a helper application to view a document's source. In these cases, you should save the Web page to disk and then load up the HTML source markup using Notepad or your favorite text editor.

LESSON #9: FILLING IN FORMS

Reading Web pages can give you a lot of information. But some pages want *you* to provide some information in return. Netscape supports forms within Web pages, allowing Webbing to be a two-way conversation.

When a page contains a form, you'll know it right away; form elements have a distinct look to them. Figure 6–8 shows an example of a form page. If you've done any work with databases, or filled out your taxes recently, you should recognize the style of most Netscape forms. A form usually consists of the following elements:

- HTML Fields: Blank boxes where you can type in a word, a sentence, or even an entire message. A field may already contain some default text. Some fields may only accept numbers, or valid dates.

- HTML Check boxes: Square boxes that can be either checked or unchecked. You can check as many options as you like. For example, a list of hobbies may be preceded by check boxes. You can check all the hobbies that interest you.

- Radio buttons: Round buttons preceding a set of options. You can choose one, and only one, of these options. For example, the words "Male" and "Female" are usually preceded by radio buttons. You can select one option or the other, not both.

- Selection List menus: A menu of available options. Just click on the applicable item. Some of these menus allow you to select more than one item by holding down the CTRL key.

- Pop-Up menus: Only one option is shown. When you click on the little arrow icon, however, a full menu of various options appears for your selection.

- Submit button: Click this button when you're done filling out your form.

- Clear button: If you want to erase all values in the form and fill out everything anew, click this button.

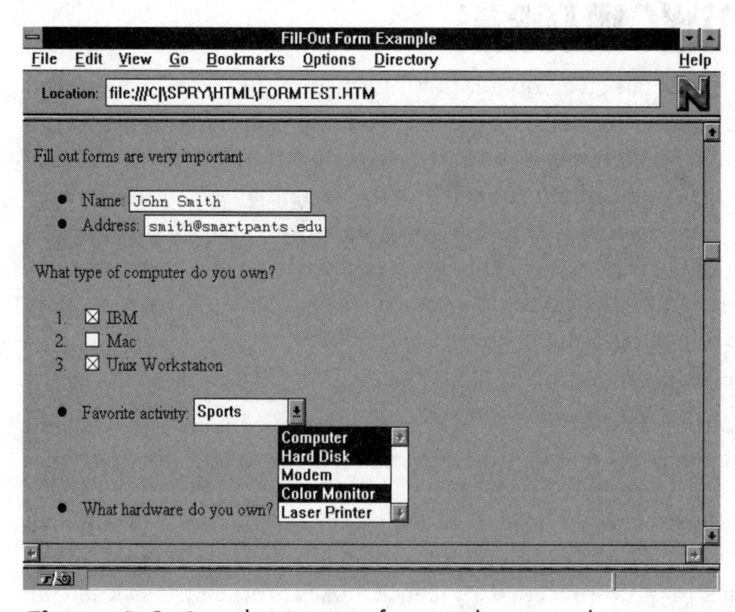

Figure 6-8 Sample Netscape form—a lot easier than taxes!

Filling 'er Out

Forms allow you to request information, fill out surveys, search for specific things, or tell people where they can reach you. One page can contain any number of different forms. If you come across a form, just click on each field to fill it in. If a checkbox is empty, for example, click on it to *X* it; if a box is already checked when you click on it, the *X* disappears.

Most forms are clearly labeled with words such as "Name," "Address," etc. If you don't understand a list of selections or a field, just leave it blank. Experiment. Check different pull-down menus to see if there's an option you forgot to select. When you've finished a form, you can send the information to the Web page's creator by clicking the Send, Done or Submit button.

If you are dealing with a secure fill-in form, a Netscape dialog box pops up to inform you. You can then feel free to write things like your credit card number, bank account numbers, etc.

User Validation

A few Web pages won't let you in without a password. This is useful for companies who want to restrict their files to their own employees, online services who want to require membership for access to their pages, etc.

If you come across a Web page that requires user validation, the Username And Password dialog box appears. Type in your Username and a valid Password and click OK. If you are an official member, you are given access to the private Web.

NOTE: Most online services have an opening screen with an option to register. You can usually fill out and submit a quick form, and get a username and password on the spot. However, your privileges may be limited until the service makes sure its billing department can find you.

LESSON #10: THE NEWS

One of Netscape's best features is its ability to act as a fully functional Usenet newsreader. Usenet is a collection of messages and replies over the Internet; there are over 7,000 different topics of discussion. Netscape has commands that allow you to select newsgroups, browse through articles, read articles, and even post articles of your own.

Each newsgroup has its own name—usually a string of words separated by periods.

Setting Up a News Server

Most every Internet provider has a special machine known as the *NNTP server* to store, handle, and otherwise take care of Usenet news. If you do not know the name of this machine, ask your Internet provider or system administrator.

To tell Netscape where to look for news, select Options, Preferences and select Directories, Applications, And News from the pop-up menu at the top of the window. In the New section, fill in the News (NNTP) Server box with the proper machine name.

You can also designate a News RC file if you want. This file contains the listings of all the newsgroups you are subscribed to. In most cases, you can just keep Netscape's default of C:\WINDOWS\NEWS.RC.

Getting the News

In some cases, a hyperlink may warp you directly into a particular newsgroup. If so, the Web page's URL should begin with the word *news:* For example: *news:alt.animals.foxes.*

If you want to access a particular newsgroup, you would access it the way you would any other URL. Select File, Open Location or press CTRL-L, and then type the word *news:* followed by the name of the newsgroup in the Location box at the top of the screen.

For example, to browse articles in the *alt.animals.foxes* newsgroup, type

```
news:alt.animals.foxes
```

in the Location box.

You can also use the wildcard asterisk (*) to view all newsgroups beginning with a certain topic. For example, to see all the different alternative sports newsgroups, you could open up the URL:

```
news:alt.sports*
```

A list of all newsgroups beginning with the phrase *alt.sports* appears. For example:

```
alt.sports.badminton
alt.sports.baseball.chicago-cubs
```

The actual list is much longer. Each newsgroup in this list is a hyperlink. To browse articles in a particular group, just click on its name.

Subscribing to Newsgroups

Subscribing to a newsgroup is similar to putting a bookmark in it. Netscape keeps a special list of your subscribed groups. It is then easy to access these groups at any time in the future.

To check out which groups you're currently subscribed to, select Directory, Go To Newsgroups. A list of your subscribed newsgroups appears, along with numbers indicating how many unread messages there are in each group. To begin browsing a group's articles, just click on the groupname.

To subscribe to a newsgroup, just type its exact name in the Subscribe To This Newsgroup box and press ENTER. The group is automatically added to your subscription list. If you're not sure where to begin, you can view all the newsgroups by opening the URL:

```
news:*
```

If you want to remove a group from your list, just check the box preceding its name. You can check as many boxes as you wish. To get rid of these groups, click the Unsubscribe From Selected Newsgroups button.

Browsing Articles

When you select a specific newsgroup, the titles of all its articles are loaded and sorted. Netscape draws a special row of browsing buttons across the top and bottom of the Web page, as shown in Figure 6–9. These buttons include:

- HTML Post Article: Write an article with a new topic to this newsgroup.
- HTML Catchup All Articles: All articles are marked as having been read. When you browse a newsgroup, Netscape usually shows you only the articles it hasn't seen you read. The Catchup All Articles button clears the entire Web page. As soon as another article is posted, it will appear.
- HTML Show All Articles: If you want to view all the articles, whether you've read them or not, click this button. If you're already reading all the articles, then this button will read Show New Articles instead; click on it to show only fresh messages.
- HTML Unsubscribe: if you're subscribed to the current newsgroup, click this button to unsubscribe yourself. If you're not yet subscribed, this button will read Subscribe; click it to add the newsgroup to your list of favorites.
- HTML Go to Newsgroups: Return to your list of subscribed newsgroups.

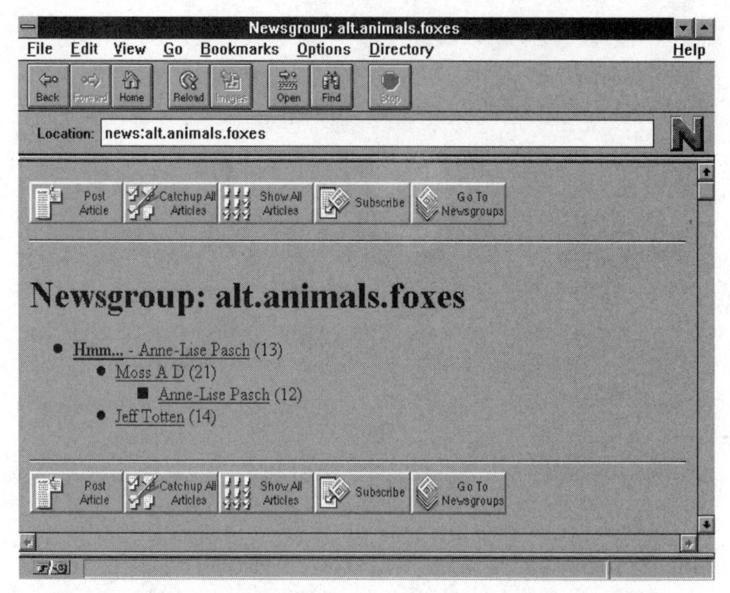

Figure 6–9 Articles in the current newsgroup are sorted so replies follow original messages

Messages themselves are sorted into *threads*. This means that each message is immediately followed by its replies. A reply, in turn, is followed by *its* replies. Each level of reply is indented as part of a bulleted list. This gives your Web pages the look of an outline. Some messages may have several layers of responses.

Each article's subject is a hyperlink. To read the article itself, just click on the subject.

Reading an Article

Figure 6–10 illustrates a sample article. Any article you read has the following information at the top:

- Title of the article
- Author
- Date the article was posted
- Organization the author posted from
- Other newsgroups the article was posted to

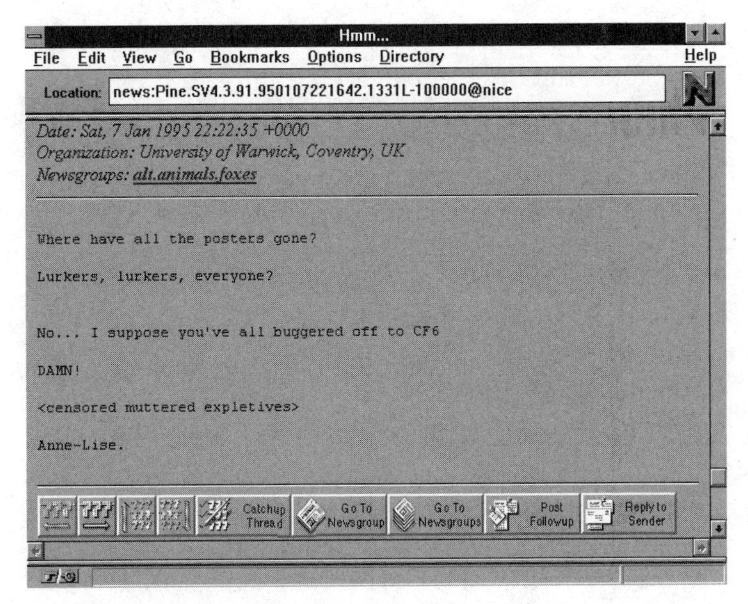

Figure 6–10 Reading a Usenet article

If you want to check out a cross-referenced newsgroup, just click on the group's name.

NOTE: If there are any e-mail addresses or URLs in a message, Netscape automatically makes these into hyperlinks.

Just like with the message-browsing screen, Netscape draws a row of buttons along the top and bottom of each message. You can use these buttons to perform any and all newsgroup-related tasks:

- Left arrow: If you are reading a particular thread, this shows you the previous article. For example, if a message has ten replies and you're reading the ninth one, this button takes you back to the eighth.
- Right arrow: Shows you the next article in the current thread, if applicable.
- Up arrow: Loads up the previous topic. The first article in that topic's thread is shown.
- Down arrow: Loads up the next topic's first article.
- Catchup Thread: The entire current thread is marked as having been read.

- Go To Newsgroup: Return to the newsgroup page where you can continue to browse through the titles of each article.
- Go To Newsgroups: Return to the main Subscribe/Unsubscribe form that lists all the newsgroups you are currently subscribed to.
- Post Followup: Post a public reply to the current message. Your reply will become part of the current topic's thread. See the next section.
- Reply To Sender: If you want to send a private message to the author of the current article, click here. The Mail Document form appears. You can include selections from the current article by pressing the Include Document Text button. The entire article is loaded into the e-mail message window. Each line of the article starts with the greater-than sign (>) to indicate that it comes from another source. See Lesson #11, E-Mailing, for more details.

Posting an Article

Whether you're kicking off a brand new topic or replying to an interesting message, Netscape makes it easy to author your own articles on the Internet. Whenever you post, the USENET News Posting form appears, as in Figure 6–11.

If you're starting a new topic, type a descriptive subject in the Subject box. If you want to *cross-post* your message to numerous newsgroups, just type each group name (separated by a comma) in the Newsgroups box.

If you are replying to a previous article, the entire article is included as part of your message. Each line starts with the greater-than sign (>) to indicate that it has been quoted. You should delete any repetitious or superfluous lines. Just keep the part of the text you actually want to respond to.

You can now type your message in the Message box. When everything looks okay, click the Post Message button at the bottom of the form. If you chicken out and decide not to send the message after all, just press the Previous arrow in the toolbar or select Go, Back.

LESSON #11: E-MAILING

A very nice Netscape feature allows you to easily send e-mail to anyone with an Internet account. Before you can work with e-mail, however, you

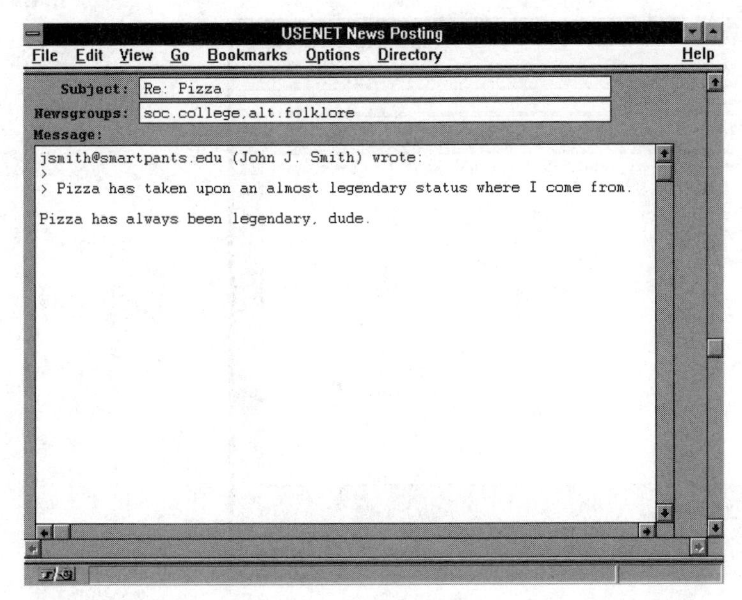

Figure 6–11 Writing an article of your own using a special Netscape form

need to set up an e-mail server. Select Options, Preferences. Choose the Mail And Proxies item from the pop-up menu at the top of the screen.

You should now fill in the following information:

- Mail Server: This is the machine on your Internet provider's network that handles e-mail. In most cases, this is the same as the *domain* of your e-mail address. For example, if your address is jsmith@chicken.smartpants.edu, then your e-mail server is usually *chicken.smartpants.edu.* If e-mailing doesn't seem to work, ask your system administrator for the name of this server.

- Your Name: Simply type in your full name, as you want it to appear on e-mail messages you send.

- Your E-mail: Type in your full e-mail address so people know where to reach you.

You can now send a letter by selecting File, Mail Document or pressing CTRL-M. The Mail Document screen in Figure 6–12 appears. This screen also appears whenever you send a private reply to a Usenet article's author.

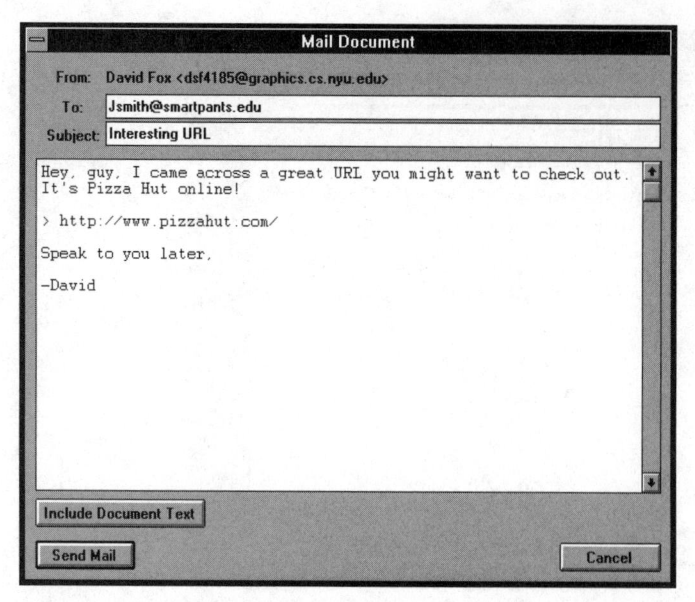

Figure 6–12 A simple e-mail form allows you to send Web pages, replies to newsgroup articles, or other comments to any address in the world

If necessary, type the full Internet e-mail address of your recipient in the To box. All Internet addresses take the form *name@location*. You can include several addresses if you separate each with a comma. If you like, you can edit the Subject of the message. In most cases, the subject line is automatically filled in with the URL of the current Web page.

If you want to include the current Web page's text, click the Include Document Text button. You probably want to go through this text and erase unnecessary lines. You can now type out your message in any blank area. When done, click the Send Mail button to ship your message away.

LESSON #12: GRABBING FTP FILES

If you'd like to retrieve a file over the Internet, Netscape can easily grab it as long as you know the file's full URL. For example, if you open the URL

```
file://ftp.smartpants.edu/pub/windows/games/bounce.zip
```

Netscape will retrieve the *bounce.zip* file (if it exists), and save it to your hard disk.

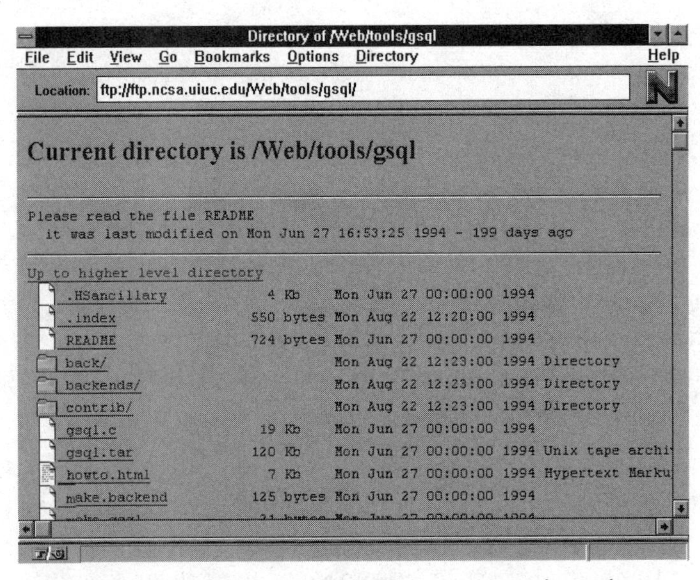

Figure 6–13 Pointing and clicking your way through an FTP archive

In some cases, however, you'd like to browse a popular FTP archive. For example, the archive at *ftp.netcom.com* has lots of great shareware, graphics, sounds, and text files. You could open the archive by using the URL

```
ftp://ftp.netcom.com/
```

Netscape allows you to browse the directories of any anonymous FTP site. Figure 6–13 shows a sample screen. Directories have yellow folder icons. Just click on any directory to view it. Text files or HTML hypertext files are tagged with an icon of a page with print on it. Again, just click on a text file to display it. Plain files have blank page icons. Netscape will either display these or save a copy to your hard disk. Binary files have icons showing a page with the word "bin" written on it. Click on one to download it.

NOTE: You can also browse private FTP sites as long as you have a valid account with a username and password. See Chapter 16 for more details.

LESSON #13: CONFIGURING VIEWERS

Netscape can handle a lot of different images, but it can't handle them all. If you come across a strange graphic format, a movie, or a sound, Netscape passes the file to a viewer. Before it can do this, however, Netscape needs to know which viewers are installed on your system.

To set up these *helper applications,* select Options, Preferences and choose Help Applications from the top pop-up menu. You should see a list with three columns. This list has the following elements:

- Mime type: These are formats of files that Netscape cannot display. MIME is a standard Internet naming format for different types of files. Whenever Netscape receives a file, the Web server tells it what MIME type to deal with. In most cases, this MIME is standard HTML hypertext or a GIF inlined image. If not, Netscape looks at this chart to figure out what to do. MIME types include video, text, images, audio, and special application files such as Microsoft Word documents.

- Action: This is the program Netscape should run to view a particular MIME type. Most actions in this default Netscape chart are listed as ?????, meaning Netscape doesn't know what to do. If an action is unknown, Netscape prompts you whenever it comes across this type of file, asking you whether you want to save the file to disk or configure a viewer.

- Extensions: This lets Netscape know how it should recognize a MIME type. Each file format has a different extension to its filename. For example, MPEG movies usually end with the letters *.MPG.* JPEG files end with *.JPG.*

To set up a viewer, just follow these steps:

1. Select the MIME type you want to deal with from the chart.

2. If the MIME type uses extensions that aren't listed in the Extensions box, add them.

3. Select an Action at the bottom of the window. If you don't have a viewer that can deal with the MIME type, click the Save button. The file will automatically be saved to disk if Netscape comes across it. Otherwise, click the Launch Application button and use Browse to find a supporting viewing program.

For example, the LView Pro viewer can handle several types of graphics: TIFFs, JPEGs, GIFs, and more. In most cases, you can just use Netscape itself to view JPEGs and GIFs. But what about TIFFs? Select the image/tiff MIME type from the list. In the Action box at the bottom of the screen, click the Launch Application button. Now click Browse and designate the Directory and Filename of LVIEWP1A.EXE. Click OK. The full pathname of LView, including LView's icon, now appears in the Launch Application box. From now on, whenever Netscape encounters a TIFF file, LView takes care of it.

LESSON #14: CUSTOMIZING YOUR NETSCAPE EXPERIENCE

Netscape offers a bunch of bells and whistles, allowing you to decide exactly how you want your Web experience to look and act. To set Netscape options, select Options, Preferences. You can now click the pop-up menu at the top of the window to edit the following settings:

- Styles: How should each Web page look?
- Directories, Applications, And News: Where are various specialty files stored?
- Network, Images, And Security: How should the network act? How should images look? What sort of security alerts should a user get?
- Mail And Proxies: Which machines handle specific Internet tasks such as e-mail, FTP, gopher, news, or WAIS?
- Helper Applications: Which viewers should Netscape call when it comes across a file type it doesn't know how to display?

You've Got the Look

Most Web pages use two general types of fonts:

- Proportional: A font where each letter gets as much space as it needs—so that *m* is much bigger than *i*—like the type usually found in books, newspapers, or magazines. This is used for most text.
- Fixed: A typewriter-like font where each letter is the same width. This is useful for tables or pictures where the spacing matters.

You can specify each of these fonts by selecting the Styles box in the Netscape Preferences window. Select the Change Proportional Font or Change Fixed Font button. The Change Font dialog box appears. You can now change the Font and Font Size of basic Web page text.

Another option allows you to specify the look of hyperlinks. Netscape colors and underlines most hyperlinks, to really emphasize them. If you don't want links to be underlined, unselect the Underline Links checkbox.

There's No Place Like Home

When you first start Netscape, the Netscape home page at

```
http://home.netscape.com/home/welcome.html
```

is loaded. But what if you don't ever really use this page? Why should you waste time waiting for a needless home page to appear? Instead, you can customize your own home page. This might be your personal home page, your company or university's home page, or a popular search index.

NOTE: You can even use a file on your own hard disk as the home page. To see the URL for this file, select Open, File and load up the file. The URL is printed in the Location box. You can then copy this URL to your preferences menu.

Select the Styles box in the Netscape Preferences window. Fill in the full URL of your desired home page in the Home Page Location box. If you don't want *any* home page at all, select the Blank Page button.

WHAT NOW?

Congratulations! You've just mastered one of the world's most advanced Web browsers. You can now take a short tour around the Web, using Chapter 8, What Can I Do?, as a guide.

If you're ready to start creating your own Web pages, flip to Part II, Creating Web Pages, which begins with Chapter 8. The next chapter covers some other commonly used Web browsers.

7

A BRIEF LOOK AT OTHER BROWSERS

7

There are dozens of Web browsers floating around. Some are simple text browsers like Lynx; others are designed for users with special needs. For example, certain browsers can display Japanese characters, others can read in complex mathematical equations, and still others can show actual moving video images embedded within a Web page.

About half the world's Web users seem to use Mosaic, with most of the other half probably using Netscape. The rest of them, by and large, make do with Lynx or SlipKnot. There are, however, a few other contenders. Some of these browsers have a lot of promise, and some of them have a lot of history behind them.

Several Internet providers or software companies give you their own browser when you sign up. These browsers may or may not be faster, easier, or more full-featured than Mosaic. In most cases, these so-called commercial browsers are actually clones of Mosaic, with similar menus, icons, and commands.

SPRY AIR MOSAIC

The Spry Corporation bought the rights to NCSA Mosaic and decided to spruce it up. The result is the AIR Mosaic. AIR is a commercial product, included in the *Internet in a Box* package or the AIR series TCP/IP package. While AIR is slightly faster than older versions of Mosaic, it still makes you wait for all images to load before you can start browsing a page. Netscape is faster, has more features, and lets you configure more options.

Features

Some of AIR Mosaic's features include:

- Kiosk mode: Empty your screen of toolbars, buttons, and menus, so you can view Web pages without interference—a great way to demonstrate Web pages to clients, friends, or classes. You can even set AIR Mosaic on autopilot so it scrolls through certain pages automatically.
- Built-in hotlists: Go directly to many important sites around the Web. To make life even easier, you can organize these hotlists into folders and subfolders, and add your favorite Web pages directly to a pull-down menu.
- Hotlist converter: Make NCSA Mosaic hotlists into AIR Mosaic hotlists with a minimum of keystrokes.
- Pull-down configuration menus: Set your preferences for viewers, fonts, color, and other preferences easily.
- Memory cache: Speed up page reloading by storing each page that is read.
- Printer support: Print hard copies of your favorite Web pages—and check them out first with the print preview option.
- Drag and drop support: Use the Mouse to drop text or HTML files into the AIR Mosaic icon instead of typing in their names.

- HTML Usenet newsreader: Read-only access to newsgroups. (Unfortunately, you cannot use AIR Mosaic to post news.)
- HTML Load-to-disk mode: Store a Web page's text or graphics on your hard disk directly, without reading it first. If you hold down the SHIFT key while clicking a link, the page is automatically loaded to disk.
- HTML Destination preview: See the type of Internet resource, the size, and other pertinent information before you jump. If you hold down CTRL while clicking a link, you get information that can help you decide whether you should bother following it.
- HTML Image selection: Save time by turning off all images, then loading the ones you want individually. If you point to an unloaded image icon and click the right mouse button, the image is automatically loaded.
- HTML Built-in AU and AIFF audio support: No external viewer is necessary.

Spry AIR Mosaic has a pretty sleek look to it, as shown in Figure 7–1. The toolbar at the top of the "console" is similar to Mosaic's. Whenever it retrieves a Web page, it shows a radar sweep rotating around the globe logo in the top right corner.

Getting It

Spry offers a demo version of AIR Mosaic at the following site:

`file://ftp.spry.com/AirMosaicDemo/AMOSDEMO.EXE`

The demo includes all of AIR Mosaic's regular features. The only catch is that after you view six Web pages, the demo becomes crippled. To view any more, you have to order a registered copy. For more details, contact Spry:

Spry Inc.
800-777-9638
info@spry.com

Spry's home page is located at:

`http://www.spry.com/`

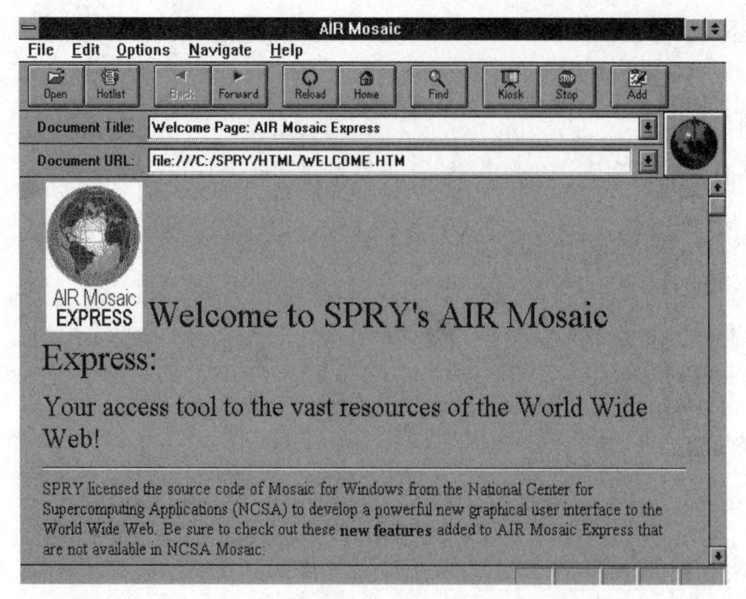

Figure 7–1 A breath of fresh AIR? The basic AIR Mosaic screen

WINWEB

ElNet's WinWeb is the Windows sister program of the popular MacWeb for the Macintosh. WinWeb is probably the most rudimentary graphical browser you can get your hands on. It offers hyperlinks, hyperimages, clickable image maps, and all the other basics. However, it has problems reading in some Web pages. It also lacks advanced features such as forms or transparent images, and can't use Internet resources such as telnet, e-mail, or WAIS.

Consider WinWeb if your computer hasn't got enough memory or disk space to support more advanced browsers—it may run when no other graphical browser will work.

Features

WinWeb offers these basic features:

- Easy printing: A print preview option lets you see what the hard copy will look like.
- Load-to-disk mode: You can have a Web page loaded to disk instead of displayed.

- HTML Image option: You can decide whether or not you want images to be loaded.
- HTML Customization: You can adjust the way your screen fonts and colors look.
- HTML History lists and hotlists: They're pretty basic, but better than nothing.

The WinWeb screen has a simple, no-nonsense look to it, as shown in Figure 7–2. Much like any other browser, it includes buttons that allow you to access a home page, view a history list, or view a hotlist. To access a hyperlink, just click on it.

Getting It

To download WinWeb, use any Web browser or FTP software to access the site:

```
ftp://ftp.einet.net/einet/pc/winweb/winweb.zip
```

You can also find out more about WinWeb by accessing EINet's home page:

```
http://www.mcc.com/
```

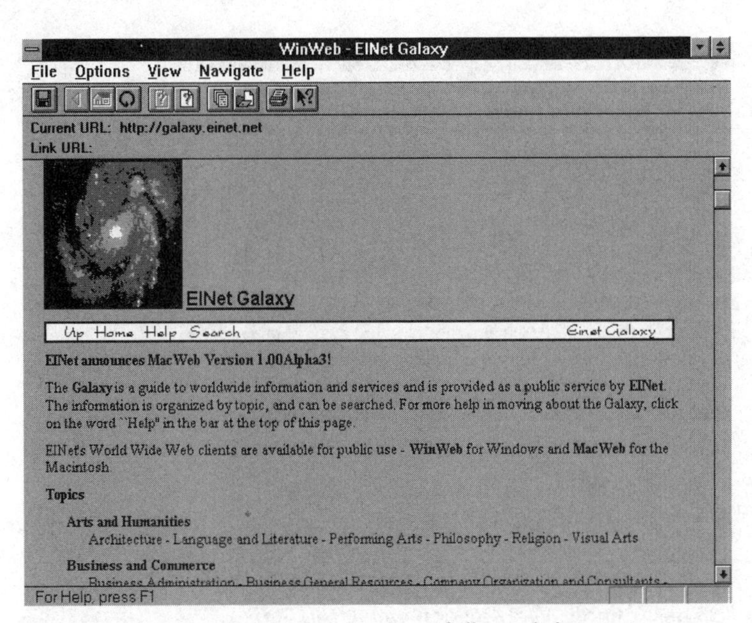

Figure 7–2 WinWeb is a good, no-frills Web browser

For more information, contact EINet:

EINet Windows Software
MCC
3500 West Balcones Center Drive
Austin TX 78759-6509
USAwinweb@mcc.com

CELLO

When Cello first came out, it was a favorite for a lot of Webbers. The screen area was large. Hyperlinks were clearly marked, surrounded by perforated boxes. Images often appeared sharper on a Cello screen than they did on other browsers. Cello also had a nice style of colors, bullets, lines, and fonts—Web pages looked more like finished documents than like haphazard Internet data. It also had more features and options than the original version of Mosaic. See Figure 7–3 for a sample Cello screen.

The Cornell University's Legal Information Institute developed Cello, and offers it absolutely free to all Internet users. Currently, however, there is little need for Cello. Mosaic Version 2 is also free, and is far superior. Cello takes quite a while to load pages and often gets confused if it runs across a strange file. The Cello menu structure is also pretty confusing to figure out.

There are some die-hard Cello fans out there, however.

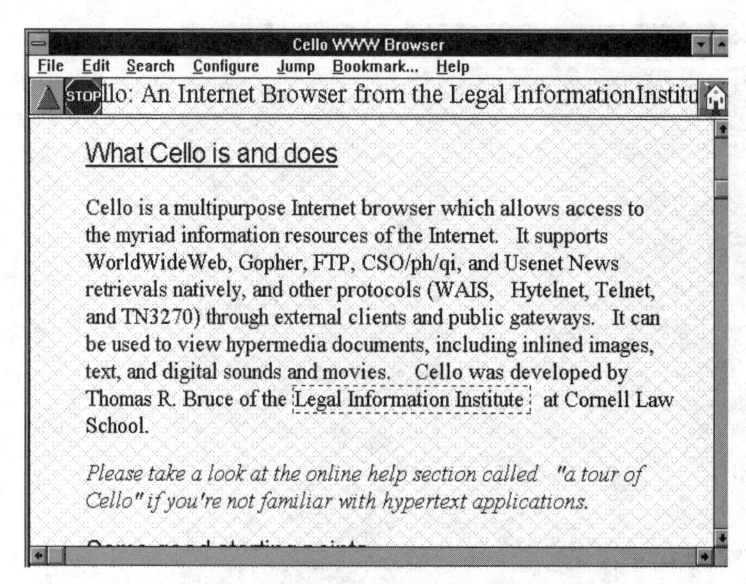

Figure 7–3 Orchestrating a Web session with Cello

Features

Cello offers the following features:

- HTML Graphics: You can use graphical imagemaps, inline graphics, and all the usual Web multimedia tricks.
- HTML Hypertext: Text links are clearly marked inside a perforated box.
- HTML Special commands: Cello acts more like an Internet tool than a basic Web browser. Rather than type in full URLs, for example, you can choose FTP, telnet, WAIS, phonebook, hytelnet, rlogin, and gopher from menus—all you type is the variable information.
- HTML Customization: Lots of configuration options allow you to adjust the look of your screen.

Getting It

The Cello file is available from

`ftp://ftp.law.cornell.edu/pub/LII/Cello/cello.zip`

The Cello home page has more information about the latest releases:

`http://www.law.cornell.edu/cello/cellotop.html`

SPYGLASS ENHANCED MOSAIC

Spyglass is yet another commercial Mosaic product based on NCSA's version. Basically, Spyglass looks and acts just like NCSA Mosaic. The Spyglass software runs on par with Mosaic, but doesn't quite match AIR Mosaic or the Netscape Navigator.

Features

If you know how to use NCSA Mosaic, then you also are an expert at the Spyglass version. Enhanced Mosaic has the following enhancements:

- HTML Speed: It runs slightly faster than standard Mosaic.
- HTML Conservation: It takes one-third less memory than the standard NCSA Mosaic program.
- HTML Support: It's fully supported by Spyglass, Inc.

Getting It

Several companies have bought licenses for Spyglass Mosaic:

- IBM
- DEC
- Firefox
- FTP Software
- O'Reilly & Associates

You will have to contact one of these publishers if you want a copy, or if you want more information about ordering the Spyglass Mosaic. Other questions can be directed to

`comments@spyglass.com`

Latest release notes and a product description can be found at the Spyglass home page:

`http://www.spyglass.com/`

NETCRUISER'S WEB BROWSER

The Netcom nationwide Internet provider has created its own Web browser known as NetCruiser.

Features

NetCruiser acts as a complete front end to all Internet services:

- Electronic mail: Reading and sending
- Usenet newsgroups: Reading and posting
- Telnet: Full support
- FTP: Full support

As far as the World Wide Web itself is concerned, NetCruiser looks and acts similar to NCSA Mosaic.

Getting It

To use NetCruiser, you need to register for Netcom's NetCruiser SLIP account. Contact Netcom at:

```
3031 Tisch Way
San Jose, CA 95128
408-983-5950 or 800-353-6600
info@netcom.com
```

Check out the home page for more information:

```
http://www.netcom.com/
```

WHAT NOW?

If you started here, pick up the basics on Web browsers from the previous four chapters. Chapter 5 covers NCSA Mosaic, the basis for most modern Web browsers, while Chapters 3, 4, and 6 talk about Lynx, SlipKnot, and Netscape, respectively.

In Chapter 8, What Can I Do? you'll start using your browser to explore a few popular Web pages.

PART II:
CREATING
WEB PAGES
8
WHAT CAN
I DO?

8

With thousands of Web servers and tens of thousands of individual pages, the Web is loaded with all sorts of goodies from all walks of life. The Web can serve up everything from a simple informative home page to a detailed customer-service database or a complete online service. Not convinced? Flip through this chapter. Sample a tasty buffet of some of the Web's best stuff. You'll find snapshots of the grooviest graphics, clippings of tremendous text, and descriptions of the most interesting ideas.

This chapter by no means covers every possible type of Web page; after all, that's what the Web itself is for. Instead, we'll go on a guided tour of pages that exemplify certain categories: navigation, publishing, entertainment, education, news, etc. These categories are arbitrary, of course. A good Web page usually fits in many categories at once, being educational, informative, entertaining, and interactive all at once.

You should walk away from this chapter full of ideas. The Web is a wide open venue, and has as many uses as it has users. If you can imagine it, you can probably do it.

NAVIGATE: PLACES TO START

More and more Web pages dealing with the Web itself seem to be cropping up. Everybody and their uncle has created an index of favorite sites. Some pages, however, have burst ahead of the game, providing spectacular indexes organized by subject. This way, if you're interested in something specific, you can browse through the listing until you find a page that meets your needs.

Best of the Web

`http://wings.buffalo.edu/contest/awards/index.html`

Each year, a bunch of Web experts meet and take a look at some of the most popular Web pages. They vote for their favorites. The winners receive prestigious Best of the Web awards. There are awards in 13 categories, such as Best Use of Interaction, Best Document Design, Best Commercial Site, Best Professional Site, and so on.

Global Network Navigator

`http://nearnet.gnn.com/gnn.html`

O'Reilly and Associates' Whole Internet Catalog (Figure 8-1) organizes the Internet by any subject or topic you can think of. A Top 25 list lets you sample some of the Web's most popular sites, and a What's New list highlights the latest Web ventures. There's also some information for Web publishers available at this site.

Einet Galaxy

`http://galaxy.einet.net/galaxy.html`

This comprehensive index includes links to all sorts of pages. The following topics are thoroughly covered:

- HTML Arts and Humanities
- HTML Business and Commerce

- HTML Community
- HTML Computer
- HTML Engineering and Technology
- HTML Government
- HTML Intellectual
- HTML Law
- HTML Leisure and Recreation
- HTML Medicine
- HTML Reference and Interdisciplinary Information
- HTML Safety
- HTML Science
- HTML Social Sciences

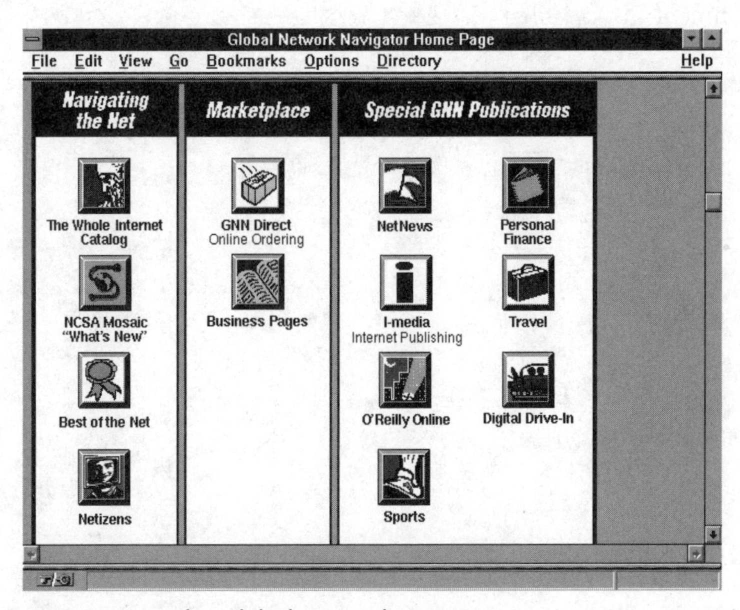

Figure 8-1 The Global Network Navigator

Yahoo

`http://akebono.stanford.edu/yahoo/`

Twirl your lasso and shout a giant "Yahoo" for this mother of all Web indexes. This site, shown in Figure 8-2, contains an eclectic list of all sorts of pages. New sites are added daily, and a special New icon lets you check out the hottest sites as soon as they're developed.

Yahoo has hundreds of links to pages in all the following categories:

- HTML Art
- HTML Business
- HTML Computers
- HTML Economy
- HTML Education
- HTML Entertainment
- HTML Environment and Nature
- HTML Events
- HTML Government
- HTML Health
- HTML Humanities
- HTML Law
- HTML News
- HTML Politics
- HTML Reference
- HTML Regional Information
- HTML Science
- HTML Social Science
- HTML Society and Culture

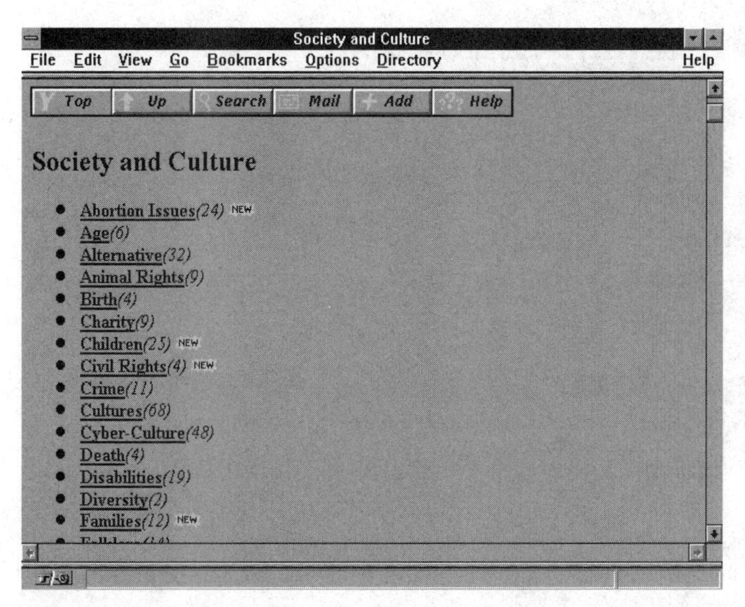

Figure 8-2 Yahoo

INFORM: TERRIFIC TEXT

Hypertext allows people to write in ways never seen before. One topic can lead to another, completely different one. An article can have deeper and deeper layers of detail. Stories can have multiple endings.

The following pages take text and use the Web to present that text in ways no book or other print medium could do. Such text is easy to read and easy to navigate using a hypertext Table of Contents, glossary, index, and such.

Manuals: NCSA Mosaic

`http://www.ncsa.uiuc.edu/SDG/Software/WinMosaic/Docs.html`

The Web is great for online reference books or manuals. A hyperlinked Table of Contents can lead to each topic, and cross references pop up at the click of a mouse.

For example, NCSA offers full online documentation for Mosaic. This neat idea lets you learn Mosaic while you use it. From any given page you can flip to the next page, review the previous page, turn to the beginning of the section, or view the entire Table of Contents.

Helpful Information: OncoLink

`http://cancer.med.upenn.edu/`

Some of the Web's information can be downright essential. Created by E. Loren Buhle, the University of Pennsylvania Medical Center's OncoLink (Figure 8-3) ties together cancer information from around the world and puts it at your fingertips. Soak up the latest research. Or scroll to one of the many sections that help parents, teachers, families, patients, and health care workers deal with cancer.

A New Type of Text

`http://www-swiss.ai.mit.edu/samantha/travels-with-samantha.html`

Travels with Samantha is a full-length travel journal. Author Philip Greenspun toured North America with his companion Samantha and came away with lots of stories, quirky characters, strange sights, and over 250 snapshots. These photographs are scattered throughout, as in Figure 8-4.

These pages allow you to see a side of a country and a culture that you probably never knew existed.

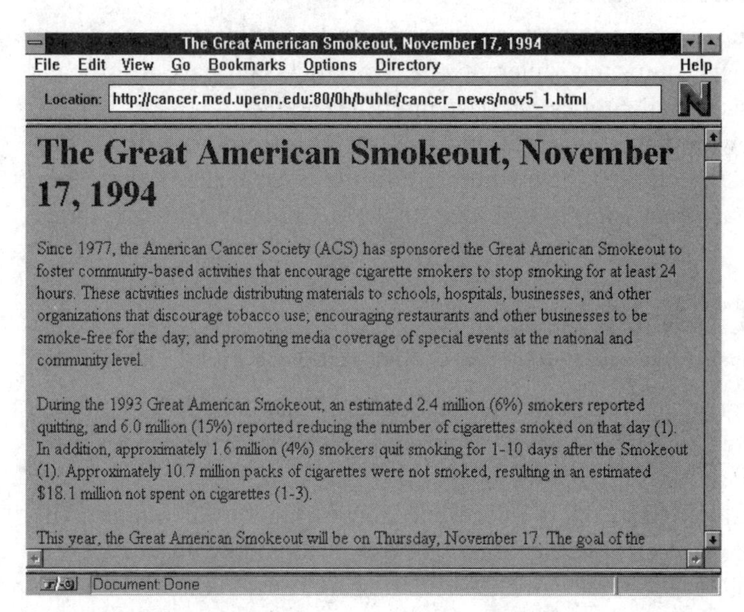

Figure 8-3 OncoLink

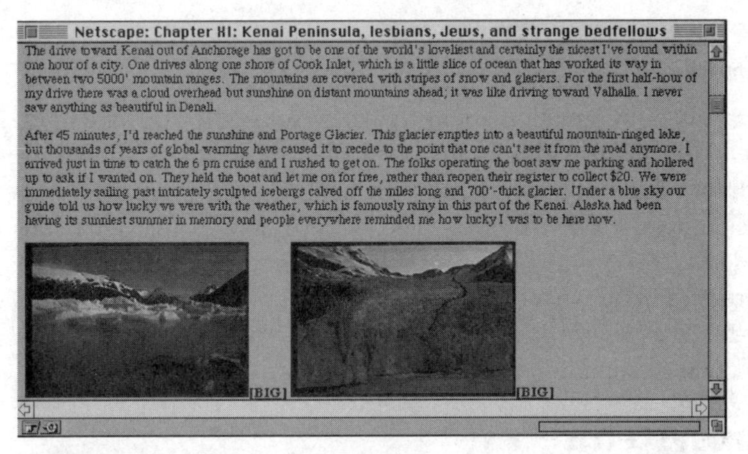

Figure 8-4 Travels with Samantha

HOME-MAKING: NO PLACE LIKE HOME PAGES

Home pages are the Web's front door to a company, organization, or person. They can serve as a home base, a starting point that leads to other related pages, a portfolio, or a sort of interactive business card.

Corporate Pages

It pays for businesses to make their presence known on the Web. Interested customers, associates, stockholders, and sellers can easily contact or read about your corporation—whether it's an international conglomerate or a company of one.

A typical corporate home page contains, or may lead to:

- HTML Corporate philosophy
- HTML Overview of products and services
- HTML Customer service or troubleshooting
- HTML Latest company news
- HTML Stock/bond reports
- HTML Research and development
- HTML Directory of employees

IBM

http://www.ibm.com

Big Blue has scads of information about the latest software, hardware, and services. There are photos, sound clips, and plenty of text, as shown in Figure 8-5. Information about quarterly dividends, stock programs, and fourth quarter results is also included. There's even an area that tells you about IBM's latest technology and research. The index is searchable, so interested parties can find what they want, quickly.

Many of IBM's pages are laid out like a company newsletter or magazine, making them easy and fun to read.

Sun Microsystems

http://www.sun.com/

The Sun page (Figure 8-6) acts as a showroom for Sun's full line of computer systems. There's a section for Product Overview, Service and Support, Company Overview, Doing Business with Sun, Technology & Research, and Solutions.

Rather than just provide a list of systems and features, Sun's Web pages seek to give in-depth solutions to specific problems.

Figure 8-5 Hello from Lou Gerstner, chairman of IBM

Figure 8-6 Sun Microsystems

University Home Pages

One of the biggest slices of the Internet pie belongs to educational institutions. Academics from around the world are among the Web's biggest customers. Many schools–indeed, many *departments*–have created their own home pages to guide, instruct, or bring together students, faculty, staff, prospective students, and researchers.

The typical university home page includes:

- HTML List of faculty, students, and staff
- HTML Course catalogs and schedules
- HTML Admissions info
- HTML Financial aid info
- HTML A map of the campus
- HTML Administration and services
- HTML Calendar of student life

- HTML Campus publications
- HTML University library catalogs
- HTML Other research resources

University of Illinois

`http://www.uiuc.edu/`

The University of Illinois home page has all the stuff you'd expect: People, class catalogs and schedules, University honors and awards, descriptions of current research, an online catalog of the university library, admissions info, financial aid, and campus policy manuals. There are also links to registered student organizations, job hunting areas, recreation, and info about the surrounding Champaign-Urbana community.

One neat section designed by a webspinner known as Ducky lets you walk around the university campus (see Figure 8-7). To get there, use the URL

`http://www.uiuc.edu/navigation/locator.html`

You can also get detailed maps of any University of Illinois campus, as well as of a specific building or even a room within a building.

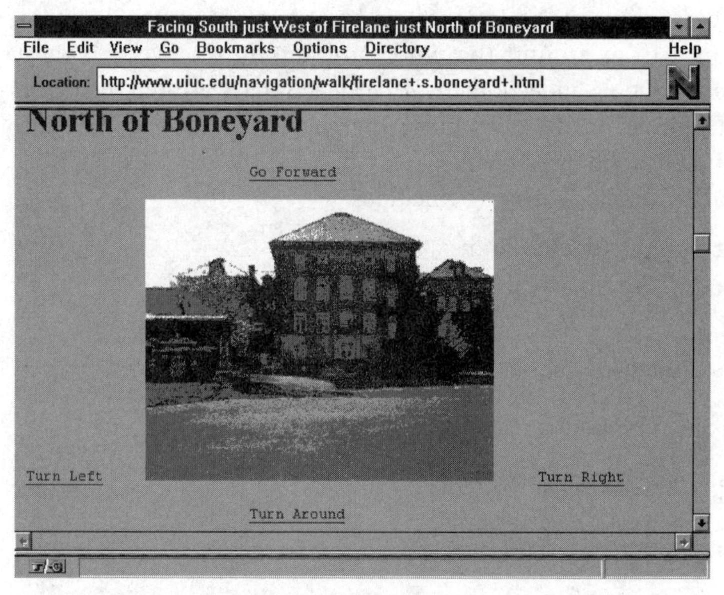

Figure 8-7 Walking around the UIUC campus from the comfort of your own home

Figure 8-8 The Computer Science department at NTUA

National Technical University of Athens (NTUA)

`http://www.ntua.gr/`

Interested in studying abroad? Colleges from around the world have made their presence known on the Web. At the National Technical University of Athens (NTUA) home page (Figure 8-8), you can read all about the NTUA people and their research activities. You can pick up an application for the grad school, find out about local weather, interactively explore a Mandelbrot fractal, see a gallery of local artwork, and read some funny documents. A treasure of information about the Web, the Internet, and Unix is also available.

If you have the right fonts on your system, you can read some of these pages in their original Greek.

Government Home Pages

`http://www.whitehouse.gov/`

Most every government bureau, division, department, and office is beginning to realize the usefulness of Web pages. Huge stores of official information are available online. Perhaps the White House Home Page in Figure 8-9 typifies

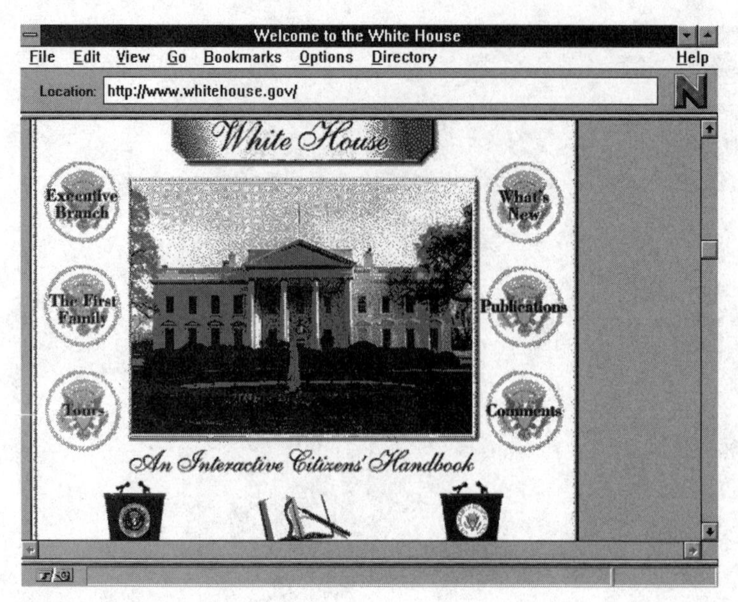

Figure 8-9 WWW White House

what a government home page should look like. It includes official addresses, tour information, an introduction and history of the White House, and a biography of the first family itself. This way, you can pay ol' Bill and Hillary (or whoever the current first couple happens to be) a visit without being frisked.

Personal Home Pages

You don't need to be famous, rich, or crazy to tell the world about yourself. Nearly anybody involved with the Web has created a personal home page. This page can be part résumé and part biography, part business and part pleasure. You can design a personal page as unique as yourself.

Personal home pages typically include a photograph or two, addresses and phone numbers, descriptions of current projects, educational or work background, some talk about your favorite hobbies or causes, links to your best friend's Web page, or any other quirky side of yourself you want to unleash upon the world.

Consultants, salespeople, or other freelancers often rely on Web pages to sell themselves. Many senators and other public servants are creating their own pages. These pages can be a great help around election time, when voters need all the help they can get to understand which issues a politician stands for and which he or she stomps on.

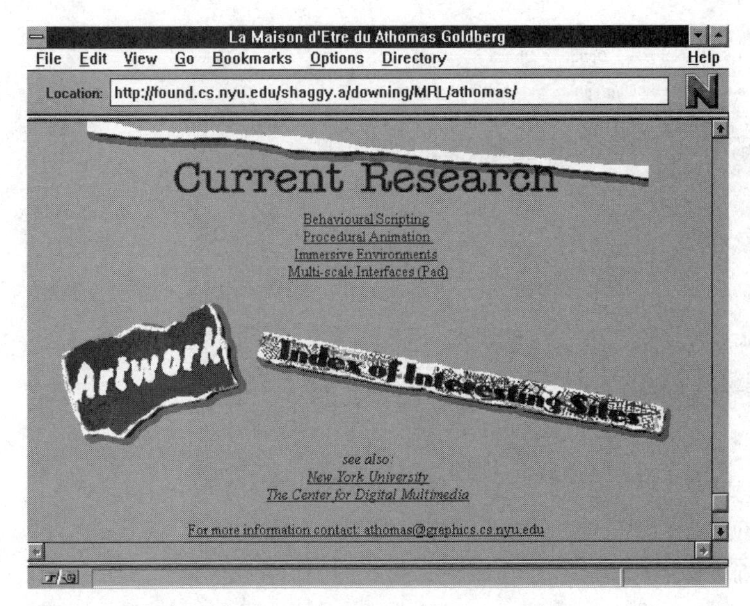

Figure 8-10 Athomas' Home Page

Athomas Goldberg

`http://found.cs.nyu.edu/athomas`

The Web page in Figure 8-10 is a sterling example of what an ultra-snazzy personal home page can look like. Design expert Athomas Goldberg's page includes links to papers he's written, projects he's been involved with, and organizations he works with. An online art gallery lets you scroll through Athomas' portfolio of oils, pastels, and even T-shirts he's designed.

David Fox

`http://found.cs.nyu.edu/dFox`

Why not? At the risk of being eponymous, Figure 8-11 shows one of your authors' own home pages. The design is simple but effective.

A Literary section talks about books and articles in press or in progress. It even includes a few sample short stories and poems to read through. An Art section lets you preview several drawings and paintings. A Computer section discusses latest research projects. And a Links section takes you to other interesting pages.

The full source code and images for this set of pages is included in the enclosed CD-ROM in the \HTML\DAVID directory. Chapters 11 and 12 use sections of this home page as examples.

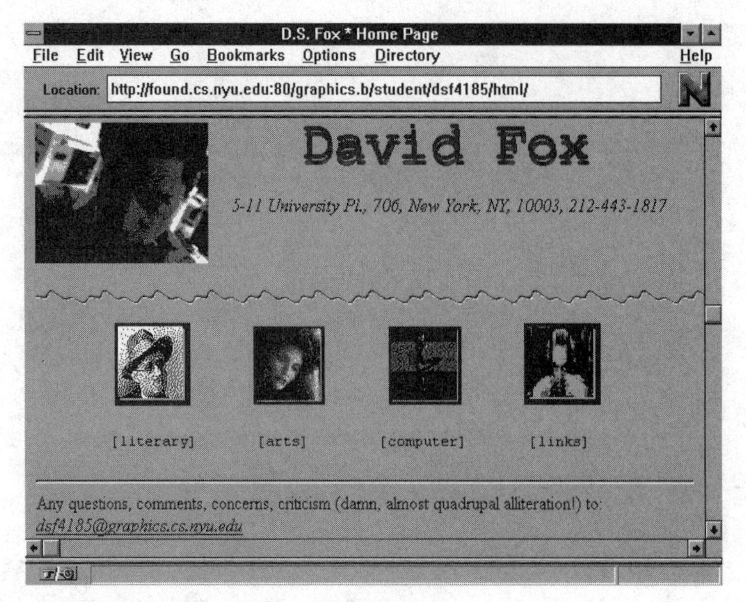

Figure 8-11 David Fox's Home Page

TEACH: EDUCATION

One of hypertext's greatest advantages is the vast amount of information that can be processed in a short period of time. This turns the Web into a fantastic learning tool. Kids (not to mention grown-ups) absolutely *love* clicking on pictures and text. By giving people some control over the information presented to them, studying becomes almost as much fun as playing video games. Almost.

Geography Skills

`http://ww.usgs.gov/education/teacher/what-do-maps-show/index.html`

The United States Geological Survey has a vast depository of cool information. One of the neatest pages in the Web is the What Do Maps Show section. This page consists of a huge "poster" consisting of several frames (see Figure 8-12). Each frame contains a different type of map—relief map, road map, aerial map, political map, etc. Clicking on each map tells you more about it. You can learn how maps are made, and which maps are good for which purposes. Parts of the poster can also be downloaded, printed, or viewed on a full screen.

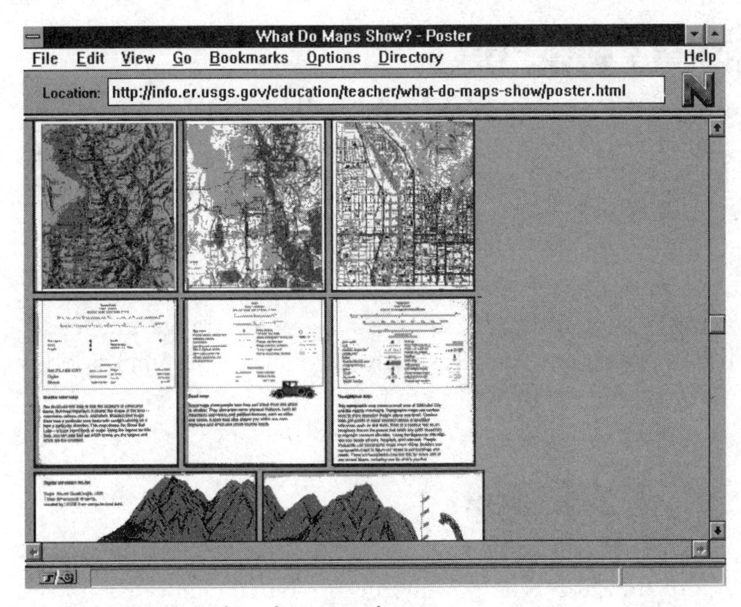

Figure 8-12 What do maps show?

ERIC

`http://ericir.syr.edu/Main.html`

The Educational Resources Information Center (ERIC) is a huge database of ideas, stories, lesson plans, educational technology, textbooks, literature, and other educational media.

The AskERIC section allows K-12 teachers, librarians, and administrators to ask any education-related question at all. ERIC experts will respond within two days with advice, a reference, or an exact answer.

Britannica Online

`http://www.eb.com/`

The world-famous *Encyclopædia Britannica* is now online–all 44 million words of it. The Britannica Online service also includes Merriam-Webster's Collegiate Dictionary and the Britannica Book of the Year. As of now, only schools or other institutions can subscribe to this service.

An online encyclopedia not only lets you look up words, but you can search the entire text for a particular term, hyperlink to related topics, and browse a vast index. Inlined images spice up the text with thousands of maps, flags, diagrams, and photos.

ENTERTAIN: GROOVY GRAPHICS

The Web may be great for business and great for learning, but the reason the Web is booming so fast and so soon is because it's downright fun. The Web helps tie together entertainment, culture, and other important pastimes, bringing the whole world into your room.

And it's much more than text–text can be terrific, but images are what really suck the eyes toward Web pages. As a result, a great variety of artistic styles spice up the Net. Some pages are abstract, with strange images or symbols that lead to even stranger places. Others go for the minimalist look. Still others ... You've got to see them for yourself!

Here are a few places that make excellent use of visual elements.

TV: Interactive TV Index

`http://www.tvnet.com/ITVG/itvg.html`

Can't get enough of the tube? The TV Internet Resource Guide has everything you could need. There's an interactive TV index, reviews of the hottest new shows, and a TVPoll with surveys about your favorite shows. Links to other television sites let you find out the plots to your favorite soaps, join the Seinfeld fan club, or gossip about one of the *Star Trek* shows.

There's even an online TV guide.

Movies: Buena Vista

`http://bvp.wdp.com/BVPM/MooVPlex.html`

The Buena Vista Movies page (Figure 8-13) gives you access to reviews, stills, and clips from some of the most popular Disney and Touchstone movies. Sample a breathtaking scene from *The Lion King* or hear some dialog from the next boy-dog movie.

Music: Underground Music Archive

`http://www.iuma.com/`

This is one of the most in-depth music sites known to humankind (see Figure 8-14). If you want to take a break from Top 40, Pop, and MTV, check these pages out. There are dozens of labels and hundreds of bands. You can read about most bands, see their album cover art, and even hear bites from their best songs.

The *Addicted To Noise* online magazine gets down and dirty about the underground music scene and lets you know about the latest success

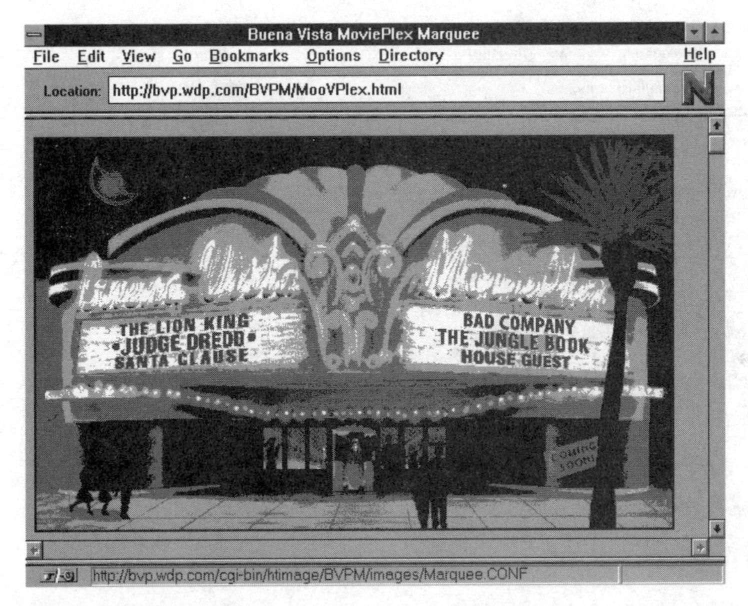

Figure 8-13 Movies

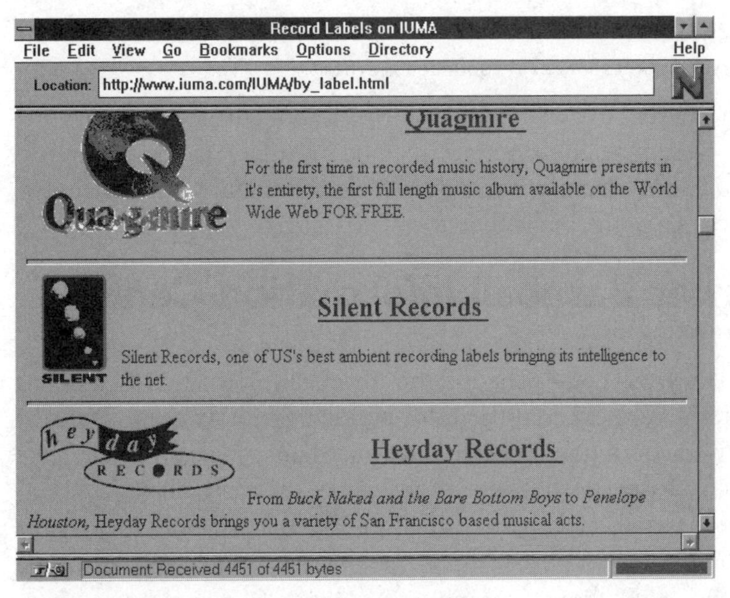

Figure 8-14 Underground Music Archive

stories, concerts, and album releases. For more information about this page, contact info@iuma.com or phone 408-426-4862.

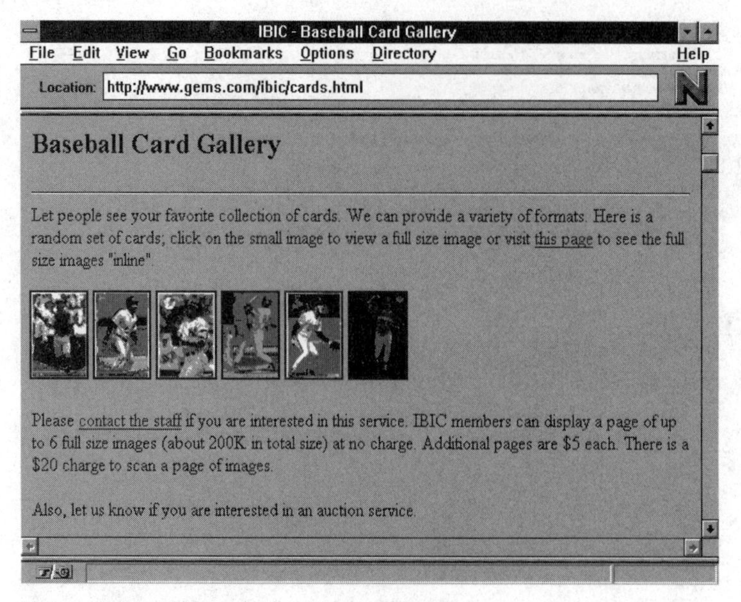

Figure 8-15 Baseball cards at the IBIC

Art: ArtSource

`http://www.uky.edu/Artsource/artsourcehome.html`

ArtSource is a gateway to all sorts of Web pages about art and architecture. You can find everything from pottery to modern art to Victorian houses. This site is growing constantly. ArtSource is selective about what it includes, and it links to some of the Web's best art-related sites.

Sports: Internet Baseball Information Center

`http://www.gems.com/ibic/`

If you click it, they will come. The Internet Baseball Information Center is a baseballer's dream. You can join the IBIC, access the full database of player statistics, view league reports, create your own fantasy league to compete against others, visit the Hall of Fame, or just shoot the baseball breeze.

An online baseball card gallery (Figure 8-15) lets you add to your virtual collection.

PUBLISH: PAPERS, BOOKS, MAGAZINES, AND MORE

Playboy, Penthouse, VIBE, Mother Jones, Saint Petersburg Press,—these are just a few of the more traditional print magazines and newspapers who've branched out to the Web. A bunch of literary journals and specialized 'zines have also been developed primarily for the Web.

From detailed technical manuals to experimental hyperpoetry, the Web can handle it.

Academic Papers

`http://www.nta.no/telektronikk/`

The Web is a great medium to publish your latest findings. Using different fonts, you can create clear papers with abstracts, summaries, and headings. Most articles have a hypertext Table of Contents leading to various sections, hypertext footnotes and references, and links to other notable sites. Some articles even offer inlined illustrations, photos, charts, and diagrams.

Norway's Telenor Research, for example, publishes the *Telektronikk* journal (Figure 8-16). This journal has a very professional, slick look to it. Articles deal with multimedia, networks, and telecommunications and can range from "SCREAM: Screen-based navigation in voice messages" to "Altruism and benefit in Cyberspace." Each article includes photos, hyperlinked Tables of Contents, and other supporting graphics.

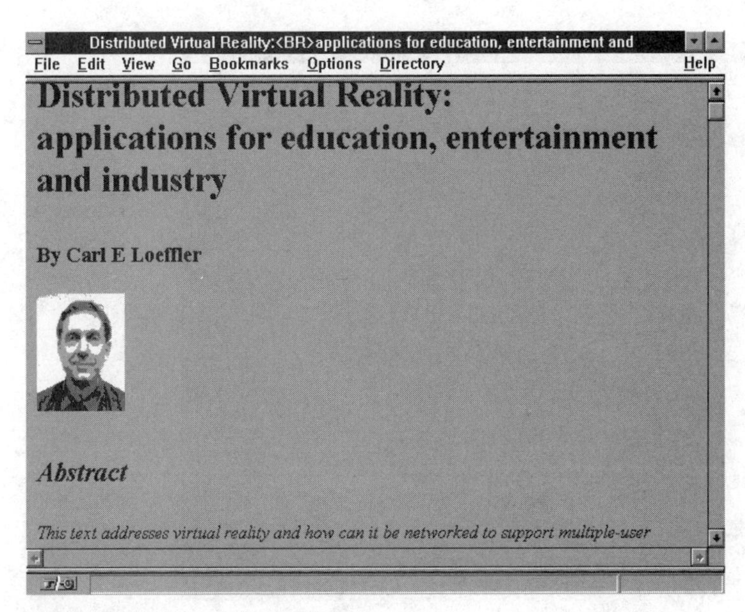

Figure 8-16 Telektronikk

Multimedia Magazines

An online magazine can have departments, timely articles, editorials, advertisements, letters to the editor, and everything else magazines are known for. However, these magazines can also offer sounds, movies, software, and lots of links to related Web pages. An online magazine, then, nearly becomes its own online service.

VIBE

`http://www.timeinc.com/vibe/`

VIBE Online, shown in Figure 8-17, has the hip look and feel of its paper counterpart. There are profiles of recording artists, actual recordings of the latest music releases, and even an interactive Dotcom Bar, where people can chat, listen to music, and pick each other up. You'll also find lots of music-related information.

WIRED

`http://www.hotwired.com/`

WIRED Magazine's HotWIRED service, designed by Max Kisman, is one of the best-dressed places in cyberspace. (See Figure 8-18.) Much like *WIRED Magazine* itself, the fonts are bold and varied, the design is irreverent and

Figure 8-17 Some good vibes

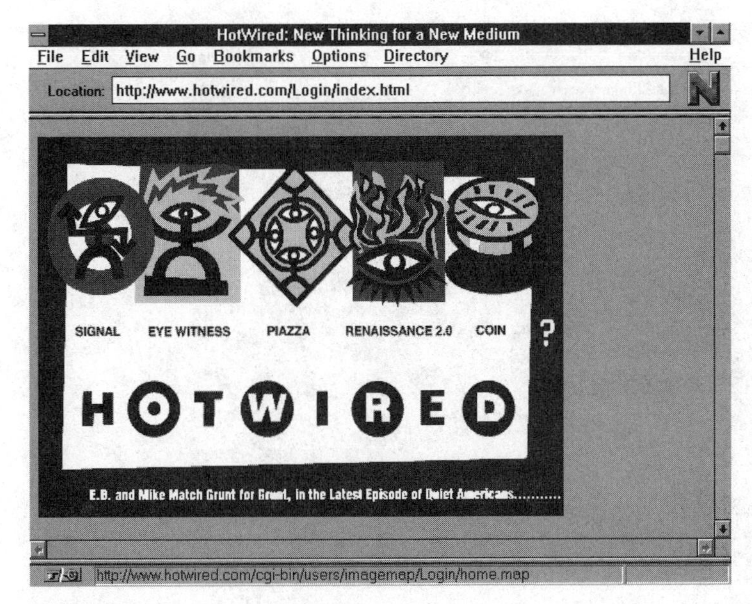

Figure 8-18 The HotWIRED service

flip, and the articles are fast-paced and hot. To "flip" through this magazine, you'll need to become a member (which, for now, is free). HotWIRED requires a username and password.

Once inside, you can read about the latest technology trends, gossip, etc. An ever-rotating selection of articles, stories, and other miscellany also awaits. A link to an MOO allows you to have real-time conversations in a text-based virtual reality. The Coin section has classified ads with some great personals, help wanted, and position wanted selections.

HotWIRED materials are copyright 1994-1995 by Wired Ventures, Ltd. All rights reserved. HotWIRED is a trademark of Wired Ventures, Ltd.

'Zines

`http://sunsite.unc.edu/shannon/ckind/title.html`

If you have a political bent, literary leer, or lascivious outlook, why not publish your own 'zine? In paper form, these 'zines are usually ratty black-and-white pamphlets. Online, however, you can use your full potential to include all sorts of graphics, fonts, lettering, and of course content.

Cyberkind, for example, features some of the Web's most interesting art, poetry, fiction, articles, and essays. The *twentyNothing* 'zine takes a hard Generation X look at life, death, sex, and other sundries.

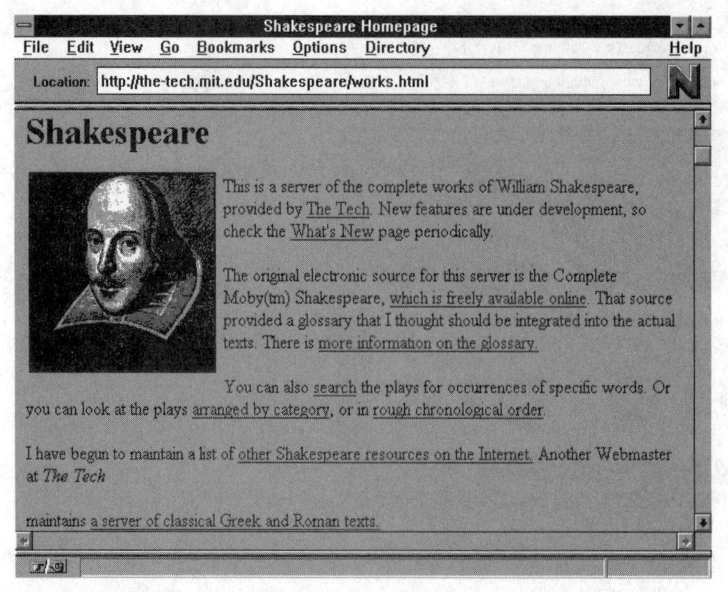

Figure 8-19 The Bard, caught asunder in thy Web

Books

`http://the-tech.mit.edu/Shakespeare.html`

More and more full-length books are appearing online. Whether your goal is to infiltrate, educate, or enlighten, online books can help spread the word. For example, the full works of Shakespeare are available on the Web (see Figure 8-19). You can search any play or sonnet for a particular word or scene or just begin reading.

SHOWCASE: PUTTING YOUR TALENTS ONLINE

`http://sunsite.unc.edu/Dave`

Whether you're a beginner or a pro, the Web is always a fitting place to strut your stuff. All sorts of artists, designers, and other folk have put the following online:

- HTML Art, sketches, paintings, cartoons
- HTML Fiction, poetry, screenplays, plays

- Videos, film trailers, dramatic scenes
- Music, singing
- Resumes
- Demo programs

U2, Tori Amos, and Kate Bush are just a few of the singers who have official (or unofficial) home pages. Lewis Carroll, Isaac Asimov, Terry Pratchett, J.R.R. Tolkien, and Bram Stoker are just a few of the authors. And many up-and-coming artists have features. Even if you're not-so-famous, the Web can be a great place to showcase your talents. For example, Figure 8-20 shows Dave Farley's Doctor Fun comic, which appears every weekday. This single-panel comic has become a cult favorite.

Agents, casting directors, employers, producers, and art dealers are beginning to realize the potential and talent available over the Web. So should you.

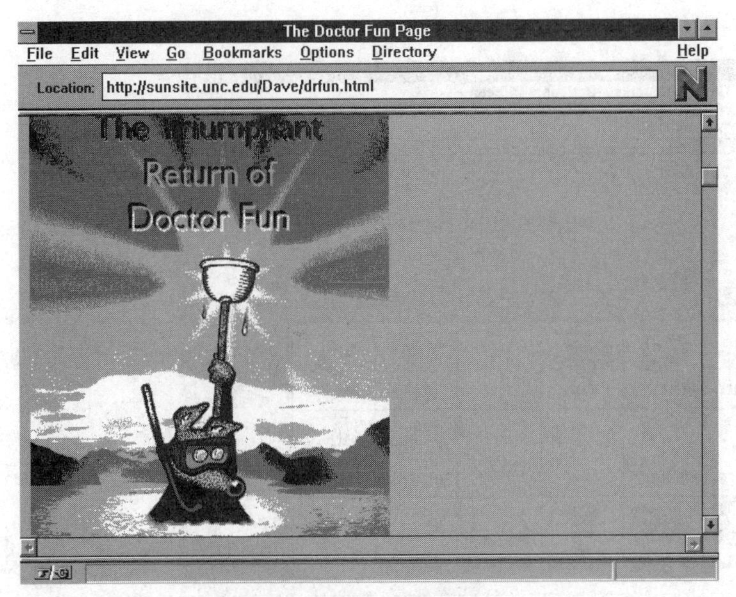

Figure 8-20 Dave Farley's Doctor Fun

SELL: TAKING CARE OF BUSINESS

Money makes the world go round, and the same can be said for the World Wide Web. A huge chunk of the Web's growth is due to large corporations and enterprising entrepreneurs hoping to turn the Web into tomorrow's most lucrative medium.

Some pages are no more than online display ads. These may or may not be interesting or fun to look at. Other financial pages, however, get much more in-depth.

Stock Quotes

`http://www.quote.com/`

QuoteCom's Web page, shown in Figure 8-21, provides the latest market data to Webbers. It offers lots of general information about the market, the stocks game, and company names. If you subscribe to the service, you can get even more detailed information—actual quotes, charts, a personal portfolio service, a PR newswire, a financial newsletter, a stock guide, and company stock histories and annual reports.

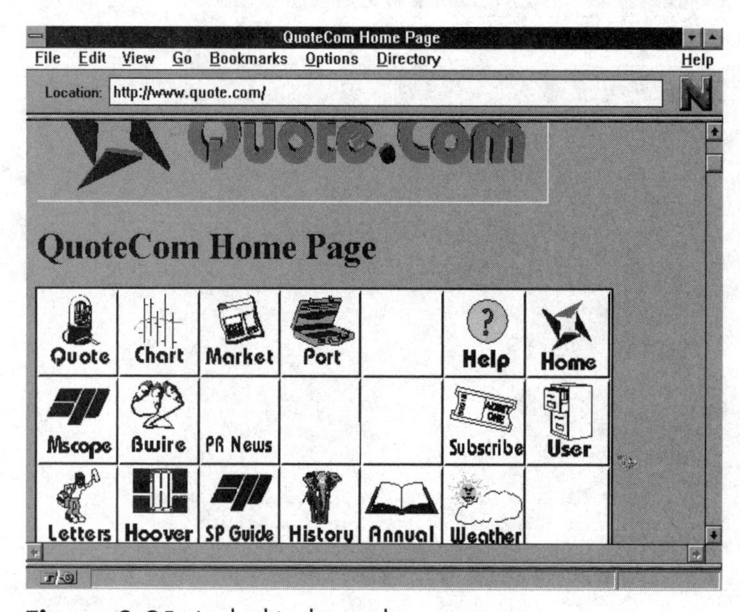

Figure 8-21 Locked in the stocks

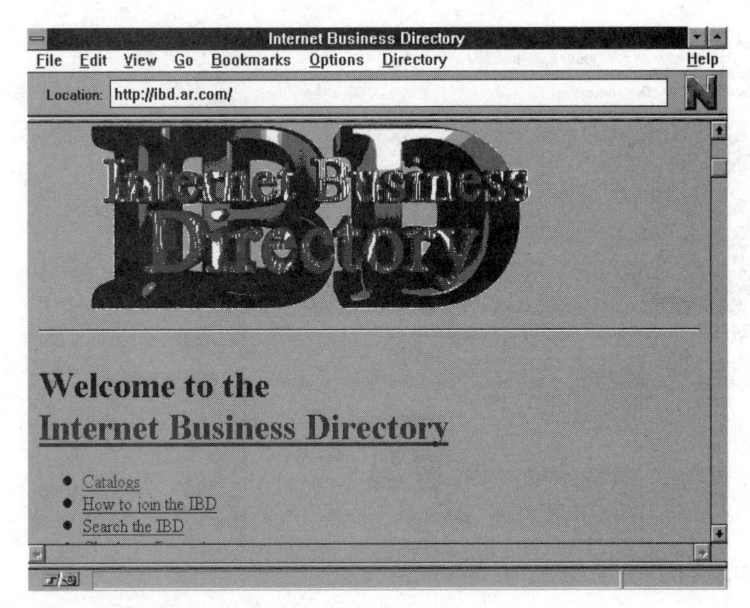

Figure 8-22 Internet Business Directory

Networking Over the Net

`http://ibd.ar.com/`

Many businesses have made a whole business of bringing other businesses together. The Internet Business Directory (Figure 8-22) contains online résumés and a full catalog of commercial Web sites.

Job Searching

`http://www.monster.com/home.html`

The Monster Board, shown in Figure 8-23, has all sorts of job-related data. There are company profiles, recruitment information for recent graduates, and a full set of employment classifieds.

BUY: SHOPPING

Ah, Web shopping. Unlike shopping malls, you can browse from the comfort of your home, any time of day, and with no hassles. Unlike traditional online shopping, you can see actual photos of whatever it is you want to buy, and read piles of detailed information. This atmosphere makes the Web a dream for shoppers and sellers alike.

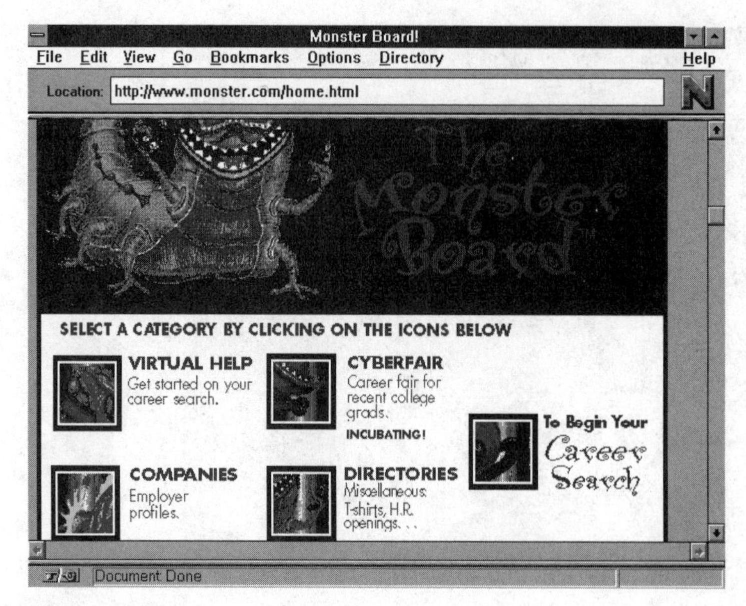

Figure 8-23 Facing the mighty Monster Board

The Internet Shopping Network

`http://shop.internet.net/`

Brought to you by the same people who run the Home Shopping Network, the Internet Shopping Network (ISN) is one of the world's biggest shopping malls. See Figure 8-24. You can browse through over 600 companies, order products, and have them delivered to you the next day.

Each company has its own look to it. And you can find everything from office supplies to flowers to cars waiting for you on the Web.

Direct Ordering

`http://www.pizzahut.com/`

If you're a small company, why not use the Web to hook in a few new customers? You can even offer direct marketing or ordering. The Pizza Hut Web page, for example (Figure 8-25) lets you order a pizza without picking up a phone. (As of now, this only works in parts of Southern California—the drivers won't go to Kansas for you....) This service is great if you get a sudden pizza attack while cruising the Web.

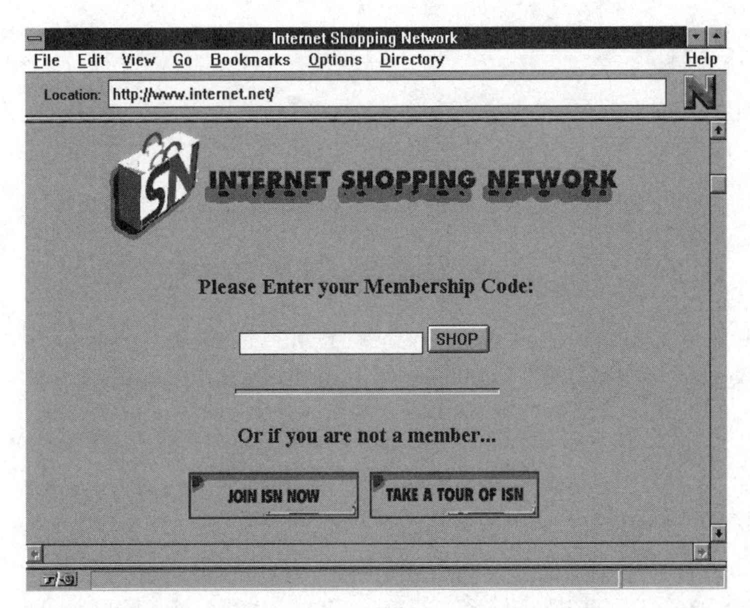

Figure 8-24 A huge cybermall for you to spend your money in

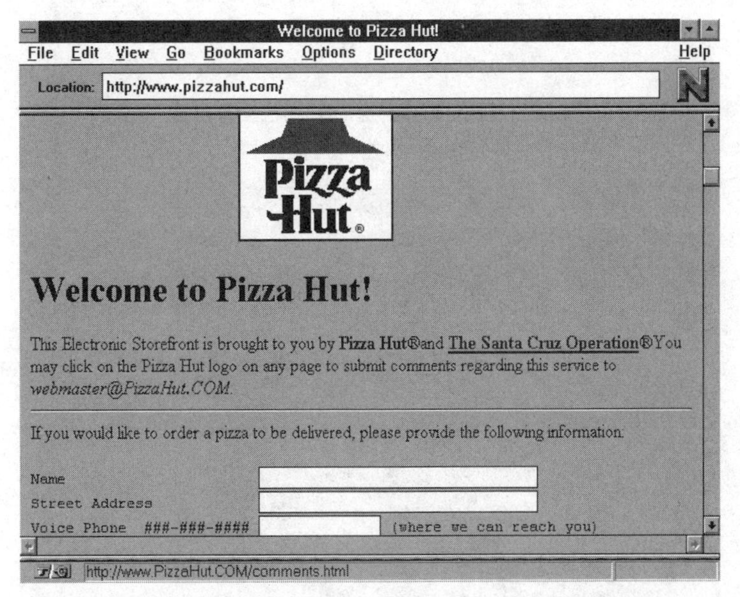

Figure 8-25 Pizza Hut Online: May I take your order?

SPEAK FREE: POLITICS

The Web can be used to spread more than information. Like all media, it attracts propagandists and activists. Lots of political viewpoints find homes on the Web.

PeaceNet

`http://www.igc.apc.org/igc/pn.html`

PeaceNet brings together social justice, human rights, and peace organizations from around the world. The latest news and information about justice, disarmament, health care, and other issues is supported.

FedWorld

`http://www.fedworld.gov/`

FedWorld, shown in Figure 8-26, is a vast depository of government stuff. There are links to Web servers, FTP archives, gopher menus, and telnet sites run by all sorts of U.S. government departments.

You can view information about topics from administration to ocean technology to the military to health care to industrial engineering to justice to urban and regional technology.

Figure 8-26 FedWorld Home Page

An Interactive Citizens' Handbook lets you browse government Web servers by agency. The National Technical Information Service (NTIS) has tons of literature, reports, and databases about governmental science and technology. A Recent U.S. Government Reports section lets you read the latest studies and findings from every government agency you could think of.

OBSERVE: THE NEWS

Since Web publishing is so fast and easy, Web pages can be replaced daily or even hourly. This makes the Web a great place to announce the latest news. If your life depends on the distribution or acquisition of accurate (or at least hot) news, the Web will surely interest you.

Headline News

`http://www.cfn.cs.dal.ca/Media/TodaysNews/TodaysNews.html`

Much of *The Daily News,* a newspaper from Halifax, Nova Scotia, is available here (Figure 8-27). Summaries of the top local and national news stories, entertainment news, sports news, weather, and business news are included. The page even comes complete with a daily comic, "Mou's Cartoon."

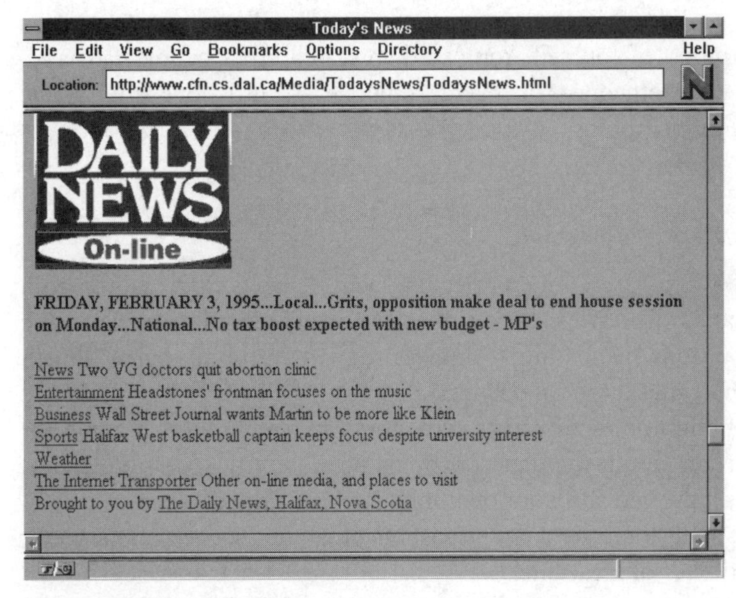

Figure 8-27 Today's News

Weather

http://www.ucar.edu/metapage.html

Nice day today, isn't it? If you're not so sure, there are tons of instant weather stats and maps. One of the most versatile sites is the National Center for Atmospheric Research (NCAR) in Boulder, Colorado. There are also links to all sorts of meteorological resources and articles.

INTERACT: FILL-IN FORMS

Interactivity allows you to talk back to the Web. You can communicate with the Web by clicking a link, clicking an imagemap, or—more likely—filling in a form. There are tons of uses for forms, ranging from shipping orders to membership information to detailed surveys and polls. Some Web pages make full use of these forms, turning the Web into an intelligent responder.

Personal Ads

http://www.mall2000.com/date/date.html

One of the most exciting aspects of the online world is the ability to meet people, whether it be business associates, friends, or even lovers. The Waite Group's *Love Bytes: The Online Dating Handbook* talks all about the potential for cyberlove. The Web offers tons of romantic resources.

The Face to Face personals page, for example, allows you to write a detailed description of yourself. You can then search other people's ads and, if interested, write someone—or several someones—a little love letter. Some ads even have inline photos.

Databases

http://www.msstate.edu/Movies/

Cardiff's movie database contains details, facts, reviews, and names from tens of thousands of movies. It covers almost every popular movie in the world, ranging from silent films to movies that are currently being filmed. Figure 8-28 illustrates a typical database page.

The full filmgraphies of actors, directors, and other film moguls are included. You can search the database by name, date, title, position, credit, and more. You can even add your own information to the database.

To top it all off, there are a few snapshots of famous scenes, some poster art, and sound bites of great lines.

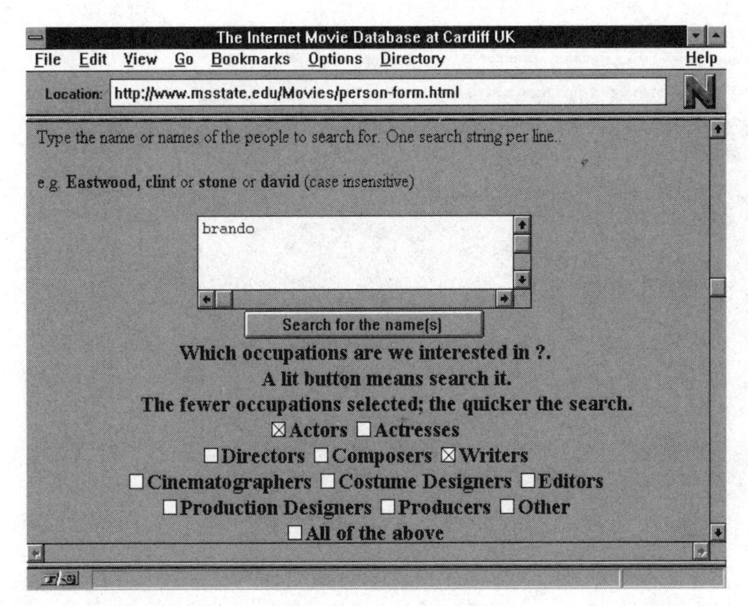

Figure 8-28 Cardiff's Movie Database

Security

The Netscape Commerce server, along with Netscape Navigator, offers transmission of secure fill-in forms. As more advanced Web browsers and servers come out, these secure forms will become much more usable and widespread.

FIND: MAPS

Since the Web can display any sort of graphic or text, it's a great resource for finding specific places. The Web sports many maps, ranging from building floor plans to the map of a campus to the map of the Milky Way.

Interactive Weather Map

`http://rs560.cl.msu.edu/weather/interactive.html`

The Interactive Weather Map server, shown in Figure 8-29, allows you to click on any state or city to view detailed satellite weather information.

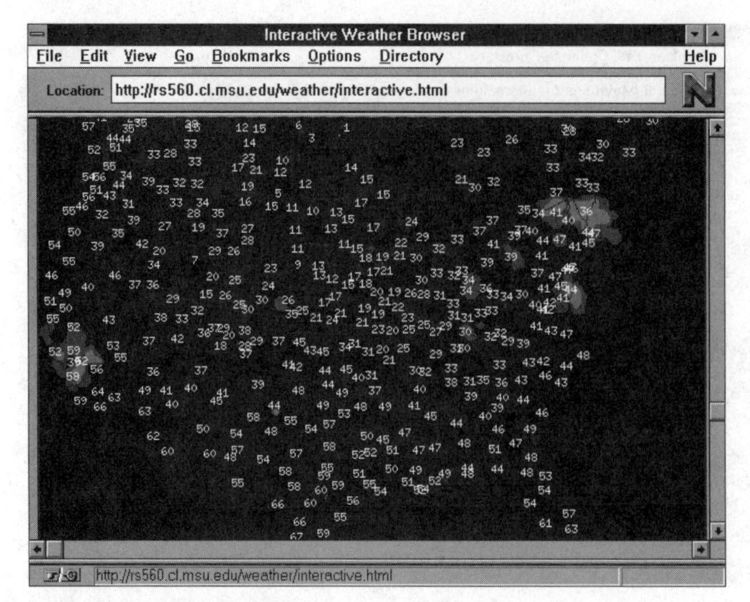

Figure 8-29 The Interactive Weather Map server

Xerox Map Server

`http://pubweb.parc.xerox.com/map`

The Map Viewer, courtesy of the Xerox Palo Alto Research Center, is one of the craftiest sites on the Web. It presents an image of the world, and you can zoom in on any point by entering a longitude and latitude. Or simply by clicking on the map, as shown in Figure 8-30. You can continue zooming until you're looking at the exact region of the globe you're interested in.

By clicking on various hyperlinks, you can adjust the look of the map. You can view borders, rivers, physical features, colors, and more. All in all, the Map Viewer allows you to design your own custom map image.

Map of Mars

`http://www.nasa.gov/nasa_online_education.html`

NASA's Mars Browser (Figure 8-31) is part of its vast educational resources. The browser is a full atlas of Mars' surface. You can rove the Mars surface by using arrow controls or picking a particular feature. There are also special color shots of famous Mars landmarks.

The NASA Web site also includes lots of multimedia presentations about topics such as space, the space shuttle, the history of the space

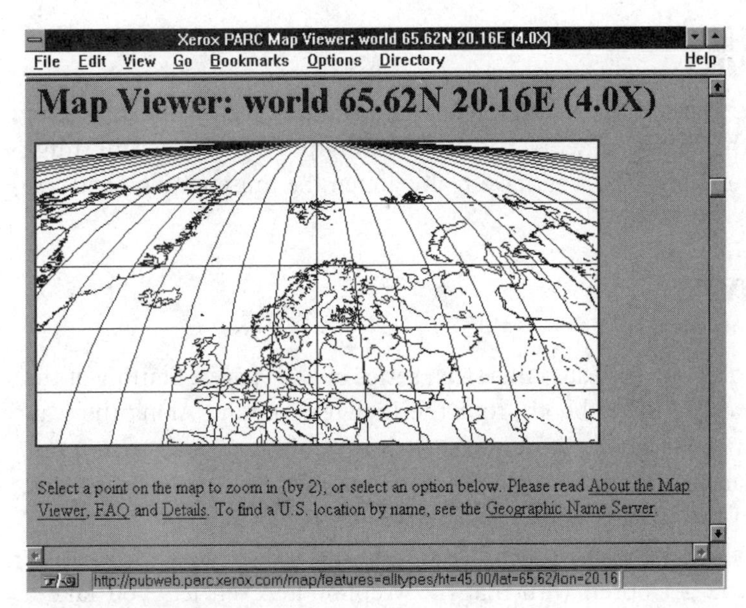

Figure 8-30 PARC Web Map Viewer

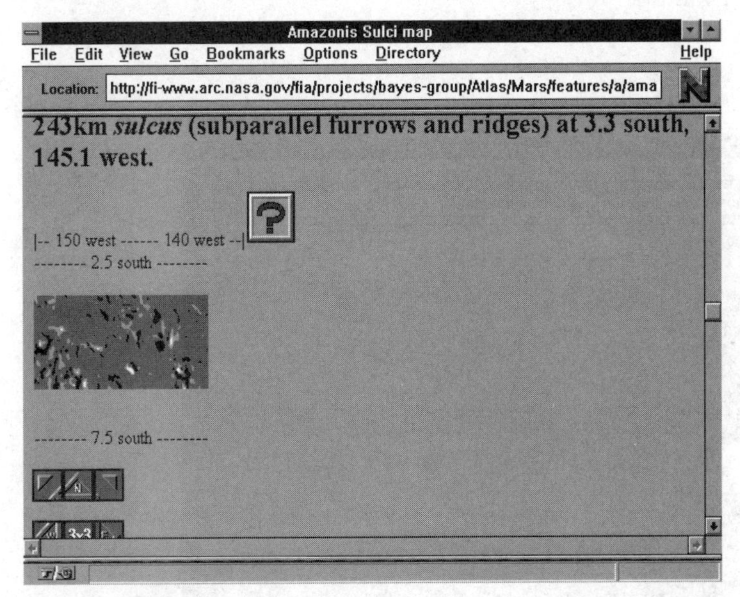

Figure 8-31 Mars Browser

program, space colonies, remote sensing, radio waves, the Hubble telescope, ocean color from space, and astronomy. A vast photo gallery lets you browse through tons of space-related images and video clips.

TOUR: MUSEUMS

Museums are places that present interesting materials, artifacts, exhibits, or artwork to the world. The Web can be thought of, then, as one huge museum. Some sites, however, have really gotten the museum look and feel down pat.

Le WebLouvre

`http://mistral.enst.fr/`

Designer Nicolas Pioch created this sleek series of Web pages. Starting at the grand Le Pyramide ticket booth, tour the Louvre museum. Along the way, you can learn about artistic movements such as cubism, surrealism, impressionism, dadaism, and modernism. Read biographies of famous artists and sample one or two of their paintings, as shown in Figure 8-32.

You can also take a leisurely stroll around the Louvre palace's beautiful grounds. If you get bored with that, Le WebLouvre even lets you take a quick trolley around Paris. Stroll the Seine, scale the Eiffel Tower, and gaze at the Arc de Triomphe.

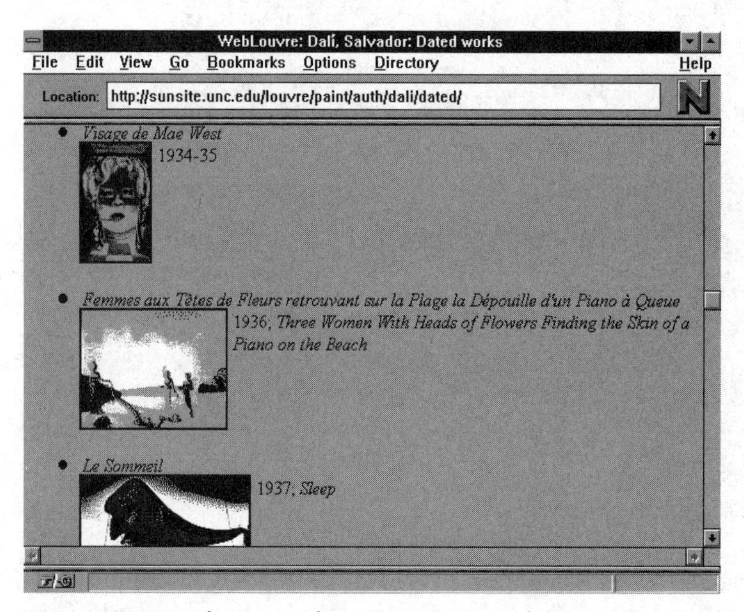

Figure 8-32 The *pièce de résistance:* Le WebLouvre

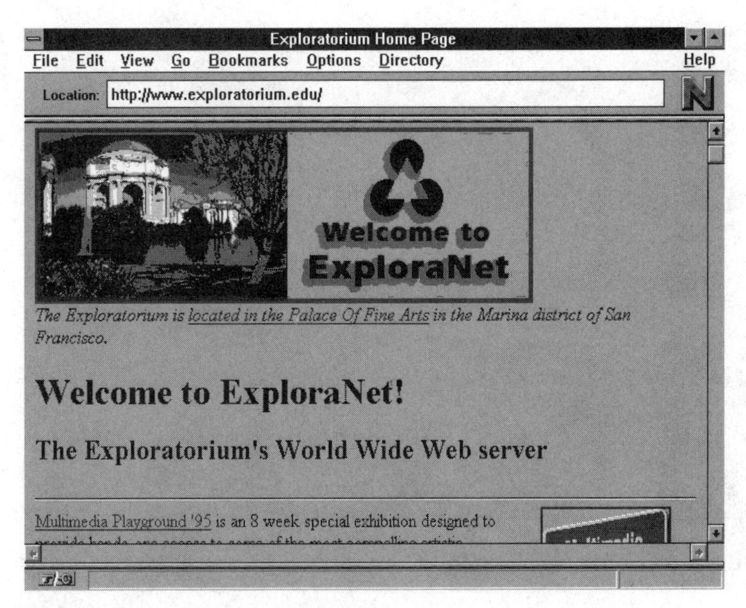

Figure 8-33 Exploratorium Home Page

Exploratorium

`http://www.exploratorium.edu/`

The Exploratorium is a real museum in California dedicated to interactivity, multimedia, and technology. Its home page (shown in Figure 8-33) opens the door to tons of online exhibits showing you the best interactive art, science, education, virtual realities, and commerce. You can also flip through the library of scientific images and sounds.

If you wish, you can find out about the Exploratorium itself or read about exhibits and tours. If you really want to make your museum trip authentic, you can even shop at the Exploratorium Store.

Museum of Paleontology

`http://ucmp1.berkeley.edu/`

The University of California at Berkeley's Museum of Paleontology has tons of photographs and text about fossils, bones, and other real old stuff (Figure 8-34). This includes plants, protists, invertebrates, and of course our good friends the vertebrates. You can also learn all about paleontology itself and read about the latest research.

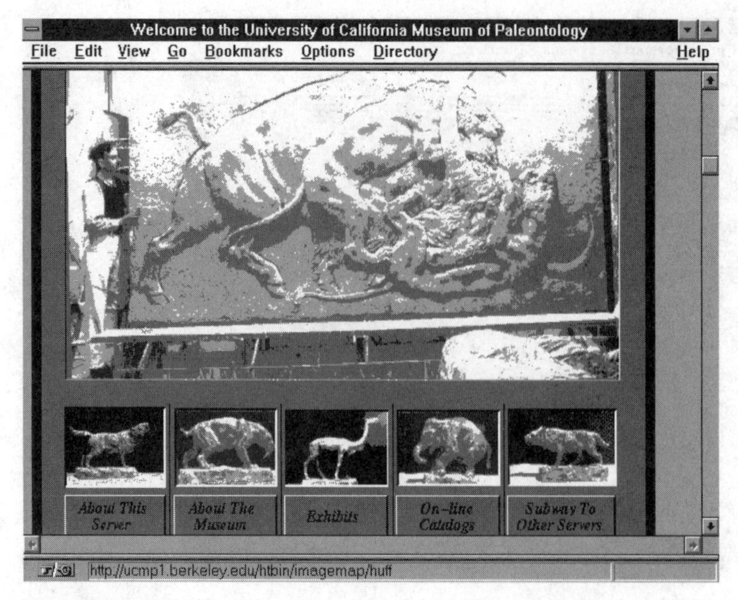

Figure 8-34 The Main Menu at the U.C. Berkeley Museum of Paleontology

You can view each exhibit by phylogeny (what it looks like) or geology. Learn about evolutionary thought or follow a species family tree. There's even a geological time machine that lets you bring the Jurassic and other epochs to your Web browser—much safer than *Jurassic Park!*

VISIT: VIRTUAL PLACES

Being worldwide, the Web can bring remote parts of this Earth to your own home. As a Web publisher, you can create entire worlds—real or fictional—for others to romp around in. If you have a tourist bureau or travel agency, or live or work someplace interesting to visit, why not duplicate the look and feel of your surroundings?

San Diego

`http://white.nosc.mil/sandiego.html`

This immense Web server tells you anything and everything you could possibly want to know about San Diego (see Figure 8-35). There are tons of maps, photos, and lists. News, finance, government, lifestyles, real estate, jobs, law, weather—it's all in here. This site is a godsend for tourists and residents alike.

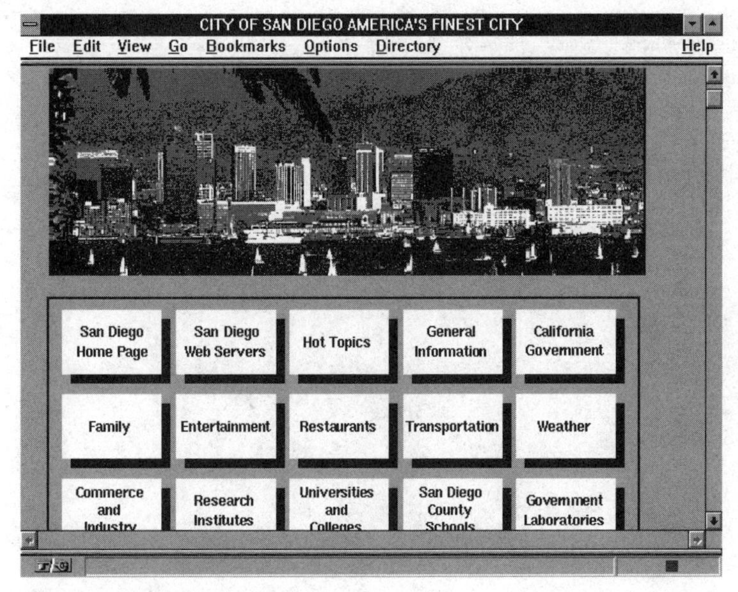

Figure 8-35 San Diego Home Page

You can easily find a cool place to tour, a hotel, an apartment, a gallery, a company, a restaurant, a TV or radio station, a park, a library, or a place to shop. The public transportation area shows you how to get where you want to go. Find out about sporting events (those poor Chargers), conventions, concerts, or special festivals.

This site also includes links to many other San-Diego-related pages.

Paris

`http://meteora.ucsd.edu/~norman/paris/`

Snap on your beret and visit the city of lights, shown in Figure 8-36. This site includes a Paris Visitor's Center, where you can get your bearings. You can then take the Metro, RER, or Bus to one of the monuments, museums, expositions, stores, or cafés. An interactive map lets you click on a location to automatically travel there.

If you want a more subdued tour, flip through the beautiful gallery of Paris scenes. You can also get tons of historical, anecdotal, and trivial information about Paris.

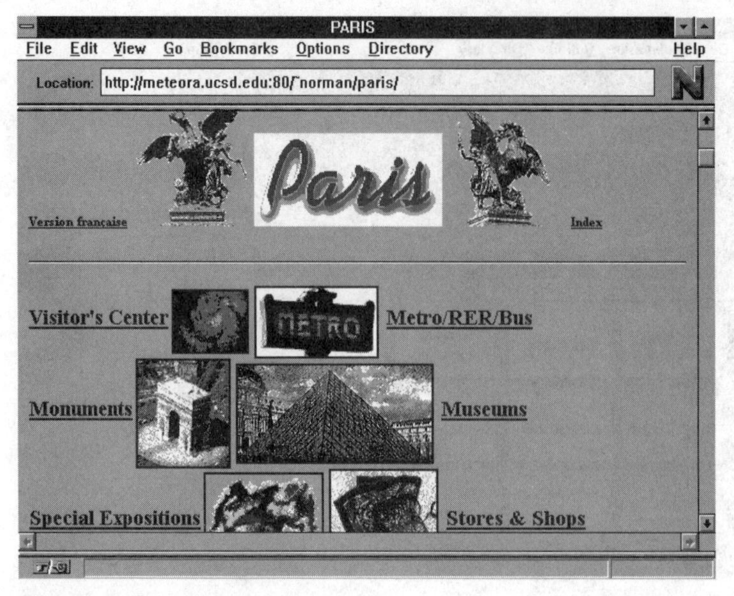

Figure 8-36 Vive Paris

EXPO Ticket Office

`http://sunsite.unc.edu/expo/expo/busstation.html`

The EXPO Ticket Office is an exhibition of some of the best sites on the Web. Click on the map of famous sites to decide where you want to visit. Grab your free ticket and take a shuttle bus to one of the following Web-wide exhibits:

- The Vatican Exhibit: Many of the Vatican Library's most valuable books, documents, and maps.
- Soviet Archive Exhibit: Read about the espionage, thrills, and hidden side of the Soviet's now-defunct Communist government.
- 1492 Exhibit: Read about conquerors and explorers who braved the New World from 1492 to 1600.
- Dead Sea Scrolls Exhibit: View the actual 2,000-year-old Dead Sea Scroll manuscripts and learn about who may have written them.
- Fossil Life Exhibit: The Museum of Paleontology's exhibit about evolution and geology.

- HTML Spalato Exhibit: Learn about the ancient Roman city of Spalato.
- HTML The Krannert Art Museum Exhibit: Sample the museum's works.
- HTML Dinosaur Exhibit: A look at the history and fossils of some Jurassic giants.
- HTML History of Prints: Learn all about printmaking.
- HTML Ansel Adams Exhibit: Photographs by the famous nature artist.
- HTML Mount Wilson Observatory Exhibit: Take a virtual reality walking tour of this observatory.

Downtown Anywhere

`http://www.awa.com/`

Downtown Anywhere (Figure 8-37) is one of the most realistic (and capitalistic) virtual places in the world. You can buy real estate space on the Internet. You can do what you want with your space—create your own Web pages (that would be my suggestion) or just keep it as an investment.

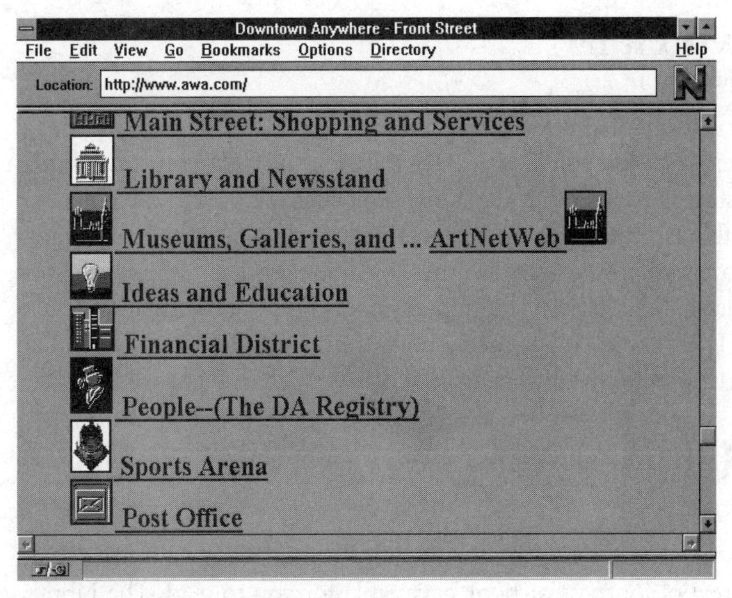

Figure 8-37 Downtown Anywhere

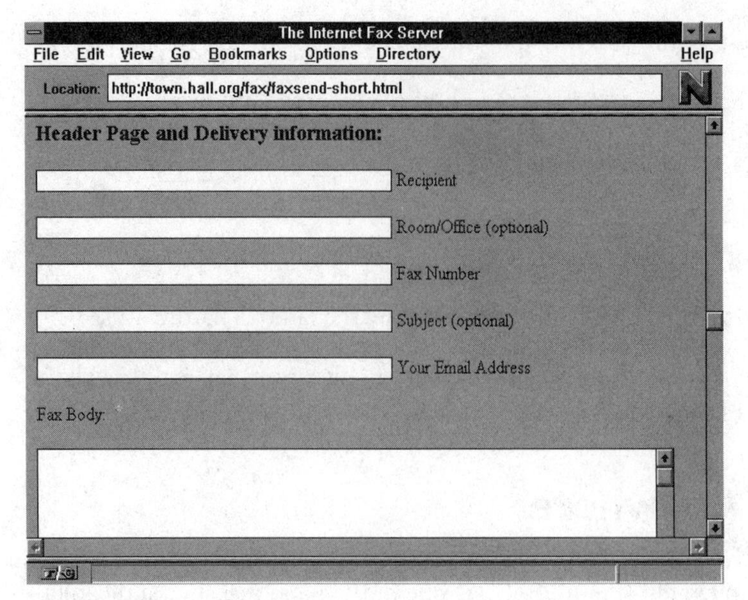

Figure 8-38 Internet Town Hall's fax utility

You can visit some of the businesses and people who have made Downtown Anywhere a home away from home. Downtown Anywhere is basically a commercial Internet provider geared toward expanding businesses.

Internet Town Hall

`http://town.hall.org/`

This friendly corner of the Web contains an eclectic collection of ideas, places, and services. You can tour the Digital Deli to tickle your taste buds, browse bookstores, or even visit the North Pole and meet a virtual Santa.

Much of this is geared toward Internet Talk Radio—a service that transmits live radio programs over the Internet. Additionally, lots of miscellaneous government databases can help you find any sort of official information you're interested in. The Internet Town Hall's Phone Company allows you to send an actual fax out to a friend just by filling in a form, shown in Figure 8-38.

BROWSE: LIBRARIES

`http://lcweb.loc.gov/`

Lots and lots of libraries and bookstores are online. Some libraries even have the full text of journals or books available for you to read. The Library of Congress has much more:

- HTML Exhibits: Documents you could see in person at the Library of Congress, such as the Dead Sea Scrolls or the original Gettysburg Address (see Figure 8-39)
- HTML American Memory: Special collections of documents and other American memorabilia
- HTML Thomas: All the legislative information you could need
- HTML Country Studies: Detailed information about any country, area, or city
- HTML POW/MIA Database: The names, ranks, and serial numbers of prisoners of war or those soldiers missing in action
- HTML LOCIS: The entire Library of Congress catalog, listing nearly every English-language book in the world

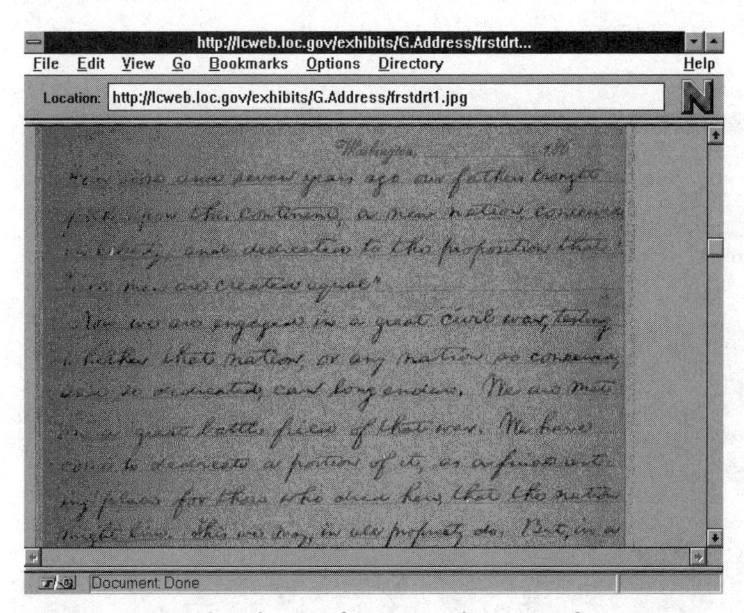

Figure 8-39 The Library of Congress has tons of treats to offer

SURPRISE: OTHER NEAT GIMMICKS

As the Web matures, various creative people are finding totally new uses for it. By hooking up Web servers to video cameras, robots, or clever software programs, the Web can serve as a global front-end for almost any local routine. Some of these gimmicks are silly, others are downright amazing. As technology gets faster and more detailed, the Web will be used to control bigger and better things. Eventually, you may be able to duck into the Web before you leave work and switch on your home porch light, turn up your thermostat, start your coffee maker, and warm up the barbecue—almost as good as having a Spousal Unit minding the home fires!

LabCam

`http://found.cs.nyu.edu/cgi-bin/rsw/labcam1`

NYU's original LabCam, shown in Figure 8-40, lets you view a frame from a live interactive movie. A robot-mounted camera points to a spot in the NYU Robotics Lab. Click on the image. The camera will now focus wherever you clicked. The Web page is reloaded and the picture is updated. You can use LabCam to gaze all around the lab. Sometimes, you and another Web user will both try to control LabCam at once. You can have some neat fights with people, trying to beat them to the draw (or the click).

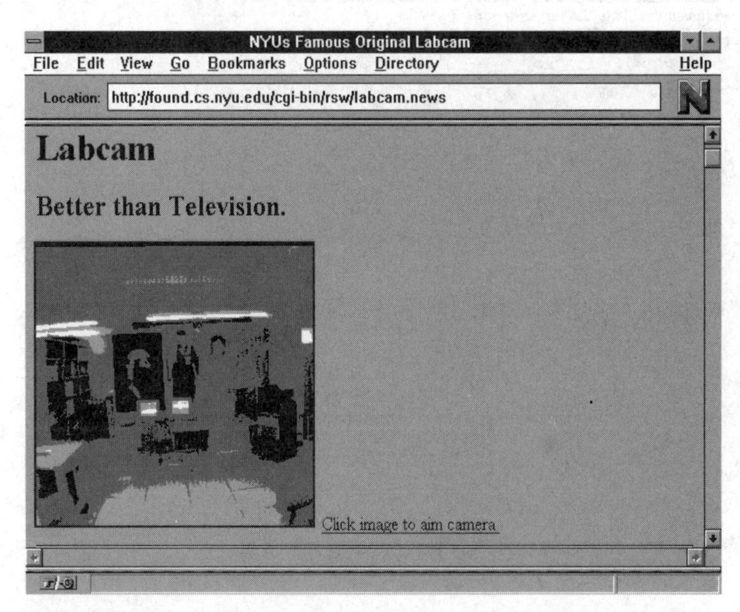

Figure 8-40 Peeking at a New York city lab with LabCam

The Cyrano Server

`http://www.nando.net/toys/cyrano.html`

Make any day Valentine's Day. Use this form to select a type of love letter (choose from Steamy, Indecisive, Surreal, Desperate, Intellectual, or Poetic). Fill in a few adjectives, verbs, or other descriptions. Tell Cyrano who the letter should be sent to. A custom love letter whizzes off to your soulmate. Results may vary. For example:

```
Dearest Lover,
My love, I can imagine myself kissing your curious body and slathering
you with various oils and ice cream. Your hairs are my anchor in the
stormy sea of life; I wonder how I ever made it through a day without
you. Please meet me dressed in your flannel shirt on Valentine's Day
and we will celebrate our tentative love together.
```

Lite-Brite

`http://www.galcit.caltech.edu/~ta/cgi-bin/asylhome-ta`

The Inmate's Asylum home page leads to all sorts of wacky areas. There's a revolving door hotlist that will toss you into a random Web site. There's a fiction therapy group. There's an online cuckoo clock.

One of the neatest Asylum areas, however, is the Web Lite-Brite machine, shown in Figure 8-41. Using small colored lights, fill in a grid

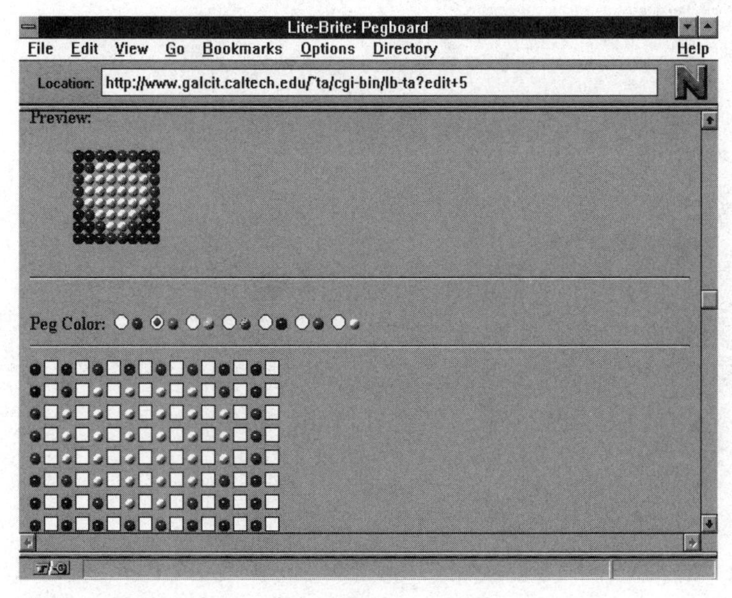

Figure 8-41 The Asylum's Lite-Brite machine

with the lights you want. Once you get used to the interface, the Lite-Brite machine gets addictive. You can create some truly beautiful, albeit primitive, scenes.

The Virtual Frog

`http://george.lbl.gov/ITG.hm.pg.docs/dissect/info.html`

Tadpoles of the world, rejoice! Squeamish biology students, eat your lunches! The virtual frog Web pages shown in Figure 8-42 allow you to "slice" through an illustrated frog, learning about all its organs and other anatomical features. You can peel away the frog's skin and remove each of its organs, one at a time. You can rotate the frog or zoom in on it. You can even create a froggy movie. Select the axis of rotation and the frog will spin on your screen, allowing you to see its innards from all angles.

The Virtual Frog Dissection Kit comes to you courtesy of Lawrence Berkeley Laboratory, University of California.

Say...

`http://www_tios.cs.utwente.nl/say/formpost/`

Want your Web to talk back? This simple but extremely neat Web page allows you to type any word or phrase, as shown in Figure 8-43. Say... will

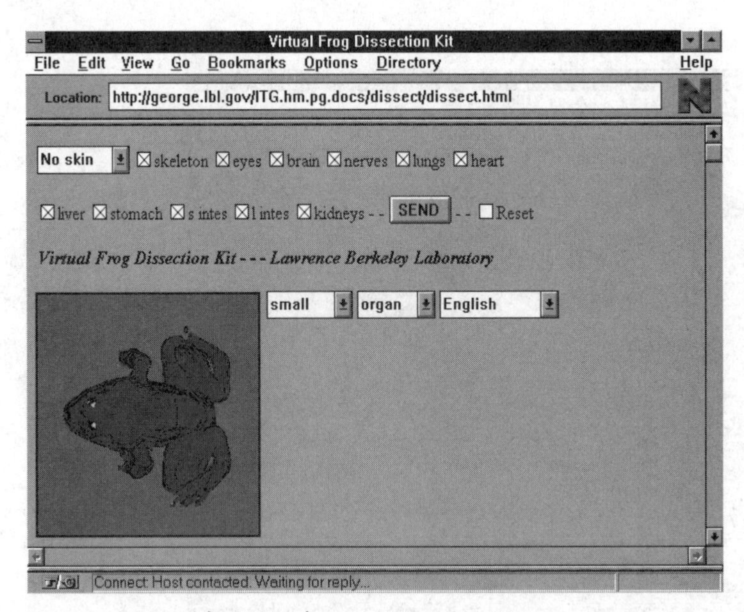

Figure 8-42 The Virtual Frog Dissection Kit

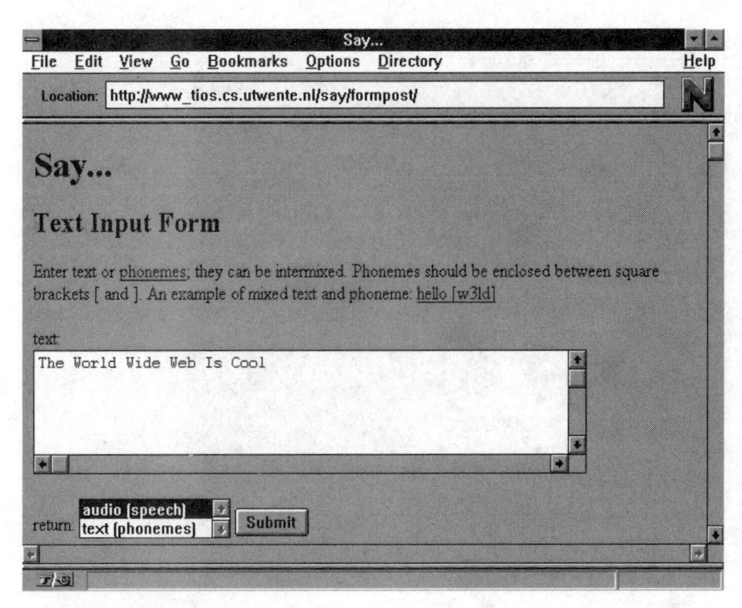

Figure 8-43 Say...

then create a special sound file containing the digitized speech and send that file to you.

Bianca's Smut Shack

`http://bianca.com/shack/index.html`

This colorful off-color Web page is a fun place to wallow in. Even better, though, are some of the neat rooms you can visit:

- **HTML** The Bathroom: Read or write graffiti on the walls, ceiling, or floor. You can use HTML commands within your message to make bold, italicized, or otherwise emphasized statements.
- **HTML** Bianca's Bedroom (and Love Chamber): Talk with a nasty-mouthed Troll. These trolls respond to whatever you say, and you may find yourself wondering whether the Troll is computer generated, human, or something else entirely.
- **HTML** The Foyer: Read about Bianca's latest exploits, and sign the guest book.
- **HTML** Hall of Fame: Gaze at Bianca's favorite photographs.

Figure 8-44 A Webbable finger puzzle

Most sections have a sort of forum area, where you can read or write comments. These comments are immediately "posted" to the Smut Shack for others to enjoy. Folks have been to known to have near-real-time conversations using these forums.

A Puzzler

`http://www.cm.cf.ac.uk/htbin/AndrewW/Puzzle/puzzle4x4image/`

Remember those cheap plastic puzzles that sometimes came as the prize in Cracker Jack boxes? There are fifteen colorful squares, arranged in a 4x4 matrix with one square missing, as shown in Figure 8-44. You can slide any square into the blank space, moving around the cubes until you form some sort of picture. It's like something between a jigsaw puzzle and Rubik's cube.

Well, now you can play the same game online. Andrew Wilson's creative Web page allows you to simply click on the tile you want to move.

WHAT NOW?

Inspired? A photo or brief description of a Web page can never do it justice. Try out some of these sites for yourself. Start thinking about your own pages—how they'll look, what they'll offer, and how you'll design all those features. The next chapter gives you some hints on what to concentrate on when you create a Web page, how to refine your view of your audience and your objective, and what pitfalls to watch out for.

Chapters 10 through 16 get down and dirty, teaching you how to pull off everything from basic hypertext to great-looking graphics to sound to full interactivity. Chapters 17 through 19 cover various editors, translators, and other utilities that can make writing a Web page a lot easier and a lot more fun.

So get started! The world is looking forward to seeing you.

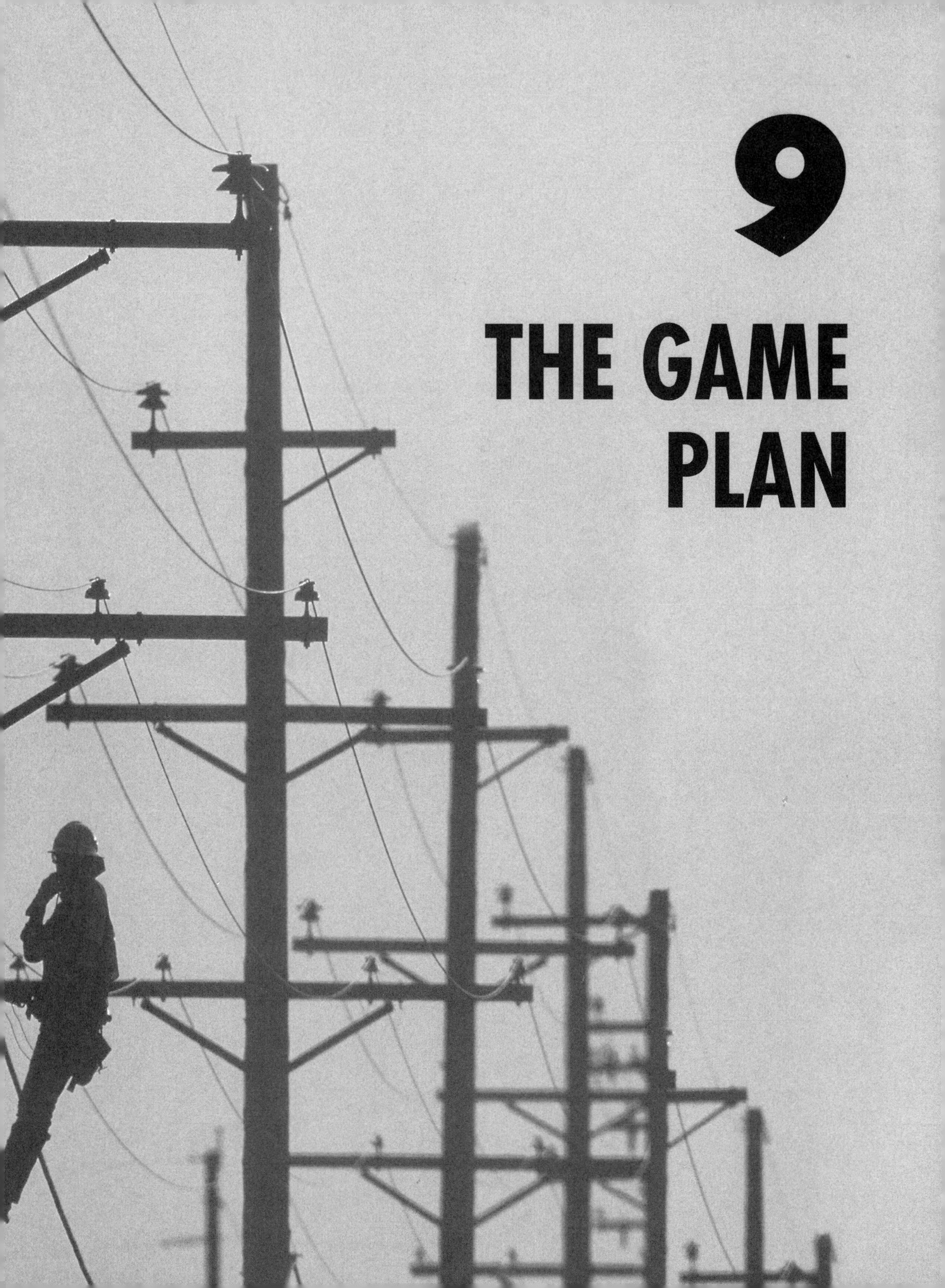

9

THE GAME PLAN

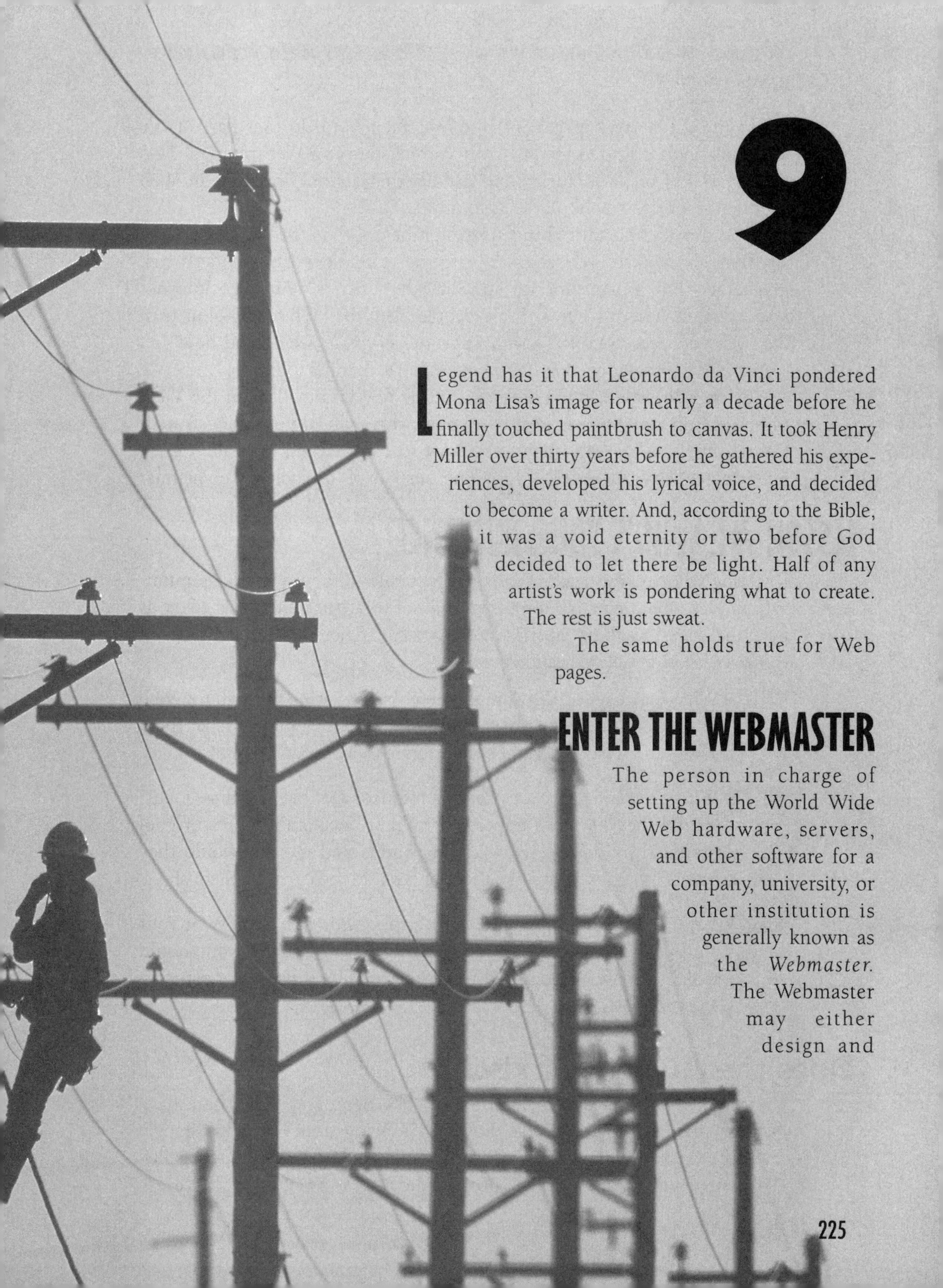

9

Legend has it that Leonardo da Vinci pondered Mona Lisa's image for nearly a decade before he finally touched paintbrush to canvas. It took Henry Miller over thirty years before he gathered his experiences, developed his lyrical voice, and decided to become a writer. And, according to the Bible, it was a void eternity or two before God decided to let there be light. Half of any artist's work is pondering what to create. The rest is just sweat.

The same holds true for Web pages.

ENTER THE WEBMASTER

The person in charge of setting up the World Wide Web hardware, servers, and other software for a company, university, or other institution is generally known as the *Webmaster*. The Webmaster may either design and create the actual Web pages, or hire *Webspinners* to do that part of the job. This book is geared toward both Webmasters and Webspinners. This chapter is full of hints, ideas, and pitfalls that anyone involved in Web production or design should keep in mind.

The most important thing to remember is that the Web isn't like anything else you've ever seen. It's tempting to think of the Web as a vast magazine—but a magazine doesn't have hyperlinks, software, Internet resources, movies, or sounds. Some people liken the Web to TV—but with the Web you have complete control over what you're seeing and how you see it; with TV the only choice you have is what channel to flip to.

Before you seriously think about putting any information on the Web, the most important step is to get to know what's already out there. Part I: Connecting To The Web, shows you how to connect and navigate. Check out Chapter 8, What Can I Do? for a tour of some of the coolest Web haunts.

LESSON #1: WHO'S YOUR AUDIENCE?

Knowing who you're speaking to is the first rule for any type of communication. Describing creative impulses to a corporate accountant is often as meaningless as speaking Japanese to a Mexican. There are three important things to know about your audience:

- What they expect. Why are these people browsing through the Web to begin with? If they reach your site, what's going to make them stay—and what's going to bore or scare them away?

- What they enjoy. Are they serious minded? Do they like dirty jokes? Would they be more impressed by hard facts and figures or cool graphics and charts? How about sounds and movies; would they like bells and whistles like these or would they consider them silly?

- What they know. How familiar are they with the Web? With your subject matter? This lets you determine how detailed you should make your Web pages, and whether you should use fancy computerese terms.

Does the Audience Exist?

Nobody knows the exact breakdown of Web demographics. There have been a bunch of recent surveys, however, ranging from the painstakingly scientific to the quick and casual. Most polls show pretty similar results. Here's a good guess of the type of people who use the Web:

- HTML About 40 percent are programmers, consultants, hackers, computer buffs, MIS professionals, software developers, hardware engineers, or other computer-type people.
- HTML About 35 percent are college or graduate students.
- HTML About 15 percent are professors, educators, librarians, or other academic types.
- HTML About 10 percent are hobbyists or casual net-surfers.

What does the typical Web user look, act, or think like? Well, there are some clear trends:

- HTML The audience is mostly male: Nearly 90 percent of Web users are men. The male/female ratio is reduced each day, however.
- HTML The audience is mostly North American: About 65 percent of Web users call from the United States or Canada.
- HTML The audience is mostly young: Over 50 percent of Webbers are 20-something.

You should remember, however, that the Web is doubling in size and traffic every two months or so. Since the Web is so lively, intuitive, easy-to-use, and fun, it will likely become a major medium, joining the ranks of TV, radio, and books. Even if your audience doesn't seem to exist yet, it might be worthwhile to start creating for tomorrow's audiences. Your Web site may even become a reason for people to decide to join the Web.

What's Already Out There?

If you want to target your Web pages to a specific group, you should check out a list of Usenet newsgroups. If a group exists, that means there are people on the Internet who find that topic interesting. You should also search for mailing lists, WAIS databases, gopher sites, *frequently-asked-question* (*FAQ*) archives, and, of course, other Web pages.

Focusing in

What, then, is the difference between a Web page written for a home computer user and one written for a Biology researcher? Here are some basic guidelines:

Hackers/Techies

Most computer-type people like their data fast and accurate. You don't need to bother defining terms like The Internet, TCP/IP, or RAM, though you may want to make these terms into hyperlinks that lead to sections in an associated glossary page.

Try to include software for as many operating systems and computer types as possible. Ideally, a user should be able to click on a hyperlink and automatically download a demo version of your product or idea.

Academics

If your Web pages are directed toward a professional or academic group, you can think of your Web pages as an online journal. You can publish articles, photographs, images, or even movies that help explain the latest research, trends, news, or other developments. Be sure to use lots of references. Don't be afraid of specific jargon, either.

Businesspeople

Businesspeople buy and sell ideas as well as goods. Your Web page should be fact filled and very convincing. You can think of the page as a proposal, brochure, or report. Your product or service can be clearly explained and supported with relevant images, tables, sounds, or movies.

Artists

The Web is a great place to showcase any sort of writing, visual art, music, film, or animation work. Other artists, agents, producers, or art dealers can then review your pages.

Think of your Web page as a multimedia portfolio. Showcase only your best work, and make it easy to get to. If you're designing an online gallery, make the design mimic the art. If the art is traditional, create simple pages with an image and a title. You may also want to include a hyperlink that explains why you created the piece, or your artistic theory behind the piece. If the art is abstract, your Web page may be most effective if it is scattered with a collage of whimsical images, hyperlinks, and wild fonts.

Hobbyists

If your page is geared toward people who share your hobbies or favorite activities, then feel free to toss in photos, sounds, movies, and lots and lots of text. When it comes to things like fan clubs, the more information available the better. You can use slang or other specialized words for people in the know, though it's a nice idea to define these words (perhaps through hyperlinks) for beginners.

Man or Woman on the Street

The man or woman on the street may be an artist, a professional, an academic, or all or none of the above. If your page is geared toward general audiences, you should simply try to be as entertaining and illuminating as possible. Chances are, if you and your friends and your family seem to enjoy a Web page, so will many others.

LESSON #2: WHAT'S YOUR OBJECTIVE?

Why are you creating a Web area to begin with? Because it's the "hot" thing to do? Because you want to contribute useful information to the world at large? Because you want to promote a product or service? Because your competitors have already created Web pages? Because you want to showcase your talents?

Be sure your objective can be handled by the Web. If you want a detailed catalog and ordering system complete with secure credit-card retrieval, live customer service representatives, thousands of video images, and complex background music, then you may be biting off more than you can chew.

The Web works best in accomplishing the following three goals:

- Familiarizing the Internet community with your name, product, service, or idea
- Publishing text, images, software, or any other computer file to a potential audience of millions
- Creating a sort of home base for any worldwide club, company, institution, or organization

The above goals are obviously very broad. Many Web pages manage to accomplish all three goals. If you have enough creativity, time, and patience, you can probably use the Web as a launching pad to meet any objective. There are, however, a few objectives that are much more difficult or risky than others.

Sound and Video

Placing an occasional video or sound clip in a Web page is a great idea. The only caveat is that huge amounts of data take a long, long, time to transmit, especially over the "high-speed" modems many Webbers have to use. This type of connection works fine for text and simple graphics, but the Web cannot as yet transmit live television, quality video, live sound, or other lengthy recordings. See Chapter 12, Graphics, and Chapter 13, Sound, for more details.

Talking Back

Thanks to fill-in forms, the Web is somewhat interactive. You can have a user give you all sorts of information. You can then store this information, run various programs, and deliver a Web page or other Internet service that fits the user's specific needs. However, this process is too slow to actually hold live typed conversations. However again, you can use the Web to telnet to an IRC or other talk site, where such "chats" can take place. Much more information about interactivity, forms, and other on-the-fly Web programs can be found in Chapter 14, Interactivity, and Chapter 15, CGI Scripts.

Security

Right now, most Web pages are not at all secure. Any credit card information, payroll data, or other sensitive names or numbers are easily captured by prying eyes. Some Web servers, however, such as the one developed by Netscape, have various levels of *encryption*. When used in conjunction with the Netscape Navigator, a Netscape Commerce Web page can be transmitted over the Internet in a scrambled fashion. Such security is not yet implemented in all servers or browsers, however.

Most Web browsers and servers also support *user validation*, which allows only people with a proper password to view your Web pages. More information about security issues can be found in Chapter 14, Interactivity, and Chapter 15, CGI Scripts.

LESSON #3: THE HARD SELL

You can certainly try selling things over the Web. Most Web pages manage to sell things: ideas, services, artwork, products, people, or companies. But, at the same time, most Webbers abhor commercials. Why would someone want to waste time visiting you if all you're trying to do is push a product?

There are enough ads in magazines, on radio, on TV, and on the sides of busses. How, then, can a Web page sell without directly selling?

Never take a boring print ad or display ad and just stick it on the Web. Not only will it generally be ignored, it will also offend some people. Instead, try to abide by the following three cardinal rules:

- Astound!
- Inform!
- Entertain!

Astound!

Why should people visit your page if they can get the same information someplace else? No matter what your objective is, always use a unique angle in presenting yourself. If you're an automotive company, don't just show a picture of your latest car. Anyone could do that! Instead, maybe create an animated car cartoon character, or maybe show exactly how your car was built—from the engine to the shell to the computer-controlled fuel injection system.

If you create a Web page that nobody has ever seen before, it will become hot in no time. If your layout is so darn cool and in-your-face, if you offer a unique interactive service, or if your page contains images or text that aren't available anywhere else in the world, then you've made your mark on the World Wide Web.

If you're creating a home page, for example, don't just stick in your name, address, and photograph. That's too standard. Instead, why not include a heap of information about your favorite hobby, or about your job, or even about your favorite rock group? For example, if you're a huge fan of Bruce Springsteen, you can create Web pages containing his album covers, lyrics, tour dates, latest gossip, etc. If you're a ballet dancer, include a list of dancing schools, ballet terms, photographs of famous ballerinas or information about upcoming shows.

By making your home page the main source for a given topic, hobby, or scene, you are not only telling the world more about yourself and your interests, you're allowing other people with similar interests to meet you and share your wealth of knowledge.

NOTE: Use a search index or list of sites to look for Web pages that sound similar to yours. Study those sites and think of a way to provide something new. Searching for similar pages also provides a good opportunity to cross-reference. When you build your page, include links to sites that deal with similar topics, and ask the makers of those sites to include links back to you.

Inform!

Being informative goes hand in hand with being unique. Take advantage of the limitless possibilities of the Web, and offer data or advice that no other page can offer.

For example, if you are an electronic surveillance company, why not include some real-life case studies? You could then tell all sort of James-Bondesque stories, explaining what equipment was used, how the equipment worked, and what the outcome was. Show pictures of your products in action. Teach the reader all about surveillance techniques. You may even want to include a directory of licensed private eyes, organized by city, where people can turn if they need to do some snooping.

NOTE: Information should be accurate and up to date. It's better to have no information than erroneous information.

Entertain!

The real reason most people prowl the Web is entertainment. Depending on what your page offers, Web users may feel like they've just tiptoed through an art museum—or stomped through a mall.

Keep the writing on your page lively and to the point. Include clear, interesting images. Be savvy, be sexy, be surprising. Traveling around the Web is sometimes *too* fast and easy. If you bore a Webber, even for a moment, he may already be off across the world, browsing through another Web page.

If you're the tourist bureau for Des Moines, for example, don't just describe your city. Include lots of maps. Show lots of great pictures. Play sounds. All in all, try to capture the entire Des Moines experience and mood with multimedia. A visit to your Web page should feel almost like a visit to the city itself.

If you're trying to promote a new band, include samples of that band's music. If you're talking about a new book, be sure to include a full scene for people to read.

LESSON #4: OVERALL DESIGN

There is no right or wrong way to create a set of Web pages. There are some issues, however, you should be aware of.

Point of Entry

Most Web sites have a home page, with graphics, hyperlinks, or even a structured Table of Contents leading the user to the other pages. The thing to remember about the Web, though, is that it's open-ended. You have no control over where users will enter your Web site. For example, you may have a home page that leads to the News page, the Sports page, and the Entertainment page. A famous Web site may decide to include a hyperlink to your Entertainment page only. You may get hundreds of people visiting your Entertainment site per hour, though only a fraction of them used your home page to get there.

Since your Web pages can have an arbitrary point of entry, keep the following in mind:

- Every page counts. Don't spend a lot of time on one page and leave the others plain, jumbled, or boring.
- Put your most important information, such as your e-mail address or phone number, on every page.
- Always make it easy to return to your home page—or to get there after arriving from someplace else. Don't leave a page stranded out in cyberspace.

The Home Page

The home page generally makes the first impression. Based on your home page, people decide whether or not to continue exploring your particular corner of the Web. Here's the essential information for a home page:

- Owner's name or company name
- Logo or photograph
- Contact address
- Statement of objective
- Description of what else can be found in this Web site

The Main Menu

If you only have a few Web pages, you should list them all on your home page. You can create a descriptive menu—usually just a list of hyperlinks. You can also create clickable icons or other hyperimages to make your menu easier to access, as shown in Figure 9–1.

Many home pages now have a clickable *imagemap*. This is one image with many different sections, each leading to a different place when a user clicks on it.

Some "menus" are hidden within a story, or within other text. For example, you could create the following paragraph:

```
Welcome to Company X. We specialize in widgets, though we also have quite
a fine line of gizmos. The President of Company X, Frank Stein, has been
in the widget business since 1982. Since then, our company has grown to be
a worldwide widget importer.
```

A user could then click on the word "widgets," to learn about X's widgets, or could click on "worldwide" to see a world map with information about each of X's offices.

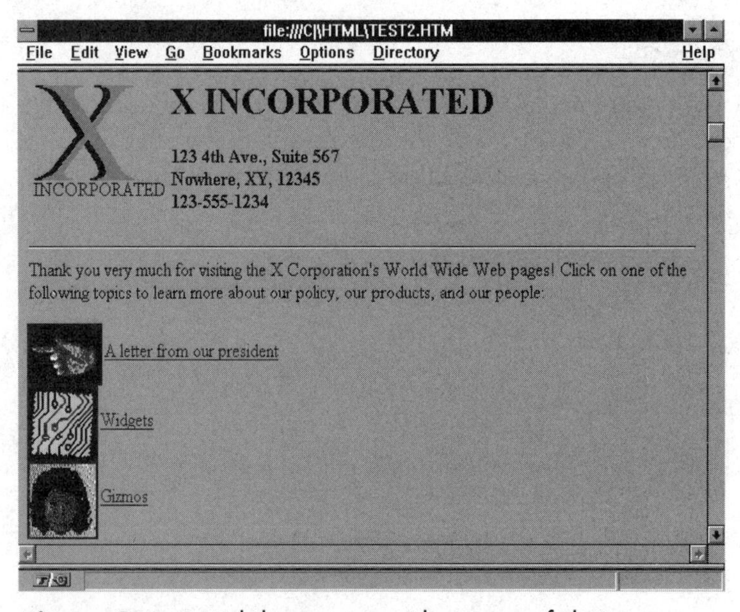

Figure 9–1 A Web home page with a menu of choices

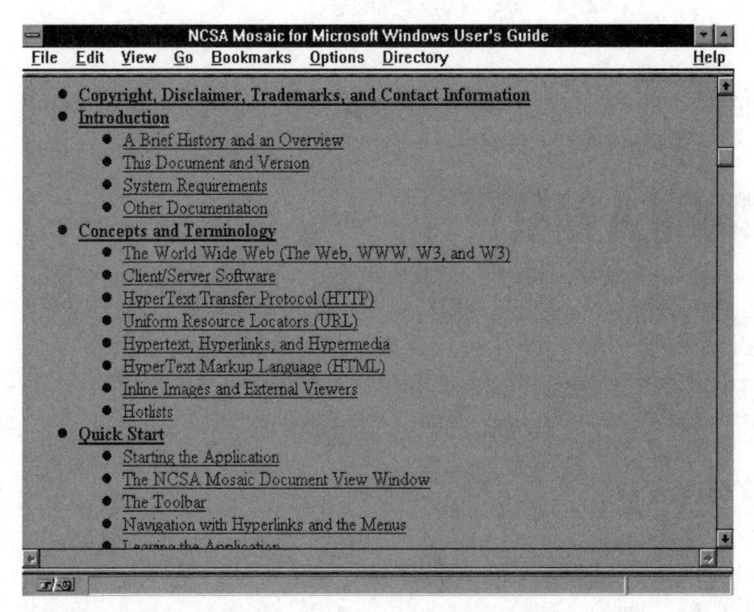

Figure 9–2 A Web home page with a Table of Contents

Table of Contents

If you have quite a few Web pages, or if you are putting a manual or book online, its a good idea to organize your pages in a Table of Contents. This is usually written in an outline-like style, as shown in Figure 9–2.

At the bottom of every page, there should be an option to return to this Table of Contents. This way, users can flip through your Web pages the same way they might use a reference book.

Search Index

If your Web site is *really* big, you may want to create a searchable index. This way, a user can type in a given word or phrase and a list of all relevant Web pages appears. Indexes can also be a great help if your Web site deals with many different types of products or issues. You'll find more information about indexes in Chapter 15, CGI Scripts.

Permanence

Does your Web page change often, like a magazine or weekly newsletter, or is it pretty much a one-time deal? If you want to create a weekly journal, for example, be sure you have the resources to design, write, and publish elaborate content week after week. If not, you may want to keep your Web page design relatively simple.

If you want to create a more permanent page, then spend the extra time ensuring that everything looks as perfect as can be.

LESSON #5: PROBLEM PAGES

Many Web pages are sparse, sloppy, and designed without any interesting graphics or layout. Other pages use up *too many* resources—and that can be an even bigger problem. You may have created an absolutely beautiful Web page, a Web page that belongs on the ceiling of the Sistine Chapel, but if it takes too long to load then nobody will stick around long enough to see it.

Art Bombardment

A few Web pages have graphic lines zooming every which way. Every headline is in a different type of font. Small graffitios and sketches always pop up interrupting the text.

Using lettering, lines, and clip art as part of your layout turns a plain Web page into something special, but too many graphical elements can quickly get annoying. Don't murk up the content of your page with an abundance of cute trimmings. If you overdo any particular style, layout, or art element, then a page can quickly lose its appeal.

Graphic Gluttony

Some pages use screen-captures of fancy styled text and custom fonts instead of plain Web text. This may indeed make the page look better, but it can take what feels like forever to load. For example, if you use a fancy paint program to create a multi-colored, shadowed headline, it can take up to a minute to load and render. If you create the headline using standard HTML heading commands, then it takes a fraction of a second!

Other pages include a full-screen photograph after every paragraph, or a piece of artwork every few inches. Not only does this make the page look cluttered, it can take tons of time to load up.

If you include graphics, be sure they're small enough to load quickly. Even icons or reduced-size artwork, however, can get out of hand if you scatter them left and right. In general, your Web page should have less than six images.

NOTE: Some pages, such as art galleries, will naturally have many more graphics of paintings, photographs, or other images. If possible, warn the user before he or she selects such a page, with a message similar to: "WARNING: The following page contains a dozen large images and may take a while to fully load." If possible, split up such pages into many smaller pages.

Multimedia Moderation

Movies, images, and sound files are always huge. Although some Web users have lightning-fast connections, many others have to use a modem. For those with 14,400 baud modems, it takes nearly ten minutes to load a megabyte of information. In other words, downloading a movie or a large sound breaks up the Web session.

Don't rely entirely on a movie or song to carry your Web page. If possible, always include stills from the movie, or snippets from the song. This way, even users with slower connections can grab a taste of what you have to offer.

Textual Terseness

Text can load in fast, but it's still a good idea not to overdo it. Whenever most people come across a long story or article, they only read the first paragraph. This trend is well known in the world of journalism, and is the reason why most news articles are written in the *pyramid style*. The most important information always goes first. After that, you get the details; the most important details first, and the other stuff at the end. You never know how long a person will stay on your Web page. Try to use the pyramid style and hit your readers with the most essential facts, figures, or ideas first.

Use lots of numbered and bulleted lists to organize concepts. These lists leap off the screen and are always easier to read than blocks of text. Split your articles into lots of headings and subheadings, so people can easily scan through and find what they want.

You should also split up any long page into several different pages. This way, a reader will never have to wait too long for a Web page to load.

LESSON #6: GETTING THE RIGHT LOOK

If they've done their job, some of the Web pages illustrated in Chapter 8, What Can I Do? have indeed given you ideas about what you can do. Many elements affect the look of a Web page:

- HTML Text layout
- HTML Hypertext and hyperimage links

- HTML Lettering
- HTML Artwork
- HTML Color
- HTML Photos
- HTML Fill-in forms or other interactivity

Placing these elements together is always a fun challenge. How you use these elements depends, of course, on your audience, your objective, and your sense of aesthetics.

If you're planning a vast Web for a big company, you may want to do what big-time film directors do for each scene: create *storyboards*. These are illustrated mockups of what you want each of the Web pages at your site to look like. You can then hold a meeting or two, and people can comment on these storyboards, add to them, or suggest other designs.

Consistent Controls

Consistency is always a key. A set of Web pages can certainly have a fresh, whimsical look to it, but if it gets too confusing, people will just drift away. Always begin each page with a similar heading. Put your address and other contact information at the bottom of every page. Links to similar areas should look the same every time you use them—don't use icons on one page and a bulleted list on another page.

The best way of achieving consistency is to use a menu bar, or a set of uniform links. You can include these navigation controls at the top or bottom of every page. For instance, many Web pages use the following links at the bottom of each document:

```
[Home]  [Next]  [Previous]
```

If a user clicks on [Home], then the home page appears. The [Next] button loads up the next page in the series, and the [Previous] button, naturally, loads up the previous page.

Figure 9–3 shows another example of a consistent menu bar. A set of custom icons at the top of the screen leads to the City Life, Nite Life, Expo, Media, or Main Menu section. This same menu is printed at the top of every page.

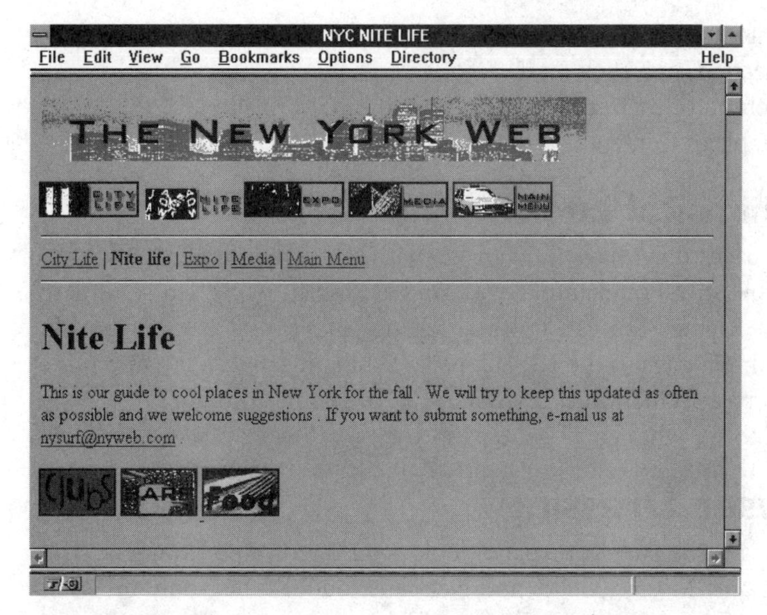

Figure 9–3 The New York Web, where each Web page contains links to other major sections

The Look Should Fit the Structure

The style of your pages depends largely on how your Web site is organized. The idea is to link all pages to each other. If you have an unlinked Web page, then it's almost impossible for anyone to reach it.

The Menu Tree Look

If you aren't dealing with too many Web pages, or if your Web pages are organized in different sections, you probably want to use menus.

A typical menu consists of a home page that leads to main sections. Each of the main sections, in turn, may have its own home page, with menus to subsections. At the top of each page are links that return the user to the previous menu, or to the main menu. The Web page shown in Figure 9–3 fits this bill.

The Book Look

If your Web pages are meant to be read in some particular order, you should probably opt for the book look. The book always begins with a

Table of Contents that points to various chapters, sections, or subsections. To access a section, just click on it.

At the bottom of each section there should be controls to take the reader back to the Table of Contents, to the next page, or to the previous page.

The Whimsical Look

If your Web pages don't have much to do with each other, you may want to link them arbitrarily. For example, you can have a page about Horses link to a page about Racing. You can link the Racing page to the Gambling page, and the Gambling page to the Nevada page. While this makes it harder for a reader to find a specific topic, it is often fun to shuffle through these types of pages just to see what you'll get next.

Cross-Browser Dressing

Finally, you must be sure your pages look good on all Web browsers. This includes not only Mosaic, Cello, and Netscape, but also text-only browsers such as Lynx. If your page includes lots of fancy images, lettering, or art, be sure to include enough text so that people without graphics won't get lost or confused. You may even want to create an alternate page, free of images altogether, designed specially for text-based browsers.

LESSON #7: LINKS TO OTHER PAGES

The only way people are going to reach your page is if other Web pages are linked to yours. The more interesting or pertinent your subject, the more links will be created. You may even get on a worldwide "Best of the Web" or "What's Cool" list, ensuring hundreds of daily visitors.

To keep this spirit of sharing alive, you should use your pages to help promote other Web pages. You should link to pages that:

- Deal with the same topic you're dealing with
- Cover a deeper or alternate angle on the topic you're dealing with
- You used as references in any paper you wrote
- You just think are darn cool

Chapter 20 discusses dozens of ways to publicize your Web site. Good publicity can draw a lot of people to your Web pages, but only permanent links will ensure a steady flow.

NOTE: Although external links are a nice gesture, once people leave your Web area, they may get so preoccupied they'll never return. To avoid losing readers, you probably want to list external links as the last option or at the end of your Web pages.

Stale Links

It's perfectly fine to use external links or to include images, sounds, or other files from other Web sites. These sites, however, may often go down. Files or Web pages may be deleted or moved. Periodically check all external links to be sure they haven't gone *stale*. If a user clicks on a stale link, a rude message similar to "Domain Not Found!" usually appears.

If you find any stale links, remove them immediately. Often, a linked-to Web page may have moved to a different locale. If so, be sure to change the linked-to URL.

Senseless Links

Another thing to watch out for are links that don't make any sense. For example, if you have a Web page about sharks and then all of a sudden have the sentence

```
Click here to go to the Fine Art page.
```

people will be confused. What in the world do sharks have to do with Monet? Instead, use some sort of logic to introduce a hyperlink:

```
Although I spend most of my time studying sharks, I'm also very interested
in fine art.
```

If you are creating a menu of links, be sure the links are parallel, and make sense adjacent to each other. For example, the following links seem strange next to each other:

```
1. Lions
2. Tigers
3. Bears
4. The socioeconomic influences of poverty
```

Instead, organize your links under various headings or listings:

```
The zoology department publishes many Web pages about animals:
1. Lions
2. Tigers
3. Bears
The sociology department also has several interesting pages:
1. The socioeconomic influences of poverty
```

LESSON #8: STUDYING THE STATS

The final task of Web design is to stick your completed pages up on the Web and analyze them. Most Web servers automatically generate statistics, letting you know how many people visited each of your Web pages, how long they stayed, and what systems they came from.

In some cases, you may find that your Web site is attracting more visitors than you can handle. If so, you should get a faster Internet line or more memory on your Web server. Otherwise, your site may get so crowded that it'll grind to a halt, or people may be refused access.

Another trend you might discover is that one Web page is getting all the attention. For example, you may come up with the following statistics:

```
The Home Page          70 visitors a day
The Entertainment Page 98 visitors a day
The Sports Page         4 visitors a day
The News Page           5 visitors a day
```

Why is the Entertainment Page so popular? Does the design of your Web make it difficult to reach the Sports Page or the News Page? In any case, you should be sure to take advantage of this fact. Be sure the Entertainment Page contains the most essential information you want to distribute.

After a while, you'll also learn which pages people avoid and which they love. This can help you know how to design and lay out any future Web pages.

WHAT NOW?

Now it's time to start spinning those pages. The next chapter introduces the language used to create most Web pages: Hypertext Markup Language (HTML). Chapter 11 tells you everything you need to know about putting together Web text. Chapter 12 gives you a comprehensive gander at Graphics. Chapter 13 screams about sound.

10

THE HYPERTEXT MARKUP LANGUAGE

10

Whoa, sounds pretty messy. Not to worry, though. The Hypertext Markup Language (HTML) is much scarier to name than it is to use. Let's try a direct analogy:

I'm writing this book using a plain word processor, with pretty much just one font, style, and format. The text may be brilliant (thank you), but the pages look downright boring. Obviously, the book isn't ready to be published en masse. An editor at my publishing house will first go through the pages, scribbling special symbols on my plain manuscript, telling the production department where to insert figures, chapter titles, main headings, subheadings, font types, and so forth. Some symbols designate what type of margins or spacing should be used. Other symbols call for cute icons or graphical lines. The production department will take the editor's chicken-scratchings and my text and produce a book that follows our guidelines. However, nobody can predict exactly what the book will look like before it's printed—that depends on exactly what equipment, fonts, paper, and so forth the production department had to work with.

HTML is the same idea applied to online text. You can think of yourself as an editor; each Web browser that processes your document is its own production department. Just as the final appearance of a book depends on the resources of its publisher, the final appearance of your Web page depends on the resources of the browser that interprets and renders it. That's the brilliance of HTML—the intelligence is built into the text itself, allowing it to be read by any Web browser worldwide.

An HTML document is just a standard text document with extra marks on it, marks that designate typeface, style, format, graphics, sounds, and so forth. Some marks, of course, link the document to other parts of the document or other resources. So there you have it: HTML is a *language* to help *markup* your *hypertext*.

WHERE TO START

HTML documents are stored as plain ASCII text. You can use pretty much any word processor or editor in the world to create an HTML document. Specialized editors such as HTML Assistant and HoTMetaL make HTML authoring easier by including many common HTML commands at the press of a button. See Chapters 18 and 19 for more details about these programs.

Read on to learn how to create unique and personalized HTML pages from scratch. However, if you're extremely eager (or under a severe deadline) and want to stick something simple on the Web ASAP, here are two of the fastest ways to begin:

Steal This Text

The best way to begin writing your own hypermedia Web pages is to steal other people's HTML like crazy. Did I say steal? Naturally, I mean *borrow.* I mean *refine.* Okay, I mean *glean ideas from.* Whatever you call it, there's no better way to learn HTML fundamentals.

Here are some of the best places to steal—or borrow—HTML:

HTML *This book.* Several HTML documents, including Web pages, manuals, catalogs, and more, are packed on the CD-ROM under the \HTML directory.

The Web itself. Most every Web browser easily allows you to see the source HTML responsible for the page you're looking at. If you're using Lynx, press the backslash \ key. If you're an NCSA Mosaic person, select Document Source from the File menu. If you're using Netscape, select View, Source (see Figure 10-1). In any case, you can then copy the text into your favorite word processor or HTML editor.

NOTE: Windows or Macintosh users can use the standard copy commands—highlight the text you're interested in, press CTRL-C to copy the text, and then later press CTRL-V to paste.

Once you've found a document that looks similar to something you'd like to create, load it up using a word processor or HTML editor. Study how the page was put together. Even if you don't understand the commands or symbols being used, you can just erase the irrelevant parts of the text and fill in your own information instead.

An editor like HoTMetaL is especially helpful since it shows you exactly which codes are doing what. See Chapter 19 to learn how to make the most of HoTMetaL.

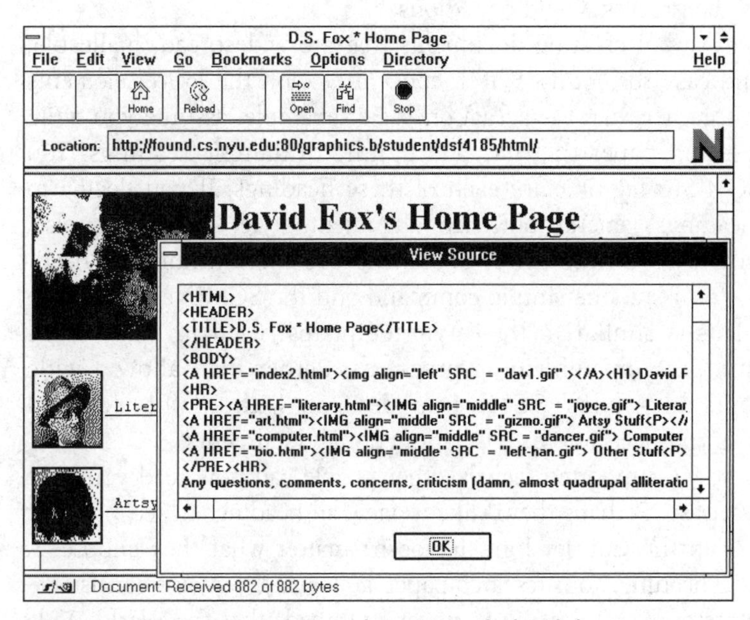

Figure 10-1 Netscape can show you a behind-the-scenes view of HTML codes for any given Web page

Convert This Text

Web browsers can display standard text files. If, however, you've written something using a popular word processor, there's probably a program out (or on the enclosed CD-ROM) that can convert your document into HTML. If you're only interested in taking information you already have and putting it on the Web, see Chapter 17 for more detailed information.

HTML HISTORY

Where did HTML come from? What is its purpose? To answer these questions we must sneak a peek at the ancient art and philosophy of the *Standard Generalized Markup Language (SGML)*. HTML was designed, in essence, using the ideals of SGML.

When people first started using the Net widely there was lots of messy file exchanges. If a friend of mine sent me a document she wrote using some strange word processor, I'd need to find a way to convert it. If and when I finally got that darn document loaded up, its margins or fonts might be much too small for my computer's window. Some elements might not be converted at all. And when a new version of my friend's word processor came out, I'd have to run around and find a new conversion program. At the very least, the process would be tedious.

SGML is a way of creating documents that are widespread, malleable, consistent, and easy to modify. SGML concentrates on the *logical* elements in a document, rather than the actual ones. For example, assume you write a detailed research paper that has one hundred different headings. You would use SGML to *tag* or *mark* each of these headings. If you decide to change the headings' general font, size, alignment, style, or anything else, you don't need to go through your document and alter all hundred headings. Instead, you issue one simple command and the SGML tags take care of the rest. This is similar to the "style templates" used in many word processors and desktop publishing programs. Rather than allow a wide variety of fonts and styles, SGML provides you with all the standard building blocks you need to create fully functional documents.

Using an SGML-supported viewer, other people can now read your text any way they please. Perhaps they'd like to view all headings in red print, or in boldface, or in the Courier font. It doesn't matter what they choose. A heading is still a heading. Your research paper, at its heart, remains consistent.

The creators of HTML knew (or sincerely hoped) that the World Wide Web would be exploited by many types of computers, operating systems, and brands of browsers. They built HTML as a SGML *document type defini-*

tion (*DTD*). The Web author simply marks up text to show what each section should contain. Then the Web browsers take over, interpreting and formatting this marked-up text so it looks as good as can be.

HTML FUNCTIONALITY

In general, HTML has the capacity to mark

- Hyperlinks: Icons, text, or pictures that, when clicked, will transport the user to a different part of the Internet, display a different Web page, load a special type of file, or perform some other action
- Formatting: Font styles, text types, even preformatted text
- Structure: Section headings, paragraphs, and line separators
- Lists: Bulleted, numbered, or definition style
- Graphics: Photographs, charts, logos, icon buttons...

HTML evolves and grows daily. New Web servers and browsers allow more and more HTML features. Already, several variants known as HTML3 or HTML+ are being used. In addition to supporting more types of hyperlinks, formatting conventions, graphics formats, and Internet resources, the latest official specification of HTML (version 3) has the following features:

- Forms: Database-type forms complete with text fields, pick-lists, menus, check boxes, and radio buttons
- Tables: Charts and tables with neatly-spaced columns
- Equations: With mathematical symbols and structures
- Figures: Precisely placed graphics with captions
- Variety: Numerous fonts, styles, and formatting options

Every new version of your favorite Web browser has the ability to incorporate more HTML+ features. Luckily, almost all versions of HTML+ are *supersets* of HTML. This means each new version of HTML supports the previous version's commands. The *World Wide Web Organization* (*W3O*) is working on standardizing HTML version 3 for browsers worldwide. This book covers all popular HTML version 3 commands currently in use, as well as some promising commands which have yet to appear.

HTML+ is not universal yet. Many of the fancy new styles, types, and additions are ignored by last year's Web browsers. However, the most advanced browsers such as Netscape can handle lots of HTML+ elements. Netscape, in fact, supports its own extended version of HTML: *Mozilla* (named, some say, after Netscape's Jurassic mascot: The Mosaic Godzilla).

LIFE, LIBERTY, AND GOOD HTML

Every Web browser displays each HTML document in its own style. For instance, Figure 10–2 shows a page in NCSA Mosaic, Figure 10–3 shows the page in Netscape, and Figure 10–4 is the same page in the text browser, Lynx. Since there are so many versions of HTML floating around, most browsers will simply skip confusing or redundant HTML commands. This means that any well-written HTML page will work, to some extent, on *any* browser on *any* system or platform worldwide. The following chapters cover exactly how to write such universal documents.

STYLE TIP: These style tips will pop up every so often, chock full of ideas and warnings to help make your HTML documents look as good as they can, no matter which Web browser finds them.

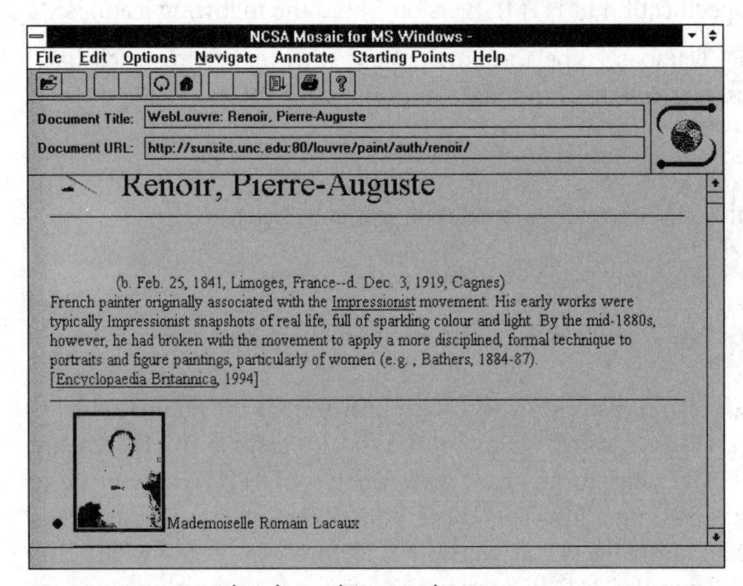

Figure 10–2 A lovely Web page shown on Mosaic

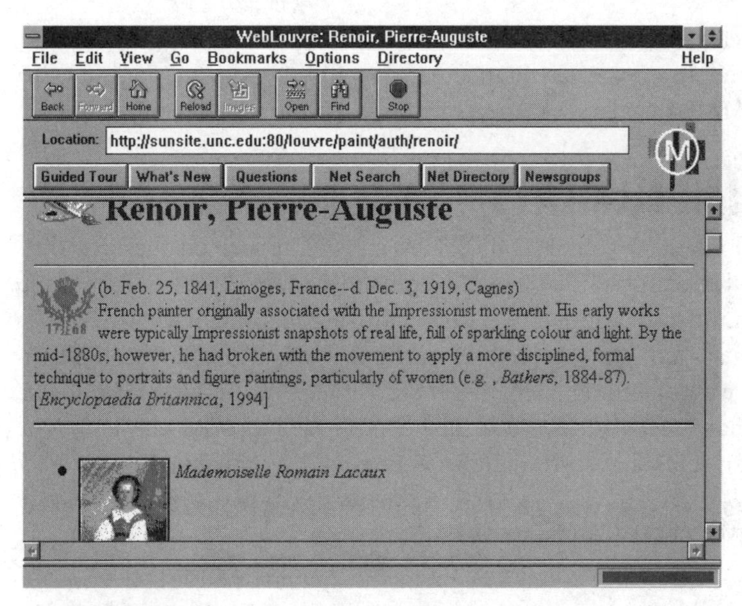

Figure 10–3 The same page on Netscape

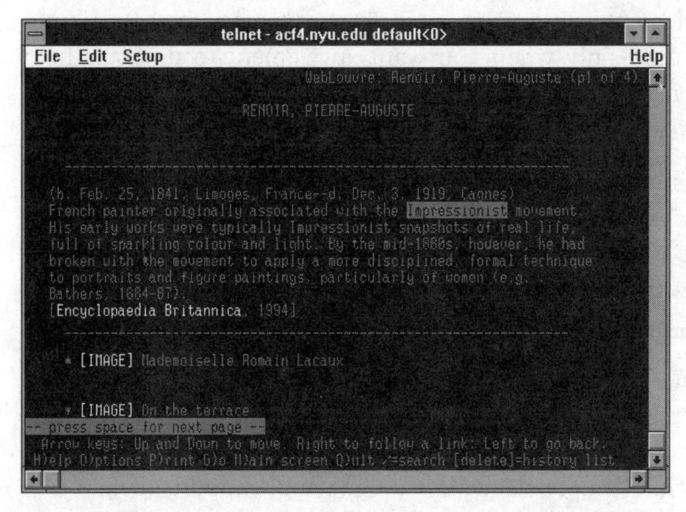

Figure 10–4 The same page, yet again, but this time seen using the text-only Lynx browser

You may be interested in designing documents that are only accessible within your company or home computer. If you're creating Web pages for just one brand of browser, then you can go crazy—make the pages look as wild as you like.

In most cases, though, you want your pages to be seen (and enjoyed) by as many people as possible. Remember that all browsers are not built the same: your HTML may look great on one browser, but hideous on another.

LESSON #1: HTML ELEMENTS

In general, any text in your HTML document will appear on the browser's screen. But what about all the HTML commands? Obviously, we don't want these commands to appear, we just want them to work. An HTML command must "talk" to the browser and tell it what to do. The browser needs some way of telling the difference between printable text and an HTML command. How does it do this? Simple: it looks for the less-than and more-than signs that surround every command. For instance:

```
This is regular text with two <B>HTML Commands</B> inserted
surrounding the phrase "HTML Commands."
```

Each set of < > symbols and its contents is known as an HTML *element*. Elements can range from one letter to several lines of detailed information. Elements can have embedded arguments, switches, and modifiers. These elements-within-elements are known as *attributes*. In most cases, attributes are optional and used only when you want an element to do something other than the norm. A typical element with attributes looks like:

```
<IMG SRC="clown.gif">
```

Most elements are like switches—one element turns a setting on and another turns things off. The off commands are preceded by a slash. For example, <TITLE> indicates that what follows is the document's title and </TITLE> indicates the title is complete.

```
<TITLE>Waite Group Press Catalog</TITLE>
```

A few elements stand on their own—things like markers to designate the end of a paragraph or the end of a line. These are called *empty* elements, because they do not affect any specific blocks of text. HTML version 3 has essentially gotten rid of empty elements, though it still supports them.

HTML is very cavalier about how it interprets elements. You can use uppercase or lowercase letters—whichever you find easier to work with. In other words,

```
<title>
```

is the same as

```
<TITLE>
```

or even

```
<tItLe>
```

NOTE: Filenames, URLs, or other addresses are still case-sensitive in HTML. In almost all cases, you should use lowercase for specific Internet resources or names.

Extraneous white space is always stripped from HTML documents. This means that you can put two HTML elements right next to each other like

```
<HEAD><TITLE>
```

or you can separate them by blank spaces or even blank lines, like

```
<HEAD>
<TITLE>
```

Either notation achieves the same result. In most cases you can write your HTML elements using whichever structure seems clearest or most intuitive to you.

STYLE TIP: Since extra white space won't show up in the final text, use as much as you need to make your HTML code easy to follow. Indentation will help you keep track of things like lists within lists, sections, blocks of text, and so forth.

Specifying HTML

The first thing each HTML document needs is a tag letting the browser know that it's looking at an HTML document. Although this is optional, and most modern browsers can do without it, inserting this tag couldn't hurt.

Simply put this element at the very beginning of your HTML document:

```
<HTML>
```

and put the closing tag at the very end:

```
</HTML>
```

The Header

Although most modern browsers don't need it, it's a good idea to give each document a header section and a body section. The header contains the title of your document, plus assorted background and indexing information that doesn't actually appear on a user's screen. Surround the header with the elements:

```
<HEAD>
```

and

```
</HEAD>
```

The Title

The title is the one part of the head that you want to use all the time. The title helps people keep track of your Web page. Most every Web browser prints the title, first thing, at the top of the screen or as the name of the window. The title also identifies a Web page saved as a bookmark or in a hotlist. For example, if you ask Mosaic to put the current Web page in its hotlist menu, the title of the page is stored for later retrieval.

Unsurprisingly, you specify a title with the tags

```
<TITLE>
```

and

```
</TITLE>
```

STYLE TIP: Make the title as descriptive as possible, but less than fifty characters long. This makes your document easier to find when its title is listed along with several others. The title must also be plain text—you may not surround it by HTML formatting commands.

So, an HTML document head with no body would look something like:

```
<HTML>
<HEAD>
<TITLE>My Web Page</TITLE>
</HEAD>
</HTML>
```

Other Elements

If you grab an HTML document off the Web, you may find a number of elements in the head besides the title. In general, you don't need to concern yourself with these additional elements. The head can give specific instructions for particular Web browsers, say, to indicate whether or not the current document has a searchable index, or to define how the current document is related to another Web document, or to do other advanced chores. See Chapters 14 and 15 for discussions of advanced header usage. Meanwhile, just for the record, here are the other header elements you're likely to see:

HTML <BASE>: This element indicates where the document's relative URLs (discussed in the next chapter) are located. It is important to specify a <BASE> if a document is moved from its original location. This way, any hypertext links in the document can be loaded from the appropriate base directory.

HTML <META>: The Web browser uses this tag to mark a document for later retrieval.

HTML <ISINDEX>: This element tells the browser that the specified document can be searched. In most cases, a box appears, asking the user to type in an Index term to be searched for. Many browsers allow you to use the <ISINDEX> element anywhere within the document.

HTML <NEXTID>: This is an ID code for the current document, most often used by HTML editors or browsers to help keep track of pages. An ID usually consists of two letters and two numbers, such as AB56.

HTML <LINK>: This element elaborates on the type of relationship the current document has to other documents. For example, if the current page is part of a long series, you can specify the previous and next pages. Many browsers have Previous and Next buttons allowing you to scroll through the series. Link elements take the form:

```
<LINK HREF="contents.html" REL="contents">
```

Where the REL attribute describes the relation to the document stored at the URL designated in the HREF attribute.

The Body

The body of the document—the part the Web browser actually displays—is marked with the

```
<BODY>
```

and

```
</BODY>
```

elements. Like the header, this marking is optional. Since there are still some Web browsers that expect the body to be defined, adding the body tags can't hurt.

The simplest HTML document in the world, then, would look something like Figure 10–5. You could slap the same eight elements onto any text file of your own, and turn it, more or less, into an instant Web page!

Start the HTML document element	`<HTML>`
Start the header element	`<HEAD>`
Designate a document title	`<TITLE>My First Web Page! </TITLE>`
End the header element	`</HEAD>`
Start the body element	`<BODY>`
The document's body	`Here's the body of my first little Web Page!`
End the body element	`</BODY>`
End the HTML document element	`</HTML>`

Figure 10–5 The most basic HTML document in the world

THE FUTURE OF HTML

The latest specification of HTML makes it much more like a programming language than a mere markup language. While simplicity is still maintained, a future version of HTML will have the capability for you to define your own elements, tags, attributes, and such.

It will be exciting to watch HTML as it grows to support things like inline sound and video, complicated foreign character sets, complete mathematical equations, calculated fields in input forms, live conferencing, and even virtual reality world construction. Like the Web itself, HTML is clearly in its infancy.

WHAT NOW?

Now it's time to put HTML into use. The magic of the Web is its hypermedia—lots of different resources strung together lots of different ways. As such, there's a chapter ahead devoted to making the most out of each medium:

HTML Chapter 11 gives you everything you need to know in order to work with text.

- Chapter 12 explains how to spice up your Web pages with graphics.
- Chapter 13 gives you another dimension: sound files—both how to use them and where to find them.
- Chapter 14 goes through the basics of interactivity, so you can set up Web page forms for other people to fill in.
- Chapter 15 explains how to use scripts to have your Web pages work with your computer's other software.
- Chapter 16 tells how to hook your document up to other Internet resources.

11
TEXT

11

Text is where it all begins. Just a year ago, Internet crawlers pretty much dealt only with text and text-based menus. Not that this was terrible—the text was good, and there was tons of it. Digital text has all sorts of magic attributes. It can be searched, stored, copied, imported, or added on to.

Today's glitzy Web mosaics may make sparser use of the printed word than before, but text always forms the backbone. When designing a Web page, think about the text first. Keep in mind:

- People browsing your Web page may only have a text browser, such as Lynx. You don't want to spurn potential clients, associates, friends, or lovers just because their Internet accounts or computer systems can't support a graphical browser.
- Although graphics add spice to documents, at the heart of your Web site is information—and nothing can present raw facts and figures better than good old text.

Luckily, HTML provides plenty of text options and formats, allowing you to design layouts as fancy as your imagination. Web text is anything but plain. You can use headings, font sizes, lists, tables, and more, giving the page a crisp, professional layout.

DESIGN FUNDAMENTALS

Until HTML+ came along, Web text was somewhat limited. You could specify the following:

- Up to six levels of headings
- Paragraphs or line breaks
- Lists (bulleted, numbered, or definition style)
- Basic styles
- Horizontal separator lines
- Hypertext links and anchors

With the advent of HTML+, you can customize many of these elements so they look or act exactly the way you want. The latest HTML also adds these new text elements:

- Font sizing
- Alignment
- Tables

STYLE TIP: Be careful when using HTML+ or Mozilla (Netscape-supported HTML commands). People who use Lynx or another primitive browser may see something completely different. If you plan on creating a fancy Web page, it's a good idea to design a simple page containing the same general information. You can then have a hypertext link at the top of your fancy page, saying something like:

```
THIS PAGE LOOK STRANGE? Click here for the simple text-based version!
```

Consistency

Use consistent punctuation, grammar, and heading styles. The more professional your page looks, the more people will enjoy it, learn from it, and not skip it. This applies to little things as well as big ones: If you use bulleted lists to organize your information on one Web page, try to use lists on all pages. If the theme of your document is particle physics, try not to get off track by talking about the history of cream cheese. If you want to discuss something else, include a separate link to it.

Signing Your Page

You should sign every Web page you create so interested parties can get in touch with you. If you change your document around a lot, you may also want to include the date of the last change. Most people put signatures at the bottom of the page, surrounded by the <ADDRESS> element (described in Lesson #6, Section Style, later in this chapter). You may also want to include a link to your e-mail address as a *mailto: URL*, so people can just click on your name to send you e-mail. You'll learn about links in Lesson #13, Hypertext, later in this chapter.

```
<ADDRESS>
<A HREF="mailto:jsmith@smartpants.edu">John Smith</A>, February 14,
1995
</ADDRESS>
```

STYLE TIP: Since the Web is viewed worldwide, don't use numerical dates. In America, for example, the date 2/1/95 means February first; in Europe it means January second. Write it out instead—February 1 or Jan 2 or whatever.

LESSON #1: SPECIAL CHARACTERS

The computer keyboard is really handy when it comes to letters of the English alphabet. But what about special currency symbols, or accent marks, or other languages altogether?

Punctuation

By now you know that HTML commands are indicated by the less-than and greater-than signs (< and >). But what if you want to include one of these signs as part of your text? HTML uses the ampersand (&) to indicate special characters, as shown in Table 11-1. To print out a special character, write the ampersand followed by a special code and a semicolon, as follows:

```
&charactercode;
```

For example, to write <WOW!> you'd use the commands:

```
&lt;WOW!&gt;
```

Table 11-1 An HTML trick for basic punctuation

HTML Text	Appears As
&	&
>	>
<	<
	A nonbreaking space; use this to force a blank space

STYLE TIP: Since HTML ignores spaces it deems unnecessary, you can use the nonbreaking space character to force white space. You can then use this white space to separate text or even graphics.

Enhanced Characters

If your Web page includes any Spanish, French, or Latin words you'll probably want to use accented characters. Using the ampersand coding system, you can output most any type of extended or enhanced character.

STYLE TIP: Not every browser supports these enhanced characters. Be wary of overusing them.

For example, to write the word café, you'd write the command:

```
caf&eacute;
```

Table 11-2 Use these codes to print extended characters on your Web pages

HTML Text	Appears As	Description
Æ	Æ	(capital AE diphthong (ligature))
Á	Á	(capital A, acute accent)
Â	Â	(capital A, circumflex accent)
À	À	(capital A, grave accent)
Å	Å	(capital A, ring)
Ã	Ã	(capital A, tilde)
Ä	Ä	(capital A, dieresis or umlaut)
Ç	Ç	(capital C, cedilla)

HTML Text	Appears As	Description
É	É	(capital E, acute accent)
Ê	Ê	(capital E, circumflex accent)
È	È	(capital E, grave accent)
Ë	Ë	(capital E, dieresis or umlaut)
Í	Í	(capital I, acute accent)
Î	Î	(capital I, circumflex accent)
Ì	Ì	(capital I, grave accent)
Ï	Ï	(capital I, dieresis or umlaut)
Ñ	Ñ	(capital N, tilde)
Ó	Ó	(capital O, acute accent)
Ô	Ô	(capital O, circumflex accent)
Ò	Ò	(capital O, grave accent)
Ø	Ø	(capital O, slash)
Õ	Õ	(capital O, tilde)
Ö	Ö	(capital O, dieresis or umlaut)
Ú	Ú	(capital U, acute accent)
Û	Û	(capital U, circumflex accent)
Ù	Ù	(capital U, grave accent)
Ü	Ü	(capital U, dieresis or umlaut)
Ý	Ý	(capital Y, acute accent)
á	á	(small a, acute accent)
â	â	(small a, circumflex accent)
æ	æ	(small ae diphthong (ligature))
à	à	(small a, grave accent)
å	å	(small a, ring)
ã	ã	(small a, tilde)
ä	ä	(small a, dieresis or umlaut mark)
ç	ç	(small c, cedilla)
é	é	(small e, acute accent)
ê	ê	(small e, circumflex accent)
è	è	(small e, grave accent)
ð	∂	(small eth, Icelandic)
ë	ë	(small e, dieresis or umlaut mark)
í	í	(small i, acute accent)
î	î	(small i, circumflex accent)
ì	ì	(small i, grave accent)
ï	ï	(small i, dieresis or umlaut mark)

Continued on next page

Continued from previous page

HTML Text	Appears As	Description
ñ	ñ	(small n, tilde)
ó	ó	(small o, acute accent)
ô	ô	(small o, circumflex accent)
ò	ò	(small o, grave accent)
ø	ø	(small o, slash)
õ	õ	(small o, tilde)
ö	ö	(small o, dieresis or umlaut mark)
ß	ß	(small sharp s, German (sz ligature))
ú	ú	(small u, acute accent)
û	û	(small u, circumflex accent)
ù	ù	(small u, grave accent)
ü	ü	(small u, dieresis or umlaut mark)
ý	ý	(small y, acute accent)
ÿ	ÿ	(small y, dieresis or umlaut mark)
®	®	(registered trademark; supported by only a few browsers)
©	©	(copyright; supported by only a few browsers)

Other Characters

If you're interested in designing a Web page in a language other than English or containing hard-to-find characters, you have a few options:

- Some computers have automatic graphic filters to convert Roman characters into things like Arabic, Hebrew, Chinese, or Japanese. You can then use the standard ASCII set to create your Web pages. For those who don't own such filters, however, the screen will read as gibberish.
- The latest version of HTML has a CHARSET attribute for paragraphs, headers, and such, which can be used to specify alternate character sets, such as Hebrew, Japanese, or any other language a browser may support.
- Create your entire page using any foreign word processor or graphic design tool and then save the entire page as a GIF graphic. You can then make this graphic transparent (see the next chapter) and place it on your page for all to see. See Figure 11-1 for an example.

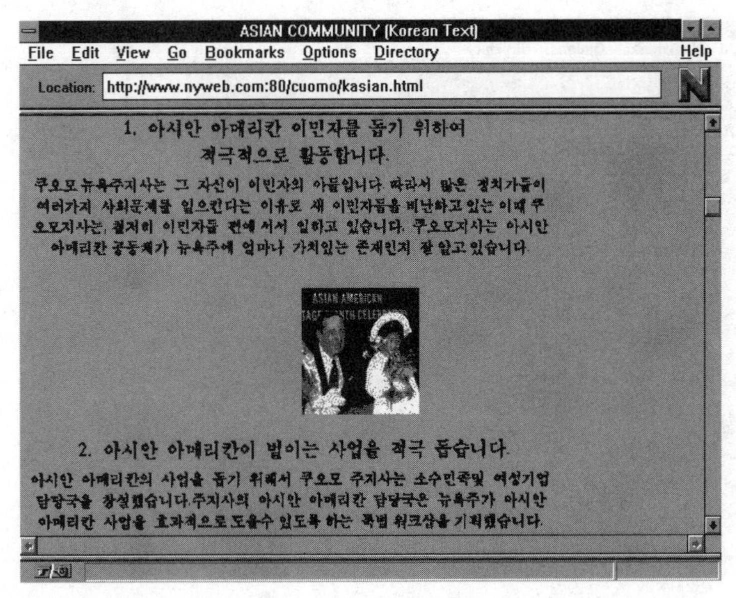

Figure 11-1 A Korean article on the New York Web

HTML You can obtain or create complete font sets with each letter stored in a separate transparent graphic file. These can be useful for foreign language headlines or small captions.

If you want to use complex mathematical equations, the latest version of HTML+ has some built-in mathematical functions. However, to be sure everybody can read your Web page, your best bet is to create the equations using a program such as LaTex. You can then use the LaTex2HTML converter (see Chapter 17) to form HTML pages.

Here are a couple of sites dedicated to multilingual servers: *http://andrew.triumf.ca/cgi-bin/country-switch/*

http://www.fer.uni-lj.si/.

LESSON #2: SECTION HEADINGS

Headings organize your document into smaller, easily-found blocks of information. Headings will generally appear as in Figure 11-2.

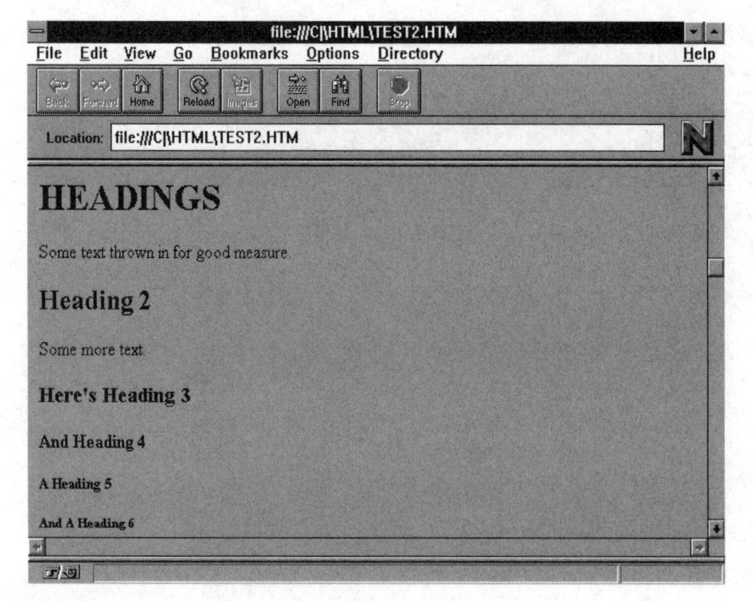

Figure 11-2 A hierarchy of headings

STYLE TIP: Although HTML supports six (and in some cases, seven) levels of headings, its a good idea to stick to four, otherwise your pages can get too complicated to wade through.

HTML headings take the form

```
<H#>heading</H#>
```

where # is the heading level—a number from one to six. For example, a document's main (largest) heading looks like:

```
<H1>Main Heading</H1>
```

STYLE TIP: The first heading is generally the same as the document title.

As in a printed document, the main headings should summarize the broadest ideas, with lower levels of headings forming a logical structure below them. Think of headings as your document's outline.

Here's the full HTML code for the headings and text in Figure 11-2:

```
<HTML>
<HEAD><TITLE>HEADINGS</TITLE></HEAD>
<BODY>
<H1>HEADINGS</H1>
Some text thrown in for good measure.
```

```
<H2>Heading 2</H2>
Some more text.
<H3>Here's Heading 3</H3>
<H4>And Heading 4</H4>
<H5>A Heading 5</H5>
<H6>And A Heading 6</H6>
</BODY>
</HTML>
```

In general, you should only use heading tags when you're actually defining a heading. In other words, don't stick a heading in the middle of a list. Although Netscape and Mosaic can handle these misplaced headings, other browsers may become confused.

Style: Drafting Good Headings

Although there's no steadfast rule, subheads generally should not stand alone. Always have at least two subheads in each section. Here's an example of good heading layout:

Desserts

Pies

Apple

Key Lime

Pumpkin

Coconut Cream

Cakes

Cheese

Chocolate

Angel Food

Whereas a less-acceptable, splotchy layout would be:

Soups

Chicken

Desserts

Pies

Apple

It also usually looks nicer if you follow each heading by at least one sentence of text instead of immediately tacking on another heading.

Describe each subsection so that the reader can decide whether or not to study, skim, or skip it. For example:

```
<H2>Desserts</H2>
There are too many popular and sumptuous desserts to name. However, the
traditional American favorites have been pies, cakes, mousses, and
various fruit dishes.<P>
```

The final caveat with headings is to be sure not to skip a level. Try not to follow an <H1> with an <H3> heading. It confuses some browsers—and some people—when you jump around like that.

Aligning Headings

More advanced browsers such as Netscape allow you to align your headings using the ALIGN attribute. You have the following alignment options:

- HTML Left (the default)
- HTML Center
- HTML Right
- HTML Justify

For instance, to center the main heading, use the command:

```
<H1 ALIGN="center">The Heading</H1>
```

LESSON #3: PARAGRAPHS

A Web browser needs to know when one paragraph ends and when a new one begins. It's essential to separate one paragraph from the next. You can do this by using a plain <P> element. This element may appear at either the beginning or end of each paragraph—you don't need to designate both. For example, the text in Figure 11-3 was achieved by the code:

```
Once upon a time there was a little man. When I say little, I mean
little. I mean real little. He was so little most people would just
pass him by. Others would see him and smirk. He felt belittled.<P>
So this little man made himself a little plan. He decided he wasn't
going to take the belittling anymore. He was going to show those
giants a thing or two!<P>
The little man waited for a foggy day. The clouds came down low. Most
everybody was blinded, but not the little man. He could walk between
the confused people's legs, and walk he did. Eventually he reached his
destination: The chainsaw store!<P>
```

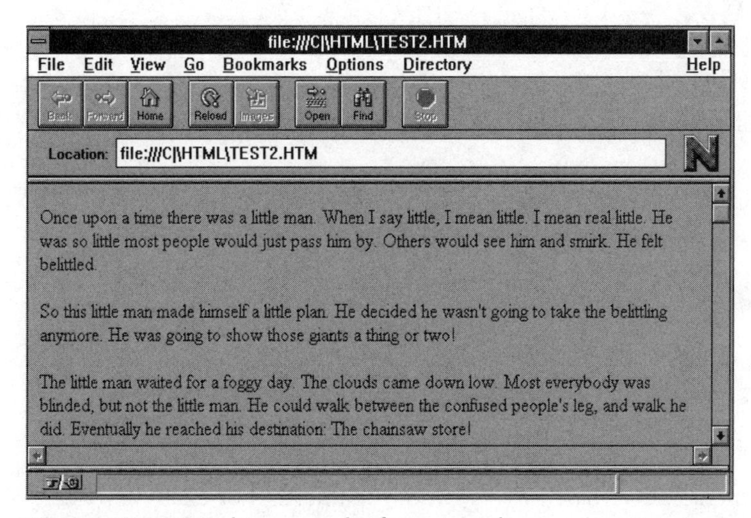
file:///C|\HTML\TEST2.HTM
File Edit View Go Bookmarks Options Directory Help
Back Forward Home Reload Images Open Find Stop
Location: file:///C|\HTML\TEST2.HTM
Once upon a time there was a little man. When I say little, I mean little. I mean real little. He was so little most people would just pass him by. Others would see him and smirk. He felt belittled.
So this little man made himself a little plan. He decided he wasn't going to take the belittling anymore. He was going to show those giants a thing or two!
The little man waited for a foggy day. The clouds came down low. Most everybody was blinded, but not the little man. He could walk between the confused people's leg, and walk he did. Eventually he reached his destination: The chainsaw store!

Figure 11-3 Picking a peck of paragraphs

NOTE: Remember, any extraneous blank spaces or lines in your HTML document are usually just ignored.

The latest HTML browsers let you define exactly how your paragraphs should look by using <P> at the beginning of your paragraph and </P> at the end. Eventually, this HTML+ paragraph *container* will allow you to define formatting attributes for each paragraph. For example, you could give each paragraph a unique ID, making it easy to reference, such as:

```
<P ID="Here">
```

More importantly, you could center align, left align, right align, justify, or indent each paragraph. For example, you would start each paragraph with the tag:

```
<P ALIGN="justify">
```

As of now, most Web browsers do not support these enhanced paragraph markers.

In general, it doesn't really matter whether you use one empty <P> marker or the <P></P> container. Use whichever technique seems most intuitive to you.

STYLE TIP: Some browsers will indent the beginning of paragraphs, others will leave a blank line or two. In any case, you don't need to worry about indentation. HTML takes care of this for you.

You do *not* need to place paragraph markings around, in, or after nonbody text, such as:

- Headings
- Lists
- Preformatted text
- Addresses
- Blockquotes
- Horizontal rule lines

These elements have their own types of separators. For example, when you define a heading, all Web browsers know to add appropriate spacing automatically.

LESSON #4: LINE BREAKS

Now your paragraphs are nice and tidy. But what if you want to put text on specific lines within the same paragraph? For example, although things like postal addresses, poems, and songs are stored in paragraphs, you want to break them up into lines. The solution is the <BR> element.

For example, if your HTML document looks like

```
Hello there, dude.
How are you today?
I surely hope you are okay.<P>
That's good to hear!
```

Then, when seen over a Web browser, the text appears like:

```
Hello there, dude. How are you today? I surely hope you are okay.
That's good to hear!
```

However, if you insert the <BR> element after each line, as follows:

```
Hello there, dude. <BR>
How are you today? <BR>
I surely hope you are okay.<P>
That's good to hear!
```

Then the Web text appears on separate lines:

```
Hello there, dude.
How are you today?
I surely hope you are okay.

That's good to hear!
```

No Break

If you have a line of text that absolutely, positively should not be broken up, you can designate this using the <NOBR> element, as follows:

```
<NOBR>
This is a piece of text that, for whatever reason, we want all on the
same line.
</NOBR>
```

As of now, only Netscape supports this function.

STYLE TIP: Be careful with this! If your no-break text is too long, it'll scroll right off the screen. This can be a pain to read.

Word Break

If you have a specific no-break section and know exactly where you wouldn't *mind* the text breaking, you can insert the <WBR> element. A word break (<WBR>) does not *force* a break the way <BR> does. Instead, it tells Netscape that, should a break be necessary, this is where it should be done.

You can use word breaks to achieve very precise blocks of text.

STYLE TIP: In general, text rolls over onto the new line once it reaches the end of the window. Be careful, because some HTML commands may break up text that is meant to be together. More advanced browsers like Netscape will only break up a line when it comes across empty space such as a space or a tab.

LESSON #5: TEXT STYLE

Most HTML browsers will display the following text emphasis styles:

- HTML Bold
- HTML Italic
- HTML Underlined
- HTML Preformatted Text

Highlighted text flows along with any neighboring text. You can also mix and match these elements to achieve, say, bold and italicized text.

There are two general style types: physical and logical. Physical styles tell the browser exactly what the text should look like. Logical styles, on the other hand, explain the *kind* of text being marked and let the browser do whatever it does with that kind of text. The next two subsections explain the differences, and you can use whichever type you feel most comfortable with.

All styles have a start tag and an end tag. To highlight a word, phrase, or entire paragraph, surround the text by tags. For example, to create boldface text you'd type:

```
<B>This text will be bold,</B> but this text won't.
```

STYLE TIP: You can usually mix and match emphasis elements to achieve, say, bold and italicized text. You should note, however, that browsers have their own rules for interpreting overlapping styles. Some browsers interpret only the innermost element, which would make

```
<B><I>Bold and Italicized Text</B></I>
```

appear in italics but not boldface. In general, you should immediately surround any text you wish to highlight with its proper physical or logical style elements.

Physical Styles

Physical styles tell the Web browser exactly how a piece of text should appear. Most word processors make use of physical styles. However, each browser will implement a physical style in its own way, and not every browser supports all physical styles.

The supported physical styles are:

HTML <B> **Bold text** </B>

HTML <I> *Italicized text* </I>

HTML <TT> `Typewriter fixed-width font text` </TT>

HTML <U> Underlined text </U>

HTML+ has specifications for the following additional styles. Most of these are currently supported by browsers such as Mosaic and Netscape:

HTML ^{^{Super}script}

HTML _{$_{\text{Sub}}$script}

HTML <S> ~~Strikethrough~~ </S>

HTML <BLINK> Blinking text </BLINK>

HTML <CHANGE> Change bar </CHANGE>

STYLE TIP: Try not to use too many different types of emphasis in a document, or your text will appear peppered. Stick to one or two styles and be consistent about what type of text you use them for.

Logical Styles

Logical styles, in most cases, get the same results as physical styles. However, a logical style will usually be more consistent from browser to browser. A logical style is more like a description of the enclosed text and is useful for writing scholarly journals, manuals, or other articles involving many types of print.

Here are the most popular logical styles:

HTML <DFN>: A word being defined. This word may later appear in a glossary. (Usually displayed as italics.)

HTML <EM>: Emphasized text. Use this to give words some oomph. (Usually displayed as italics.)

HTML <CITE>: A citation. Used around titles of books, journals, movies, poems, etc. (Usually displayed as italics.)

HTML <CODE>: Computer code. If you include a program's source code listing, you may want to surround it by this element. (Usually displayed as a fixed-width font.)

HTML <KBD>: Keyboard entry. If you tell a user to type a specific set of commands, surround the commands with this element. (Usually displayed as a bold, fixed-width font.)

HTML <SAMP>: Sample status messages. (Usually displayed as a fixed-width font.)

HTML <STRONG>: Strong emphasis. Good for warnings or other text that you want to leap off the screen. (Usually displayed as bold.)

HTML <VAR>: A variable. If you show a command, you can use this element to designate parts of the command that the user should replace with a legal parameter. (Usually displayed as fixed-width italics.)

HTML <Q>: An inline quote. (Only Netscape supports this tag, surrounding the text by proper open and closed quotation marks.)

For example, if you wanted to emulate the following text:

```
To change directories in Unix, use the cd command, as follows:
cd directory-name
```

You would type the HTML sequence:

```
To change <DFN>directories</DFN> in Unix, use the cd command, as
follows:<P>
<KBD>cd <VAR>directory-name</VAR></KBD><P>
```

LESSON #6: SECTION STYLE

Giving individual words a particular emphasis is a great way to clarify your text. HTML also offers the ability to mark entire paragraphs or text sections with a particular style.

Preformatted Text

If you have a table, indented program listing, a free-form poem, or a tiny piece of ASCII art, you want it to appear over the Web the same way it appears on your screen. The *<PRE>* element allows you to mark a section of text as preformatted. This text is then printed using the same line breaks, and fixed-width characters. For example the poem:

```
<PRE>
This is a poem,
                          I'm not sure why I wrote it.
But it's a poem nonetheless,
                          Try not to over-quote it.
</PRE>
```

Would appear exactly as you entered it:

```
This is a poem,
                          I'm not sure why I wrote it.
But it's a poem nonetheless,
                          Try not to over-quote it.
```

STYLE TIP: Hyperlinks can be used within <PRE> sections without any problems. You should avoid using other HTML tags within preformatted text, however, since there's no telling how they'll appear. Since line breaks are automatically interpreted, there's no need for <P> paragraph tags or <BR> line break tags. You should also avoid tabs, since every Web browser may have different tab settings. Use several blank spaces instead, which will always line up in a fixed-width font.

The Joy of Fixed-Width Fonts

Fixed-width fonts make each character the exact same size. With most other fonts, spaces, periods, and dashes are much shorter than alphanumeric characters—this usually gives the text a nice cosmetic appearance, but it can also make it hard to align different lines. For example, <PRE> lets you draw this cute little animal head:

If you don't use the preformatted text style, such a picture would come out skewed:

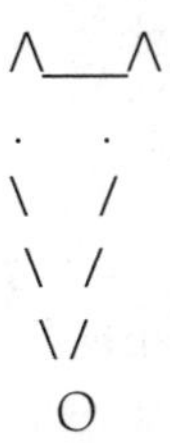

WIDTH

You can use the *WIDTH* attribute to let a Web browser know how long each line of text should be. The default is 80 lines. For example:

```
<PRE WIDTH=40>
This text will automatically be wrapped around after every forty char-
acters. This can be useful if you're trying to create a small block of
text, or some other similar effect.
</PRE>
```

will produce:

```
This text will automatically be wrapped
around after every forty characters.
This can be useful if you're trying to
create a small block of text, or some
other similar effect.
```

Blockquotes

The *<BLOCKQUOTE>* element is useful for any sort of quoted text. This text will usually appear italicized and centered as a block in the middle of the page, as shown in Figure 11-4.

For example, if you're writing a paper about René Descartes, you could include:

```
Descartes writes:
<BLOCKQUOTE>
Thus I lived, in appearance, just like those who have nothing to do
but live a pleasant and innocent life and attempt to obtain the plea-
sures without the vices, to enjoy their leisure without ennui, and to
occupy their time with all the respectable amusements available. But
in reality I never desisted from my design and continued to achieve
greater acquaintance with truth.
</BLOCKQUOTE>
```

The latest specification of HTML (version 3) has abbreviated the <BLOCKQUOTE> element to just <QUOTE> and </QUOTE>. These shortened elements do not work with many browsers yet.

Addresses

You should surround any home address, office address, e-mail address, signature, or other personal information with the *<ADDRESS>* element. An address is generally put at the bottom of a document as a signature, or at the top as a sort of byline.

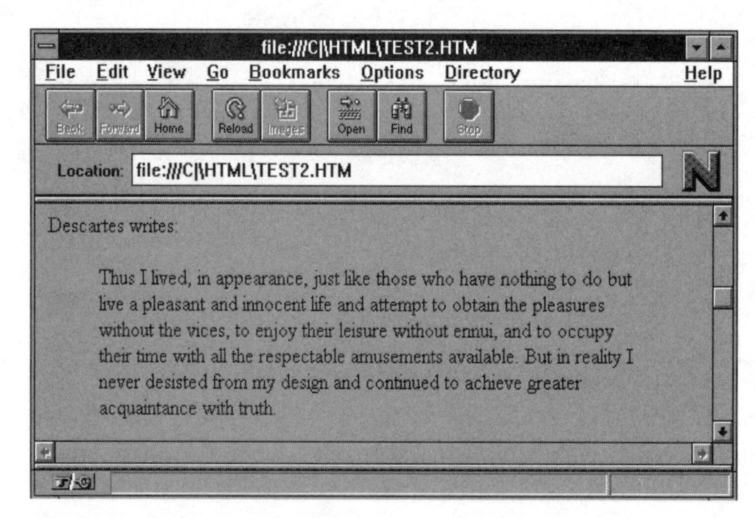

Figure 11-4 A nice way to quote a source

An address is usually printed in italics. It may also be aligned to the right or otherwise indented. For example, you might sign your documents:

```
<ADDRESS>
John Smith<BR>
123 No Way<BR>
Metropolis, IN 12345<BR>
TEL: (000)555-1234
</ADDRESS>
```

STYLE TIP: It's a good idea to include your e-mail address at the bottom of every Web page you create, so interested parties can reach you easily. You may want to use the mailto: URL (supported by most of the latest browsers) to turn your address into an automatic e-mailer. See Chapter 16 for more information.

Styles to Watch Out For

The latest HTML specification includes several additional styles, such as footnotes, margin notes, abstracts, notes, and iconized blocks. While no commercial browsers support these styles yet, they probably soon will.

Footnotes

If you have a source, or some additional information that may ruin the flow of your narrative, you'll soon be able to designate it as a footnote with the *<FOOTNOTE>* element. A footnote may appear at the end of the text, or may even show up in a pop-up box.

For example, the code:

```
Most Biblical sources give no exact year for Armageddon.
<FOOTNOTE>
A handful of mystics throughout the ages, such as Nostradamus, have
marked the year 2000 to herald the end of the world.
</FOOTNOTE>
This "judgment day" is supposed to be characterized by natural disas-
ters, fire and brimstone falling from the sky, and general turmoil.
```

Would create something that looked like the following:

```
Most Biblical sources give no exact year for Armageddon.* This "judg-
ment day" is supposed to be characterized by natural disasters, fire
and brimstone falling from the sky, and general turmoil.
```

You could then click on the asterisk to read the additional information.

Margin Notes

The *<MARGIN>* element will be similar to a footnote. Marginized text appears to the left or right of the current paragraph, or as a separate paragraph. You'll be able to use this method to stick important warnings, notes, or tips in the margins.

For example:

```
The Colt .38 Special revolver contains the typical 6 bullets.
<MARGIN>
When loading a gun be sure to face it away from you!
</MARGIN>
```

Abstract

The *<ABSTRACT>* element will be useful when you write a scholarly paper. If you surround the summary or article abstract by this element, you should get an abstract that looks like the one in a formal paper: in a small font, centered and justified beneath the paper's title. For example:

```
<H1>The Vicissitudes Of Neo-Templar Restructuring in a Postmodern
Era</H1>
<ABSTRACT>
I have no idea what this paper is about but I'm sure it's interesting.
No, really!
</ABSTRACT>
```

Note

You'll be able to use the *<NOTE>* element for notes, tips, or warnings. A note will then be set off in a special box or bold font. For example:

```
<NOTE>Be sure not to touch the two wires together!</NOTE>
```

Role

The *<ROLE>* element will mark a specific piece of text with an icon. You'll be able to give a role the following attributes, each of which displays a different icon:

HTML *Simple*: No icon

HTML *Tip*: A pointing finger

HTML *Note*: The blue information circle

HTML *Warning*: A yellow traffic warning sign

HTML *Error*: A stop sign

For example, the command:

```
<ROLE TIP>Counting to ten is much easier if you use your
fingers.</ROLE>
```

You'll also be able to use the *SRC* attribute to include your own icons. For example:

```
<ROLE SRC="caution.gif">Be careful not to touch the wires
together!</ROLE>
```

See the next chapter for details about including graphics.

LESSON #7: FONT SIZE

As of now, only the Netscape browser allows you to adjust font size. Adjusting fonts lets you design all sorts of special effects, as shown in Figure 11-5.

To change a font's size, just use the command:

```
<FONT SIZE=size>
```

The *size* value must be between 1 and 7. In general, a basic font is size 3. So, if you wanted to create a word that appeared to be shrinking, you could type:

```
<FONT SIZE=7>S<FONT SIZE=6>h<FONT SIZE=5>r<FONT SIZE=4>i<FONT
SIZE=3>n<FONT SIZE=2>k
```

You can use the </FONT> closing element to return to the default base font. For instance:

```
<FONT SIZE=7>This is big.</FONT> Let's go back to normal.
```

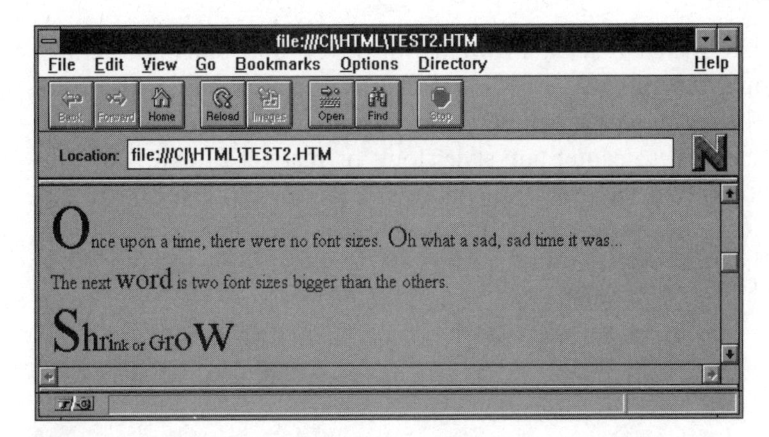

Figure 11-5 Changing font size to spice up your Web page

STYLE TIP: Be careful when embedding different-sized fonts alongside other text, especially if the text is more than one line long. The disparity in font size will mess up the vertical spacing between the lines.

Relative Font Size

You can also use the plus or minus character to change a font relative to the document's base font. For example, if you wanted a word to be two sizes bigger than the rest of the text, you would type:

```
The next <FONT SIZE=+2>word</FONT> is two font sizes bigger than the
others.
```

The Base Font

The default font size is 3. If you want a document (or a section) to appear in a larger or smaller font, you can set the base font using the <BASEFONT> element. For example, to draw all text in the largest possible font, type:

```
<BASEFONT SIZE=7>
```

LESSON #8: CENTERING

Perhaps the most typically used style of text alignment is centering. Centered text is flashy, professional, and easy to read.

In previous sections, you learned about how you could alter the alignment of a paragraph or a heading by using the

```
<P ALIGN="center">
```

or

```
<H1 ALIGN="center">
```

attributes. This format is a bit unwieldy, however, and does not center everything you'd want it to.

Netscape has come up with a more convenient *<CENTER>* element. You can use this element to center any style, font, or manner of text. You can even use <CENTER> to center graphic images. Centering is simple:

```
<CENTER>
This text will be centered.<BR>
As will this!<P>
And this!<P>
</CENTER>
```

LESSON #9: COMMENTS

Putting comments in your HTML code helps others steal from you more effectively. The public structure of the Web encourages people to borrow each other's Web pages and improve on them, customizing them to their own needs. Everybody learns from everybody else.

Anything placed within comments will not be printed by a Web browser. The only way for somebody to see your comments is to download a listing of your HTML source.

To begin a comment, use the

```
<!--
```

tag. At the end of each comment use the

```
-->
```

tag.

A typical comment, then, would look like this:

```
<!-- This section jumps to a random home page. -->
```

Most browsers do not allow you to nest comments (use a comment within a comment). They also get very confused if you use a double-dash (--) anywhere in your comment. And although Netscape and other advanced browsers let you comment out several lines of actual HTML markup, other browsers will read commands inside of comments anyway and output a big mess.

STYLE TIP: In general, then, try to restrict your comments to simple one-liners preceding each section. If you absolutely need to use multiline comments, put a <!-- at the start and a --> at the end of each line.

LESSON #10: LISTS

There are several types of HTML lists:

- HTML *Ordered:* a numbered list
- HTML *Unordered:* a bulleted list
- HTML *Definition:* a list with a term followed by a few words or sentences of description
- HTML *Plain:* a list with no numbers, bullets, or definitions

Menu: a short list of items, like a plain list, but tighter

Directory: a thin listing of many items in several columns

Lists can be mixed, matched, nested, and combined. In other words, you can have an unordered list within an ordered list, as shown in Figure 11-6.

STYLE TIP: You usually add a period to the end of a list item if it's a complete sentence. If not, lists usually look better with no punctuation.

Ordered Lists

One of the most common ways to express a number of items is to give them all numbers. These numerical, or ordered, lists are great for describing a series of instructions or set of problems.

An ordered list begins with the *<OL>* element and ends with *</OL>*. Each list item itself is preceded by the empty *<LI>* element. For example, to make this list:

```
1. Remove the cat from the box.
2. Pet the cat.
3. Feed the cat.
4. Place the cat back in the box.
```

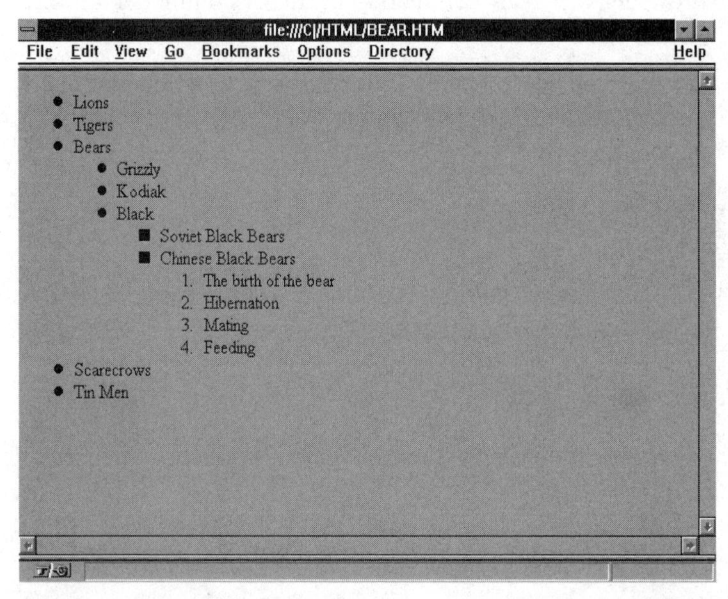

Figure 11-6 Nesting lists together to achieve an outline effect

You would use the following HTML instructions:

```
<OL>
  <LI>Remove the cat from the box.
  <LI>Pet the cat.
  <LI>Feed the cat.
  <LI>Place the cat back in the box.
</OL>
```

STYLE TIP: You can create a list without <LI> list elements to indent a block of text. This trick works with most browsers. For example, if you want to indent a special tip or idea, you could use the following code:

```
<UL>
This text will be indented, no matter how long the paragraph stretches
on. Pretty cool, eh?
</UL>
```

List Type

By default, an ordered list will count using standard numbers starting from 1, continuing with 2, *ad infinitum.* More advanced versions of HTML, such as Netscape's Mozilla, allow you to define the type of counting system you want. Use the *TYPE* attribute, as follows:

```
<OL TYPE=t>
```

In place of *t* you can fill in one of the following:

- HTML *A:* capital letters
- HTML *a:* lowercase letters
- HTML *I:* large Roman numerals
- HTML *i:* small Roman numerals
- HTML *1:* standard numbers (the default)

So, for example, if you used the HTML sequence:

```
<OL TYPE=a>
  <LI>Remove the cat from the box.
  <LI>Pet the cat.
  <LI>Feed the cat.
  <LI>Place the cat back in the box.
</OL>
```

Your list would appear as follows:

```
a. Remove the cat from the box.
b. Pet the cat.
```

Continued on next page

Continued from previous page

```
c. Feed the cat.
d. Place the cat back in the box.
```

Why Start at One?

In some cases, you don't want your ordered list to begin with the number 1. You may be continuing a list from a previous section, or discussing a group of items from another list.

Using the *START* attribute, you can begin a list from any number you wish. For example, type

```
<OL START=4>
```

to begin your list with the number 4. The actual value of the list will still depend on the TYPE attribute. So, for example, if you designate:

```
<OL TYPE=I START=10>
  <LI>Remove the cat from the box.
  <LI>Pet the cat.
  <LI>Feed the cat.
  <LI>Place the cat back in the box.
</OL>
```

You'll get a list that looks like this:

```
X. Remove the cat from the box.
XI. Pet the cat.
XII. Feed the cat.
XIII. Place the cat back in the box.
```

Unordered Lists

The bulleted, or unordered, list is one of the best ways to express a series of points quickly. You can use bullets to list features, names, things in an inventory, or just about anything else. An unordered list begins with *<UL>* and ends with *</UL>*. Just like the ordered list, each list element is preceded by the *<LI>* element.

To create the statement

```
The biggest tourist sites in New York City are:
· The Statue of Liberty
· The World Trade Center
· The Empire State Building
· Rockefeller Center
· Central Park
· The Metropolitan Museum of Art
```

You would use this sequence:

```
The biggest tourist sites in New York City are:
<UL>
  <LI> The Statue of Liberty
  <LI> The World Trade Center
```

```
  <LI> The Empire State Building
  <LI> Rockefeller Center
  <LI> Central Park
  <LI> The Metropolitan Museum of Art
</UL>
```

Nesting Unordered Lists

You can easily create lists within lists, if you like, to achieve an "outline" effect. You can even mix and match unordered and ordered lists:

```
<UL>
  <LI> an item
  <LI> another item
  <LI> here's a nested list:
   <UL>
     <LI> a nested item
     <LI> another nested list:
     <OL>
       <LI> ordered item 1
       <LI> ordered item 2
     </OL>
   </UL>
  <LI> the last item
</UL>
```

STYLE TIP: Although you can nest as many lists together as you wish, try to curb the nesting to three levels. Beyond this, a list becomes hard to read.

In most cases, your browser draws a small black circle as the first-level bullet. Lynx uses asterisks, and a browser like Netscape uses a small solid disc. As you nest lists, the bullets become indented and the style of bullet changes. Figure 11-6 shows a sample Netscape nested list: circular bullets mark the first and second unordered levels, and squares mark the next two levels.

STYLE TIP: As with headings, no nested list item should stand alone. It always looks much better to make each level of your list have two or more entries. Why else would it be called a list?

Pick Your Own Bullet

Using the TYPE attribute, Netscape and several other HTML+ browsers allow you to designate different styles of bullets. You have three choices, no matter which level of the unordered list you're at:

HTML disc

HTML circle

HTML square

So, to make a short list preceded by two squares:

```
<UL TYPE=square>
  <LI> Item 1
  <LI> Item 2
</UL>
```

Customizing Lists

You now have quite a bit of control over how your lists can look. But Netscape supports an even further level of list customizing. By adding the TYPE or VALUE attribute to the *<LI>* element, you can combine bullets and numbers within the same list, combine various types of numbers, or use various types of bullets.

For example, to make a list that counts backward by twos, using different types of numbers:

```
<OL START=8>
  <LI>Remove the cat from the box.
  <LI VALUE=6 TYPE=I>Pet the cat.
  <LI VALUE=4 TYPE=a>Feed the cat.
  <LI VALUE=2 TYPE=i>Place the cat back in the box.
</OL>
```

This code would produce:

```
8. Remove the cat from the box.
VI. Pet the cat.
d. Feed the cat.
ii. Place the cat back in the box.
```

To make a list with three different types of bullets, you could write:

```
<UL>
   <LI TYPE=disc> Item 1
   <LI TYPE=circle> Item 2
   <LI TYPE=square> Item 3
</UL>
```

Definition Lists

Definition lists are useful for any sort of listing that contains a piece of additional information for each list item. This is great for glossaries, detailed outlines, or even play scripts (where each speech appears as a "definition" for the name of the character saying the words). The list itself starts with the *<DL>* element and closes with the *</DL>* element.

Each item in a definition list has two parts, the term—designated by *<DT>*—and the definition—*<DD>*. The term—usually one word or phrase—must fit on a single line. The definition itself can take up as many lines as you like.

Figure 11-7 shows a sample definition list. Here's the markup to create that list:

```
<DL>
  <DT> <B>The Statue of Liberty</B>
   <DD> This symbol of liberty and goodwill to all women and men was
donated to the United States by France. Situated on Liberty Island in
the New York Harbor, the statue is a sight which greeted American
immigrants for decades.
  <DT> <B>The World Trade Center</B>
   <DD> The tallest building in New York, and the second-tallest
building in the world. Also known as the Twin Towers.
  <DT> <B>The Empire State Building</B>
   <DD> Once the world's tallest building, it now ranks third. The
needle-like architecture makes this building a distinct New York land-
mark.
  <DT> <B>The Metropolitan Museum of Art</B>
   <DD> One of the world's premiere art museums, spanning most every
era and culture.
</DL>
```

STYLE TIP: It generally looks good to set the definition term in bold, italic, or some other sort of enhanced print. Note how each <DT> element in the above code is also surrounded by the <B> attribute.

The <DL> element also has the optional *COMPACT* attribute. You can use this to create a list that appears condensed on some browsers.

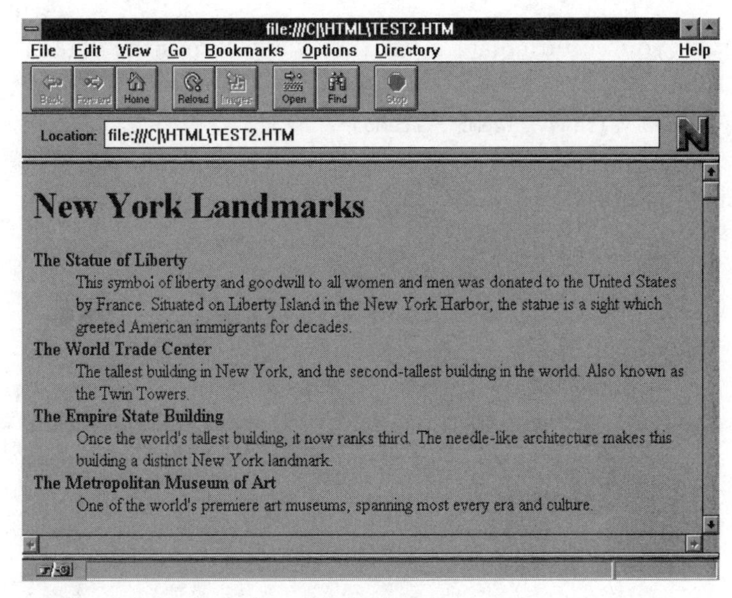

Figure 11-7 A standard definition list

STYLE TIP: Officially, you're not supposed to use more than one definition (<DD>) for each term (<DT>). If you want a definition that is longer than one paragraph, just use the <P> element and continue writing. Some browsers may get confused if you create a definition without an associated term. You can, however, list a term without including a definition for it.

Plain Lists

If you want to list items without using any fancy bullets, numbers, or definitions, you can easily create a plain list. Simply add the *PLAIN* attribute to any unordered list container. For example:

```
<UL PLAIN>
  <LI>First item
  <LI>Second item
  <LI>The Third
</UL>
```

A plain list can either shoot straight down the screen, or wrap over from line to line. This way, a list of twenty elements will be ordered in columns across the screen rather than wasting many pages. To wrap a list, use the WRAP attribute, with one of the following tags:

- HTML vert
- HTML horiz

For example, you could create a list that went across the screen horizontally:

```
Item1   Item2   Item3   Item4   Item5   Item6
Item7   Item8   Item9   Item10
```

by using the markup:

```
<UL PLAIN WRAP=horiz>
  <LI>Item1
  <LI>Item2
  ...
  <LI>Item10
</UL>
```

If you specified the wrap as vert, then the items would be listed vertically instead:

```
Item1   Item4   Item7   Item10
Item2   Item5   Item8
Item3   Item6   Item9
```

The <MENU> list and the <DIR> list, described in the next two sections, are a shorthand representation for popular plain lists. Try to use <MENU> and <DIR> whenever you can, since some browsers do not support the PLAIN attribute.

STYLE TIP: You can use the COMPACT attribute to give your plain lists a tighter appearance.

Menu Lists

A menu list looks very similar to an unordered list, except it usually consists of smaller paragraphs. The <MENU> element generally gets the same results as a plain list. You can use it to create a list that appears tighter, smaller, and with more white space:

```
<MENU>
  <LI>Caviar
  <LI>Champagne
  <LI>Beef Wellington
  <LI>Cheez Whiz
</MENU>
```

Directory Lists

The *<DIR>* element gives you a quick list of short words or phrases that wrap across the screen. In most cases, <DIR> gets the same results as the <UL PLAIN WRAP=vert> element. Each item in a directory list should be less than 20 characters long:

```
<DIR>
  <LI>John
  <LI>Mary
  <LI>Sue
  <LI>Bob
  <LI>Billy
  <LI>Kathy
  <LI>Frank
  <LI>Tim
  <LI>Elliot
  <LI>Mark
  <LI>Carlos
</DIR>
```

This would create something similar to the following:

```
John    Billy   Elliot
Mary    Kathy   Mark
Sue     Frank   Carlos
Bob     Tim
```

Some browsers make no distinction between plain lists, menu lists, and directory lists.

LESSON #11: HORIZONTAL LINES

Having lots of text together on a screen can be difficult to read. Luckily, most every Web browser supports horizontal rule lines. Anytime you write <HR> the browser draws a thin line completely across the screen. You can use these lines to mark the beginning or end of sections, to make headings look snazzy, to begin a footnote section, or to separate text from inline graphics or icons.

In Netscape and Mosaic the horizontal rule looks like a thin engraved line. Lynx uses a string of dashes.

STYLE TIP: Do not overuse horizontal rules. Too many lines muddle up the page with empty space, and make things hard to read.

In Thickness and in Health

Netscape and several other HTML+ browsers allow you to adjust the thickness of each horizontal line. Usually the line is 1 unit thick, but you can make it as thick as you like. Simply use the *SIZE* attribute. To make a line 5 units thick, type:

```
<HR SIZE=5>
```

Setting the Line's Width

What if you don't want your line to stretch all the way across the screen? Many times it's nice to have lines that are just as long as a nearby heading. Another nice Netscape feature allows you determine a line's width by using the *WIDTH* attribute.

If you want, you can determine the exact width in pixels. When you decide how long to make a line, keep in mind that an average VGA screen is about 640 pixels wide. Here's what the element looks like:

```
<HR WIDTH=200>
```

Or, even more easily, you can just determine what percentage of the screen the line should take up:

```
<HR WIDTH=50%>
```

Aligning Your Lines

Finally, Netscape gives you the ability to easily align your lines. Since lines can be any width, why not push them against the right margin or center them? By setting the *ALIGN* attribute you can achieve some nice results.

There are three ways to align your lines:

- HTML Left (the default)
- HTML Right
- HTML Center

For example, this element creates a half-sized line in the center of the screen:

```
<HR WIDTH=50% ALIGN=center>
```

Using a Solid Bar

The standard Netscape horizontal line looks as if it was carved into the monitor with a laser beam. If you want a more traditional solid line, simply specify the *NOSHADE* attribute as follows:

```
<HR NOSHADE>
```

Figure 11-8 shows the results of setting various thicknesses, widths, alignments, and solidities, as follows:

```
<HR>
<HR SIZE=2>
<HR SIZE=5>
<HR SIZE=3 WIDTH=50%>
<HR SIZE=3 WIDTH=50% ALIGN=right>
<HR SIZE=3 WIDTH=50% ALIGN=left>
<HR SIZE=4 WIDTH=60% ALIGN=center>
<HR SIZE=6 WIDTH=40% ALIGN=center>
<HR SIZE=8 WIDTH=10% ALIGN=center>
<HR WIDTH=10% ALIGN=center NOSHADE>
<HR NOSHADE>
<HR SIZE=4 WIDTH=60% ALIGN=center NOSHADE>
<HR SIZE=6 WIDTH=40% ALIGN=center NOSHADE>
<HR SIZE=8 WIDTH=10% ALIGN=center NOSHADE>
```

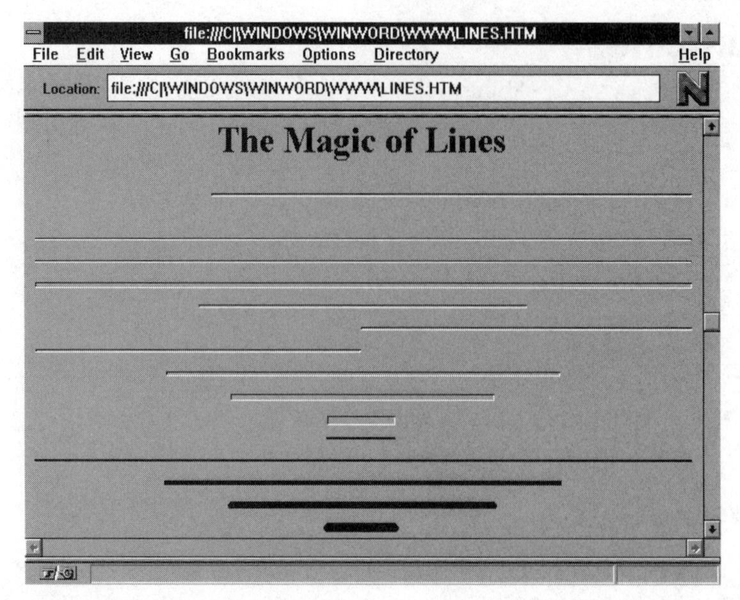

Figure 11-8 Going crazy with customized lines

LESSON #12: TABLES

There are three ways to create tables:

- Using preformatted text
- Using graphics
- Using HTML+ commands

Text Tables

Every browser has the ability to use preformatted text. Remember, this type of fixed-width text is designated by the <PRE> tag and closed by the </PRE> element.

You can create your table by hand, then, using ASCII characters, as follows:

```
+--------+----------+-------+
+  Name  |  Date    | Score |
+========+==========+=======+
| Ralph  | January  | 10    |
| George | February | 20    |
| Mary   | March    | 15    |
| Sara   | April    | 25    |
+--------+----------+-------+
Table 3: Each contestant's final score.
```

This may not be the most professional look in the world, but it gets the job done.

Graphical Tables

You can use any software you'd like to create your table. Then capture the screen, convert the image into a GIF graphic file, and display this image on your Web page. See the next chapter for the specifics.

HTML+ Tables

The latest version of Mosaic and Netscape fully supports HTML+ table commands. Eventually, most browsers should support this feature. HTML table elements allow you to quickly slap together a very professional and sleek-looking table.

STYLE TIP: Since table commands are a relatively new feature, be sure to include a link to a standard preformatted text table. This way, people with browsers who can't view tables can still see your data.

You designate the start of a table using the *<TABLE>* element and end a table with *</TABLE>*. Within a table you can specify captions using the *<CAPTION>* element. Begin each row with the *<TR>* element. Header cells are designated using the *<TH>* element, and data cells are marked by the *<TD>* element.

Each cell can contain a word or a phrase, or entire paragraphs, lists, and headers—even graphical images. Figure 11-9 shows a sample table, which was created using the following code:

```
<TABLE BORDER>
  <CAPTION>Table 3: Each contestant's final score.</CAPTION>
  <TR><TH>NAME</TH><TH>DATE</TH><TH>SCORE</TH></TR>
  <TR><TD>Ralph</TD><TD>January</TD><TD>10</TD></TR>
  <TR><TD>George</TD><TD>February</TD><TD>20</TD></TR>
  <TR><TD>Mary</TD><TD>March</TD><TD>15</TD></TR>
  <TR><TD>Sara</TD><TD>April</TD><TD>25</TD></TR>
</TABLE>
```

Table Cells

Each row in a table begins with the <TR> element. If you like, you can end rows with </TR> though this is optional.

Any text that you want to head up your table begins with the <TH> element, and may end with the </TH> element. This text appears in a bigger, bolder font. Each cell of the table's actual data begins with the <TD> element, and may end with the optional </TD> element. Headings are usually created at the top or to the left of the data.

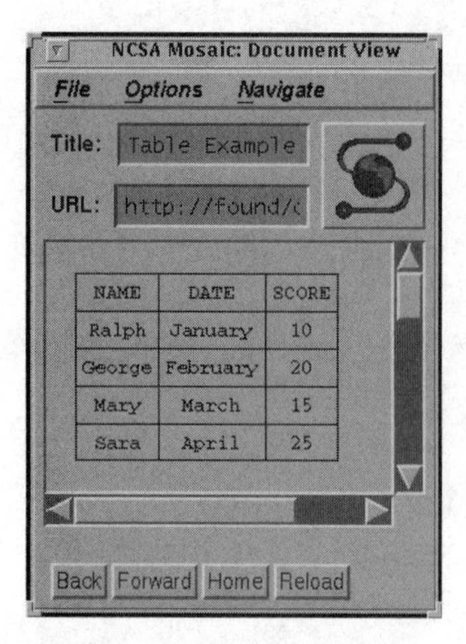

Figure 11-9 A simple but great-looking table created with HTML

NOTE: Rows can have different numbers of cells. The table is drawn accordingly.

STYLE TIP: When your Web browser comes across a table, it tries to figure out the table's size before it fills in any values. If the table is too wide to fit on the screen, it usually wraps text over within each cell. In this way, each cell acts as its own little window. Since this might make a table look awkward, try to limit the size of each cell. If you have too much data in one particular cell, you may want to use two separate tables.

A table's headings and data do not have to be plain text. You can place nearly anything within a table:

- HTML Images
- HTML Formatted text
- HTML Various text styles
- HTML Lists
- HTML Hyperlink anchors
- HTML Forms

For example, you could make a table as complicated as the following:

```
<TABLE BORDER>
  <CAPTION ALIGN=top>Table 6: Birds</CAPTION>
  <TR><TH>Famous Birds</TH><TH>Color</TH></TR>  <TR>  <TD>   <OL>
  <I><LI> The Roadrunner</I>
  <I><LI> Big Bird</I>
  <I><LI> Chilly Willie</I>
  <I><LI> Tweety Bird <IMG SRC= "Tweety.gif"></I>
  </OL>  </TD>  <TD>   <UL>
  <LI> Green and blue   <LI> Yellow    <LI> Black and white    <LI>Yellow
  </UL>  </TD>  </TR>
</TABLE>
```

The Caption

Always designate the *<CAPTION>* element as the first command in your table. The caption is usually placed directly above the table in a separate font. You can also position the caption using the ALIGN attribute. For example:

```
<CAPTION ALIGN=bottom>Table 5. A neat table.</CAPTION>
```

would print the caption at the bottom of the table. To print the caption at the top, you'd use:

```
<CAPTION ALIGN=top>Table 5. A neat table.</CAPTION>
```

The Border

If you want to give your table a border, be sure to specify the *BORDER* attribute:

```
<TABLE BORDER>
```

STYLE TIP: In general, you can keep small tables free of borders. However, large tables can be hard to read unless each cell has a border.

Alignment

Data is usually centered within each cell. You can use the ALIGN attribute, however, to specify the horizontal alignment of cell headings or cell data:

- HTML Left
- HTML Center (the default)
- HTML Right

Use *VALIGN* to specify the vertical alignment:

- HTML Top

HTML Middle (default)

HTML Bottom

For example, to place the words "Top left" at the top left corner of a cell:

```
<TD ALIGN=LEFT VALIGN=TOP>Top left</TD>
```

NOWRAP

Use NOWRAP to specify whether or not text within cells should wrap around. If you don't want text-wrapping, use markup similar to the following:

```
<TD NOWRAP>
```

Merging Cells

Two cells can be merged to form one cell; this way you can create one header cell for two columns. To make a cell span more than one row, use the *ROWSPAN* attribute; use *COLSPAN* to make the cell larger than one column. You can make any cell heading or cell data as wide or as tall as you wish.

For example, the code:

```
<TABLE BORDER>
  <CAPTION>Wide rows</CAPTION>
  <TR><TH ROWSPAN=2></TH>
      <TH ROWSPAN=2>NUMBER OF<BR>CONTESTANTS</TH>
      <TH COLSPAN=2>SCORE</TH>
  </TR>
  <TR><TH>HIGHEST</TH>
      <TH>LOWEST</TH>
  </TR>
  <TR><TH ALIGN=LEFT>MALES</TH>
      <TD>20</TD>
      <TD>101</TD>
      <TD>23</TD>
  <TR><TH ALIGN=LEFT>FEMALES</TH>
      <TD>823</TD>
      <TD>103</TD>
      <TD>12</TD>
</TABLE>
```

produces the table in Figure 11-10.

In other words, if you designate a cell with ROWSPAN=2, then it becomes two units high, merging with the cell directly below it. You only need to create one heading for a set of merged cells. If you make a cell with COLSPAN=2 then it becomes two units wide, merging with the cell to the immediate right. Your Web browser automatically centers all headings, making merged cells easy to read.

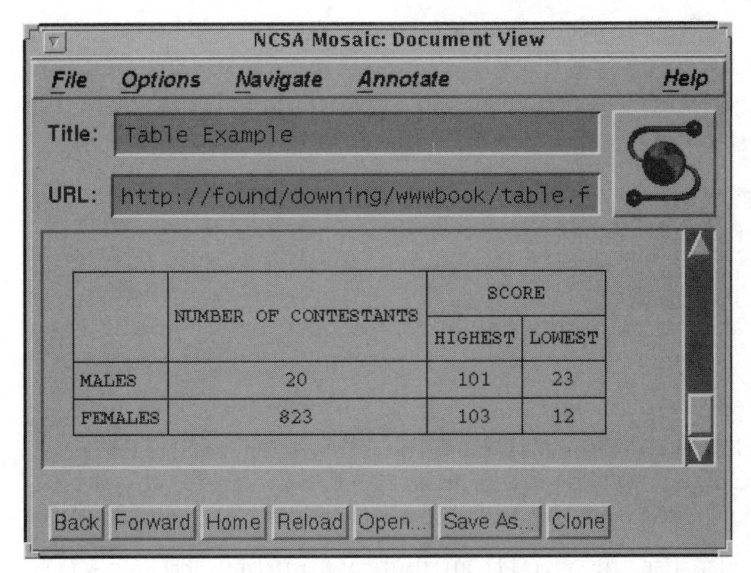

Figure 11-10 A table with merged cells

In cases where you have labels along the top and side of a table, you can create an empty cell in the upper-left corner just by typing <TH> twice.

When merging a column of cells, you can force an entry to take up more than one line by using the <BR> element.

STYLE TIP: Be sure you don't create row and column spans that cause cells to overlap. The resulting table is usually pretty hard to read.

Netscape's Table Extensions

Netscape creates lovely-looking tables, with three-dimensational borders, colors, and tight layouts. Some additional Netscape attributes let you customize the look of a table even further. For example, Mozilla HTML allows you to assign the table's BORDER attribute a value, giving different tables different looks. To create a table with a border four units thick:

```
<TABLE BORDER=4>
```

Spacing and Padding

Netscape also allows a CELLSPACING and CELLPADDING attribute as part of your <TABLE> element. By default, there are two units of space between each cell. If you want to tighten or loosen up a table, you can use markup similar to the following:

```
<TABLE CELLSPACING=4>
```

Padding is the space between a cell's border and it's contents. Netscape usually pads a cell by one unit. If you want your cell's contents to be surrounded by more free space, you could use markup similar to:

```
<TABLE CELLPADDING=3>
```

Table or Cell Width

Finally, Netscape allows you to set the exact WIDTH of your table or of each cell. You can set a value (in pixels) or a percentage. For example, if you want your table to go across half the Web page, you could use the command:

```
<TABLE WIDTH=50%>
```

STYLE TIP: Usually Netscape tries to create a table width that looks as good as possible. Only use WIDTH if your table is relatively small and you have an exact layout look in mind. Big tables can end up looking squashed.

You can also use the WIDTH attribute within the <TH> or <TD> elements. This lets you determine the size of a given cell. If you want a cell to take up a quarter of the table, you could use the markup:

```
<TD WIDTH=25%>Big ol' Cell</TD>
```

Design Hints

You might find it helpful to design your tables using a sort of graph, as shown in Figure 11-11. Each square on the graph is a cell. The thick lines represent the sizes of each cell. The bold print represents headings. You can then go through each cell with HTML commands, using the appropriate COLSPAN and ROWSPAN attributes and filling the cells with appropriate data. Each time you design a cell, cross it out, along with any other affected cells in the table. This prevents you from declaring the same cell twice, skewing the entire table.

For example, here's the code for a table based on the graph in Figure 11-11. Note that the caption doesn't show up on the graph, because it doesn't affect cell size or contents.

```
<TABLE>
  <CAPTION ALIGN=bottom>Each month's winners.</CAPTION>
  <TR><TH ROWSPAN=2><TH COLSPAN=2>SIZE<TH ROWSPAN=2>BEST<BR>SCORE
  <TR><TH>HEIGHT<TH>WEIGHT
  <TR><TH>JOHN<TD>5'10"<TD>150<TD>983
  <TR><TH>SARA<TD>6'0"<TD>164<TD>901
</TABLE>
```

		Size	
	Height	Weight	Best Score
John	5'10"	150	983
Sara	6'0"	164	901

Figure 11-11 Designing a complicated HTML table

LESSON #13: HYPERTEXT

Let's review how hypertext works: You click on a word or phrase or image and then you're magically transported to a wonderful new world. In other words, the Web browser needs to know two pieces of information about each hypertext link:

- Which part of the document is the link?
- Where does the link lead?

The answer to the first question is the <A> *link* element. The answer to the second question is a URL (covered in detail in Chapter 1) and an *anchor.*

The Anchor Element

The anchor element puts the hyper in hypermedia. A link designates that the next piece of text or graphics is actually a hypertext doorway to a strange, new, and wonderful place. You designate an anchor or link using the

```
<A>
```

element.

When your link text is finished, you designate that using the closing element:

```
</A>
```

Link text can take many formats. In some cases it is the exact address, file name, or location of the place the user will be zapped to, as in the top half of Figure 11-12.

In most cases, though, a link can be much more subtle, as in the bottom half of Figure 11-12. The word "aquarium" can whisk the user to an online store specializing in aquariums and tropical fish supplies. The style of your document link is completely up to you.

STYLE TIP: Try to create links that don't muck up the flow of the text. People may convert your hypertext document into a plain text document so they can refer to it offline. Your text should stand on its own. You might want to avoid words like "click your mouse on this sentence to read about the history of skyscrapers." Every Web user should know how to click. You're also being "mouseist"– some sensitive person who doesn't use a mouse may be offended. Instead, say something like, "There's an excellent article on the history of skyscrapers by T.O. Tall"–and make the word "skyscraper" your link.

Links do not have to be plain body text. You can generally turn any sort of text–headings, lists, italicized or bold text, or anything else into a link. It's perfectly fine to put an anchor within another HTML element. For example:

```
<H2><A HREF = "fishstore.html">Fish Stores</A></H2>
```

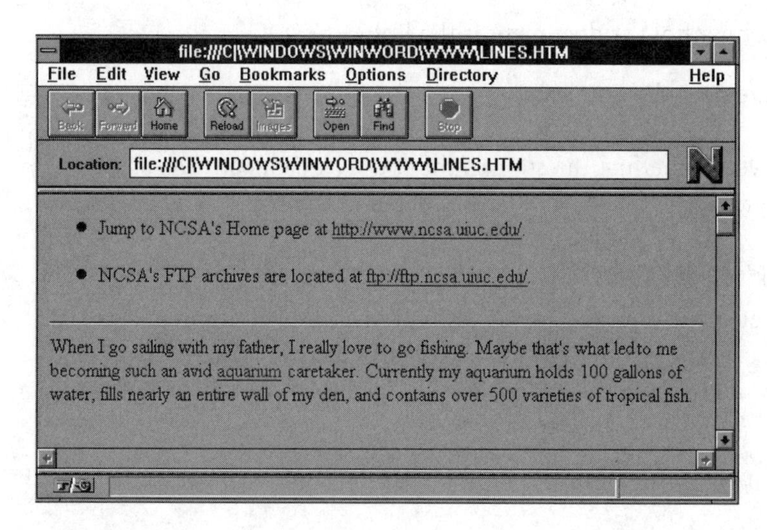

Figure 11-12 You can make anchors large and obvious (top) or subtle (bottom)

You should not, however, embed other HTML elements within an anchor, since some browsers may become confused. This is a no-no:

```
<A HREF = "fishstore.html"><H2>Fish Stores</H2></A>
```

You can even make a graphic into a hyperlink. The next chapter talks about how to do this.

The anchor element has a number of optional attributes, including:

- HTML *HREF:* jump to another Web page or resource
- HTML *NAME:* Destination for jumps from another part of the current document
- HTML *TITLE:* Title of document
- HTML *REL* and *REV:* Relationship between objects
- HTML *METHODS:* How to link

An anchor is meaningless, however, unless it has either an HREF or a NAME.

Links: HREF

The HREF attribute is the hyperlink reference: the place where you want to jump to. The anchor takes the form

```
<A HREF="url.html">clickable link text goes here</A>
```

Replace "url.html" with the full URL of the destination document (inside the quotes). Any text or graphics between the <A> and the </A> becomes an anchor, and most browsers will highlight it in blue. The user can then click on this blue text and automatically jump to the HREF location. See Figure 11-13 for a breakdown of a complete link.

WARNING: Do not create an anchor that doesn't lead to a valid location. Users will get confused and fed up clicking on links that don't exist. If you're not sure of a URL, you can either use empty quotes or just underline your link text: <U>Link Text</U>. You can then come back later and easily insert the real link. Also be sure to periodically check your remote links, since hypertext can often go *stale* as pages move or are erased.

HREFs often include *absolute URLs*—the specific addresses of distant Web documents, pictures, sounds, FTP files, gopher menus, telnet sites, newsgroups, e-mail, WAIS databases, and more. Any URL on the Internet

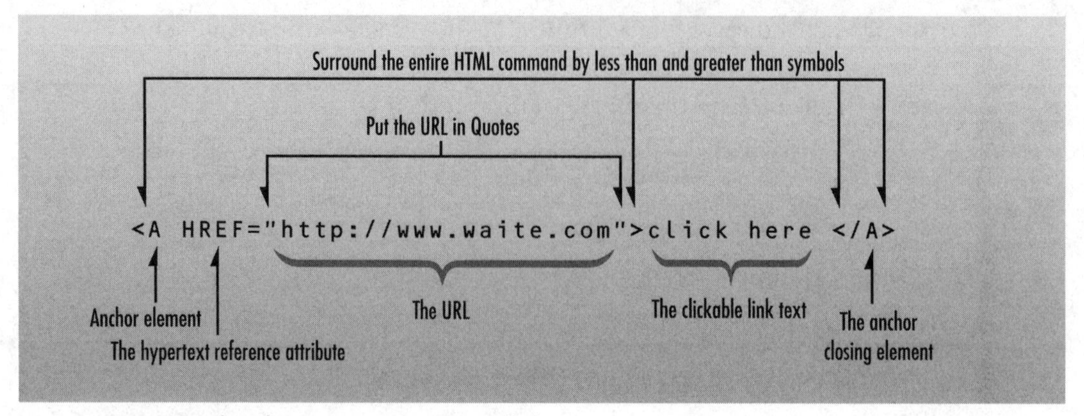

Figure 11-13 The elements in a hypertext link

can be jumped to. Most URLs are https, leading to another Web server. For example:

```
<A HREF="http://www.cern.edu/dsd/sd">CERN's home page.</A>
```

You can also jump to an FTP site, however:

```
<A HREF="ftp://ftp.netcom.com">Netcom's public FTP archives.</A>
```

Or even telnet to a remote computer:

```
<A HREF="telnet://world.com">Visit the World system.</A>
```

Most HREFs, however, are expressed as *relative URLs*—identifying documents, images, or other files that are available in the current directory. You can also indicate a relative URL location if you'd like to jump to an HTML document that is stored somewhere on the current Web server. For example, you can have users easily return to your own home page by using the anchor:

```
<A HREF="index.html">Click here to return to the home page.</A>
```

Or, if the file is stored in a different directory, you could indicate the entire pathname:

```
You should visit my friend <A HREF="/web/smith/public-
html/home.html">John Smith's</A> home page.
```

NOTE: Unix directories are separated by slashes, whereas DOS directories are separated by backslashes. If your HTML server is on a Windows or DOS PC, express filenames the way you normally would. If you are using a Unix machine, be sure to use a Unix directory structure. You may need to check with your system administrator if you're interested in using files in a directory different from your own. See Chapter 21 for detailed information about Web servers.

Relative URLS

When you can, stick to relative URLs. They're easier to type and easier to locate. All relative URLs consist of a simple filename. That file—whether it be a graphic, sound, movie, text file, or another HTML document—must be stored in the same directory as your Web page.

Relative URLs are especially useful if you must move your Web page to another location. For example, if your Internet provider goes out of business, you can transfer your entire Web directory to another machine. All relative URLs will still be valid—you won't need to retype a thing. Simply notify people of your new Web address.

When writing a relative URL, you don't need any slashes as long as the document you're linking to is in the current directory. If you call a URL that is in a different directory on the same machine, simply include the file's full pathname, which usually begins with a slash.

WARNING: Be careful not to use partial pathnames. Such a setup may load up when you use it, but won't work for remote users.

Absolute URLS

You should link to an absolute URL when:

- You didn't create the document being jumped to.
- The document, for space or copyright reasons, is stored on a distant server.
- You're linking to a document that often moves around.

In most cases, you create a link to a distant URL because it fits in with the theme of your page. For example, if I'm interested in tango dancing, I may include a link to the official Tango Page in France. If you're involved with fractal research and there's an interesting movie about fractal animations in a colleague's directory at another university, use that person's complete URL.

STYLE TIP: Don't be shy when it comes to using absolute URLs. Distant hyperlinks are what makes the Web a web. Many people create a special Web page with links to their favorite places. In fact, you can convert your Lynx, Netscape, or Mosaic bookmark lists into HTML. Turn to Chapter 17 to find out how.

An absolute URL must take the form

```
protocol://www.domain/directory/filename
```

See the section on URLs in Chapter 1 for details.

Anchors: The Name Attribute

Suppose you have a hundred-page document. Are you going to force readers to scroll down through the entire thing if they're only interested in one section?

The NAME attribute turns the anchored text into an actual hypertext destination. In other words, if you designate a piece of text with a certain name, you can build in explicit jumps to it. This attribute takes the form:

```
<A NAME="label">Optional Text</A>
```

In the corresponding HREF, precede the anchor name with the pound sign (#), so the attribute takes the form:

```
<A HREF="#label">Put your jump text here</A>
```

Once you designate a named anchor, you can jump to it from anywhere within the document (an *internal link*), or even from another document (an *external link*). See Figure 11-14.

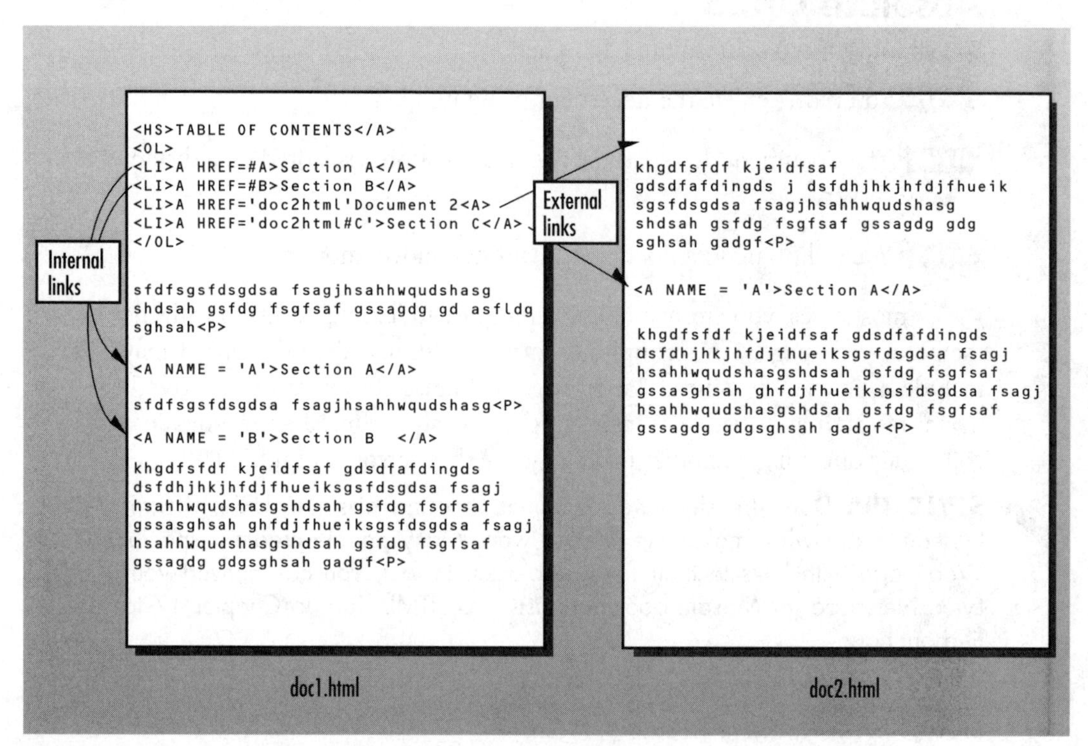

Figure 11-14 The difference between an internal link and an external one

STYLE TIP: Since some browsers can get confused by messy anchors, be sure to create anchors at the left margin of a given line. Try to limit your anchors to one word. Anchor names are case sensitive, so be sure to be consistent.

Internal Links: Creating a Table of Contents

The NAME attribute comes in most useful if you set up a table of contents as shown in Figure 11-15. Each line of this table can be a link to a heading that appears later in the same document.

For example, if you have a heading buried deep in some long document:

```
<H2>Judaism</H2>
```

you can mark it as a link by giving it an anchor name:

```
<H2><A NAME="jew">Judaism</A></H2>
```

You can then create a jump from the table of contents by setting up the entries there in a form like this:

```
<OL>
  <LI><A HREF="#christ">Christianity</A>
  <LI><A HREF="#jew">Judaism</A>
  <LI><A HREF="#hindu">Hinduism</A>
</OL>
```

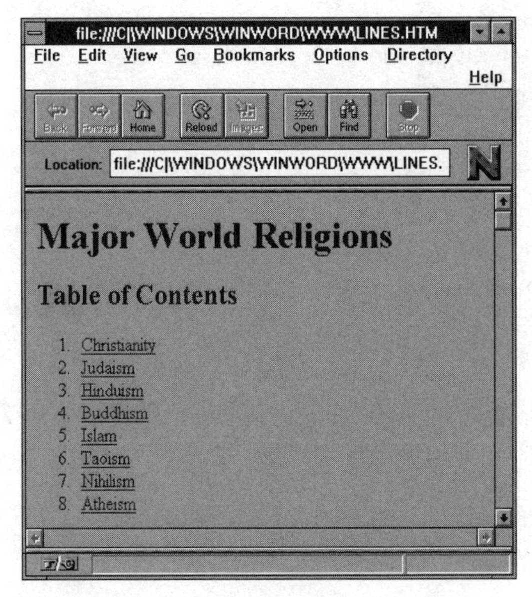

Figure 11-15 A hypertable of contents

When someone clicks on the word Judaism in your table of contents they'll be warped to the appropriate section of your document.

NOTE: The <LI> element precedes the <A> link because most tables of contents are created using ordered lists.

External Links: The Guts of Another Document

Normally, when you jump to another document using the HREF attribute, you are taken to the beginning of the text. If the name attribute is also included, however, you can begin reading a document from any particular point. This is very useful. Simply append the *#NAME* text to the end of the URL.

Suppose, for example, you're creating a document about the Middle East. It might be useful to create a link to your document about Major World Religions. When you got to talking about Israel's Jewish populace, for example, you could include the following hyperlink:

```
<A HREF="religions.html#jew">Click here to read some more about
Judaism</A>.
```

Assuming there's a properly labeled <A NAME="jew"> section in the *religions.html* document, your readers will be warped directly there.

STYLE TIP: If you have many Web pages dealing with the same topic, you may want to create one master Table Of Contents page with external links to each section of each document. You could then include a button at the bottom of every Web page that returns the user to your table of contents. This makes a lot of material easy to flip through.

You can even create external links to distant absolute URLs. For example, if you find a huge article about marine life on some distant system, you can scan that article's HTML source code until you find a NAME tag. For example, you may find:

```
<H1><A NAME="sharks">Sharks: Deep Sea Killers</A></H1>
```

If you happen to be discussing sharks within your own Web page, you can create a link to the shark section of the marine life article:

```
An <A HREF="http://www.sea.org/marinelife.html#sharks>excellent
article</A> about sharks is published by the SEA Organization.
```

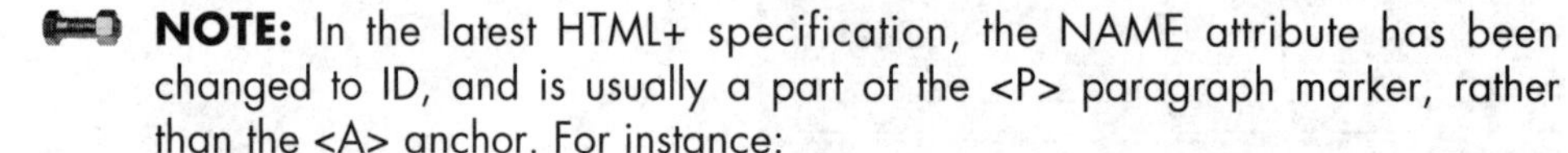

NOTE: In the latest HTML+ specification, the NAME attribute has been changed to ID, and is usually a part of the <P> paragraph marker, rather than the <A> anchor. For instance:

```
<P ID="jew">
```

However, for the time being, most browsers do not support this. You should stick to the NAME attribute.

Title

The *TITLE* attribute is optional, and usually not necessary. TITLE should be used only when creating a link to a non-HTML document. Every HTML document should have its own title. However, telnet sites, Gopher menus, FTP files, and text files do not have official Web titles. Inserting a title in the anchor displays a title at the top of the browser's screen.

This takes the form:

```
<A HREF="plaintext.txt" TITLE="A Plain Text Document">Click here</A>
```

A TITLE is usually informational, acting more as a comment than a useful tag.

Defining Relationships

The REL and REV attributes are used within advanced HTML documents. These two markers define the exact relationship between the linked document and the current document. REL and REV are only used *in addition to* the HREF attribute.

Most hypertext links consist of a *source document* (yours) and the *destination document* (the URL specified in HREF).

REL

The REL attribute expresses a forward relationship between the source and the destination. You can use REL as follows:

```
<A HREF="http://www.here.there/path/crazy.html" REL="Useindex">Click
here</A>
```

Here are the most useful relationships you can create between documents:

- HTML Acyclic: You cannot return to the source document from the destination document.
- HTML Annotation: The destination document just contains notes, edits, or small additions to the source document.
- HTML Approves: The destination document has been approved by the source.
- HTML Embed: The destination document is included in the source document. Some browsers use this to display two documents at once.

- HTML History: The destination document lists the many versions of the source.
- HTML Includes: The source document includes the destination within some sort of group.
- HTML Interested: The owner of the source document is interested in the destination.
- HTML Made: The source document is a home page or description of the destination's author.
- HTML Owns: The person who owns the current source document also owns the destination document.
- HTML Precedes: The source document precedes the destination document. This is useful if you have a book or manual consisting of a string of many Web pages. Often, you can click the browser's Next or Previous arrows to navigate. Each document can be preceded by only one other document.
- HTML Present: Whenever the source document is presented, the destination document must also be retrieved.
- HTML Refutes: The destination document refutes an argument made in the source. See Supports.
- HTML Reply: The destination document is a reply to a question or issue raised in the source.
- HTML Search: The destination document should be searched, not shown. Most browsers will ask the user to type in a search term. This allows you to create an index or database.
- HTML Supersedes: The destination document is a previous version of the source.
- HTML Supports: The destination document supports an argument made in the source. See Refutes.
- HTML UseGlossary: The destination has the glossary definition of terms that are listed in the source.

- Useindex: The destination document is a search index.

Most REL tags are pretty much arbitrary and can be used by you to keep track of your Web documents.

REV

The REV attribute is the exact opposite of REL. For example, a link from the source to the destination with:

```
<A HREF="document2.html" REL="Precedes">Click here to view the next
document in the series.</A>
```

Is the same as a link from the destination to the source with:

```
<A HREF="document1.html" REV="Precedes">Click here to view the
previous document in the series.</A>
```

Methods

You almost never need to worry about this attribute. The METHODS tag tells the httpd server which method types the linked-to URL supports.

LESSON #14: RELATIONSHIPS AND HYPERPATHS

You now know how to jump to another document. But what if you want the jump to be automatic? You can create an ordered list of several documents, forming a sort of guided tour of your Web pages.

Once you create a hyperpath, a user would have two ways of accessing adjacent documents along the path:

- Clicking on the anchor, as usual
- Pressing the Next or Previous button in the browser's toolbar

STYLE TIP: Many browsers won't support forward and backward links. If you're presenting a multipage document, it's always a good idea to include a set of buttons or phrases at the bottom of your page that can take the user to and fro. For example:

```
[Table Of Contents] [Next] [Previous]
```

Which can be created using HTML similar to the following:

```
<A HREF="toc.html" REL="Precedes"> [Table Of Contents] </A>
<A HREF="page5.html" REL="Precedes"> [Next] </A>
<A HREF="page3.html" REV="Precedes"> [Previous] </A><P>
```

Using Link

HTML has a <LINK> element which uses the REL and REV attributes, similarly to the <A> element. For example:

```
<LINK HREF=URL REL="next">
```

The REL attribute takes arguments similar to:

- HTML Contents: The destination document is a Table of Contents.
- HTML Next: The destination document is the next document in the sequence.
- HTML Previous: The destination document is the previous document in the sequence.
- HTML Parent: The destination document is the parent of the current document.
- HTML Help: The destination document has lots of help for topics in the current document.

The best way to make one document automatically follow another is to use the <LINK> element's REL attribute. The LINK is usually placed in the document's <HEAD>. For example, if you have three documents: doc1.html, doc2.html, and doc3.html, you could put these links at the beginning of your third document:

```
<HEAD>
<TITLE>Sample Document 3 of 10</TITLE>
<LINK HREF="doc2.html" REL="previous">
<LINK HREF="doc4.html" REL="next">
<LINK HREF="toc.html" REL="contents">
</HEAD>
```

and this set of links at the beginning of document 4:

```
<HEAD>
<TITLE>Sample Document 4 of 10</TITLE>
<LINK HREF="doc3.html" REL="previous">
<LINK HREF="doc5.html" REL="next">
<LINK HREF="toc.html" REL="contents">
</HEAD>
```

You could continue doing this for all the documents. Some browsers then allow you to press the Next or Previous buttons to cycle between these ten documents. In the future, browsers may even include an automatic Table of Contents button.

Nodes

The latest specification of HTML also has commands that will make it easy to develop complex hypertext paths. To create stepping stones along a hypertext river, use the <A> anchor's *NODE* attribute. You can create as many nodes as you like. You usually want to put your nodes in a list for a user to see:

```
<UL>
  <LI><A HREF="node1.html" NODE>The first stop on our tour.
  <LI><A HREF="node2.html" NODE>The second stop.
</UL>
```

A browser reads these nodes, in order, and places them in its own list. A user can then use the Next and Previous button to cycle between the nodes.

NOTE: Modern browsers do not yet support the NODES command.

Path

Eventually, you'll be able to use NODES to create a special HTML document which lines up a specific path. If you want to call this path document, you could use the anchor's *PATH* attribute. For example, if you have a set of paths listed in the file paths2.html, you could use the command:

```
<A HREF="paths2.html" PATH>Another path</A>
```

The second path would then be added onto any existing nodes.

LESSON #15: MATHEMATICAL EQUATIONS

As of now, there are no widespread Web browsers that can handle equations. However, the proposed new HTML version 3 format has some great mathematical additions. Since the next generation of browsers will most likely implement these elements, it's worth going over them.

HTML+ has elements for all basic mathematical functions. To designate an equation, you would type the *$* element. To end the equation, use *$*.

A browser that supports mathematical symbols would have a set of common escape characters, such as:

HTML *∫*: Integral symbol

HTML *∞*: Infinity

HTML *&tanh;*: Tangent

HTML *α*: Greek Alpha

HTML *β*: Greek Beta

HTML *θ*: Greek Theta

HTML *κ*: Greek Kappa

You can create an equation, then, using a command similar to the following:

```
<math>
  F(t) = &int;<sub>n</sub><sup>&infin;</sup> j<sup>t</sup> dt
</math>
```

which would create the equation in Figure 11-16. The subscript and superscript would automatically center the appropriate numbers over and under the integral sign.

Netscape and Mosaic already support <SUB> subscripts and <SUP> superscripts, making it possible to create simple exponents and such.

The HTML+ math specification also calls for the *<BOX>* element to group a set of numbers of equations together. The *<OVER>* element could be used to create fractions with a numerator and a denominator. An *<ARRAY>* element would print out nice-looking matrices. A *<ROOT>* element would be used to express various roots.

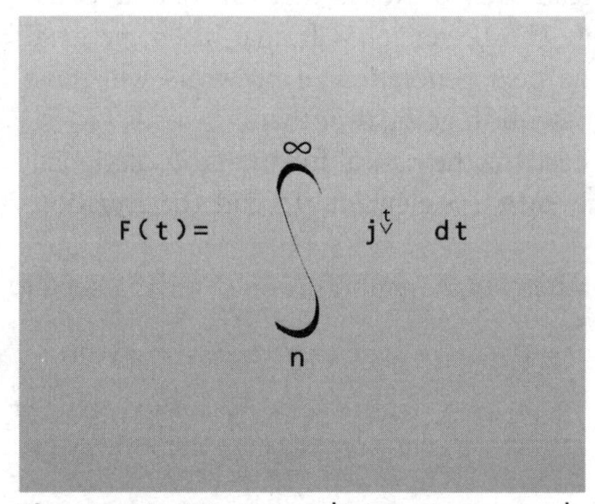

Figure 11-16 A sample equation created by HTML+

You can read more about HTML+ math commands and other HTML+ specifications by jumping to:

```
http://www11.w3.org/hypertext/WWW/MarkUp/HTMLPlus/
```

LESSON #16: DYNAMIC DOCUMENTS: PUSH OR PULL?

The latest version of Netscape Navigator supports dynamic documents by using the *server push* and *client pull*. This lets your Web browser receieve new data periodically. For example, a Web page with the latest weather map could be updated every ten minutes, or a Web page with stocks could be updated any time a stock's price changed. A video camera can even be used to send the latest frame to your Web browser, forming a live animation or movie.

Server Push

Server push is when the Web server delivers information to a Web page. Unlike a standard Web page, however, the connection between the server and the Web client remains intact. This way, whenever the server decides to update information, the Web page is immediately reloaded.

You can use server push to create very detailed sets of dynamic documents. You can even dynamically change a single image within a Web page, providing video or animation (albeit with a very slow frame rate) within an otherwise unchanging page.

To find out more about how to create CGI scripts which promote server pushing, check out the following URL:

```
http://home.netscape.com/home/demo/1.1b1/pushpull.html
```

Client Pull

Client pull is similar to server push, but gives the Web page itself more power. A Web page can be programmed to tell a server to reload its data after a given amount of time. The server waits and then automatically gives the Web page the new information.

Client pull is accomplished by using the HTTP-EQUIV="Refresh" attribute in the META element (an HTML3 element that simulates a document's header). The number of seconds to wait is specificed using the CONTENT attribute. For example, the following markup should be the first line of your HTML document if you want the Web page to reload itself after 3 seconds:

```
<META HTTP-EQUIV="Refresh" CONTENT=3>
```

The Web page will continue to reload every three seconds.

NOTE: You can use a CONTENT of 0 seconds to load up the given document as quickly as possible.

To load up a different document after a set amount of seconds, simply specify a full URL using the URL attribute. For example, to load the page at *http://www.smartpants.edu/sample.html* after a minute, use the following markup as the first line in your HTML document:

```
<META HTTP-EQUIV="Refresh" CONTENT=60
URL=http://www.smartpants.edu/sample.html>
```

You can use this trick to flip between two documents, animate a sequence of images, or create an automatic "slide show" of many Web pages.

NOTE: To stop a dynamic document while it is loading, a user needs to either close the window, click on a hyperlink, or use the history list to return to a previous document.

LESSON #17: POLISHING

Proofread your pages for spelling and grammar errors. The page will be seen by millions of adoring fans around the world. Don't publish something flawed.

You should also double-check your HTML syntax, keeping a sharp eye out for these common problems:

- Unpaired elements—that is, start-something elements with no corresponding closings (it's easy to forget the slash "/" in </H1>).
- Missing opening or closing quotes around URLs (<A HREF="http://www.sillyme.com>)
- Never-ending comments (<!--How come nothing else on my Web page is getting displayed?!?!?)
- HTML elements with no closing greater-than bracket (<A NAME="hello")
- Using the less-than, greater-than, or ampersand sign as part of your text (<, >, &).
- Special characters with no semicolon (>)

- URLs with uppercase letters when the system wants lowercase (<A HREF="HTTP://A.EDU/C/D/E/FILE.HTML">) or vice versa

There are several programs and services that run through your HTML code, checking for such errors. You can read about them in Chapter 20, Where to Place Your HTML Documents.

STYLE TIP: Remember, a Web page is always a work in progress. Polish it and polish it again 'til it shines.

WHAT NOW?

Your Web page already looks pretty good, doesn't it? Well, just wait until you add graphics. Flip to the next chapter. Now that you can create hyperlinks, you can read about interesting things to link to in Chapter 15.

If you can hardly wait to put your pages on the Web, check out Chapter 20, Where to Place Your HTML Documents.

12 GRAPHICS

12

A magazine without illustrations of any kind. A newspaper devoid of news photos. A report empty of graphs. Plain, cold text against a plain white background. In a word: Boring.

Before the Web, there was no easy way of viewing graphics over the Internet. Not only do images add spice to online text, but they often replace it. Here's just a tiny sample of common Web graphics:

- Huge billboard-like display ads
- Logos
- Borders, lines, or other page-enhancing designs
- Signatures
- Icon buttons
- Custom fonts
- Photos, drawings, paintings, or other helpful illustrations
- Charts, graphs, and tables

Basically, using graphics, a Web page can look exactly the way you want it. If you can sketch, scan, or design it, the Web can shoot it all over the world. This chapter covers everything you need to know about grabbing, creating, converting, designing, and placing graphics over the Web.

GRAPHIC FORMATS

There are dozens of ways to store graphics. Some formats deal with black and white images, others can hold photographic-quality pictures, while others contain video. See Table 2-1 in Chapter 2 for a list of the most common graphic types. Since graphics are generally stored as a plain sequence of numbers, they can easily be shared across various types of computers and operating systems. Graphics viewers can usually read in several types of images and then write out the image in the format of your choosing.

The Web generally deals with two types of images: GIFs and JPEGs.

GIF

The Graphical Interchange Format is a very basic table of colors. This table can hold most any resolution of graphics, though it is limited to 256 colors. Since GIFs use a very modest form of compression, GIFs are generally quite large. You should use GIFs for the following types of images:

- Icons, buttons, or bullets for lists
- Small illustrations

- Graphical lines or separator bars
- Charts, tables, or graphs you want to place alongside your Web text
- Thumbnails (see the Thumbnails section, later in this chapter)

JPEG

The JPEG format squeezes and compresses images, and thus graphics take up much less room to store (though they take longer to interpret). JPEG can also deal with images containing millions of colors. JPEG is known as a *lossy* format because the compressed images generally lose some data and sharpness. The general rule of thumb is to use JPEGs for:

- Photographic-quality or other "real life" images
- Large images
- Complex images that use more than 256 colors
- Images you don't need to include directly on the Web page

When you store a JPEG, you can usually designate the amount of compression you'd like to use. The more you compress, the more data the image loses.

GRAPHIC VIEWERS

Every multimedia browser can display some images alongside blocks of text. However, there are many types of graphics that your browser can't load up on-the-fly. To see these you'll need a separate graphic viewer.

Graphic viewers can do more than display images, they can help manipulate them. Before you start to work with graphics, you should install two important Windows viewers: LView and WinGIF. Each browser allows you to configure viewers for popular types of files.

LView

The most popular and versatile Windows viewer is probably LView Pro, by Leonardo Loureiro. LView can only run on a 386 or better, and a Super VGA card and monitor are recommended. There is also a commercial LView version that needs a 486 running 32-bit Windows or Windows NT. LView can read or write the following graphics formats:

- .JPG JPEG JFIF
- .GIF GIF87a GIF-89a
- .TGA Truevision Targa
- .BMP Windows and OS/2
- .PCX Zsoft and Microsoft Paint Pixelmap
- .PPM and .PGM by PBMPLUS
- .TIF TIFF

To install LView Pro, copy the entire \WINDOWS\VIEWERS\LVIEWP directory from your CD-ROM and place it on your own hard disk. You can now configure Mosaic or Netscape to use LView as the native graphic viewer. You should also set up an LView icon in the Windows Program Manager, since it's a program you'll probably use often.

Tweaking the Image

Depending on the image you load and the type of video hardware you have, you may want to adjust LView's settings. Load up a sample image by selecting File, Open. Select the graphic format by clicking on the List Files Of Type box.

If the image doesn't look very good, this may just be a limitation of Windows. Try tweaking the image to look its best by selecting tools from the Retouch menu. You can perform a Gamma Correction (if all colors seem slightly skewed), an Interactive RGB session, Color Balance, Contrast, etc.

Flipping Out

LView makes it easy to rotate, flip, or even take the photographic negative of an image. Select Flip Horizontal!, Flip Vertical!, Rotate Left!, or Rotate Right! from the Edit menu.

Adding Text

Another useful feature of LView is the ability to add text onto an image. This lets you scribble in company names beneath logos, descriptions on top of buttons, or captions or credits alongside photos.

Using the mouse, click on a spot where you want your text to begin. Holding down the mouse button, create a rectangle to show LView where

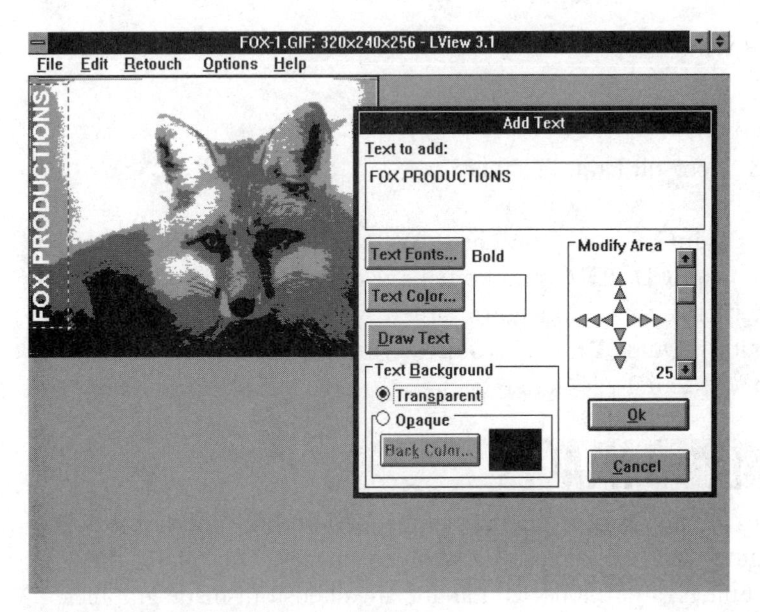

Figure 12-1 Putting text on an image

your text should be. Let go of the mouse button. Select Edit, Add Text. The Add Text dialog appears, as in Figure 12-1.

Click Text Fonts to choose a font's Name and Points size. Select the Bold, Italic, Underline, or Strikeout style if desired. You can also align the text Left, Right, or Centered. If you like, you can even create vertical text. Click the Vertical Up button to create vertical text that runs up the screen, click Vertical Down for text running downward.

Click Foreground and pick any text color from the palette. In most cases you want your text's Background to be Transparent; be sure Transparent Text Background is checked. If not, click Background and select the text's background color. As you play around with different ideas, click Exec to preview what the print will look like. When the text appears the way you want, click OK.

To finalize the text, click anywhere on your image.

WinGIF

WinGIF is an easy-to-use graphics viewer that also contains some basic image manipulation commands. WinGIF can handle most popular graphics formats:

HTML .GIF GIF 87a GIF89a

- HTML .BMP Windows
- HTML .RLE
- HTML .PCX Microsoft Paint Pixelmap

To install WinGIF, copy the entire \WINDOWS\VIEWERS\WINGIF directory from the CD-ROM onto your hard disk. WinGIF is a basic, no-frills viewer. If the image on your screen is difficult to make out, try selecting Options, Quick Dither. This uses Windows colors to emulate what the image should actually look like.

LESSON #1: INLINED IMAGES

Inlined images are any sort of graphics embedded within the Web text. For example, Figure 12-2 contains several inlined images. The photo, the icon buttons, the bullets, and the horizontal line are all custom-made graphics.

Almost all inlined graphics are in the popular GIF format, though some are stored in the JPEG or X-Windows binary map style. Every multimedia browser can display GIFs along with text, and most can display XBM images. Some browsers, like Netscape, can also inline JPEGs. Other graphic formats

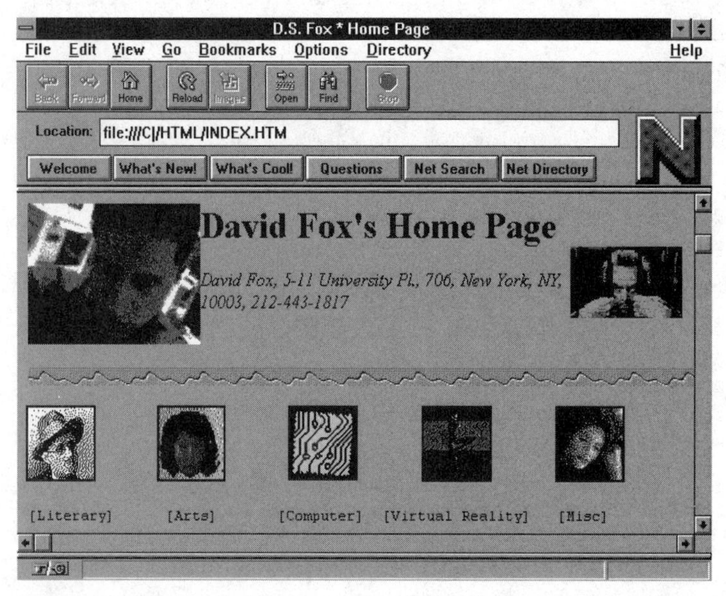

Figure 12-2 A Web page just wouldn't be much of a page without inlined graphics.

can be downloaded and shown using a viewer. Chapters 4, 5, and 6 discuss how to install a graphical viewer with SlipKnot, Mosaic, or Netscape.

The IMG Command

Once you have a nice collection of GIF images, choose the ones you'll want to use. Copy all the necessary image files to the same directory as your HTML document.

To insert an image in your Web page, use the HTML *<IMG>* command at the place you want the image to appear. Designate the name of the source image file using the SRC attribute. For example, typing

```
<IMG SRC="image.gif">
```

immediately displays the image in the IMAGE.GIF file.

The "image.gif" filename is a relative URL and must be located in the current directory. You can also use images from different directories, by designating the entire pathname:

```
<IMG SRC="/design/icons/image.gif">
```

Distant Images

Using full URLs, you can even grab images from anywhere else on the Internet. Suppose you're designing a Web page about astronomy. You browse around and find a great photo of Jupiter at the Smartpants University archives. If the file is publicly available, you can request it, download it, and place it in your own directory. Otherwise, you can just insert it using this command:

```
<IMG SRC="http://www.smartpants.edu/astronomy/planets/Jupiter.gif">
```

NOTE: Since distant images involve extra Internet connections, loading them is generally slower than using a local image.

Hyperimages

One of the nicest things about inlined images is the ability to use them as buttons. You can develop your own interactive screens full of icons. To create a hyperimage, use the HTML anchor command as usual, inserting an image in the middle:

```
<A HREF="jumphere.html"> <IMG SRC="jump.gif"></A>A really cool Web
page.
```

Most browsers draw a blue border around a hyperimage to let people know they can click it.

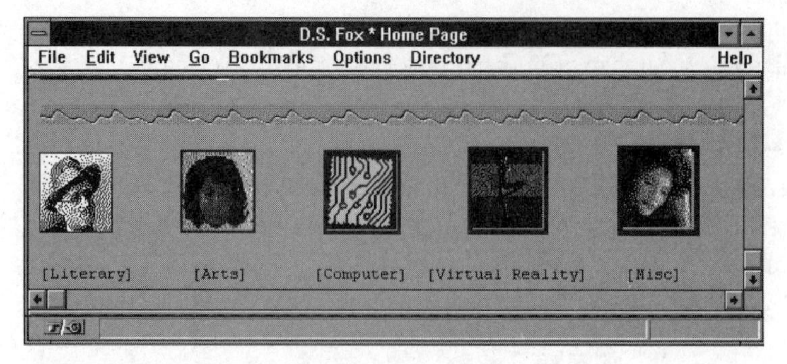

Figure 12-3 A set of buttons with border sizes ranging from size 1 to 5

Crossing the Border

More advanced versions of HTML, such as Netscape's Mozilla, allow you to specify the size of an image's border using the BORDER attribute:

```
<IMG SRC="image.gif" BORDER=2>
```

Generally, Web browsers automatically draw blue borders of size 1 around hyperimages. If you want, however, you can draw a border around any image at all. Various sizes of borders can add a nice cosmetic effect to your Web pages. For example, if you have several buttons on your page, you may want to surround the default button with a thicker border than the others. Figure 12-3 shows some sample borders.

NOTE: If you set a hyperimage's border to 0, users have no way of knowing that the image is, indeed, an anchor. You may or may not desire this effect. For example, if the image is quite obviously a button, most users will try pressing it, whether or not it's surrounded by a blue border.

LESSON #2: ALIGNMENT

Sprinkling images around your text is definitely a great way to snazz things up. In most cases, an image is accompanied by some sort of text. This may be a caption, a heading, or just the body of an article. If you randomly insert an image, there's no telling how adjacent text will appear.

Most browsers allow you to suggest an alignment location for your inlined images. All you need is the *ALIGN* attribute:

```
<IMG ALIGN="top" SRC="/image.gif">This text appears next to the top of
the image.
```

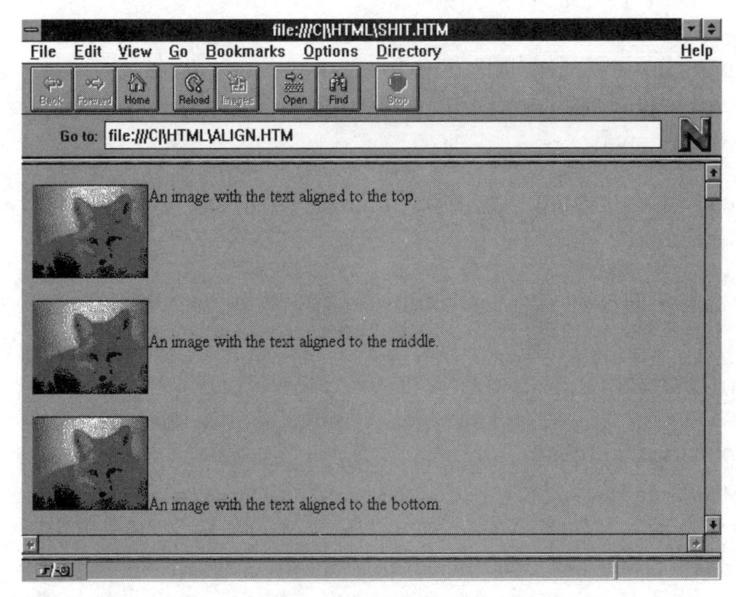

Figure 12-4 Top, middle, and bottom-aligned images

The adjacent text then appears toward the top of the image. Likewise, you can specify *ALIGN="bottom"* or *ALIGN="middle"*. By bottom-aligning an image, text appears next to the bottom of the image:

```
<IMG ALIGN="bottom" SRC="image.gif">This text appears next to the
bottom of the image.
```

Similarly, you can middle-align the text:

```
<IMG ALIGN="middle" SRC="image.gif">This text appears next to the
middle of the image.
```

Figure 12-4 shows three images, each using a different type of alignment.

Absolute Alignment

If you want, you can get *really* precise with your alignment options. This is useful if you're developing a Web page that uses several images nestled together. You may also want to use absolute alignment if you're dealing with fancy text made up of various fonts or styles.

NOTE: Only advanced browsers such as Netscape support these additional ALIGN attributes.

The absolute alignment attributes are:

- HTML *texttop:* Aligns the image with the top of the tallest piece of *text* in the given line. This is different from the standard *ALIGN="top"* attribute, which lines up the image with the tallest *item* in the line, whatever it may be.
- HTML *absmiddle:* This lines up the exact middle of the current line with the exact middle of the image.
- HTML *baseline:* Essentially the same as *ALIGN="bottom"*.
- HTML *absbottom:* Aligns the exact bottom of the image with the exact bottom of the current line.

For example, the command

```
<IMG ALIGN="absmiddle" SRC="photo.gif"><IMG ALIGN="absmiddle"
SRC="photo2.gif">
```

is a great way to precisely align two images to each other.

Floating Alignment

Most versions of HTML+, including Netscape's Mozilla, support more useful types of image alignment. These alignment techniques make use of a *floating image,* which allows you to align the image itself, not just the surrounding text. Your graphic floats in the area you specify (against the right margin, the left margin, or even smack in the middle of the page) and any nearby text lines or other images flow smoothly alongside.

Right and left alignment of graphics is a recently introduced function, allowing you to create newspaper-like text that wraps around your images. For example, the Web page shown in Figure 12-5 was created using the following code:

```
<IMG ALIGN="right" SRC="dav1.gif" VSPACE=1 HSPACE=2>
<CENTER>
<H2>Aligning</H2>
</CENTER>
Notice how nicely this text wraps around the photograph. You can wrap
around text of any sort, size, or style. You can even wrap other
images. It's like magic! The text continues here. When we reach the
bottom of the photo, the text continues as usual. You can use right
and left image alignment to make your pages look like professional
newspaper or magazine articles. You would, of course, have to have
more interesting text (and a handsomer photo) in place of what's
here.<P>
```

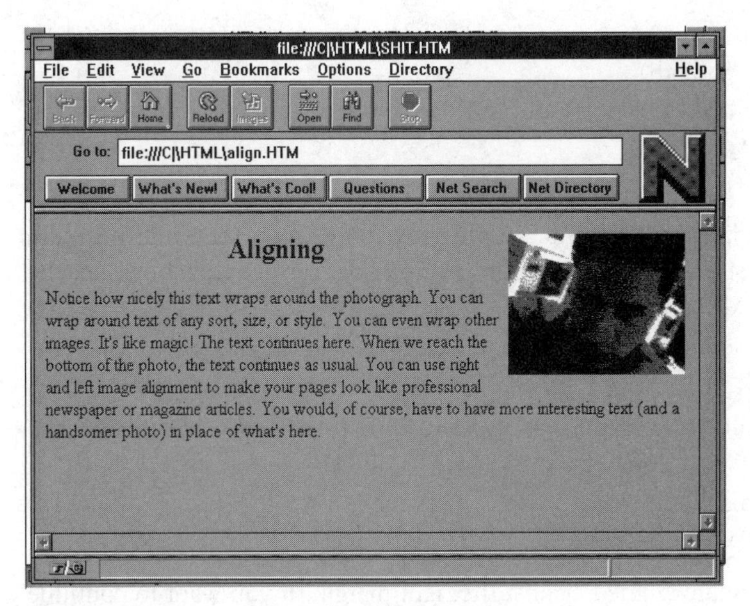

Figure 12-5 An image aligned to the right

Mino in the Gutter

You probably don't want your wrap-around text crowding up against a neighboring image. Mozilla allows you specify a *gutter,* forcing text to keep away from an image. You can specify the vertical space above and below an image by using the *VSPACE* attribute. The *HSPACE* attribute takes care of space to the left and right of the image.

For example, the command

```
<IMG SRC="image.gif" ALIGN="left" VSPACE=5 HSPACE=5>
```

pushes the surrounding text five spaces away.

Clearing Space After Line Breaks

Thanks to floating images, lots of text can now share the same space as a graphic. However, what if you want to place a certain piece of text next to an image (such as a caption), and place other text beneath the image?

The <BR> line break element won't do the trick alone. For example,

```
<IMG SRC="image.gif" ALIGN="left">This text here should be to the left
of the image.<BR>
But what about this text here? We want this to be below the image!<P>
```

results in all the text being placed to the immediate right of the image (if the image is large enough).

Netscape makes use of the *CLEAR* attribute to solve this problem. You can designate

```
<BR CLEAR=left>
```

to break the line and continue writing text only when there are no more images against the left margin. For example, we can fix the above text by using the HTML sequence:

```
<IMG SRC="image.gif" ALIGN="left">This text here should be to the left
of the image.
<BR CLEAR=left>
But what about this text here? We want this to be below the image! And
now it is!<P>
```

You can also designate

```
<BR CLEAR=right>
```

for images that are aligned against the right margin. If you want to continue only after *both* the right and left margins are clear, use the command:

```
<BR CLEAR=both>
```

LESSON #3: TEXT ALTERNATIVES

Graphics are great for those who can see them, but what about the rest of the world? Due to slow modems, limited Internet connections, or sheer preference, thousands of people surf the Web using Lynx or other text-based browsers. Is it fair to just forget about these folks?

In most cases, text browsers simply skip images. Lynx displays a replacement tag instead, surrounded by brackets. The default is

```
[IMAGE]
```

Using the *ALT* attribute, you can suggest an alternate word or symbol to be shown. For example, if your HTML code was:

```
<IMG ALT=" [Hot Air Balloon] " SRC="/balloon.gif">
```

Lynx would display

```
[Hot Air Balloon]
```

STYLE TIP: Often, inlined graphics are just whimsical ways to spice up a document, but are otherwise optional. If an image is not important, it's a good idea to tell the text-based browser to ignore it. If you don't want any alternate text at all, just use a blank:

```
<IMG ALT=" " SRC="image.gif">
```

Alternate text is especially important for hyperimages, such as icons or buttons. If all a user sees is the word [IMAGE], how is she supposed to know whether or not it's worth clicking on? For example, if you have a row of icons as in Figure 12-2:

```
<IMG ALT=" [Literary] " SRC="joyce.gif">
<IMG ALT=" [Art] " SRC="gizmo.gif">
<IMG ALT=" [Computers] " SRC="computer.gif">
<IMG ALT=" [VR] " SRC="dancer.gif">
<IMG ALT=" [Misc] " SRC="girl.gif">
```

A text-bound user would then see:

```
[Literary] [Art] [Computers] [VR] [Misc]
```

If you wish, you can use the ALT attribute alone, without specifying a source. Browsers of the future may even display icons for special key words, such as "Home," "Next," or "Previous."

LESSON #4: IMAGE SIZING

Images can take a long time to load, even with browsers like Netscape that support multiple image loads. This is because the browser must read through the image, determining its height and width, before it can lay out the rest of the document. The browser first draws a properly sized box and then it fills the image in, row by row.

What if the browser knew the exact size of a graphical element before it so much as loaded a single byte? The answer: Performance could be increased by up to 50 percent.

Netscape lets you solve this problem with the *HEIGHT* and *WIDTH* attributes. You specify the image's size in pixels, as follows:

```
<IMG SRC="image.gif" WIDTH=150 HEIGHT=200>
```

Netscape then uses this information to predraw the image box. That lets it load the rest of the Web page immediately.

NOTE: This speed-up technique only works for the Netscape browser. Of course, other browsers will just skip this sizing information, so including it could never hurt.

To determine an image's size, load it up using LView. Select Edit, Resize or press CTRL-R. The Resize dialog box appears, with the image's size—width times height—printed in the Current Size or Current Dimensions box.

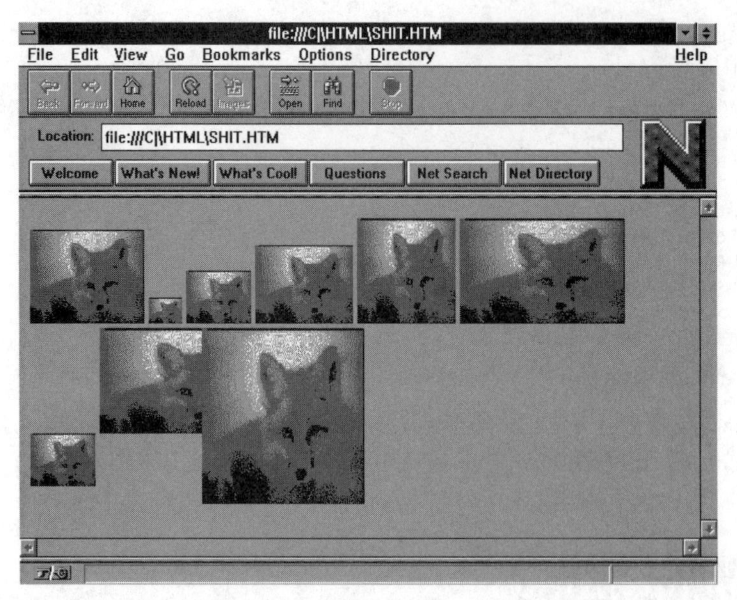

Figure 12-6 Using auto-scaling to show several sizes of the same image

Auto-Scaling

The sizing attributes can serve another function: scaling your images as they're loaded. This allows you to use several sizes of the same image. See Figure 12-6 for an example.

All you need to do is use WIDTH and HEIGHT specs that are different from the image's actual dimensions. The image can then be ballooned, stretched, or shrunken. If you want the image to appear with similar proportions, be sure to keep up the *aspect ratio* by multiplying the height and width by the same number. For example, if you have an image that is 25x30, you can load it in at four times its size by using the command:

```
<IMG SRC="smallimg.gif" WIDTH=100 HEIGHT=120>
```

Scaling is also useful for patterns, small photos, or other images that take up a lot of disk space. You can quickly load up a tiny image and have it fill the entire screen.

NOTE: Browsers other than Netscape will display a scaled image at its usual size.

Percentage Auto-Scaling

If you don't feel like calculating out the exact size of a scaled image's height and width in pixels, you can have Netscape do the work for you. Simply specify the HEIGHT or WIDTH as a percentage of the available screen. This way, the image always appears relative to the rest of the Netscape page. If you make your Netscape window bigger, the image will grow bigger; if you compress your window, the image will shrink.

In general, you want to scale an image according to how wide it is. So, if you have a small 25 by 25 image, you can triple its height and have it fill half the screen by using the command:

```
<IMG SRC="smallimg.gif" WIDTH="50%" HEIGHT=75>
```

If you only type in one dimension attribute, the image will always keep the same aspect ratio. For example, use the command

```
<IMG SRC="fox.gif" WIDTH="75%">
```

The image's width fills up three-quarters of the screen, as shown in Figure 12-7. The height will change as the size of the screen changes, always corresponding to the dimensions of the original image.

Figure 12-7 Using percentage auto-scaling to make small images leap off the screen

LESSON #5: TRANSPARENT GIFS

Sneak a peek at Figure 12-8. Which fox looks better, the block-like, splotched-out one on the top or the floating, snazzy, cute little one on the bottom? (Can you tell the question is loaded?)

When dealing with logos, buttons, icons, or any other simple graphics, *transparent background images* are the only way to go. Most browsers support transparent images, automatically setting the image's background color to match the color of the browser's window—no matter what it is.

To make an image transparent, it must be in the latest GIF format—*GIF89a*. This format has the ability to mark a single color as the transparent one. Making an image transparent may take a bit of work, but the sleek results often speak for themselves.

STEP 1: Isolate the Background

The first thing you need to do to create a transparent GIF is to paint the image's background all one color. Most icons, buttons, and such are already set against a solid white or black background, in which case no isolating is necessary. If an image's background color isn't used anywhere else in the image, you can skip immediately to Step 3. However, if you'd like to make a photograph transparent (to design a floating face, for example), this process is much more difficult.

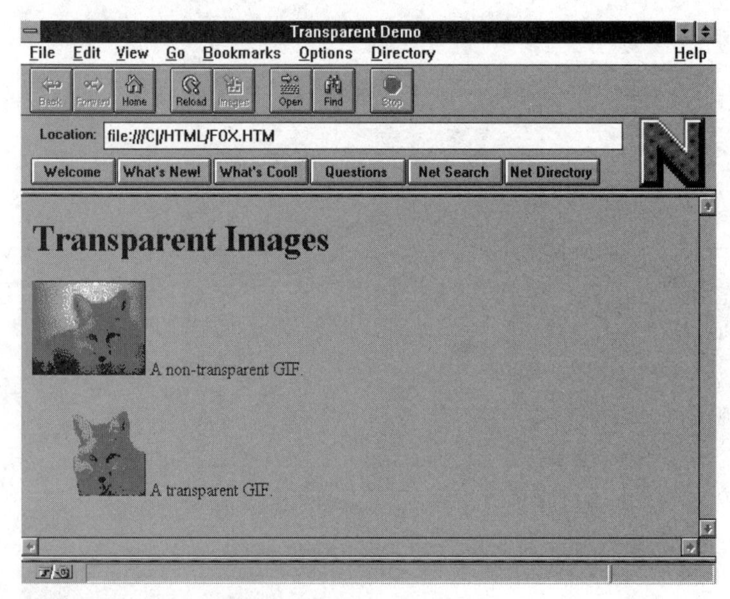

Figure 12-8 Which image is foxier?

Professional tools such as Adobe Photoshop are built to create just such effects. However, you can often do a pretty good job of background isolation by using something as simple as the Windows Paintbrush program.

First, use WinGIF or LView to convert your image to the PCX or BMP format. To convert a file, you need to load it (using File, Open) and then save it under a different filename and file type (using File, Save As).

You can now load up the image using the Windows Paintbrush, which should be located in the Accessories group in your Program Manager. Select File, Open. The image appears on your screen. You now need to cut away the image's background, or any other parts of the picture that you wish to be transparent.

Select the Polygon Cut tool—the scissors cutting away the star. Remember kindergarten, where you had to cut out a doll outline from construction paper? Those skills are now put to the test. Click on the place where you'd like to start cutting and hold down the mouse button. Holding your hand steady and moving the mouse very slowly, you can now draw a line around the entire image. Pretend you're holding an X-acto knife, or directing a laser beam. Be sure to include the borders of the image as part of your outline. At the end, you should have a shape that corresponds to the part of the picture you wish to cut away. Figure 12-9, for example, shows the results of isolating a fox' face.

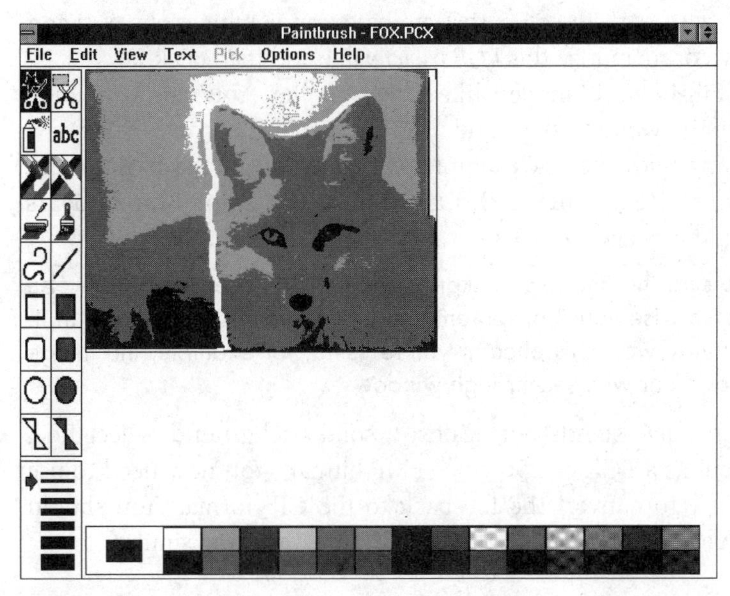

Figure 12-9 Cutting away an image's background

To cut away what you've just selected, choose Edit, Cut or press CTRL-X. Your image should appear to be floating against a white background. If not, select Edit, Undo and try again.

If the image is bigger than your screen, you need to use the scroll bars to deal with the rest of the picture. Continue scrolling and cutting until the entire background is cleared. You can preview the entire image by selecting View, View Picture or pressing CTRL-P.

NOTE: Most every drawing package has similar tools, and most can handle more colors or graphics types than Windows Paintbrush. Experiment until you find the package most comfortable for you.

STEP 2: Selecting a Background Color

You're now ready to fill in a unique background color. Try to pick a basic, primary color that isn't used anywhere else in the image. Usually solid black or solid white works just fine. If not, select yellow, red, green, or blue.

STYLE TIP: If possible, use light grey as your background color. Not only is it the easiest color to work with, but if a browser doesn't support transparent images, grey usually blends in well with that browser's background anyway.

Once you've decided on a color, double-click on the color from the palette at the bottom of the screen. A dialog box appears showing you the color's Red, Green, and Blue *(RGB)* composition values. For example, black is comprised of 0,0,0. White is 255,255,255. Green is 0,255,0. Blue is 0,0,255. For simplicity, try to stick to colors that are based on combinations of 0 and 255. Write down or memorize this *RGB triplet* value and then click OK.

Click the Fill-in tool, shaped like a paint roller. You can now click anywhere along the white background. The background becomes your new color. Continuing with the fox example, we could fill in the background with Blue (whose RGB value is 0,0,255) since the color Blue appears nowhere else in the image.

STYLE TIP: Be sure the image's background color isn't used anywhere else in the image, otherwise your transparent image will seem to have holes in it. Of course, you may want this effect if you're using, for example, the image of a doughnut or a car with see-through windows.

When your image stands out against a solid background, select File, Save As to save it as a PCX or 256-color BMP bitmap. You now need to use WinGIF or LView to convert the file back to the GIF format. You should now have an image file named TRAN-FOX.GIF or something similar.

STYLE TIP: When defining a background color, you may also want to draw a border around the image using that same color. You can do this easily using any drawing package's rectangle tool. This way, there will be a small transparent border around your entire image. Since most browsers draw a blue border around hyperimages, this invisible border will give your image the appearance of floating within a button.

STEP 3: Making the Background Transparent

Now comes the final step: Transforming your uniform-background GIF87a image into a transparent GIF89a image. If your computer can run LView Pro, then this step is easy. If not, you'll need to use a small DOS command called GIFTRANS.EXE.

LView Pro

Load up the image you just created by selecting File, Open. You now need to tell LView which color should be transparent. Select Options, Background Color. You see the Select Color Palette Entry window, shown in Figure 12-10.

You now need to try to find the background color from the palette. Depending on your image, this palette index may be 16 colors, 256, or more. If you isolated the background color using Window Paintbrush, then your background color is probably located in the top row. Click the background color. To be sure you've selected the right color, check the Mask Selection Using box. Every color *other* than the background color is shown in black (or white). A silhouette of your image should appear. Everything other than this silhouette now acts as a transparent background.

If you picked the right color, select OK. If not, guess again. Sometimes an image is made up of fifty shades of blue, and it can be difficult to find the right one. You can use the Current Selection Info RGB at the bottom of the dialog box to help you find the actual background color. Keep selecting possible colors until the RGB index matches the one you found in Step 2. Mask the image to be sure and then select OK.

NOTE: If you want your image to be interlaced, be sure to check Options, Save GIFs Interlaced. Lesson #9, later in this chapter, explains interlaced images.

You're now ready to save your new image. Select File, Save As. Be sure to Save File as Type GIF89a—*not* GIF87a. Once you save a GIF89a file, LView automatically designates the background color as the transparent

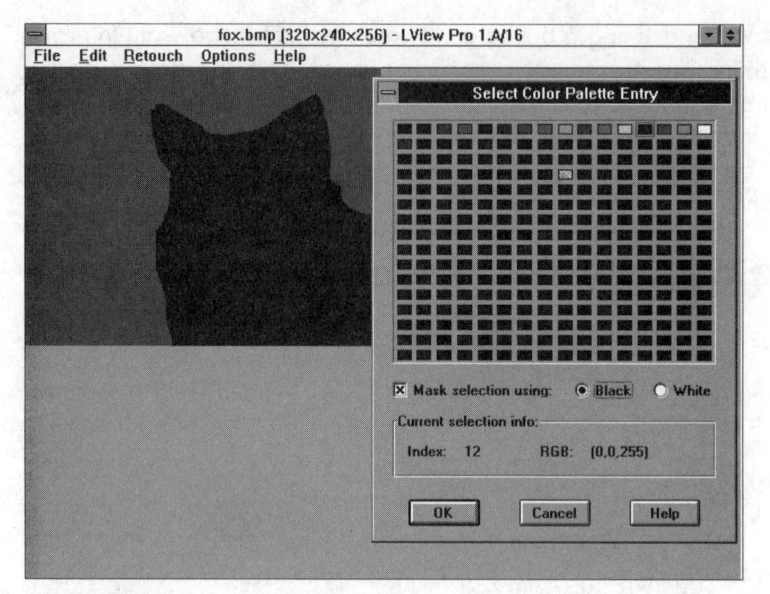

Figure 12-10 Masking out the background color to be sure you have the right one

color. That's all there is to it. If you saved your file as FOX2.GIF, then, you could put the image on your Web page using the markup:

```
<IMG SRC="fox2.gif">
```

GIFTRANS

Another way of designating a transparent background color is a utility called GIFTRANS. GIFTRANS can be downloaded from the site listed in Appendix D. Unzip the file and copy GIFTRANS.EXE to any convenient directory along your path, such as the C:\WINDOWS directory.

GIFTRANS is a simple DOS filter that converts standard GIF87a images into GIF89a format. To exit to the DOS prompt, select the DOS icon from the Main group in the Windows Program Manager. Move to the directory where your TRANS.GIF file is stored. For example, if the file is in the C:\HTML\IMAGES directory, type

```
cd c:\html\images ENTER
```

at the DOS prompt.

You can now use GIFTRANS, which takes the form:

```
giftrans -t index source.GIF > destination.GIF
```

Instead of *index* you'll need to type in the background color's RGB value in the hexadecimal form:

```
#rrggbb
```

Here's why we told you to only use RGB values of 0 or 255. The hexadecimal representation of 0 is *00,* the hexadecimal representation of 255 is *ff*. Your index, then, is comprised of three *00*s or *ff*s. Table 12-1 contains a short listing of sample color values:

Table 12-1 RGB index values for various colors

Color	RGB Value	Hexadecimal Index
White	255,255,255	#ffffff
Black	0,0,0	#000000
Red	255,0,0	#ff0000
Green	0,255,0	#00ff00
Blue	0,0,255	#0000ff
Yellow	255,255,0	#ffff00
Magenta	255,0,255	#ff00ff
Dark red	191,0,0	#bf0000
Dark yellow	191,191,0	#bfbf00
Dark green	0,191,0	#00bf00
Medium blue	0,191,191	#00bfbf
Light blue	0,255,255	#00ffff
Dark blue	0,0,191	#0000bf
Dark magenta	191,0,191	#bf00bf
Dark grey	128,128,128	#808080
Grey	192,192,192	#c0c0c0

NOTE: If you're familiar with hexadecimal notation, feel free to use any value at all as your background color.

For example, to convert our TRAN-FOX.GIF image into a transparent image, we'd type

```
giftrans -t #0000ff tran-fox.gif > fox2.gif
```

We use the index #0000ff because the background color was Blue. The final product is now stored in the FOX2.GIF file. So, the next time we felt like sticking a transparent fox head in our Web page, we'd type:

```
<IMG SRC="fox2.gif">
```

LESSON #6: CREATING SPACERS

Suppose you want to position two or more images next to each other. How can you determine the exact spacing? For example, suppose you want to create a pyramid of images, as in Figure 12-11. How does the Web browser know? The solution is to use transparent images to create, in essence, an invisible image. This image can then act as a *spacer.*

Spacers should only be one pixel high–like an invisible horizontal line. That way, they'll load in lightning fast while still serving their purpose. You can use LView to create a spacer:

1. Select File, New.
2. Type the image's width in pixels in the first box of the New Image Dialog, and type 1 for the image's height in the second box.
3. By default, the line should be drawn in the background index color. Select Options, Background Color to be sure.
4. Select File, Save and save your spacer. Type in a filename such as SPACE100.GIF. Be sure to specify the GIF89a format.
5. You can now use the spacer as you would any other image. For example, to create the pyramid shown in Figure 12-11:

```
<IMG SRC="space50.gif"><IMG SRC="gizmo.gif"><BR>
<IMG SRC="girl.gif"><IMG SRC="space50.gif"><IMG SRC="joyce.gif><P>
```

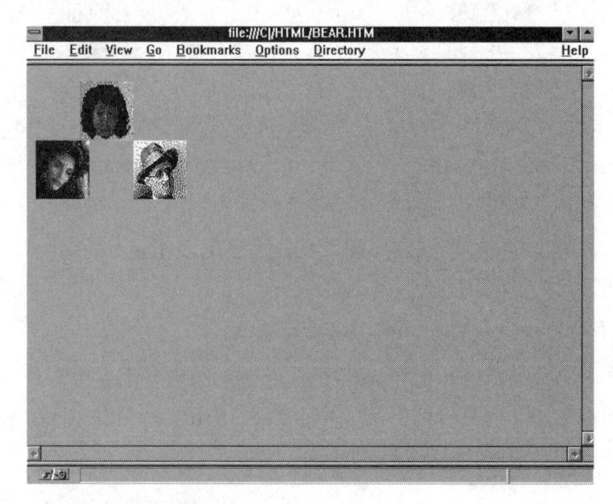

Figure 12-11 A pyramid of images

LESSON #7: PERKS, GIZMOS, AND FRILLS

Many browsers do a good job with things like <HR> horizontal lines, <UL> bullets, and other tiny graphics. But why not customize these yourself? Look at the difference between Figure 12-12 and Figure 12-13.

Bullets

The CD-ROM has a whole collection of bullets stored in the \CLIPMDIA\BULLETS directory. Normally, the HTML code for a bulleted list looks like:

```
<UL>
  <LI>One
  <LI>Two
  <LI>Three
</UL>
```

To insert your own bullets, you'd typically use code like the following sample instead of the standard list format:

```
<UL>
<IMG SRC="bullet.gif" ALT="*"> One<BR>
<IMG SRC="bullet.gif" ALT="*"> Two<BR>
<IMG SRC="bullet.gif" ALT="*"> Three<P>
</UL>
```

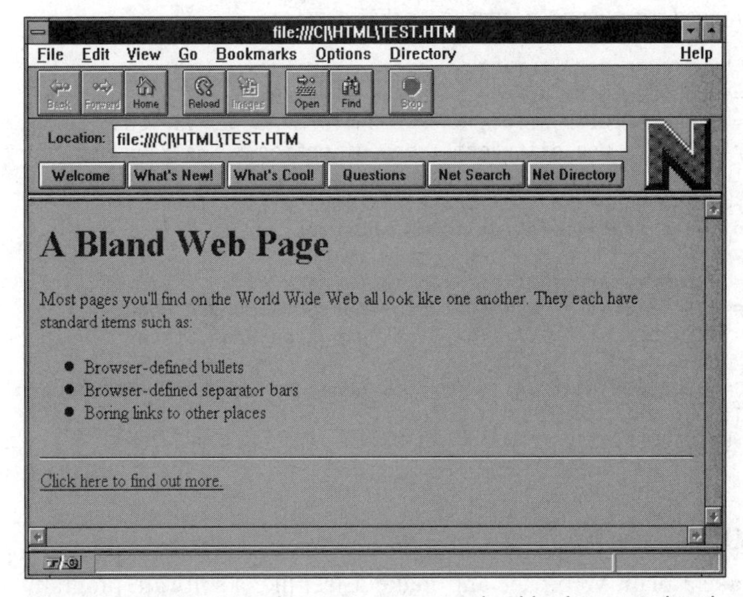

Figure 12-12 A Web page using standard built-in graphical elements

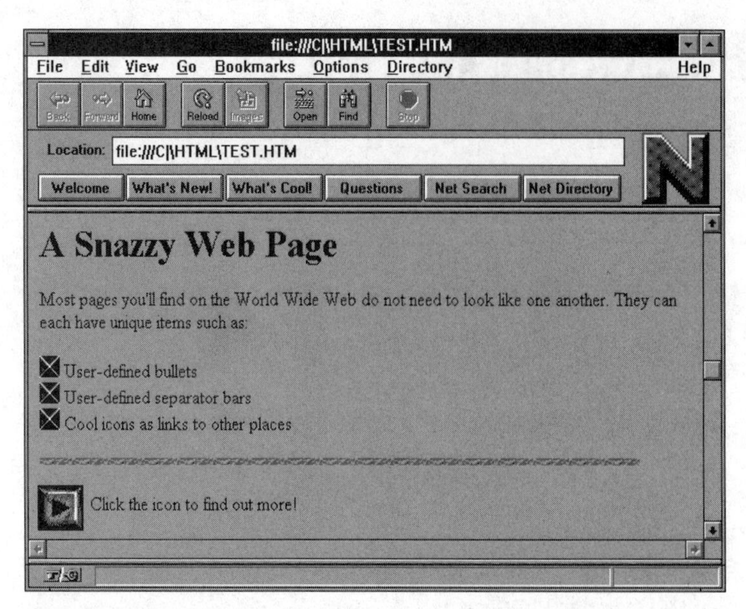

Figure 12-13 A totally rad Web page with unique graphics of its very own

You can also get fancy with custom bullets, making your own nested definition lists, as in Figure 12-14. Here's the code for it:

```
Things you'll need to pursue a career in kickboxing:
<DL>
<DT><IMG SRC="BLUECUBE.GIF" ALT="*"> <B>Shin Pads</B>
<DT><IMG SRC="BLUECUBE.GIF" ALT="*"> <B>Arm Pads</B>
<DT><IMG SRC="BLUECUBE.GIF" ALT="*"> <B>A Uniform</B><DD>Various
styles of martial arts use different types of uniforms. Many modern
kickboxing studios are very liberal about this, accepting sweatpants
and tank top or any other sort of loose-fitting outfit. There are
three types of more traditional uniforms, however:
<DL>
<DT><IMG SRC="GRENBULL.GIF" ALT="+"> Cotton V-Neck
<DT><IMG SRC="GRENBULL.GIF" ALT="+"> Open-fronted Japanese Hogu
<DT><IMG SRC="GRENBULL.GIF" ALT="+"> Black Ninjitsu-Wrap Style
</DL>
<DT><IMG SRC="BLUECUBE.GIF" ALT="*"> <B>Men: A Cup</B> <DD>Never
leave home without it!
<DT><IMG SRC="BLUECUBE.GIF" ALT="*"> <B>Women: A Sports Bra</B>
</DL>
```

Buttons / Icons

Buttons can take a plain Web page and make it feel like a software program of its very own. By giving the user a set of buttons to press, you make access

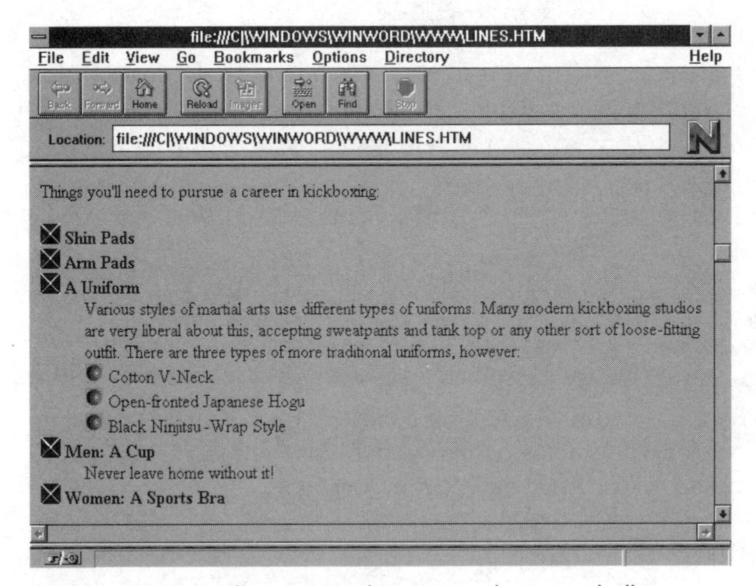

Figure 12-14 Shooting up the page with custom bullets

to your information more interesting and more customized: users can select the specific items they're interested in.

You'll find a large selection of standard buttons and icons in the CD-ROM \CLIPMDIA\BUTTONS directory.

You can arrange buttons any way your heart desires. However, there are two basic layouts:

- HTML The toolbar: a row of buttons stretching across the screen. See Figure 12-3.
- HTML The list: A vertical list of icons or buttons alongside some sort of description.

STYLE TIP: It's a good idea to include some sort of description next to each button, since the functions of certain icons may not be obvious.

Code for a toolbar of buttons would typically take the form:

```
<A HREF="home.html"><IMG SRC="home.gif" ALT="[H]"></A>
<IMG SRC="spacer.gif">
<A HREF="forward.html"><IMG SRC="next.gif" ALT="[>>]"></A>
<IMG SRC="spacer.gif">
<A HREF="back.html"><IMG SRC="previous.gif" ALT="[<<]"></A><P>
<PRE>[Home]     [ >> ]     [ << ]</PRE>
```

Notice the small spacer (see Lesson #6) between each image. If you want your icons to appear right next to each other, remove the spacer. Also notice that the descriptive text along the bottom has to be carefully spaced out so it appears beneath each icon. Preformatted text is usually the best way to accomplish this.

Code for a list of buttons, on the other hand, would look something like:

```
Click one of the following buttons to move to another Web page:
<A HREF="home.html"><IMG SRC="home.gif" ALT="[H]">Home</A><P>
<A HREF="forward.html"><IMG SRC="next.gif" ALT="[>>]">Next</A><P>
<A HREF="back.html"><IMG SRC="previous.gif" ALT="[<<]">Previous</A><P>
```

STYLE TIP: Be sure to use the ALT attribute to name your buttons. For example, [H] can lead to a home page and [>>] can lead to the next page. This way, text-based users can "press" your buttons too.

Bars

The HTML <HR> command is a great way to separate sections, or to designate the end of a document. However, this line is always gray, straight, and monotonous. Why not use your own colors or line designs? The CD-ROM has a bunch of sample bars in the \CLIPMDIA\BARS directory.

To use a bar, just type

```
<CENTER>  <IMG SRC="bar.gif"><P>
</CENTER>
```

STYLE TIP: You can use Netscape's image sizing or alignment commands to center bars in the middle of the screen, offset them to the right or left, make them act as vertical graphical lines, or even separate columns of text.

LESSON #8: MAKING GRAPHICS HUMBLE

It's tempting to use oodles of graphics in your Web pages. Be wary, however, of overloading the Web with data. Graphic files are usually pretty large. If someone has a slow modem or Internet connection, the page may take almost hours to load. Although some users may use their browsers to turn off graphics, others may just get fed up and skip your page altogether.

There are several ways of making your graphics gentler, kinder, and faster to load:

- HTML Reduce the resolution of the image by shrinking it.
- HTML Use compressed graphic types like JPEGs, perhaps with GIF thumbnails.

HTML Use Netscape's flip trick.

STYLE TIP: Many PC users have monitors that can display only 256 colors (as opposed to the millions and millions of colors available with an enhanced graphics card). For them, complex images will not appear as crisp or defined as you'd like. When posting images on the Web, try to use the clearest, most basic images you can and steer clear of images using tons of different colors. Even with high-powered monitors, there's a potential problem when you try to display two complex color images at once. If one image has 256 shades of blue and the other uses 256 shades of red, which colors will actually be displayed? Windows will usually try to share the colors, making both images seem splotchy and discolored. If you must put two complex images near each other, try to stick to a similar color scheme.

Shrink Me

You can easily use LView or WinGIF to change the size of any given image. Using either program, select File, Open and load up the image.

STYLE TIP: It's a good idea to change an image's size if it seems out of place, or unwieldy. You should also resize images to give your Web page some uniformity. If you have several buttons, for example, it looks much nicer to make them all the exact same size.

LView

If you're using LView, select Edit, Resize or press CTRL-R. The Resize dialog box appears. Type in either a new width or a new height. As long as the Preserve Aspect Ratio check box is checked, the image will keep its scale. If you'd like to stretch an image, you can deselect the Preserve Aspect Ratio checkbox and type in any values you wish. If you're going to be changing an image's aspect ratio, however, it's a good idea to crop the image first.

Suppose, for example, you want to take a full-sized rectangular image and make it into a square 50x50 button. First, you'd crop the image to make it square. Move your mouse to the top corner of the square, hold down the mouse button, and then create a box around the part of the image you want to keep. Release the mouse button. There should be a perforated box drawn around your image, as in Figure 12-15. Now select Edit, Crop! to throw the rest of the image away.

You can now resize the image. Select Edit, Resize or press CTRL-R. Deselect the Preserve Aspect Ratio checkbox and fill in 50s in the two boxes. The result is a postage-stamp-sized image that you can then save (File, Save As) as a GIF and use throughout your HTML documents.

Figure 12-15 Cropping an image

WinGIF

Resizing an image works pretty much the same in WinGIF. Hold down the mouse to select a rectangular part of the image. As you create the cropping square in WinGIF, the square's dimensions are printed in the middle of the screen. This is a nice feature, allowing you to create perfectly scaled crops.

Once your cropping square looks the way you want it, let go of the mouse button. Select Edit, Trim to crop it. Select Edit, Resize or press F4. The Resize dialog box appears. Type in the image's new width and/or height. If you don't want to maintain the aspect ratio, deselect the Resize To Scale checkbox.

Thumbnails

GIF images are large and often take too long to load in. A better way to share photos or other detailed artwork would be to use the JPEG format. Unfortunately, most browsers cannot inline this format with the rest of the text. A solution to this problem is *thumbnails,* or tiny previews of larger or more intricate images. Using hyperimages, you can set up thumbnails to lead the way to actual full-sized images. Thumbnails take only a second or two to load. Figure 12-16 shows a few sample thumbnails.

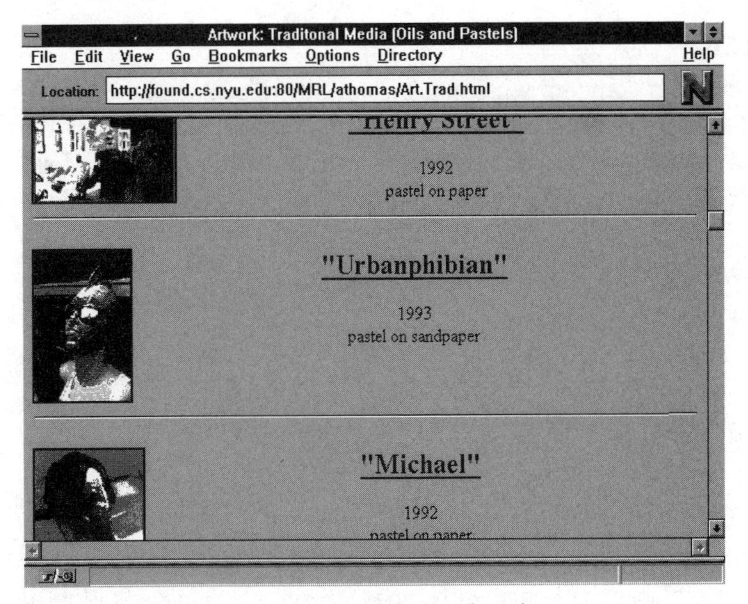

Figure 12-16 Twiddling through thumbnails

For example, if I had a high-resolution, thousand-color GIF image of New York City, it would take a while for any Web browser to display it. It would be much smarter to store the picture as a JPEG. Using LView or WinGIF, load up the picture of New York and resize it to 100x100 (or thereabouts). If you're using many thumbnails on one page, you may want to make them even smaller. Save this new image as a separate GIF.

To place a thumbnail in your HTML document, you'd typically use the form:

```
<A HREF="bigimage.jpg"> <IMG SRC="littleimage.gif" ALT="Big Image"
ALIGN=MIDDLE></A>
Click on this thumbnail image to retrieve the full high-resolution
JPEG.
```

Users could then click on littleimage.gif to load up the bigimage.jpg. If you want, you can emulate thumbnails using Netscape's sizing attribute, as follows:

```
<A HREF="bigimage.jpg"> <IMG SRC="bigimage.jpg" ALT="Big Image"
ALIGN=MIDDLE WIDTH=10%></A>
```

Click on this thumbnail image to retrieve the full high-resolution JPEG.
The image, however, will be full sized on other browsers.

The Flip Trick

Netscape Mozilla has come up with an excellent function that allows you to quickly load in a low-resolution preview of an image, depending on the capabilities of your browser. This way, users with Netscape can see a low-resolution JPEG image as soon as your Web page loads. Eventually, this low-res JPEG will be replaced by a higher resolution GIF.

NOTE: For people who don't use Netscape, the high-res GIF is simply loaded as usual.

The *LOWSRC* attribute makes this possible. Create two copies of your high-resolution images, such as photographs or other full-screen images: one GIF and one JPEG. To call up the images, then, use the HTML command:

```
<IMG SRC="highres.gif" LOWSRC="lowres.jpg">
```

Netscape loads up small *lowres.jpg* first. After it gets the rest of the document loaded, it replaces the image with the *highres.gif* file. This acts kind of like an instant thumbnail. A user who likes the image will stay on your page and wait for the high-res image to fade in. Otherwise, she'll be off to another part of the Web.

NOTE: Remember, you can specify the *WIDTH* and *HEIGHT* attributes, in which case both low-res and high-res images will load in to the same scale. If you don't specify the image size, the high-res image will load in at the same scale as the low-res image regardless of what you meant it to be, since the rest of the document has already been laid out.

STYLE TIP: You can use this trick to perform some neat special effects, such as limited animation. Create the first frame as the LOWSRC and the second frame as the SRC. The second frame will appear to fade in from the first frame. This effect turns out even nicer if the GIF is interlaced (see the next section).

For example, if you have a 500,000-byte 800x600 GIF of New York City and a tiny 5,000-byte 50x50 JPEG copy, you can quickly load up a blurry, scaled-up version of the JPEG and then gradually replace it with the actual image:

```
<IMG SRC="nyc.gif" LOWSRC="nyc.jpg" WIDTH=800 HEIGHT=600>
```

LESSON #9: INTERLACED GIF IMAGES

Different browsers load up graphics in different ways. Mosaic, for example, loads one image at a time, only displaying the image once the entire thing is loaded. Netscape and similar browsers are much more sophisticated, featuring *incremental* graphic loading. Netscape reads in all images at once, displaying each image as it loads. You can watch an image take shape like a curtain dropping, starting from the top, line by line.

The GIF format can store image data in an *interlaced* style. All this technobabble means is that a graphic appears to fade in as it loads. Instead of a curtain dropping, an interlaced GIF looks more like a set of venetian blinds opening. The latest version of Netscape goes even further, offering the *progressive enhancement* effect. As an interlaced GIF loads, Netscape fills in the blanks with an educated guess of what the color should be. This gives the impression of a blurry image, constantly being sharpened.

Interlaced GIFs do not load faster or more accurately than noninterlaced GIFs, but many people prefer them because they make more sense sooner. For example, it takes a quarter of the time for a large image to appear—in primitive form—on the screen. Often, this is enough for the user to decide whether it's worth waiting for the rest of the image.

The WinGIF program makes it easy to create interlaced images. Simply follow these steps:

1. Load up the GIF (or other image format) you want to interlace.
2. Select File, Save.
3. Click the Format>> button.
4. Select the GIF radio button.
5. Be sure the Interlace GIF box is checked, as in Figure 12-17.
6. Make sure the proper filename is filled in (the GIF extension is automatically added).
7. Click Save.
8. You may be asked if you'd like to overwrite the existing file. Click OK.

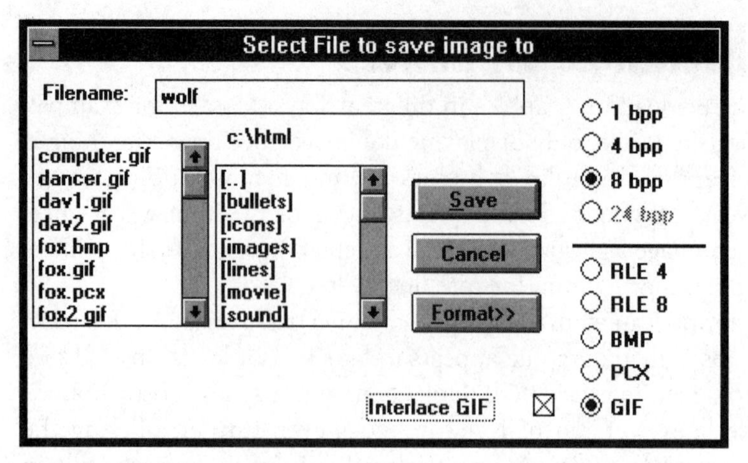

Figure 12-17 Saving a GIF in the interlaced style to create extra-snazzy Web images

You can also interlace images with LView Pro. Just be sure the Options, Save GIFs interlaced is checked before you save any GIF.

LESSON #10: CLICKABLE IMAGEMAPS

So far we've seen graphics do some pretty amazing things, acting as text aids, design elements, and even buttons. But how about creating an entire custom Web page consisting of one huge graphic. How about having that graphic be smart enough to know what part of it is being clicked, and smart enough to perform several distinct actions.

An example: You load up a Web page and see the front view of what seems to be a shopping mall. You click on the doorway of the Sporting Goods store and can now shop for baseballs or tennis shoes. If you clicked on the Software store you could've browsed the latest CD-ROMs.

Another example: You see a floor plan of a museum. You click on Renaissance and images by Leonardo DaVinci and Raphael suddenly appear. You click on Roman Sculpture and a huge close-up of Zeus fills your screen.

Yet another: The graphic on your screen seems to be of several photographs, each of a different person, all tossed together on a table. You click on Mary's face and are transported to her home page. Bob's face takes you to his page. Likewise with Ralph.

One last one: A map of the world fills your screen. You click on a red dot near London and are transported to your company's British offices.

Click on Denver and you visit the Mile High City. Click on the Mexico City dot and the next thing you know pages full of Spanish fill your screen.

As you can see, these *imagemaps* allow your creativity to jump off the deep end. Although the above scenarios could've been accomplished using several different hyperimages, the interface just wouldn't have been as intuitive or as fun.

Imagemaps allow you to make a hyperimage interactive. It's much like a patchwork of many little hyperimages, all strung together. Depending on where on the graphic you click, you'll be linked to different URLs. Given a graphic, you can use imagemaps to designate polygons, circles, or rectangles as their own anchors.

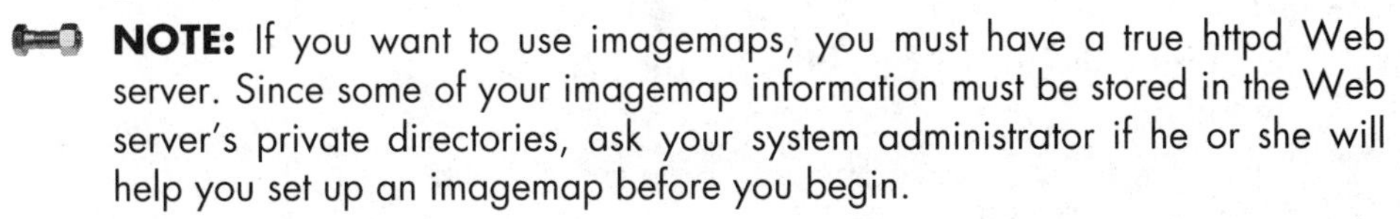

NOTE: If you want to use imagemaps, you must have a true httpd Web server. Since some of your imagemap information must be stored in the Web server's private directories, ask your system administrator if he or she will help you set up an imagemap before you begin.

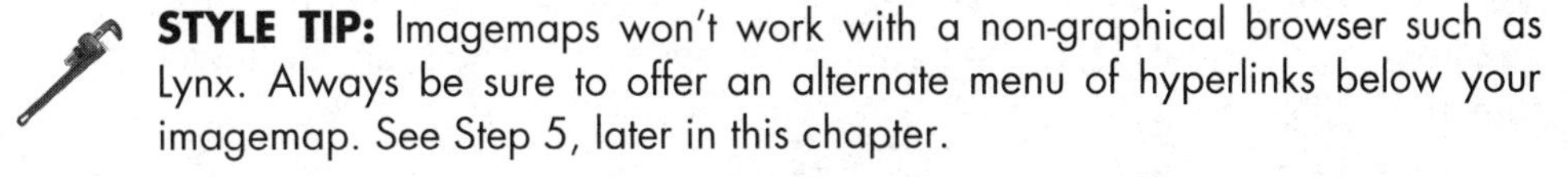

STYLE TIP: Imagemaps won't work with a non-graphical browser such as Lynx. Always be sure to offer an alternate menu of hyperlinks below your imagemap. See Step 5, later in this chapter.

STEP 1: Create the Image

There is no one way to create imagemaps. You may want to use one big image, such as a floor plan or a map, or you may want to combine several smaller images together. Although you can use a simple tool like the Windows Paintbrush, you can design much nicer and professional images using a commercial package such as Adobe Photoshop or Illustrator.

One common method of imagemap design is to create several distinct buttons or images. You can then load these all onto one canvas and scatter them around, combine them, draw arrows, or create other logical connections. Browse through Chapter 8 for some more sample imagemap ideas.

Another idea is to take a photograph of any typical object associated with your subject, such as a filing cabinet, an office desk, or even an entire building. You can then scan in the image and create hot spots for various drawers, doors, windows, appliances, etc.

In any case, you generally want to label each hot spot clearly. Write some descriptive text beneath, atop, or embedded in each hot spot. You can use LView to add pretty clear horizontal or vertical text to most images. If you have a tool like Adobe Photoshop or Adobe Illustrator, you can even create *anti-aliased* text that blends right into the image, making the print seem flawless.

STYLE TIP: Design your map so the boundaries of clickable items are pretty obvious. Space your hot spots to make it easy for the user to tell where to click. Try not to overlap too many hot spots.

STEP 2: Create the Map

The key to imagemaps is the map file itself. When you click an imagemap, your browser sends the coordinates of that click to a special imagemap program. This software then performs the following steps:

1. It notes exactly where on the image the mouse was clicked.
2. It looks up these *hot-spot* coordinates in a map file.
3. It jumps to the URL specified in the map file.

Maps files always have the *.map* extension. They can be stored anywhere, but it's usually most convenient to just place them in the same directory with your HTML code and the image itself. The map file looks something like this:

```
default http://www.smartpants.edu/righthere.html
#The Home Page
poly (10,75) (29,65) (21,57) (29,42) (36,43) (45,35) (65,41) (56,21)
(69,7) (87,11) (105,11) (121,16) (137,26) (159,21) (174,66) (167,98)
(163,110) (157,110) (144,135) (122,142) (124,152) (112,152) (111,157)
(106,151) (77,151) (73,148) (65,148) (52,137) (47,140) (43,138)
(31,143) (6,79) http://www.smartpants.edu/home.html
#The Computers Page
rect (500,95) (588,234) http://www.smartpants.edu/computers.html
#The Graphics Page
circle (223,85) 30 http://www.smartpants.edu/graphics.edu
```

For NCSA servers, the map file looks more like:

```
default http://www.smartpants.edu/righthere.html
#The Home Page
poly http://www.smartpants.edu/home.html 24,125 17,124 17,270 113,272
115,172 205,172 203,126 150,124 144,136 122,144 125,157 108,153 69,152
59,144 57,137 42,137 35,139 26,126
#The Computers Page
rect http://www.smartpants.edu/computers.html 500,95 588,234
#The Graphics Page
circle http://www.smartpants.edu/graphics.edu 67,50 48,30
```

In either case, the file contains:

- HTML Comments (prefaced by the # character)
- HTML A default URL for clicks that don't fall into any specified range

HTML Hot-spot circles with affiliated URLs

HTML Hot-spot rectangles with affiliated URLs

HTML Hot-spot polygons with affiliated URLs

How in the world, you might wonder, do you know where to specify the coordinates of a given image's hot spots? Luckily, there's a Windows program that does it all for you: MapEdit.

MapEdit 1.1.2

To create an accurate imagemap, you'd need to be able to point to the image itself and know exactly which coordinate is which. Luckily, Thomas Boutell created the MapEdit program, which does just that, and more. All in all, MapEdit makes imagemaps a snap.

You'll find MapEdit in the \WINDOWS\TOOLS\MAPEDIT directory of the enclosed CD-ROM. Copy it to any directory on your hard disk, then set up an icon for MapEdit in the Windows Program Manager.

NOTE: MapEdit is not in the public domain. Be sure to register for MapEdit if you do end up using it. Commercial users need to pay $25, but nonprofit and education users can just send the author a postcard. Read the licensing terms included with the software for more information.

MapEdit loads up your GIF image and places it in a neat window. You can then use the mouse to draw rectangles, circles, or intricate polygons around certain parts of the image. You can then specify a URL for each of these hot spots.

Loading an Image

Once you've created a suitable image for your imagemap, you can load it into MapEdit by selecting File, Open/Create. The Open/Create Map dialog box appears, as in Figure 12-18. Type the GIF filename in the box or click Browse to search your hard disk for the proper file.

If you're creating a new map, just type any name (with the *.map* extension). In general, it's easier to keep track of things if you use the same name for your map as you do for your image.

NOTE: You can also edit an existing imagemap by designating its name in the Map Filename box.

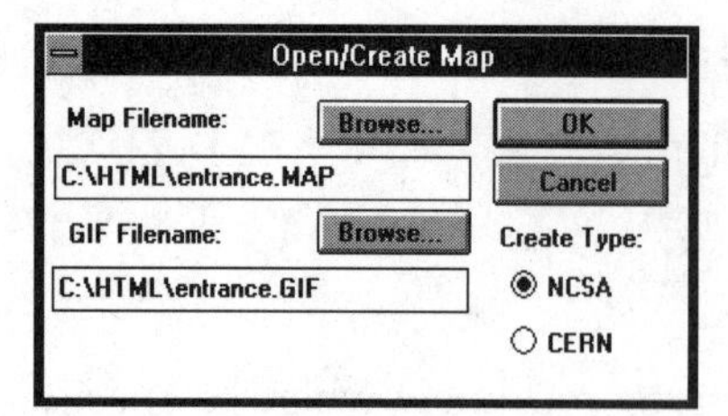

Figure 12-18 Designate the name of the GIF image and the map file

By default, MapEdit creates an NCSA map file. If your system is using the CERN Web server, then click the CERN radio button.

When you're done, click OK. Click OK again when the system asks if you'd like to create the given map file. It takes quite a while for MapEdit to load your GIF into memory. Eventually, it appears on the screen. If your image is larger than the screen, you may need to adjust the window or use the scrollbars.

The Default URL

If somebody clicks a *cold* area of your imagemap (one that isn't covered by a hot spot), what happens? If you don't designate a default URL, then most browsers display a message telling the user that the area they clicked has no link.

It's a good idea to set up a default URL instead, which can take the user to the most likely or popular page. Select File, Edit Default URL. The Default URL dialog box appears. Fill in the default and click OK.

Drawing Hot Spots

Creating polygonal, circular, or rectangular hot spots is simple. For example, select Tools, Rectangle to designate a rectangular region. Click the left mouse button on one of the rectangle's corners and then move the mouse to the rectangle's opposite corner. If you want to abort this rectangle, click the left mouse button again. Otherwise click the *right* mouse button.

The Object URL dialog box appears. Fill in this hot spot's URL (the way you would designate HREF in an anchor) in the URL for clicks on the object box, as shown in Figure 12-19. You can also type in a description of the URL or other comments in the Comments box. When done, click OK.

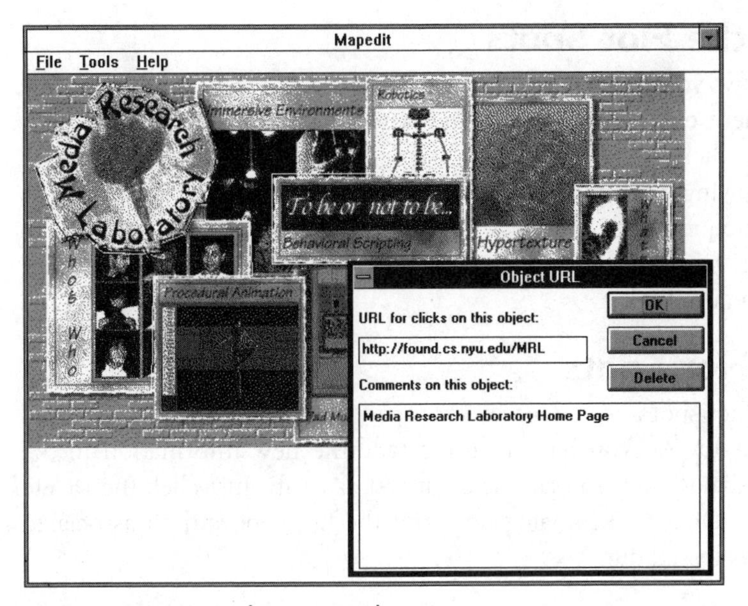

Figure 12-19 Making a spot hot

NOTE: If you don't know the URL yet, just type in some sort of guess. Later, you can use MapEdit to change the URL. See the Editing Hot Spots section of this chapter.

Creating a circle works the same. Just select Tools, Circle. Move the mouse cursor to where you want the center of your circle to be and click the left mouse button. Now move the mouse, lengthening the circle's radius. When you have the circle you want, press the *right* mouse button. Fill in the Object URL dialog box, as before.

Finally, you can create polygons with as many sides as you wish. This allows you to specify very specific shapes and patterns. Click on where you want the polygon to begin. You can now draw little lines connected to each other until your polygon is formed. Just keep clicking at strategic spots around the area you wish to define: a blob, a starfish, whatever. Continue until you've outlined the entire area. To cancel the polygon, press the left mouse button again. If you like the way it looks, click the *right* mouse button and fill in the Object URL dialog box.

NOTE: If hot spots overlap, the first one you created will control where the user goes.

Testing the Hot Spots

MapEdit allows you to try before you buy. Just select Tools, Test+Edit. Now click anywhere on the image, the way a user at your Web page would. Anytime you click on a hot rectangle, circle, or polygon, the URL window pops up, showing you the link you've just defined. The current hot spot is also highlighted in green.

Click OK to continue testing. MapEdit remains in testing mode until you choose a new Tool.

Editing Hot Spots

If you test a hot spot and it doesn't work the way you wanted it to, you can edit it on-the-fly. All you have to do is type the new information in the Object URL dialog box. You can delete it just as easily. Just click the Delete button in the Object URL dialog box, and the hot spot and all associated information is tossed out.

Saving the Map File

When your imagemap works just the way you want it to, you can save the map file. Select File, Save. The map file you first specified is created or updated.

That's all there is to it. Keep track of where your map file is located; you'll need it for the next steps.

NOTE: You can use the File, Save As command to save your map to a different file, or in a different format.

STEP 3: Write the HTML

To use an imagemap, just create a suitable GIF image and display it as usual using the IMG element. However, you need to add the *ISMAP* attribute letting the browser know that the image is a clickable map. Once ISMAP is declared, your browser automatically passes the coordinates you clicked on to the imagemap program.

For example, if your image is called *entrance.gif* and your map file is *entrance.map,* you would type:

```
<A HREF="http://www.smartpants.edu/cgi-bin/imagemap/entrance">
<IMG SRC="entrance.gif" ISMAP></A>
```

The anchor, then, should point to the imagemap script itself. If you do not know where your imagemap program is located, ask your system administrator. The entrance "subdirectory" designates the name of your imagemap program, as designated in the *imagemap.conf* file. See the next section for instructions on setting up your imagemap configuration file.

NOTE: With some systems, instead of designating just the name of your map, you need to include the map's exact location.

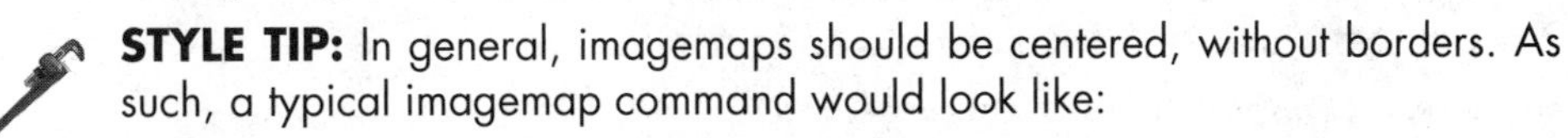

STYLE TIP: In general, imagemaps should be centered, without borders. As such, a typical imagemap command would look like:

```
<CENTER><A HREF="http://found.cs.nyu.edu/cgi-
bin/imagemap/homepage"><IMG BORDER = 0
SRC="http://found.cs.nyu.edu/MRL/Homepage2.gif" ISMAP></A><P>
</CENTER>
```

STEP 4: Set Up the Server

Most of the action with imagemaps takes place in the background. Your http server (usually on a Unix system) performs the tasks using cgi-bin programs. See Chapter 15 for details about CGI and Chapter 21 for information about Web servers. However, you don't really need to understand how servers work—you just need to have access to one.

NOTE: If you don't have access to your own Web server, ask your system administrator to perform the following steps for you. Most commercial Internet providers should be happy to set up their imagemap software to include your personal map.

To use imagemaps, you need the *imagemap cgi* program. If this program isn't already compiled and installed in your cgi-bin directory, be sure to do so. Both CERN and NCSA http servers have versions of this program, usually included with their server. When your Web browser comes across an imagemap (designated by the ISMAP attribute) it automatically runs the imagemap software.

NOTE: If you're using a server other than CERN or NCSA http, check with the server's distributor for details. In most cases, the steps for creating an imagemap are exactly the same.

If you have access to your NCSA http directories, then you can easily set up your imagemap. Simply switch to your server's *conf* subdirectory. In other words, if your server is located at

```
/www/httpd
```

change to the *conf* directory by typing

```
cd /www/http/conf
```

There should be a file here called *imagemap.conf*. If not, you may need to create it. You now need to add a line to this file telling the server where your imagemap's map file is located. This takes the form

```
mapname: map's full directory
```

For example, if the map's name is *entrance.map* and it's located in the */www/http/htdocs* directory, you would add the line

```
entrance: /www/http/htdocs/entrance.map
```

That's all there is to it, on the server side.

STEP 5: The Text-Based Index

Whenever you use an imagemap, be sure to include a text-based index for those folks who can't—or don't have the time to—display graphics. For example, suppose your imagemap contains a bunch of flags each leading to one of the following areas:

- English
- Japanese
- French
- Russian
- Hebrew
- Arabic
- Greek

In this case, you should include a few lines of HTML (or a hyperlink to a separate HTML document) as follows:

```
Here's the text-based index:<P>
<UL>
<LI><A HREF="english.html">English</A>
<LI><A HREF="japanese.html">Japanese</A>
<LI><A HREF="french.html">French</A>
<LI><A HREF="russian.html">Russian</A>
<LI><A HREF="hebrew.html">Hebrew</A>
<LI><A HREF="arabic.html">Arabic</A>
<LI><A HREF="greek.html">Greek</A>
</UL>
```

LESSON #11: WHAT'S YOUR BACKGROUND?

Hold onto your hat. One of the neatest features in HTML3 has just been announced: the BACKGROUND attribute. This allows you to take a small picture, pattern, or color, and use it as a texture for the entire Web page's background. This way, your Web page can appear to be printed on sandpaper, stucco, metal, rock, water, or against any type of wallpaper you can imagine. See Figure 12-20 for an example.

NOTE: Currently, only Netscape supports the BACKGROUND attribute, though it is within the current HTML3 specification.

The attribute itself is very simple. Just specify the GIF image file for your background in your Web page's <BODY> element:

```
<BODY BACKGROUND="pattern.gif">
```

NOTE: Your background images should be as small as possible, since nothing can be loaded until the background has been painted. Small (less than 150x150) backgrounds can be loaded and rendered quite quickly, however.

STYLE TIP: Try not to mix transparent images and background patterns, since your custom background will not show through the transparent spots.

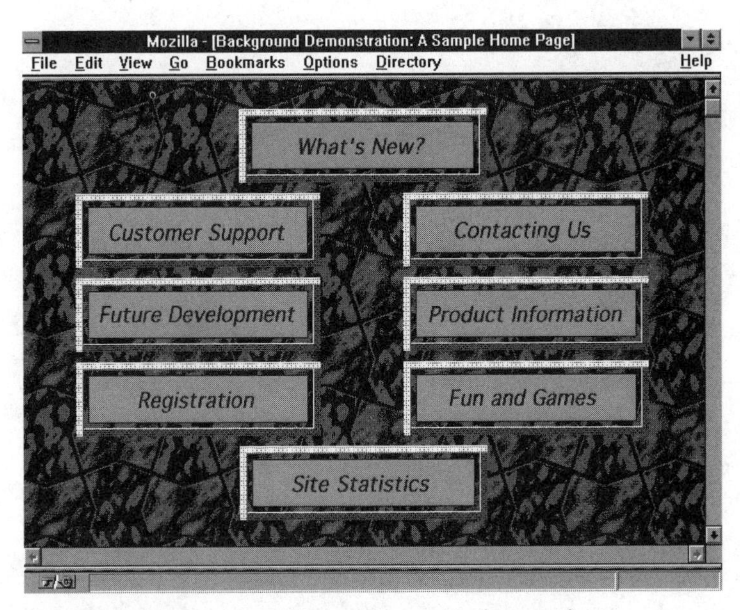

Figure 12-20 A custom Web page background

Background Color

Netscape has come up with a quick and easy attribute which allows you to change the color of your background. This way, you can use the same pattern for a rainbow of different pages.

The BGCOLOR attribute is also part of the <BODY> element. Simply specify the color as a hexidecimal RGB color triplet, which always begins with the pound sign (#). For example, the color black is #000000 and white is #FFFFFF. See Table 12-1 earlier in this chapter for a listing of several sample colors. For example, to make the background black, you would use the markup:

```
<BODY BACKGROUND="image.gif" BGCOLOR="#000000">
```

Foreground Color

Usually, the text on your Web page is printed in black. However, if your background is dark, black text may very well be illegible. Wisely, Netscape allows you to specify the foreground color.

Text Color

To change the color of the document's standard text, use the TEXT attribute along with an RGB triplet. For example, if you want light-gray text, use the markup:

```
<BODY TEXT="#F0F0F0">
```

Hyperlink Color

Normally, a hyperlink is blue, a visited link is purple, and active links are red. Netscape also allows you to specify the color for each hyperlink, visited link (a link which was already loaded), and active link (a link currently being loaded). Simply use the LINK, VLINK, and ALINK attributes, respectively. These attributes are also expressed within the <BODY> element. For example, if you want yellow links, use the markup:

```
<BODY LINK="#FFFF00">
```

A typical <BODY> element, then, might look something like:

```
<BODY BACKGROUND="pattern.gif" BGCOLOR="#FFFFFF" LINK="#FFFF00"
VLINK="#000000" ALINK="#00FFFF">
```

Getting Backgrounds

The Netscape Communications Corporation has many sample backgrounds at:

```
http://home.netscape.com/home/bg/index.html
```

You can point to these images directly or copy them and use them as a base for your own backgrounds.

Many groovy backgrounds are also stored on the enclosed CD-ROM in the \CLIPMDIA\BKGRNDS directory.

LESSON #12: EMBEDDING

The latest version of Windows Netscape allows you to use the new <EMBED> element to drop most any kind of document directly in your Web page. As long as a user has a viewer for the document on his or her computer, an embedded file appears as some sort of icon. A user need only click on the icon to see or access the document.

You can use EMBED to insert word-processed documents, movies, sounds, or nearly any type of graphic. For example:

```
<EMBED SRC="bird.tif">
```

You can also use the WIDTH and HEIGHT attributes to fit the embedded object within a certain space. Simply specify the dimensions in pixels. For example, to create an image which appears in a 100X50 box:

```
<EMBED SRC="bird.tif" WIDTH=100 HEIGHT=50>
```

THE SILVER SCREEN

The Web can handle any sort of file—even movies. On a computer, "movies" can be animations, multimedia presentations, film clips, sequences of images, or even just soundtracks. Two main movie/multimedia formats are popular on the Web:

- HTML QuickTime .MOV files
- HTML Multimedia .MPEG files

Additional types of movies and animations are listed in Table 2-1 in Chapter 2. Most Web browsers don't have built-in movie-display software, but you can find movie viewers for most every format, operating system, or computer type. Viewers are discussed further on in this section. In most cases, you should be able to download a supported viewer at the site where you retrieve the movie or animation.

WARNING: Video runs very, very slowly on machines without at least 8 MB of memory. And if your machine doesn't have a Super-VGA monitor or better, the video will probably look pretty splotchy.

Lights, Camera... Action?

To add a movie to your Web page you need to set up an anchor that leads to the movie file. For instance, to play the movie *rocket.mov*, just include the line:

```
<A HREF="rocket.mov">Click here to see the Rocket movie. (2.2M)</A>
```

The rocket.mov file must be stored in the same directory as the rest of your HTML documents.

It's a good idea to use a preview frame from your movie instead of a simple text anchor like the one above. Most video capture tools—such as Adobe Premiere and MovieMaker—allow you to do this. This makes a "poster" for the movie, to help the user decide if it's worthwhile to view or download the movie itself. For example, if you captured a frame of the rocket movie as *rocket.gif*, you would type:

```
<A HREF="rocket.mov"><IMG SRC="rocket.gif"></A>Click here to see the
Rocket movie. (2.2M)
```

STYLE TIP: Since movies are terribly long, be sure to adequately describe each movie. Otherwise, people may waste many minutes downloading movies they don't really care to see. It's also somewhat of a convention to tag how long each movie is, in megabytes. This way, someone with a slow modem will know not to bother checking out your enormous 10-megabyte film.

You can, of course, also include movies that aren't stored in your local HTML directory. You can use movies located anywhere else on your system, or even anywhere else on the Internet. For example, if you come across a movie at the *http://www.movieland.com/rocket.mov* URL, then your link would look like:

```
<A HREF="http://www.movieland.com/rocket.mov">Click here to see the
Rocket movie. (2.2M)</A>
```

You can browse around the Internet, finding movies that fit the theme of your Web page. When you come across something interesting, you can check the link's complete URL at the bottom of the screen in Mosaic or Netscape simply by touching the link with your mouse arrow. In Lynx, just highlight the link and press =.

NOTE: A distant movie generally takes longer to load and play, due to the time it takes to leap across the network.

QuickTime

QuickTime is the Macintosh video and sound capture tool. Movie files generally end with the .MOV extension. There are also several Windows quicktime viewers, one of which is found at the site listed in Appendix D. Unzip and copy the files to a convenient directory on your hard disk. You can now configure Mosaic or Netscape to call this viewer whenever they have to present a QuickTime movie.

NOTE: If you grab a QuickTime movie from a Macintosh system, you may have to *flatten* it before you can play it on another operating system. Mac users should flatten movies before putting them on the Web. When you flatten a movie, all the resources, image data, and QuickTime sound are placed into one file. Try to search the Web for the shareware *flattmoov* file. You can also flatten a flick using the commercial Adobe Premiere software.

MPEGPLAY

MPEG stands for the Moving Pictures Experts Group, a body of people who work with digital video compression, storage, and viewing. The MPEG format is perhaps the most popular format of computerized video and multimedia.

There's a very good shareware MPEG player available (called, appropriately, MPEGPLAY) in the CD-ROM's \WINDOWS\VIEWERS\MPEGPLAY directory. Copy the entire directory to your hard disk and configure your Web browser to use MPEGPLAY as your MPEG viewer. See Chapters 4, 5, and 6 for instructions on setting up viewers.

The next time you download a movie from the Web, MPEGPLAY pops up. You can use the VCR-type controls to Rewind, Stop, Advance the movie one frame, or Play the entire movie. These same controls can be selected from the Movie menu. Figure 12-21 shows a sample movie being played.

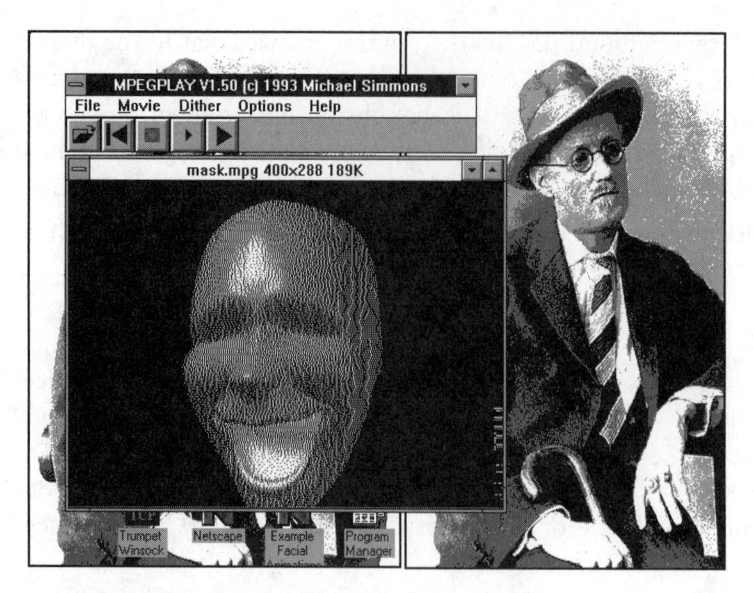

Figure 12-21 Watching a Web flick

GRABBING GRAPHICS

Where do images come from? Spend just a few minutes browsing the Web and you'll realize that there's no lack of graphics in cyberspace. There are three basic ways of building up your collection of images: you can create them, capture them, or download them.

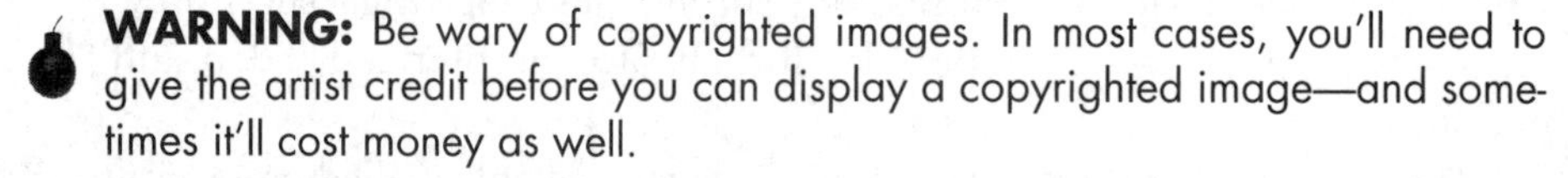

WARNING: Be wary of copyrighted images. In most cases, you'll need to give the artist credit before you can display a copyrighted image—and sometimes it'll cost money as well.

Playing Picasso

If you're a bit of an artist you can, of course, design your own images. Tools for this range from the simple Windows Paintbrush to the painterly Adobe Illustrator or Fractal Painter. There are also plenty of computer design firms who can create just the logo, backdrop, or style you've been picturing.

If you're interested in creating video, you'll need more sophisticated resources. Not just a video camera, either; your computer needs a video digitizer card and some sort of video capture software such as Adobe Premiere.

WARNING: Movie files are huge. Try to edit your movies to be as short as possible while still preserving their quality and impact. You may want to save your movies in black-and-white format, since this often takes up less space.

There are many software packages capable of producing animations or multimedia presentations. Check out Autodesk Animator or Macromedia Director if you're interested in creating professional quality cartoons or other animations.

Capturing

If you come across an image you'd like to use, you can easily capture it. In general, there are three capture methods. Depending on the image you want and the browser you're using, one of these methods should work like a charm.

Load to Disk

Most browsers have a Load to Local Disk option. Turn this option on and then reload the page. As the image loads up, the browser asks for a filename. In this way, you can save any inlined GIF to your hard disk. When you're done capturing, be sure to turn the Local Disk option off.

Loading the Image's URL

If your browser doesn't offer the Load to Local Disk command, there's a slightly more troublesome method: Display the current page's HTML source. Browse through the markup until you find the <IMG> command that corresponds to the image you want to snag. Copy the SRC's URL to your clipboard or write it down. If the SRC is local, you can just append this filename to the current Web page's URL. You can then instruct your browser to load up this specific URL. Select File, Save As and you should be able to save the image onto your hard disk.

For example, suppose you're browsing a page at:

```
http://graphics.smartpants.edu/webstuff/cool.html
```

and you come across a great picture of a pickle. You view the HTML source and find the line:

```
<IMG SRC="pickle.gif">
```

You can download the pickle by opening the URL:

```
http://graphics.smartpants.edu/webstuff/pickle.gif
```

Full Screen Capture

If you like, you can grab an entire screen itself. Windows has a built-in screen capture utility that allows you store the current screen in the clipboard: Just press ALT-PRT-SC.

You can now load up the Windows Paintbrush, or any other paint program, and paste this screen image onto the canvas. You can now work with the image, erasing the parts you don't want, changing colors, or touching things up.

Image Hunting

The enclosed CD-ROM contains a library of images to get you started. General images are in the \CLIPMDIA\IMAGES directory. There's also a directory for bullets, icons, and bars.

If you don't find what you need, you can search cyberspace for a suitable image. The only problem with downloading images from the Internet is that there are too many places to look. There are literally hundreds of Web pages, FTP sites, or other archives full of GIFs, JPEGs, movies, animations, and more.

Table 12-2 lists some of the best places to get general images. Table 12-3 lists archives full of icons, bullets, buttons, bars, and other Web spices. And, finally, Table 12-4 contains a full list of animations, videos, and other movies. Happy hunting!

Table 12-2 Just a few places to find images over the Web

Archive Name	URL
Internet Image Finder	http://www.cm.cf.ac.uk/Misc/wustl.html
Yahoo Server Index	http://akebono.stanford.edu/yahoo/Computers/Multimedia/Pictures/
WWW Power Index	http://www.webcom.com/power/multimedia.html
Archive Image Archive	ftp://archie.au/graphics/gifs
Flinux Image Archive	ftp://flinux.tu-graz.ac.at/pub/graphics
Funet Image Archive	ftp://ftp.funet.fi/pub/pics
Informatik Image Archive	ftp://ftp.informatik.tu-muenchen.de/pub/rec/images
Isca Image Archive	ftp://grind.isca.uiowa.edu/images
Nic Image Archive	ftp://nic.uakom.sk/pub/multimedia
Smithsonian Archive	gopher://bramble.er.usgs.gov/1ftp%3aphoto1.si.edu%40/
Stuttgart Image Archive	ftp://ftp.uni-stuttgart.de/pub/graphics/pictures
Sunet Image Archive	ftp://ftp.sunet.se/pub/pictures
Sunsite Image Archive	file://sunsite.unc.edu/pub/multimedia/pictures/

Archive Name	URL
UIUC Image Archive	http://www.acm.uiuc.edu:80/rml/Gifs/
WUArchive Images	ftp://wuarchive.wustl.edu/
Newsgroup Archives	http://web.cnam.fr/Images/Usenet/abpm/summaries/
Space Image Archive	http://www.jsc.nasa.gov/~mccoy/Images/"> Daniel's Space Image Archive
Another Space Archive	ftp://tezuka.rest.ri.cmu.edu/usr/anon/pub/space
More Space Images	http://info.cern.ch/Space/Overview.html
Astonomy Pictures	http://www.univ-rennes1.fr/ASTRO/astro.english.html
NASA Space Images	ftp://explorer.arc.nasa.gov/pub/SPACE/GIF
Data Visualization	http://www.nhgs.tec.va.us/GovSch/datavisual.html
MRI Images	http://www-mri.uta.edu/"> Magnetic Resonance Imaging
Historical NASA Archive	http://www.ksc.nasa.gov/history/history.html
Ansel Adams Photos	http://bookweb.cwis.uci.edu:8042/AdamsHome.html
America Images	http://rs6.loc.gov/amhome.html
Arizona Images	gopher://miles.library.arizona.edu:70/1
Brazil Images	http://guarani.cos.ufrj.br:8000/Rio/Todas.html
California Images	http://www.water.ca.gov/Calif.images.html
California Photo Museum	http://cmp1.ucr.edu/
Hawaii Images	http://www.mhpcc.edu/tour/Tour.html
Hypatia Images	http://hypatia.gsfc.nasa.gov/Images
Indiana Images	gopher://enif.astro.indiana.edu:70/11/images
New Mexico Images	http://www-swiss.ai.mit.edu/philg/new-mexico/album.html
Utah Images	http://wings.buffalo.edu/staff/plewe/so-utah/images.html
Washington DC Images	gopher://calypso.oit.unc.edu:70/11/sunsite.d/politics.d/multimedia.d
WWW Images Examples	http://www.cit.gu.edu.au/images/Images.html
Index of Banners	http://strauss.ce.cmu.edu:2000/cgi-bin/banner
Fractal Art Gallery	http://www.cnam.fr/fractals.html
Mathemartical Art	http://sunsite.unc.edu/pics/mathgif.html
Aviation Art	http://146.245.2.151/rec/air/air.html

Table 12-3 Icons, buttons, bars, bullets, and flags

Archive Name	URL
Yahoo Server Icons	http://akebono.stanford.edu/yahoo/Computers/World_Wide_Web/Programming/Icons/
Yahoo Server Flags	http://akebono.stanford.edu/yahoo/Reference/Flags/
WWW Power Index	http://www.webcom.com/power/icons.html
Anthony's Icon Library	http://www.cit.gu.edu.au/~anthony/icons/
Daniel's Icon Archive	http://www.jsc.nasa.gov/~mccoy/Icons/index.html

Continued on next page

Continued from previous page

Archive Name	URL
Example WWW Icons	http://www.cit.gu.edu.au/images/Images.html
Icon Archive (Trancv1)	http://ivory.nosc.mil/html/trancv/html/icons-hcc.html
Icon Browser	http://www.di.unipi.it/iconbrowser/icons.html
Index of Flags	http://155.187.10.12/images/flags/
Index of Icons	http://www.bsdi.com/icons/AIcons/
Index of NCSA Icons	http://www.ncsa.uiuc.edu/General/Icons/
Network Services	http://www-ns.rutgers.edu/doc-images
Space Icons	ftp://explorer.arc.nasa.gov/pub/SPACE/LOGOS
Standard Icons	http://www.cs.indiana.edu/elisp/w3/icons.html
Virtual Icon Collection	http://inls.ucsd.edu/y/OhBoy/icons.html
World Flags	http://www.adfa.oz.au/CS/flg/

Table 12-4 Your source for Web movies and animations of all sorts

Archive Name	URL
Thant's Animations Index	http://mambo.ucsc.edu/psl/thant/thant.html
Andrew Tong's Archive	http://www.ugcs.caltech.edu/~werdna/mpegs.html
Index of MPEGs	http://www-psrg.lcs.mit.edu/~rweiss/mpeg.html
MPEG Movie Archive	http://www.acm.uiuc.edu:80/rml/Mpeg/
Another MPEG Archive	http://www.eeb.ele.tue.nl/mpeg/index.html
A 3D Frog	http://george.lbl.gov/ITG.hm.pg.docs/Whole.Frog/Whole.Frog.html
Aquarium Movies	http://www.actwin.com/fish/index.html
Army Computing	http://www.arc.umn.edu/html/ahpcrc.html
Berkeley Quicktimes	http://oms1.berkeley.edu/Video/QTlist.html
Big Bang Animation	http://www.ncsa.uiuc.edu/evl/cosmic/cosmic.html
Buena Vista Pictures	http://bvp.wdp.com/
Calypso	gopher://calypso.oit.unc.edu:70/11/../.pub/multimedia/animation/mpeg
Cocteau Twins Videos	http://garnet.berkeley.edu:8080/cocteau.html
Collection of Videos	http://www.st.nepean.uws.edu.au/pub/movies/mpeg/
Computer Graphics	http://mambo.ucsc.edu/psl/cg.html
Cornell Visualizations	http://www.tc.cornell.edu/Visualization/vis.html
CRS4 Animation Gallery	http://www.crs4.it:/Animate/Animations.html
Facial Animations	http://www.cs.ubc.ca/nest/imager/contributions/forsey/dragon/top.html
Figure Skating	http://www.cs.yale.edu/HTML/YALE/CS/HyPlans/loosemore-sandra/skate.html
Formula 1 Racing	http://www.abekrd.co.uk/Formula1/bin.html
Fractal Animations	http://www.cnam.fr/fractals.html

Archive Name	URL
Galaxy Animations	http://zebu.uoregon.edu/movie.html
Hang Gliding	http://cougar.stanford.edu:7878/MoviePage.html
Japanese Quicktime	ftp://ftp.iij.ad.jp/pub/info-mac/grf/Quicktime
Juggling Movies	http://www.hal.com/services/juggle/animations/
Kaleidospace Movies	http://kspace.com/KM/screen.sys/screenlist.html
Kylie Minogue's Videos	http://www.eia.brad.ac.uk/kylie/index.html
Married with Children	http://www.eia.brad.ac.uk/mwc/index.html
MCNC Quicktime Library	http://www.cnidr.org:5050/quicktime.html
Military Animations	file://dsn-sgi.nosc.mil/pub/movies
NASA's F-16 Project	http://dval-www.larc.nasa.gov/F16XL/index.html
Pearl Jam	http://fiasco.snre.umich.edu/users/galvin/mpeg/pjmpeg.html
Pixel Motion Gallery	http://aton.hypercomp.ns.ca/pix/pix_dragon_gal.html
Planet Earth MPEGs	http://white.nosc.mil/movies.html
Public FTP Archive	http://ftp.arl.mil/images.html
Quicktime Collection	gopher://informns.k12.mn.us/11/best-k12/images/Quicktime%20Movies
Quicktime Guide	http://www.ncsa.uiuc.edu/SDG/Software/MacMosaic/QuickTimeGuide.html
Raytraced MPEGs	http://www.santafe.edu/~nelson/mpeg/
Ren and Stimpy	gopher://kazak.nmsu.edu/11/Public/Ren%20%26%20Stimpy/movies/quicktime
Rob's Multimedia Lab	http://www.acm.uiuc.edu/rml/Mpeg/
Rugby	http://rugby.phys.uidaho.edu/rugby/Action/edwards.html
Science Theatre	http://www.ncsa.uiuc.edu/SDG/DigitalGallery/DG_science_theater.html
SIGGRAPH Showcase	http://www.ncsa.uiuc.edu/evl/showcase.html
Silicon Graphics Movies	http://www.sgi.com/free/gallery.html#movie
Space Movies	ftp://bozo.lpl.arizona.edu
Space Movies	http://www.univ-rennes1.fr/ASTRO/anim-e.html
Star Trek	http://sherlock.berkeley.edu/docs/info/star_trek/trek.html
Sumex Quicktimes	gopher://sumex-aim.stanford.edu/11/info-mac/Graphic/Quicktime
Sunet Animations	ftp://ftp.sunet.se/pub/movies
Sunsite Multimedia	file://sunsite.unc.edu/pub/multimedia/
Supermodels	http://www.cs.buffalo.edu/~skumar/video.html
Tango Movies	http://litsun35.epfl.ch:8001/tango/
The Beatles Quicktime	http://orathost.cfa.ilstu.edu/oratGopherHome/oratClasses/
The MPEG Group	http://www.crs4.it/HTML/LUIGI/MPEG/mpegfaq.html
Tori Amos Videos	http://www.mit.edu:8001/people/nocturne/tori/quicktime.html
USC Quicktime Archives	http://cwis.usc.edu:80/dept/etc/hollynet/movies/
Virtual Reality	http://www.sics.se/dce/dive/dive.html

WHAT NOW?

What now, you ask? Well, you can turn to the next chapter and add sound to your already multimedia Web page. Chapter 15 covers CGI Scripts—various programs you can run using your Web page. Many of these programs can be used hand-in-hand with graphics, achieving super-special effects.

If you want to start putting your pages in the world-wide limelight, turn to Chapter 20, Where to Place Your HTML Documents.

13
SOUND

13

Why in the World Wide Web would you want to stick audio in cyberspace?

- Greetings in your own voice personalize your home page.
- Snippets of talk, music, or commentary bring life to a theme. For example, if you have a Web page about civil rights, you might want to play part of Martin Luther King's "I Have a Dream" speech.
- Your talents can find a new showcase on the Net. If you've got the ability to sing, play an instrument, or make amazing underarm noises, why not flaunt it?
- Sound bites in online interviews bring the participants to life.
- Cool sound effects spice up an otherwise plain page.
- Your company's message is more memorable with its jingle or theme song attached.
- Your online presentation can include a verbal narrative along with charts, graphs, and tables.

Until the Web and Mosaic came along, the Net was almost entirely visual. You could transfer sound files back and forth, but there was no easy way to listen to them. These days, though, the ear gets a chance to take part in the action. Incorporating noises with your text and graphic creations provides a true multimedia experience.

HEARING AIDS

Before you start to work with audio, you should make sure your computer isn't mute. Most Macintoshes and Unix workstations come with sound hardware built in. If you have any sort of sound card installed in your PC, then you're all set. Your Windows sound driver is probably already configured. If not, check out the documentation or software that came with your sound board.

But what if you have a plain old run-of-the-mill multimedia-challenged PC? Luckily, Microsoft provides a utility called SPEAK.EXE to supercharge the PC's 25-cent speaker, making it act like a fancy sound board. The output is kind of grungy, and speech in particular is almost impossible to make out, but it's certainly better than nothing. Results vary depending on exactly how your hardware is set up.

Installing SPEAK.EXE

SPEAK.EXE can be found at the site listed in Appendix D. Download the file and copy it into your windows directory. Then, run the

```
SPEAK.EXE
```

program to extract the speak driver.

To install the driver itself, select the Control Panel icon from the Main group in your Windows Program Manager. Now select Drivers. Click on Add, and select Unlisted Or Updated Drivers from the list that appears. Type in the path of your Windows directory, which is usually

```
C:\WINDOWS
```

and click OK.

The Sound Driver For PC Speaker option should appear. Select this and click OK. You should hear a clutter of strange sounds, which indicates the driver SPEAKER.DRV has been installed.

Configuring SPEAKER.DRV

The first time you install the driver, a dialog box appears allowing you to play with the PC speaker's options. You can return to this Setup box at any time by choosing the Drivers icon in the Control Panel, selecting Sound Driver For PC-Speaker, and then clicking the Setup button.

You can now adjust Speed, Volume, and Limit, as shown in Figure 13-1. It's a good idea to set Seconds To Limit Playback to No Limit; this way, audio files of any length can be played. Click Test every so often until you've tweaked out the best sound.

Since the speaker driver requires lots of memory to do what it does, it generally disables interrupts. This means when a sound plays, your

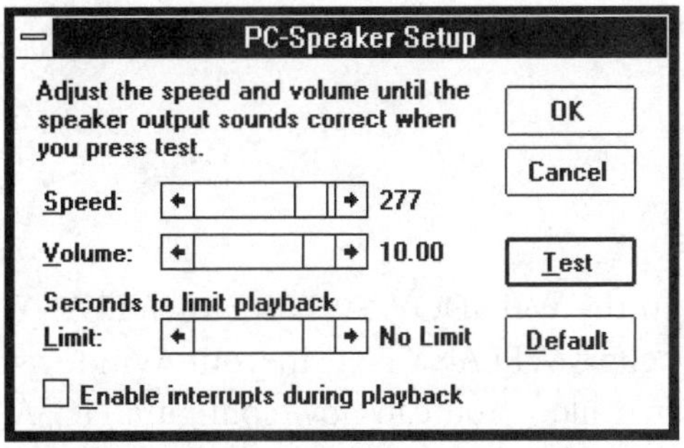

Figure 13-1 Tweaking your speaker to sound just right

Since the speaker driver requires lots of memory to do what it does, it generally disables interrupts. This means when a sound plays, your computer must wait for the sound to finish before it performs another task. If you don't want your computer to freeze, check the Enable Interrupts During Playback check box. If you enable interrupts, however, the sound quality will be even worse than it already is.

When you're done setting up the driver, click OK. You now need to restart Windows for your new sound driver to take effect.

NOTE: Windows automatically plays sounds every so often. For example, if there's some sort of error, Windows notifies you with a bell. To disable or change these system sounds, select the Sounds icon from the Control Panel.

JAMMIN'

As with any other type of fancy media, your Web browser needs a viewer if it wants to play audio. ("Viewing" sounds may seem odd, but that's what it's called!) See the Installing Viewers sections in Chapters 4, 5, and 6 for help. Two of the most popular sound programs for Windows are WPLANY and WHAM. WHAM is also a full sound editing program.

WPLANY

WPLANY, which is short for something like "Windows Play Anything," is perhaps the easiest and most versatile sound viewer available. This no-frills program reads in any sound and pipes it through your speakers. It supports these audio formats:

- .VOC SoundBlaster
- .AU Sun/NeXT/DEC
- .WAV Windows Waveforms
- .SND Sounder/Soundtools
- .IFF Amiga .8SVX

The WPLANY.EXE program is in the \WINDOWS\VIEWERS\WPLANY directory of the CD-ROM. Simply copy WPLANY.EXE to your Windows directory (or any other directory you'd like). You can now configure NCSA Mosaic, Netscape, or any other multimedia Web browser to call WPLANY any time you encounter a sound.

WHAM

WHAM is short for Waveform Hold and Modify. WHAM 1.31 supports the following formats:

- HTML .VOC Creative Voice
- HTML .AU Sun/NeXT/DEC
- HTML .IFF Amiga IFF/8SVX
- HTML .WAV Windows Waveforms
- HTML .IFF Amiga .8SVX
- HTML .AIF Apple/SGI
- HTML Raw 8-bit sound

WHAM is much more than a player. A host of professional tools allow you to manipulate, splice, or convert existing sound files. You'll find the WHAM files in the CD-ROM's \WINDOWS\VIEWERS\WHAM directory. Copy the files (or the entire directory) to your own hard disk. You can now configure your favorite Web browser to call WHAM any time you encounter a sound. It's also worthwhile to put the WHAM.EXE file in your Windows Program Manager.

To load an audio file with WHAM, select File, Open. Select the List Files Of Type pull-down list and choose the file format you want to retrieve. You can then switch directories until you find the file you want.

Selecting a Chunk of Sound

WHAM allows you to modify your sound, piece by piece. The easiest way to deal with an audio file is to view the entire structure at once. Select View, Entire Sound or press CTRL-O.

You can now select part of the current sound. Simply use the mouse to point to the beginning of the chunk, hold down the left mouse button, and drag the mouse to the end of the chunk you want to select. Release the mouse button. The chunk appears highlighted, as in Figure 13-2.

Beneath the actual image of the sound is a ruler-type line that shows you how long your sound is. Two triangle markers on the ruler designate where your selected chunk begins and ends. You can drag these markers right or left to increase or decrease the selected chunk.

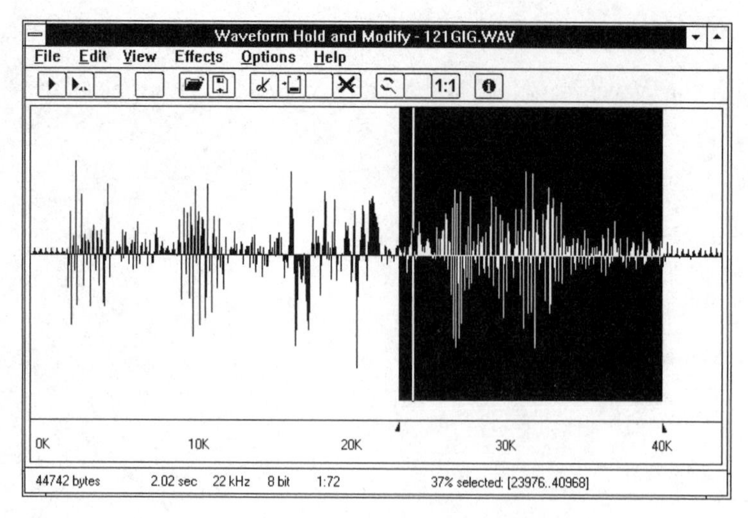

Figure 13-2 Using WHAM to customize a sound file

Playing It

To play the entire sound, press P or select the Play VCR-Type button. To only hear the selected chunk of sound press CTRL-P or click the Play Selection button. In this way, you can break up your sound into precise chunks, deleting those you don't want to hear or saving various chunks separately.

Deleting a Chunk of Sound

If you record your own audio there will often be a few seconds of random noise or silence before and after the actual sound. To shorten your sound file, it's a good idea to cut out this noise. Select these silent chunks of sound—they should appear as flat lines on the sound graph. Select Delete from the Edit menu.

You may also want to take an excerpt from a long speech or piece of music. If this is the case, select the chunk of audio that you wish to keep. To throw away everything else, select Delete Unselected from the Edit menu.

LESSON #1: HYPERSOUND

To stick sound in your HTML documents, then, all you need to do is include an anchor to the sound file. Here's an example:

```
<A HREF="blab.wav">Hear me blab (75K).</A>
```

The file BLAB.WAV must be in the same directory as the rest of your HTML documents.

STYLE TIP: It's a nice idea to briefly describe the sound—this way people will know what to expect before they click. Since audio files can be tremendously long, it's also considered polite to tag how long each sound is, in kilobytes or megabytes. This way, someone with a slow modem will know not to bother retrieving your sound.

One of the best things about the Web is the ability to share other people's resources. Suppose you're surfing around and find a page full of songs sung by Elvis impersonators. Maybe you love the rendition of "Don't Be Cruel" so darned much you want to include it on your own home page. No problem—just note the song's URL. Remember, you can see a link's URL on the bottom of the screen in NCSA Mosaic or Netscape simply by touching the link with your mouse arrow. In Lynx, just highlight the link and press =. The URL is generally shown in its complete form, something like:

```
http://www.graceland.com/cruel.au
```

in which case you can just create an anchor that points directly to the song. For example:

```
Click<A HREF="http://www.graceland.com/cruel.au"> here </A>to listen
to a great version of "Don't Be Cruel" (950K).
```

You can also download the song yourself and place it on your local hard disk. See the Searching For That Right Sound section later in this chapter for more details.

NOTE: A linked-to sound generally takes longer to load and play, due to the time it takes to leap across the network.

You might want to attach your sound to some sort of speaker or audio-play icon, as shown in Figure 13-3, so Web users know that this link is, indeed, an audio one. For example:

```
<A HREF="blab.mod"><IMG SRC="speaker.gif" ALT="(>"></A> Me Blabbing
(75K)
```

You can also attach an audio file to any other inlined image. For example, a user could click on your picture to hear you speak, or could click on an album's cover art to hear a particular song.

Music files—in most any format–are very long and often unwieldy. To avoid cluttering the Web, it's a good idea to use sound selectively—as a spice rather than as a main dish.

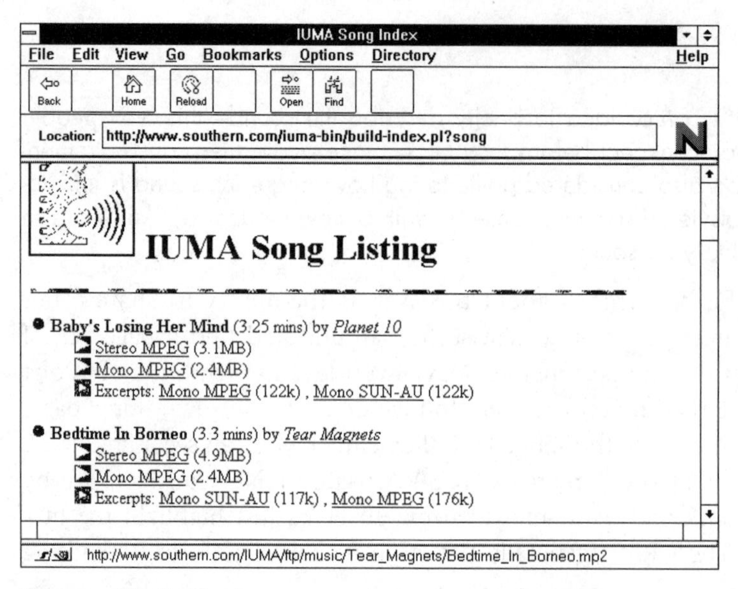

Figure 13-3 Getting your ear's worth over the Web

When posting a sound on the Net, use WHAM or Windows Sound Recorder to edit the sound so it's as clear as can be. Instead of including the entire recording of Martin Luther King's most famous speech, for instance, you may want to just give a flavor of the speech by including the words "I have a dream today." Also be sure to use WHAM or Sound Recorder to cut out any unnecessary static, since this only takes extra time to download.

SOUNDING OFF

So where does this audio come from? Whether you're interested in riffs, sound effects, speech, notes from various instruments, or entire musical scores, there's no lack of sound resources over the Internet.

Audio Formats

Sound formats abound. Most every computer type, operating system, and music-composition software stores audio in its own special way. Luckily, these formats are pretty similar. It's not too hard to convert from format to format. Most good audio viewers (such as WPLANY or WHAM) can handle most any type of audio.

It's important to recognize a sound when you come across one. Table 2-1 in Chapter 2 lists all the common types of sounds you're liable to run across. The most common audio format over the Web is probably the Unix workstation's .au Audio. The .WAV format is almost always used on Windows systems.

You can generally use whichever format you feel most comfortable with, since most operating systems have their own viewers like WPLANY that are capable of booming any popular style of sound.

Recording It Yourself

To record your own voice or music, you'll need specialized hardware. Most multimedia PCs are now equipped with microphones and input jacks. If you've got multimedia, you can probably plug your keyboard (piano keyboard, that is), CD player, or boom box right into your PC. Either the Windows Sound Recorder or WHAM will do a good job of capturing sound for you, once you've set up the hardware to talk to them.

NOTE: Due to memory constraints, it's generally best to limit your own sounds to one minute.

Sound Recorder

The Windows Sound Recorder makes it easy to capture bits of sound and then manipulate or store them. Select the Sound Recorder from your Program Manager's Accessories group. Click the Record microphone icon. You can now speak or sing into the microphone or press Play on your cassette or CD-player. When finished, click Stop.

If you like the sound and want to save it, select File, Save As. Your new sound is saved in the .MOD format.

WHAM

The WHAM program also supports sound recording. To capture a sound using WHAM, select File, Record New or click the Record microphone icon. The Recording dialog box appears. Click the Record button to begin. WHAM takes a second to search for free memory. Wait until the "Recording Commenced" message appears. You can now speak into your microphone or press Play on your tape or CD-player.

When you've finished recording, click Stop. Click Play to hear your sound. If you like the way the sound turned out, click OK. Otherwise, record it again. You can now edit your sound or save it to disk by selecting File, Save As. You can store your sound in any format you wish.

Searching For That Right Sound

The best way to get music is to go hunting for it over the Web. Just like with clip art, clip icons, clip movies, and clip animations, the Internet is home to samples of every sound imaginable. Use your favorite search utility and type in the name of your favorite band, recording artist, style of music, or just the word "sound" itself (if you have several hours to spare).

Once a sound is retrieved, most Web browsers pump the audio through a default sound player. If the player is WHAM, you can edit and save the sound as soon as you grab it. Otherwise, you can usually select File, Save from the browser's pull-down menu and save the sound file directly to your disk.

Table 13-1 contains some interesting FTP sites with all sorts of music snippets. The newsgroup *news://alt.binaries.sounds* also contains a constant new collection of various tunes, quips, and effects.

Table 13-1 Various FTP sites chock full of groovy tunes

ftp://plaza.aamet.edu.au/Simtel-20/micros/pc/oak/music
ftp://elof.iit.edu/pub/drum/acoustics
ftp://euler.math.usma.edu/pub/acoustic
ftp://f.ms.uky.edu/pub/atari/music
ftp://ftp.eu.net/comp/mac/sound
ftp://ftp.udel.edu/pub/midi/software
ftp://nic.funet.fi/pub/msdos/sound
ftp://ux1.cso.uiuc.edu/amiga/mirror/mods
ftp://ftp.brad.ac.uk/misc/mods
ftp://uni-kl.de/pub/amiga/mods
ftp://gdr.bath.ac.uk/msdos/music
ftp://media-lab.media.mit.edu/music/midi
ftp://sunsite.unc.edu/pub/multimedia/chinese-music
ftp://nic.funet.fi/pub/culture/music/middle-eastem,
ftp://nic.funet.fi/pub/culture/music/samples
ftp://snake.mcs.kent.edu//pub/SB-Adlib

WHAT NOW?

Your Web pages can scream, rattle, jeer, narrate, or yodel. All in all, you have enough tools under your belt to design fully functional hypermedia documents. The next chapter shows you how to design pages that people can interact with. This way, you can speak *with* people, not just at them.

If you're ready to put your pages on the Web as is, check out Part III: Weaving a Web of Your Own; you'll find a list of places where you can strut your hypertextual stuff. You'll also learn how to start your very own Web site.

14

INTERACTIVITY

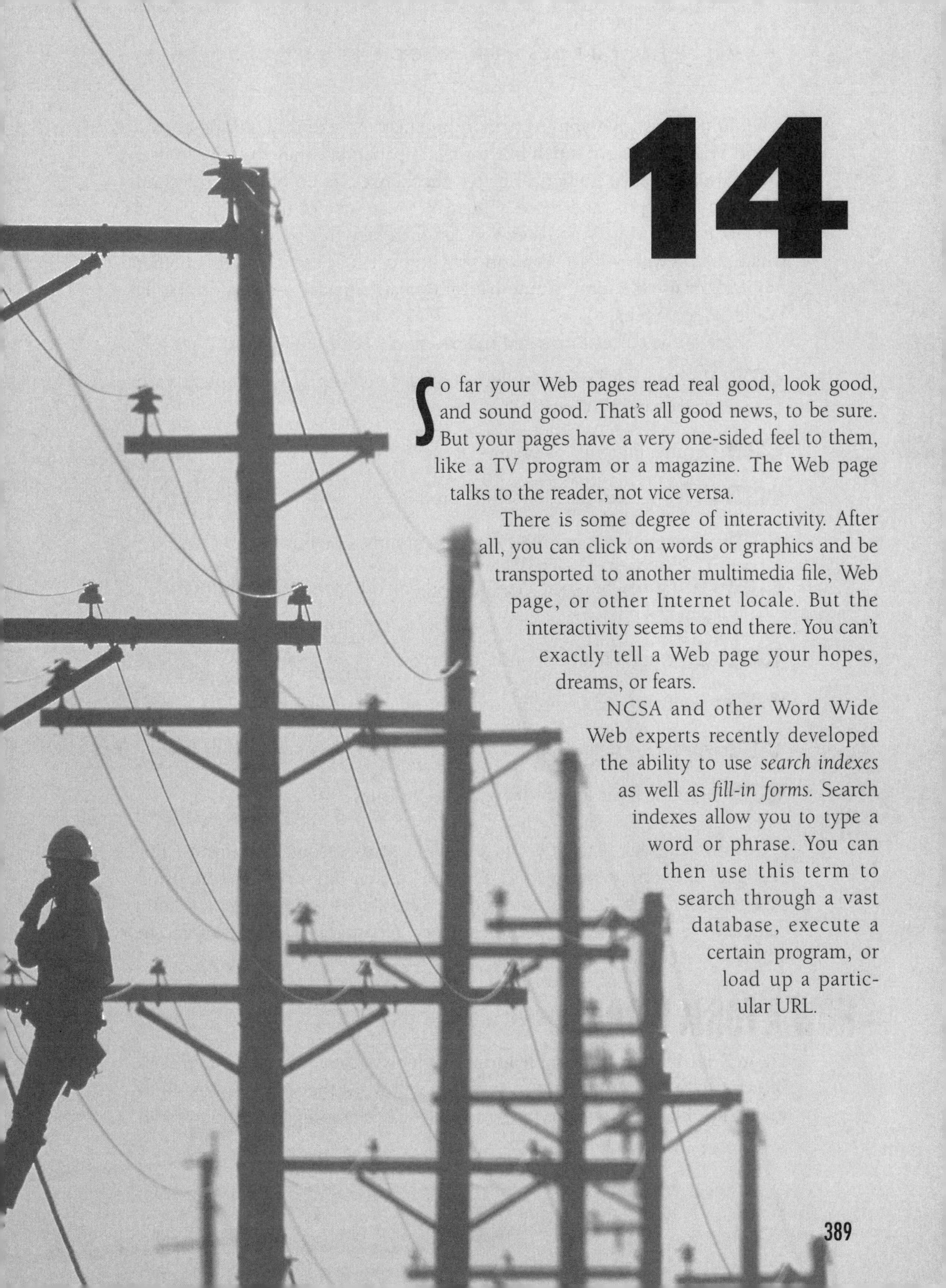

14

So far your Web pages read real good, look good, and sound good. That's all good news, to be sure. But your pages have a very one-sided feel to them, like a TV program or a magazine. The Web page talks to the reader, not vice versa.

There is some degree of interactivity. After all, you can click on words or graphics and be transported to another multimedia file, Web page, or other Internet locale. But the interactivity seems to end there. You can't exactly tell a Web page your hopes, dreams, or fears.

NCSA and other Word Wide Web experts recently developed the ability to use *search indexes* as well as *fill-in forms.* Search indexes allow you to type a word or phrase. You can then use this term to search through a vast database, execute a certain program, or load up a particular URL.

Fill-in forms give you even more interactive flexibility. Forms on the World Wide Web work much like forms on paper, but they're easier to use. There are text fields, numerical fields, checkboxes, radio buttons, selection lists, pop-up menus, and more. Once you create one of these forms, users can talk back to your Web page. You can then take this information and do whatever you wish with it. You can save it, process it, use it to steer another program, or use the form to automatically create a made-to-order, on-the-fly World Wide Web page.

Some of the places forms and indexes have been used include:

- Holding nearly-live bulletin-board conversations, complete with articles and replies
- Conducting polls or surveys of the World Wide Web community
- Ordering, shipping, or selling products
- Signing up to join online services, groups, or clubs
- Placing newly-typed classified ads or other messages on the Web immediately
- Collecting e-mail responses to surveys
- Specifying exact search criteria for online indexes or databases
- Directing Archie searches to find files somewhere on the Internet
- Running basic adventure or strategy games

Forms can get really complex and do some fascinating things. For example, one form allows you to design a custom "lite-brite" picture using tiny colorful circles. Another form on the Web allows you to direct a robotic camera toward a particular piece of scenery. Yet another form allows you to add text to a collaborative hyperfiction novel.

HOW A FORM WORKS

Figure 14-1 illustrates a sample form. The look of the form varies from Web browser to Web browser, but in theory it will work the same way on all of them. You fill out a form, typing in values, checking boxes, clicking radio

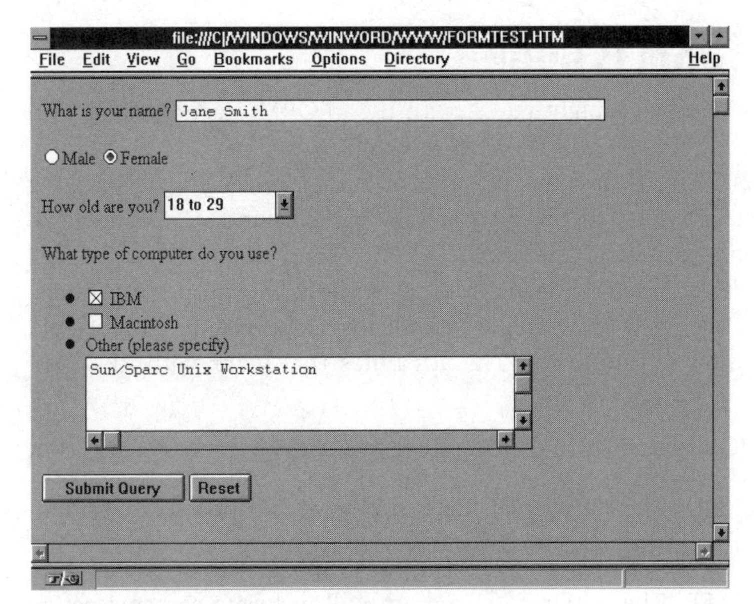

Figure 14-1 A fully functional fill-in form

buttons, or selecting items from menus. You then usually click some sort of Submit or Send button. The form's data is then sent to a specified Web server, converted into a special list of names and values.

The server then passes on these values to a special *CGI script,* which is a program running on the Web server. It can be a shell script, a C program, a batch file, whatever makes sense to the person writing the program. CGI is short for Common Gateway Interface, a standard way of communicating between the Web server and your computer. A detailed description of CGI programming is given in Chapter 15, CGI Scripts.

The script can read the values from the form and analyze, save, or otherwise use them. Writing forms, then, requires two important steps:

- Writing the Web page form itself in HTML. This chapter covers the ins and outs, the ups and downs.

- Writing the CGI script or program to interpret the form entries. The next chapter discusses CGI scripts in detail, with sections on how to extract data from a form, what to do with that data, and how to create customized forms on-the-fly.

LESSON #1: A FORM IS BORN

All forms begin, as you might guess, with the <FORM> tag, and end with the </FORM> tag.

You can have more than one fill-in form in the same Web page, as long as each form is located between its own <FORM> and </FORM> tags. Forms cannot be nested or combined.

The <FORM> element means nothing without the proper attributes. Attributes tell the Web browser the type of form, the way it should look, and exactly what it should do. The attributes that work with <FORM> include:

- HTML ACTION: The URL of the computer that actually processes the form
- HTML METHOD: The http server method that should be used to submit the fill-in form
- HTML ENCTYPE: The option to encode the fill-in form's contents before they're sent to the server

STYLE TIP: Not all browsers clearly delineate forms from the rest of the Web page. You should draw a horizontal rule with <HR> before and after each form, to clearly mark it as a separate entity. This is especially important if you have more than one form on the page.

ACTION

The ACTION attribute lets the Web browser know where to send the form's contents. In most cases, this is a specific cgi-bin script or other program. These server scripts are discussed in more detail in the next chapter.

If your server script is called *formprog*, for example, and is stored in the *cgi-bin* directory of the current *www.smartpants.edu* server, then your ACTION attribute would look like:

```
<FORM ACTION="http://www.smartpants.edu/cgi-bin/formprog">
```

The ACTION attribute is optional. If you omit it, then the current Web page's URL will be used.

METHOD

When a form is filled out and submitted, the data can be sent in one of two methods:

- GET: The form's contents are appended to the URL with a question mark, similar to a search query.
- POST: The form's contents are sent to the server as a message.

The METHOD attribute lets the Web browser know exactly how the data should be sent. The default is GET. Most modern servers, however, can handle the POST method, which is usually more reliable. The GET method often causes errors when it tries to send too much information. To specify the POST method in HTML, you would type:

```
<FORM ACTION="http://www.smartpants.edu/cgi-bin/formprog" METHOD=POST>
```

ENCTYPE

Use the ENCTYPE attribute if you want to encode the data you send. You can only encode the form's contents if your METHOD is set to POST. As of now, there is only one type of supported encoding (application/x-www-form-urlencoded). In most cases, you do not need to use this attribute.

LESSON #2: INPUT FIELDS

Once you let your Web page know it's dealing with a fill-in form, you can start creating fields. Most fields are specified using the <INPUT> element.

The <INPUT> tag is an empty element (there is no </INPUT> tag, though some people insert one for clarity). You can have as many input fields within a given form as you wish.

The most important attribute for any input field is the NAME; a unique name assigned to each field. Input tags can be used to create text fields, checkboxes, radio buttons, submit buttons, or reset buttons. These various fields are specified using the TYPE attribute. Finally, the DISABLED attribute lets you create a field that doesn't actually accept data.

Other possible attributes are used only in specific situations, and are generally optional. These attributes will be discussed later in this chapter, as they become relevant, but here is a quick reference list:

- ID: The field ID number
- CHARSET: The character set
- SIZE: The size of the field

- HTML MIN: The minimum value
- HTML MAX: The maximum value
- HTML MAXLENGTH: The maximum length
- HTML VALUE: The default value for the field
- HTML CHECKED: The default state of a check box or radio button (checked or unchecked)
- HTML ERROR: The error-testing flag
- HTML SRC: The source filename or URL for an image to be used instead of a button
- HTML ALT: The alternative text for text-based browsers
- HTML ALIGN: The placement of the image (can be set to Top, Middle, or Bottom)

TYPE

Each INPUT tag should include the TYPE attribute. You can choose from the following types of fields:

- HTML Text: A plain text entry field
- HTML Password: A text entry field where any letters the user types are printed as asterisks
- HTML Int: An entry field that only accepts integers
- HTML Check box: A box that can either be checked or unchecked
- HTML Radio: A radio button that precedes several items; the user can choose one, and only one, of these items
- HTML Submit: A button to press when the form is completely filled out
- HTML Reset: A button that erases all fields and snaps everything back to their default values

HTML Hidden: A field name and value that is not visible to the user. The "hidden" TYPE is useful for sending parameters in a form that are not input by the form user.

Each of these types is discussed in its own section later in this chapter.

NOTE: When you define a TYPE you can enclose in it quotes, such as TYPE="hidden" or just leave it bare, as in TYPE=hidden. Any browser that supports forms should not care. Use whichever style you're most comfortable with.

Other input types are currently being developed for HTML3. Most Web browsers and servers do not support them yet, but it's useful to know what you may be able to do in the near future. These types include:

HTML Float: A field that can hold a floating point (decimal) number

HTML Date: A field that only accepts a legal date

HTML URL: A field that only accepts a legal URL

HTML Range: A control bar, similar to a thermostat control, allowing a user to pick a number between specified low and high values

HTML Audio: An input field that would allow sound bites

HTML File: The filename of a file stored on the user's computer

HTML Scribble: A blank field that would allow the user to scrawl a message using a lightpen, mouse, or image tablet

HTML Image: An input field that would allow an image

NAME

The NAME attribute is mandatory for every type of input field except for the Submit and Reset buttons. Every question you want to ask a fill-in form user must be designated by a unique name, specified by the NAME attribute. This name should ideally describe the field. For example, if you're creating a field for your readers to type their last names, your markup would begin with:

```
<INPUT NAME="lastname">
```

A field's name is not actually displayed to the user. This information is merely sent to the server script where it can be processed.

DISABLED

If you include the DISABLED attribute with any field, it usually appears grayed out. Users cannot type or select a disabled field. The DISABLED attribute is specified in HTML3. You should note, however, that most current browsers do not support disabled input fields.

Disabled fields are useful for complex forms that you distribute to many different people. If a given question isn't applicable to a specific person or situation, you can gray out the field. This way, people will know that the question *exists,* just not for them.

For example, a user may fill out one form only to be returned another form. In the first form, the user might have specified that he isn't married. The second form could then have a disabled field:

```
<P>What is your spouse's name? <INPUT DISABLED NAME="spousename">
```

STYLE TIP: Disabling makes things easier for the Web developer, as well. Instead of going through an HTML document and deleting unused fields, changing the look of your Web page, you can just gray these fields out.

MIN/MAX

Some browsers allow you to specify a minimum and maximum value for integer fields. This way, you can limit the numbers that people can actually submit. Simply specify a MIN and MAX attribute.

For example, if you want people to enter a number between 90 and 100, you could type:

```
<P>Type a number between 90 and 100: <INPUT NAME="number" TYPE=int
MIN=90 MAX=100>
```

LESSON #3: TEXT FIELDS

A text field is a box where a user can type some information. You can get fancy with text fields, specifying values for them to take if the user doesn't enter anything, masking the input with asterisks for added security, or limiting input to a numerical value. Figure 14-2 shows several types of text fields.

Text Field Variations

To specify a *plain text* field, all you have to do is use the <INPUT> element and name the field. You could use the TYPE=text attribute, but it's easier to

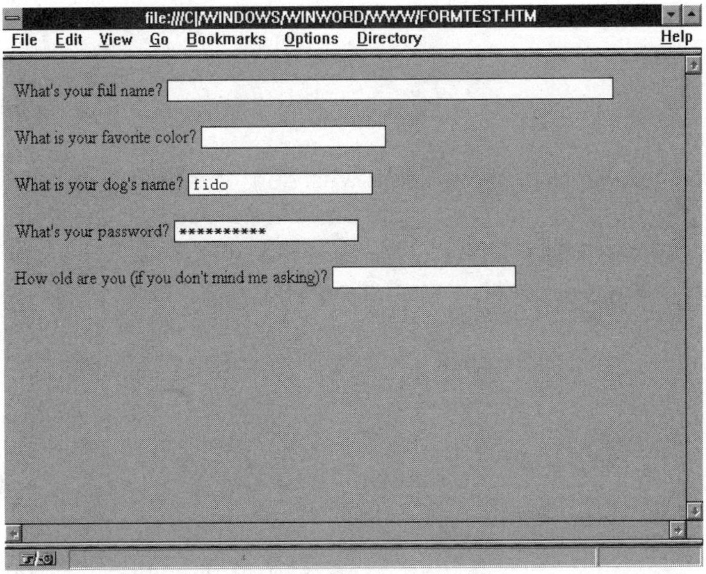

Figure 14-2 Two plain text fields, a text field with a default value, a password field, and an integer field

leave it out; plain text is the default TYPE, so that's what you get unless you specify something else. For example, to create a field that asks for somebody's favorite color, you would type:

```
<P>What is your favorite color? <INPUT NAME="color">
```

When you're dealing with credit card numbers, passwords, or any other secure information, you don't want them left out in the open, so you use *password* fields. As a user types in this kind of field, asterisks hide the values. This way, if somebody is peeping over the typist's shoulders, the intruder won't be able to tell what was just typed. You create a password field by adding TYPE=password to the <INPUT> element. So, to create a field that asks a person for a password, you would type something similar to:

```
<P>What's your password? <INPUT NAME="password" TYPE=password>
```

If you want to make sure you don't get alphabet soup, you can use the last type of "text" field: the *integer* field. This field only accepts integers (whole numbers, negative or positive). To create an integer field, you use TYPE=int in the <INPUT> element. A typical integer field might look like:

```
<P>How old are you (if you don't mind me asking)? <INPUT NAME="age"
TYPE=int>
```

VALUE

The VALUE attribute lets you assign a default value to a text, password, or integer field. When the form first appears, or when the form is Reset, this value is already written in the input box.

You can also use values to show a user what sort of information he or she needs to type. For example, when you ask for the name of the user's dog, you can include a common name as the default value:

```
<P>What is your dog's name? <INPUT NAME="dogname" VALUE="Fido">
```

SIZE

You can designate how long the input box should be by using the SIZE attribute. The default size is 20 characters. If you want to create an extra-big text entry field, you could type something similar to:

```
<P>What's your full name? <INPUT NAME="name" SIZE=50>
```

If you want your text entry field to be more than one line long, you should use a textarea, which is discussed later in this chapter.

MAXLENGTH

No matter how big your input box is, a user can usually continue typing as much text as he or she wants. The text scrolls within the box. If you want to limit the length of the input, specify this limit with the MAXLENGTH attribute. If a user tries typing beyond your MAXLENGTH, the browser will usually beep or display some sort of error message.

For instance, to limit a number to three digits, you could type:

```
<P>Enter your age: <INPUT NAME="age" TYPE=int SIZE=4 MAXLENGTH=3>
```

STYLE TIP: Since scrolling text is often difficult to read, it's a good idea to set MAXLENGTH less than the SIZE of a field.

LESSON #4: CHECKBOXES OR RADIO BUTTONS

Checkboxes or radio buttons can be used to quickly express a lot of information. Figure 14-3 illustrates several checkboxes and radio buttons.

VALUE

Each radio button should have its own value, as expressed with the VALUE attribute. If the button is selected, this value is then sent to the Web server along with the radio button's NAME.

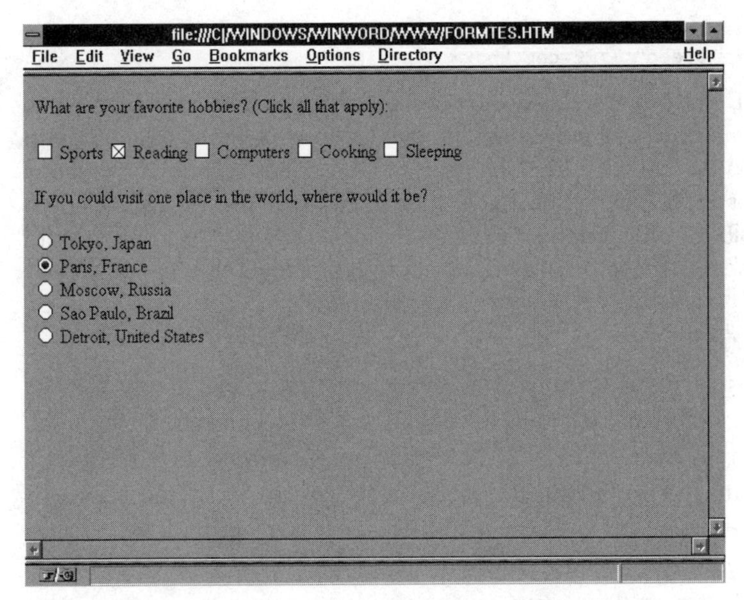

Figure 14-3 A selection of checkboxes and radio buttons

If you want, you can specify a VALUE for each checkbox as well. Checkboxes have two default values (on or off), but you can define other values for them if you wish. Each checkbox must have a NAME. If a checkbox is selected, this name is sent to the Web server along with any given value; if no value was specified, then the word "on" is simply sent. If a box is unselected, then nothing at all is sent to the server. If you desire, you can give several checkboxes the same NAME and different VALUEs. A group of radio buttons should *always* have the same NAME and different VALUEs.

In any case, the VALUE is usually a descriptive word or short phrase. When you create your cgi-script, you will need to refer to this value. Use something obvious.

Checkboxes

A checkbox usually precedes any item or value that is either true or false. For example, you can list several hobbies and allow users to check any hobby they're interested in. If you wanted the hobbies to be listed on the same line, the markup to do this would be:

```
What are your favorite hobbies? (Click all that apply):<P>
  <INPUT NAME="sport" TYPE=checkbox> Sports
  <INPUT NAME="read" TYPE=checkbox> Reading
  <INPUT NAME="computer" TYPE=checkbox> Computers
```

Continued on next page

Continued from previous page

```
  <INPUT NAME="cook" TYPE=checkbox> Cooking
  <INPUT NAME="sleep" TYPE=checkbox> Sleeping<P>
```

STYLE TIP: Don't put too many checkboxes or radio buttons on the same line, since some browsers may scroll the text to the next line. You may get a checkbox on a different line from the label that describes it. If you have many checkboxes or radio buttons, or if your labels are long, you should include a line break <BR> or paragraph <P> after each item. You may also want to list a bunch of checkboxes in a bulleted, numbered, or menu list.

Radio Buttons

Radio buttons are used to select between several exclusive items, like the tuning buttons on your car radio. Each item in a group preceded by a radio button should have the same NAME attribute and its own VALUE attribute.

You should use radio buttons for any list where only one choice is allowed. For example, if you want a user to select one option from a list of hot tourist sites, you could use the markup:

```
If you could visit one place in the world, where would it be?<P>
  <INPUT NAME="place" TYPE=radio VALUE="japan"> Tokyo, Japan<BR>
  <INPUT NAME="place" TYPE=radio VALUE="paris"> Paris, France<BR>
  <INPUT NAME="place" TYPE=radio VALUE="moscow"> Moscow, Russia<BR>
  <INPUT NAME="place" TYPE=radio VALUE="saopaulo"> Sao Paulo,
Brazil<BR>
  <INPUT NAME="place" TYPE=radio VALUE="detroit"> Detroit, United
States<BR>
```

You can have as many groups of radio buttons on a form as you wish. For example, the following markup is perfectly legal:

```
Sex: <INPUT NAME="sex" TYPE=radio VALE="male"> Male <INPUT NAME="sex"
TYPE=radio VALE="female"> Female<P>
What amount of schooling have you had:<P>
<INPUT NAME="degree" TYPE=radio VALE="hs"> High School<BR>
<INPUT NAME="degree" TYPE=radio VALE="bs"> College<BR>
<INPUT NAME="degree" TYPE=radio VALE="ma"> Graduate School
(Masters)<BR>
<INPUT NAME="degree" TYPE=radio VALE="phd"> Graduate School
(Doctorate)<BR>
```

Prechecked

The CHECKED attribute allows you to set the default value for any checkbox or radio button. If you want to check any checkbox or select any given radio button, just include the CHECKED attribute:

```
<INPUT NAME="computer" TYPE=checkbox CHECKED> Computers
```

STYLE TIP: You shouldn't use the CHECKED attribute for more than one radio button within a given NAME group.

LESSON #5: THE RESET AND SUBMIT BUTTONS

No form is complete without a Reset button and a Submit button. The Reset button erases any values already filled in and returns all checkboxes, radio buttons, menus, or textareas to their default values. The Submit button gathers up all the data in the form and sends it off to the server to be processed.

These two buttons are usually placed at the bottom of a form, as shown in Figure 14-4. The markup to create these buttons is:

```
<INPUT TYPE=submit> <INPUT TYPE=reset><P>
```

STYLE TIP: You can place the Submit and Reset buttons anywhere you wish within a form. In some cases, they might look good next to a text entry field or at the top of a form.

As soon as the user clicks the Submit button, the browser sends off the form's entries. You can include several Submit buttons if you wish, each one performing a different action with the same data. For example, you can have a form that asks the user for a search term. You can then have several Submit buttons for various types of databases or search indexes. Each Submit button should have its own NAME attribute.

Customizing the Label

Different browsers use different labels for these buttons. Where some say "Submit," others use "Send," and many use "Submit Query." The Reset button sometimes says "Reset" and sometimes says "Clear."

HTML If you don't want to take your chances with the user's browser, you can use the VALUE attribute to easily replace the labels of these push buttons with your own text.

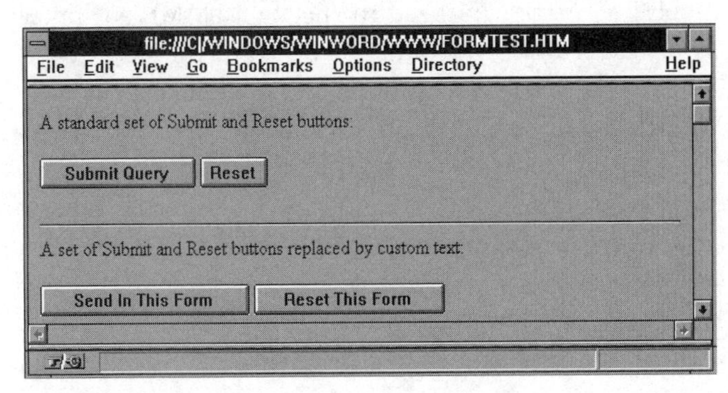

Figure 14-4 The Submit and Reset buttons

For example, if you want your Submit button to read "Send In This Form," just use the markup:

```
<INPUT TYPE=submit VALUE="Send In This Form">
```

Using Icons

The latest specification of HTML+ allows you to use a special icon instead of the browser's default Submit or Clear buttons. Just specify a SRC, ALT, and ALIGN attribute, the way you would for the <IMG> element. You can even use an imagemap, if you want to get really fancy.

Most browsers do not currently allow you to use an icon. Once iconed buttons become more popular, however, you can use markup similar to the following:

```
<INPUT TYPE=submit SRC="submit.gif" ALIGN=middle ALT="[Submit]">
Submit<P>
```

This would allow you to use the picture of a pointing finger, a green GO sign, or any other graphic you wanted. Such Submit buttons would make a form look spiffy, and be easy for the user to understand.

NOTE: Any SRC attributes within the submit INPUT element are usually just ignored if the browser doesn't support HTML3.

LESSON #6: TEXTAREAS

If you want to create a multiline text entry field, you should use the <TEXTAREA> element. The element requires a </TEXTAREA> closing tag.

A textarea can be used as the message box for e-mail or newsgroup articles, for short answers to questions, or for entire addresses. Textarea fields have both vertical and horizontal scroll bars; you can type as much information as you want.

Much like the INPUT element, you need to specify a NAME attribute. You can also specify the DISABLED attribute if you want the field to be grayed out. If you want your textarea to contain any default text, write it between your <TEXTAREA> and </TEXTAREA> elements. You don't need to specify a line break or paragraph, just press ENTER at the end of each line. For example, to create the textarea shown in Figure 14-5, you would type:

```
<TEXTAREA NAME="address" ROWS=5 COLS=50> ENTER
John Smith ENTER
Biology Department ENTER
Smartpants University ENTER
Anytown, AW 12345 ENTER
</TEXTAREA> ENTER
```

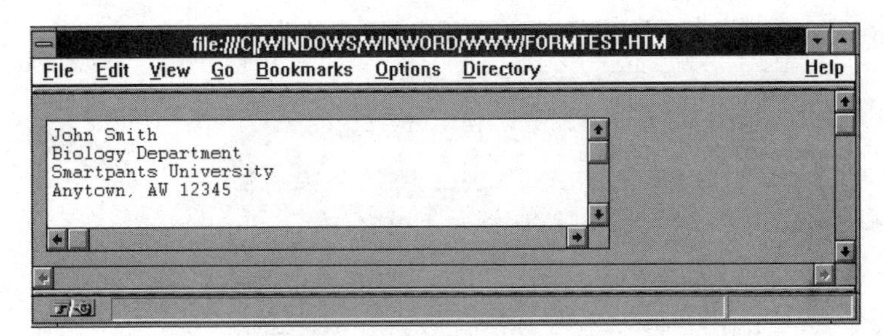

Figure 14-5 A textarea with a default address filled in

Size

By default, a textarea is only 1 line high and 40 characters wide. In most cases, you want to create a custom size for your textarea. Specify the height of your box with the ROWS attribute, and specify the width with the COLS attribute.

For example, to create a huge box that fills much of the screen (20 characters high by 70 characters wide), you would use the markup:

```
Type your message in the following box:<BR>
<TEXTAREA NAME="message" ROWS=20 COLS=70></TEXTAREA>
```

WRAP

Another useful attribute for the TEXTAREA element is WRAP. If you select WRAP, the textarea has no horizontal scroll bar. Whenever the typist gets to the end of the line, the next word automatically wraps around. This HTML+ attribute does not work with some browsers, in which case the TEXTAREA will function as usual.

As an example:

```
<TEXTAREA NAME="message" ROWS=20 COLS=70 WRAP></TEXTAREA>
```

LESSON #7: SELECTION LISTS

The last type of input field you can create is a selection list. A selection list can be an open menu of several items, a pop-up menu, or any other sort of menu list you could hope to design. The look of a selection list depends on the browser. Figure 14-6 shows some sample lists.

You can include as many selection lists as you like. Each selection list is designated by the <SELECT> element and must be closed with the </SELECT> element.

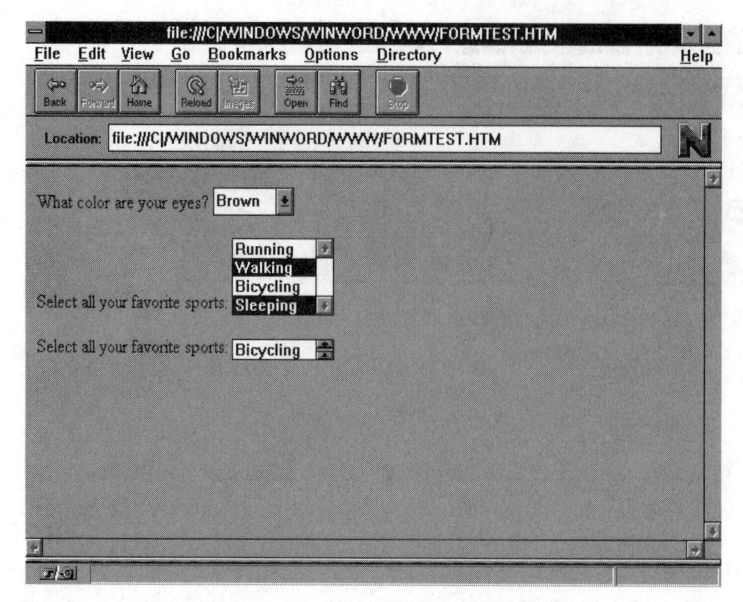

Figure 14-6 A nice selection of selection lists

Your selection list, like any other input type, must have a NAME attribute with a unique identifying name. Each item within a selection list must begin with the <OPTION> element. Although you can leave it out, it usually makes the HTML markup easier to read by closing each option with </OPTION> element.

For example, a basic selection list could look like:

```
What color are your eyes?
<SELECT NAME="color">
  <OPTION>Green</OPTION>
  <OPTION>Brown</OPTION>
  <OPTION>Blue</OPTION>
  <OPTION>Black</OPTION>
</SELECT>
```

SIZE

The size of a selection list can drastically change its look. If the SIZE attribute is omitted, or if the size is set to 1, then the selection list looks like a pop-up menu, as shown at the top of Figure 14-6. Only one item is shown. The user can click on a little arrow to the right of the item to see the full list pop up on the screen. Here's the markup to create a pop up menu:

```
What color are your eyes?
<SELECT NAME="color" SIZE=1>
```

```
  <OPTION>Green</OPTION>
  <OPTION>Brown</OPTION>
  <OPTION>Blue</OPTION>
  <OPTION>Black</OPTION>
</SELECT>
```

If the SIZE is 2 or more, then the selection list appears as a scrollable menu. For example, if your list has 15 options and a size of 5, then only the first 5 options are shown. To see the remaining options, a user could scroll down through the list using the scroll bar. The size of the list, for obvious reasons, should not be larger than the number of options.

STYLE TIP: You can't place selection lists next to each other or next to more than one line of text. If your SIZE matches the number of list elements, then all items will be visible. This is often a good idea for short lists. If a selection list is very long, however, it takes up many rows and leaves a lot of white space on your Web page screen. You can prevent this by making your lists smaller, and having people scroll through them using the scroll bar.

Multiple Selections

Can users select more than one option from the current list? If your list topic has several possible answers, you should use the MULTIPLE attribute. For example, if you have a list of several hobbies, you may want to allow a user to select several of them:

```
Select all your favorite sports:
<SELECT NAME="sports" SIZE=4 MULTIPLE>
  <OPTION>Running</OPTION>
  <OPTION>Walking</OPTION>
  <OPTION>Bicycling</OPTION>
  <OPTION>Sleeping</OPTION>
</SELECT>
```

STYLE TIP: If you use the MULTIPLE attribute, your selection list cannot be a pop-up menu. It may, however, be scrollable.

Options Attributes

Each <OPTION> element can have its own attributes, including SELECTED and DISABLED.

SELECTED

If you'd like an option to be selected by default, use the SELECTED attribute. If your selection list is MULTIPLE, then you can select several options as defaults.

For example, in the following markup the "Running" and "Sleeping" options will be selected:

```
Select all your favorite sports:
<SELECT NAME="sports" SIZE=4 MULTIPLE>
  <OPTION SELECTED>Running</OPTION>
  <OPTION>Walking</OPTION>
  <OPTION>Bicycling</OPTION>
  <OPTION SELECTED>Sleeping</OPTION>
</SELECT>
```

DISABLED

As with any other input field, you can disable any option in a selection list by using the DISABLED attribute. Any disabled attribute appears grayed-out and cannot be selected. For example:

```
<OPTION DISABLED>Bicycling</OPTION>
```

STYLE TIP: Many browsers do not understand the DISABLED attribute, so do not rely on disabled options; use these options only for cosmetic reasons, to help suggest which options to avoid.

SHAPE

The latest specification of HTML3 allows you to specify the SHAPE attribute for each option. This would allow you to design the graphical look of the option. Currently, however, there are no browsers that understand this attribute.

LESSON #8: PUTTING IT ALL TOGETHER

To actually create your form, first plan it out on paper. A form can have any text style, headings, or paragraph styles. Don't neglect to use plenty of <BR> line breaks and <P> paragraphs to provide enough spacing between each input field or each caption and the next one. If your form is long, break it up into sections with horizontal lines. Use bulleted or menu lists (perhaps without the <LI> bullet element) for a series of checkboxes or radio buttons. All in all, try to make your form as intuitive as possible to fill out.

STYLE TIP: When you have a list of options, you can present them either as a bunch of checkboxes or as a multiple selection list. In most cases, you should make options that relate to each other into a list and arrange options that are independent from each other as check boxes.

A Basic Form

The form shown at the beginning of the chapter, in Figure 14-1, was created using the following HTML code:

```
<FORM ACTION="http://www.smartpants.edu/cgi-bin/survey">
   <P>What is your name? <INPUT NAME="name" SIZE="48">
   <P><INPUT NAME="sex"TYPE=radio VALUE="male">Male
   <INPUT NAME="sex" TYPE=radio VALUE="female">Female
   <P>How old are you?
   <SELECT NAME="age">
      <OPTION>Less than 18</OPTION>
      <OPTION>18 to 29</OPTION>
      <OPTION>29 to 39</OPTION>
      <OPTION>More than 40</OPTION>
   </SELECT>
   <P>What type of computer do you use?
   <UL>
       <LI><INPUT NAME="ibm" TYPE=checkbox VALUE="ibm"> IBM
       <LI><INPUT NAME="mac" TYPE=checkbox VALUE="mac"> Macintosh
       <LI><INPUT NAME="other" TYPE=checkbox VALUE="other"> Other
(please specify)<BR>
         <TEXTAREA NAME="others" COLS=48 ROWS=4></TEXTAREA>
   </UL>
    <P><INPUT TYPE=submit> <INPUT TYPE=reset>
</FORM>
```

A Sample Message Form

The easiest and quickest way to start understanding and producing your own forms is to take a look at other forms that contain features that you are interested in using. Once you've looked at the code, you can start cutting, pasting, refining, personalizing...doing whatever you need to make the form do what you want.

The following HTML code describes a page that contains a single form. This form contains most of the major form features, including other common HTML statements. See Figure 14-7 to get an idea of what this form would look like to a client using the X-Windows version of Mosaic. The markup for the entire page is as follows:

```
<HTML>
<HEAD>
 <TITLE>Comment Form</TITLE>
</HEAD>
<BODY>
<H1>Troy's feedback page</H1>
<IMG SRC="/shaggy.a/downing/public-html/face.xbm"><BR>
Let me know what's on your mind....<BR>
```

Continued on next page

Continued from previous page

```
<HR>
<FORM ACTION="http://found.cs.nyu.edu/cgi-bin/testtbd" METHOD="POST">
Who's calling?<BR>
<PRE>
First Name <INPUT TYPE="text" NAME="first" SIZE=10>
Last<INPUT TYPE="text" NAME="second" size=20>
E-Mail <INPUT TYPE "text" NAME="email" VALUE="yourname@youradd.edu"
SIZE=25>
<INPUT TYPE="checkbox" VALUE="list">Check here to be added to my
mailing list.
</PRE>
<HR>
Select message type:
<SELECT NAME="urgency">
   <OPTION>Urgent!
   <OPTION>Important
   <OPTION>No Hurry
   <OPTION>FYI
</SELECT>
<BR>
   <INPUT TYPE="radio" NAME="Menu" CHECKED VALUE="complain">Complaint
   <INPUT TYPE="radio" NAME="Menu" VALUE="joke">Joke
   <INPUT TYPE="radio" NAME="Menu" VALUE="quote">Quote
   <INPUT TYPE="radio" NAME="Menu" VALUE="greet">Greeting
   <INPUT TYPE="radio" NAME="Menu" VALUE="offer">Offer
   <INPUT TYPE="radio" NAME="Menu" VALUE="suggest">Suggestion
<BR>
<HR>
Tell me about it...<BR>
<TEXTAREA NAME="textbox" ROWS="3" COLS="60">Type your message here...
</TEXTAREA>
<BR>
<INPUT TYPE="submit" VALUE="Submit"><INPUT TYPE="reset" VALIE="Clear
Entries">
</FORM>
<BODY>
</HTML>
```

The CGI script to handle this form is included in the next chapter.

LESSON #9: INCLUDING HIDDEN TEXT

At times, it is important to include variable information without having it appear as part of the form. This information can be a user ID number, a time stamp, or whatever makes sense in each particular case. These cases will be much more apparent after you read the next chapter. To send form data that a user does not explicitly type or select, you can use a hidden field.

NOTE: Users can see a hidden field by viewing the source for the Web page, but the field won't show up in the normal Web browser.

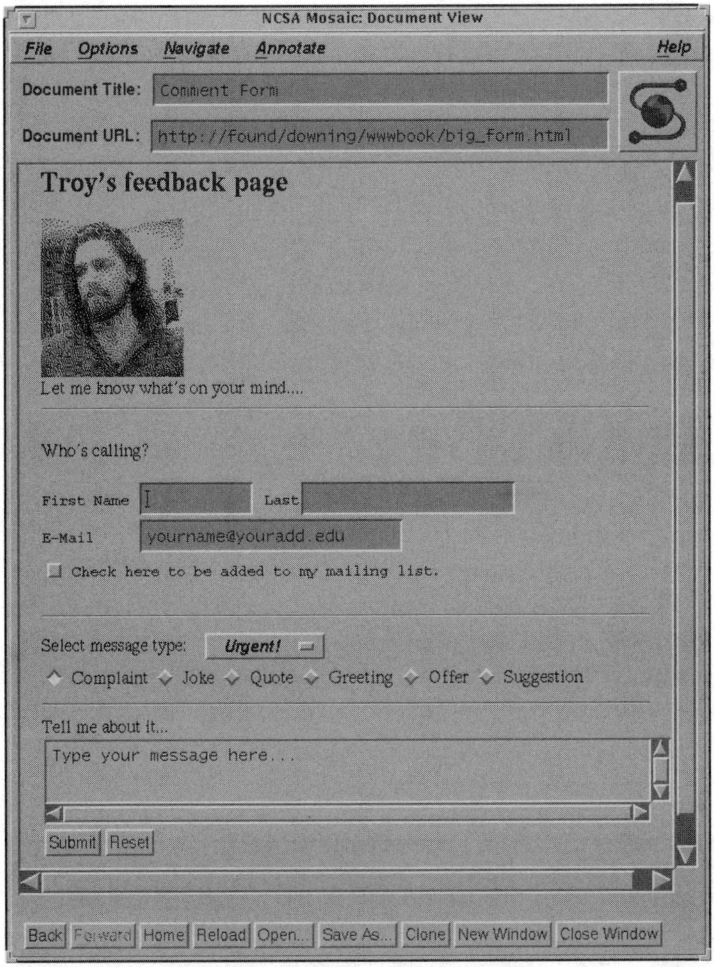

Figure 14-7 A groovy message form

Hidden fields are particularly useful if you want to track a user who is using multiple forms without asking the user to input a name or ID at each level or step of the form. Hidden fields can be created using the INPUT element:

```
<INPUT TYPE=hidden NAME="invisible" VALUE="samplevalue">
```

When a user submits this form, the value pair "invisible=samplevalue" is automatically included. Hidden fields are most useful when you have their values dynamically assigned and included in your forms. Chapter 15, CGI Scripts, will explain how to do this.

Sometimes it is useful to be able to include static hidden variables as well. One example would be a time or version stamp. If you wanted to keep track of which version of a form a user was accessing your server with, you could include something like:

```
<INPUT TYPE=hidden NAME="version" VALUE="6.1">
```

Now, every time you edited the HTML file that contained this form, you could increment the value "6.1" to the new version number. The CGI script side of your form could evaluate this version number and make a decision based on the version number such as sending a message like

```
"Version number not valid, please reload form."
```

LESSON #10: SEARCH INDEXES

Let's go back in time a bit. Before fill-in forms were created, there was the search index. A search index is basically similar to a form text input field. The user simply types in a word or phrase and presses ENTER. This search term can then be used to look up information in an index file. Index files themselves are discussed in the next chapter.

If your collection of Web pages is huge, a good index is essential. Figure 14-8 shows a typical index. Some browsers, such as Mosaic version 1, will display the search index box at the bottom of the screen. Other browsers display the index field anywhere within the Web page.

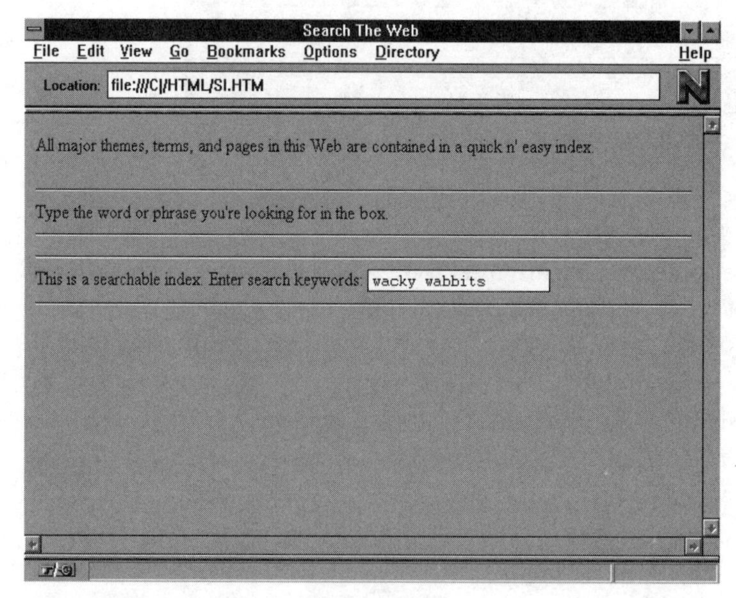

Figure 14-8 A simple search index

ISINDEX

To prompt the user for a search term, use the <ISINDEX> element.

The index query is usually placed in the <HEAD> section of a document, though the latest specification of HTML+ allows you to place an index request anywhere in the Web page.

HREF

You can use <ISINDEX> by itself, in which case the current Web page must be a search index of some sort; in other words, your Web page is actually a CGI program. You can learn how to create these hybrid cgi-script/Web pages in the next chapter. In most cases, however, your index should point to the script designated by the HREF attribute:

```
<ISINDEX HREF="http://smartpants.edu/cgi-bin/vastindex">
```

PROMPT

By default, the message "This is a searchable index. Enter search keywords:" precedes an index field. You can use the PROMPT attribute to change this label. For example, to ask for a book title, you could use a tag similar to:

```
<ISINDEX PROMPT="Enter a book title here:">
```

Currently, only Netscape understands this attribute, though it has been defined for HTML3.

Book-Like Index Documents

The latest specification of HTML+ allows you to create text-only index documents, similar to the index in a book. An HTML+ index document would list every topic or keyword and include a hyperlink to places where that word appears. These indexes could then be viewed directly, or can be searched. Unfortunately, no current browsers support these indexes.

Whenever you wanted to create an indexed term, you could just use the INDEX attribute, as part of a heading, paragraph, blockquote, or other type of text block:

```
<h3 id="a99" index="Horses/Ponies">Ponies</h3>
```

These indexes could then be used to automatically create an index file with segments like this:

```
Horses
   caring for
   feeding
   history of
```

Continued on next page

Continued from previous page

```
   ponies
   racehorses
Iguanas
```

Users could then view this index directly, or search it using <ISINDEX>. Once indexes like these become widely accepted, it will be easy to organize vast amounts of text or even sounds, video, and graphics.

LESSON #11: TESTING IT OUT

You can quickly and easily test out your HTML fill-in forms using one of NCSA's public server scripts. If you want to use the POST method, use the following format for your form:

```
<FORM METHOD="POST" ACTION="http://hoohoo.ncsa.uiuc.edu/htbin-
post/post-query">
```

If you want to try out the GET method, use a different server script:

```
<FORM METHOD="GET" ACTION="http://hoohoo.ncsa.uiuc.edu/htbin/query">
```

This gets you a returned Web page that shows exactly what you submitted, and lists the names and values of each of your input fields. A sample page for the message form shown in Figure 14-7 might look like:

```
Query Results
You submitted the following name/value pairs:
· first = David
· second = Fox
· email = dfox@graphics.cs.nyu.edu
· urgency = Important
· Menu = joke
· textbox = Why did the chicken cross the road? Because there was an
earthquake!
```

LESSON #12: WHAT THE DATA LOOKS LIKE

When you submit a form or an index query, every field's name and value is sent to the specified ACTION server or HREF. The data format differs depending on whether you use the GET or POST method.

With search indexes, the browser sends the actual text string the user typed. With fill-in forms, the values that go to the Web server correspond to the input fields. Each input field sends a different type of information:

- HTML Text, integer, and password fields: The name of the field, along with whatever the user typed. (If the user typed nothing, then a blank string follows the field name.)

- HTML Checkboxes: The name and value of any checked box. (If the box has no individual value, the browser sends the default value—"on". It sends nothing at all if the box isn't checked.)
- HTML Radio buttons: The name of the radio button group, along with the selected value. (It sends nothing if none of the buttons are checked.)
- HTML Textareas: The name of the textarea along with any typed text.
- HTML Selection lists: The name of the selection list along with the value (text) of the selected option. (If the user selects more than one option, an additional name/value pair is sent for each choice.)

In general, the NAME of each entry in the form is paired with the VALUE of that entry, along with an equals sign (=). Each of these entries is then separated by the ampersand (&). For example, a form with two entries would send data similar to the following:

```
name=value&name=value
```

If the value of a field contains unusual characters such as the ampersand (&) or the equals sign (=), these characters are *escaped*. Escaped characters are represented by a percent sign (%) followed by the hexadecimal (base 16) ASCII number for that character.

In addition to these special characters, spaces embedded in text fields are changed to the plus sign (+). This way, your stream contains no spaces or other strange gaps.

Search Indexes

The value the user types in the search index is known as the *query*. This query is sent tacked on the URL specified with the HREF attribute. For example, you can create an index as follows:

```
<ISINDEX HREF="http://www.smartpants.edu/cgi-bin/index">
```

A user may then type a query, such as "jack daniels." The browser creates the following URL and jumps to it:

```
http://www.smartpants.edu/cgi-bin/index?jack+daniels
```

The GET Method

Much like an index query, The GET method sends all your form's data as part of the URL, which takes the form:

```
action?name=value&name=value&name=value
```

For example, if your ACTION server is *http://www.smartpants.edu/cgi-bin/survey* and your form asks for a name and phone number, the URL might look like this:

```
http://www.smartpants.edu/cgibin/survey?lname=smith&fname=john&phone=1
23-555-1234
```

Since different operating systems have different limits for the size of the URL, the URL is often truncated if you send a lot of data.

The Web server on the receiving side assigns the string passed by the form to an environmental variable called QUERY_STRING. The CGI script processing the form can then access the data by reading the contents of QUERY_STRING and parsing it into its component parts. See the next chapter for details.

POST

The POST method sends a special data stream to the server (specified by the ACTION attribute). The POST stream looks similar to the GET query. A typical POST may take a form similar to the following:

```
lname=smith&fname=john&phone=123-555-1234
```

The POST method allows you to send an arbitrary amount of data. There is no need to worry about it being too long and getting cut off. The string goes to the receiving URL as a standard *input stream* to the specified CGI script. The length of the string is stored in an environment variable called CONTENT_LENGTH, so the CGI script can access the names and values by reading the number of characters stored in CONTENT_LENGTH from the standard input stream. The CGI program can then break up the string into its component parts and process the data. The next chapter gets into all this nitty-gritty.

THE FUTURE OF FORMS

Right now, forms are somewhat limited. It would be nice to have calculated fields, so you could turn a Web page into an instant spreadsheet. The values of some fields should also be able to affect the defaults or status of others. If you wanted to have the server control these calculated fields, forms would take way too long to process. As a result, people are developing a special *application program interface (API)* to allow live fill-in form processing to work hand-in-hand with all Web browsers.

Date fields, file fields, and URL fields would also be useful things to have. Eventually, fields could be created that allow you to pop in graphics, say something into a microphone, or scribble something using a pen. This would allow you to send as well as retrieve multimedia using the Web. All in all, a Web page could become a full-fledged piece of software in its own right.

Such developments are underway, and will probably arrive sooner than you can click Submit.

WHAT NOW?

The next essential step in form creation is to write a CGI script or other program to handle your form data and do something useful with it. All sorts of examples, suggestions, and ideas can be found in the next chapter.

If you haven't yet installed a Web server, then all this information about dealing with forms can seem pretty useless. Read up about Web servers in Chapter 21, Starting Your Own Web Site.

15

CGI SCRIPTS

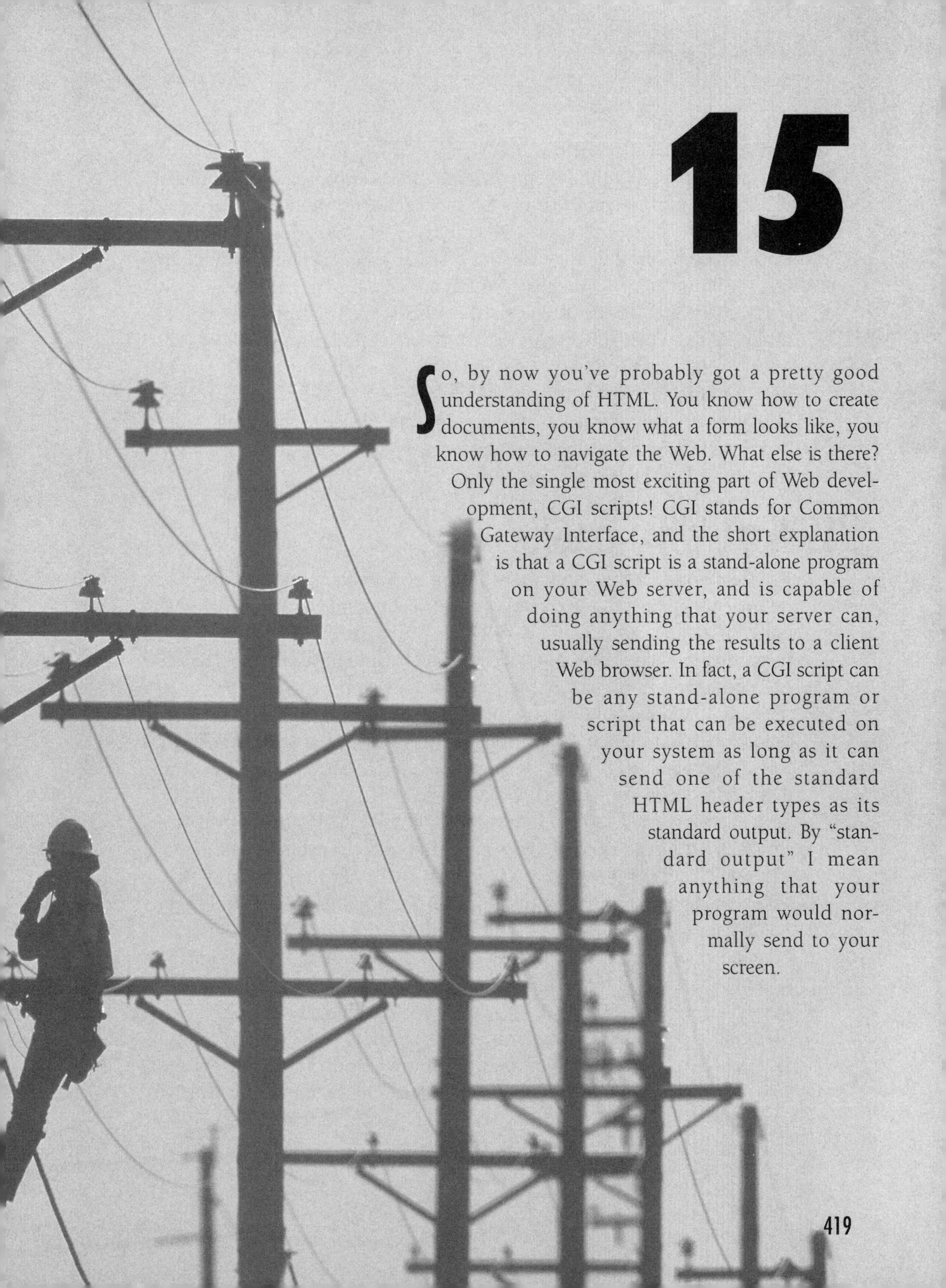

15

So, by now you've probably got a pretty good understanding of HTML. You know how to create documents, you know what a form looks like, you know how to navigate the Web. What else is there? Only the single most exciting part of Web development, CGI scripts! CGI stands for Common Gateway Interface, and the short explanation is that a CGI script is a stand-alone program on your Web server, and is capable of doing anything that your server can, usually sending the results to a client Web browser. In fact, a CGI script can be any stand-alone program or script that can be executed on your system as long as it can send one of the standard HTML header types as its standard output. By "standard output" I mean anything that your program would normally send to your screen.

Sounds pretty exciting, doesn't it? In this chapter, you'll get a description of what a CGI script can do, what it can use as its input, and how it can format its output, and then you'll see some sample scripts that you can edit to suit your needs or just use as is. For the most part, the samples will be written in C and will assume that your server is running on a standard Unix platform, but if you are running a server on a Macintosh or Windows PC, you'll find a few tidbits that you can use as well. The main reason Unix is given preferential treatment as the Web server platform of choice is simple: Unix HTTP servers are the most common and most robust HTTP servers available as of this writing. That's not to say that you can't get satisfactory results from a Macintosh or Windows server; in fact there are many intriguing Web sites that are running on both of these platforms. It's just that the Unix side works better at this point in the history of the Web. Well, enough on that, let's get started.

LESSON #1: WHAT IS CGI?

The Common Gateway Interface—or CGI—is a method that lets you access external programs on a Web server and usually send the results to a Web browser. (There are situations in which you want the script to do some processing on your server, but not send data back to the client.)

These programs can be any executable code, script, or program supported by the operating system that runs your server. The CGI code to call an external program can be a shell script, or a batch file, an AppleScript file, a C program, a PASCAL program, compiled BASIC ... literally anything that will run as a stand-alone executable Script on your system. Many CGI developers use shell scripts; others prefer Perl and C. Choose what works best for you! Just to make things simple, this chapter refers to all CGI code files as CGI scripts—or simply as "scripts"—whether they are written in a scripting language or in a compiled or interpreted programming language.

A server executes a CGI script based on a user request from a Web browser, as diagrammed in Figure 15-1. This request can be as simple as selecting a hyperlink that points to an executable item, or it can be a search request using the <ISINDEX> tag, or it can involve clicking the Submit button from within an HTML form. The parameters the script has available to it depend on how it was accessed. There are also many parameters available to scripts via environment variables that are set by the server. You'll get details on all of this in the Writing Your Own Scripts section.

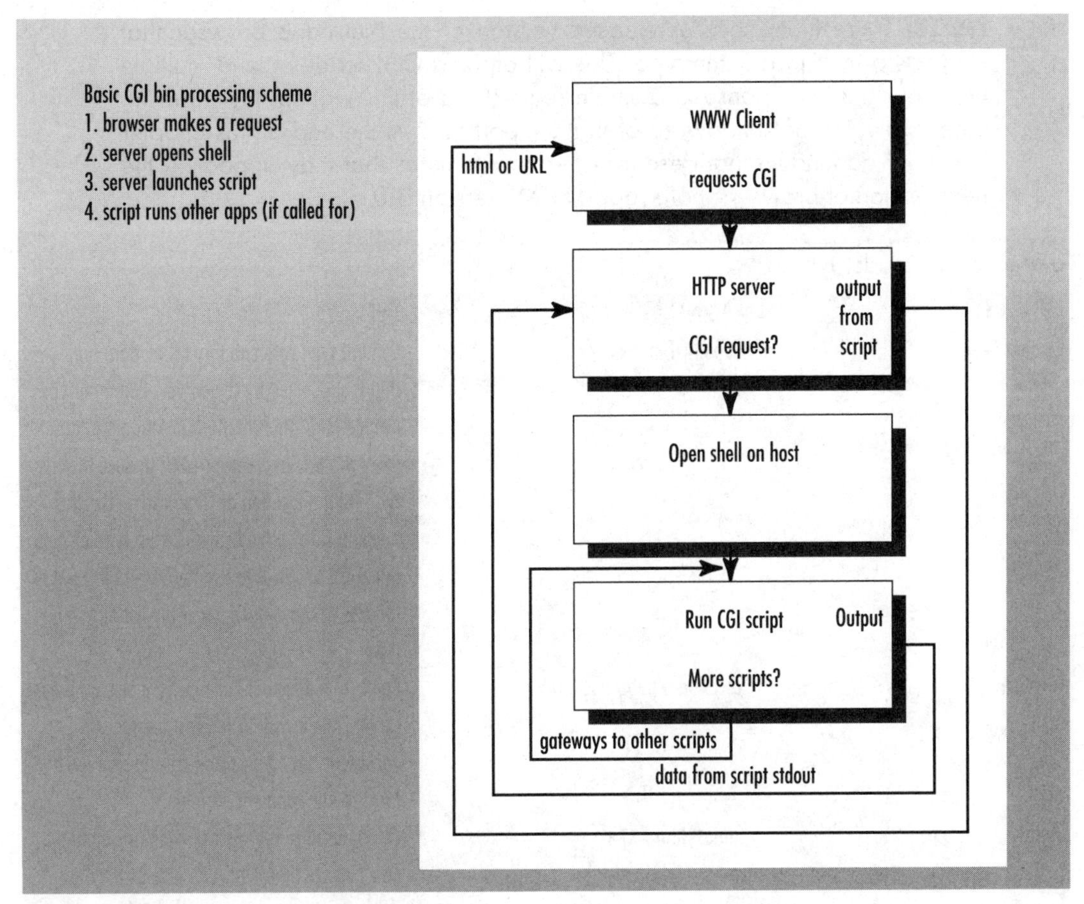

Figure 15-1 Diagram of a CGI session

A CGI script must produce an output header even if no data is to be forwarded to the Web browser. The HTML header must be the first thing that a script sends as output and must be followed by a blank line or carriage return. The header tells the server what kind of data to expect, if any; the server in turn tells the client that invoked the script what to expect. Currently, there are three types of headers. These headers are mutually exclusive—that is, you can't have more than one header for any one request. (See note for exception.) Valid header types are Content-Type, Location, and Status (see Table 15-1).

 **NOTE:** There is a recently released version of the Netscape browser that supports a multi-part mime type. This will allow a CGI script to send multiple types of data in response to a single request. As of this writing, there are no other browsers that I'm aware of that support this. At the end of this chapter is a brief addendum that describes the new features that may appear in the next version of browsers that support HTML version 3.0.

Table 15-1 Header types

Header Type	Format	Description
Content-Type	Content-Type: xxx/xxx	Content type refers to any MIME data type that is supported by the server. Common types include text/html, text/plain, and data/gif. Since the browser/server can't deduce the file type from a location or filename suffix, this heading will tell the browser what type of data to expect and how to use it. (See Table 15-4 at the end of the chapter for a full list of MIME types.)
Location	Location: /path/doc	Points to a document somewhere else on the server. Allows you to redirect requests to documents based on some criteria sent via a form or environment variable.
Status	Status: nnn XXXX	Can be used to run a script, without sending a new page to the client. Can also be used to send an error message or other information to the client.

What Can I Do with a CGI Script?

A CGI script can do anything allowed on the host system as long as it sends one of the three header types listed in Table 15-1. It can access other programs, open files, read from files, create graphics, dial your modem, call your mother, do database searches, send e-mail, you name it. The only rules are:

HTML The script has to be in a place designated by the server for CGI scripts, or it has to have a special suffix that the server is configured to recognize as a legal CGI script. Most systems store CGI scripts in a directory relative to the root directory of the HTTP server called cgi-bin, which is set up so that only certain trusted users can write to it. This avoids the obvious security problems of allowing anonymous remote users to execute anything they want on your system.

- The script can take its parameters from the standard input (by standard input, I mean what would normally be typed in at the keyboard), the environment variables, or both. (It is not necessary to take user input at all, the script can simply execute without needing any more information.)
- The script must output one of the three standard header types as a normal text string.
- The script must be runable by the user that the server is configured to run as. (On a Unix machine every directory, file, and program has a set of permissions attached to it. These permissions specify who can read, change, or execute different files. These permissions are divided into three groups, owner, group, and world. Also, every process must run as some user. There is a special user called "nobody" that is the default user for most Web servers. You must make sure that the user "nobody", or the user that your server is configured to run as, has permission to execute your scripts and read/write to any files that the script may use.)

CGI scripts are used for doing all of the "cool" stuff on the Net. There are sites that have interactive robots you can control with a Web browser, sites that allow you to control cameras and take pictures of remote places, sites that create graphic images on-the-fly, serve maps, open X clients on your machine and send you live video feeds, access huge databases, order submarine sandwiches, and ask questions of the Web's own version of the Magic Eightball, as shown in Figure 15-2. All of this is possible through the use of CGI scripts.

LESSON #2: THE STANDARD CGI SCRIPTS

As you read this, CGI scripts are coming to life all over the world. Some are special purpose, some are useful utilities, some are interesting, and some are just plain silly. Among these scripts, there are a handful that have become standard at most Web sites. If you download NCSA's HTTPD or copy it from the CD-ROM that came with this book, you'll find that it includes two CGI directories, cgi-bin and cgi-src. The cgi-bin directory contains many

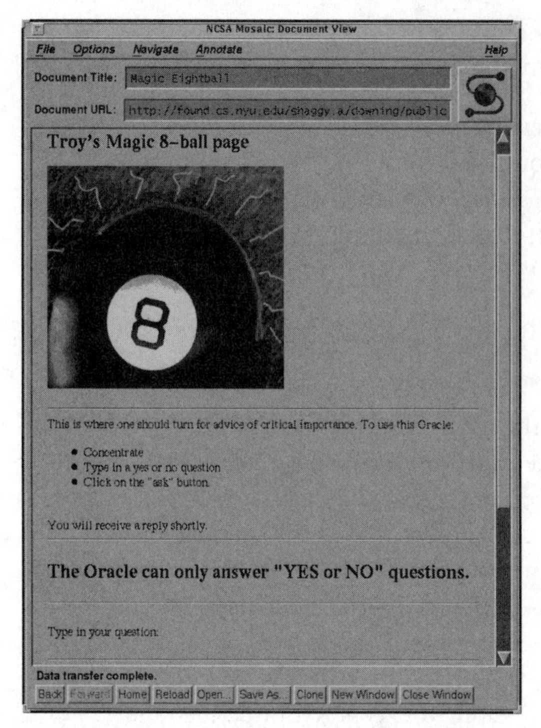

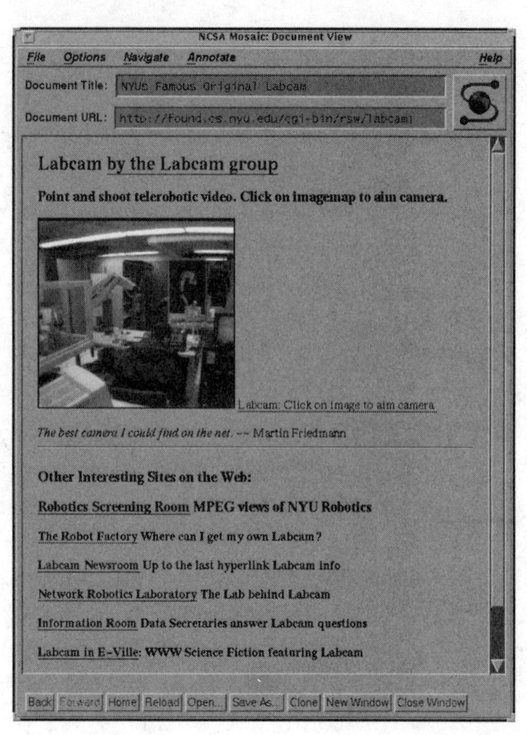

Figure 15-2 Two nifty services, courtesy of CGI scripts

demos and useful CGI scripts, and cgi-src contains the source code for these scripts so you can customize them—or just learn from them.

The CD-ROM scripts include C programs, shell scripts, and Perl scripts that do a few helpful little tasks for you. A few of them are even necessary for your server to have all the utility that you expect of it, like processing image maps. Table 15-2 describes all the scripts in the cgi-bin directory that comes standard with NCSA's HTTPD.

Table 15-2 Standard CGI scripts

Name	Type	Description
archie	shell script	Gateway to an archie server.
calendar	shell script	Gateway to the Unix calendar utility.
date	shell script	Calls the system date and sends it as an HTML doc.
finger	shell script	Gateway to the Unix finger utility.
fortune	shell script	Gateway to the Unix fortune utility.

Name	Type	Description
imagemap	C program	Handles imagemaps in HTML documents, taking the X and Y coordinates from the user, and forwarding a URL based on a map file created by the map developer.
ii	C program	Processes an order form from a submarine sandwich shop, then opens a pipe to a mailer, and faxes the order out of a fax modem. (A useful example, even if you're not selling sandwiches.)
nph-test-cgi	shell script	Echoes back the names and values of the environment variables. (Good for testing forms, or just figuring out what's going on.)
phf*	C program	Creates a fill-in form interface for a CSO ph database. (Great for looking up names/addresses on ph servers.)
post-query*	C program	Echoes the name/value pairs of a form that uses the POST method.
query*	C program	Echoes the name/value pairs of a form that uses the GET method.
test-cgi*	shell script	Echoes the names and contents of the environment variables.
test-cgi.tcl*	tclsh script	Echoes the names and contents of the environment variables.
uptime*	shell script	Gateway to the Unix uptime command. Will print the time that the system has been running.
wais.pl*	perl script	Provides an <ISINDEX> front end for WAIS searches.

Some of these are C programs, some are TCL scripts, and some are Perl scripts, but they all function in the same way. They get executed by the HTTP server, take their parameters (if any) from standard input or environment variables, and output at least a header when they're done.

As you can see, there are a few utilities here that you may find useful, such as a WAIS or finger gateway, and some that are necessary in some form to allow valuable utilities like imagemap, and still others that are intended simply as learning tools to demonstrate how to write a CGI script in the

TCL scripting language. They all come standard with the NCSA HTTPD server software, and it's good to know what's there and how it can be used, either as a learning tool or utility. Later on, this chapter will describe many other special-purpose and form-handling scripts.

LESSON #3: HOW TO USE PRE-EXISTING SCRIPTS

OK, I know what a CGI script is, I know what one looks like, I know the names of a few standard scripts, now how do I use them?

The answer to this is simple. You access a CGI script in the same way you access any other URL: create a hyperlink in a document that points to a CGI script, or use the "open URL" option on your browser, or include the URL in the METHOD attribute of a form (as described in Chapter 14). Since most installations require all CGI scripts to be in one protected directory (namely cgi-bin), the following examples all use this convention.

Constructing a CGI URL

A URL that points to a CGI script follows the same conventions as other URLs that point to HTTP servers. It contains a protocol type (HTTP), the name of the server that will execute the script and forward the results, and the name and path of the CGI script to be executed. The simple generic format to create a CGI script URL is:

```
http://machinename/cgi-bin/myprogram
```

In this form, the URL will open an HTTP connection to the "machinename" server, the server will then invoke the "myprogram" script from the standard cgi-bin directory, and will forward the results of the execution of "myprogram" back to the Web browser. There are also ways to include query and path information along with the URL. Query information can be appended to the URL separated by a question mark (?).

```
http://machinename/cgi-bin/myprogram?whoareyou
```

Here the HTTP server sets the environment variable QUERY_STRING to the value "whoareyou" when it executes the "myprogram" script. The script can then access the query data through the environment and make a decision based on the "whoareyou" value that was stored in the QUERY_STRING variable.

To include path information in the URL, simply append the relative path to the URL. For example:

```
http://machinename/cgi-bin/myprogram/people/docs
```

This will invoke the script and assign the value "people/docs" to the environment variable PATH_INFO. It will also resolve the address from a virtual path to a physical path and store that value into PATH_TRANSLATED. For example, if your server root is set to "/usr/httpd" and "/people/docs" is sent along with the CGI URL, the server will assign PATH_INFO the value "people/docs" and "/usr/httpd/people/docs" is assigned to PATH_TRANSLATED.

The following listing is a sample HTML document that calls a CGI script called test-cgi on a server called myserver.com. If you have a standard HTTPD installation like the one on the CD-ROM that comes with this book, you should be able to replace "myserver.com" with the name of the machine running the server software and use this document.

```
<TITLE>test-cgi</TITLE>
<H1>Test CGI</H1>
<HR>
<A HREF="http://myserver.com/cgi-bin/test_cgi">Click here to run test-
cgi</A><BR>
<HR>
test-cgi should return a virtual HTML document that contains the names
of environment variables and their values on the HTTP server speci-
fied.<BR>
```

Specifying a Script Within a Form

When specifying a script to act on form data submitted from a client, construct the URL in the same way as before, that is:

```
http://machinename/cgi-bin/programname
```

The only difference is where to place it within the HTML document. Specifically, include the script URL in the ACTION attribute of the <FORM> tag.

```
<FORM ACTION="http://machinename/cgi-bin/programname">
```

Later in this chapter, the section headed Handling Form Data will give you the details on creating a CGI script that will process the HTML form.

Specifying a Script from the "Open URL" Interface

Executing a script directly from your Web browser is as simple as selecting the Open URL or Open Location option in your browser and entering the URL for the script. The URL can contain any of the standard URL conventions—see Chapter 1 if you need a review. In particular, you can include optional port numbers if you need them, and you have to escape any special characters that may be required to specify the path or filename of the CGI script.

LESSON #4: HOW TO USE A SCRIPT TO ACCESS OTHER APPLICATIONS

Why is it called the Common "Gateway" Interface? Well, the answer is simple: the Common Gateway Interface was originally intended as a "gateway" between WWW clients and other programs that could be run remotely on your server. Many CGI scripts, especially those that access databases, simply execute another application on the server and redirect its output with whatever formatting changes are required to the HTTP server and then to the client that requested the script.

As a simple example, let's take a quick look at the finger script that was mentioned in the standard script table (Table 15-2). Finger is a standard Unix utility that allows you to locate users and/or machines and retrieve information about them. Don't worry if you don't understand the entire script, we'll cover that in the next section.

The finger gateway is written in the Unix shell scripting language, so first we give it a shell script header, and define a constant that points to the actual finger program in the Unix filesystem.

```
#! /bin/sh

FINGER=/usr/ucb/finger
```

Notice that the FINGER constant is assigned the entire path of the program that it will be running. Next, we send the server a standard header. We'll use the Content-Type header and specify the "text/html" MIME type. (For a complete list of MIME types, see Table 15-4 at the end of the chapter.) This will inform the client that we plan on sending it straight ASCII text, and that the text should be interpreted as HTML code. It is important to specify a header of some type, as most servers and browsers will return an error message if they don't get a header. We send the header to the server simply by writing it to the standard output. (In the examples of this chapter, standard output is the same as printing directly to the screen or console. The HTTPD server intercepts and redirects this output as necessary.) An easy way to do this in a shell script is with the "echo" command. Note the blank echo line after the header. This is necessary with most servers and should always be included.

```
echo Content-type: text/html
echo
```

Now we are ready to start sending the output from the finger script to the server. Just to make it look a little nicer, we add a <TITLE> tag and a short description of the output as follows.

```
echo <TITLE>Finger Gateway</TITLE>
echo <H1>Finger Gateway</H1>
echo This will finger our HTTP server
echo
```

Now, we execute finger, with a <PRE> tag added just before and a </PRE> right after to make it look a little nicer to the user:

```
echo <PRE>
$FINGER
echo</PRE>
```

Since finger will automatically send its results to the standard output, this text goes to the server and then to the browser as part of an HTML document. This simplified finger gateway looks like this:

```
#! /bin/sh
FINGER = /usr/ucb/finger
echo Content-type: text/html
echo
echo <TITLE>Finger Gateway</TITLE>
echo <H1>Finger Gateway</H1>
echo This will finger our HTTP server
echo
<PRE>
$FINGER
</PRE>
```

Since finger usually works best with parameters, such as user@machine, it's nice to be able to pass along a parameter supplied by the user. The full finger gateway uses the <ISINDEX> tag to get a username and machine-name from the user, and passes these along to the Unix finger utility. A listing of the complete finger gateway is listed below. Some parts may be unfamiliar, but these will be discussed in the Writing Your Own Scripts section.

```
#! /bin/sh
#This script comes standard with NCSA's HTTPD
FINGER=/usr/ucb/finger
echo Content-type: text/html
```

Continued on next page

Continued from previous page

```
echo
if [ -x $FINGER ]; then
       if [ $# = 0 ]; then
               cat << EOM
<TITLE>Finger Gateway</TITLE>
<H1>Finger Gateway</H1>
<ISINDEX>
This is a gateway to "finger". Type a user@host combination in your
browser's search dialog.<P>
EOM
       else
               echo \<PRE\>
               $FINGER "$*"
       fi
else
       echo Cannot find finger on this system.
fi
```

WARNING! Remember to make your shell scripts executable. In Unix this means that you must type:

```
chmod o+x scriptname
```

for any new shell script you create.

It should start becoming clear how simple and powerful a gateway script can be. A script can point to any executable file on your server and execute it. All data sent to the standard output–either your script or the file(s) it executes–will be forwarded to the client and interpreted as the MIME type specified in the Content-Type header. This is a lot of power and should be used with caution. You don't want users imposing potentially (or deliberately) destructive scripts on your server, so it is usually a good idea, on a shared system, to allow only a few trusted users to create CGI scripts.

There are a few mechanisms in place to help protect you. One is the ability to require CGI scripts to be in a specific directory, and the other is the ability to require CGI scripts to have a specific suffix. Either method prevents anonymous users from being able to write URLs that point to your server and run whatever they want (Say, rm -r * for example. Not a pleasant thought.) Don't worry! The risk potential is there, but if you install your server with some thought, you should be able to avoid such mishaps. If you are concerned about security, read the security section in Chapter 21.

LESSON #5: WRITING YOUR OWN SCRIPTS

OK, enough talk, let's see some action. We're going to try the learning-by-example method here, so let's just get a few things out of the way first. In order to run CGI scripts, make sure the following infrastructure is in place:

- You have an HTTP server installed at your site.
- The HTTP server has been configured to allow CGI scripts.
- You, or someone you know, has write permission in the cgi-bin directory on this server, unless the server has been configured to allow CGI scripts elsewhere.

That in mind, writing a CGI script is a six-step process:

1. Write the script and compile it if necessary. (Obviously, you don't compile a shell script.)
2. Have the script moved into the cgi-bin directory (or equivalent).
3. Make sure the script is executable. (The Unix command is *chmod o+x scriptname*.)
4. Write a reference URL or form to access the script.
5. Debug the script.
6. Publish the script. (Tell your audience about it, or create links to it.)

Writing a Simple Script

Let's start with a simple script: an interactive <ISINDEX> form that will ask the user to input his or her name, and then echo back a short greeting to the user's browser. This example assumes that you are using the NCSA HTTPD server software from the CD-ROM that came with the book.

We will use the Unix shell scripting language to write it. To start, using your favorite text editor, create the following file:

```
echoname.sh
```

Since this is a shell script, we will start it with a standard shell script header. The first line is:

```
#! /bin/sh
```

Now, to avoid having problems interpreting the data, or getting error messages for not being specific, we add the HTML header. In this case, we are returning text that we want interpreted as HTML code. The header for this type of data is just the MIME type for HTML code. Add the following to your file to print the header information:

```
echo Content-Type: text/html
echo
```

The extra "echo" is necessary, as most installations require a blank line after the header. Next, we want to create the HTML code that is sent to the browser. We will share some code, and the rest will be unique depending on whether there was user input or not. First we create the common HTML. Notice that in a shell script, the greater-than and less-than brackets (< >) are reserved symbols and must be escaped with backslashes (\). So if you want to print a less-than symbol using echo, you would use "echo \<"—"echo <" won't work by itself. You can avoid messing with backslashes by enclosing the entire string in double-quotes. With that in mind, add the following lines to your file:

```
echo "<TITLE>Echoname example</TITLE>"
echo "<ISINDEX>"
echo "<H1>CGI script example</H1>"
echo Any name typed into the query window will be echoed to the
screen.
echo "<HR>"
```

Now we want to create a fork—one side allows the user to input a name, and the other displays a message if the user types in a name. In this example, since we are using the <ISINDEX> tag, we can assume that the command line parameter count is greater than zero if the user entered a value, and zero if not. The following lines will check for a value on the command line and print a prompt message if there were no parameters.

```
if [ $# = 0] ; then
        echo Please enter your name in the query window.\<BR\>
else
        echo Hello $*, Welcome to our server.
fi
```

Now, if this script is called without parameters, it will print the message "Please enter your name in the query window." When called with parameters, it will print the message "Hello [parameters], Welcome to our server." The entire script looks like this:

```
#! /bin/sh
echo Content-Type: text/html
echo
echo "<TITLE>Echoname example</TITLE>"
echo "<ISINDEX>"
echo "<H1>CGI script example</H1>"
echo Any name typed into the query window will be echoed to the
screen.
echo "<HR>"
if [ $# = 0 ]; then
        echo Please enter your name in the query window.\<BR\>
else
        echo Hello $*, Welcome to our server.\<BR\>
fi
```

NOTE: The <ISINDEX> tag uses the GET method to pass data from the browser to the calling script. This means that the encoded input data is stored in the QUERY_STRING environment variable. But the <ISINDEX> query will also list the unencoded values on the command line of the calling script.

Before we can test the script, we need to make sure it is executable. At the Unix command prompt, type:

```
chmod +x echoname.sh
```

This will make the shell script executable, a necessity if you want to be able to run this script. Now to test it, type:

```
echoname.sh
```

This should produce the results:

```
Content-Type: text/html

<TITLE>Echoname example</TITLE>
<ISINDEX>
<H1>CGI script example</H1>
Any name typed into the query window will be echoed to the screen.
<HR>
Please enter your name in the query window. <BR>
```

Now test the script with a command line argument. Try the following:

```
echoname.sh Troy
```

The result should be:

```
Content-Type: text/html

<TITLE>Echoname example</TITLE>
<ISINDEX>
<H1>CGI script example</H1>
Any name typed into the query window will be echoed to the screen.
<HR>
Hello Troy, Welcome to our server.
```

We are now ready to place the file into the correct directory and try it out with a Web browser. Copy the file into the appropriate directory for CGI scripts on your server. If you're using NCSA HTTPD from the CD-ROM, this is the cgi-bin directory. In any case, the command will be something like:

```
cp echoname.sh /usr/httpd/cgi-bin
```

Now, let's try it out with a browser. Take your favorite Web browser and open the following URL, substituting the name of your server and the exact path to your CGI directory as necessary:

```
http://yourserver/cgi-bin/echoname.sh
```

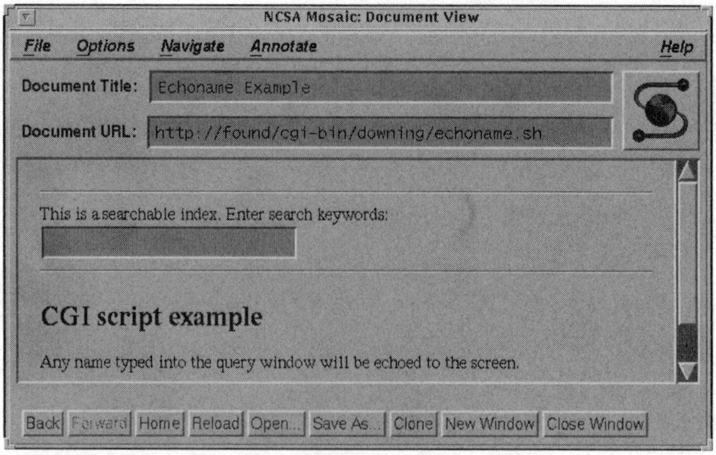

Figure 15-3 echoname.sh with no arguments

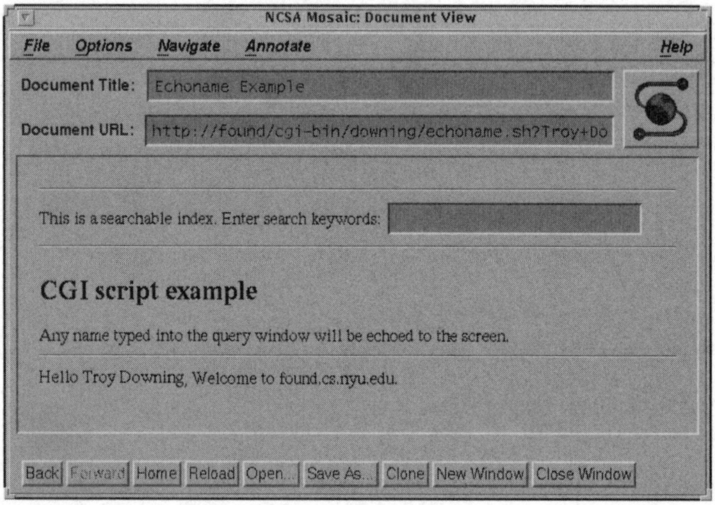

Figure 15-4 echoname.sh with "Troy Downing" as the argument

Opening this URL should cause your HTTP server to execute the script "echoname.sh" and send back an HTML page with a query window as in Figure 15-3.

Now try typing a name into the query window. The resulting screen should look something like Figure 15-4.

Congratulations! You've just created your first CGI script. Doesn't do a whole lot, but it shows how simple script writing can be. This script could have been created just as easily in another scripting language or a compiled language such as C or PASCAL. The next example will show how to use environment variables to get information about the user and the user's environment.

Using Environment Variables in Scripts

Whenever a server launches a CGI script, a number of environment variables are set with information about the data being sent, the client software, the client machine, even the username in some authentication schemes. See Table 15-3 for a list of environment variables set on the NCSA HTTPD server. As a simple exercise, we are going to add a few lines of code to the previous echoname.sh script to make use of some environment variables. The only lines we are going to change are the few at the end that print the "hello" message. The two variables we will use to demonstrate this are SERVER_NAME and REMOTE_HOST. SERVER_NAME is set to the name of the machine that is running the HTTP server and REMOTE_HOST is the name of the machine that is making the HTTP request. Let's make the following changes to echoname.sh:

```
#!/bin/sh
echo Content-Type: text/html
echo
echo "<TITLE>Echoname example</TITLE>"
echo "<ISINDEX>"
echo "<H1>CGI script example</H1>"
echo Any name typed into the query window will be echoed to the
screen.
echo "<HR>"
if [ $# = 0 ]; then
        echo "Please enter your name in the query window.<BR>"
else
        echo Hello $* from $REMOTE_HOST, Welcome to \
        $SERVER_NAME.\<BR\>
fi
```

Notice the addition to the last "echo" line. We've added the two environment variables to our greeting. Now execution of this file should result in a reply string that looks something like:

```
Hello Troy from play.cs.nyu.edu. Welcome to www.nyu.edu.
```

You may or may not want to use the environment variables in this way. Environment variables are particularly useful when processing forms. In many cases, you need them for retrieving data from forms using the GET method, and for determining the length of the data block when using the POST method. This will all be explained in greater detail in the section on form handling coming up next. Before going on to forms, let's take a look at a few more scripts.

Table 15-3 Environment Variables

Variable Name	Description
SERVER_SOFTWARE	The name and version number of the server software that is serving the request, and running the CGI script. Format: name/version.
SERVER_NAME	The server's hostname, alias, or IP address depending on the particular installation.
GATEWAY_INTERFACE	Revision number of the gateway interface. Format: CGI/revision #.
SERVER_PROTOCOL	The protocol name and revision of the protocol that the request came in with. Format: protocol/revision.
SERVER_PORT	The port number that the server is accepting requests through. (Usually port 80.)
REQUEST_METHOD	The method of the request. Normally POST or GET.
PATH_INFO	The path information that came along with the request. Normally, this information was appended to the end of the URL that called the CGI script.
PATH_TRANSLATED	The physical mapping that is derived from the virtual path supplied in PATH_INFO.
SCRIPT_NAME	The path and file name of the script.
QUERY_STRING	The value of a query URL or a form that was sent using the GET method is stored here. The QUERY_STRING is url-encoded, unless the query was invoked with the <ISINDEX> tag, then the "name" of the field is omitted and only the value is assigned to QUERY_STRING variable. In <ISINDEX> calls, the unencoded value will also be passed along to the script as command line parameters.
REMOTE_HOST	The host name of the machine making the request. Either the DNS name or alias.
REMOTE_ADDR	The IP address of the REMOTE_HOST.
AUTH_TYPE	The authentication method used to validate users for protected scripts.
REMOTE_USER	The user name making the request. This value is only set if user authentication has been used.
REMOTE_IDENT	The user ID for a remote user in some authentication schemes.
CONTENT_TYPE	The MIME type of the data being served.
CONTENT_LENGTH	The number of bytes of content being sent by the client.
HTTP_ACCEPT	The MIME types that the client will accept. Format type/type, type/type,...
HTTP_USER_AGENT	The browser that the client is using.

As an exercise and a utility to see what your environment variables are being set to, we will write a short shell script that simply returns the values of all the main environment variables.

```
#!/bin/sh
#simple script to return the values of environment variables.
echo Content-Type: text/html
echo
#simple header info
echo "<TITLE>env_vars.sh</TITLE>"
echo "<H1>env_vars.sh</H1>"
```

```
echo "Below are the values of environment variables that were set"
echo "when this script was launched.<b><HR><LISTING>"
#were there any command-line arguments?
echo number of args: $#
echo value of args: $*
echo
#now the variables
echo SERVER_SOFTWARE:          $SERVER_SOFTWARE
echo SERVER_NAME:              $SERVER_NAME
echo GATEWAY_INTERFACE:        $GATEWAY_INTERFACE
echo SERVER_PROTOCOL:          $SERVER_PROTOCOL
echo SERVER_PORT:              $SERVER_PORT
echo REQUEST_METHOD:           $REQUEST_METHOD
echo PATH_INFO:                $PATH_INFO
echo PATH_TRANSLATED:          $PATH_TRANSLATED
echo SCRIPT_NAME:              $SCRIPT_NAME
echo QUERY_STRING:             $QUERY_STRING
echo REMOTE_HOST:              $REMOTE_HOST
echo REMOTE_ADDR:              $REMOTE_ADDR
echo AUTH_TYPE:                $AUTH_TYPE
echo REMOTE_USER:              $REMOTE_USER
echo REMOTE_IDENT:             $REMOTE_IDENT
echo CONTENT_TYPE:             $CONTENT_TYPE
echo CONTENT_LENGTH:           $CONTENT_LENGTH
echo HTTP_ACCEPT:              $HTTP_ACCEPT
echo HTTP_USER_AGENT:          $HTTP_USER_AGENT
```

Be sure to make this script executable and to put it into the correct directory for CGI scripts. If you include this script as the action for a form, or just call the script directly from your favorite browser, it will list the contents of the environment variables that we listed in the script. Typically, the results will look something like Figure 15-5.

Location and Status Headers

The Content-Type header we've been discussing tells the browser to expect a stream of data of a certain type, but sometimes you don't want to create a data stream at all. If you want your script to simply redirect clients to a different location based on the machine they are connecting from or the browser they are using, use the Location header. You can also use a Location header to point the browser to a different file somewhere on the server. The format is simple:

```
Location: path/newfile
```

Like the Content-Type header, the Location header requires a blank line after it. To use this header in a shell script, it would look something like:

```
echo Location: ../downing/funstuff.html
echo
```

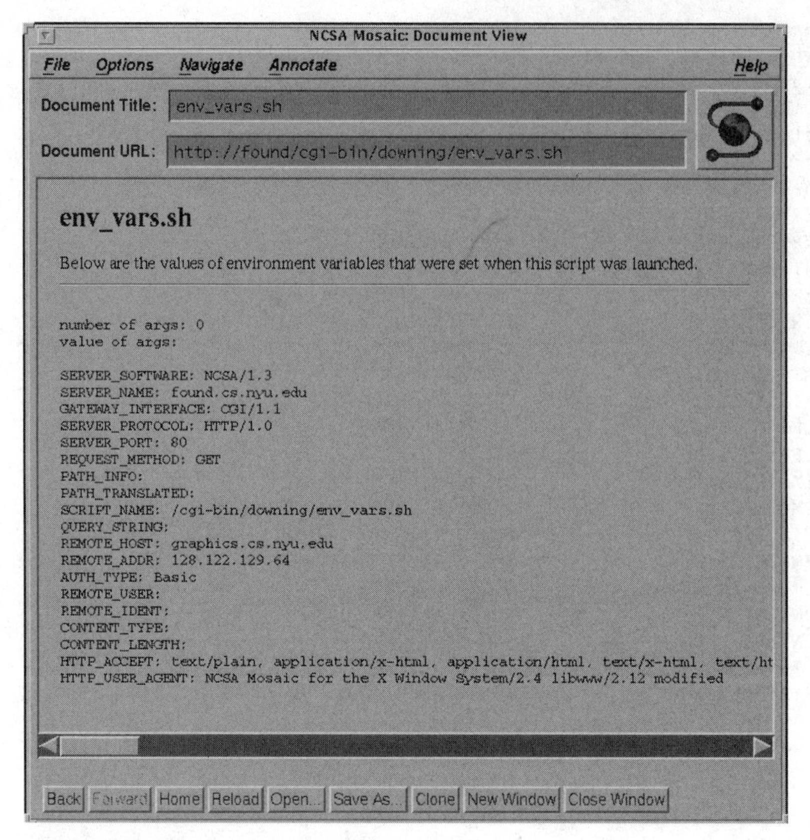

Figure 15-5 env_vars.sh results

NOTE: You cannot mix header types. Every header must be either Content-Type, or Location, or Status.

The following script will redirect a request based on the browser making it. A Netscape browser will get a file formatted for Netscape, other browsers will get a default page.

```
#!/bin/sh
#This will send the location of a file based on the
#client browser
FILENAME="default.html"
#default.html is the standard HTML file we want to serve
#if the user is using Netscape, we will redirect to
#nsversion.html
if [ "$HTTP_USER_AGENT" = "Mozilla"]; then
```

```
        FILENAME="nsversion.html"
fi
        echo Location: ../htdocs/$FILENAME
        echo
```

If you want to run a CGI script without having any change appear on the user's browser, use the Status header. If the script returns a Status header with the status number set to 204 and the string "No Response" attached, the calling browser will simply stay on the page that the request was made from. In other words, the browser does nothing, even though the server ran a remote script based on the browser's request. We can take care of some task, say add a line to a database, without changing the user's current page. The following script will add the machine name that the request came from, and the name of the browser used, to a database in the "logs" directory relative to the cgi-bin directory.

```
#! /bin/sh
#This will add the machine name and browser
#name of a client to a database
LOGPATH="../logs/browser.dat"
echo $REMOTE_HOST $HTTP_USER_AGENT >> $LOGPATH
#now send the status to the browser
echo Status: 204 No Response
echo
```

Assuming that you have created a file called /logs/browser.dat, this script will add the remote host name and the browser name to this file and terminate, sending a status code back to the client. The client will stay on the page where the call came from. There are a number of status codes that are sent from a server to a browser. Most of them aren't very useful in cgi scripts but are used to tell the browser that a file was not found or that the user doesn't have permission to access a certain file. I'm sure you've all seen the "404 Not Found" error message—this was status number 404.

Security with CGI Scripts

BEWARE! Watch out for characters that have special meanings to the shell, such as %.<,>... A client can enter these characters into input fields and sometimes compromise your system if you don't handle them carefully. Any user-supplied data that is used as a command line argument can take advantage of this problem. An easy, but not foolproof way to handle some of these problems is to include the command line parameters in double quotes so that any special characters will be treated as literals rather than shell directives. See Chapter 21 for more information on server security.

Most HTTP servers and clients have certain security features built in, but you may occasionally want to try protecting a document by having a CGI script ask the user for a password of some sort. The following script will give very rudimentary security to a script; it's listed here as an example of how you might implement such a scheme, even though it's not necessarily a completely secure solution. It will print a message prompting the user to input a password. Since this is a single field of input, we will use the <ISINDEX> tag.

NOTE: If you wanted to add a more secure password field in a form, it would make sense to use <FORM> tags instead of the <ISINDEX> tag and use the <INPUT TYPE="password"> tag to prevent characters from being echoed to the screen.

This script will return a "failure" page if it receives an incorrect password. If it gets the correct password, it will redirect the browser to another location.

```
#!/bin/sh
#simple password script
PASSWORD=Schmoo
PROTECTEDFILE=/usr/me/securefile.html
if [ $# = 0 ]
then
        cat << EOM
                Content-Type: text/html
                <TITLE>Password script</TITLE>
                <ISINDEX>
                <H1>This page is protected. Enter password</H1>
EOM
elif [ "$#" = "$PASSWORD" ]
then
        echo Location: $PROTECTEDFILE
        echo
else
        cat << EOM2
                Content-Type: text/html

                <TITLE> FAIL!</TITLE>
                <ISINDEX>
                <H1>Password failed! Try again.</H1>
EOM2
fi
```

Remember—passwd.sh is meant as a demonstration to base other schemes on; it's far from the most secure way to protect a page or server. If you are interested in security, read the security section in Chapter 21.

LESSON #6: HANDLING FORM DATA

And now, (drum roll please), the moment you have all been waiting for... Form Handling! In Chapter 14, we learned all about one half of the form scheme: how to write the HTML code that describes a form interface and how the form sends its data. Unfortunately, you can't do much with a form without having some sort of program that can accept the data that is passed by a form and do something with it. To clear the air about using form data, there is some good news and some bad news. The bad news: the form data is sent in an encoded data block that can be a pain to decode into its component parts. The good news, this is such a common task among CGI scripters that people have already written a number of form-decoding utilities. A useful little collection of C functions comes with NCSA's HTTPD; you can just plug these functions into your C programs, and voilà! the task is done. For those of you who are not C programmers, there are also plenty of utilities that can be used with shell scripts, TCL scripts, and most of the common scripting and programming languages.

What Does Form Data Look Like?

There are two methods that a form can use to pass data to a script, GET and POST. As a quick guideline, use POST whenever possible, and use GET only for indices and single-parameter forms.

When a form sends its data using the GET method, the data is encoded and stored in the environment variable QUERY_STRING. With the POST method, data is sent along through the standard in stream of the script. (By standard in, I mean what would normally be typed in from the keyboard. The HTTPD server redirects that data to the script as if it were being typed in.) In either case, the string is URL encoded. All variables and their values are paired together with equals (=) signs, then all of the name/value pairs are concatenated and separated with ampersands (&). The spaces are replaced with plus (+) signs, and the special characters are escaped. (Backslashes don't work here as they did in shell scripts); in this context, "escaped" means the character is represented by a percent sign (%) followed by the hexadecimal ASCII representation for that character.)

NOTE: Some definitions may be useful here. *American Standard Code for Information Interchange (ASCII)* is a code assigning unique numbers to the standard printable and control characters. This code can be read by virtually any computer in operation today. *Hexadecimal,* or base 16, is a numbering system using 16 as the base instead of 10. Numbers from 10 to 15 are represented by the first five letters of the alphabet.)

Encoding example: If a form had the following text input fields in its description: <INPUT TYPE="text" NAME="VAR1"> and <INPUT TYPE="text" NAME="VAR2">, and the strings typed into these text fields were "Troy Downing" and "Boo{TAB}Radley", the resulting encoded string would look like:

```
VAR1=Troy+Downing&VAR2=Boo%09Radley
```

To interpret the contents of the string, you would want to parse it into name/value pairs, replace the "+" with a space, and replace %09 with the {Tab} character. Simple enough? The following code has a number of C routines to do just that. It's based on the NCSA distribution version, but has a few comments added to the code and a header file to go with it.

```
/* util.c standard utility functions for parsing encoded
  strings, and other related CGI tasks. */
#include <stdio.h>
#define LF 10
#define CR 13
/* getword separates two words separated by the "stop"
  character */
void getword(char *word, char *line, char stop) {
   int x = 0,y;

   for(x=0;((line[x]) && (line[x] != stop));x++)
       word[x] = line[x];

   word[x] = '\0';
   if(line[x]) ++x;
   y=0;

   while(line[y++] = line[x++]);
}
char *makeword(char *line, char stop) {
   int x = 0,y;
   char *word = (char *) malloc(sizeof(char) * (strlen(line) + 1));

   for(x=0;((line[x]) && (line[x] != stop));x++)
       word[x] = line[x];

   word[x] = '\0';
   if(line[x]) ++x;
   y=0;

   while(line[y++] = line[x++]);
   return word;
```

```
}
char *fmakeword(FILE *f, char stop, int *cl) {
   int wsize;
   char *word;
   int ll;

   wsize = 102400;
   ll=0;
   word = (char *) malloc(sizeof(char) * (wsize + 1));

   while(1) {
       word[ll] = (char)fgetc(f);
       if(ll==wsize) {
           word[ll+1] = '\0';
           wsize+=102400;
           word = (char *)realloc(word,sizeof(char)*(wsize+1));
       }
       --(*cl);
       if((word[ll] == stop) || (feof(f)) || (!(*cl))) {
           if(word[ll] != stop) ll++;
           word[ll] = '\0';
           return word;
       }
       ++ll;
   }
}
char x2c(char *what) {
   register char digit;

   digit = (what[0] >= 'A' ? ((what[0] & 0xdf) - 'A')+10 : (what[0] -
'0'));
   digit *= 16;
   digit += (what[1] >= 'A' ? ((what[1] & 0xdf) - 'A')+10 : (what[1] -
'0'));
   return(digit);
}
void unescape_url(char *url) {
   register int x,y;

   for(x=0,y=0;url[y];++x,++y) {
       if((url[x] = url[y]) == '%') {
           url[x] = x2c(&url[y+1]);
           y+=2;
       }
   }
   url[x] = '\0';
}
/* plustospace turns the '+' characters into spaces
  in an encoded string */
void plustospace(char *str) {
   register int x;

   for(x=0;str[x];x++) if(str[x] == '+') str[x] = ' ';
```

Continued on next page

Continued from previous page

```
}
/* plusto_ is similar to plustospace, but replaces the '+'
  with an underscore character */
void plusto_(char *str) {
   register int x;

   for(x=0;str[x];x++) if(str[x] == '+') str[x] = '_';
}

int rind(char *s, char c) {
   register int x;
   for(x=strlen(s) - 1;x != -1; x--)
       if(s[x] == c) return x;
   return -1;
}
int getline(char *s, int n, FILE *f) {
   register int i=0;

   while(1) {
       s[i] = (char)fgetc(f);

       if(s[i] == CR)
           s[i] = fgetc(f);

       if((s[i] == 0x4) || (s[i] == LF) || (i == (n-1))) {
           s[i] = '\0';
           return (feof(f) ? 1 : 0);
       }
       ++i;
   }
}
void send_fd(FILE *f, FILE *fd)
{
   int num_chars=0;
   char c;

   while (1) {
       c = fgetc(f);
       if(feof(f))
           return;
       fputc(c,fd);
   }
}
/* util.h simple header file with the prototypes used in util.c. */
#ifndef __util.h
#define __util.h
extern void getword(char *word, char *line, char stop);
extern char *makeword(char *line, char stop);
extern char *fmakeword(FILE *f, char stop, int *cl);
extern char x2c(char *what);
extern void unescape_url(char *url);
extern void plustospace(char *str);
extern void plusto_(char *str);
```

```
extern int rind(char *s, char c);
extern int getline(char *s, int n, FILE *f);
extern void send_fd(FILE *f, FILE *fd);
#endif
```

Right now, you're probably thinking, "Wow, what a mess! What am I supposed to do with all of that stuff?" Well, don't worry, you don't have to look at the util.c code again. All we will do is compile it into an object file once, then link it to whatever programs we write that use its functions. So, let's get that out of the way. You should create a directory somewhere to contain the source code for your CGI scripts. Move the util.c and util.h files into this directory. Now, using your favorite C compiler, compile the util.c file into an object file called util.o. If you use the gcc compiler, all you have to type to create this object file is

```
gcc -c util.c -o util.o
```

This would compile the code and save it in the same directory as util.c. OK, that's taken care of. Now, the best way to show how to use these functions is to demonstrate them in a CGI script example. The following program will create a Magic Eightball game on your server. For those of you who have never heard of the Magic Eightball, it is a black plastic ball full of blue liquid, with an icosahedron floating inside. The bottom of the ball has a window, in which one of the sides of the icosahedron is visible. There are 20 different answers to "Yes" or "No" questions written on the sides of the icosahedron. The user asks the Eightball a question, shakes the ball, and then turns it upside down to read its response.

In this version of the Eightball, the user types a question into a form on their Web browser. A click of the Submit button encodes the question and sends it to a server. The server randomly picks one of the 20 replies that would normally be written on the icosahedron, and returns an HTML document with the answer. This CGI script also adds the question and answer to a log file so that users can select the "log" page and look at all of the extremely useful advice that the Eightball has given.

Forms generally have two parts, an HTML part and a CGI script part. This example lists the CGI script first since that's what we're working on here, then it gives a few notes on how to compile the script, and finally lists the corresponding HTML form description.

```
#include <stdio.h>
#include "util.h"
#define CHOICES         20
#define LOG             "/usr/httpd/logs/eightball_log.html"
#define LF              10
```

Continued on next page

Continued from previous page

```
int main(void)
{

        int cont_len;   /* number of bytes to read from stdin*/
        unsigned char rn; /* random number */
        FILE *questions; /* pointer to the log file */
        char *entry;     /* value of the data string */
           /* 20 answers of the icosahedron */
        static char *message[]={
          "Yes",
          "No",
          "Maybe",
          "My reply is YES",
          "Reply Hazy try again",
          "Concentrate and ask again",
          "Definitely",
          "Signs point to YES",
          "Ask again later",
          "Without a doubt",
          "It is certain",
          "Outlook not so good",
          "My reply is NO!",
          "Don't count on it",
          "Outlook good",
          "Most likely",
          "VERY doubtful",
          "My sources say no",
          "You may rely on it",
          "It is decidedly so"

        };
           /* getstring length */
        cont_len = atoi(getenv("CONTENT_LENGTH"));
           /* store data string in entry */
           entry = fmakeword(stdin, '&', &cont_len);
           /* replace +s with spaces */
        plustospace(entry);
        /* unescape any special character
        unescape_url(entry);
           /* store value of name/value pair in entry */
        makeword(entry,'=');
           /* print standard MIME header */
        printf("Content-type: text/html%c%c",LF,LF);

        if (!(questions=fopen(LOG,"a")))
                printf(stderr,"unable to open log file");
           /* seed the random generator */
        srand(getpid());

        rn = rand()%20; /* take a random number between 0..19*/
           /* add the question and answer to the log */
        fprintf(questions, "<pre>%s </pre>",entry);
```

```
        fprintf(questions, "<B> %s</B><hr>\n",message[rn]);

        fclose(questions);
           /* return the answer page to the user */
        printf("<title>Magic 8-ball reply</title>%c",LF);
        printf("The Magic Eight Ball has thought long");
        printf(" and hard about your question and has come");
        printf(" to the following answer:<p>%c<hr>%c",LF,LF);
        printf("<H1>%s</H1>%c<hr>",message[rn],LF);
        printf("<a
href=\"http://found.cs.nyu.edu/shaggy.a/downing/public-html/e
ightball.html\">Return to 8-ball</a><p>");
        printf("<a
href=\"http://found.cs.nyu.edu/shaggy.a/downing/public-html/i
ndex.html\">Troy's page</a><p><hr>%c",LF);
        printf("If you find public/anonymous postings in a log format
%c",LF);
        printf("offensive, or embarrassing, ");
        printf("then please do not read the 8-ball log <p>%c",LF);
        printf("<a href=\"logs/eightball_log.html\"> Read 8-ball
log</a><p>");
        printf("%c<hr>",LF);
}
```

Note that you will have to change the path names and filenames to match the ones your system uses. For example, if you put the log file in a different location, you will have to change the HREF that points to it in the bottom of the file.

To install this file, compile it and link it with the util.o object file that we created earlier in this section. If you're following the example exactly, type:

```
gcc eightball.c util.o -o /usr/httpd/cgi-bin/eightball
```

Note the path to the cgi-bin directory. This eliminates the step of moving the compiled program into the correct directory. If you compile your version locally, remember to either move it into the correct directory, or ask your system administrator to move it for you if you don't have write privileges to make changes there.

Now, let's take a look at the form that calls this script. Remember that you will have to change the machine name and path to match your own installation.

```
<TITLE>Magic Eightball</TITLE>
<H1>Troy's Magic 8-ball page</H1>
<IMG SRC="/shaggy.a/downing/public-html/8-ball.gif"><P>
<HR>
This is where one should turn for advice of critical
importance. To use this Oracle:
<UL>
```

Continued on next page

Continued from previous page

```
<LI>Concentrate
<LI>Type in a yes or no question
<LI>Click on the "ask" button.
</UL><BR>
You will receive a reply shortly.<BR>
<HR>
<H1> The Oracle can only answer "YES or NO" questions.</H1>
<HR>
<FORM ACTION="http://found.cs.nyu.edu/cgi-bin/downing/eightball"
METHOD="POST">
Type in your question:<P>
<HR>
<TEXTAREA NAME="question" ROWS=2 COLS=60></TEXTAREA>
<HR>
<INPUT TYPE="submit" VALUE="Ask 8-ball"><INPUT TYPE="reset"
VALUE="Clear Entry">
</FORM>
<HR>
<H5>I can't be held responsible for bad advice given
by this oracle</H5>
<H4>Accept no imitations! This is the Original WWW 8Ball and not a
cheap imitation!</H4>
<A href=/logs/eightball_log.html>Read Log</A>
```

To make this work, you must make sure that all of the hrefs are pointing to the path/names of the files you created on your system. The paths and filenames listed here are only examples. To see the Eightball in action in its original home, point your Web browser at:

```
http://found.cs.nyu.edu/downing/eightball.html
```

The Eightball example only deals with a single variable that contains the question string. What happens when we need to deal with several name/value pairs? Well, the following example works with the basic "feed-back" page form that was described in Chapter 14, which allows a user to submit comments via their browser. This version adds the comments to a database, but this could easily be changed to a mailer that would mail the results to the form's owner.

The technique used for dealing with multiple name/value fields in this example is not necessarily the best. It assumes that the name/value pairs will arrive in a specific order, trusting that the form will control the order and eliminate the need to bother checking the names of the variables. To take a simple example, if a form has the following code bits in it:

```
<INPUT TYPE="text" NAME="Foo">
<INPUT TYPE="text" NAME="bar>
```

The CGI script can assume that the encoded string will be something like:

```
Foo=foovalue&bar=barvalue
```

If you separate the values and index them in an array of strings, you can assume that string 0 will contain the value of Foo and string 1 will contain the value of bar. This method falls apart if the input fields are reordered in the form description, but let's assume, for now, that they are not.

Here is the description of the database handler that goes with the form description in Chapter 14. It will take the form data, return an HTML page to the browser confirming receipt of the data, write the data to a database, and send e-mail informing the author that new data has been added.

```
#include <stdio.h>
#include <stdlib.h>
#include "util.h"
#define MAILER  "/usr/ucb/mail"
#define LOGFILE "/usr/pub/feedback.log"
#define LF      10
#define MAX_ENT 1000                   /*  max number of variables
                                        that can be used */
#define MY_EMAIL     "downing@nyu.edu"
/* header index. used to index the struct array containing the
  variables passed from mosaic */
#define FIRST   0
#define SECOND  1
#define EMAIL   2
#define LIST    3
#define URGENCY 4
#define MENU    5
#define TEXTBOX 6
typedef struct {
              char *name;
              char *val;
              } entry;

void main(void)
{

       entry entries[MAX_ENT];
       int cont_len,index,marker;
       char address[256];
       FILE *mdata, *log;

       index=marker=0;

       cont_len = atoi(getenv("CONTENT_LENGTH"));

    /*separate values and put into entries structure */
   for(index=0;cont_len&& (!feof(stdin));index++)
   {
       marker=index;
       entries[index].val = fmakeword(stdin,'&',&cont_len);

       if ( index == BODY)
```

Continued on next page

Continued from previous page

```
                plustospace(entries[index].val);
        else
                plusto_(entries[index].val);

        unescape_url(entries[index].val);
        entries[index].name = makeword(entries[index].val,'=');
    }

        printf("Content-type: text/html%c%c",LF,LF);

        /* put together e-mail address */

        sprintf(address, "%s -s \"%s\" %s",
                     MAILER,entries[LIST].val,MY_EMAIL);

        if (!(mdata=popen(address,"w"))){
                printf("<h1>Unable to open mail pipe</h1>%c",LF);
                exit(-1); }
            fprintf(mdata,"New message from %s %s arrived.",
                entries[FIRST].val,entries[SECOND].val);
/* return html code to browser */
        printf("<h1>Message sent!</h1> %c",LF);
        printf("content follows:<p><hr>%c",LF);

    log=fopen(LOGFILE, "a");
        fprintf(log,"----------\n");

    for(index=0; index <= marker; index++)
        {
        printf("%s:  %s<p>",entries[index].name,
               entries[index].val);
        fprintf(log,"%s:  %s\n",entries[index].name,
               entries[index].val);
        }

    fprintf(log,"----------end--\n");

        pclose(mdata);
        fclose(log);
        exit(0);
}
```

Here's an exercise. To get an idea of what your encoded strings look like to your CGI scripts, write the following shell script:

```
#include <stdio.h>
#include <stdlib.h>
#define LF 10
void main(int argc, char *argv[])
{
```

```
        int cont_len,index;
        char c;

        cont_len = atoi(getenv("CONTENT_LENGTH"));

        printf("Content-type: text/html%c%c",LF,LF);
        printf("<listing>\n");
    for(index=0;index<cont_len;index++)
    {
        c = getchar();
        printf("%c",c);
    }
}
```

Compile this program and place it in the cgi-bin directory. Now, using one of the forms you've created, or one of the forms described in this book, change the <ACTION> tag to point at this program. (You must use the POST method for this to work.) Now, when you submit a form that points to this script, it should return the entire encoded string that your form sent it. This can be a useful tool if your decoding algorithms aren't doing what you expect.

LESSON #7: SAMPLE SCRIPTS FOR UNIX, WINDOWS, AND MACINTOSH SERVERS

This final section offers a number of educational, useful, and/or interesting CGI scripts, with something for whatever platform you're likely to be using. Most of them come from public archive sites around the Internet community, and their authors deserve great thanks for making them publicly available.

Unix

Unix is generally the CGI programmer's operating system of choice. Most of the more intriguing scripts seem to have been written for Unix servers. This doesn't mean that they can't be revised to run on other servers; in fact, many of them can be modified to run on other platforms with very little work. It may take some doing to convert a shell script to an AppleScript program, but the C programs should port quite nicely. Note that any C programs that are listed below that contain "#include "util.h"" must be linked with the util.c functions listed earlier in this chapter. Well, enjoy!

fax_mailer.c

```
/*      This works with a specific fax-modem terminal that the author
runs locally. The fax modem takes e-mail as its input. This may need
to be modified to work on your system.

        HTML Fax Utility. Should be run as a cgi file under
        HTTPD. Takes the variable string supplied from the
        HTML "Form" submittal and parses it into an e-mail
        address.... The order that the variables appear in the
        html form is important. They must appear in the form
        in the same order that they are listed in the defines
        below, that is, AT..FROM. (Not the best approach for the
        job; it'll get fixed at some point.) This will produce an
        e-mail message of the form:

        /FN=995-4122/AT=Troy_Downing/O=NYU/@text-fax.nyu.edu

        text-fax.nyu will parse the "to" line and create a fax
        cover page and attempt to fax it to the number listed
        after /FN=. Currently, all spaces are converted to
        underscores in the address but not in the body.

        The fax is mailed from nobody@yourserver.com and this
        will appear on the header as the sender. So, It's
        important to include the FROM string so that the
        recipient will know who it came from....

*/

#include <stdio.h>
#include <stdlib.h>
#include "util.h"
#define MAILER  "/usr/ucb/mail"
#define LOGFILE "/usr/logs/fax.log"
#define LF      10
#define MAX_ENT 1000                    /*  max number of variables
                                            that can be sent from form*/
#define FAX     "@text-fax.myserver.com"

/* header index. used to index the struct array containing the
  variables passed from mosaic */
#define AT      0
#define SUBJECT 1
#define FN      2
#define O       3
#define OU      4
#define BODY    5
#define FROM    6
typedef struct {
            char *name;
            char *val;
```

```
            } entry;

void main(int argc, char *argv[])
{

        entry entries[MAX_ENT];
        int cont_len,index,marker;
        char address[256];
        FILE *mdata, *log;

        index=marker=0;

        cont_len = atoi(getenv("CONTENT_LENGTH"));

    for(index=0;cont_len&& (!feof(stdin));index++)
    {
        marker=index;
        entries[index].val = fmakeword(stdin,'&',&cont_len);

        if ( index == BODY)
                plustospace(entries[index].val);
        else
                plusto_(entries[index].val);

        unescape_url(entries[index].val);
        entries[index].name = makeword(entries[index].val,'=');
    }

        printf("Content-type: text/html%c%c",LF,LF);

        /* put together e-mail address */

        sprintf(address, "%s -s %s /FN=%s/AT=%s/O=%s/OU=%s/%s",
                MAILER, entries[SUBJECT].val, entries[FN].val,
                entries[AT].val, entries[O].val, entries[OU].val,FAX);

        if (!(mdata=popen(address,"w"))){
                printf("<h1>Unable to open mail pipe</h1>%c",LF);
                exit(-1); }

        fprintf(mdata,"%s %c",entries[BODY].val,LF);
        fprintf(mdata,"%c%cMessage Sender:
%s",LF,LF,entries[FROM].val);

        printf("<h1>Mail sent!</h1> %c",LF);
        printf("content follows:<p><hr>%c",LF);

    log=fopen(LOGFILE, "a");
        fprintf(log,"----------\n");

    for(index=0; index <= marker; index++)
        {
```

Continued on next page

Continued from previous page

```
        printf("%s:  %s<p>",entries[index].name,
              entries[index].val);
        fprintf(log,"%s:  %s\n",entries[index].name,
              entries[index].val);
        }

    fprintf(log,"----------end--\n");

        pclose(mdata);
        fclose(log);
        exit(0);
}
```

mailer.c

This next script will send e-mail submitted via a form. It can be useful if users can't use mailto: URLs with their browsers.

```
#include <stdio.h>
#include <stdlib.h>
#include "util.h"
#define MAILER              "/usr/ucb/mail"
#define USER                "you@youraddress.edu"
#define SUBJECT             "Webpage_Reply"
#define LF                  10
#define MAX_ENT             10000       /*  max number of variables
                                            that can be sent from form*/
#define FROM                0
#define EMAIL               1
#define USUBJECT            2
#define BODY                3
typedef struct {
               char *name;
               char *val;
               } entry;

void main(int argc, char *argv[])
{

        entry entries[MAX_ENT];
        int cont_len,index,marker;
        char address[256];
        FILE *mdata, *log;

        index=marker=0;

        cont_len = atoi(getenv("CONTENT_LENGTH"));

    for(index=0;cont_len&& (!feof(stdin));index++)
    {
        marker=index;
        entries[index].val = fmakeword(stdin,'&',&cont_len);
```

```
                plustospace(entries[index].val);

        unescape_url(entries[index].val);
        entries[index].name = makeword(entries[index].val,'=');
    }

        /* put together e-mail address */

        sprintf(address, "%s -s %s %s",
                MAILER, SUBJECT, USER);

        /* open pipe to mailer */

        if (!(mdata=popen(address,"w"))){
                printf("<h1>Unable to open mail pipe</h1>%c",LF);
                exit(-1); }

        /* send data to mailer */

        fprintf(mdata,"Subject: %s%c%c",entries[USUBJECT].val,LF,LF);
        fprintf(mdata,"%s %c",entries[BODY].val,LF);
        fprintf(mdata,"%c%cMessage Sender:
%s",LF,LF,entries[FROM].val);
        fprintf(mdata,"%c%cEmail: %s",LF,LF,entries[EMAIL].val);

        /* put together HTML confirmation for mosaic user */

        printf("Content-type: text/html%c%c",LF,LF);

        printf("<h1>Mail sent!</h1> %c",LF);
        printf("<h2>If you included an e-mail address you should
receive
                a reply shortly.</h2>");
        printf("content follows:<p><hr>%c",LF);

    for(index=0; index <= marker; index++)
        printf("%s:  %s<p>",entries[index].name,
               entries[index].val);
    printf("<p><a href=\"http://found.cs.nyu.edu/\">RETURN</a><p>");

        pclose(mdata);
        exit(0);
}
```

mailer.html

```
<HEAD>
<TITLE>Mailer form</TITLE>
<H1> Mailer </H1>
<br>
<hr>
<i>Please send us your problems/questions/comments and we'll get back
to you as soon as we can</I>
```

Continued on next page

Continued from previous page

```
<hr>
<form action="http://yourserver.com/cgi-bin/mailer" METHOD="POST">
<pre>
<B>NAME:   </B><input type="text" name="sender" size=30><p>
<B>EMAIL:  </B><input type="text" name="Email" size=30><p>
<B>SUBJECT:</B><input type="text" name="subject" size=30><p>
</pre>
<hr>
<h2>Message...</h2>
<textarea name="body" rows = 15 cols = 55></textarea><br>
<input type="submit" value="Submit Message"><br>
</form>
<hr>
<br>
If your mosaic browser does not support forms, send comments to:<p>
<B>your @email.address</B>.
<P>
```

names.c

```
/* This program parses a form that contains 3 input fields: a name
suggestion for my expected new baby, a sex which could be
male/female/either, and a comment. The suggestions are added to a data-
base that I'm keeping until I actually have to name the kid. */
#include <stdio.h>
#include <stdlib.h>
#include "util.h"
#define LF              10
#define MAX_ENT         100
#define NAME            0
#define SEX             1
#define COMMENT         2
#define NAMES           "/usr/pub/names"
typedef struct {
                char *name;
                char *val;
                } entry;

void main(int argc, char *argv[])
{

        entry entries[MAX_ENT];
        int cont_len,index,marker;
        char address[256];
        FILE *names;

        index=marker=0;

        cont_len = atoi(getenv("CONTENT_LENGTH"));
    for(index=0;cont_len&& (!feof(stdin));index++)
    {
        marker=index;
```

```
        entries[index].val = fmakeword(stdin,'&',&cont_len);
                plustospace(entries[index].val);
        unescape_url(entries[index].val);
        entries[index].name = makeword(entries[index].val,'=');
    }
        printf("Content-type: text/html%c%c",LF,LF);
        names = fopen(NAMES, "a");

fprintf(names,"%s\t\t%s\t%s\n",entries[NAME].val,entries[SEX].val,
                entries[COMMENT].val);
        fclose(names);
        system("/usr/bin/sort /shaggy.a/downing/pub/names >
/shaggy.a/downing/pu
b/tmp");
        system("/usr/bin/mv /shaggy.a/downing/pub/tmp
/shaggy.a/downing/pub/names");
        printf("<h1>Thanks for your suggestion!</h1> %c",LF);
        printf("<h2>I will take the name \"%s\" into serious
consideration!<p>"entries[NAME].val);
        printf("<a
href=\"http://found.cs.nyu.edu/shaggy.a/downing/pub/names\">"
);
        printf("List of names</a><p>");
        printf("<a
href=\"http://found.cs.nyu.edu/downing\">return</a><p>");
        exit(0);
}
```

names.form

```
<form action="http://myserver.com/cgi-bin/names" METHOD="POST">
Please help suggest a name. Enter a name, comment if you want, and
sex.<BR>
name:<input type="text" NAME="name" size=15>
<select name="sex">
 <option>Male
 <option>Female
 <option>Either
</select>
comment:<input type="text" name="comment" size=30>
<input type="submit" value="submit name">
<a href="/usr/pub/names">List of names so far...</a>
</form>
```

Neat Tricks for HTML 3 Browsers

Recently, Netscape Communications released version 1.1 of their Web Browser. This was the first commercial release of an HTML 3 compliant browser that I am aware of. There are a couple of neat things this browser allows CGI programmers to do that I'm sure will be supported by the other major Web browsers shortly. Namely, the server push and the client pull. What the server push allows you to do is send a series of objects to the client rather than a single one. Normally, a CGI script sends a single type of data, say a text/html document or a GIF image and once this object has been passed on to the client, the connection is broken. With a server push, the connection is left open while the server sends a series of objects and is not closed until the script terminates. This is particularly useful using the multipart/x-mixed-replace MIME type with graphic images. This will allow you to send a graphic image to the client browser and then immediately replace it with another. By stringing a series of images like this together, you can create a sort of inline animation on the client's browser without using an external "helper application."

The client pull is similar to the server push but rather than having the server send another object, the client requests a series of objects after a specified interval. This comes in handy if you want the client to keep checking a document or script for changes automatically and for orchestrating "guided tours" without requiring user intervention. The client pull is implemented as an HTML tag that is interpreted by the client's browser. An example of a server push and a client pull follow.

Slide Show Animation— The following is the code for an inline animation script. It will send a series of GIF files to a browser, replacing each image with a subsequent one. It can easily be modified to use JPEG or XBM images as well. To work as intended, it should be called with an HTML document similar to the one that follows.

movie.c

```
/*      Multipart-mixed cgi demo.

        Troy Downing 1995

        This was written to demonstrate the multipart/mixed-replace
        capabilities that are now available with HTML 3.0 compliant
        browsers.

        This will send a series of images to a browser. Each image
        will replace the previous image giving the illusion of an
        animation. This will work best on fast networks with small
        images of the same size/resolution.

        Just to make things simple, I've named the images 1..8.gif;
        this could be easily modified to deal with other
        filenames/types.
*/
```

```
#include <stdio.h>


#define BOUNDARY       "--ThisRandomString\n"     /*marks beginning of
file*/
#define ENDING         "--ThisRandomString--\n"  /*marks end of file*/
#define HEADER "Content-type: multipart/x-mixed-
replace;boundary=ThisRandomString"
#define TYPE           "Content-type: image/gif"  /*mime type of file*/
#define IMAGETYPE      "gif"                 /*filename suffix*/
#define IMAGEDIR       "/usr/downing/gifs/"          /*contains  the
images*/
#define NAMELEN        256
#define REPEAT         8                        /*number  of  images  to
send*/
#define BUF_SIZE       1024                     /*number of bytes to read
at once*/


void main(void)
{
       FILE   *f_spew;        /*points to image files*/
       char   file[NAMELEN]; /*holds  image  file  name  for  use  with
fopen()*/
       char   buffer[BUF_SIZE]; /*buffer for reading file*/
       int counter,count,tries;

       printf("%s\n\n",HEADER);       /*print the multipart header*/

       counter=REPEAT+1;
       while(counter--)               /*cycle through images*/
       {
          printf("%s",BOUNDARY);      /*print beginning boundary*/
          printf("%s\n\n",TYPE);      /*print mime type for image*/

            sprintf(file,"%s%d.%s",IMAGEDIR,counter,IMAGETYPE);
/*construct filename*/
           while((f_spew = fopen(file,"r"))==NULL) /*open file*/
           {
               if(tries--<0) break;
           }
          while (!feof(f_spew))       /*send data while not EOF*/
           {
              count = fread(buffer, 1, BUF_SIZE, f_spew);
              fwrite(buffer, 1, count, stdout);
           }

           fclose(f_spew);

           printf("%s",ENDING);       /*print ending boundary*/
       }

}
```

Now, here is the HTML page that calls this program. I'm assuming that the code was compiled as "movie.cgi" and placed in the cgi-bin directory.

```
<HTML>
<HEAD>
<TITLE>Movie Test</TITLE>
</HEAD>
<body>
The following box should show a series of images. Click the
"reload" button to restart it.<BR>
<CENTER>
<TABLE border = 10><td><img src = "http://yourserver.com/cgi-bin/
movie.cgi"></td>
</TABLE>
</CENTER>
</BODY>
```

The following is an example of a client pull. The client pull is specified with an HTML <META> tag. For more information on the HTML 3 specs, see Chapter 10. This page will automatically reload itself every 30 seconds.

```
<HTML>
<HEAD>
<TITLE> Client Pull demo </TITLE>
<META http-equiv="Refresh" content=30>
</HEAD>
<BODY>
The following is a picture of our lab. It will
refresh every 30 seconds.<BR>
<IMG SRC="HTTP://ourserver.com/cgi-bin/take_pic.cgi">
</BODY>
```

DOS/Windows Scripts

There are a number of DOS and Windows scripts available on the Internet archives. Many are written as batch files, C programs, compiled BASIC programs, or PASCAL programs. Since most of the C programs written for Unix can easily be modified to work on a DOS system, this section will concentrate on the batch files.

A few notes about file location: The standard directory for CGI scripts on a Unix server is in the cgi-bin directory relative to the server root directory. As described in Chapter 21, the HTTPD server is installed relative to a directory specified in the configuration files for a particular installation. This directory is usually something like C:\HTTPD and all of the document, configuration, and CGI files are in directories relative to this. Any reference to "server root" is referring to this directory. For example: Given the above installation, to say that the cgi-bin directory is relative to the server root directory is the same as saying C:\HTTPD\CGI-BIN. Likewise, the document root directory is the directory that you have configured your server to look for HTML documents in. Normally this would be something like C:\HTTPD\HTDOCS. The HTTPD server for Windows is very similar to the Unix version. Relative to server root, there is normally a cgi-win and a cgi-dos directory. You should place your DOS and Windows CGI scripts into one of these corresponding directories.

args.bat

```
rem
rem ************
rem * ARGS.BAT *
rem ************
rem
rem Script used in args.htm to illustrate argument transfer
rem
rem Bob Denny <rdenny@netcom.com>
rem 30-Apr-94
rem
rem Echo is OFF at script entry
rem
set of=%output_file%
echo Content-type:text/plain > %of%
echo. >> %of%
echo CGI/1.0 test script report: >> %of%
echo. >> %of%
echo argc = %#  argv: >> %of%
if NOT %#==0  echo %1 %2 %3 %4 %5 %6 %7 %8 >> %of%
if %#==0  echo {empty} >> %of%
echo. >> %of%
echo environment variables: >> %of%
echo REQUEST_METHOD=%REQUEST_METHOD% >> %of%
echo SCRIPT_NAME=%SCRIPT_NAME% >> %of%
echo QUERY_STRING=%QUERY_STRING% >> %of%
echo PATH_INFO=%PATH_INFO% >> %of%
echo PATH_TRANSLATED=%PATH_TRANSLATED% >> %of%
echo. >> %of%
if NOT %REQUEST_METHOD%==POST goto done
echo CONTENT_TYPE=%CONTENT_TYPE% >> %of%
echo CONTENT_FILE=%CONTENT_FILE% >> %of%
echo CONTENT_LENGTH=%CONTENT_LENGTH >> %of%
echo ---- begin content ---- >> %of%
type %CONTENT_FILE% >> %of%
echo. >> %of%
echo ----- end content ----- >> %of%
echo. >> %of%
:done
echo -- end of report -- >> %of%
```

demoindx.bat

```
rem
rem ****************
rem * DEMOINDX.BAT *
rem ****************
rem
rem Offers an ISINDEX document if no query arguments,
rem else reports on the "results" of the query.
rem
rem Bob Denny <rdenny@netcom.com>
rem 28-Apr-94
rem
set of=%output_file%
if NOT %#==0 goto shoquery
rem
rem No query, signal server to do redirect to ISINDEX demo doc.
rem
echo Location: /demo/isindex.htm > %of%
echo. >> %of%
goto done
rem
rem There were query arguments. Generate plain text report
(COMMAND.COM: BAH!)
rem
:shoquery
echo Content-type:text/plain > %of%
echo. >> %of%
echo Here is what the server would have fed to the back-end program:
>> %of%
echo. >> %of%
echo Number of query arguments = %# >> %of%
echo. >> %of%
echo Arguments: >> %of%
echo %1 %2 %3 %4 %5 %6 %7 %8 %9 >> %of%
:done
echo -- end of report -- >> %of%
```

Macintosh Scripts

Most Macintosh scripts are written as AppleScript programs. Here is an AppleScript CGI script and an HTML file to give you an idea of how Macintosh CGI scripting works. Dennis Wilkinson wrote the code you see here as an example of how to get MacHTTP to deal with data from forms supported by clients like XMosaic 2.0.

query.applescript

```
tell window 1 of application "Scriptable Text Editor"
       set contents to http_search_args
```

```
        return "<title>Server Query Response</title><h1>Hi!</h1>We get
        the picture. Thanks for the feedback.<P><address>Here</Address>"
end tell
```

query.html

```
<title>Feedback Form</title>
<h2>Submit your feedback</h2>
<form method=GET action="http:/form.script">
Name: <input name="username"><p>
E-Mail: <input name="usermail"><p>
<select name="feedback">
<option selected>I Love It!
<option>I'm Lost!
<option>I Hate It!
</select><p>
<input type=submit value="Submit your feedback now"><p>
<input type=reset value="Reset this form"><p>
```

Table 15-4 MIME Types

</form>MIME Type	File Extension(s)
application/activemessage	
application/andrew-inset	
application/applefile	
application/atomicmail	
application/dca-rft	
application/dec-dx	
application/mac-binhex40	
application/macwriteii	
application/msword	
application/news-message-id	
application/news-transmission	
application/octet-stream	bin
application/oda	oda
application/pdf	pdf
application/postscript	ai eps ps
application/remote-printing	
application/rtf	rtf
application/slate	
application/x-mif	mif
application/wita	

Continued on next page

Continued from previous page

</form>MIME Type	File Extension(s)
application/wordperfect5.1	
application/x-csh	csh
application/x-dvi	dv
application/x-hdf	hdf
application/x-latex	latex
application/x-netcdf	nc cdf
application/x-sh	sh
application/x-tcl	tcl
application/x-tex	tex
application/x-texinfo	texinfo texi
application/x-troff	t tr roff
application/x-troff-man	man
application/x-troff-me	me
application/x-troff-ms	ms
application/x-wais-source	src
application/zip	zip
application/x-bcpio	bcpio
application/x-cpio	cpio
application/x-gtar	gtar
application/x-shar	shar
application/x-sv4cpio	sv4cpio
application/x-sv4crc	sv4crc
application/x-tar	tar
application/x-ustar	ustar
audio/basic	au snd
audio/x-aiff	aif aiff aifc
audio/x-wav	wav
image/gif	gif
image/ief	ief
image/jpeg	jpeg jpg jpe
image/tiff	tiff tif
image/x-cmu-raster	ras
image/x-portable-anymap	pnm
image/x-portable-bitmap	pbm
image/x-portable-graymap	pgm
image/x-portable-pixmap	ppm

</form>MIME Type	File Extension(s)
image/x-rgb	rgb
image/x-xbitmap	xbm
image/x-xpixmap	xpm
image/x-xwindowdump	xwd
message/external-body	
message/news	
message/partial	
message/rfc822	
multipart/alternative	
multipart/appledouble	
multipart/digest	
multipart/mixed	
multipart/parallel	
text/html	html
text/plain	txt
text/richtext	rtx
text/tab-separated-values	tsv
text/x-setext	etx
video/mpeg	mpeg mpg mpe
video/quicktime	qt mov
video/x-msvideo	avi
video/x-sgi-movie	movie

WHAT NOW?

There are popular services that you can use in your Web publishing. The next chapter looks at some of the major non-HTTP services available through WWW browsers.

16

OTHER WEB RESOURCES

16

The Hypertext Transfer Protocol (HTTP) and the World Wide Web are relatively new concepts on the Internet. Long before the World Wide Web became popular, Internet users were using Internet information services like Usenet, WAIS, gopher, e-mail, FTP, and a number of others for retrieving data, sending messages, or just wasting time. Many of these services have been around longer than graphic computer terminals, so for the most part these are text-based services. Many now have graphic front ends, but they are still basically text services. Fortunately, most WWW browsers still let you access these services. You can connect via hypertext links in an HTML document, or access them directly through an "Open URL" option by constructing URLs that point to these services. This chapter will discuss the main non-

HTTP services available through a WWW browser. You can connect to any of the URLs discussed below with a text-only Web browser such as Lynx, but the illustrations will show how they look and feel with a graphic Web browser–that's the way to go if you have any choice.

LESSON #1: GOPHER

Gopher services are popular among many educational institutions. Gopher is a nongraphic, menu-based information service that may also include external services such as telnet and FTP, and usually allows searches or queries of databases. A gopher server doesn't require the user to have any special kind of terminal or graphics capability, which is a big help for people with limited resources.

There are a few ways to connect to a gopher server from a WWW browser. You can construct a gopher URL and enter it into the "open URL", "Go to", or "open location" option in your browser, you can select a link to a gopher server from within someone else's HTML document, or you can add a link to a gopher URL in one of your own HTML documents. The generic form for a gopher URL is *gopher://servername[:port number][/type/path]*

The simplest way to connect to the root level of a gopher server is to use just *gopher://servername*. For example, to connect to the gopher server at gopher.nyu.edu, you could use the URL *gopher://gopher.nyu.edu*. This should open a gopher connection to gopher.nyu.edu using the standard port for gopher services. Usually, it is best to leave out the port number when you construct the URL. The browser will use the standard port number for the service you are requesting if you don't provide one, and it usually works just fine. You can assume a service uses its standard port unless the administrator or someone else with information about the server tells you otherwise.

Most browsers will list the root menu as a series of hyperlinks preceded by some standard icon (see Figure 16-1). To access any of these submenus, just select them as you would any other hyperlink in an HTML document. If you choose a searchable database or index, the browser should automatically generate an input field for you, using the standard query input for that particular browser (see Figure 16-2).

Accessing specific items within the gopher hierarchy can be a little messy. As with all URLs, *nonstandard characters*–that is, anything but upper or lowercase letters, forward slashes, underscores, or parts of the URL scheme such as colons–require special treatment. If you want to use spaces,

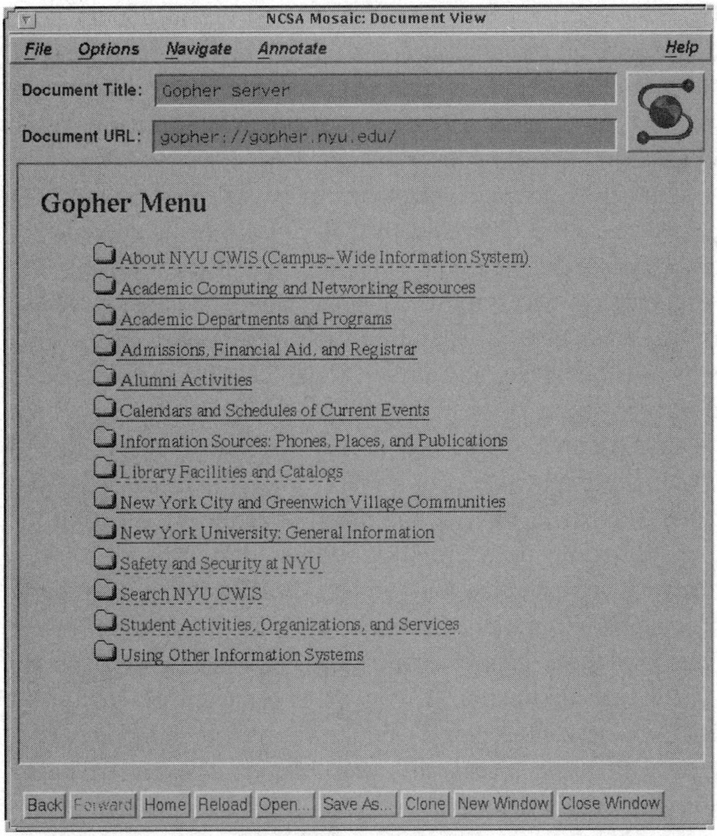

NCSA Mosaic: Document View

File Options Navigate Annotate Help

Document Title: Gopher server

Document URL: gopher://gopher.nyu.edu/

Gopher Menu

- About NYU CWIS (Campus-Wide Information System)
- Academic Computing and Networking Resources
- Academic Departments and Programs
- Admissions, Financial Aid, and Registrar
- Alumni Activities
- Calendars and Schedules of Current Events
- Information Sources: Phones, Places, and Publications
- Library Facilities and Catalogs
- New York City and Greenwich Village Communities
- New York University: General Information
- Safety and Security at NYU
- Search NYU CWIS
- Student Activities, Organizations, and Services
- Using Other Information Systems

Back | Forward | Home | Reload | Open... | Save As... | Clone | New Window | Close Window

Figure 16-1 The Mosaic menu for gopher://gopher.nyu.edu

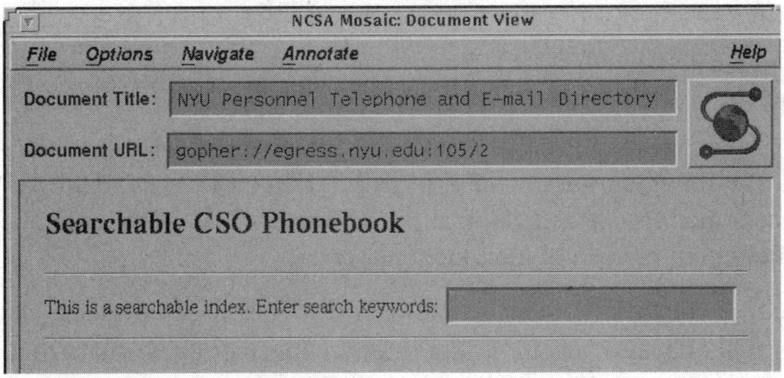

NCSA Mosaic: Document View

File Options Navigate Annotate Help

Document Title: NYU Personnel Telephone and E-mail Directory

Document URL: gopher://egress.nyu.edu:105/2

Searchable CSO Phonebook

This is a searchable index. Enter search keywords:

Figure 16-2 X-Windows Mosaic Query prompt

tabs, or any other characters necessary to point at a particular document in your URL, you must use an *escape sequence*–a percent sign (%) followed by the two hexadecimal characters that represent that special character. (See "Handling Form Data" in Chapter 15 for more information on using escape sequences in URLs).

There are a number of gopher types that can be specified in a gopher URL. The "type" refers to the type of item that you are being served. For example, a directory has a different type number than a text document. The gopher type is generally not necessary when connecting to a gopher server, so I won't go into the details here. If you simply specify a gopher URL with a machine name that is running a gopher server, it will fill in the type for you as you traverse directory structure. If you want to reference a gopher item directly, save the URL information that may or may not contain a type. To find the type for a document request on your server, you can connect to the root level of the gopher server and traverse the menu structure by selecting the associated hyperlinks, then note the URL address that appears in your browser. Alternatively, you can ask your server administrator what type to specify for the document in question. Generally, it is quicker and easier just to connect to the root level of the gopher server and click on the hyperlinks until you've reached your final destination. If you want to reference a document called "information" using gopher type 11 on a server called gopher.nyu.edu, you would use the URL *gopher://gopher.nyu.edu/11/information.* Here type 11 refers to a directory on the gopher server.

LESSON #2: NET NEWS

Net News has been around a long time on the Internet. It's a widely distributed public forum where participants can discuss everything from the latest innovations in microprocessor technology to how to brew beer in a home kitchen. Normally, you can't access news URLs unless you have a news feed or NNTP server somewhere in your local network.

NOTE: There is a recent version of the Netscape browser that will allow you to specify remote news servers. The syntax for a remote news URL is: *news://machinename/newsgroup.* Not all news Servers will allow connections that originate from outside of their local networks.

In HTML version 2, news URLs do not allow you to specify a news server, so you will normally have to specify it as a local environment variable. On a

Unix workstation, this is done by typing the following string at the Unix shell prompt (not in your Web Browser):

```
setenv NNTPSERVER your_news_server.your_net.domain
```

There are two ways to construct a news URL. The first form points to a newsgroup, the second points to a specific article. To point to a newsgroup you use the form "news:newsgroup."

Here, newsgroup is one of the valid Usenet newsgroups, say alt.beer, or comp.binaries.mac. Figure 16-3 shows a typical listing of alt.beer. Since this type of URL depends on a local news feed, the machine is always assumed to be the local NNTP server. (So you never use the machine name preceded by a double slash (//) to construct it. See above note for exception.)

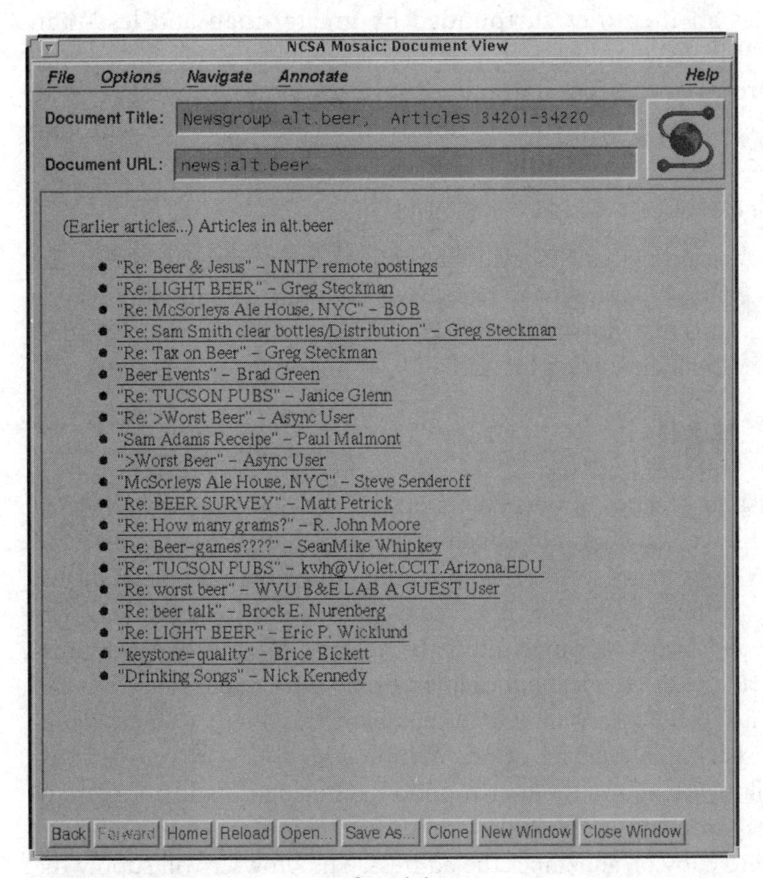

Figure 16-3 Mosaic menu for alt.beer

The asterisk (*) can be used as a wildcard character to list all groups instead of one particular newsgroup. Using the wildcard (news:*) will produce a list of all of the newsgroups available from your local news server.

When connecting to a newsgroup, the browser will display a list of hyperlinks to all the current messages of that group. The links are made up of the subject line and the name of the person who posted that message. Selecting a link will display the contents of the message along with links to newsgroups and other referenced messages (if they exist).

NOTE: It is not very useful to point to a specific article in a newsgroup. Messages have a relatively short life span, and a URL that points to a specific message will quickly become obsolete.

To construct a URL that points to a specific message within a newsgroup, include the message-id instead of the name of the newsgroup. A message-id is an identifier surrounded by greater-than and less-than brackets, so it looks a lot like an HTML tag. It points to a specific message in a newsgroup and will eventually expire. A sample message-id is *<Zlzaioa.ewelgat@delphi.com>,* and is shown in Figure 16-4. The URL that points to this message would be *news:Zlzaioa.ewelgat@delphi.com.*

NOTE: Omit the < and > brackets in the URL.

A user who selects this URL will see the message it refers to–unless the message has expired. For the most part, news URLs are a convenient way to access newsgroups that you are interested in. They are not commonly found in public HTML documents on the Web.

LESSON #3: E-MAIL

When publishing a series of documents on the Web, it is usually expected that you will leave some kind of e-mail address so that people can get hold of you if they want to ask for more information, to report a problem, or just to say "Hi!" Sometimes this will be your personal e-mail address, the address of your system administrator, the address of your web administrator, or an address to request information from your organization. You can set up a *mailto* URL if you want a convenient way for a user to send you e-mail without having to leave his or her Web browser.

The mailto URL allows the user to send mail using a standard interface to the address specified in the URL without having to use a separate application or try to copy or remember the address. The browser will supply the

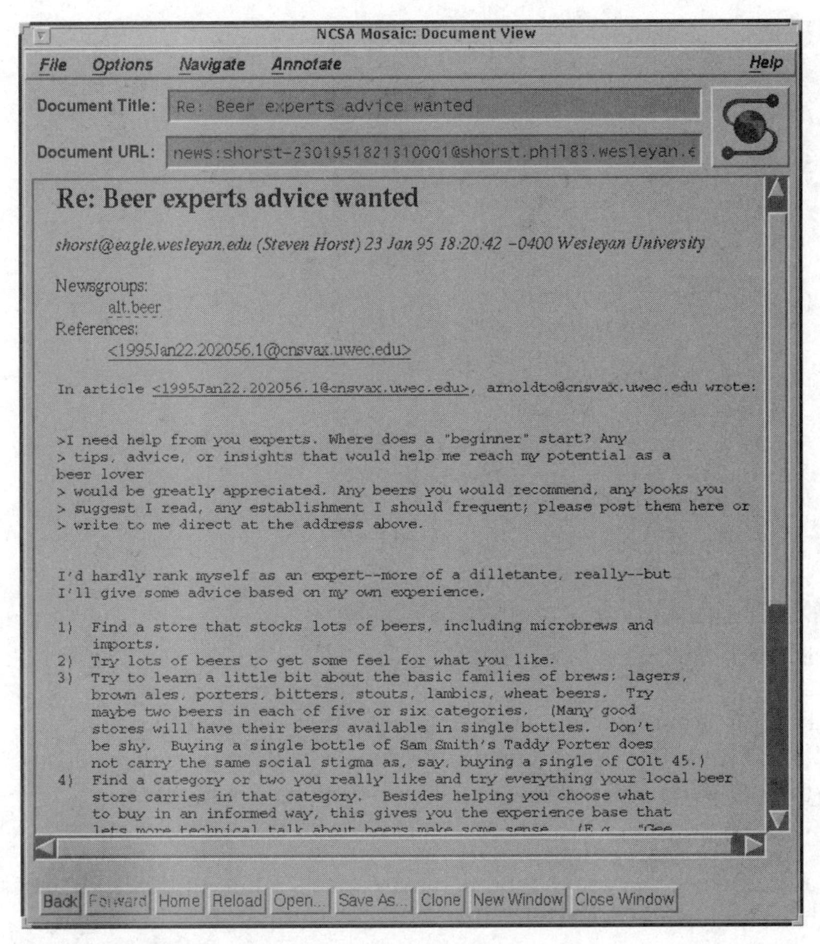

Figure 16-4 news:Zlzaioa.ewelgat@delphi.com

user with fill-in fields and a means to submit the message. An example of the Mailto interface is shown in Figure 16-5. The browser will then forward the message to the address specified in the URL. To enter a mailto URL, all you have to do is type

```
mailto:
```

followed by an Internet-style address.

NOTE: Some Web browsers do not support the mailto URL! Be sure to list your e-mail address elsewhere in the Web page so that users can send messages with a separate e-mail facility. It may be a good idea to include your snail-mail address as well, so people can reach you via the post office.

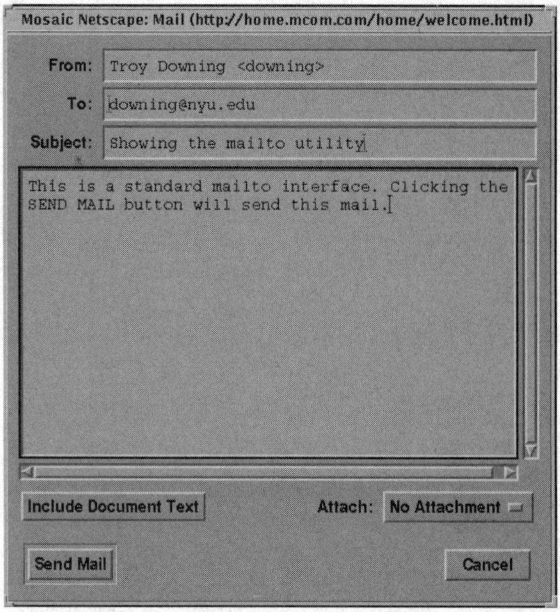

Figure 16-5 Mailto Interface

Take a "typical" Internet address: *downing@nyu.edu* (which belongs to one of the authors). If Troy wanted to include a URL in one of his documents that allowed users to easily send him e-mail, he would insert

```
mailto:downing@nyu.edu
```

If a user whose browser supports mailto selects a link to this URL, the user's browser would prompt for the message text and offer the option to send or abort the message. If the user selects the "send" option, the message would go off to Troy at his nyu.edu account. See Figure 16-5 for an example of a mailto input screen. The entire reference to this URL in the document would look something like:

```
<A HREF="mailto:downing@nyu.edu">Troy Downing downing@nyu.edu</A>
```

The browser would then print

```
Troy Downing downing@nyu.edu
```

as a link. When a user selected this link, the browser would initiate its mail input mechanism if it had one. And if it didn't, the user would have enough information to send ordinary e-mail.

There is an alternative to using the mailto URL. It is possible to write a CGI script that takes its information from an HTML form and mails the message. This is a good alternative if you want to customize the user mail interface or allow a mail interface for those who have form support but not mailto support. In Chapter 15, CGI Scripts, you'll see a sample form and CGI script that will request information and e-mail it.

LESSON #4: WIDE AREA INFORMATION SERVICE

Most browsers allow an easy interface to the Wide Area Information Service (WAIS). WAIS is a text-based information server similar to gopher. WAIS servers are normally set up as searchable databases. The WAIS URL is either constructed as a query or as a pointer to a specific document. The document form of the URL is *wais://hostname/database/document_name.*

If the database name is used alone without naming a specific document, the browser produces its standard query input field and constructs a query URL with the value of that field. If you want to construct a WAIS URL that contains a query value, separate the database and the query value with a question mark. For example, to search a database called "index-of-servers" for the value "index" on a WAIS server named "cnidr.org", you'd type this URL:

```
wais://cnidr.org/index-of-servers?index
```

The results of the search appear as hyperlinks to the documents referenced in the database (see Figure 16-6).

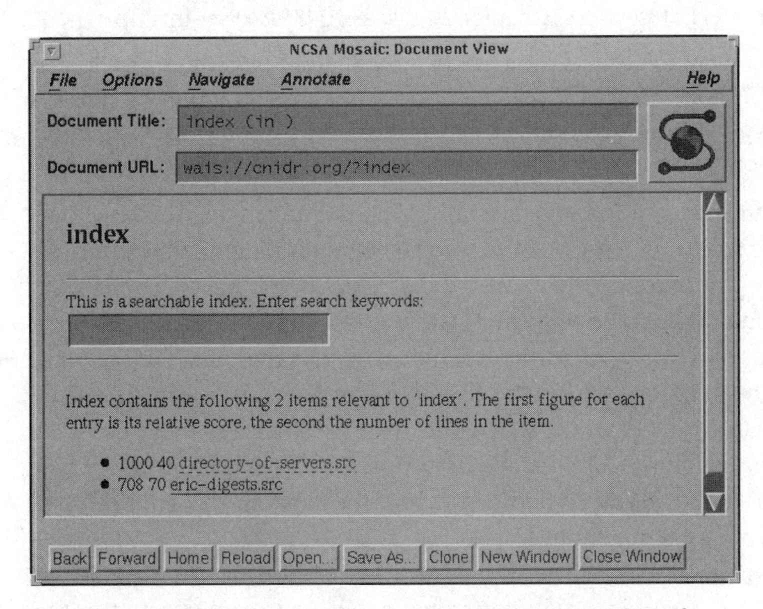

Figure 16-6 Mosaic search screen for cnidr.org/index-of-servers?index

LESSON #5: FILE TRANSFER PROTOCOL

The most common way to move files from one part of the Internet to another is by using the File Transfer Protocol (FTP). FTP is still one of the best ways of moving files from a remote archive site to your local machine. There are huge archive sites with terabytes of programs, games, documents, utilities, images, sound bites, source code, you name it! All just sitting there waiting to be downloaded. Free for the asking. See Appendix B for a list of popular FTP sites.

Most sites that allow public downloading of files follow a standard convention for logging in, which is generally called *anonymous FTP* because the user types in "anonymous" when prompted for a username. The server will often ask for your Internet e-mail address as the password. However, you normally do not have to provide the information; it is only a courtesy so that the administrators of the archive have some idea of who's using their site. Some installations ask for your e-mail address but don't use it at all–it is merely a formality. As you will see later, the easiest FTP servers to access as a URL are the ones that follow the standard "anonymous" convention.

FTP URLs are great for including demos, source code, documents, and other files that you want people to copy to their own machines. FTP URLs can also be used to publish HTML documents on the Web from sites that have FTP services but not HTTP services. Chapter 20 discusses how to set this up.

NOTE: If you want to serve documents to the general public, it is best to use the standard "anonymous FTP" scheme of allowing users to log in as "anonymous" and type in an e-mail address as the password. The browser will insert this information automatically unless you specify otherwise.

So, what can you do to enhance your Web documents with FTP URLs? Say you have a great video game that you've been working on and you have a description of it on one of your Web documents. If you have a copy of the software sitting on an anonymous FTP server, you can create a link to your software and allow users to easily download your game and take it for a test-drive. The same is true for any files that you keep and want people to be able to grab easily. To make this work, the one crucial element is access to a machine that allows anonymous FTP. Most Unix machines come with a standard FTP utility. If you are in doubt about the capability of your system, check with your system administrator.

It is possible to use FTP user/password authentication, but not advisable. First of all, if you include information about your own account in the URL, it is easy for anyone who sees the link to figure out your login name and password. Posting this kind of information usually ends in frowning system administrators disabling your account after some unneighborly Internet community member has logged into your account, deleted your files, and sent nasty mail to other people on your system with your signature attached. Well, enough said about that. The alternative is to set up a guest account that allows FTP downloads, but has normal logins disabled. You can use this scheme if you have to, but using the standard anonymous scheme really works out better in the long run. If you really want to use authentication, ask your system administrator to set up an account that allows FTP connections, but disables logins.

A standard FTP URL contains the URL name, machine name, path, and document name. If you wanted to construct a URL that would download a file named "whatsnew.tar" that existed on a server named "www.cern.ch" in the directory named "/pub/www94", the URL would be *ftp://www.cern.ch/pub/www94/whatsnew.tar.* The generic anonymous FTP URL is *ftp://servername/directory/file.* This form will allow you to transfer files from any FTP server that uses the standard anonymous FTP scheme. If a server uses a nonstandard port, you can include it after the servername, separated by a colon.

If you want to "browse" an FTP site, you can construct the URL with the servername and omit the file name. This allows you to browse the site and traverse the directory structure by selecting hyperlinks that point to them (see Figure 16-7). If you select a link to a file, an FTP session will be initiated and the file will be transferred to your local machine.

The format for an *authenticated* FTP URL (one that uses a specific login name and password) looks like *ftp://accountname:passwd@servername/directory/file.*

Notice that the account name and password come before the machine name and are separated by a colon. This form of the URL will try to initiate an FTP session with the machine named "servername" and log into the "accountname" account using the password "passwd". As mentioned earlier, the main problem with this type of URL is that if it is used as a link in an HTML document, anyone using that document can easily gain access to the account specified.

What Happens to Downloaded Files?

Once you select an FTP URL in your browser, the browser tries to initiate an FTP session with the FTP server specified. If all goes well, the server will start sending the requested file to the browser. Once the file has been

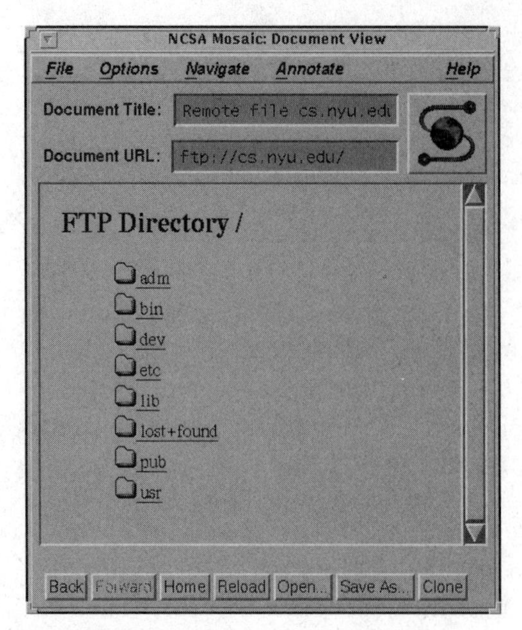

Figure 16-7 Mosaic menu for ftp://cs.nyu.edu

successfully downloaded, most browsers will store the file in one of three ways. Some browsers will store the file in a default download directory. Usually the name of this directory is specified in a preference file somewhere depending on the particular browser. This is the most common scheme on Windows and Macintosh browsers. Unix browsers normally ask for a path relative to your home directory or the directory that the browser was launched from. Either way, you'll quickly get the hang of what ends up where on your particular installation.

The second way that a browser may store a downloaded file is by prompting the user for a path and filename. The user then has the option of renaming the file and saving it somewhere on the local system. This is nice if you want to dynamically store incoming files, but can be a bother if you want everything automatically stored in a default directory.

The third scheme doesn't really store the file, it serves it. If the filename has an .html or .htm suffix and is a text file containing HTML code, most browsers will treat the incoming data in the same manner that they would treat an HTTP URL. In other words, you will have all of the normal features of an HTML document (with a few exceptions) without having to install an HTTP server.

How Can I Send a File Using FTP?

Currently, there is no standard way of sending files to an FTP server with a Web browser. There is work underway that will allow a document author to request a file from the user and then upload it, but this is not yet in common usage.

If you need to send files using the FTP protocols to other machines, you will need to use some other FTP facility like ftp in Unix, or Fetch on the Mac or PC.

LESSON #6: TELNET

The standard way to initiate remote interactive sessions on other machines is with a protocol called telnet. Telnet allows you to have a local window that is actually a shell running on some remote machine. There are several applications that use the same or similar means to run processes on other machines, including rlogin or rsh and other terminal emulators.

What Does Telnet Allow Me to Do?

Telnet allows you to have interactive sessions on a remote machine as if you were logged in locally. Usually a telnet session is text-based and not very fancy. But it does allow you to use a lot of databases and useful applications that were not designed for the HTTP protocol.

Many public libraries have their card catalogs "computerized" and allow access to these catalogs from other machines on the Internet. The New York Public Library is an example. They allow users to log into their machines using a public "guest" account, and search for books and other library materials via telnet. Fortunately, most WWW browsers allow telnet URLs. This makes it simple for the Web user to initiate a telnet session to another machine by selecting the hyperlink that points to a telnet URL. The URL scheme for a telnet URL is *telnet://username:passwd@machinename.*

The username and passwd elements are optional in the URL, but required for virtually all accounts that you would normally log into. (It is uncommon to allow telnet sessions on a machine without authentication).

What Happens When I Initiate a Telnet Session?

When you select a telnet URL, most browsers will spawn a separate shell or terminal emulator. The current version of Mosaic for X-Windows, as of this

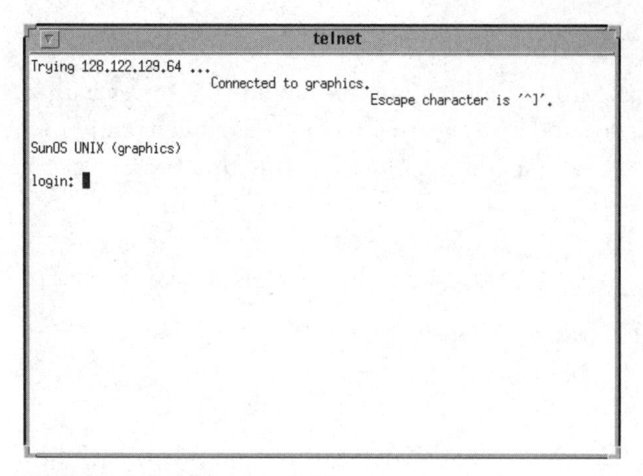
telnet
Trying 128.122.129.64 ...
Connected to graphics.
Escape character is '^]'.
SunOS UNIX (graphics)
login:

Figure 16-8 A typical telnet session

writing, will then give you a pop-up window that tells you what login name to use once the session connects to the machine that was specified in the URL. Once the remote machine accepts your login, it will run whatever shell or software that it was configured for. You will normally have a text-only interface to the remote machine, and you generally can't use a mouse or other pointing device to interact with it. Figure 16-8 shows a typical telnet session.

Most public telnet services automatically give you a menu of services offered through the specific account that you used to log in. If it is well designed, it will give you an obvious way of terminating the session as well (but this may not always be the case). The termination procedure for a telnet session depends on the actual software used by a particular system and the operating system that it is running on. Check the documentation for your specific installation for details.

LESSON # 7: ACCESSING LOCAL FILES

If you are browsing files that are on your local filesystem, there is a much faster way than going through an HTTP server. Use a "File" URL. A File URL points to any of the standard file types including .html, .gif, .jpeg, and .txt files but opens them locally rather than communicating over the network with the added overhead of client-server protocols.

This URL type comes in handy when you are debugging and troubleshooting your HTML documents. You can quickly make changes to your files and almost instantly see the effect. The URL format is quite simple, the URL identifier "File" followed by the path of the item you wish to access. An example File URL would be *file:/usr/people/mydir/myfile.html*.

Beware that users outside of your network won't be able to access this type of URL on your system, in fact, only those running on machines that have direct access to your files will be able to access in this manner.

LESSON #8: URL SCHEMES

This section gives you a summary list of URL naming schemes. In the list, optional items are surrounded by brackets, and exclusive ORs are separated by a vertical bar (|) surrounded by spaces. (Where the | code appears, use only one of the choices.) Remember that although the port number position appears in the list, port numbers are optional, and should only be used if the server is using a nonstandard port setting for that particular service.

If you come across part of a URL address that includes special characters not specific to the URL scheme, use escape sequences to identify them. That is, represent the character by a percent sign (%) and the two hexadecimal digits that correspond to its ASCII number. When typing in a URL, you'll generally use one of the following patterns:

HTML http://machinename[:port]/[path]/[document][?query]

HTML ftp://[[loginname][:password]][@]machinename[:port]/path/filename

HTML news:groupname | messageID | *

HTML mailto:localaddress | Internetaddress

HTML wais://machinename[:port]/database[?query]

HTML gopher://machinename[:port][/gophertype][/command]]

HTML telnet://[[username][:password]@]machinename[:port]

HTML file:/path/[filename]

WHAT NOW?

The next chapter covers formatting and translation of text files.

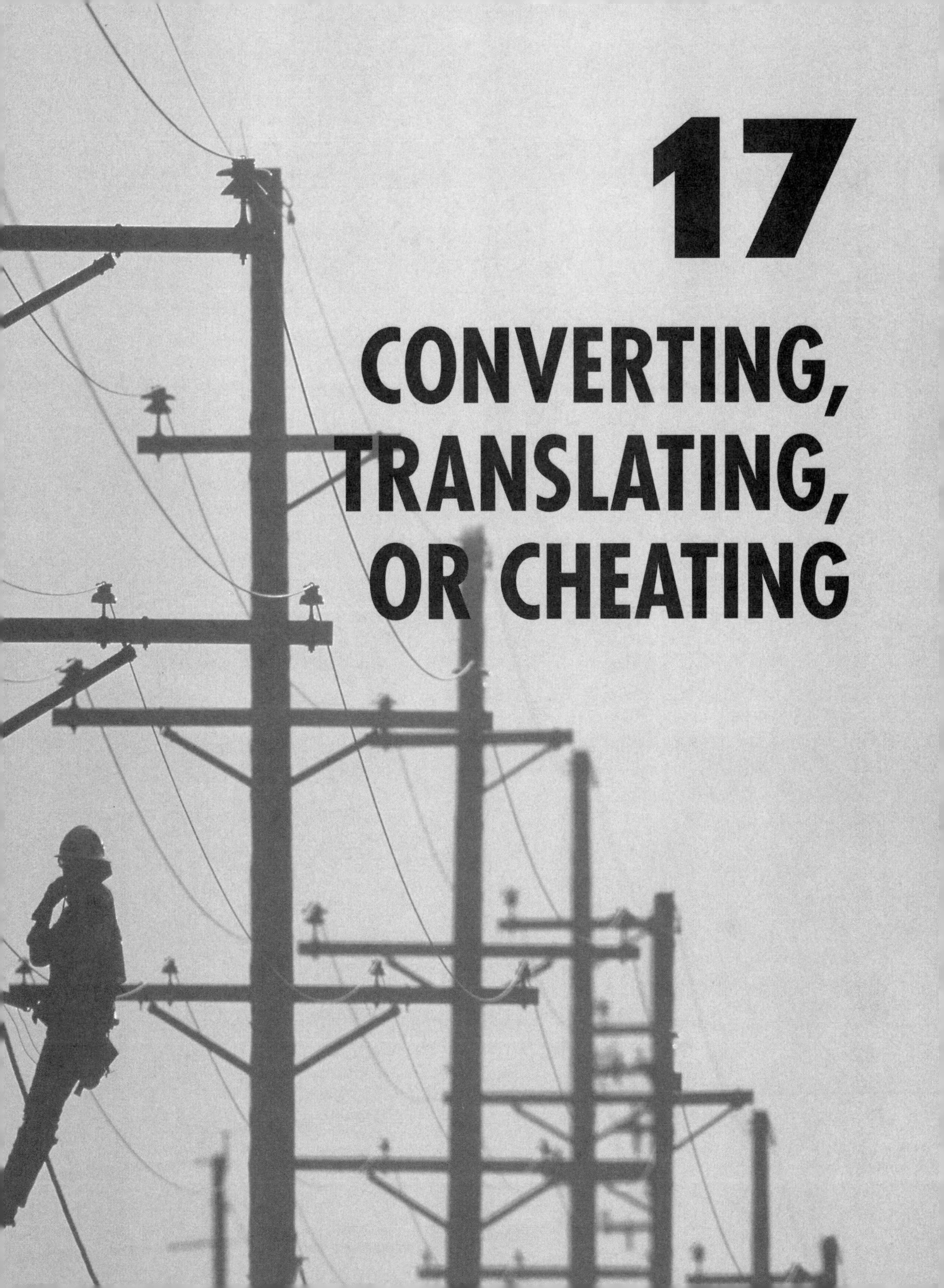

17

CONVERTING, TRANSLATING, OR CHEATING

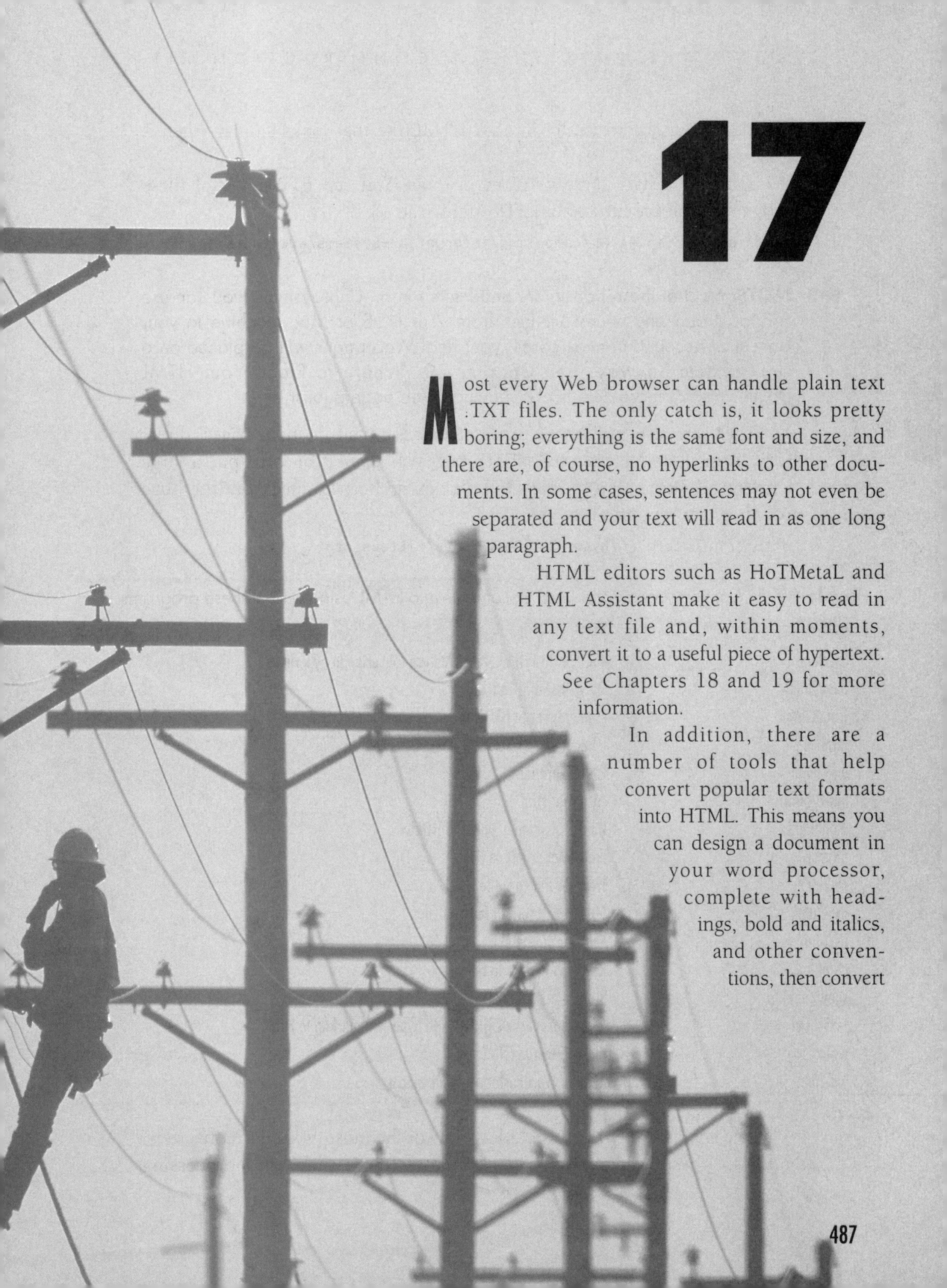

17

Most every Web browser can handle plain text .TXT files. The only catch is, it looks pretty boring; everything is the same font and size, and there are, of course, no hyperlinks to other documents. In some cases, sentences may not even be separated and your text will read in as one long paragraph.

HTML editors such as HoTMetaL and HTML Assistant make it easy to read in any text file and, within moments, convert it to a useful piece of hypertext. See Chapters 18 and 19 for more information.

In addition, there are a number of tools that help convert popular text formats into HTML. This means you can design a document in your word processor, complete with headings, bold and italics, and other conventions, then convert this document automatically into an HTML file that looks similar when it loads up.

Table 17-1 lists some conversion tools. You can FTP many of these programs from the British SunSITE Archive at:

```
ftp://src.doc.ic.ac.uk/computing/information-systems/WWW/tools/trans-
lators
```

NOTE: Most of these translators and filters run on Unix systems; you can use FTP to upload any necessary files from your DOS or Mac machine to your Unix shell account. In most cases, your final Web pages will be placed on a Unix system anyway. See Chapter 20, Where to Place Your HTML Documents, for more details about actual Web page publishing.

There are also utilities to turn databases, e-mail, manual pages, directory listings, and more into HTML pages. If your goal is to put a large amount of information on the Web quickly and easily, check out the huge list of converters and filters at CERN:

```
http://info.cern.ch/hypertext/WWW/Tools/Filters.html
```

Table 17-1 Convert your existing text documents into HTML using one of these programs

Format	What it does
asc2html	ASCII text to HTML. Any URLs are converted to hyperlinks
decw2html	DecWrite SGML to HTML
frame2html	Framemaker to HTML, including embedded graphics
html2asc	HTML to plain ASCII
info2html	EMACS info files to HTML
latex2html	LaTeX to HTML
man2html	Unix man manual pages to HTML
miftran	FrameMaker MIF to HTML
ms2html	Troff MS macro set to HTML
nse2html	FOLIO .NFO format to HTML files
ps2html	Postscript to HTML
rtftohtml	Rich Text Format to HTML
sgmltohtml	SGML markups to HTML DTDs
texi2html	Convert from the GNU TeXinfo hypertext markup to HTML
wp2x	WordPerfect to HTML
wp2html	Another WordPerfect-to-HTML macro

The enclosed CD-ROM includes a few of the most useful PC converters. Many of these act as macros or templates to existing word processing programs. This way, you can use your favorite word processor as its own HTML editor. This gives you What You See Is What You Get (WYSIWYG) functionality. It also lets you do nifty things like spell check your HTML documents, run search-and-replaces, use macros, etc.

WORDPERFECT TO HTML

The WPTOHTML files by Hunter Monroe are macros that make it easy to convert standard WordPerfect files into HTML files. Even if you have no idea how to use HTML, you can use this utility to create nice-looking Web pages.

WPTOHTML has the following features:

- Table conversion: WordPerfect tables turn into readable HTML tables.
- Automatic hypertext: Tables of contents, cross-references, indexes, footnotes, and endnotes turn into hypertext links.
- Character conversion: Any extended ASCII or Latin characters turn into their HTML equivalents.
- Special commands: You can easily create hypertext, references to inline images, horizontal lines, block quotes, addresses, headings, or fixed-width fonts.

Note that you *cannot* use WPTOHTML to edit existing HTML files. The current version of WPTOHTML also has no support for bulleted (unordered) or numbered (ordered) lists or inline graphics. You can always touch up a generated HTML document with another editor, however, such as HTML Assistant or HoTMetaL.

Installing It

The enclosed CD-ROM has the version of WPTOHTML for WordPerfect 6.0 in the \WINDOWS\EDITORS\WP2HTML\60 directory, and the one for WordPerfect 5.1 in the \WINDOWS\EDITORS\WP2HTML\51 directory. Both versions work only with DOS WordPerfect files.

Copy the file WPTOHTML.WPM to your WordPerfect Macro Files directory, which is usually called C:\WP60\MACROS or C:\WP51\MACROS.

NOTE: If you have WordPerfect for Windows, you can easily convert your files to WordPerfect for DOS format.

Writing Your Document

You can now load up any WordPerfect document or start writing one from scratch. The WPTOHTML macro automatically takes care of the following styles:

- Bold text stays bold
- Italic text stays italicized
- Underline, double underline, and redline come out as underlined text
- Extra large, very large, large, small, and fine text turn into various levels of headings
- Left/right indented paragraphs become blockquotes
- A WordPerfect graphic line becomes a horizontal line
- Latin or extended characters acquire the corresponding HTML codes
- Outline headings 1 through 7 become HTML headings
- Tables of contents, lists, or indexes become internal hyperlinks
- Cross-references and targets also become internal hyperlinks
- Tables stay properly arranged. You can either use the WordPerfect table commands or create tables by separating columns of data with the TAB key—in either case they turn into preformatted text
- Endnotes become hypertext links—just click on an endnoted word and the proper endnote appears

The one thing WPTOHTML won't do automatically is convert footnotes for you from scratch. WordPerfect footnotes appear at the end of each page, so an HTML document has no place for footnotes—it's not divided into pages. All you have to do is make your footnotes into endnotes before you convert them to HTML; WordPerfect comes with a FOOTEND.WPM macro that does just this. To run this macro, press ALT-F10 and then type

FOOTEND

Converting

To convert the WordPerfect document to HTML, first save your document to disk as usual. Then press ALT-F10 to run the macro. Type

```
WPTOHTML
```

The macro runs through your WordPerfect text, automatically inserting the proper commands. For example, it puts the <I> and </I> elements around italicized text. When it's done, it asks if you want to save your document to disk with the .HTM extension. Select Yes.

MICROSOFT WORD TO HTML

The most popular word processor for Windows is Microsoft Word. Two excellent macros allow you to compose near-WYSIWYG HTML documents simply by using Word's familiar commands.

ANT_HTML

The ANT_HTML utilities, created by Jill Swift, can turn Word for Windows 6 into a tour de force HTML editor. The "ANT" has the following features:

- A comprehensive toolbar for most styles
- Support for all logical HTML styles
- Easy list creation
- GIF images (or placeholders) inlined on your Word screen
- Easy creation of internal or external links
- HTML document editing
- Automatic conversion for WinWord "smartquotes" and other confusing characters
- Simple one-step process for converting and saving files

NOTE: The professional version of ANT_HTML allows you to read in existing HTML documents and view them, add material, or edit them in a complete WYSIWYG manner. The shareware version allows you to load HTML documents, but styles do not appear the way they actually will when the Web page is published. To order ANT-PRO, please contact the author: jswift@freenet.fsu.edu.

Installing the ANT

You'll find shareware ANT files at the site listed in Appendix D. Unzip the file and copy the ANT_HTML.DOT file to your WinWord template directory, which is usually called:

```
C:\WINWORD\TEMPLATE\
```

Writing the Document

To create a Web page from scratch, select File, New from the Word menu. Select the ANT_HTML template from the Use Template list and choose OK.

To edit or convert an existing Word, plain text, or HTML document, first create a new document based on the ANT_HTML template, as described in the previous paragraph. You can now load up the file you wish to convert by selecting File, Open. Copy the entire file to your clipboard by selecting Edit, Select All and then selecting Edit, Copy. Switch to your empty ANT_HTML template and select Edit, Paste. This pastes the contents of your old document into the new space.

You can now create HTML paragraphs, headings, or other styles. ANT gives you three ways to insert HTML formatting in your document:

- Using ANT toolbar buttons or items from the ANT tools menu
- Selecting styles from the Style pop-up menus
- Selecting extended styles from a special Style dialog box

Most popular paragraph styles can be created by using the full-featured ANT toolbar, shown in Figure 17-1. These tools can be used by clicking on the ANT toolbar, or by selecting the tool from the AntTools pull-down menu. To use a tool, click on the paragraph you wish to format and then click on the appropriate tool. If your cursor is located at a blank line, clicking on a tool inserts the proper HTML codes directly before and after the cursor; anything you now type is automatically formatted.

NOTE: If the ANT toolbar isn't on your screen, select View, Toolbars, ANT_HTML and then click OK.

The ANT tools include:

- Title: Click the T icon to specify the HTML document's title.

HTML Headings: Click the 1 through 6 icon to create a heading.

HTML Address: The A icon marks the highlighted text as an address.

HTML Normal: The N icon marks text as plain ol' text.

HTML Pre: The slash icon creates preformatted text.

HTML Horizontal line: The line icon creates a horizontal ruled line.

HTML Paragraph: The <P> icon inserts a paragraph marker at the given location.

HTML Break: The BR icon inserts a line break marker at the current cursor location.

HTML Unordered list: Word's Bulleted List icon creates an unordered list. Each paragraph in the currently selected block of text becomes an element in the list.

HTML Ordered list: Word's Numbered List icon creates an ordered list. All the text in the list must be selected. Each paragraph then becomes its own numbered list element.

HTML Definition list: The uneven-lines icon turns the currently selected text into a definition list. Each paragraph becomes a definition. ANT asks if you want to create a Definition Term or Title entry (a <DT>). If so, type in the text in the dialog box.

NOTE: To mark text as bold or italic, use the standard Word B and I icons. If you want to mark a heading, a blockquote, or any other style as bold or italic, use the ANT tools to format the text as that style before you bold or italicize it.

To designate special HTML logical styles, you can use the Style tool (the S button). Use your mouse to highlight the text you wish to format. A dialog box appears with a full selection of HTML elements:

HTML <quote>

HTML <comment>

HTML <directory>

HTML <cite>

HTML <code>

HTML <fixed>

HTML <keyboard>

HTML <sample>

HTML <strong>

HTML <variable>

Select an element to mark up the highlighted text.

All of these HTML styles can also be found under the Style pop-up menu in the top left corner of the Word screen. Simply highlight the text you wish to mark, click the Style menu, and select the style you want.

NOTE: No HTML markup will actually be inserted until you use the Check Styles For HTML Codes tool. See the Converting It section.

Creating Links

ANT has three tools that let you create any type of hyperlink.

To create a link to another Web page or any other external URL, highlight the text you want to be hyper and select the URL Link tool (the icon of two arrows). A dialog box appears, asking you to enter the full URL. Select OK. The selected text is now hypertext.

If you want to jump around within the current HTML document, you need to create a named anchor. Highlight the text that should act as the destination for your anchor and select the Local Anchor Destination icon (the target). Type a short, descriptive name for your anchor and choose OK. To create a hyperlink to that anchor, highlight the text that you want to be hyper and select the Local Anchor Reference icon (the anchor). Type in the name of your destination anchor and click OK. Word now asks you if you'd like to install the anchor destination. If you haven't already done so, select Yes. This lets you search the document for the destination text and then create an anchor.

Inserting Inlined Graphics

Whenever you want to add a GIF image to the current HTML document, move to where you want the image to appear and select the GIF tool (the icon of the mountain and the moon). You now have three options:

HTML Insert the appropriate .GIF (graphic) reference and a graphic placeholder into the current document. The image itself does not appear in your Word HTML document, but a placeholder box lets you know that an image has been inserted. Since GIFs take a while to load and will slow things down, this option is a good idea if you're inserting many images.

HTML Insert the appropriate .GIF reference and the actual picture into the current document. The actual picture is embedded in the current document.

HTML Insert only the appropriate codes. No placeholder or picture is inserted in the file, but you type the name of the .GIF reference into a text box, and the actual HTML markup is created.

In any case, you are asked to type in the full name of the GIF. If the GIF is located in the current directory (a good idea), just type the GIF's filename. If not, you need to enter the GIF's entire pathname.

Viewing the Hidden Codes

As ANT creates HTML codes, it hides them from your view. This way, you don't see annoying markup like <B> or <BLOCKQUOTE>; instead, you see a Web page similar to the way it will actually look.

Sometimes, however, it's a good idea to check or edit the actual HTML markup, as in Figure 17-1. To view the markup, select the View Hidden Codes tool (the spectacles icon). Click this icon again to hide the markup.

Removing Markup

If you change your mind, or if you selected the wrong style or tool, you can easily delete hidden HTML markup. To clean up a given piece of text, highlight the text and select Ant Tools, Zap Codes From The Selection. If you want to erase all the markup throughout the entire document, select Ant Tools, Zap Codes From Document.

Converting It

If you have been marking up your document using the Word Style pop-up menu, some HTML codes may have been omitted. Click the Check Styles For HTML Codes tool (the checkmark icon) to automatically convert all styles into official HTML markup.

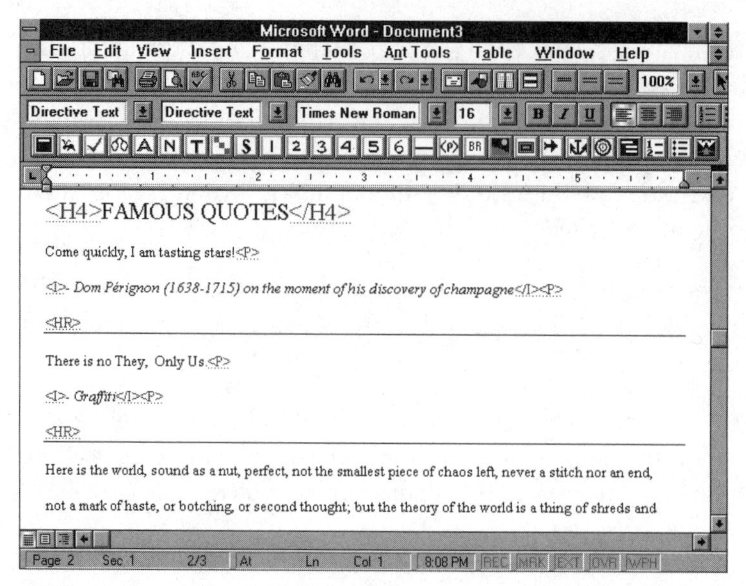

Figure 17-1 A typical ANT screen, with all markup shown

When you're finally ready to save your completed HTML document, select the Convert And Save tool (the icon of a box with a little label on it). A dialog box appears, allowing you to specify the conversion options:

- Do you want the <P> paragraph tags automatically inserted after every paragraph or have you already done this manually? It's much easier to have ANT take care of paragraphs for you.
- Do you want text which has been marked as bold and italic to be converted to the <B> and <I> HTML styles or have you already done this manually?

You must now specify a filename. The ANT automatically converts all styles into HTML and saves your document with the .HTM extension. Then it asks if you want to save the original document as well. This is a good idea, in case you ever want to edit or add on to your Web page. If you're using ANT-PRO, of course, you can easily load up any .HTM document the same way you would a WinWord .DOC file.

NOTE: If you use ANT_HTML regularly, you should register it for $15.

CU_HTML

The CU_HTML package by Kenneth Wong and Anton Lam is similar to ANT_HTML, except it runs on Word for Windows version 2 as well as version 6. CU cannot edit existing HTML documents, but it does a pretty solid job of creating them. What you see is truly what you get when you use CU_HTML. The macro includes the following features:

- GIF images inlined in your Word screen
- Easy creation of hypertext or hyperimage links
- Buttons for applying text styles to selected paragraphs

Installing It

You'll find the CU_HTML files in the \WINDOWS\EDITORS\CU_HTML directory of the enclosed CD-ROM. Copy the following files to your Windows directory (C:\WINDOWS):

- CU_HTML.DLL
- CU_HTML.INI
- GIF.DLL

To set up the template file, Word for Windows version 2 users should copy the CU_HTML2.DOT file as CU_HTML.DOT. Version 6 users should copy CU_HTML6.DOT as CU_HTML.DOT instead. In either case, CU_HTML.DOT goes in the Word template directory.

Writing It

To create an HTML document from scratch, select File, New from your Word menu. Select CU_HTML from the Use Template list. Your toolbar will have six new buttons or several new menu entries, as shown in Figure 17-2. If you're using Word 6, then a new HTML menu is created. WinWord 2 users can look under the Tools menu for a bunch of new HTML commands.

To convert an existing text file or Word document, just load it up and select Edit, Select All. Then select Edit, Cut to put the entire text of the document in the clipboard. You can now create a new HTML workspace as explained in the previous paragraph. Paste your document into this workspace by selecting Edit, Paste.

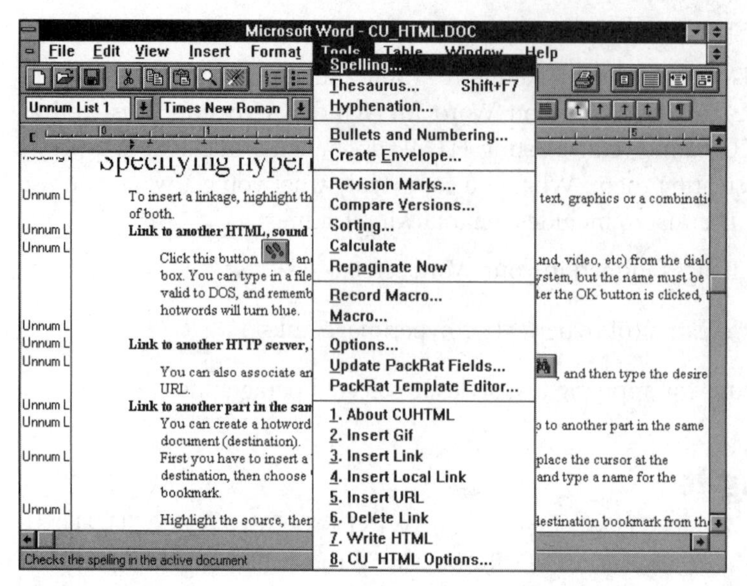

Figure 17-2 CU turns Word into a basic HTML editor

The CU_HTML macro can handle the following styles automatically:

- HTML CTRL-B: Create bold text as usual
- HTML CTRL-I: Create italic text as usual
- HTML CTRL-U: Create underlined text as usual

Most other styles can be found under the Style pull-down list, in the top left corner of your Word screen. To create a style, just highlight the text you want with your mouse, click the pull-down menu, and then select the given style. The following HTML styles are available:

- HTML Address text
- HTML Heading 1 through Heading 6
- HTML Horizontal rule lines
- HTML Normal text
- HTML Num List 1 through 4; the List 1 style applies to your first numbered list, if you nest a second list then it should be marked as List 2, if you nest yet another list it should be List 3, etc.

HTML Preformatted text

HTML Title

HTML Unnum (bulleted) List 1 through 4

Inserting an Inlined Image

To drop an inlined GIF image, just move to where you want the image to appear and click the Graphics shapes button or select Insert GIF from the Tools or HTML pull-down menu. A dialog box appears, asking you for the full filename of the GIF file. Specify the Drive, Directory, and Filename and then choose OK. The GIF appears in your Word document.

NOTE: If you have lots of inlined images, your Word document may scroll by very slowly. To speed things up, you can replace images by rectangular placeholders. Select Tools, Options, and check the Picture Placeholders check box in the View category.

Creating Hyperlinks

To create a hypertext link, highlight the word or phrase you want to make into the link. You can also highlight an inlined GIF image.

To link to a graphic, sound, movie, or other multimedia file, click the Link button (the footprint) or select Insert Link from the Tools or HTML menu. Select HTML Hypertext, Graphics, Audio, or Movies from the List Files Of Type pop-up menu. You can now specify the Drive, Directory, and Filename of the multimedia resource you want to load. Select OK. The hypertext or hyperimage is now colored blue.

NOTE: The filename does not actually have to exist. This comes in useful if you're linking to pages which you haven't yet created, or which aren't stored on your home system. Be sure, however, to check all your links for accuracy before unleashing your Web page on the unsuspecting public.

To link to another Web page or any other URL, click the Link URL button (the binoculars) or select the Insert URL item from the Tools or HTML pull-down menu. Type in the full URL (this should usually be lower-case) and then click OK.

To create an internal link to another part of the current Word document you need to first specify a destination by using Word's bookmark command. Move the cursor to the anchor destination and select Insert, Bookmark. Type in a name for the bookmark and click OK. You can now highlight the source hypertext or hyperimage. Click the Insert Local Link button (arrow pointing to page) or select Insert Local Link from the Tools or HTML menu. Specify the name of the destination bookmark and then click OK.

To delete any hyperlink, click on the hypertext or hyperimage and click the Delete button (the trash can) or select Delete Link from the Tools or HTML menu. Select Yes. The link text or image turns black again.

Converting It

When your Word document looks as good as can be, save it to disk. If possible, all GIF images, external Web pages, and Word documents should be saved in the same directory. This helps the CU macro create easy-to-use relative URLs.

You are now ready to press the Write button (the loop arrow) or select Write HTML from the Tools or HTML menu. The Web page is then saved with the current name as the current Word document, only with the .HTM extension instead of the .DOC extension.

Setting Options

Since your final Web pages will probably be stored on a Unix system, things like backslashes, filenames ending in *.HTM* instead of *.html*, and other DOS terminology will need to be changed. You can either edit these yourself using an HTML editor or text editor, or you can have CU take care of some of these cleanup features for you.

To set CU's options, select CU_HTML Options from the Tools or HTML menu. You can then select from the following:

- HTML *Assume HTML files have .html extension:* On Unix, HTML files have the *.html* extension, not *.HTM*. If this option is selected, all filenames within URLs are automatically converted to the Unix standard.

- HTML *Verify path after selecting from dialog:* Whenever you insert a link, a dialog box shows you how the path will look. You can then edit this relative URL. For example, on your DOS system a file may be stored as *c:\www\html\page.htm,* whereas on the final Unix system the file will actually be stored in the same directory and thus needs no pathname. You can then edit the URL to be simply *page.html.*

The Internet Assistant

Microsoft has recently released the beta version for a rather unique attachment for Word for Windows 6 known as the Internet Assistant. The Internet Assistant turns Word into its own Web browser, similar to Mosaic. Currently this browser is extremely slow and lacks many of the latest features.

More usefully, the Internet Assistant lets you use standard Word commands to write basic HTML documents.

Using It

You can use the Internet Assistant to create a Web page just by typing it up—complete with graphics, headings, tables, and styles. Hyperlinks can be created by dragging the icon of one document into another document. A new Save As feature allows you to write the file in HTML format.

The Internet Assistant makes switching between editing mode and Web browsing mode easy, allowing for instant testing of your Web pages.

Perhaps the nicest feature of Internet Assistant is that it lets you load up HTML documents, automatically converting them into WinWord styles. This turns Word into a full-fledged HTML editor.

Getting It

If the Internet Assistant sounds interesting, contact Microsoft at 800-426-9400 or check out the "What's New" section of the Microsoft Web server at:

```
http://www.microsoft.com/
```

Other Tools

Many companies are now coming out with WinWord HTML add ons. Quarterdeck, for example, is planning the release of HTML Authoring Tools which support HTML version 2 commands (such as forms), a custom HTML dictionary, easy URL entry, and custom online help. You can contact Quarterdeck at 310-392-9851.

BOOKMARKS TO HTML

Many times, you want to create a Web page that consists of nothing more than links to other pages. One of the best places to grab this collection of links is your Mosaic hotlist or Netscape bookmark file.

Lynx

Lynx stores its bookmarks in a separate HTML document. This file is usually called *lynx_bookmarks.html* and stored in your Unix home directory. You can create a copy of this file using the Unix *cp* command. For example, to make a file called *mymarks.html,* type, at your Unix prompt:

```
cp lynx_bookmarks.html mymarks.html
```

You can now edit the *mymarks.html* file using your favorite Unix text editor. Each line consists of a Web page's title, surrounded by the <A> anchor element, and pointing to that Web page's URL.

Mosaic

All of Mosaic's hotlists are stored in the MOSAIC.INI file, usually located in the C:\WINDOWS directory. Each hotlist item takes a form similar to:

```
Item2=NCSA Mosaic Demo
Document,http://www.ncsa.uiuc.edu/demoweb/demo.html
```

If you wish, you can edit this file from scratch, inserting the <A HREF> link element around every item, putting the URL in quotes, and formatting everything correctly. A much easier option, however, is to use HTML Assistant to automatically convert the MOSAIC.INI file into a nice-looking HTML file. See the next chapter for instructions.

Netscape

Netscape can be used to automatically generate an HTML document complete with your bookmarks. While in Netscape, select Bookmarks, View Bookmarks. You can now click the Export Bookmarks button. A dialog box appears, asking you to specify the Drive, Directory, and Filename for your new HTML file. Do so and click OK.

Cello

HTML Assistant can automatically convert a Cello bookmark file into an HTML file. See the next chapter for instructions.

WHAT NOW?

Now that you've created a basic HTML document, you may want to use a full-featured HTML editor to edit things further. For example, you could align your paragraphs and images, add fill-in forms, work with HTML tables, or create special lists, horizontal lines, or text styles. See the following chapter, HTML Assistant, and Chapter 19, HoTMetaL, for the details.

Or perhaps you're ready to stick your HTML documents online for the world to cherish. If so, turn to Chapter 20, Where to Place Your HTML Documents.

18 HTML ASSISTANT

18

HTML itself is quite a straightforward language. You can use most any word processor or text editor to create great Web pages. There are, however, some confusing elements and attributes, which are often difficult to memorize and tricky to implement. HTML Assistant by Howard Harawitz makes Web page creation almost brainless. The program is a souped-up text editor that can quickly and easily insert and arrange most popular HTML markup elements. Some of HTML Assistant's features are:

- Context-sensitive online help
- Point-and-click access to most HTML commands
- Direct Web browser interface, so you can test your HTML documents as you create them
- Simultaneous editing of several HTML files, making it easy to cut and paste between documents
- HTML Hypertext or plain text conversion for Cello bookmark, Mosaic hotlist, and URL text files
- Easy-access storage for lists of common URLs
- User-defined toolbox, so you can create quick macros for your favorite HTML+ elements
- Text file printing

NOTE: HTML Assistant is graciously provided as freeware. You can also get a professional version of HTML Assistant for $59.95. HTML Assistant Pro includes an automatic page creator to interactively and quickly create simple Web pages in a snap, a code-hidden mode so you can view your HTML documents without all the extraneous markup, and a text file converter to switch Unix to DOS files and vice versa. It also comes with a manual and full support.

INSTALLING THE ASSISTANT

You can find the HTML Assistant files in the \WINDOWS\EDITORS\HTMLASST\ directory of the enclosed CD-ROM. Copy the entire directory to your hard drive. To run the Assistant, you need to run the HTMLASST.EXE file. You should set up a Windows Program Manager icon if you plan on using HTML Assistant often.

NOTE: HTML Assistant is a Visual Basic file. If you already have a copy of the VBRUN300.DLL library in your C:\WINDOWS or C:\WINDOWS\SYSTEM directory, you can erase this file from the HTML Assistant directory.

LESSON #1: FROM TEXT TO HTML

The HTML Assistant has several handy utilities that make it a snap to take a plain text file and create a nice-looking HTML page.

To load up the text file, select File, Open. Click the List Files Of Type pop-up menu and select Text Files (*.txt). Specify the Drive, Directory, and Filename of your text file and then choose OK.

If you load a standard text file using a Web browser, it usually appears like one huge paragraph. The browser has no idea where to break up paragraphs. HTML Assistant has a quick fix for this. Load up your plain text file. Highlight all the text by selecting Edit, Select All. Now select Command, Autoinsert Paragraph Markings or press CTRL-P. The <P> paragraph tag is added to the end of every paragraph. You can now save the text file as an HTML file by selecting File, Save As and specifying a Filename. If you want to add headings, hypertext, or other HTML elements, simply continue editing the file as usual.

To load up an existing HTML file, select File, Open and specify the Drive, Directory, and Filename. Click OK. You can open many HTML documents at once, each one appearing in its own edit window, as shown in Figure 18-1. You can switch between documents by using the Windows menu. If you'd like a document to fill the entire screen, select the Maximize arrow in the upper right corner of the window.

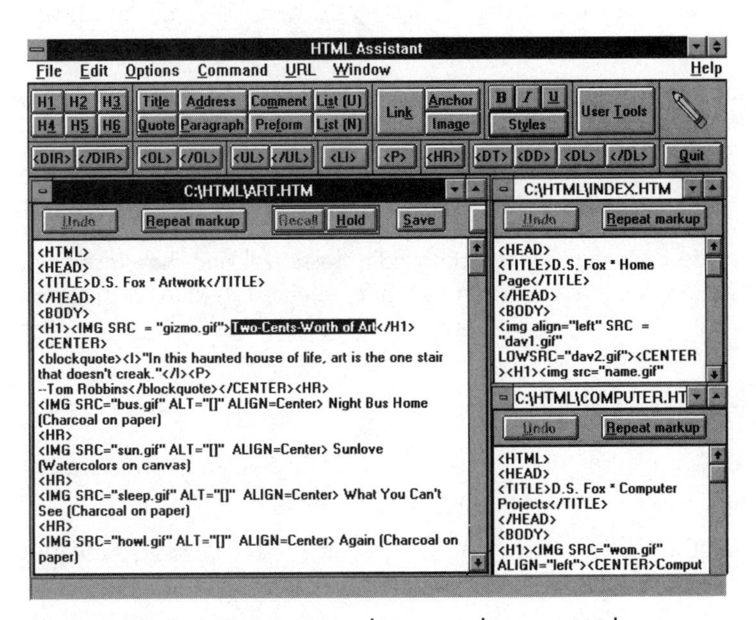

Figure 18-1 HTML Assistant lets you edit many Web pages at once

LESSON #2: CREATING FROM SCRATCH

If you're composing a Web page from scratch or converting a basic text file, HTML Assistant can automatically create the basic heading and body elements. Load up the text file as described in the previous section or create a brand new file by selecting File, New.

Select Command, Display Standard Document Wrapper or press CTRL-W. The following markup appears:

```
<HTML>
<HEAD>
</HEAD>
<BODY>
</BODY>
</HTML>
```

You can now begin typing between these elements or move these elements to their appropriate locations. For example, you'll probably want to begin by inserting a title in the Web page's header section. Move the cursor between the <HEAD> and </HEAD> elements and type a short title. Highlight the title using your mouse or the cursor keys and then click the Title button in the toolbar. The <TITLE> and </TITLE> elements are automatically inserted around the title.

You can now move between the <BODY> and </BODY> tags and begin creating your text.

NOTE: You may find it more intuitive to create the body, header, and HTML elements as the *last* thing you do, instead of the first. Use your mouse to highlight the main body of your HTML document and then select Command, Mark Selected Text As BODY (or press CTRL-Y). Highlight the head and select Command, Mark Selected Text As HEAD (or press CTRL-D). Finally, you can highlight the entire document by selecting Edit, Select All and then insert the <HTML> tags by selecting Command, Mark Selected Text As HTML (or pressing CTRL-T).

LESSON #3: THE TOOLBAR

Most every HTML element is available in HTML Assistant's toolbar, as shown in Figure 18-2. There are two ways to use most tools:

- Highlight a chunk of text and then click the tool to surround the text with the proper HTML elements (selection tools).
- Move the cursor to the location where you want the element to be inserted and then click the tool (insertion tools).

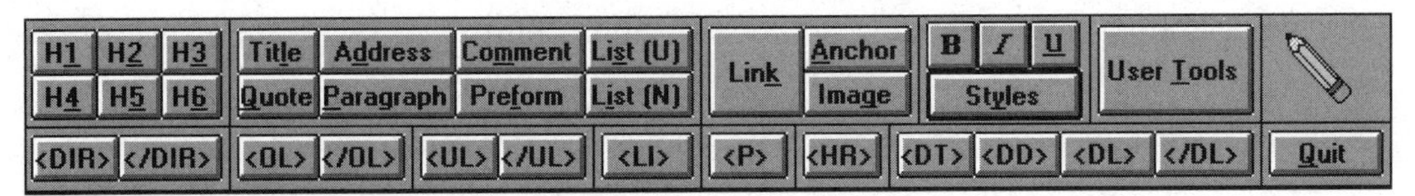

Figure 18-2 HTML Assistant's comprehensive toolbar

The toolbar is divided into two sections. The upper section contains mostly selection tools, the lower section contains tools to insert a lone HTML element.

Selection Tools

The selection tools include:

- H1 through H6: Turns the currently selected text into a level 1 through level 6 heading.
- Title: Turns the current text into the Web page title (there should be only one title per Web page).
- Quote: Formats the current text as a blockquote.
- Address: Formats the current text as an address.
- Comment: Formats the current text as a comment.
- Preform: Defines the selection as preformatted text.
- List (U): Creates an unordered (bulleted) list from the current text, which should include several lines. Before you create a list, be sure to press ENTER after every list item. Each line of text will then become an element in the list.
- List (N): Creates an ordered (numbered) list from the current text, with each line of text becoming an element in the list.
- B: Marks the current text as bold print.
- I: Marks the current text as italicized print.
- U: Marks the current text as underlined print.

Additionally, you can click on the Styles button to select from the following HTML styles:

HTML Bold

HTML Cite (citation)

HTML Code

HTML Fixed

HTML Italic

HTML Keyboard

HTML Sample

HTML Strong

HTML Underline

HTML Variable

For example, to create a bulleted list that looks like this:

```
• Dog
• Cat
• Mouse
```

you would first type the word "Dog," press ENTER, type "Cat," press ENTER, and then type "Mouse," and press ENTER as follows:

```
Dog ENTER
Cat ENTER
Mouse ENTER
```

You would then click on the *D* in "Dog," hold down your mouse button, and move your mouse cursor to the *e* in "Mouse," and let go of the mouse button. This would highlight all three words. You would then click on the List (U) button. With no further effort, this would give you the following markup:

```
<UL>
<LI>Dog
<LI>Cat
<LI>Mouse
</UL>
```

Insertion Tools

The remaining tools are insertion tools, acting as macros. Instead of typing an HTML element, you need only move the cursor to the place where you want the element to appear and then click on one of the following:

HTML <DIR>: Beginning of a directory list

HTML </DIR>: End of a directory list

HTML <OL>: Beginning of an ordered list

HTML </OL>: End of ordered list

HTML <UL>: Beginning of an unordered list

HTML </UL>: End of unordered list

HTML <LI>: A list item

HTML <P>: A paragraph separator

HTML <HR>: A horizontal rule line

HTML <DT>: A term in a definition list

HTML <DD>: A definition in a definition list

HTML <DL>: Beginning of a definition list

HTML </DL>: End of definition list

NOTE: It is often easier to use the List(U) and List(N) buttons to create a list, rather than the individual <UL>, <OL>, and <LI> elements.

This way, you can create directory lists, definition lists with terms and definitions, horizontal rule lines, and paragraph endings. For example, at the end of every plain-text paragraph you type you should make it a habit to click <P>.

LESSON #4: INSERTING HYPERLINKS

HTML Assistant has a rich hyperlink system that allows you to create links and anchors easily. You can even keep a list of common or routine URLs and automatically link to these with the click of a few buttons.

External Links

To create a link to another Web page or other Internet resource, just highlight the text you wish to be the hyperlink. You can also highlight any <IMG SRC="image.gif"> element to turn the selected graphic into a hyperimage. Once you select your link area, click the Link button. The Enter A URL Link dialog box appears, as in Figure 18-3.

To specify a remote link, click the URL Prefixes pop-up menu. A list of URL services such as http, ftp, telnet, and gopher appears. Select the service you want. Now click on the URL Text box. The service is already filled in. Type the rest of the URL, including the domain name, directory path, and/or filename. When done, click OK.

To specify a relative URL, just type the name of the Web page, graphic, movie, or sound in the URL Text box. You can even use the Browse button to locate and insert a Drive, Directory, and Filename from your own hard disk.

NOTE: If you eventually post your Web page to a Unix system, be sure all relative URLs are listed correctly. In most cases, a relative URL should consist of just a lowercase filename. See Chapter 20, Where to Place Your HTML Documents, for more information about posting Web pages on Unix systems.

For example, if you want to turn the word "Mosaic" into a hyperlink leading to the NCSA Mosaic home page, highlight the word "Mosaic" and click the Link button. Type the following URL in the URL Text box:

```
http://www.ncsa.uiuc.edu/SDG/Software/Mosaic/NCSAMosaicHome.html
```

Click OK. HTML Assistant then creates the proper hyperlink in your HTML document:

```
<A
HREF="http://www.ncsa.uiuc.edu/SDG/Software/Mosaic/NCSAMosaicHome.html
>
Mosaic</A>
```

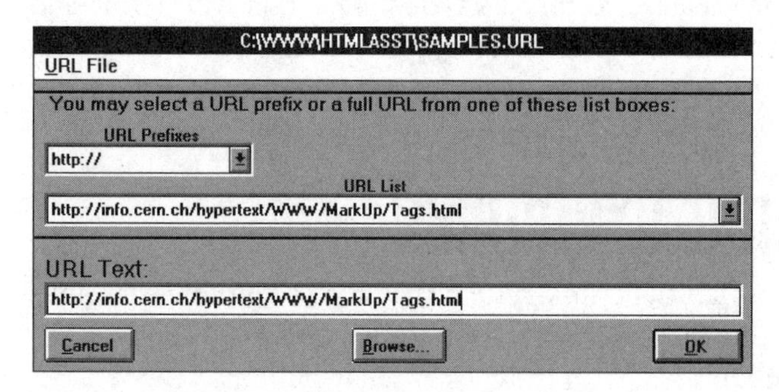

Figure 18-3 Defining a hyperlink using HTML Assistant

If you want the word "football" to bring up a picture of a football (BALL.JPG), be sure the picture is stored in the same directory as your Web page. You can then highlight the word "football" and click on the Link button. Type the relative URL in the URL Text box:

```
ball.jpg
```

Click OK. HTML Assistant creates a relative hyperlink:

```
<A HREF="football.jpg">football</A>
```

Internal Links

To jump to a different section within the current Web page, you can easily specify an anchor and a link. First, move to the part of your HTML document that you want to be the destination for the jump. Highlight some key text and then click the Anchor button. A dialog box appears, asking you for the name of your anchor (see Figure 18-4). Type in a short, descriptive name.

You can now create the link leading to that anchor. Highlight the text or <IMG> image that you want to be hyper. Click the Link button. In the URL Text box, type the hash sign followed by the name of the anchor you wish to jump to.

For example, if you have a section in your HTML document with the heading "Oak Trees," you can highlight this heading and click the Anchor button. Type *oak* as the anchor name. The heading now looks as follows:

```
<A NAME="oak"><H2>Oak Trees</H2></A>
```

You can now move to the top of the document, where you have a Table of Contents with the line:

```
Chapter 5: Oak Trees
```

Highlight the "Oak Trees" item in the listing and click the Link button. Type

```
#oak
```

in the URL Text box and click OK. You now have a functional internal hyperlink:

```
Chapter 5: <A HREF="#oak">Oak Trees</A>
```

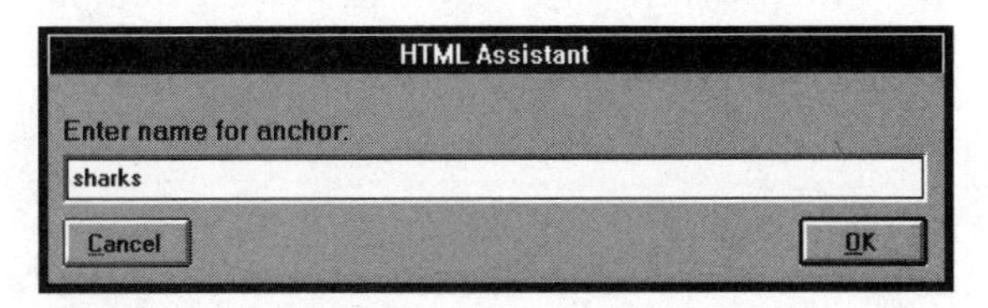

Figure 18-4 Naming an anchor that can be jumped to using an internal link

Recycling URLs

Each time you enter a new URL, HTML Assistant saves it in a special URL list. The next time you create a hyperlink, you can access a previously typed URL by selecting it from the URL List in the Enter A URL Link dialog box. This allows you to create complex hyperlinks with only a few clicks of your mouse.

You can save this list for future use by selecting URL File, Save URL List To File. Specify a Drive, Directory, and Filename. An HTML Assistant URL file usually ends in the .URL extension.

Likewise, you can load up a URL list at any time by selecting URL File, Load URL List To File. Specify the Drive, Directory, and Filename of the URL file. A list of URLs appears for you to work with.

NOTE: You can even convert Mosaic hotlist or Cello bookmark files into HTML Assistant URL files. See the Converting a Bookmark, Hotlist, or URL File to HTML section, later in this chapter. This allows you to use your browser to bounce around the Web. Whenever you come across a page you're likely to call, just hotlist it.

LESSON #5: IMAGES

To insert an inlined image (usually a GIF), simply click the Image button. The Enter A URL For The Image dialog box appears. Type in the image's URL in the URL Text box. If the image is located in the same directory as your Web page, just type the image's filename (i.e. image.html). Always be sure to use lowercase letters.

You can also browse your hard disk until you find the proper image. Click the Browse button. You can now sift though Drives, Directories, and Filenames until you find the image file you want. Select the image and click OK. The full pathname of the image is now printed in the URL Text box. This full pathname works great for testing your Web page; however, if you eventually put this Web page on a Unix system, the pathname will no longer be valid. When you actually post a Web page, be sure to change all image URLs so that they are valid within your Unix file and directory system. See Chapter 20 for more information.

LESSON #6: USER TOOLS

HTML Assistant has buttons for most every HTML element, but not for all of them. What about <MENU>, for example? And what about table elements like <TABLE> and <TD>? And there's no support for fill-in forms elements either.

Luckily, HTML Assistant lets you overcome this by creating your own quick-and-easy tool buttons. You can specify up to ten of these user tools. Simply click the User Tools button. The User Tools palette appears. You can move this palette to the side of your screen and keep it open for easy access. To use a tool, just click its button. If you want to hide the palette, click Close or click the User Tools button again.

Creating a User Tool

To create a tool, click Modify. The Modify Tools dialog box appears, as in Figure 18-5. There are ten slots. Simply type any text you wish into each of these ten slots. The caption you type becomes the actual command. When you click on one of these buttons, the caption is inserted in your HTML document. When you're done modifying the tools, click OK to save your settings.

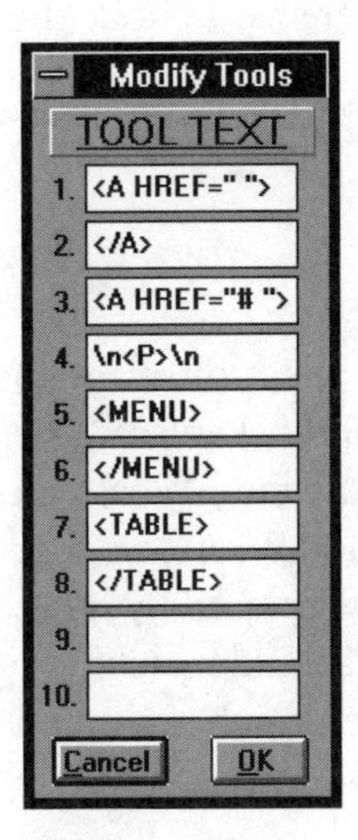

Figure 18-5
Using user tools to create quick buttons for commonly used elements

Entering Enter

If you want a tool to automatically insert a carriage return, just type *\n*.

For example, this user tool:

```
\n<HR>\n
```

would be the same as pressing ENTER, typing *<HR>*, and pressing ENTER again.

LESSON #7: FINDING OR REPLACING

If your HTML documents start getting pretty lengthy, you may find the Find command useful. This allows you to search for any word, term, or HTML markup command. A replace function lets you replace each item you find with an alternate.

Finding

To find the next occurrence of a word, select Edit, Find or press CTRL-F. The Find dialog box appears. Fill in the word, phrase, or markup in the Find What box. If you want to search from the current location down, be sure the Down Direction is selected. Otherwise click Up. If you'd like to search for an exact match—upper and lowercase making a difference—check the Match Case checkbox. To start the search, click Find.

If you'd like to find the next occurrence of your search term, select Edit, Find Next or press F3.

Replacing

Another useful function is Replace. Suppose, for example, you want to change all bold print into italicized print. Simply select Edit, Replace. The Replace dialog appears. Fill in the text to be replaced in the Find What box and type what it should be replaced with in the Replace With box. For instance, all *<B>*s should be replaced by *<I>*s and all *</B>*s replaced by *</I>*s. You can also select Direction and whether or not the case should match.

Click Verify; you are shown each occurrence of the search term and asked if you'd like to replace it. If so, click Yes, if not, choose No. If you're sure you want to replace each occurrence, click Replace All.

LESSON #8: TOOLING WITH TOOLS

HTML Assistant includes a few advanced features that allow you to undo, repeat, or experiment with different tools.

Undo

If you highlight text and then select a tool, the text is now marked up with some sort of HTML element. If you decide you want to use different elements, or you want to select different text, simply select the Undo button at the top of each HTML document. You can also select Edit, Undo Last Command or press CTRL-U.

Auto Repeat

Whether you just used a surround tool, an insert tool, or a user tool, you can easily repeat the last action you performed by pressing CTRL-R or by selecting Command, Repeat Last Command. You can also press the Repeat Markup button at the top of any HTML document.

Putting an HTML Document on Hold

If you spent a long time marking up an HTML document, you may want to hold the contents of the document before you add any more sections, elements, or other markup. Just click the Hold button at the top of your document.

You can now experiment, search and replace, or play around with the markup. If everything seems okay, click Hold again to keep things as they are. If you don't like the results of your edit, you can turn back time by pressing the Recall button. Your Web page warps back to the way it looked when you first clicked Hold. You can also recall a recall, if you wish, by clicking Undo.

LESSON #9: TESTING 'ER OUT

A marked-up HTML document looks like a mess. Imagining how a Web page will actually turn out is all well and good, but HTML Assistant lets you go one step further and makes it easy to test a Web page as you develop it.

Before you test an HTML document, you need to save it. Click the Save button at the top of your HTML document or select File, Save. If you haven't yet created a filename for your Web page, you'll need to specify a Drive, Directory, and Filename.

NOTE: Be sure any hyperlinked files or inlined graphics are located in the same directory as the HTML document itself. Also double-check all HREFs and SRCs to be sure the filenames are accurate. In general, the filenames should be lowercase and shouldn't include any path or directory names.

Specifying a Browser

The first time you test out an HTML document, you need to tell HTML Assistant which browser you are using and where it is located. Select File, Enter Test Program Name. Specify the Drive, Directory, and Filename of your browser. Most any browser works well with HTML Assistant. The program has been tested extensively with Cello, Mosaic, and Netscape without any problems.

The Final Test

To see exactly what your Web page looks like, click the Test button at the top of your document or select File, Test. You may be asked if you'd like to save your file; select Yes.

NOTE: You can automatically save files each time you test them by selecting Options, Autosave Before Testing.

Your browser is now launched. If you're using Netscape, Mosaic, Cello, or any other SLIP-based browser, be sure that your Winsock program is running in the background. You can now flip through your Web page, see all inlined images, and even click the hypertext and hyperimages and see the results.

LESSON #10: PRINTING

You may want a hard copy of your HTML document for reference, to study, or to show to other people. If so, you can easily print your page by selecting File, Print. A dialog box appears for each open HTML document, asking you if you want to print it. If you do, select Yes.

LESSON #11: URL FILES

HTML Assistant has some powerful commands that allow you to convert, copy, comment, append, or edit URLs. All in all, the Assistant makes it easy to keep large lists of common Internet sites, Web pages, or multimedia files. You can then refer to this list any time you insert a hyperlink.

Select URL, Edit/Build URL File or press CTRL-E to bring up the URL Manager window, as shown in Figure 18-6.

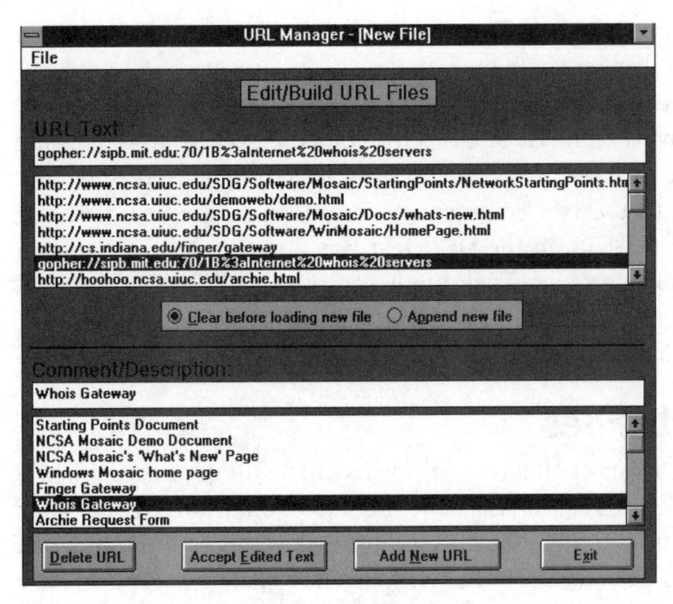

Figure 18-6 The built-in URL file editor

Grabbing URLs

If you have an existing URL file, a Mosaic hotlist, or a Cello bookmark list, you can load up the URLs from one or more of these sources. Select one of the following options from the File menu:

HTML CTRL-B: Open Cello Bookmark File

HTML CTRL-A: Open HTML Assistant URL File

HTML CTRL-M: Open URLs in MOSAIC.INI File

You can now specify the Drive, Directory, and Filename for the file you wish to open.

Editing URLs

Once you open a file, you are shown a list of all URLs. The top listing shows you the actual URL Text. The bottom listing shows you a Comment/Description, which is usually the title of the URL's Web page. You can select any URL Text or

Comment/Description and edit it. Be sure to click the Accept Edited Text button before you select another item from the list.

To delete a URL, select it and click the Delete URL button.

If you have a hard copy list of URLs, or you come across an interesting URL in a magazine or book, you can add it by selecting the Add New URL button. You can also use this command to begin creating a new URL file from scratch. Type the URL in the URL Text box and type a description in the Comment/Description box. Click the Accept New URL button. You can continue typing in new URLs and associated comments. When you're done, click the Go To Edit Mode button.

Combining URL Files

Maybe you have a nice collection of URLs that you've created while building hyperlinks in HTML Assistant. Perhaps you'd like to add your Mosaic hotlist to this URL file. The URL Editor makes this easy. Simply load up the information in your MOSAIC.INI file. Then click the Append New File radio button in the middle of the window. You can now load up any URL file. The information from the second file is tacked on to the information from the first, yielding a super-dooper URL list.

Saving It

Once you're happy with your collection of URLs, you can easily save it. Select File, Save to save an already open file or select File, Save As to save your information to a new file. Specify the Drive, Directory, and Filename for your new URL file.

NOTE: You can automatically save your information as a Cello bookmark file by selecting File, Save As Cello Bookmark File.

LESSON #12: CONVERTING A BOOKMARK, HOTLIST, OR URL FILE TO HTML

If you've developed a great list of URLs, why not offer these links to the world? You can create a Web page consisting entirely of hyperlinks to other interesting pages. HTML Assistant makes this process nearly automatic.

You can easily convert a URL file, a Mosaic hotlist, or a Cello bookmark file into a clean HTML document. You can then organize this HTML document by date, size, or topic. You can even break the HTML document up into several Web pages, if you like.

To convert, simply select URL, Autoconvert File To HTML. The following submenu appears:

- Cello Bookmark File {CTRL-B}
- HTML Assistant URL File {CTRL-A}
- URLs in Mosaic.ini File {CTRL-M}

Select the type of file you want to convert. You can now specify a Drive, Directory, and Filename. Cello bookmark files are usually located in the Cello directory, with the extension .BMK. The MOSAIC.INI file is usually in your Windows directory. HTML Assistant URL files are generally in your HTML Assistant directory. Once you've found the proper file, choose OK.

The Assistant quickly converts the data, leaving your original URL File, Cello bookmark file, or MOSAIC.INI file untouched. A new HTML document is created. All URLs now appear on your screen as proper HTML links, separated by paragraph tags.

WHAT NOW?

You now are armed with a powerful tool that lets you create great Web pages quickly and accurately. To save your Web page, just select File, Save and specify a Drive, Directory and Filename. The filename should always have the .HTM extension.

Once you've cobbled together a few HTML documents, you're ready to put them online for the world to see. Flip to Chapter 20, Where to Place Your HTML Documents, for the scoop. The next chapter explores the HoTMetaL editor.

19

HoTMetaL

19

SoftQuad's HoTMetaL is a powerhouse HTML editor. You never actually have to type in HTML elements or attributes when you use HoTMetaL. Instead, you just select styles, formats, and other elements from a comprehensive menu. Markup appears graphically on your screen as shown in Figure 19-1, and you can choose to hide this markup if you wish. HoTMetaL then displays your Web page in a near What You See Is What You Get (WYSIWYG) manner. This allows you to preview what your Web page will look like (more or less) as you create it.

HoTMetaL also includes full rules checking. If you try to use an HTML element in an illegal way, HoTMetaL won't let you. An opening element will always automatically have an associated

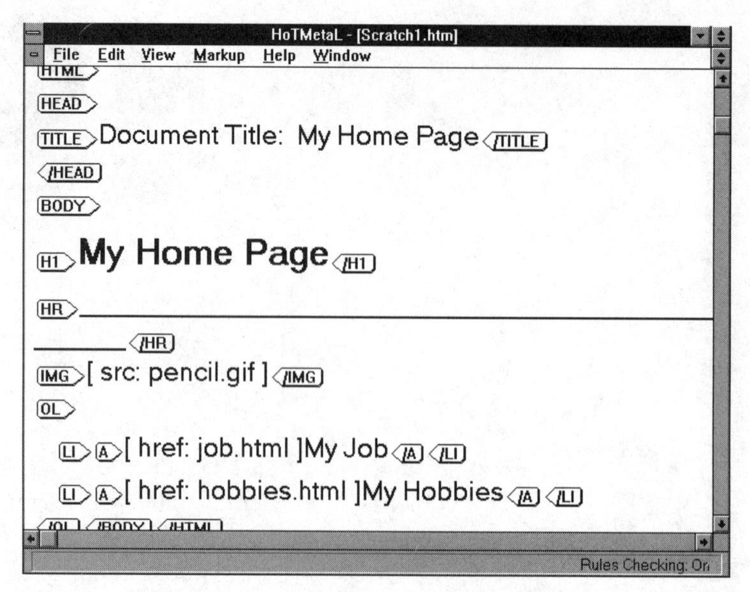

Figure 19-1 A typical HoTMetaL editing session

closing element. This guarantees your Web page will work without tripping up the browser.

Sometimes HoTMetaL's ease and strictness works against itself: HoTMetaL won't allow you to type in your own elements or attributes, even if you want to. Although HoTMetaL has full support for forms and most text styles, HoTMetaL has no way of creating certain HTML3 or Mozilla commands, such as alignment or tables. The HoTMetaL software also runs very slowly if your Web page gets too long or cumbersome.

However, for the design of a basic, simple Web page, nothing could be easier than HoTMetaL. You can load up a template, fill in a few values, press a few keys, and voilà, you've just completed a Web page.

INSTALLING IT

You'll find the HoTMetaL software in the \WINDOWS\EDITOR\HOTMETAL\ directory of the enclosed CD-ROM. This includes six subdirectories: \DOC, \DTDS, \LIB, \RULES, \STYLES, and \TEMPLATE. To install HoTMetaL, copy the entire HoTMetaL directory and its subdirectories to your hard disk.

You can create a new Program Item in the Windows Program Manager by selecting File, New and pressing OK. Fill in the following values:

```
Description: SoftQuad HoTMetaL
Command Line: C:\HOTMETAL\BIN\SQHM.EXE -sqdir C:\hotmetal
Directory: C:\HOTMETAL
```

NOTE: Read the COPYRIGHT.TXT file for information about SoftQuad's license. A Pro Version of HoTMetaL is also available. Contact SoftQuad at hotmetal@sq.com or by phone at 416-239-4801.

LESSON #1: STARTING WITH A TEXT FILE

HoTMetaL can open any ASCII file, whether it be HTML or plain text. In general, however, HoTMetaL is not the best tool to use for plain text conversion. If you use a text file, you will need to go through it, paragraph by paragraph, inserting the paragraph elements or other styles. A better idea is to use HTML Assistant to convert a text file into a simple HTML file, as described in Chapter 18. You can then load up this HTML file with HoTMetaL and spruce it up.

To open a file, select File, Open, or press CTRL-O. Specify a Drive, Directory, and Filename and choose OK.

NOTE: HoTMetaL cannot handle messy HTML files or files that contain advanced Mozilla or HTML3 commands such as <CENTER> or <TABLE>. HoTMetaL often goes ahead and opens such files, with its rules-checking routines turned off. If you turn rules checking on (see the section on Rules later in this chapter) then your HTML document will cause errors. Sometimes, HoTMetaL all-out refuses to open a document. If you want to use HoTMetaL to edit a complicated HTML file, go through it with a text editor first and remove any nonstandard HTML markup.

You can open many files at once. Each document appears in its own editing window. You can Tile, Cascade, or Switch between active windows by selecting commands from the Window pull-down menu. You can also minimize a window by clicking the Minimize box in the upper right corner; the HTML document appears as a small icon at the bottom of the screen.

LESSON #2: STARTING FROM SCRATCH

To begin anew, select File, New. A document called SCRATCH1.HTM appears. You can now start inserting HTML elements or typing other text.

Templates

An even faster way of creating your own Web page is to use an existing template. A template is a sample HTML document that includes all the markup you could need. A template's text is explanatory, with simple phrases such as "Replace this text with title" or "Level 1 Heading." You can easily replace or delete any of these samples.

To get started, select File, Open Template. HoTMetaL comes with the following templates:

- HTML CUSTREG: A customer mailing list form
- HTML DEFLIST: A sample definition list
- HTML H1: A sample document with just one heading
- HTML H2: A sample document with two levels of headings
- HTML H3: A sample document with three levels of headings
- HTML HOMEPAGE: A basic corporate home page
- HTML IMG: A sample inlined image
- HTML IMGS: A document with a few inlined images
- HTML LOLIST: A long ordered list
- HTML LULIST: A long unordered list
- HTML PARAS: A bunch of paragraphs
- HTML README: A description of each template
- HTML SOLIST: A short order list
- HTML SULIST: A short unordered list

Select a template and choose OK. The template loads up, as shown in Figure 19-2. You now have a basic building block that you can use to create full-featured Web pages. Go through the document, changing hyperlinks, renaming graphic file sources, and adding text to best suit your needs.

Templates also come in handy if you want to create a simple list, layout, or image, but aren't quite sure how to do it. Just load the template and use

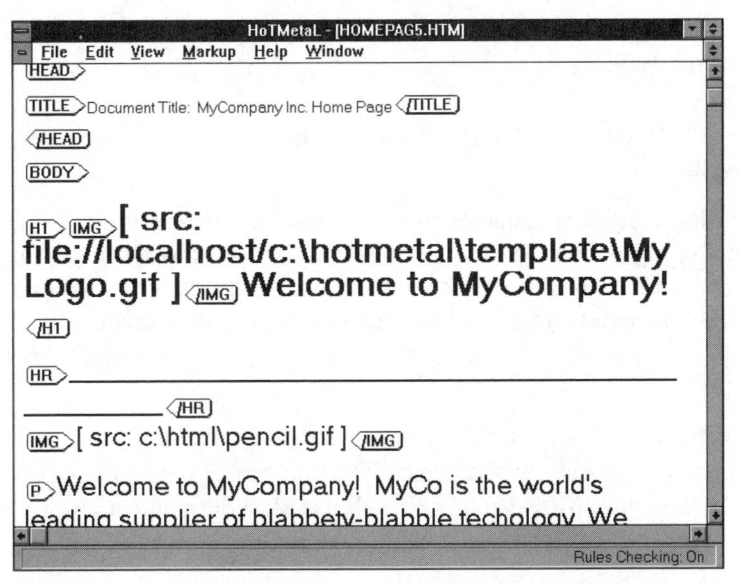

Figure 19-2 HoTMetaL's Home Page template. Just fill in the blanks!

the Edit menu's Cut and Paste commands to cut the markup from the template and drop it in your actual HTML document. You can also learn a lot by glancing over a template's structure.

NOTE: You can easily create your own templates. When you put together a basic Web page that you might want to use again, save it in HoTMetaL's \TEMPLATES directory.

Saving

No matter how you create your HTML document, you can easily save it by selecting File, Save As, or pressing CTRL-S. If you're saving a Web page for the first time, you need to specify a Drive, Directory, and Filename. Your file should always end with the .HTM extension.

LESSON #3: MARKING IT UP

There are two ways to mark up your HTML document with styles, links, or other elements:

- Insert the markup and then type the appropriate text between the starting tag and the closing tag.

HTML Type some text first, highlight it, and then surround it with the proper markup.

For most HTML elements, you can use whichever procedure you find most comfortable.

NOTE: HoTMetaL uses most elements as containers, not as empty elements, even if the closing tag is optional. For instance, paragraphs always start with the <P> tag and end with </P>. Each element of a list starts with <LI> and ends with </LI>. This makes your HTML source easier to read through.

Inserting

To insert an element in the current cursor location, select Markup, Insert Element, or press CTRL-I. The Insert Element dialog box appears, as shown in Figure 19-3. This box lists every applicable HTML command, in alphabetical order, along with a short description of what the command does.

Paragraph Styles

If you try typing text in some blank area of your HTML document, HoTMetaL often gives you an error message: "Text is not allowed here!" The solution is to tell HoTMetaL what *type* of text to insert. The Insert Element commands let HoTMetaL know whether it's working with a blockquote, a hyperlink, a plain paragraph, a heading, or a list.

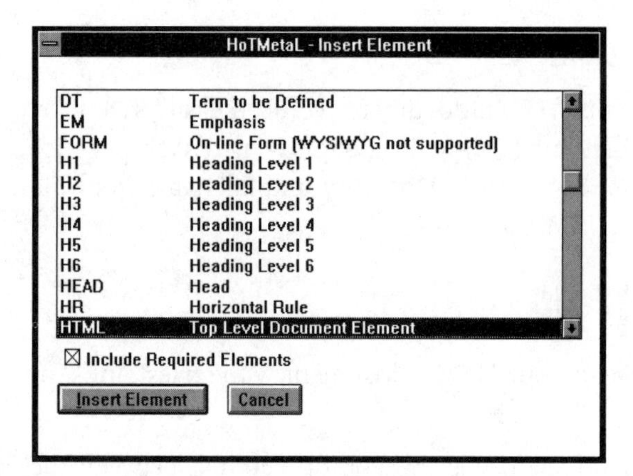

Figure 19-3 Inserting an HTML element

When you are at the start of a paragraph, you have the following HTML commands to choose from:

HTML A: Anchor

HTML ADDRESS: Address

HTML BLOCKQUOTE: A blockquote paragraph

HTML DL: A definition list

HTML FORM: A fill-in form

HTML H1 through H6: Heading levels 1 through 6

HTML HR: A horizontal rule line

HTML IMG: An image

HTML LISTING: A listing

HTML OL: An ordered (numbered) list

HTML P: A paragraph

HTML PRE: A section with preformatted text

HTML UL: An unordered list

HTML XMP: An example

To select an element, just double-click on it or select it and press the Insert Element button. You can also type the first letter of any element to automatically scroll to it in the list. For example, to start writing a paragraph of text, double-click on P. The <P> and </P> tags are automatically created in your HTML document, with the cursor positioned between them. You can now type your paragraph text.

As another example, to create a bulleted list you would select UL. The following tags appear:

```
<UL><LI> </LI></UL>
```

The cursor is positioned between the <LI> and </LI> elements, ready for you to type your first list item. Move the cursor past the </LI> tag (before the </UL> tag) and then press CTRL-I again. The Insert Element dialog appears with only once choice: LI. Select this. You can now define your second list item. Continue like this until your list is complete. You can then move the cursor past the </UL> tag, which exits you from the list and allows you to create any other type of paragraph style.

Text Styles

When you are in the middle of a paragraph, heading, or other paragraph style, you have a different set of text formatting commands to work with. These allow you to change the style or look of a given piece of text:

HTML B: Bold text

HTML BR: Forced line break

HTML CITE: Citation

HTML CODE: Example of program code

HTML DFN: Definition instance of a term

HTML EM: Emphasized text

HTML I: Italicized text

HTML INPUT: Input for a fill-in form

HTML KBD: Keyboard (something a user would type)

HTML SAMP: A sample sequence of literal characters

HTML SELECT: A selection list in a fill-in form

HTML STRONG: Strong emphasis

HTML TEXTAREA: A multiline text field in a fill-in form

HTML TT: Teletype fixed-width font

HTML U: Underlined text

HTML VAR: A sample variable (named place holder)

If you select B, for example, the marks <B> and </B> appear, with the cursor between them. Any text you now type will appear in bold print.

Surrounding

Surrounding text with HTML elements works similar to inserting, except the procedure is reversed: First you type the text you want to modify or define, then you select the HTML element you wish to define it. You cannot surround entire paragraphs; you can only use the Surround command to define text styles.

NOTE: If you like, you can select a few paragraphs of text and use the Surround command to define the selection as an address, a blockquote, or a form.

To bring up the Surround dialog box, use your mouse to highlight the text you want to define. Select Markup, Surround, or press CTRL-U. Much like the text styles in the Insert Element box, the Surround box (shown in Figure 19-4) lists valid HTML elements with short descriptions of each one. Double-click the element you want or select the element and click the Surround button.

Changing

Once you define a paragraph or a piece of text, you may change your mind. For example, you may have some italicized text that you think should be bold instead.

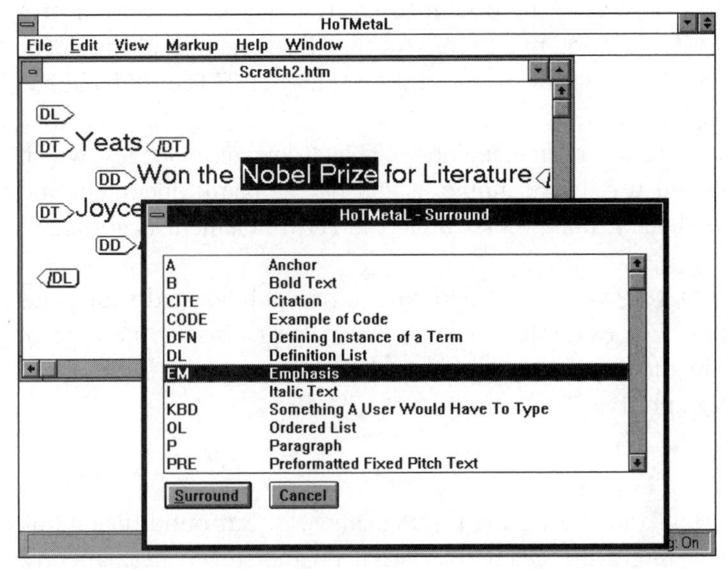

Figure 19-4 Surrounding existing text with HTML elements

Move the cursor into the section you want to change and select Markup, Change, or press CTRL-L. The Change dialog box appears, identical to the Surround box. Select the new element from the list and click the Change button. The Change command allows you to quickly substitute one set of elements for another.

Deleting

To erase an HTML element, move the cursor after the opening element and press BACKSPACE. Backspacing over a closing element has no effect. For example, if you want to un-bold the following phrase:

```
<B>This is bold</B>
```

move the cursor before the *T* in "This" and press BACKSPACE to delete the <B> element. The closing </B> element automatically disappears as well.

HoTMetaL only lets you delete paragraph elements such as <PRE> or <P> if you highlight the tag and then press DEL. This protects you from messing up your document by backing over these crucial tags by accident.

The Smart List

HoTMetaL's list of elements is intelligent. The Insert Element box usually contains only those HTML elements that are valid for the current situation. For example, if you're inserting an element while working within a definition list, you will only have the option to create either a <DT> term or a <DD> definition itself. If you're currently in the HEAD section of the document, you will have the option to insert a <BASE>, <TITLE>, <ISINDEX>, <LINK>, or <META> element.

When you opt to insert an element, HoTMetaL may also suggest which element you should use. For example, if you have a blank document and try inserting an element for the first time, the HTML element is automatically selected.

If the element you want isn't listed, you're probably located someplace you shouldn't be. For example, you may be trying to insert one type of paragraph within another. Or you may be trying to insert a text style before inserting a paragraph style.

Pinning

If you find yourself bringing up the Insert Element or Surround dialog box pretty often, you might just want to paste it on the screen permanently. Select the control box in the box's upper left corner and choose the Pin item. The Insert Element box becomes a window, permanently "pinned" on your screen. You can resize your HTML document and work with both windows simultaneously.

LESSON #4: SPECIAL CHARACTERS

HTML does not allow you to use the less-than, greater-than, or ampersand characters directly. You can still have them, though. Whenever you type &, <, or >, HoTMetaL automatically replaces these characters by small box icons: [amp], [lt], or [gt]. When your Web page is displayed, these characters will look the way you want them to—but Web browsers won't confuse them with real HTML markup.

In addition, there may be times when you want to insert characters with French or Spanish accents, the copyright symbol, the currency symbol for pounds or yen, or other typical characters. HoTMetaL comes with several libraries of typical characters. Select Markup, Insert Character Entity or press CTRL-E. To choose a category, click the Entity Set pop-up menu at the bottom of the window. You can select from the following sets of characters:

- Local & Active
- Rules File
- Added Latin
- Numeric and Special Graphic
- Diacritical Marks

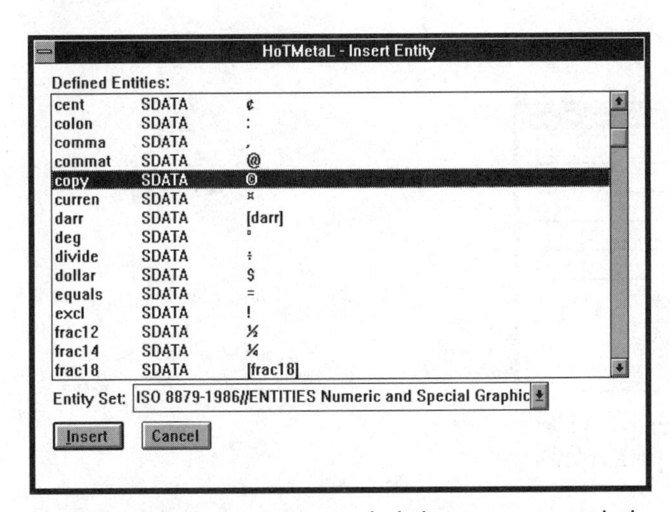

Figure 19-5 Inserting extended characters or symbols into your HTML document

Double-click the character you want or select it and click the Insert button. This special character is now embedded in your HTML document, surrounded by a rectangle.

LESSON #5: WORKING WITH HYPERLINKS

Often the trickiest part of Web page creation is how to format or specify your hyperlinks. HoTMetaL makes this process relatively simple. In most cases, you can create perfect links with the click of a few keys.

Creating External Links

You can create a hyperlink using either the Insert Element or Surround commands. To insert a hyperlink, press CTRL-I and select A. If you've already created your hyperimage or hypertext, highlight it, press CTRL-U, and select A. The following markup appears:

```
<A>[ href: ]</A>
```

By itself, the anchor element doesn't mean much. You need to insert attributes, such as link references or names. To work with these attributes, select Markup, Edit Links And Attributes, or press F6. The Edit Attributes dialog box in Figure 19-6 appears.

The only important attribute is the HREF. Fill in the full (or relative) URL of your hyperlink destination in the HREF box. You do not need to surround this reference with quotes. For example, if you have a Web page called *stats.html* in the same directory as your current Web page, just type

```
stats.html
```

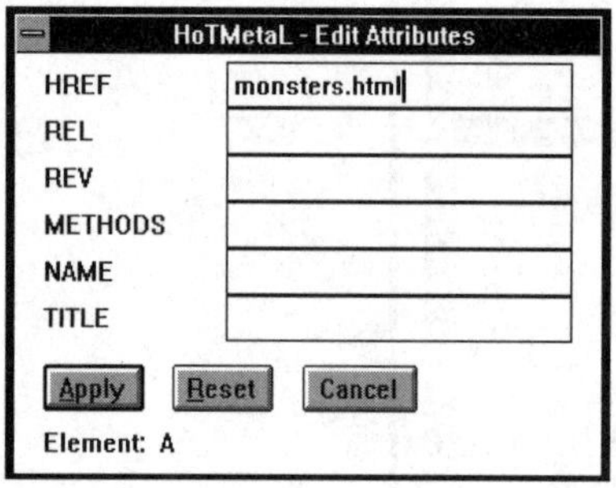

HoTMetaL - Edit Attributes

HREF	monsters.html
REL	
REV	
METHODS	
NAME	
TITLE	

Apply · Reset · Cancel

Element: A

Figure 19-6 Customizing the attributes for your hypertext links

If you want to reference a distant document, multimedia file, or other Internet resource, just type the full URL, for example:

```
http://www.ncsa.uiuc.edu/SDG/Software/Mosaic
```

If you like, you can define the REL, REV, METHODS, NAME, or TITLE attribute. In most cases, however, none of these are necessary. When you're done defining attributes, click the Apply button. You can change or edit these attributes at any time by moving between the <A> and </A> elements and clicking F6.

Creating Internal Links

To create an internal link, you need to set up two anchor sections: a link and an anchor. The anchor should have the NAME attribute filled out, and the link itself should have a HREF attribute with the hash sign (#) followed by the name of the anchor.

For example, if you have a long document about home furnishings (a wild topic, no doubt), you may want to include an internal link at the beginning of your document that jumps to the section on sofas. First you need to define the anchor. Scroll through your document until you find the Sofa section, which probably has a heading similar to:

```
<H2>Sofas</H2>
```

Highlight the word "Sofas" and then press CTRL-U to bring up the Surround box. Select A and click Surround. Press F6 to edit the attributes. Move to the NAME box and type

```
sofa
```

and click Apply. You have now created an anchor.

Now move to the top of your document and type up some sort of Table of Contents. One of the lines in the Contents should be something like:

```
<LI>Sofas</LI>
```

Highlight the word "Sofas," press CTRL-U, select A, and click Surround. Your line should now look like this:

```
<LI><A>[href: ]Sofas</A></LI>
```

Press F6 to define the attributes. In the HREF box, type

```
#sofa
```

and then click Apply. Your final internal link would look like this:

```
<LI><A>[href: #sofa]Sofas</A></LI>
```

LESSON #6: WORKING WITH GRAPHICS

To insert an inlined image, move your cursor to the place where you want the image to appear and press CTRL-I. Select IMG from the list and click Insert Element. The Edit Attributes dialog box appears, as in Figure 19-7.

Image Attributes

The most important attribute is the SRC, which is required. This is the local filename or full URL of your image file. Type this in without quotes. If the graphic file is stored in the same directory as your current Web page, just type the filename, such as:

```
image.gif
```

If the image is stored on another part of the Internet, specify the full URL:

```
file://www.smartpants.edu/graphics/myimage.gif
```

If you like, you can also click the ALIGN pop-up menu to align your image's adjacent text to the Top, Middle, or Bottom (but not Left or Right—HoTMetaL doesn't support those codes). It's also a good idea to type some alternative text in the ALT box. If your image is a clickable imagemap, then be sure to select ISMAP from the ISMAP pop-up menu.

When you're done, click Apply. The following markup appears in your HTML document:

```
<IMG> [src: image.gif]</IMG>
```

You can edit your image attributes at any time by moving the cursor between the <IMG> and </IMG> tags and pressing F6.

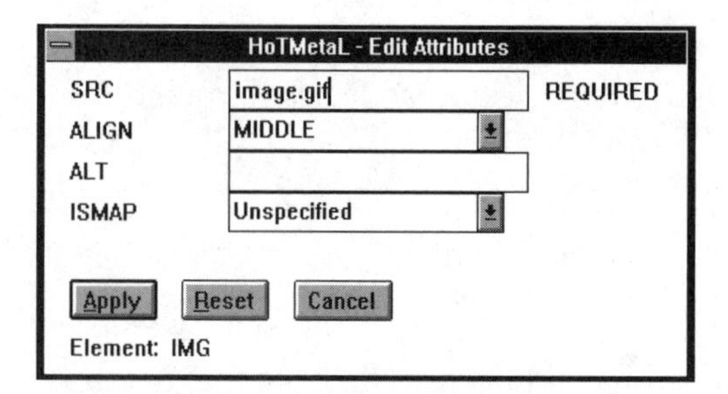

Figure 19-7 Specifying the filename and/or URL of your inlined image

Viewing Images

You can have HoTMetaL quickly display any inlined image to be sure you're using the one you want. To do so, however, HoTMetaL needs its own helper application, such as WinGIF or LView. Edit the SQHM.INI file using Notepad or any other text editor:

```
view_gif                  = c:\lview\lviewp1a
view_bmp                  = c:\windows\pbrush
```

You can now display any image by moving the cursor between the <IMG> and </IMG> tags. Select View, Show Image. The image is loaded up and displayed.

LESSON #7: WORKING WITH FORMS

HoTMetaL has full support for all forms elements and attributes. First select FORM from the Insert Element or Surround dialog box. The following markup appears:

```
<FORM> </FORM>
```

Press F6 to define the form's attributes. An attribute dialog box appears. You can alter the following options:

- HTML ACTION: A CGI script or other action that should happen after this form is filled out
- HTML SCRIPT: The script file that should be run
- HTML METHOD: The method of the form (POST or GET)
- HTML ENCTYPE: The encoding type
- HTML ID: The unique ID number for the form
- HTML CHARSET: The character set for the form

In most cases, you need only define ACTION and METHOD. The other options are HTML3 attributes, and do not currently work with most browsers. When done, click Apply.

Input Field

You can now start creating your form. First create a <P> paragraph or a heading. You can now type any captions or other explanatory text. To insert

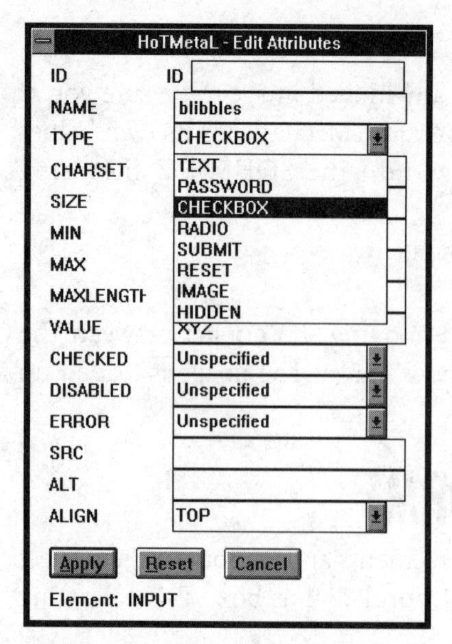

Figure 19-8 Fiddling with fill-in forms; defining an input field

an input field, select INPUT from the Insert Element dialog box. The input field appears:

```
<INPUT> </INPUT>
```

You can now press F6 while between the <INPUT> and </INPUT> tags to specify the input field's options. The attribute dialog box appears as in Figure 19-8. You can define all or none of the following attributes:

- HTML ID: The field ID number
- HTML NAME: The field name
- HTML TYPE: The kind of field: text, password text, checkbox, radio button, submit button, reset button, image, or hidden
- HTML CHARSET: The character set
- HTML SIZE: The size of the field
- HTML MIN: The minimum value
- HTML MAX: The maximum value

- MAXLENGTH: The maximum length
- VALUE: The default value for the field
- CHECKED: The default on/off state (for checkboxes or radio buttons)
- DISABLED: Should the field appear disabled?
- ERROR: Should the field return an error?
- SRC: The source filename or URL for an image
- ALT: The alternative text for text-based browsers
- ALIGN: Should this input field be aligned Top, Middle, or Bottom relative to the image?

In most cases, all you'll need to define is the TYPE of the field and the field's unique NAME. Most browsers don't support the other attributes yet.

TEXTAREA

You can easily create an input area for text by selecting TEXTAREA from the Insert Element dialog box. Be sure your cursor is currently between <P> and </P> or some other paragraph element. The proper markup appears:

```
<TEXTAREA> </TEXTAREA>
```

You can now type any default textarea text. To specify textarea options, press F6. You can work with the following attributes, as shown in Figure 19-9:

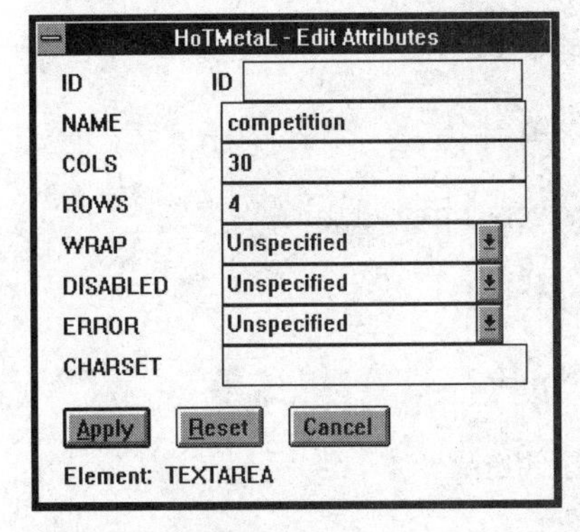

Figure 19-9 Defining the look and functionality of a text box

- HTML ID: The unique ID number for the area
- HTML NAME: The unique name for the area
- HTML COLS: The width of the area
- HTML ROWS: The height of the area
- HTML WRAP: Should text be automatically wrapped?
- HTML DISABLED: Should this area appear disabled?
- HTML ERROR: Should this area return an error?
- HTML CHARSET: The character set for the area

In most cases, all you need to worry about specifying is the NAME. You should also define the size of your textarea by typing values in COLS and ROWS.

Selection Lists

Selection lists are probably the trickiest form elements to create. First you need to create the list itself by selecting SELECT from the Insert Element dialog box. The list elements appear in your HTML document:

```
<SELECT> <OPTION> </OPTION> </SELECT>
```

The cursor appears between the <OPTION> and </OPTION> tags. Type in the text for your list's first item. Press F6 to specify the details about the item. Each item in the selection list can have its own attributes, all of which are optional:

- HTML ID: The unique ID number for the item
- HTML VALUE: The default value of the item
- HTML SELECTED: Should this item be selected by default?
- HTML DISABLED: Should this item be disabled?
- HTML SHAPE: What shape should the item be?
- HTML CHARSET: The character set for the item

To define another item, move your cursor to the right, past the </OPTION> tag but not past the </SELECT> tag. Select OPTION from the Insert menu (it should be the only choice). Continue like this until you've created your whole list of items, and your markup looks something like this:

```
<SELECT>
<OPTION>Item1</OPTION>
<OPTION>Item2</OPTION>
</SELECT>
```

Finally, move your cursor so that it is directly before the </SELECT> tag or directly after the <SELECT> tag. Press F6 to define the attributes for the selection list itself. These attributes include:

- HTML SRC: The source for the image or file to be loaded
- HTML ID: The unique ID number for the list
- HTML NAME: The unique name for the list
- HTML EDIT: The edit criteria for the list
- HTML MULTIPLE: Can multiple options be selected?
- HTML ERROR: Should the list return an error?
- HTML CHARSET: The character set for the list

You should specify a NAME. Unfortunately, HoTMetaL doesn't give you the ability to specify a SIZE.

LESSON #8: FINDING SOMETHING

After a little while, your HTML document may get quite long. Luckily, HoTMetaL has a complete search utility that allows you to easily search, find, and even replace any text. To look for a given word or phrase, select Edit, Find And Replace.

The Search Term

Type the term or phrase to search for in the Find box. If you want to replace each occurrence of the term with another word or phrase, type that replacement text in the Replace box.

You can also search for special entities. For example, if your element begins with the less-than sign (<) and a valid element name, then you can search for that particular element. For example, if you want to replace all <B> bold elements with <I> italics, you could type

```
<B
```

in the Find box, then move to the Replace box and type

```
<I
```

You can also search for text within a certain element. For example, if you want to change all boldface "Hello"s to "Goodbye"s you would go to the Find box and type

```
<B>Hello
```

In the Replace box you would type simply

```
Goodbye
```

The Find In box lets you restrict a search further, and only search for text located within a certain element. This way, you can search for a bold search term within, say, an unordered list. To restrict your search to unordered lists, you would go to the Find In box and type

```
<UL
```

Search Options

You can now specify any of the following options by clicking the associated checkbox:

- Whole Words: The search term must be its own word. For example, if you search for "cat," then "catastrophe" or "implicate" are *not* found.

- Case Sensitive: The search term must appear exactly as you typed it. For example, if you search for "Big," the words "big," "bigotry" or "ambiguous" are *not* found, but "Bigfoot" is.

- Wrap: The search will continue at the beginning of the document after HoTMetaL reaches the end. (Normally, it goes to the end and stops.)

- Backward Search: The search will proceed from the current cursor location upward to the beginning of the document. (This option is handy if you're at the end of the file. Normally, HoTMetaL searches from the current cursor location downward.)

HTML Find Patterns: The search will look for specified patterns using the *regular expression* format. (For example, you can use the ampersand (&) to search for two words or use the OR line (|) to search for one word *or* another.)

Searching

You can now search for the term you specified by clicking Find. HoTMetaL locates the first occurrence of your term and highlights it. You can then overwrite it with your specified Replace word by clicking Replace. You can also click Replace Then Find to replace the current word and immediately find the next occurrence. To replace every occurrence of the term, click Replace All.

You can also find a previously specified word by selecting Edit, Find Next. This allows you to hide or close the Find & Replace dialog box.

NOTE: All text you specify must be within the same element. For example, if you try to look for the phrase "Big Trouble" when the word "Big" is marked as bold print, HoTMetaL won't find the phrase.

LESSON #9: BREAKING THE RULES

You might notice, as you try to develop an HTML document, that HoTMetaL is very strict. It won't let you emphasize text until you create a paragraph type. It won't let you insert text in the middle of nowhere. It won't let you start any element without finishing it. When you try to insert or surround text with an element, you have to choose from a list of valid elements.

If you find these rules too rigid, you can turn them off by selecting Markup, Turn Rules Checking Off, or pressing CTRL-K. Often, you may want to insert an element or tag that HoTMetaL doesn't like. Turning off rules is usually the easiest way to do this.

If you press CTRL-K again or select Markup, Turn Rules Checking On, your document is reviewed and checked for faulty HTML commands or syntax. Any errors are flagged for you to fix. Fix the error (if it is indeed an error) and try turning on rules checking again.

LESSON #10: STYLES

As you design your Web page, you can have each element look exactly the way you wish. HoTMetaL is a WYSIWYG editor. By customizing styles, you can see exactly what you want to see. Any styles you set are automatically saved along with the HTML document.

NOTE: When you actually put an HTML document on the Web, its specific styles are dictated by the Web browser itself. HoTMetaL styles are only valid during the editing session.

Character

The first thing you want to customize is each element's *character-based properties.* This is the way the element's text appears as you edit it. Put the cursor in a paragraph style such as <P>, <H1>, <BLOCKQUOTE>, or <PRE> and then select View, Character. The Character dialog box appears. The element you are modifying appears in the lower left corner of the box. You can now change various properties:

- Font: Choose from any font family on your system.
- Font Size: Select any point size you wish.
- Style: Select Bold, Italic, Underline, Superscript, or Subscript. You can click as few or as many styles as you wish. Select Adopt Current to use the default style. The current element's style then depends on the element that surrounds it. Select Toggle if you want the current element to stand out, no matter where it's placed. For example, if you designate an element as both Bold and Toggle, then it will appear in bold print when it is surrounded by plain text, and in plain text if it is surrounded by bold print.
- Line height: How much vertical space should the element take up? If your element takes up more than one line, how much space should be between each line? Select Single, Double, or Triple. You can also specify line height as a percentage. For example, if you want half the usual space between lines, type 50.
- Justification: Do you want the text to be aligned Left, Right, Center, or Both (fully justified)?
- Fill mode: If fill mode is on, carriage returns are treated like blank spaces, otherwise they'll act like true new-line characters and cause the text to break over into the next line.

- Format type: Should the element appear Inline or start on its own Block? Inlined elements do not cause adjacent elements to be pushed away and are useful for text emphasis (bold, italic, and so on) or inlined graphics. Block elements always start on their own line and cause any following element to be put on a new line.

For all style types, you can usually select Adopt Current. This uses the same font, size, line height, or justification as the last element you edited. This allows you to quickly give many elements the same general look.

Separation

You can now determine how much space should appear before and after each element. Move the cursor to the element you wish to define and select View, Separation. Enter the amount of space that should frame the element. You can also force an element to be indented. The options include:

- Top Space: The amount of white space that should precede the element's text. This can be a specific number of lines (1, 2, 3, etc.) or a percentage. For example, if you want half a line of white space between elements, you could set the top space to 50%.

- Bottom Space: The minimum amout of white space that should follow the element's text.

- Tabbed: The element's text should begin with a tab, to make it slightly indented.

Load Styles

HoTMetaL comes with four preconfigured styles:

- HTML-HID.ASF: A nice set of fonts for HTML editing, with hidden tags.

- HTML.ASF: HTML editing with visible tags.

- REAL-HID.ASF: A realistic view of what a Web page might actually look like, with tags hidden.

- REAL.ASF: A realistic view, with tags shown.

To select any of these, select View, Load Styles. Move to HoTMetaL's \STYLES directory. All HoTMetaL styles end with the .ASF extension.

LESSON #11: TESTING IT OUT

Okay, you've created your paragraph types, surrounded your text with interesting style elements, and carefully crafted a bunch of hyperlinks and images. Is your page still difficult to read? Whatever happened to WYSIWYG? Well you ain't seen nothing yet.

Hiding Tags

As you design your Web page, HoTMetaL inserts tons of arrow icons, boxes, and other markup. If you want a better indication of what your Web page will look like, you can make all this markup invisible. Simply select View, Hide Tags. All HTML elements disappear, as shown in Figure 19-10. You can continue adding tags, if you wish—they just won't show on the screen. To see the tags again, select View, Show Tags.

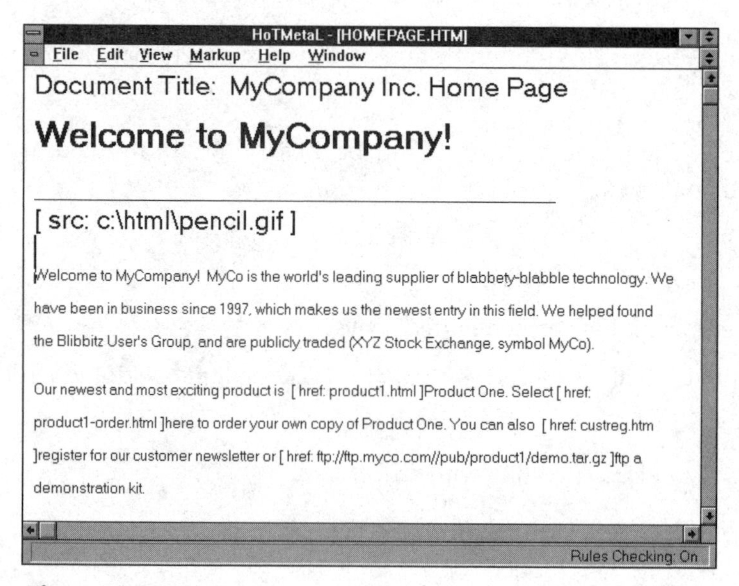

Figure 19-10 Viewing an HTML document without the HTML muck

Publishing

While you're developing a Web document on your local Windows system, your hyperlinks and images have URLs that look similar to: *file://c|/images/test.gif*. When you move your HTML documents to a Unix server, however, these URLs will probably need to change to be something like *http://smartpants.edu/images/test.gif*.

HoTMetaL lets you do this in a flash by selecting File, Publish. By default, this allows you to change URLs from *file://* to *http://*. Type the part of each URL you want to change in Change From box. The appropriate replacement text should appear in the Change To box. Go ahead and find the first occurrence by pressing Find. HoTMetaL selects the next occurrence of your Change From text. Click Replace if you want to replace it with the Change To text. Click Find Next to find the next occurrence. Continue like this. If you want to replace all occurrences of file:// to http://, just click Replace All.

Previewing

HoTMetaL gives you a pretty good indication of what your page will look like, but it's not perfect. Things like graphics, forms, and specific layout are not shown. Launching Mosaic, SlipKnot, Netscape, or another browser lets you see *exactly* what your page looks like.

Before you can preview, you need to edit the following line in the SQHM.INI file, inserting the full path of your Web browser:

```
HTML_BROWSER       = MOSAIC
```

For example, if you want to preview your page using Netscape, you could write something similar to:

```
HTML_BROWSER       = C:\NSCAPE\NETSCAPE
```

The SQHM.INI file is usually located in the \HOTMETAL directory.

To preview a Web page, all you have to do now is select File, Preview, or press CTRL-M.

LESSON #12: THE HTML BACKBONE

HTML documents can get messy. HoTMetaL comes with a few neat commands that make it much easier to organize or understand a muddled Web page. The Context window and the Structure window give you the backbone of your HTML document, showing you in the ins and outs of each element in relation to the others.

The Context Window

Sometimes you may have elements within elements within elements. If things get confusing, you can use the Context window to help figure out where you stand. Move your cursor to the part of your HTML document you want help with. Select View, Show Context Window or press F12.

The Context window appears, showing you the hierarchical sequence of elements. You see all opening tags leading up to your current location. If you have any nested lists, these are clearly delineated. You can keep this window open. As your cursor position changes, so will the contents of the window.

One of the nicest things about this window is that it shows you all attributes. For example, if you move to a hyperlink, you see its HREF URL displayed in full. If you move to a form's INPUT element, you see its NAME and TYPE. This lets you review the actual HTML markup. You cannot edit items in the Context window.

The Structure Window

To see the structure of the entire Web document, select View, Show Structure Window, or press F11. An outlined structure view of your document appears. Each line shows you the start and ending tags of each element in your HTML document. If an element is nested within another element, it is hidden in the structure view.

When you first use this window, only a few elements may appear. This is because each element is closed. Any indented subelements are hidden. To expand a given element, just click on its icon. All its subelements appear. To expand any of these, simply click on them. Click on an expanded element to hide the subelements again. A sample HTML document structure view might look like:

```
<HTML> Document Title: Sample Document        </HTML>
       <HEAD> Document Title: Sample Document              </HEAD>
              <TITLE>  Document Title: Sample Document     </TITLE>
       <BODY> My Sample Document              </BODY>
              <H1> My Sample Document                </H1>
              <P> This is a pretty neat document, huh? In fact...</P>
              <UL> One                        </UL>
                            <LI> One                       </LI>
                            <LI> Two                       </LI>
```

You cannot edit these elements directly, but you can use the Insert or Surround commands from the Markup menu. You can also cut and paste elements. To select an element, move your cursor to the left of the starting-tag element and double-click. Any changes you make to the Structure window are automatically repeated in the actual HTML document.

The Structure window is perhaps most useful when it comes to first planning out your HTML document. You can create a sort of outline in this window and then move to the main document window to type in the specifics.

WHAT NOW?

Now you have a fully functional Web page. You might want to spruce it up even more, especially if you're interested in using Netscape or more obscure HTML3 commands such as the one that aligns graphics to the left, or specifies the width of a horizontal rule line. You can further edit your page using HTML Assistant (see the previous chapter) or any other text editor or word processor.

You've come a long way, baby. You're probably keen to put your own pages online at last. Turn to the next chapter to find out how.

20

WHERE TO PLACE YOUR HTML DOCUMENTS

20

The Web is growing at such a phenomenal rate that by the time this goes to press, there will undoubtedly be an increase in Web sites of exponential proportion. Right now, there are individuals and institutions creating their own sites, there are commercial services that will create a site for you, consultants who will tell you how to write HTML or do it for you, there are commercial sites that will publish an HTML document, there are free sites that will post or advertise your pages, educational institutions that allow students and staff to create their own pages ... it's a virtual free-for-all and it's going to be a while before the dust settles and everyone subscribes to some standard of where things should be and who the providers are, and more importantly, who will pay for it. The reality is that there are already big corporate advertisements showing up in places you would never expect—everything from Zima ads to mail-order brownies to order-a-pizza from Pizza Hut pages. So, the question is, where should you post your HTML documents? Well, a lot of that depends on who you are and who your target audience is. Are you big enough to install your own server and does that make sense for your goals? Or will you get all the exposure you need simply by posting a page with some free provider?

This chapter will describe how you can troubleshoot your HTML documents, how to use them locally, where you can post them for free, and what services are available to post your pages for a fee.

LESSON #1: TROUBLESHOOTING YOUR HTML DOCUMENTS

The number of incomplete, miscoded, and poorly styled HTML documents on the Net is amazing. Most of the problems are simple spelling mistakes, or just carelessness on the part of the authors. And it's easy to avoid problems like these. Before you advertise your pages or make them available on the Net, make sure they say what you think they say. It can be very frustrating for a user to select a link on one of your pages that points to something very interesting, only to find that the link points nowhere. HTML tags are often left open or misspelled, and countless documents have nonexistent or poorly referenced inline images. (If an <IMG> tag can't find the image it is referencing, a standard image marker appears in most Web browsers). The worst thing about this whole situation is that mistakes like these are so easy to avoid. *Test!* Make sure your documents work! First, just run a quick visual check of the HTML code.

- HTML Make sure that all start tags have matching end tags—that is, every <PRE> has its </PRE>, and so on.

- HTML Check your spelling. Thank god for spell-checkers! Use one if you join your authors among the spelling impaired. If you plan on writing a lot of HTML code, add the tag names to your personal dictionary—words like IMG, HTML, HTTP, and the rest.

- HTML Check the paths and filenames of references in your document. If you have a reference to an image such as <IMG

SRC=/usr/pictures/mydog.gif>, make sure that “mydog.gif” really exists in the directory /usr/pictures.

Make sure that files and directories are readable to your server. Most HTTP servers run as the special user “nobody.” If “nobody” doesn’t have read permission for the files and documents you reference, the server will be unable to access these documents. To make a file or directory “world-readable” on a Unix system, type:

```
chmod w+r your_filename
```

(Be sure to replace “your_filename” with the name of the file you want to affect.) Also, you must make sure that the server can execute all directories in the path name of a reference. To make a directory executable, type:

```
chmod w+x directory
```

Make sure that your brackets and quotes match. Every “<” should have a “>” and every open quote should have a close quote. (And as before, make sure to replace “directory” with the name of the directory you want to allow access to.)

The next order of business is to make sure that you are following the HTML spec. Unfortunately, the spec is a living, breathing entity and will continue to grow and be refined and redefined in the months and years to come. Many of the organizations involved in the development of HTTP and HTML have publicly available drafts of new HTML and HTTP specs. One good place to look is on the CERN server. Their URL is:

```
HTTP://www.cern.ch
```

If you don’t have access to this, don’t worry. Most new drafts of a specification are backward compatible. It’s pretty unlikely that a browser or server will come out anytime soon that doesn’t handle last year’s HTML specification.

Once you have done this spot check, open your document with a browser. Does it look the way you expected? If not, modify the code and recheck it. There are a number of browsers out there, and many of these format HTML code with slight differences. Actually, there are sometimes major differences, so it is probably a good idea to look at your HTML documents with a couple of different browsers. The most common browsers you are likely to see are Netscape, Mosaic, and Lynx. If you browse your documents with these three, it should give you a good idea of what most of your clients are seeing, as well as give you insight in how to effectively format your documents for a wide viewing audience. Using a document locally is different from using it remotely, so beware—some links may not work the same as they will when run off of a server. We'll worry about that later. Right now, let's just make sure that the HTML code does what we intended. You can get an informative online HTML style guide that also lists many of the HTML common mistakes and pitfalls by looking at:

```
http://www.willamette.edu/html-composition/strict-html.html
```

LESSON #2: HTML DOCUMENT ANALYSIS SERVICES

There are people out there writing HTML analyzers. Some analyzers are available already, and you can expect more in the months to come. At least one site has set up a free service that allows you to submit your HTML documents and have them reviewed for proper HTML syntax and grammar. They check for pitfalls and return an analysis of your document—all for free. Their URL is:

```
http://www.halsoft.com/html-val-svc/
```

You can expect many commercial services that offer the same or similar analyses in the months to come. Everyone is scrambling to carve their niche in the Web market—either as big commercial service providers, or as high-quality, cutting-edge providers, that offer free services in the public interest or for personal notoriety. Wow, that said, let's take a look at some HTML analyzing services.

One such service is available from

```
http://www.halsoft.com/html-val-svc/
```

At this location, you'll find a set of HTML validation tools that you can download for most major platforms. These tools were developed by Dan Connelly and Mark Gaither, and advertise the following benefits:

- Increase the consistency and quality of the HTML documents at your site.
- Gain an understanding of the HTML 2.0 standard through trial and error with immediate feedback.

Also available at this site is an interactive HTML validation service where you can submit your documents or pieces of HTML code for immediate feedback on your HTML. The submissions are made via a form that allows

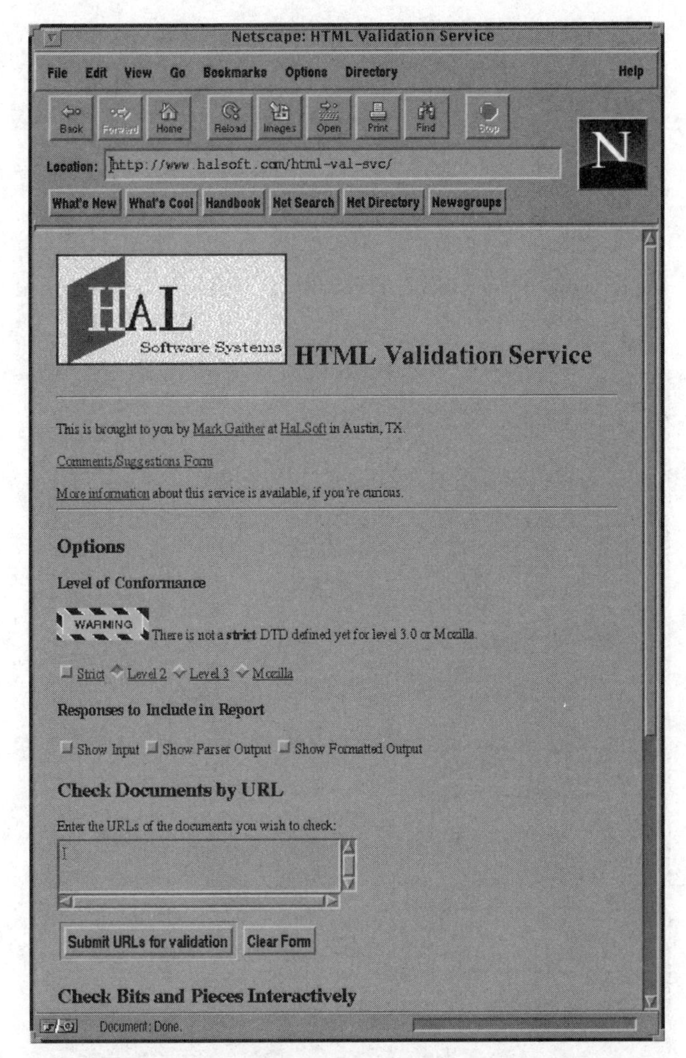

Figure 20-1 http://www.halsoft.com/html-val-svc/

you to enter a URL or input your code fragments as well as make other selections about how you want your code analyzed. You can specify the strictness of the review and the version of HTML or the "Mozilla" extensions to be used by the Netscape browser. (See Figure 20-1.)

There are a few other sites that offer HTML checking utilities. This site offers a Perl script that will check your HTML:

```
http://www.w3.org/hypertext/WWW/tools/weblint.html
```

The next URL offers a similar utility in the form of an AWK script:

```
http://www.w3.org/hypertext/WWW/tools/htmlchek.html
```

If you would like to update old HTML into the newer SGML-abiding code, try the Perl script at this site:

```
http://www.w3.org/hypertext/WWW/tools/fix-html
```

Yet another HTML analyzer can be found at:

```
http://www.gatech.edu/pitkow/html_analyzer/README.html
```

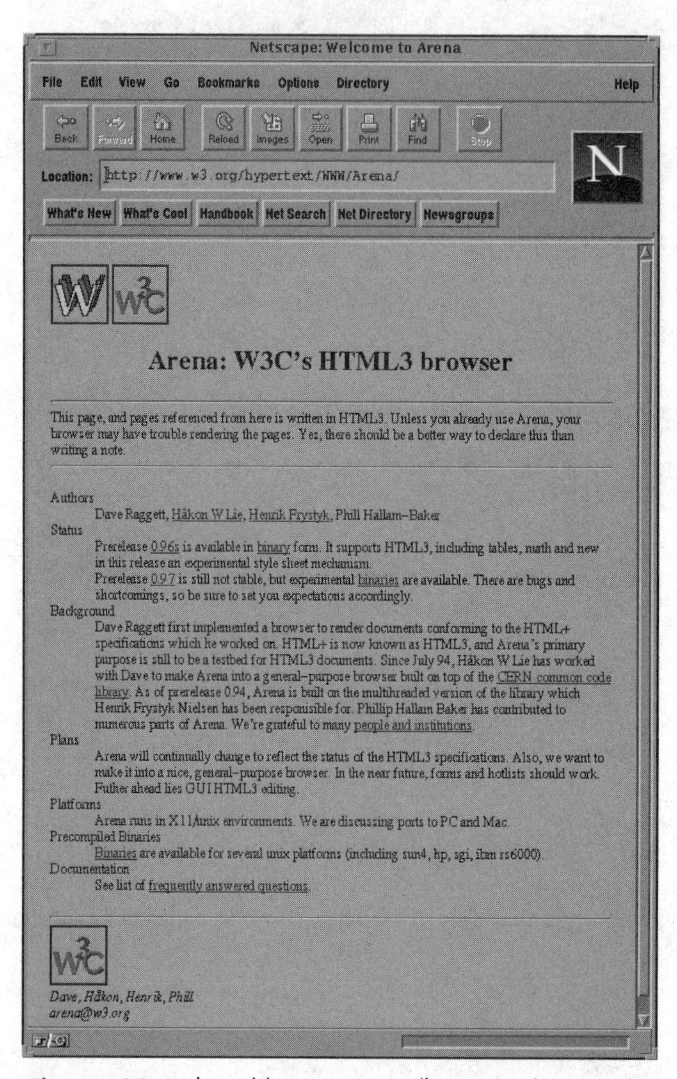

Figure 20-2 http://www.w3.org/hypertext/WWW/Arena/

Finally, here is a browser, as shown in Figure 20-2, that will check HTML3 code-flagging and commenting out bad HTML:

`http://www.w3.org/hypertext/WWW/Arena/`

Many commercial services that develop and/or post HTML documents for you also offer services to analyze your documents for syntax and style problems. Ask about such services when you are shopping around for service providers. Actually, we're probably not far off from having huge ad agencies developing content as well. For a listing of commercial services, see the Web Space for Sale section later in this chapter.

LESSON #3: FREE WEB POSTING SPOTS

Luckily, there are a few free entry points where you can get documents published on the Web. Here are the most obvious solutions to the space problem:

- If you are affiliated with an educational institution, inquire about Web services that might be available to you through your institution. The largest point of entry for free Web pages is your friendly local university. So, if you are affiliated with an educational institution that has Internet connections, ask about getting Web space. If your institution isn't on the Net, go bang on someone's door and demand they get moving on this!
- If you are affiliated with a commercial institution with Internet access, ask about getting space on the company Web server if there is one, and ask about having one installed if not.
- Some local governments and communities have Web sites and will allow the publication of documents that meet requirements for community-related content.
- There are a few "special purpose" Web sites that will publish for you if you meet certain criteria. For example, some local art groups will publish digital art for you in their WWW art galleries. There are certain other institutions that will publish for nonprofit organizations. Look around, there may be some little niche that your pages will fit into.

If you don't fall into one of these categories, don't fret! There are still a few alternatives for free Web publishing that may be available to you. (See Table 20-1 and Figure 20-3.) In addition to this list, you should keep your eyes open while Web surfing, and watch for new public sites that may have a place for your pages.

In addition to the sites that will publish your document for you, there are many others that allow you to leave references to your pages, leave graffiti, images, pointers, poetry, you name it.

Table 20-1 Free and very low-fee Web publication sites

Name	URL	Who Is Eligible
NYU Center for Advanced Technology	http://found.cs.nyu.edu/	non-profit NY businesses (small fee)
World Access	http://www.csn.net/way/docs/free.html	anyone
wizard.com	http://snark.wizard.com/wwpr.html	anyone (small fee)
wisc.edu	http://www.bocklabs.wisc.edu/ims/writers.html	writers

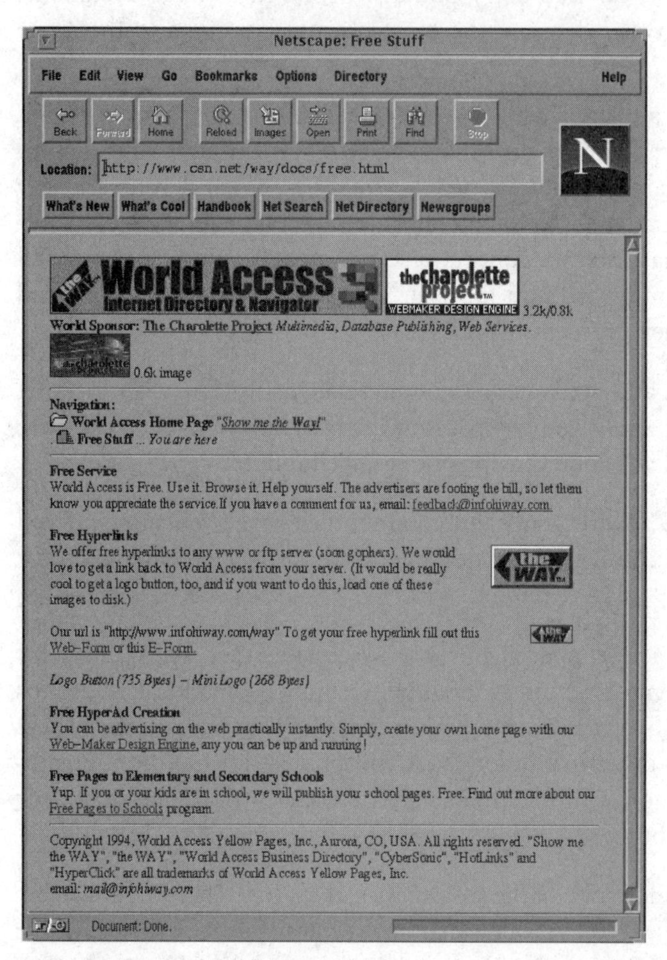

Figure 20-3 World Access

LESSON #4: WEB SPACE FOR SALE

It seems that every day there are more commercial sites popping up that will sell, rent, or offer consultation to would-be Web publishers. These range from Mom-and-Pop services running out of someone's kitchen in Pocatello, Idaho, to huge corporate enterprises like America Online and Prodigy. Since the race has just begun, many of the large providers are offering services not much different from the smaller start-ups and entrepreneurs. Prices range from a few dollars a month for publishing a page to several hundred thousand to start a full-blown commercial site. A reasonably priced site that will set you up with your own domain name and web site for a modest start-up and monthly maintenance fee is Network Wizards. They can be reached by

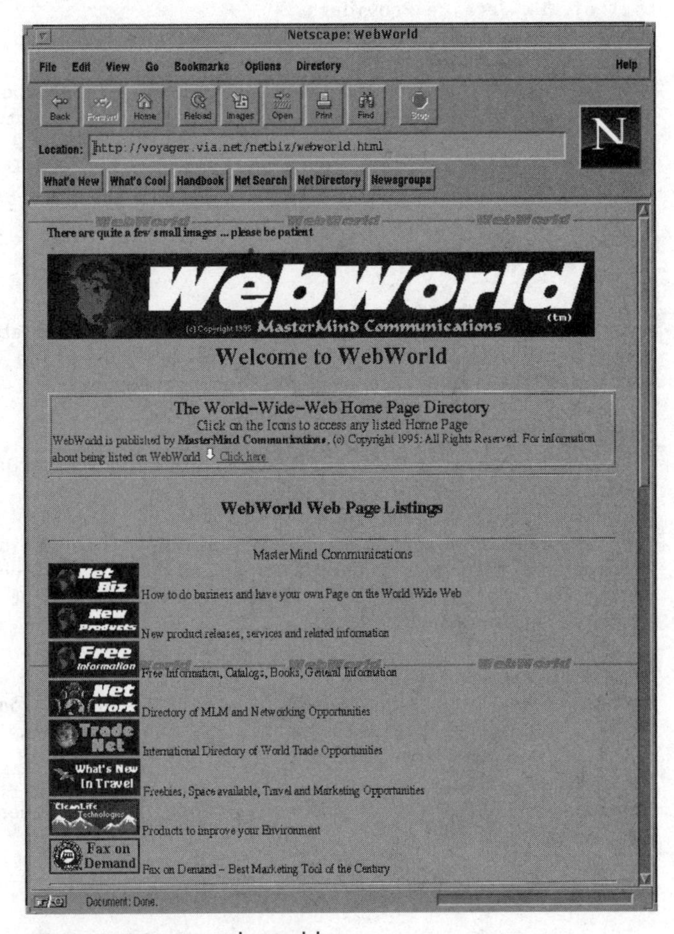

Figure 20-4 WebWorld

telephone at (415) 326-2060. Another site that will set up Web services for a fee is WebWorld (see Figure 20-4). The URL for WebWorld is:

```
http://voyager.via.net/netbiz/webworld.html
```

A few online lists of Internet service providers can also be found at the following URLs:

```
http://sensemedia.net/crisp/crisp
http://www.teleport.com/~/cci/directories/pocia/pocia.html
```

There are a number of places that offer "clearing house" services for would-be providers, and keep current lists of who's out there and what they do. One such list is maintained by Mary Morris at:

```
http://union.ncsa.uiuc.edu/HyperNews/get/www/leasing.html
```

A modified version of this list is as follows:

```
List of WWW Service Providers
=============================
Active Window Productions
Offers WWW consulting services including HTML authoring, multimedia
artwork design, and web server space rental. (info@actwin.com)

Applied Computer Services
Offers a full range of value added services (gregg@acsil.com)
Atlantic Computing Technology Corporation
 (info@atlantic.com)

BizWeb
A commercial business directory service. Contact us about listing your
commercial web page in our listing or for price information for
leasing space on our web server. (bob@bizweb.com)

CERFnet
Provides a Web server via a T3 connection. (webmaster@cerf.net)

Commerce Bulletin Board System
Provides small and large businesses alike with a national presence via
WWW and the Internet. Advertising space on the Commerce Bulletin Board
System can cost as little as $20 per month for a full screen including
graphics and/or forms. (info@nis.net)

CyberMall VirtualNet
Establishing Digital Storefronts for Internet commerce via WWW,
Gopher, and searchable WAIS indexes. (services@cybermall.com)

Demon Internet Services Ltd.
Provides WWW server space and consultancy. (sales@demon.net)
```

Digital Express Group
Provides a mid-level World Wide Web service known as Express Advertising. Express Advertising also offers Usenet News posting and email robots. (sales@digex.net or call (301) 220-2020)

Digital Marketing (DigiMark)
Now online. (info@digimark.net)

ElectriCiti
Offers a T1 connection to the Internet, with a Unix operating system. (dknight@powergrid.electriciti.com)

EmeraldNet
An Internet Presence provider for groups and organizations looking for a creative presence on the INTERNET, but don't wish to invest the time and money required to have a dedicated line. (INFO@Emerald.NET)

EntertainNet
Offers WWW leased services and consulting; full internet access. (dwatson@entertain.com)

Fentonnet
A Twin Cities based WWW service provider. Reasonable pricing, Quality service. (mfenton@fentonnet.com)

Flightpath Communications of Austin, TX
Offers a low-cost, flexible option for serving information on the Internet via WWW, FTP, and Gopher servers and an online conference center. (info@flightpath.com)

Gastown Webspace - A virtual town
Offers space for $7 per month.(gastown@xmission.com)

The Global City
A gathering place for merchants and aspiring writers. (oquinn@bga.com)

Global On-Line Directory
Has WWW space for lease in Cambridge, UK. (tony@cityscape.co.uk)

IAGIweb (Internet Access Group, Inc)
Provides ISDN internet connections, web space on IAGIweb, business & trade resource listing, and our own service catalog. (adhir@iagi.net)

Ieunet
The Irish branch of EUnet, ieunet provides a full range of communication services including Electronic Mail, Network News and Internet Access. (info@ieunet.ie)

iMALL
Offers free classified advertising and competative rates on a broad range of services. (jardine@imall.com)

Continued on next page

Continued from previous page

InterAccess
Chicagoland's Full-Service Internet Provider (www@interaccess.com)

Internet Ad Emporium
Multimedia Ink Designs CEO. (rdegel@ctsnet.cts.com)

The Internet Group
Helps companies develop direct Internet Marketing Channels. (bauer@tig.com)

Internet Information Systems
Web document creation, server space, consultancy. (info@internet-is.com).

The Internet Plaza(tm)
Dedicated to providing Internet services for companies interested in selling or providing information about their products online. (plaza@plaza.xor.com)

Khera Communications
Provides Internet Consulting, Training, and World Wide Web Services. (khera@kciLink.com)

Lightside Inc.
Offers WWW space. (dennish@lightside.com)

MagicNet Services
Offers dial-up slip and shell connections. (info@magicnet.net)

/MouseTracks/
Has two sections related to WWW leasing. There is the Hall of Malls listing as well as the marketing services directory called the MetaMarket. (chofack@nsns.com)

Netcom's Internet Distribution Services
(marcf@netcom.com)

Net Effects InfoNow! Internet Services
(jshunter@netcom.com)

The NetMarket Company
Specializes in dynamic pages which create stateful connections, for example, allowing automated shopping lists. We also support simpler, HTML-based advertising. (info@netmarket.com)

Nyx
A free public-access system. They offer web server services to all registered users. Telnet to nyx.cs.du.edu and follow instructions to sign up.

PIPEX
The Public IP Exchange Ltd, is the UK's leading supplier of commercial internet connectivity. We provide internet connectivity, web space,

consulting, authoring and training. We also have a number of international partners. (sales@pipex.net)

Primenet
Offers low cost commercial web services. (web-sales@primenet.com)

RCI
offers WWW server, online catalog, and personal internet services. Custom document authoring and graphic design available. (kadokev@ripco.com)

Sell-it on the WWW
offers space for as little as $10 per month. (wwwads@xmission.com)

Sierra-Net
ISP's providing web space, virtual servers, etc (giles@sierra.net)

South Valley Internet
Provides all of our subscribers with some WWW space if they so desire. Larger spaces are also available for reasonable prices. (info@garlic.com)

The Sphere Information Services
Services include World Wide Web presence, FTP service, and electronic mailing list. (dlp@thesphere.com)

The Spiderweb
offers free home pages (limited time offer) and Hyperclassifieds. (support@spiderweb.com)

SSNet, Inc.
WWW space leasing, doc creation. (russ@ssnet.com)

Studio X
(webmaster@nets.com)

SunSITE
(jem@sunsite.unc.edu)

The TAG Online Mall
Leases web server space and offers advertising and publishing services. (office@tagsys.com)

Telerama Public Access Internet
Offers WWW, FTP, Gopher, and email server space, and provides a holistic approach to marketing presence on the global network. (info@telerama.lm.com)

The Tenagra Corporation
Our Houston based company offers commercial grade servers, HTML development, CGI scripting and a full range of Internet consulting, marketing, and advertising support. Check our listing of Print Publications on Business Use of the Internet. (info@tenagra.com)

Continued on next page

Continued from previous page

```
ThoughtPort Web Services
Create a virtual image for your company via the World Wide Web.
(trout@thoughtport.com)

Turku Telephone Company
A member of the Telegroup of Finland, the Turku Telephone Company
provides all kinds of communication services from cellular networks
and picture transfer to World Wide Web based information services and
high capacity Internet connections. (www@utu.fi)

Visualogic, Inc.
provides consulting on all aspects of WWW operation, from HTML
authoring through setting up your own server. (info@visualogic.com)

Voicenet
is a commercial service provider for Philadelphia and the Delaware
Valley. We operate a combined gopher/web server with a special focus
on the region and make available commercial space on our server. We
also offer a full range of network connectivity options as well as
design and programming support to suit your business needs.
(webmaster@www.voicenet.com)

Web Communications
provides high performance, self-service, affordable and easy-to-use
facilities, tutorials, online help, and technical support for creating
a WWW or FTP site and/or using electronic mailing lists.
(info@webcom.com)

WorldWide Access
A full-service Internet provider specializing in commercial World Wide
Web services, including our MagicServer (SM) virtual server service.
(support@wwa.com)

xxLINK Services
Provides Dutch companies, institutions and individuals with a means to
present themselves internationally on the Internet. (info@xxlink.nl)
```

Another site that lists commercial providers is:

`http://www.netusa.net/ISP/`

Netusa has a list of worldwide Internet service providers, many of which offer WWW services. The list is sorted by telephone country codes, then regional area codes, then local phone number prefixes.

LESSON #5: POSTING

HTTP is not the only protocol that can transport HTML documents. Many Web sites don't use HTTP servers at all. There are certain services that are available only with an HTTP server, but for the most part, you can get away with quite a lot if you have anonymous FTP services on your system.

Serving your HTML documents with an FTP server is much the same as posting them via an HTTP server. The big difference is the lack of CGI support. This means no CGI scripts, and no imagemaps. But if you can deal with publishing documents that don't use special scripts or imagemaps, an FTP server will work just fine. In fact, you may already be using sites that are served solely by FTP servers. Any HTML documents that you have been accessing that have URLs prefaced with "ftp://" are being served with an FTP server rather than an HTTP server.

If you want to publish your pages with an FTP server, first make sure that your FTP server allows anonymous login. The standard scheme for this is to have the server accept the user "anonymous" and the user's e-mail address as the password. It is possible to have HTML documents served with authenticated login to an FTP server, but this makes offering pages much more complicated. If you are interested in authenticated login to your FTP server, see the section on the File Transfer Protocol in Chapter 16 for the URL format to use.

The first thing to do is write your HTML documents. Be sure that any references to other documents on your server use the FTP URL format and not the HTTP format. Next, make sure that you have privileges to save documents in a directory that is accessible to anonymous users of your FTP server. Create a directory structure that makes sense for your needs relative to this directory and copy your files into these directories. Now test your documents by accessing them with a Web browser, being sure to specify the FTP URL for the document. As a reminder, if your HTML document is called "index.html" and resides on a FTP server named "myserver.com" in a directory called "/pub/my_html_docs", then the FTP URL would look like:

```
ftp://myserver.com/pub/my_html_docs/index.html
```

Once you have tested your documents and all the links they contain, your final step is to notify users of the information you are providing, including the exact URL of your home page.

Here are the basic steps for installing an FTP Web site:

- Install an anonymous FTP server if you don't already have one.
- Create a directory that is publicly readable for storing your HTML documents.
- Create and debug your HTML documents.
- Move your HTML documents into the correct directories on your FTP server if you have not already done so.

- Test your documents and their links with a Web browser.
- Notify the Web community of your new services.

Sometimes FTP servers will not allow normal logins for users who have accounts on them. In this case, it may be necessary to create your documents on one machine, and then transfer them to the machine that is running the FTP server software. The obvious choice for transferring these files is the File Transfer Protocol—your friend FTP. Just make sure that you have some sort of FTP client software on your development machine: "ftp" on a Unix machine, or Fetch on a Mac or PC, or one of the other free or commercial ftp clients. You can find at least one available for virtually any of the major computer platforms.

When transferring your files from your local machine to your FTP server, make sure that you choose the correct transfer mode for the type of file you are transferring. HTML documents are basically ASCII text and can be transferred using the ASCII transfer mode. Most images (including .GIF and .JPEG files) must be transferred using the binary or image transfer protocol. The way you specify the protocol differs among FTP clients, so you will have to check the documentation for your specific software package.

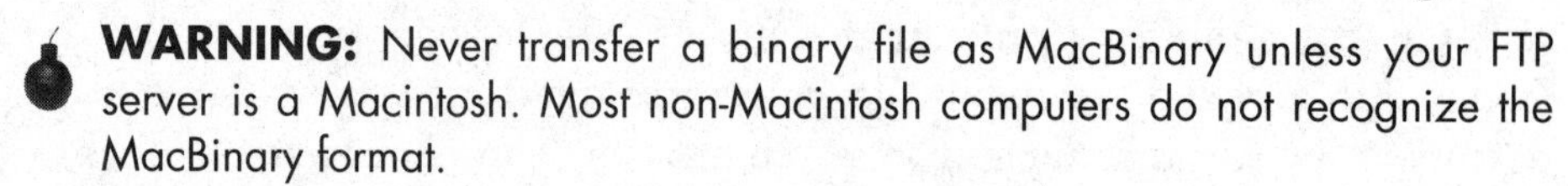

WARNING: Never transfer a binary file as MacBinary unless your FTP server is a Macintosh. Most non-Macintosh computers do not recognize the MacBinary format.

LESSON #6: UPLOADING DOCUMENTS

Uploading is the process of transferring a document from a local machine to a remote machine, often the server. How you upload depends on what types of machines you are transferring from and to, and what kind of software you are using. If you are using a machine that is connected to the same network as your server, and both of these machines can communicate via TCP/IP (Transmission Control Protocol/Internet Protocol, the standard protocol of the Internet), then your best bet for transferring files is probably FTP. FTP is also a good candidate if you are connected via SLIP or PPP (Serial Line Internet Protocol and Point to Point Protocol, which are commonly used for dial-up services). If you are connected via a standard dial-up connection with some sort of terminal emulator, you will probably have to use another transfer protocol such as Xmodem or Kermit.

Uploading via FTP

If you are using the Unix ftp command and want to transfer your documents to your FTP and/or HTTP server, do the following:

1. Make sure you have an FTP account on the server in question. If you don't know, ask your system administrator.

2. From the Unix prompt on your local machine, type:

   ```
   ftp servername
   ```

   Servername is the name of the server you want to transfer your files to.

3. Once connected, the server will ask for a username. Type in the name for your account on that machine.

4. When prompted, type in a password.

5. Change the current directory to the one you want to transfer files into. Use the "cd" command. For example, to change to "mydirectory" in "pub," type:

   ```
   cd /pub/mydirectory
   ```

6. Set the transfer mode to match the type of file you are sending. If you are sending a text-only file like .html, the transfer mode is "ASCII", you can change to this transfer mode by typing the word "ascii;" if the file is an image or other binary file such as .GIF or .JPEG, the transfer mode is "binary", likewise, you set this transfer mode by typing the word "binary."

7. Send the file to your server by typing the following line, substituting filenames where necessary:

   ```
   put /path/myfile.html
   ```

8. Repeat steps 5 through 7 for each file that you want to transfer.

9. Terminate your FTP session. The usual commands are "bye" or "exit."

Since each software package is slightly different, you may have to modify these steps slightly for your particular installation. Check your documentation for details.

Transferring Files with a Modem

There are a number of different terminal emulator packages out there. Unfortunately, they're all slightly different and they use a lot of different protocols. The most common protocols for sending files from a PC or Macintosh over a modem are Xmodem, Kermit, Zmodem, and Compuserve B. You must find out what protocols your terminal software and server have in common. Then connect to your server using your terminal emulator, and transfer the files using a protocol supported by both machines. Unfortunately, the different software packages and protocols are too numerous to list here, so you will have to check the documentation for your software to determine how file transfers work for that particular package.

LESSON #7: INSTALLING PAGES ON AN EXISTING WEB SERVER

If you already have access to an installed HTTP server, you are one of the lucky ones. Publishing your pages is as simple as copying your HTML documents into some publicly readable directory, and creating a link to them from your Web server's document root directory. The document root directory is the directory you specified as the base directory for all of your HTML documents. All paths to documents on your server are relative to this directory. (Normally, it will be something like /usr/htdocs or /usr/httpd/htdocs.)

There are two different ways to link your directories to the document root directory. The first is to physically move your directories into the document root; the second, which is a little more common, is to create links in the document root that point to your directories. This way, you can keep your directories relative to your home directory, and still have them accessed by the outside world relative to the document root.

One way that many Web sites use is to declare some common directory name relative to a user's home directory such as public-html. That way, the Web administrator can assume that any Web pages that a user creates are relative to ~user/public-html. For example, if your home directory is in /usr/people/downing, then the Web administrator can assume that you will have a directory called public-html in your home directory and that all of your HTML documents will be in /usr/people/downing/public-html. Different sites will differ slightly, and you should check with your administrator if you are unsure of the conventions used in your particular installation.

Call your home page "index.html" if you want people to get that page in your directory as the default. What that means is that a user can get the home page by selecting the URL ~downing and not have to specify the filename such as ~downing/index.html. Users can get to the rest of the pages by selecting links on this home page. Or—if they prefer (and have the information)—they can request them specifically by giving the whole path and filename in the URL.

Once you've created your HTML directory and documents, the next step is to have your directory linked in the document root. This is something that your system or Web administrator will probably have to do. To help keep things straight, it's a good idea to follow the convention of making a symbolic link in the document root directory for each user directory that has Web pages. For example, say your home directory is /usr/people/downing and you've put your HTML documents in a directory called public-html relative to your home directory (/usr/people/downing/public-html, to be specific). Let's also assume that the HTTP server that is running on your system has the document root set to /usr/httpd/htdocs. The easiest way to create a link to your HTML documents is to change to the document root directory and then create a symbolic link that points to your public-html directory. The commands to do this are:

```
cd /usr/httpd/htdocs
ln -s /usr/people/downing/public-html downing
```

The first line changes directories, and the second creates a link in htdocs called "downing" that will act as your "public-html" directory. The link will just point to the public-html directory and not actually duplicate it, so any changes in the local files will also be changed if accessed via this link. Once this link is in place, a user can find your home page (called index.html) by selecting the following URL:

```
http://mymachine.edu/downing
```

Since "downing" really points to "/usr/people/downing/public-html," users will see the pages in that directory without having to type out that huge pathname when specifying the URL.

To recap:

1. Create a directory in your home directory structure using some standard naming convention such as "public-html."
2. Place your HTML documents into your "public-html" directory.
3. Name your default HTML document or home page "index.html."

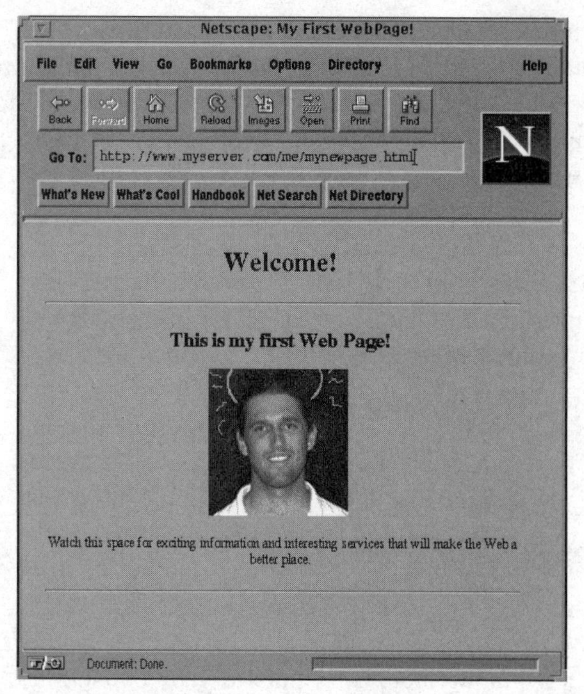

Figure 20-5 http://www.myserver.com/me/mynewpage.html

4. Have your system or Web administrator create a symbolic link in the document root directory of your server that points to your "public-html" directory.

It's that simple. The only other thing that you may want to do is have a link to your home page added to the home page or root document of your institution. That will let people find your home page for themselves. If you don't do that, the only way people will know about your pages is if they happen to see whatever you do to advertise them.

What Now?

So, there you have it. You are now part of the rapidly growing Internet community with a Web page. At the time of this writing, it is estimated that 250 people per day are surfing the Web for the first time, and most of them will be envious that you have a Web page of your own and they don't. Just remember that only a few years ago, none of us had Web pages...

Coming up in Chapter 21, you will learn how to install your own Web server. Everything from picking the right server platform for your needs to dealing with the growing complexity of security issues on the Internet is explained in detail for you. Even if you don't plan on installing your own server, Chapter 21 will give you a little insight on what's involved, and should give you a better understanding of the internal workings of the World Wide Web.

21

STARTING YOUR OWN WEB SITE

21

So, you've decided that you are tired of being a hitchhiker on the Information Superhighway, and you want to try your hand at driving for a while. Well, it's not as difficult as you may think. There are many HTTP server packages that are as simple to configure as copying software and executing it. As long as you have a machine that is capable of running the software, a reliable connection to the Internet that allows you to start such services, and a little bit of time, you should be up and running.

The sections to follow will explain what sort of hardware you will need, what software, and what types of connectivity are adequate for running a Web site.

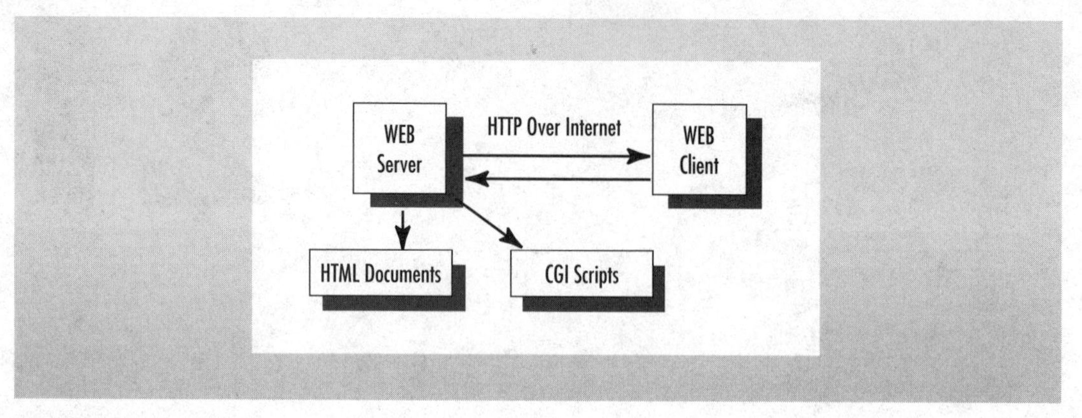

Figure 21-1 HTTP server

LESSON #1: YOUR WEB SERVER

A Web server can be a machine that supplies any of a number of services—gopher, news, WAIS, and so on. But in the context of this chapter, a Web server is a machine connected to the Internet that can serve hypermedia documents using the Hypertext Transfer Protocol (HTTP).

In the simplest form, a Web server listens to a port on the network and transfers HTML documents when it hears a request. Most Web servers can service multiple requests for multiple documents. Typically, a Web server also allows clients to browse directories on your server and execute certain programs on the server, forwarding the results to a client in the form of HTML documents. These may include images, imagemaps, forms, and any of the standard HTML documents discussed earlier in this book (see Figure 21-1).

LESSON #2: WEB SERVER SOFTWARE

As of this writing, there are three major HTTP server packages in use. There are two different packages called HTTPD—one from CERN in Geneva, Switzerland, and the other from the National Center for Supercomputing Applications (NCSA)—and a third called Netsite, from Netscape Communications. There are a number of other server packages, as well, but the three listed here are the most prevalent on the Net at this time. You will find several server packages (including NCSA's HTTPD) on the CD-ROM that came with this book.

Historically, the Internet has been very Unix-centric. Most of the servers, and for a long time most of the clients, have been Unix boxes. Consequently, most of the best server software for running HTTP, FTP, Gopher, WAIS, and other similar services was written for Unix computers. This is not to say that there is no hope if you want to install a Web server on your Macintosh or Windows PC. They are just a little behind in the Web server race. There are a number of reasons for this that are, for the most part, beyond the scope of this book, but the main reason a Web server runs best on top of Unix is the ability of Unix to run true multithreaded applications and the advanced built-in networking capabilities that come standard with Unix installation. A multithreaded architecture makes a Unix server much more capable of handling multiple simultaneous requests without having to queue requests and slow everyone down. Imagine having a CGI script running on your Macintosh that must launch, run, and terminate, sending its data to a client before another client can request the same service. This might be fine if you have a very light load on your server, but in terms of what people expect of an Internet server, it's just not acceptable.

For those of you determined to run your server on a Windows machine, there is much promise with Windows 95, which allows multithreaded applications. You just need a little patience. And the service you get with the current technology might work fine for you in the meantime, depending on the services you plan on providing.

Of the three servers listed above, two are freeware and the third is a commercial product. Both HTTPD products (CERN and NCSA) are freely available. They can either be FTPd from their respective sites, or you can copy the NCSA product from the companion CD-ROM. Both of these products are similar in design and function, though they have some minor differences. The CERN server can be easily configured to run as a proxy. This means that if your site uses a gateway machine or firewall that is your connection to the Internet, the proxy can be installed on this gateway machine and forward requests from the Internet to your machine(s) on the other side of the firewall. The CERN product can also be used to cache a number of requests and the most common HTML documents that are requested. This can speed things up for your clients, especially if there are certain services on your system that are requested frequently. HTTPD is available in most flavors of Unix in addition to a version for the Macintosh platform.

Netscape Communications has two commercial HTTP server products: the Netsite Information server and the Netsite Commerce server. The

Netsite Information server is similar to the CERN and NCSA products, but has some advantages—mainly customer support and some speed-up for user accesses. The Commerce server is a somewhat different beast. Intended for doing business over the Net, it allows secure, encrypted transmission of data. This makes it an obvious choice for those who want to be able to do financial transactions over the Net that might contain sensitive data or credit card numbers.

Other servers you may see are SERWEB for Windows, MacHTTP for Macintosh, and a few other products for other platforms. Here is a list of some other servers that you may see around:

Unix:

EIT httpd

GN (a gopher/HTTP httpd server)

Plexus

Perl server

WebWorks Enterprise server

httpds

PC (DOS/Windows):

Novell httpd NLM

Web4Ham

NetPublisher

OS/2:

GoServ

GoHTTP

Others:

HTTP for VM

Region 6 (VMS)

For a good list of server software available, and where you can find it, take a look at:

http://www.yahoo.com/Computers/World_Wide_Web/HTTP/Servers/

LESSON #3: SERVER SOFTWARE SOURCES

If you are connected to the Internet and have a machine that can transfer files using FTP, obtaining software is as easy as FTPing it from another machine. If you don't have FTP access, you can either purchase the commercial versions of some HTTP products, copy the HTTPD server from the CD-ROM that came with this book, or try retrieving it from local BBSs that may keep archives of such software. This discussion assumes that you'll copy NCSA's HTTPD server from the CD-ROM. If, for some reason, you don't want NCSA HTTPD, SERWEB, or any of the other bundled software, or you don't have access to the CD-ROM or to a CD-ROM reader, try connecting to the following sites as an anonymous FTP client:

Table 21-1 HTTPD Software Sources

Product	Site
CERN HTTPD	ftp.cern.ch
NCSA HTTPD	ftp.ncsa.uiuc.edu
SERWEB	ftp.mcp.com
MacHTTP	sumex-aim.stanford.edu/info-mac/comm/tcp/mac-http

Connect to one of these machines using your favorite FTP client. Log in as "anonymous" and type in your e-mail address as the password. Once there, read the local documentation to find out what versions are there and where you can find them on that particular server. If you are downloading binaries or compressed files, be sure to set the FTP file type to "binary" or "image". You can normally do this by just typing the word "binary" at the FTP prompt. If you try to transfer a binary file using the ASCII transfer protocol, your FTP client will interpret the programs and compressed data as characters and punctuation marks. Basically, it will seem like you transferred the files, only they will contain garbage and most likely won't work.

Netscape Communications also runs an FTP site that allows you to download some of its products. However, if you are interested in installing one of the Netsite server products, you will have to purchase it. They offer certain discounts for educational and research institutions, but you will have to get that information from them directly. Via e-mail, Netscape Communications can be reached at sales@mcom.com. Or if you just want information on their products, you can write to info@mcom.com.

LESSON #4: TIPS AND CAUTIONS

Before you start ... here are a few things to consider when planning an HTTP installation.

When you add a server to the World Wide Web, it quickly becomes entangled with the thousands of other servers out there. Users you may be entirely unaware of will begin referencing your services in their own documents. As HTML documents are created and referenced all over the Net, tiny tears in the Web fabric may appear when servers are brought down, renamed, or restructured. As users begin to depend on the services you are providing, it becomes increasingly troublesome to make changes to either the machine name or the directory structure of the documents that your server supplies. The point is, decide before you go public what machine you want to install your server on and what it will be called.

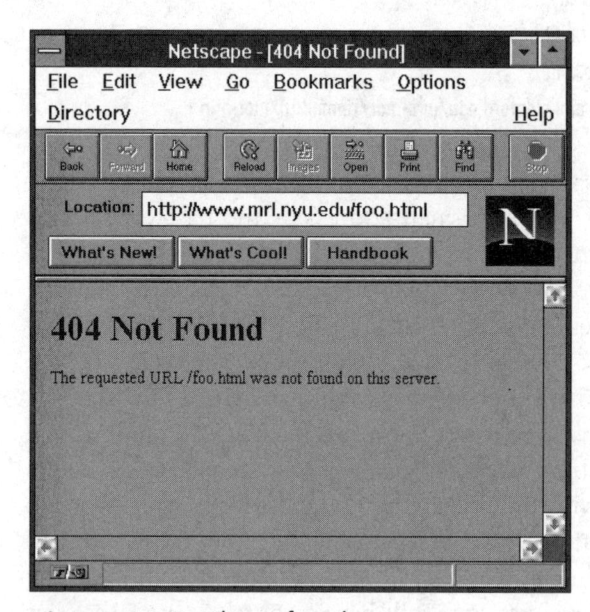

Figure 21-2 File not found

Type of Machine

You will need to decide whether you want to dedicate a machine as a full-time HTTP server, or whether you want to run the HTTP server in the background on a workstation. Depending on how popular your services become, it may become necessary to dedicate a machine at some time in the future in order to keep up with the volume of requests your server receives. This brings us back to the first point: it is not good Web citizenship to rename services. The type of service you plan on providing is an important factor in deciding what type of machine to use. Obviously, a server that is only serving text-based HTML documents will be less heavily burdened than a server that is offering documents laden with inline images and fancy CGI scripts generating on-the-fly MPEG movies of what's happening down the hall from your office. If this is what you see in the future of your Web services, you should strongly consider dedicating a high-end server. Even machines like midrange Sparcs grind to a halt under the stress of trying to service multiple HTTP requests that include excessive graphics and CGI processes.

Currently the best candidates for high-volume HTTP requests are Unix workstations. If you plan on having lots of graphic content in your documents and services, you will also need adequate physical storage space on your machine. You can gauge the amount of space you need by estimating the number and size of files you think your services will require over the next few years and multiply by three.

NOTE: A Unix workstation can be a number of types of physical hardware. PCs based on the Intel 80x86 and Pentium processors can be set up to run a version of Unix instead of DOS or OS/2, and Macintosh computers can run certain versions of Unix instead of MacOS. Some of the options are: Linux, BSD, AUX, and Solaris.

Memory

Random Access Memory (RAM) is also something to consider. Your workstation should have enough RAM to run multiple processes simultaneously. Once in service, your server will start creating processes for each service request that comes in over the line. These can start to add up at peak access times. You need to be able to run the daemon process for the server (that is, the process that "hangs out" waiting for HTTP requests), a server process for each request that comes in, a process for each shell that is initiated by a CGI script, and processes for each program that a CGI script may execute. It really does add up quickly. If a user attempts to access a service on your machine, and your machine's process space is all used up by other processes, the user will get an error message saying something in the order of "The machine is unable to service your request." It's difficult to say exactly how much RAM is enough. There are many flavors of Unix out there and different types of hardware that all have different requirements. A starting point would be to figure out how much your machine's operating system needs to run, and then figure out how much memory your server software takes and multiply it by the number of processes you want to be able to run simultaneously. A good starting point is to set your server to process 16 simultaneous requests. If you notice that your load tends to be higher than that, you can adjust the process ceiling as needed.

Another thing to consider when deciding how much RAM you need for your server machine is whether your machine is a dedicated server, or doubles as a workstation. Obviously, your machine will need more resources if it is compiling code, running EMACS, and displaying digital images in addition to acting as your HTTP server.

If you are determined to run your server on a Windows PC or a Macintosh running MacOS, that's fine. Just keep in mind that at this point in Web time, these aren't going to be your fastest or most efficient options as Web servers.

LESSON #5: SECURITY!

Security. That's a pretty big word when dealing with any Internet-connected services. It seems to be even more on Unix adminstrators' minds in the wake of the recent release of SATAN. (SATAN is a tool that you access through a Web browser to find security holes in Unix systems.) Unfortunately, there are people out there who get satisfaction from breaking things. It's hard to imagine why people would want to destroy someone else's work, usually someone they don't even know. But the fact remains that such people are out there and you need to be prepared, especially if you have sensitive, financial, or personal data on your server that you don't want to lose or release into the public domain.

Security has always been an issue in the Unix world as well as the Internet community, so fortunately, most of the security issues have been thought out reasonably thoroughly. (On the other hand, remember that the would-be data terrorists have been digging for holes in security mechanisms just as long....)

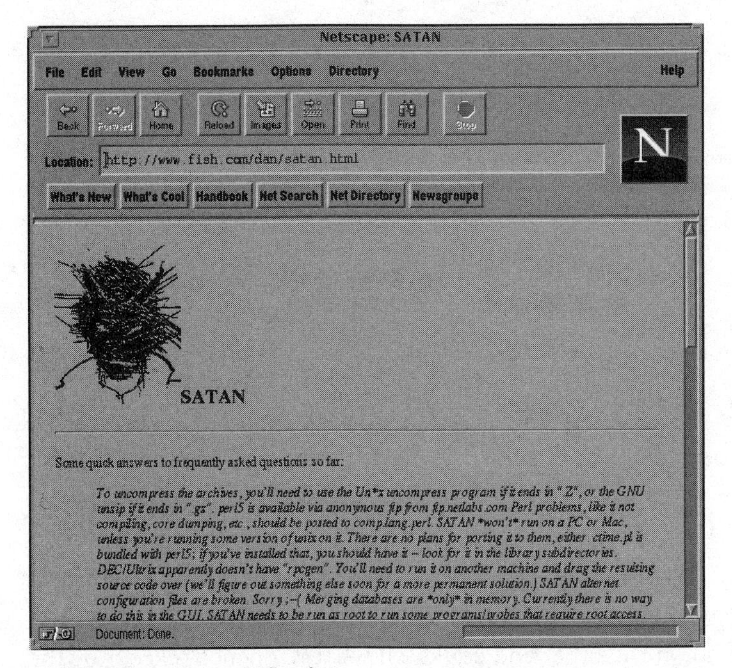

Figure 21-3 satan.html

There are two types of security that are common in Web discussions: transmission security and access control. *Transmission security* is protecting the data that is traveling from a legitimate server to a legitimate client over a public wire. *Access control* is restricting or allowing access to certain individuals or groups of people.

Transmission Security and Data Encryption

The way that the Internet is structured makes it pretty easy to tap into conversations over the Net. When a message is sent over the Internet, it is essentially broadcast to a number of machines. The first part of the message contains an address specifying who the message is intended for. If (as is almost certain) the message passes through a machine it is not intended for, the intermediate machine looks at the destination address, decides it is not interested, and forwards it, ignoring the message contents. Basically this is true for every machine on the same wire between the sender and recipient. What this means is that a user with enough control and machine know-how can "listen" to other people's conversations just by accepting message packets that are intended for someone else. The other problem is that this makes it easy to pretend to *be* someone else. If your machine passes

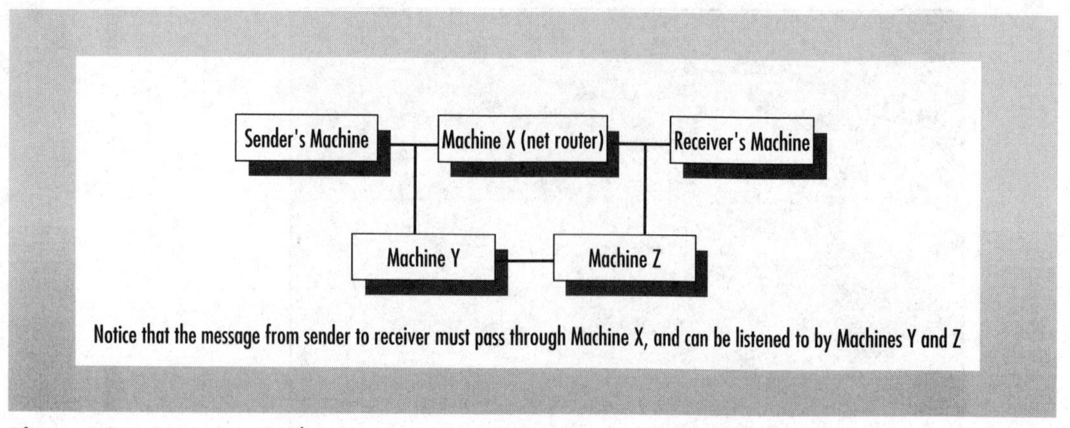
Sender's Machine
Machine X (net router)
Receiver's Machine
Machine Y
Machine Z
Notice that the message from sender to receiver must pass through Machine X, and can be listened to by Machines Y and Z

Figure 21-4 Internet outline

messages from one machine to another, it makes sense that you could generate messages that look like they came from the first machine and send them on—and no one at either end could tell what happened, except by the resulting chaos.

This may sound scary, but *don't worry!* Things have been this way for a long time. The volume of messages bouncing around makes it pretty unlikely that someone will be listening to your transactions. Banks use this method for transferring funds. They even use it for communicating with the Automatic Teller Machines that you find on every other corner these days.

Most people don't worry about Internet eavesdroppers. They figure that anyone who wants to intercept routine e-mail is welcome to it. On the other hand, anyone conducting business over the Internet that includes money transfers, online sales transactions, or trade secrets does need to be concerned about the potential for disaster. Banks, businesses, and even the U.S. Department of Defense deal with this concern by using data encryption.

Data encryption is the process of running your messages through some mathematical algorithm that effectively makes them unreadable unless you know the deciphering algorithm. (An *algorithm* is simply a series of steps used to produce some result). The most common algorithm for encrypting messages in the United States is the Data Encryption Standard (DES) algorithm of RSA Data Security Inc. This is the same algorithm used by the U.S. government, banks, insurance companies, you name it.

The way it works is by using a public and private key to encrypt data. A *key* is simply a number used when encrypting the messages. If you encrypt with a certain key, the message is effectively indecipherable to anyone who doesn't know this key. If this all sounds complicated, don't worry, it's all done in software, you don't have to do any calculations or complex mathematical algorithms yourself. It's all done for you.

The big selling point for Netscape's Netsite Commerce product is that they offer secure transmission using the DES model. If you want to do business on the Internet and require data transmission security with user authentication, this product may be just what you need–take a close look at it. Netscape Communications can be reached by e-mail at info@mcom.com or by phone at 800-NETSITE.

Access Control, Passwords, and Other Filters

Access control involves restricting access to documents or services to certain individuals or groups of individuals. The most common way to do this is to require a password in order to access a certain service, like the password that you probably use when you log into your Unix or e-mail account. Password systems involve a master list of users and passwords maintained by a system administrator, and checked automatically every time someone logs in. All of the major HTTP server packages give you the ability to restrict access to certain documents.

At the top level, if your server is running on a Unix system, you can prevent access to your documents by using the standard Unix control mechanisms. File permissions set to 700 will disallow the reading, changing, or execution of a file or directory to anyone except you and the super-user on your system (file permissions are normally represented in octal or "base 8" notation. 700 would expand to -rwx------ giving read/write/execute permissions to the file owner, but nobody else). Use this only if you want to have a file that is in an HTTP-server-accessible directory that you don't want anyone to see.

A more flexible approach is to use the built-in security features of your HTTP server. When your server is installed, there are a number of parameters that can be adjusted to allow the inclusion or exclusion of certain directories or files on your system, and can also implement authentication schemes for certain areas of your server.

Specifying directories: In the configuration files for HTTPD, you can specify what directories may contain CGI scripts, HTML documents, and certain other files that your server needs. Once you specify a document root directory, your server will disallow access to any files on your system that are not either in the document root directory, a subdirectory of the document root, or linked to the document root. In the same manner, if you set /usr/local/httpd/cgi-bin (or some other directory) as the sole directory for gateway scripts, your server will not allow programs to be run that exist anywhere else on the system. This is an important consideration. If you allow CGI scripts to reside anywhere on your server, any client can write a URL and run commands on your server—including destructive commands that you have every reason to keep off your system, no matter how trusting and user-friendly you want to be.

You can also limit CGI script access without specifying certain directories, by specifying a suffix that a CGI script must have in order to be executed by the server. Common CGI suffixes are .cgi or .shtml. If you set your server to only recognize files with these suffixes as CGI scripts, then the scripts can exist anywhere on your server, but will not execute unless they have one of the valid suffixes attached to the name of the file. This is acceptable for many installations, but if you are concerned about the users on your system, and want to limit their ability to create CGI scripts, you may want to specify a "cgi-bin" directory and restrict access to it to users that you trust.

Directory Access Control by User Authentication

Probably the most useful general access control scheme involves setting rules for particular directories and subdirectories. This lets you compile lists of users and groups of users that have access privileges within certain directories. Say you have two directories on your HTTP server, "research" and "secrets." You may want anyone on your research staff to be able to access files in the "research" directory, while allowing only your company executives to access files in the "secrets" directory. Let's also say that you have a list of users: joe, president, bob, vp, and einstein. If we want bob, joe, and einstein to have access to the research pages, it would make sense to create a group file called "researchers" that contains the members bob, joe, and einstein. Likewise, you could have a second group that contains the users president and vp. You could call this group "important_people". Now, you simply say that only people in the "researchers" group have access to the "research" directory and only members of the "important_people" group have access to the "secrets" directory.

This is the basic scheme that NCSA HTTPD uses for controlling access to HTML documents. You create a password file that contains user's names and passwords, and you optionally create a group file that contains the names of groups of users. You can allow access to directories based on individuals or on groups.

NOTE: You should put your password and group files in a directory other than the ones they are protecting.

The first order of business is to create a password file. The password file contains usernames and encoded passwords separated by colons. The passwords are encoded in the standard way that Unix machines encode their user passwords. The file contents will look something like this:

```
bob:CgiaaKmJBy.k
joe:gFdEEErftBy
einstein:oPPojUh.Mbb
vp:KJMnhBhCvAQ
president:GjjKnMMbtrF
```

Luckily, HTTPD comes with a utility that can easily generate this file. The program is called htpasswd and is located in the support/directory relative to the httpd directory. You specify a password filename and username on the command line, and the program asks you to input a password twice. (The second time is for verification.) The htpasswd program will then encrypt the password and create an entry for that user in the named password file. There is also an optional flag, -c, that allows you to create a new password file.

So let's create a new password file. First select a place to put the file. This can be pretty much anywhere, but let's say we want to use a directory called "mydir/http_stuff". To create a password file called ".htpasswd" in this directory, we would run the htpasswd program with the following parameters (here we are adding an entry for a user named bob):

```
htpasswd -c /mydir/http_stuff/.htpasswd bob
```

The htpasswd program will now ask for a password, and you'll have to type it in blind, as the characters will not be echoed to the screen. The htpasswd program will then ask you to type the password a second time to verify that you typed what you think you typed. Now, if all went well, we have created a password file called .htpasswd in the directory /mydir/http_stuff that contains one entry—for user "bob"—that looks something like

```
bob:UgFhCv/KK.gf
```

To add other users to this file, we type the command and omit the -c flag. For example, to add a user "einstein" to this password file, we would type:

```
htpasswd /mydir/http_stuff/.htpasswd einstein
```

and go through the same password entry steps. Make sure that your privileges are set correctly for this file. You should disallow changes by unauthorized people, but the file must be readable by the user that your server is running as. Normally this is the special user "nobody". Don't worry about others on your Unix system being able to read the password file. The passwords are encrypted and close to impossible to decode.

NOTE: Make sure that your password file is readable by the user that your HTTP server is running as—probably "nobody."

Next order of business is to create a group file. A group file is a list of groups of users. It is much easier to give privileges for a directory by listing a few groups rather than listing all of the individuals separately. This way, once you are set up, you only need to add or remove users from the group file instead of changing the permissions of the directory that they have access to. This is what we did in the example above, where we used two groups of users who had access to different directories.

The group file is similar in format to the password file. The entries consist of a group name followed by a colon and a list of users. The group file that defines our two groups, "researchers" and "important_people," would look something like this:

```
researchers: joe bob einstein
important_people: president vp
```

You should create this file using your favorite text editor. You can place the file wherever it makes sense to you, but it is a good idea to put it in the same directory as the password file. The following examples assume that you named your group file ".htgroup" and put it in the directory "/mydir/http_stuff."

Okay, now you know how to add users and groups, so what do you do with them? Well, when HTTPD serves a document requested by a user, it first checks for an access file to see if the files in that directory have restricted access. In the default configuration for HTTPD, ".htaccess" is the name of the access file. The .htaccess file lists the permissions for all files and subdirectories relative to the directory containing the .htaccess file. So, if only joe has access to the files in somedir/, then only joe can access files in somedir/papers and somedir/notes and somedir/notes/january.

The .htaccess file contains the name of the password file, the name of the group file, a name for itself, and the list of permissions. A standard access file will look something like this:

```
AuthUserFile /mydir/http_stuff/.htpasswd
AuthGroupFile /mydir/http_stuff/.htgroup
AuthName Research_Directory
```

```
AuthType Basic
<Limit GET>
require group researchers
</Limit>
```

Here AuthUserFile is followed by the path and name of the password file we created, AuthGroupFile is followed by the name of the group file that is being used, AuthName is an arbitrary name that will appear in the input window on many browsers when they request password information, and AuthType is set to Basic. (Basic seems to be the only authorization type currently in use.)

The <Limit> tag describes how you want access limited. The GET attribute limits GETs of documents in the directory of this access file or its subdirectories. Between the <Limit> tags, you list the names of users, groups, or networks that can access these files. Valid attributes in a <Limit> tag are GET, PUT, and POST. As of now, PUT and POST have not been fully implemented, but may be by the time of publication.

Within the <Limit> tag, you are allowed the following directives: order, deny, allow, and require. *Order* is the order in which deny and allow are evaluated. For example, "order deny, allow" will evaluate the machines that are denied access before allowing access to the machines specified in the allow statement. Allow and deny are followed by the machine names, network names, IP addresses, or partial IP addresses of machines and networks that are either allowed or denied access. Finally, *require* is followed by one of three terms: *user* and a specific user that appears in the password file specified, *group* and the name of a group that appears in the specified group file, or *valid-user* (which will allow any user that appears in the named password file to have access).

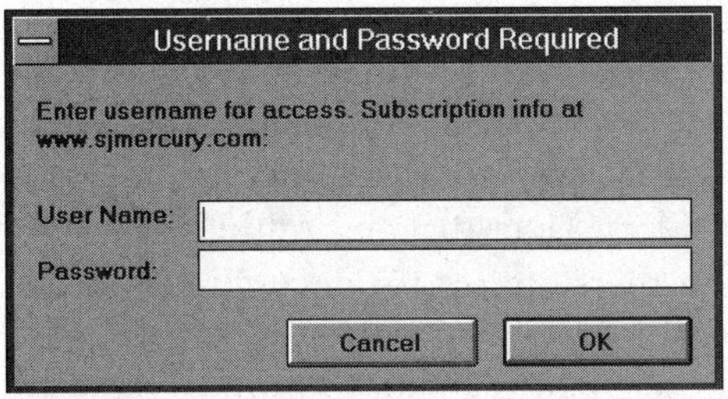

Figure 21-5 A sample authentication interface

In the above example, we are excluding everyone except members of the "researchers" group. When a person attempts to access a file in this directory, the HTTPD server will check to see if the client has been authenticated, if not, the client's browser will prompt for a username and a password. If the username and password matches the entries for a particular user that is a member of the researchers group, the server will allow access. Otherwise, access will be denied.

You can also allow access based on a single user. Instead of listing "require group researchers" between the <Limit> tags, you could change this to something like "require user joe". The files in this directory will now only be accessible to someone who requests them as "joe" and enters the correct password.

Restricting Access by Machine or Network

It is also possible to restrict access by machine name or network. The basic scheme is the same except you don't need to list a password or group file. Whenever omitting a password or group file, you should replace the path and filename with /dev/null. This tells the server that the file doesn't exist or is not needed.

Let's say that you had some internal documents that you only wanted people from within your organization to access. We will assume that your network domain name is spamnet.com. If you want to allow access only to machines within this domain, say toast.spamnet.com, blip.spamnet.com, and whatever other machines you have within this domain, you would create a text file called .htaccess in the root level of the directory you want to protect. The .htaccess file would look something like this:

```
AuthUserFile /dev/null
AuthGroupFile /dev/null
AuthName Spamnet_internal_pages
AuthType Basic
<Limit GET>
order deny, allow
deny from all
allow from .spamnet.com
</Limit>
```

This will allow any of your local machines to access the documents in this directory, and keep out all outsiders. Note that the AuthUserFile and AuthGroupFile are not used and are therefore set to /dev/null. The order line tells the order that the server will check privileges. First, the server will deny access for anybody. This keeps outsiders out, but unfortunately keeps you out as well, so the next entry supersedes the deny and allows connections from anyone in spamnet.com.

Now, say that you want to allow access to a directory from anywhere except a certain network or machine. Say you want anyone in the world to be able to read your documents except people from your competitor's network. You can just reverse the order, allow from all, and then deny from your competitor. For example, say your competitor is on comp.com and you want to restrict their access, the .htaccess file for this directory would look like:

```
AuthUserFile /dev/null
AuthGroupFile /dev/null
AuthName Spamnet_internal_pages
AuthType Basic
<Limit GET>
order allow, deny
allow from all
deny from .comp.com
</Limit>
```

Finally, say there is some user out there that is really taxing your system. This user keeps logging into your system and putting garbage in your HTML forms, and you want to deny access while letting everyone else in. Well, the only way you can restrict a person's access is by restricting the machine that person uses. The .htaccess file would be exactly the same as above, with the addition of a machine name rather than a network. For example, if the pest was accessing from a machine called bug.supersurfer.org, your .htaccess file would look like this:

```
AuthUserFile /dev/null
AuthGroupFile /dev/null
AuthName Spamnet_internal_pages
AuthType Basic
<Limit GET>
order deny, allow from all
deny from bug.supersurfer.com
</Limit>
```

Access Authorization Recap

1. In each directory that you want to have access control for, create a text file called .htaccess that contains the names of machines and/or networks allowed or denied access, or the names of users and groups that are allowed access.

2. Create a password file with an entry for each user that you want to give access to and a corresponding password. The easiest way to create this file is with the htpasswd program that is in the support directory of your server's root directory.

3. Create a group file that names groups and lists the members of each group.

4. Make sure that your server can read the password and group files.

LESSON #6: HARDWARE

There is a lot of room for deciding what type of CPU and what operating system you can use for a Web server, but there is one crucial criterion that must be met. You *must* be connected to a network. If you want your services to be part of the World Wide Web, then your network must be connected to the Internet.

The best way to be connected is via an Ethernet or token ring network, although some AppleTalk networks that can route TCP/IP packets can also be used. Serial Line Internet Protocol (SLIP) connections can also be used, but normally don't have the bandwidth capacity to run a server. So, if you don't have a network connection or if your network isn't connected to the Internet, you should check with commercial providers to get such service. It may also be possible to get this service for free if you are part of an educational institution that provides Internet service.

The type of CPU you use depends on your particular situation. If you are planning on building a huge, high-capacity server that will service thousands of accesses an hour, you may consider purchasing a reasonably fast Unix workstation with lots of RAM. The more RAM you install, the more processes you can run simultaneously, and the better the probable performance on high-traffic situations. If you don't have the money for such a server, or if this seems like overkill for the services you plan on providing, that Macintosh sitting on your desk may work fine for you. Or maybe you have a 386 lying around that you want to use—as long as it can run Windows, OS/2, or some flavor of Unix, it may work fine for you; you have to make the judgment call for your particular installation.

Obviously, the machine you use will need some sort of network interface. This may be the built-in Ethernet on a Unix workstation or Macintosh, or may be an Ethernet add-in card in your PC, or may be the serial port on your machine if you are using a SLIP connection. You will see the best performance if you are connected directly via an Ethernet or token ring adapter of some sort.

Disk, disk, disk.... As the computing world becomes increasingly graphic, storage requirements increase at the same rate. Fortunately, hard disks have been getting cheaper over the years as they have been getting denser, smaller, and faster. People want to see pictures. They want to see movies. They want to hear sound bites. All of these take up disk space. If you are planning on providing content with lots of graphic, video, and sound elements, plan on buying a high-capacity hard drive for your system. It's amazing how quickly you can run out of space. It's also impossible to give a general ballpark number for the size of disk you should buy. It depends on the amount of content you want to provide, and how laden it is with different imagemaps, GIFs, MPEG movies, and recorded audio. Just buy the largest disk that makes sense for your needs. It's better to have a little extra space than not to have enough.

LESSON #7: INSTALLING A WEB SERVER

As noted earlier, there are a number of options for HTTP server software. Most of them are free, with a few commercial products available as well. The software you install depends mostly on your needs and the equipment you have. For a full-service, high-performance machine, it's best to install your software on a Unix server of some flavor. If you require secure transactions for doing business or similar activities on the Web, the Netsite Commerce server is the best choice currently available. If you only plan on serving HTML documents, and not doing any heavy form or CGI-script-based content, and the only machine available to you is a Macintosh or Windows PC, then you'll probably do fine with MacHTTP or HTTPD for Windows. In any case, this section is divided into three parts, dealing with server installations on the three major platforms: Unix, Windows, and Macintosh.

Unix Server Installation

Since NCSA HTTPD server software is bundled with this book, this chapter uses NCSA installation as a model. If you would prefer the CERN version, the installation is very similar. You should have no problems with it if you skim the following text and then read the documentation that comes with the CERN software. Installing the NCSA software is a three-part process:

- Getting the software onto your server.

- Editing the configuration files.
- Editing local files as needed.

Getting the Software onto Your Server

You have a few options as to how to get the software onto your server. If you plan on using the HTTPD from the companion CD-ROM, and you have a CD-ROM drive connected to your computer, you can do the following:

1. Mount the CD-ROM on your file system. The way you do this is slightly different on each machine. Most likely, the command will be something similar to the following command: mount /cdrom. If you are unsure how to mount a CD-ROM on your system, check with your system documentation or your system administrator.

2. Decide where you want to place your HTTP server software. This is entirely a preference matter—just place the software in whatever directory makes sense on your system. If nothing better occurs to you, install the HTTP server software in /usr/local/httpd—that's what we'll be using in the examples.

3. Copy the software from the CD-ROM to the destination directory. There are a number of versions of the HTTPD software for different hardware. You should copy the version that matches the CPU type of the machine that will run the server. For example, if your CD-ROM is mounted on /cdrom and you want to copy the Sun version of the server software to /usr/local/httpd, you would type something like:

```
cp/cdrom/unix/servers/httpd_1.4/httpd_1.4.1_sunos4.1.3.tar.2 /usr/local/httpd
```

If you don't have a CD-ROM reader, the next best thing is to download the files via FTP. There are FTP clients for virtually every machine capable of running an HTTP server, and "ftp" is standard software with a Unix system. To transfer the files, you first have to establish an FTP connection. In order to do this, you need to know the name of the machine you are connecting to. NCSA runs an anonymous FTP server that allows you to download the latest versions of HTTPD and Mosaic, among other things. The address of their FTP server is ftp.ncsa.uiuc.edu. To connect to this server, at the Unix command line type the following:

```
ftp ftp.ncsa.uiuc.edu
```

Once you're connected, the server will prompt you for a username. Type in the word *anonymous* for the username. Next the server will prompt for a password. You should type your Internet e-mail address when prompted for the password. Now, if all went well, you have established a connection with the NCSA anonymous FTP server. The next step is to find the directory containing the software you are looking for.

When connected to an FTP server, you can navigate the directory structure in the same manner that you would navigate the directories on your local Unix system. The executable versions of the HTTPD software are in /Web/httpd/Unix/ncsa_httpd. Change the current directory to this by typing the following line at the ftp> prompt:

```
cd /Web/httpd/Unix/ncsa_httpd
```

Once you are there, take a look at the files and directories in this directory. You can do this by typing dir. You should see a listing of files and directories including a few httpd_X.X directories. The X.X will be the version and revision numbers of the software. At this writing, the latest version of HTTPD is 1.4. So, to get to the 1.4 version, type:

```
cd httpd_1.4
```

Once you are in the directory, take a look at the files contained there. There should be several versions for different types of CPUs. Find the version that matches your CPU. For example, if you are planning on running your server on a SUN Sparc 2 running SunOs, you would want to download the httpd_sun4.tar.Z version.

Since these are all binary files, you should make sure that your FTP client is prepared to transfer binary data. To change the transfer mode, simply type the word *binary* at the ftp> prompt. You should get a message that says something like "Type set to I". (The "I" stands for "Image.")

Once the transfer mode is set, you are ready to transfer the file. To transfer the file mentioned above, type:

```
get httpd_sun4.tar.Z
```

This should transfer the file to your local machine. Once the transfer is complete, you can exit ftp by typing "bye" at the prompt. (If you want a different file, all you have to do is change the filename to match the file that corresponds to your hardware. For example, replace the "sun4" with "sgi" if you want the Silicon Graphics version, or with "linux" if you want the Linux version. It should be reasonably evident which files are for which platforms by the filename.)

The file you just transferred is in a special format. It was first *tared* and then it was compressed. To make the files useful, we have to uncompress and then untar them into the proper directory. First, if the file is not in the directory that we want to use, you can move it there using mv. For example, to move the file from the current directory into /usr/local, just type:

```
mv httpd_sun4.tar.Z /usr/local
```

Once the file is where you want it, change the working directory to the one containing the new file (for example, cd /usr/local).

To unpack the files, type the following line at the Unix prompt (changing filenames where necessary, of course):

```
zcat httpd_sun4.tar.Z | tar xf -
```

This should unpack the HTTPD software into a directory called httpd relative to the working directory that you unpacked the files from.

Configuring the Software

Once you have moved the server software onto your system, you may want to edit the configuration files. They will be relative to the httpd directory that you created in a subdirectory called conf.

The following files are contained in the conf directory:

- access.conf-dist
- httpd.conf-dist
- mime.types
- srm.conf-dist

Most of the parameters in these files can be left as is—actually, in a normal installation, pretty much all of them can be left as defaults. The first thing you should do is copy the files. All the files with a -dist suffix are intended to be used as templates. The server will be looking for access.conf not access.conf-dist, so make copies of each of these files (in the same directory) without the -dist suffix. Below are the contents of these files with brief descriptions of their entries. Please note that any line that begins with a pound sign (#) is a comment and will be ignored by the server software.

The access.conf file contains parameters relating to how your server may be accessed. It also specifies the directories and filenames for the documents and programs that your server uses.

```
access.conf
# access.conf: Global access configuration
# Online docs at http://hoohoo.ncsa.uiuc.edu/
# I suggest you consult them; this is important and confusing stuff.

# /usr/local/etc/httpd/ should be changed to whatever you set
# ServerRoot to.
<Directory /usr/local/etc/httpd/cgi-bin>
Options Indexes FollowSymLinks
</Directory>

# This should be changed to whatever you set DocumentRoot to.

<Directory /usr/local/etc/httpd/htdocs>

# This may also be "None", "All", or any combination of "Indexes",
# "Includes", or "FollowSymLinks"

Options Indexes FollowSymLinks

# This controls which options the .htaccess files in directories can
# override. Can also be "None", or any combination of "Options",
# "FileInfo", "AuthConfig", and "Limit"

AllowOverride All

# Controls who can get stuff from this server.

<Limit GET>
order allow,deny
allow from all
</Limit>

</Directory>

# You may place any other directories you wish to have access
# information for after this one.
```

The srm.conf file contains information about where files are stored on your server and default directory names that are appended to user directories that contain HTML documents.

```
srm.conf
# With this document, you define the name space that users see of your
# http server.

# See the tutorials at http://hoohoo.ncsa.uiuc.edu/docs/tutorials/ for
# more information.

# NCSA httpd (httpd@ncsa.uiuc.edu)
```

Continued on next page

Continued from previous page

```
# DocumentRoot: The directory out of which you will serve your
# documents. By default, all requests are taken from this directory,
# but symbolic links and aliases may be used to point to other locations.

DocumentRoot /usr/local/etc/httpd/htdocs

# UserDir: The name of the directory which is appended onto a user's
# home directory if a ~user request is received.

UserDir public_html

# DirectoryIndex: Name of the file to use as a pre-written HTML
# directory index

DirectoryIndex index.html

# FancyIndexing is whether you want fancy directory indexing or standard

FancyIndexing on

# AddIcon tells the server which icon to show for different files or
# filename extensions

AddIconByType (TXT,/icons/text.xbm) text/*
AddIconByType (IMG,/icons/image.xbm) image/*
AddIconByType (SND,/icons/sound.xbm) audio/*
AddIcon /icons/movie.xbm .mpg .qt
AddIcon /icons/binary.xbm .bin

AddIcon /icons/back.xbm ..
AddIcon /icons/menu.xbm ^^DIRECTORY^^
AddIcon /icons/blank.xbm ^^BLANKICON^^

# DefaultIcon is which icon to show for files which do not have an icon
# explicitly set.

DefaultIcon /icons/unknown.xbm

# AddDescription allows you to place a short description after a file
# in server-generated indexes.
# Format: AddDescription "description" filename

# ReadmeName is the name of the README file the server will look for by
# default. Format: ReadmeName name
#
# The server will first look for name.html, include it if found, and
# it will then look for name and include it as plaintext if found.
#
# HeaderName is the name of a file which should be prepended to
# directory indexes.
```

```
ReadmeName README
HeaderName HEADER

# IndexIgnore is a set of filenames which directory indexing should
# ignore
# Format: IndexIgnore name1 name2...

IndexIgnore */.??* *~ *# */HEADER* */README*

# AccessFileName: The name of the file to look for in each directory
# for access control information.

AccessFileName .htaccess

# DefaultType is the default MIME type for documents which the server
# cannot find the type of from filename extensions.

DefaultType text/plain

# AddType allows you to tweak mime.types without actually editing it,
# or to make certain files to be certain types.
# Format: AddType type/subtype ext1

# AddEncoding allows you to have certain browsers (Mosaic/X 2.1+)
# uncompress information on the fly. Note: Not all browsers support this.

AddEncoding x-compress Z
AddEncoding x-gzip gz

# Redirect allows you to tell clients about documents which used to
# exist in your server's namespace, but do not anymore. This allows you to tell the
# clients where to look for the relocated document.
# Format: Redirect fakename url


# Aliases: Add here as many aliases as you need, up to 20. The format is
# Alias fakename realname

Alias /icons/ /usr/local/etc/httpd/icons/

# ScriptAlias: This controls which directories contain server scripts.
# Format: ScriptAlias fakename realname

ScriptAlias /cgi-bin/ /usr/local/etc/httpd/cgi-bin/

# If you want to use server side includes, or CGI outside
# ScriptAliased directories, uncomment the following lines.

#AddType text/x-server-parsed-html .shtml
```

Continued on next page

Continued from previous page

```
#AddType application/x-httpd-cgi .cgi

# If you want to have files/scripts sent instead of the built-in version
# in case of errors, uncomment the following lines and set them as you
# will.  Note: scripts must be able to be run as if they were called
# directly (in ScriptAlias directory, for instance)

# 302 - REDIRECT
# 400 - BAD_REQUEST
# 401 - AUTH_REQUIRED
# 403 - FORBIDDEN
# 404 - NOT_FOUND
# 500 - SERVER_ERROR
# 501 - NOT_IMPLEMENTED

#ErrorDocument 302 /cgi-bin/redirect.cgi
#ErrorDocument 500 /errors/server.html
#ErrorDocument 403 /errors/forbidden.html
```

The httpd.conf file is the main server configuration file. In most installations, this file can be left as is with only one or two changes. It sets the port number to be port 80, the standard HTTP port. You must be a superuser when you launch the server if you want it to run on port 80. Otherwise, you should change this number to be something above 5000. What this will mean to the clients is that they must specify the alternate port number in their URLs pointing to any services on your server. For example, if you set the port number to be 8080, then the URL that points to your home page will look something like: http://yourserver.dom:8080/. This file also specifies the name of your Web administrator so that users that encounter problems know who to ask for help.

```
httpd.conf
# This is the main server configuration file. It is best to
# leave the directives in this file in the order they are in, or
# things may not go the way you'd like. See URL
# http://hoohoo.ncsa.uiuc.edu/
# for instructions.

# Do NOT simply read the instructions in here without understanding
# what they do, if you are unsure consult the online docs. You have been
# warned.

# NCSA httpd (comments, questions to httpd@ncsa.uiuc.edu)

# ServerType is either inetd, or standalone.

ServerType standalone
```

```
# If you are running from inetd, go to "ServerAdmin".

# Port: The port the standalone listens to. For ports < 1023, you will
# need httpd to be run as root initially.

Port 80

# StartServers: The number of servers to launch at startup.  Must be
# compiled without the NO_PASS compile option

StartServers 5

# MaxServers: The number of servers to launch until mimic'ing the 1.3
# scheme (new server for each connection).  These servers will stay
# around until the server is restarted.  They will be reused as needed,
# however. See the documentation on hoohoo.ncsa.uiuc.edu for more information.

MaxServers 20

# If you wish httpd to run as a different user or group, you must run
# httpd as root initially and it will switch.

# User/Group: The name (or #number) of the user/group to run httpd as.

User nobody
Group #-1

# ServerAdmin: Your address, where problems with the server should be
# e-mailed.

ServerAdmin webmaster@yourserver.com

# ServerRoot: The directory the server's config, error, and log files
# are kept in

ServerRoot /usr/local/etc/httpd

# ErrorLog: The location of the error log file. If this does not start
# with /, ServerRoot is prepended to it.

ErrorLog logs/error_log

# TransferLog: The location of the transfer log file. If this does not
# start with /, ServerRoot is prepended to it.

TransferLog logs/access_log

# AgentLog: The location of the agent log file.  If this does not start
# with /, ServerRoot is prepended to it.
```

Continued on next page

Continued from previous page

```
AgentLog logs/agent_log

# RefererLog: The location of the referer log file.  If this does not
# start with /, ServerRoot is prepended to it.

RefererLog logs/referer_log

# RefererIgnore: If you don't want to keep track of links from certain
# servers (like your own), place it here.  If you want to log them all,
# keep this line commented.

#RefererIgnore servername

# PidFile: The file the server should log its pid to

PidFile logs/httpd.pid

# ServerName allows you to set a host name which is sent back to clients for
# your server if it's different than the one the program would get
# (i.e. use "www" instead of the host's real name).
#
# Note: You cannot just invent host names and hope they work. The name you
# define here must be a valid DNS name for your host. If you don't
# understand this, ask your network administrator.

#ServerName www.myserver.com
```

The mime.types file lists the MIME types that your server knows about. You will probably never have to look at this file. But, just in case, here is a listing.

```
mime.types

application/activemessage
application/andrew-inset
application/applefile
application/atomicmail
application/dca-rft
application/dec-dx
application/mac-binhex40
application/macwriteii
application/msword
application/news-message-id
application/news-transmission
application/octet-stream        bin
application/oda                 oda
application/pdf                 pdf
application/postscript          ai eps ps
application/remote-printing
```

```
application/rtf                rtf
application/slate
application/x-mif      mif
application/wita
application/wordperfect5.1
application/x-csh              csh
application/x-dvi              dvi
application/x-hdf              hdf
application/x-latex            latex
application/x-netcdf           nc cdf
application/x-sh               sh
application/x-tcl              tcl
application/x-tex              tex
application/x-texinfo          texinfo texi
application/x-troff            t tr roff
application/x-troff-man        man
application/x-troff-me         me
application/x-troff-ms         ms
application/x-wais-source      src
application/zip                zip
application/x-bcpio            bcpio
application/x-cpio             cpio
application/x-gtar             gtar
application/x-shar             shar
application/x-sv4cpio          sv4cpio
application/x-sv4crc           sv4crc
application/x-tar              tar
application/x-ustar            ustar
audio/basic                    au snd
audio/x-aiff                   aif aiff aifc
audio/x-wav                    wav
image/gif                      gif
image/ief                      ief
image/jpeg                     jpeg jpg jpe
image/tiff                     tiff tif
image/x-cmu-raster             ras
image/x-portable-anymap        pnm
image/x-portable-bitmap        pbm
image/x-portable-graymap       pgm
image/x-portable-pixmap        ppm
image/x-rgb                    rgb
image/x-xbitmap                xbm
image/x-xpixmap                xpm
image/x-xwindowdump            xwd
message/external-body
message/news
message/partial
message/rfc822
multipart/alternative
```

Continued on next page

Continued from previous page

```
multipart/appledouble
multipart/digest
multipart/mixed
multipart/parallel
text/html                         html
text/plain                        txt
text/richtext                     rtx
text/tab-separated-values         tsv
text/x-setext                     etx
video/mpeg                        mpeg mpg mpe
video/quicktime                   qt mov
video/x-msvideo                   avi
video/x-sgi-movie                 movie
```

Editing Local Files

Once you have installed and edited your server and configuration files, you may want to make an entry in your /etc/rc.local file that will start the server whenever your machine is booted. An example entry in the /etc/rc.local would be:

```
#Start up HTTPD
if [-f /usr/local/etc/httpd/httpd ]; then
        /usr/local/etc/httpd/httpd -d /usr/local/etc/httpd & (echo -n '
httpd') > /dev/console
```

This will start the HTTPD server when the machine goes through its bootstrap routines. The -d flag lists the ServerRoot directory. This tells the server where to look for its configuration and related files.

NOTE: On a Unix system there is a special user called root. This is often refered to as Super-User. The root account has access to everything on the machine, regardless of how users have set their permissions. Many programs need to access restricted resources and restricted port addresses and can only be started by someone logged in as root. Any network port number below 1024 is considered a restricted port. If you are running your server on the default port 80, then you must be logged in as root to start the server.

Once all of this is in place, you can start your server by typing the following at the command line:

```
/usr/local/etc/httpd/httpd -d /usr/local/etc/httpd
```

Please note that you must "su" to root before you start the server if you are running your server on port 80. The "su" command is the Unix command to "substitute user". If you type "su" at the Unix command line without parameters, you will be prompted for the root password (if any). If you supply the correct password, you will be effectively logged in as root. See the man page on su for more information.

Netsite

This book won't go into details about the Netsite servers, but here is some useful information about these commercial products.

First of all, a Netsite server is configured almost entirely via a Web browser. When you copy the Netsite software to your machine, you simply execute an install program and then connect to the machine with the browser of your choice to configure and install your server. It makes setting up this server very simple and straightforward. All the post-installation server administration is done in a similar manner; you just connect to the server and request the URL for the administration pages. The server will ask you for a password, and if you pass authentication, will allow you to change the server configuration or shut it down, and so on.

Netscape Communications claims that their server is faster than the NCSA and CERN products. This may well be true, as the Netsite server sets up a shortcut by asking you how many simultaneous requests you want it to be able to service. Then, when the server is started, it forks that many extra processes that "hang out" waiting for requests, and this cuts down a little bit of the overhead that it takes to spawn a child process on demand.

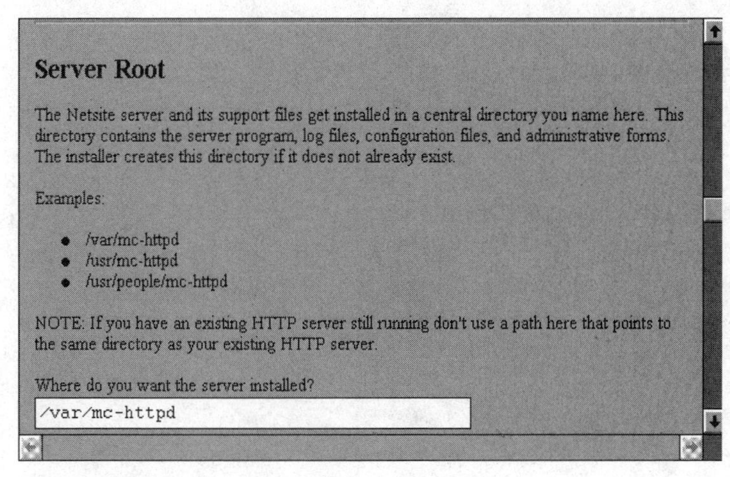

Figure 21-6 Netsite installation page

Unfortunately, it can also fill your proc table with processes that aren't doing anything. Once your proc table is full, your machine can't start any more processes until one of the running processes terminates and releases an address. This means that you can't log in, open a shell, or literally do anything on this machine until some process terminates. (The way the earlier versions of the NCSA server work, by contrast, has the server run as a daemon. When a request comes in, the NCSA server forks a process that services the request until the request is fulfilled. The child process then terminates and frees up the space it was taking in the proc table. Versions of NCSA HTTPD greater than 1.4 allow you to use either scheme. You can specify in the config files how many processes you want to start at runtime, and the maximum number of child processes that can be created.)

The really big difference between server products is with the Netscape Commerce server. This server allows public/private key data encryption based on the DES standard. If you plan on implementing a site that serves privileged information, or if you want to do online transactions, this is the server for you. Netsite and Netsite Commerce are products of Netscape Communications, which can be reached at info@mcom.com.

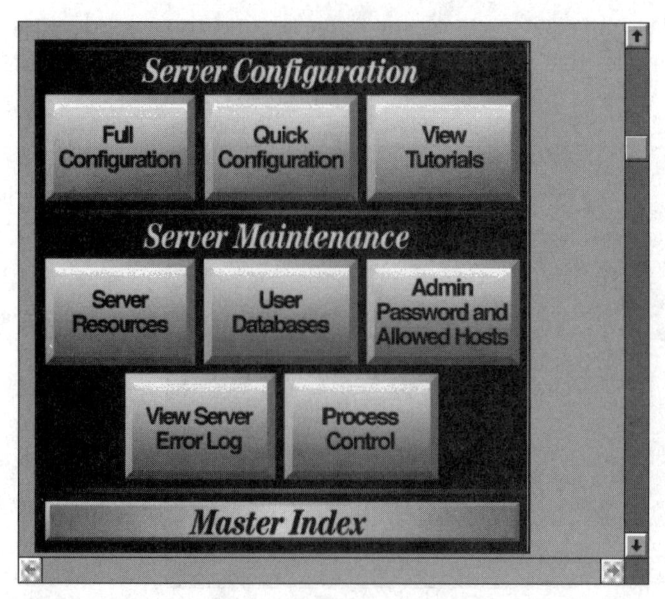

Figure 21-7 Netsite administration page

Windows Server Installation

I don't know of any DOS versions of Web servers out there yet, but there are a number of servers that will run under Windows. Many of these are reasonably functional with the exception of the Common Gateway Interface (CGI.) The current state of the Windows operating system doesn't allow true multithreaded applications. This is something that is important if you expect much traffic on your system and want to use CGI scripts. This will, however, change with the new versions of Windows NT and similar PC operating systems that allow multithreaded applications. The other drawback is that there aren't a lot of good CGI scripts written for Windows servers in the public domain. Most of the scripts that you are likely to see were written as DOS batch files (a scripting language of very limited ability), or as Visual Basic programs.

On the other hand, there are a few Windows-based servers out there that can get you up and running with a very small time investment, and most of them are free. There are two HTTP servers on the CD-ROM that came with this book. These are WIN_HTTP and SERWEB. WIN_HTTP is much more functional and better supported, but SERWEB with it's limited functionality, is very simple to set up and comes with source code for you would-be Web hacks that might want to play around with writing your own server software.

Installing WIN_HTTP

You need to first get the software onto your Windows machine. If you have a CD-ROM drive, then mount the CD-ROM on your machine. For the examples to follow, I'm going to use the drive specifier F: for the CD-ROM drive and the specifier C: for your local hard drive. Change C: and F: to match the drive labels on your particular system.

First, you need to create a directory that the server will be installed into. I suggest you use C:\HTTPD, but you may put this directory elsewhere if it suits your needs. Next, you need to unpack the files on the CD-ROM into this directory. The files on the CD-ROM are in a compressed file format. They must be uncompressed in order to use them. To unpack them, you need PKUNZIP, UNZIP, or a similar utility. Make sure that the directory containing the PKUNZIP.EXE utility is in your PATH variable. (The PATH variable is a variable that contains a list of directories that your system will search in for executable files).

Now copy the WIN_HTTP software onto your local hard drive. At a DOS prompt you may do this by typing:

```
xcopy f:\servers\windows\win_http.zip c:\httpd
```

This will copy the file WIN_HTTP.ZIP into the directory HTTPD on drive C:. Once there, you should change your working directory to C:\HTTPD by typing:

```
cd c:\httpd
```

Now unpack the files by typing:

```
pkunzip win_http.zip
```

You should see a list of messages scroll down the screen as each file is expanded. If all goes well, all of the files will be expanded into the proper directories relative to HTTPD.

Editing the autoexec.bat

The HTTP server you just unpacked *will not run* unless you have an environment variable named TZ set to a valid time zone. There are two ways to do this, you can either type: set tz=EST4EDT every time you start your machine, or you can add this line to the AUTOEXEC.BAT file on your system.

The AUTOEXEC.BAT file is a script that is automatically run every time you start up your machine. It sets a number of environment variables including your path. The AUTOEXEC.BAT file is in the root directory of your boot drive. So, if your machine boots off of drive C:, then you can find the autoexec.bat file in C:\AUTOEXEC.BAT. Open this file for editing with your favorite editor, such as EDIT. Now add the following line to the end of your autoexec.bat file:

set tz=EST4EDT

Be sure to put you local time zone here. The first three letters represent your normal time zone such as EST for Eastern Standard Time, or PST for Pacific Standard Time. The second number represents hours from Greenwich Mean Time. The third part represents your daylight savings time. Don't worry too much if this seems too complicated for you. This variable must be set to something, but the only thing that it will affect is your log file, so the server will still work if you live in New York, but set your time zone to be PST1PDT.

Once you have changed your AUTOEXEC.BAT file, save your changes, and restart your computer. The changes won't take effect until you do this.

Figure 21-8 WIN-HTTPD startup screen

Now you are ready to run Windows and start your server. There are a number of configuration files in your server directory. Your server should run fine without editing any of these. But, before we start the server, lets take a look at a few.

The HTTPD.CNF file contains information that your server uses to configure itself. This is the main configuration file for your server.

HTTPD.CNF

```
#-----------------------------------------------------------------------
-
#
#   HTTPD.CNF
#
# Main server configuration for NCSA WinHttpd V1.2 (Windows)
#
# This is the main server configuration file. It is best to
# leave the directives in this file in the order they are in, or
# things may not go the way you'd like.
#
# Do NOT simply read the instructions in here without understanding
# what they do, if you are unsure consult the online docs. You have
# been warned.
#
# NOTE: path defaults are relative to the server's installation
#       directory (ServerRoot). Paths may be given in Unix or
#       DOS format (using '/' or '\').
#
# Bob Denny <rdenny@netcom.com> 31-Mar-94
```

Continued on next page

Continued from previous page

```
#
#-----------------------------------------------------------------------
-

# ServerRoot: The directory the server's config, error, and log files
# are kept in. This should be specified on the startup command line.
#
# Format: ServerRoot <path>
#
# ServerRoot c:/httpd/

# Port: The port the standalone listens to. 80 is the network standard.
#
# Port 80

# Timeout: The timeout applied to all network operations. If you are on
# a slow network, or are using a SLIP or PPP connection, you might try
# increasing this to 60 sec.
#
# Format: Timeout nn    (seconds)
#
# Timeout 30

# ServerAdmin: Your address, where problems with the server should be
# e-mailed.
#
# Format: ServerAdmin <email addr>
#
# ServerAdmin www-admin

# ErrorLog: The location of the error log file. If this does not start
# with / or a drive spec (recommended!), ServerRoot is prepended to it.
#
# Format: ErrorLog <path/file>
#
# ErrorLog logs/error.log

# TransferLog: The location of the transfer log file. If this does not
# start with / or a drive spec (recommended!), ServerRoot is prepended
# to it.
#
# Format: TransferLog <path/file>
#
# TransferLog logs/access.log

# ServerName allows you to set a host name which is sent back to clients for
# your server if it's different than the one the program would get (i.e. use
# "www" instead of the host's real name). Make sure your DNS is set up to
# alias the name to your system!
#
```

```
# Format: ServerName <domain name>
#
# no default
```

The second configuration file is ACCESS.CNF. This file is used to set access privledges and methods on your server.

ACCESS.CNF

```
#-----------------------------------------------------------------
-
#
#  ACCESS.CNF
#
# Global access configuration for NCSA WinHttpd V1.2 (Windows)
#
# This is server global access configuration file. It is best to
# leave the directives in this file in the order they are in, or
# things may not go the way you'd like.
#
# Do NOT simply read the instructions in here without understanding
# what they do, if you are unsure consult the online docs. You have
# been warned.
#
# Bob Denny <rdenny@netcom.com> 31-Mar-94
#
#-----------------------------------------------------------------
-
#
# The following access configuration establishes unrestricted access
# to the server's document tree. There is no default access config, so
# _something_ must be present and correct for the server to operate.
#
# This should be changed to whatever you set ServerRoot to.
#
<Directory c:/httpd>
Options Indexes
</Directory>

# This should be changed to whatever you set DocumentRoot to.

<Directory c:/httpd/htdocs>

# This may also be "None", "All", or "Indexes"

Options Indexes

# This controls which options the #HACCESS.CTL files in directories can
# override. Can also be "None", or any combination of "Options", "FileInfo",
# "AuthConfig", and "Limit"
```

Continued on next page

Continued from previous page

```
AllowOverride All

# Controls who can get stuff from this server.

<Limit GET>
order allow,deny
allow from all
</Limit>

</Directory>

# You may place any other directories you wish to have access
# information for after this one.
```

Finally we will take a look at the SRM.CNF file. This is the server resource configuration file.

SRM.CNF

```
#-------------------------------------------------------------------
-
#
#   SRM.CNF
#
# Server resource configuration for NCSA WinHttpd V1.2 (Windows)
#
# The settings in this file control the document layout and name specs
# that your server makes visible to users. The values in the comments
# are the defaults built into the server.
#
# NOTE: path defaults are relative to the server's installation
#       directory (ServerRoot). Paths may be given in Unix or
#       DOS format (using '/' or '\').
#
# Bob Denny <rdenny@netcom.com> 21-May-94
#
#-------------------------------------------------------------------
-
#
# DocumentRoot: The directory out of which you will serve your
# documents. By default, all requests are taken from this directory, but
# aliases may be used to point to other locations.
#
# DocumentRoot c:/httpd/htdocs

# DirectoryIndex: Name of the file to use as a pre-written HTML
# directory index. This document, if present, will be opened when the
# server receives a request containing a URL for the directory, instead
# of generating a directory index.
#
# DirectoryIndex index.htm
```

```
# AccessFileName: The name of the file to look for in each directory
# for access control information. This file should have a name which is
# blocked from appearing in server-generated indexes!
#
# AccessFileName #haccess.ctl

# ========================
# Aliasing and Redirection
# ========================
#
# Redirect allows you to tell clients about documents which used to exist in
# your server's namespace, but do not anymore. This allows you to tell the
# clients where to look for the relocated document.
#
# Format: Redirect fakename url
#

# Aliases: Add here as many aliases as you need, up to 20. One useful
# alias to have is one for the path to the icons used for the server-
# generated directory indexes. The paths given below in the AddIcon
# statements are relative.
#
# Format: Alias fakename realname
#
Alias /icons/ c:/httpd/icons/

# ScriptAlias: This controls which directories contain DOS server
#              scripts.
#
# Format: ScriptAlias fakename realname
#
ScriptAlias /cgi-dos/ c:/httpd/cgi-dos/
ScriptAlias /cgi-bin/ c:/httpd/cgi-dos/

# WinScriptAlias: This controls which directories contain Windows
#                 server scripts.
#
# Format: WinScriptAlias fakename realname
#
WinScriptAlias /cgi-win/ c:/httpd/cgi-win/

# =========================
# MIME Content Type Control
# =========================
#
# DefaultType is the default MIME type for documents which the server
# cannot find the type of from filename extensions.
#
# DefaultType text/html
DefaultType text/plain
```

Continued on next page

Continued from previous page

```
# AddType allows you to tweak MIME.TYP without actually editing it, or to
# make certain files to be certain types.
#
# Format: AddType type/subtype ext1
#


# ReadmeName is the name of the README file the server will look for by
# default.  The server will first look for name.html, include it if found,
# and it will then look for name and include it as plaintext if found.
#
# Format: ReadmeName name
#
ReadmeName #readme.htm

# ============================
# AUTOMATIC DIRECTORY INDEXING
# ============================
#
# The server generates a directory index if there is no file in the
# directory whose name matches DirectoryIndex.
#
# FancyIndexing: Whether you want fancy directory indexing or standard
#
# FancyIndexing on

# IconsAreLinks: Whether the icons in a fancy index are links as
# well as the file names.
#
# IconsAreLinks off

# AddIcon tells the server which icon to show for different files or
# filename extensions. In preparation for the upcoming Chicago version, you
# should include explicit 3 character truncations for 4-character endings.
# Don't rely on the DOS underpinnings to silently truncate for you.
#
AddIcon /icons/text.gif     .html   .htm    .txt    .ini
AddIcon /icons/image.gif    .gif    .jpg    .jpe    .jpeg   .xbm
.tiff   .tif    .pic    .pict .bmp
AddIcon /icons/sound.gif    .au     .wav    .snd
AddIcon /icons/movie.gif    .mpg    .mpe    .mpeg
AddIcon /icons/binary.gif   .bin    .exe    .bat    .dll
AddIcon /icons/back.gif     ..
AddIcon /icons/menu.gif     ^^DIRECTORY^^
AddIcon /icons/dblank.gif      ^^BLANKICON^^

# DefaultIcon is which icon to show for files which do not have an icon
```

```
# explicitly set.
#
DefaultIcon /icons/unknown.gif

# AddDescription allows you to place a short description after a file in
# server-generated indexes. A better place for these are in individual
# "#haccess.ctl" files in individual directories.
#
# Format: AddDescription "description" filename
#

# IndexIgnore is a set of filenames which directory indexing should
# ignore. Here, I've disabled display of our readme and access control files,
# plus anything that starts with a "~", which I use for annotation
# HTML documents. I also have disabled some common editor backup file
# names. Match is on file NAME.EXT only, and the usual * and ? meta-chars
# apply.
#
# WARNING: Be sure to set an ignore for your access control file(s)!!
#
# Format: IndexIgnore name1 name2...
#
IndexIgnore  ~* *.bak *.{* #readme.htm #haccess.ctl

## END ##
```

Starting your server

Once you have made any changes to the configuration files that make sense on your system, you are ready to start your server. First, if you are not already running Windows, then start Windows. Once Windows is running, you can start your server by selecting Run from the File menu in the Program Manager. In the entry field, type:

```
c:\httpd\httpd
```

You should see a window pop up with the HTTPD icon. Your server is now running. Test your server by accessing it with your favorite Web browser. If you just select your machine name in the URL and get the default home page, there are a number of tutorials about maintaining and configuring your server. Once you have read through these, start placing your HTML documents on the server and you are now the latest Web site.

Installing SerWeb

SerWeb is a very simple HTTP server. It can serve HTML documents, but its functionality does not go much beyond that. It is included for two reasons, first because it is basically ready to go with little or no configuration, and secondly because it comes with source code for those who may want to write their own HTTP server and want some reference points.

To install SerWeb, first copy the software onto your local hard drive. Follow the directions listed above for copying the WIN_HTTP software above just substituting SerWeb for WIN_HTTP and putting the files in a directory called C:\SERWEB instead of C:\HTTPD.

Once the files are in place start Windows (if you haven't already done so). Now, select Run from the File menu from the Program Manager and type:

```
c:\serweb\serweb
```

into the input field. This should launch the SerWeb server. Once it is running, test it with your Web browser, and if it is working, you can start placing your HTML documents into its directory.

As with the other server packages, there is also a configuration file that you may edit if you chose. The configuration file for SerWeb is called SERWEB.INI and is listed below:

SERWEB.INI

```
[SERWEB]

PortNumber      = 80        ; Which Port to listen into
HowManyClients  =  5       ; Allow up to 5 people to be on at the same
                           ; time.

ClosedServer    =  0       ; 0 = OK to log in, 1 = not OK
PeriodAllowed   =  1       ; 0 = allow .. on the filenames, else don't..
PrintOut        =  1       ; Send output to status window: 1 = Yes, 0 = No

; Where to start sending from (ex - if you specify c:\data as your
; send dir, you can get c:\data\test, c:\data\other\test, but not
; c:\test
SendDir             = c:

; Message files to send specific information ......
FileNotExistMsg   = c:\serweb\nofile.htm
ClosedServerMsg   = c:\serweb\closed.htm
PeriodAllowedMsg  = c:\serweb\period.htm
```

Macintosh Server Installation

The Macintosh computer is known mostly for its interface and its ease of use. It is true that Macintosh HTTP server software is also very easy to install—though it has a couple of drawbacks that may or may not matter to you.

The first concern is speed. The server software available on the Macintosh just isn't as fast as its Unix counterparts. Not to say that it's unusable; it is actually adequate for most people. However, Unix servers and Unix clients tend to be much more responsive than their Macintosh counterparts at present, though the difference will almost certainly even out over time.

The second concern is with CGI extensions. The common way that the CGI interface is implemented is via Apple Events sent to AppleScript programs. (AppleScript is a scripting language specific to Macintosh computers). When a client requests a CGI script on a MacHTTP server, the server sends an Apple Event to the script. The script then executes based on this event. The problem is that if many users request this same script at or about the same time, the Apple Events are queued. If the script isn't written very carefully, it may drop some of these events as it terminates from a previous invocation. And even if you aren't losing events, the queued-request system may not be acceptable to you or your users. Queued events are put in an ordered line, and so your users will all have to wait in line for the requested script to service all the clients ahead of them. This isn't necessarily a problem in a low-volume or low-urgency situation, but it's a good idea to think about it before you get started.

Installing MacHTTP

This is probably one of the easiest Web servers to install. First, you must copy the software onto your Macintosh. This is probably easiest to do simply by downloading MacHTTP from the site listed in Appendix D, and unstuff it. Locate the MacHTTP folder, and drag it onto your local hard disk. Once it is there, you may edit the MacHTTP.conf file with the text editor or word processor of your choice (although you probably won't need to), and then double-click on the MacHTTP icon.

MacHTTP will now go through its initialization and wait for clients. There are a few menu-bar options that allow you to change parameters, but basically you are ready for business. The only thing left to do is add your HTML documents into the MacHTTP folder, or subfolders thereof.

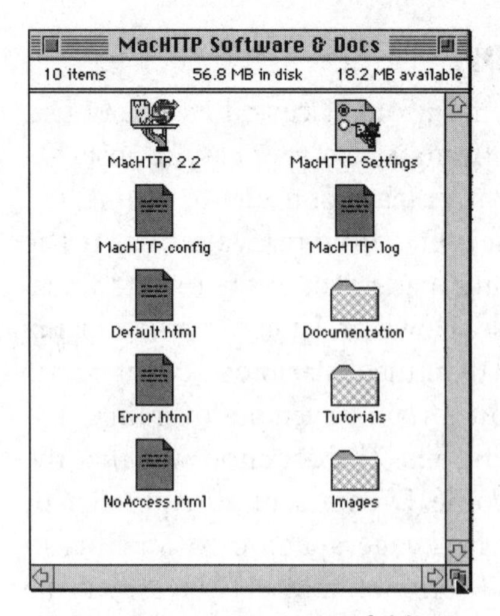

Figure 21-9 MacHTTP folder

For those who may want to know what parameters they can tweak in the configuration file, here is a listing of MacHTTP.conf:

```
MacHTTP.conf
#MacHTTP Configuration file, v. 2.0
#
#The format of this file is free form, with a few exceptions. Lines not
#starting with a recognized keyword are ignored.
#Note, all entries are converted to upper case by MacHTTP, so the config file
#isn't case sensitive, with the exception of Mac file types and creators below.

#Note that any text styles like bold or underline in this file are purely
#cosmetic and are only intended to make the file easier to read. The styles are not
#required. Legal config file keywords will appear as BOLD text if this file is
# viewed with SimpleText or TeachText.

# The version number below must match MacHTTP's version number
VERSION 2.0

###################################################
# "Special" Files
#
#The following line defines the default file type if a suffix match
#isn't found.
#The syntax is: DEFAULT <default transfer type> <default MIME type>
DEFAULT TEXT text/html
```

```
#The following lines specify where to find HTML files for error messages,
#the default home (or index) page, the name of the log file, and the message
#returned for security violations. Any of these three file directives
#point to a HTML document, script, or CGI application.
#
#NOTE!!! INDEX must be a simple file name, not a path like the other
#files.
INDEX    Default.html
ERROR    :Error.html
NOACCESS :NoAccess.html

#If the LOG file directive is missing or commented out, no logging
#will occur.
LOG      :MacHTTP.log

########################################################
# The following commands can be used to adjust MacHTTP's behavior and
# performance. Most of them can be adjusted via AppleScript and
# AppleEvents as well.

#Sets the timeout for inactive connections to 60 seconds
TIMEOUT 60

#Sets the max number of simultaneous users to 10.
#The minimum value is 3, the maximum is 48
#For larger values, you should monitor memory usage and increase
#MacHTTP's memory allocation in the Finder accordingly.
MAXUSERS 10

#Sets the number of "listens" MacHTTP performs simultaneously. For
#busy servers with clients that report "Unable to connect" errors,
#this number should be increased. If the "Listening" statistic in
#the status window ever drops to 1, some clients may miss connecting.
#Default is 5, minimum is 3, maximum is 48. Never set the number of
#listens to be more than the MAXUSERS!
MAXLISTENS 6

#A single copy of MacHTTP only listens on a single port for multiple
#connections. The HTTP standard port is 80. Users may define any port
#they'd like to listen on, but Internet standards say that ports
#numbered 1024 and below are reserved for "Well known services" that
#are pre-defined. That means if you change MacHTTP's port from 80,
#you should pick a number greater than 1024 to avoid conflicting with
#things like telnet, gopher, ftp, nfs, pop, etc. that all have ports
#assigned below 1024.
PORT 80

# This is the number of ticks that MacHTTP will "steal" from other processes
```

Continued on next page

Continued from previous page

```
# while sending data to clients. This equates directly to how much time
# MacHTTP will spend processing connections. Your Mac will effectively be
# dedicated to MacHTTP for this period of time. The argument is in
# "ticks", which are 60ths of a second. The default
# is .5 seconds. (30 ticks) Values can range between 0 and 120.
PIG_DELAY 30

# This is the chunk size that MacHTTP will divide file transfers into. The
# larger the chunk, the longer it will take to transmit over slow connections.
# The smaller it is, the more times MacHTTP will be able to swap between
# servicing multiple connections and
# freeing the Mac to work on other processes. The argument represents the
# max number of bytes to be sent in a single MacTCP write to the client.
# The min is 256, the max is 10240.
DUMP_BUF_SIZE 4096

# MacHTTP can be configured to eliminate DNS accesses. For best performance,
# uncomment the following line. MacHTTP will log IP addresses rather than
# host names, but the software will perform much faster when used with
# slow domain name servers.
#NO_DNS

##########################################################
#These lines define the suffix and file type mappings for MIME types.
#The syntax is <type> <suffix> <mac file type> <mac creator> <mime
#type>
#
#Unspecified parameters should be replaced with "*".  MacHTTP tries to match
#a file suffix first. Failing that, it tries to match Mac file type info,
#and if it can, Mac creator info as well. Matching either suffix or
#type/creator determines
#the transfer type and MIME type. If the client supports HTTP/1.0, the
#appropriate MIME header will be constructed and returned, based on the info
#below. Scripts are responsible for generating their own HTTP/1.0
headers!!!

TEXT    .HTML TEXT * text/html
BINARY  .GIF  GIFf * image/gif
CGI .CGI APPL * text/html
ACGI .ACGI APPL * text/html
SCRIPT  .SCRIPT TEXT * text/html
SCRIPT  * TEXT ToyS text/html
APPL    .EXE APPL * text/html
TEXT    .TEXT TEXT * text/plain
TEXT    .TXT TEXT * text/plain
```

```
TEXT   .HQX TEXT * application/mac-binhex40
BINARY  .JPG JPEG * image/jpeg
BINARY  .JPEG JPEG * image/jpeg
BINARY  .PICT PICT * image/pict
BINARY .AU * * audio/basic
BINARY .AIFF * * audio/x-aiff
BINARY .XBM * * image/x-xbm
BINARY  .MOV MOOV * video/quicktime
BINARY .MPEG MPEG * video/mpeg
BINARY .WORD WDBN MSWD application/msword
BINARY .XL XLS3 * application/excel
BINARY .SIT SITD * application/x-stuffit
BINARY .PDF PDF%20 * application/pdf

#####################################################
# Security configuration
#

# Security realms - see the Security tutorial for more details
#REALM workers Co-Workers
#REALM cust Customers

#IP and domain name security. There is an implied "DENY *" that is
#evaluated prior to any address security specifications if they are present.
#Otherwise, the default is an implied "ALLOW *". End complete host IP
#addresses with a "." for an exact match.
#Otherwise a statement like "ALLOW 129.106.3" would match hosts 129.106.30.*,
#129.106.31.*, 129.106.32.*, etc.
#
#You may also specify domain names for ALLOW and DENY statements.
#The domain names are matched from right to left, as opposed to the
#left to right matches done for IP address ALLOW and DENY statements.
#Also, the domain names you specify are case-sensitive and MUST end with a
#period (.). For example:
#  ALLOW abc.edu.
#  DENY mac22.abc.edu.
#would deny all hosts (implicit DENY *), allow any abc.edu node, and
#deny the specific host, mac22.abc.edu.

#NOTE!!! "ALLOW *" and "DENY *" are not valid syntax!

#ALLOW 123.45.6.
#DENY 123.45.6.7.
```

LESSON #8: HYPERMEDIA GATEWAYS

Many organizations like to isolate themselves from the rest of the Internet. They disallow all communication between their machines and machines at large. This helps protect them from snoops and vandals who may try to gain unauthorized access to their machines or data. Unfortunately, even those who value privacy often want to be able to communicate with other machines and to send e-mail from their machines to users on the Internet. The most common way to deal with this is by using a gateway machine that restricts access between the Internet and the local machine. The gateway machine acts as a firewall protecting the organization from unauthorized access. Normally, these gateway machines only allow certain types of data to pass from one network to another, such as e-mail.

Certain HTTP servers can run as proxies on networks that are behind firewalls. Basically, a proxy is set up on the gateway machine that accepts and forwards HTTP requests for services on the other side. This way, you don't have to allow access to your entire network, leaving it vulnerable to attack, but you can still enjoy the wonders of the World Wide Web.

Currently, the CERN server seems to be the only public-domain server that can be configured as a proxy. One nice thing about the CERN server is that it can cache HTTP requests and lighten the load on your local network if certain services are requested often.

The Netsite servers can also be configured as proxies and have similar advantages.

WHAT NOW?

Once your server is in place and you have started creating HTML documents, you need to let others know about your site—unless, of course, your site is for internal use only.... Where you advertise your services depends on what services you are providing, or more importantly, who you want to attract.

Tell your clients about your site and services. You would be surprised at the number of people who now have access to and normally use the Web. Many people have begun to put the URL to their home pages on business cards and letterhead.

If you are interested in attracting lots of people in general, you should also list your site in all the "What's new" and "New servers" lists on the Web. Some popular places to post links to your pages are:

HTML http://www.biotech.washington.edu/WebCrawler/WebCrawler.html

HTML http://www.cs.colorado.edu/home/mcbryan/WWWW.html

HTML http://akebono.stanford.edu/yahoo/

HTML http://www.ncsa.uiuc.edu/SDG/Software/Mosaic/Docs/whats-new.html

Once you start adding your links to these services, people will start looking at your server. If they find it interesting, they will create links to it on their pages, or tell others about it. Before you know it, your site will be an integral part of the information superhighway–pretty soon, you may want to set up your own tollbooth....

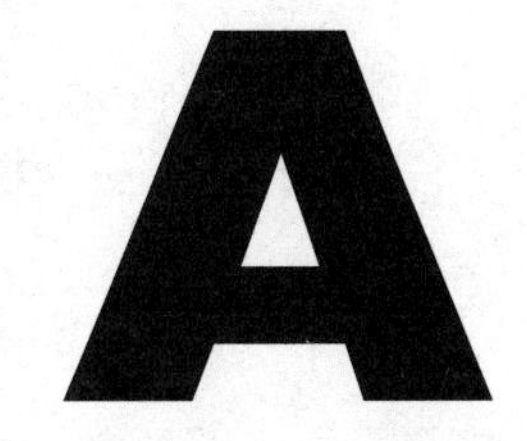

SLIP INTERNET PROVIDERS

Some Internet services charge you an exorbitant sign-up fee to cover commercial SLIP software or Web browsers. In most cases, you won't need these packages since all the software you need for the Web comes with this book. Shop around before you settle down.

COMMERCIAL SERVICES

The following services provide SLIP-based access to the Internet. On average, these services charge $20 or so a month. Check out the prices for all services in your area code. Some nationwide and worldwide servers are also included; these providers are tagged with a *(g)* for global.

The Black Box (info@blkbox.com)
Modem: 713-480-2686
Voice: 713-480-2684

Communications Accessibles Montreal (info@CAM.ORG)
Modem: 514-931-7178, 514-931-2333
Voice: 514-931-0749

Clark Internet Services, Inc. (ClarkNet) (info@clark.net)
Modem: 410-730-9786, 410-995-0271, 301-596-1626, 301-854-0446, 301-621-5216
Voice: 800-735-2258, 410-730-9764

(g) Colorado SuperNet, Inc. (info@csn.org)
Voice: 800-748-0800, 303-273-3471

Connect.com.au pty ltd: Australia (connect@connect.com.au)
Voice: +61 3 5282239

CTS Network Services (CTSNET) (info@crash.cts.com)
Modem: 619-637-3640, 619-637-3660, 619-637-3680
Voice: 619-637-3637

CR Laboratories Dialup Internet Access (info@crl.com)
Modem: 415-389-UNIX
Voice: 415-381-2800

Demon Internet Systems (DIS): Great Britain (internet@demon.co.uk)
Modem: +44 (0)81 343 4848
Voice: +44 (0)81 349 0063

(g) DIAL n' CERF or DIAL n' CERF AYC (help@cerf.net)
Voice: 800-876-2373, 619-455-3900

Echo Communications (horn@echonyc.com)
Modem: 212-989-8411
Voice: 212-255-3839

(g) Express Access: A service of Digital Express Group (info@digex.net)
Modem: 301-220-0462, 410-766-1855, 703-281-7997, 714-377-9784, 908-937-9481
Voice: 800-969-9090, 301-220-2020

Freelance Systems Programming (fsp@dayton.fsp.com)
Modem: 513-258-7745
Voice: 513-254-7246

CyberGate, Inc. (info@gate.net or sales@gate.net)
Modem: 305-425-0200
Voice: 305-428-GATE

HookUp Communication Corporation: Canada (info@hookup.net)
Voice: 519-747-4110

The IDS World Network (sysadmin@ids.net)
Modem: 401-884-9002, 401-785-1067
Voice: 401-884-7856

IEunet Ltd., Ireland's Internet Services Supplier (info@ieunet.ie, info@Ireland.eu.net)
Modem: +353 1 6790830, +353 1 6798600
Voice: +353 1 6790832

Internet Direct, Inc. (info@indirect.com (automated); support@indirect.com (human))
Modem: 602-274-9600 (Phoenix), 602-321-9600 (Tucson)
Voice: 602-274-0100 (Phoenix), 602-324-0100 (Tucson)

Individual Network e.V.: Germany (in-info@individual.net)
Modem: +49-69-39048414, +49-69-6312934 (+ others)
Voice: +49-69-39048413, +49 2131 64190

(g) Institute for Global Communications (support@igc.apc.org)
Voice: 415-442-0220

(g) InterAccess (info@interaccess.com)
Modem: 708-671-0237
Voice: 800-967-1580

(g) IQuest Internet
Voice: 317-259-5050, 800-844-8649

KAIWAN Public Access Internet Online Services (info@kaiwan.com)
Modem: 714-539-5726, 310-527-7358
Voice: 714-638-2139

Texas Metronet (info@metronet.com)
Modem: 214-705-2901, 817-261-1127
Voice: 214-705-2900, 817-543-8756

Merit Network, Inc.–MichNet project (info@merit.edu)
Voice: 313-764-9430

MSen (info@msen.com)
Voice: 313-998-4562

MV Communications, Inc. (info@mv.com)
Voice: 603-429-2223

(g) Netcom Online Communication Services (info@netcom.com)
Modem: 206-547-5992, 214-753-0045, 303-758-0101, 310-842-8835, 312-380-0340, 404-303-9765, 408-241-9760, 408-459-9851, 415-328-9940, 415-985-5650, 503-626-6833, 510-274-2900,

510-426-6610, 510-865-9004, 617-237-8600, 619-234-0524, 703-255-5951, 714-708-3800, 818-585-3400, 916-965-1371
Voice: 408-554-8649, 800-501-8649

Nuance Network Services (staff@nuance.com)
Voice: 205-533-4296

(g) Performance Systems International (info@psi.com)
Voice: 703-620-6651

South Coast Computing Services, Inc. (info@sccsi.com)
Modem: 713-661-8593 (v.32), 713-661-8595 (v.32bis)
Voice: 713-661-3301

Northwest Nexus Inc. (info@nwnexus.wa.com)
Voice: 206-455-3505

RealTime Communications (wixer) (hosts@wixer.bga.com)
Modem: 512-459-4391
Voice: 512-451-0046 (11 A.M. – 6 P.M. Central Time, weekdays)

Systems Solutions (sharris@marlin.ssnet.com)
Voice: 302-378-1386, 800-331-1386

(g) UUNET Canada, Inc. (info@uunet.ca)
Voice: 416-368-6621

UUnorth (uunorth@uunorth.north.net)
Voice: 416-225-8649

Vnet Internet Access, Inc. (info@char.vnet.net)
Modem: 704-347-8839, 919-406-1544, 919-851-1526
Voice: 704-374-0779

XNet Information Systems (info@xnet.com)
Modem: 708-983-6435
Voice: 708-983-6064

LISTS

There are lots of resources online if you're on the hunt for a cheap, reliable, accessible Internet provider. If you'd rather use a standard Unix shell account, for example, there are many great places to turn. Check out Internet books, such as The Waite Group's *Internet How-To*.

If you're already online, or have a friend who's online, check out the following lists:

- PDIAL: Public Dial List. Send e-mail to *info-deli-server@netcom.com* containing the message: *SEND PDIAL*
- FSLIST: The Forgotten Site List. ftp://freedom.nmsu.edu/pub/docs/fslist/ or ftp://login.qc.ca/pub/fslist/
- NIXPUB: Public Access Unixes. Go to ftp://VFL.Paramax.COM/pub/pubnetc/nixpub.long or send e-mail to *mail-server@bts.com* containing the message: *get PUB nixpub.long*

Also be sure to check out the following Usenet newsgroups:

- alt.internet.access.wanted
- comp.bbs.mis
- alt.bbs

B

OTHER SOFTWARE SOURCES

True, this book comes with all the software you need to connect to, cruise, create, or serve the World Wide Web. But maybe you're interested in having your own e-mail client. Or perhaps you'd like to play around with a full-featured newsreader program. This appendix tells you where to snag most available Internet software. This includes basic Internet software, other browsers, other HTML editors, and other servers.

WINSOCKS

Along with Trumpet Winsock, the NetManage company also offers a shareware Winsock: Chameleon. Contact NetManage at 408-973-7171 or:

```
http://www.netmanage.com/
```

SLIP INTERNET SOFTWARE

As long as you have a SLIP account, you might as well take advantage of it. Besides Web browsers, you can run graphical Finger clients, Usenet newsreaders, e-mail programs, Talk programs, IRC clients, etc.

Most every major FTP site has a collection of SLIP software. Check out the following archives:

```
ftp://marketplace.com/tia/steve/tia/shareware/windows/
ftp://gatekeeper.dec.com/pub/micro/msdos/win3/winsock/
```

```
http://www.ncsa.uiuc.edu/SDG/Software/WinMosaic/
ftp://oak.oakland.edu:/pub/win3/winsock/
ftp://ftp.tidbits.com/pub/slip/
ftp://ftp.cica.indiana.edu/pub/pc/win3/winsock/
```

Newsreaders

Popular newsreader clients include:

- HTML WinVN: Mark Riordan's WinVN is a full-featured Windows newsreader.
- HTML Trumpet Winsock: Another great newsreader, brought to you by Trumpet's Peter Tattam.
- HTML NewsXpress: Another fine newsreader to check out.

FTP

The best Windows FTP client is WS_FTP by John A. Junod. It includes listings of many popular FTP sites, so you can start exploring the Internet right away.

Gopher

Some of the best gopher clients include:

- HTML HGopher: A fully functional gopher client, with pretty icons and a fast interface
- HTML GopherBook: A ToolBook-based gopher program for Winsock
- HTML WSGopher: Yet another gopher client
- HTML WinGopher: And another

E-Mail

The slickest shareware e-mail program for Windows is clearly Eudora 1.4. Eudora lets you create multiple mailboxes, nickname lists, file inclusion types, and signatures. Most every command is available at the touch of an icon.

Other e-mail clients include:

- HTML dMail: A fully functional Windows mail program

HTML WinElm: An Elm e-mail reader for Winsock

Telnet

There are tons of telnet clients available. To name a few:

HTML NCSA Telnet (WinTel)

HTML Trumpet Telnet

HTML WinQVT Telnet (includes FTP, news, and e-mail features)

HTML EWAN Telnet

HTML TelW

HTML COMt

HTML QWS3270 (telnet3270 client)

HTML Tektonix Terminal Emulation

HTML Yet Another Windows Telnet (YAWTEL)

Archie

An archie client lets you search the Internet for a particular file. Two good archies are:

HTML WinArch: The Windows archie client

HTML WS-Arch: The archie client for Winsock

Finger

There are a number of finger utilities:

HTML FingerD: The Windows Finger Daemon

HTML WS-Finger: A Winsock Finger Client

IRC

The WS-IRC client is a full-featured IRC client that lets you perform all IRC functions at the click of an icon.

WAIS

The EINet WAIS client application for Winsock is a good standard.

VIEWERS

Viewers put much of the multi in multimedia. Most any viewer you'll need comes with this book. However, you may want to check for the latest updates of LView Pro, MPEGPlay, QuickTime for Windows, Wham, WPLANY, and other included viewers. Check out these NCSA Viewers pages:

HTML For Windows:

`http://www.ncsa.uiuc.edu/SDG/Software/WinMosaic/viewers.html`

HTML For Mac:

`http://www.ncsa.uiuc.edu/SDG/Software/MacMosaic/HelperApps.html`

HTML For X-Windows:

`http://www.ncsa.uiuc.edu/SDG/Software/XMosaic/faqsoftware.html#multimedia`

HTML Other good viewer archives:

```
ftp://ftp.ncsa.uiuc.edu/Mosaic/Windows/viewers/
http://home.mcom.com/MCOM/tricks_docs/helper_docs/index.html
ftp://ftp.cica.indiana.edu
ftp://gatekeeper.dec.com/pub/micro/msdos/win3/
```

Video

As computers and modems get faster, video will become more and more important. There are many good shareware video players available.

QuickTime

The Chinese University at Hong Kong has created a set of files that plug into the Windows Media Player (MPLAYER.EXE) and allow it to run QuickTime movies. You can get the files at:

`ftp://ftp.cukh.hk/pub/mov/qtw11.zip`

AVI

The new Video for Windows AVI format is constantly becoming more popular. A Video for Windows viewer is available at:

```
ftp.microsoft.com:/developer/drg/Multimedia/VfW11a/vfw11a.zip
```

MPEG

Other than MPEGPlay, there's the VTMotion Scalable MPEG Player. You can find it at:

```
ftp://gatekeeper.dec.com/pub/micro/msdos/win3/desktop/mpegxing.zip
```

PostScript

The majority of laser printers use PostScript commands to put ink to paper. Many people save formatted text in a PostScript file and make this available over the Web. It's easy to download these files and quickly dump them to your nearest laser printer—voilà! instant manual!

But what if you don't have a laser printer? Or what if you just want to browse a couple of pages on your screen? The GhostScript and GhostView programs allow you to do this, letting you view the graphics and fonts of a PS PostScript file. The GhostScript files are long (over 1 MB), and kind of slow, but can come in really useful. One source of these files is:

```
ftp://ftp.law.cornell.edu/pub/LII/Cello/gs261exe.zip
```

Acrobat

Adobe has come up with a format similar to PostScript that allows you to save printable graphic files. Most Acrobat files are in the PDF (Portable Document Format) format. Although Acrobat files are relatively rare, if you come across one the Acrobat Viewer could come in quite handy. It allows you breeze through an Acrobat document online. Get it at:

```
ftp://ftp.ncsa.uiuc.edu/Mosaic/Windows/viewers/acroread.exe
```

OTHER WEB BROWSERS

Check out Chapter 7 for places to get Windows Web browsers such as Spry AIR Mosaic, WinWeb, and Cello. There are a few other browsers you may want to check out:

The SAM (Stand Alone Mosaic) program is yet another Mosaic-like hack. It can be found at:

```
ftp://ftp.cis.ufl.edu/pub/sam/
```

Booklink is a $99 commercial browser. A demonstration version is available at:

ftp://ftp.booklink.com/lite/

Mac Browsers

CERN's Samba browser has some neat features. Grab it at:

ftp://info.cern.ch/ftp/pub/www/bin/mac

MacWeb is EINet's Macintosh version of WinWeb. It's available at:

ftp://ftp.einet.net/einet/mac/macweb/

AMIGA Browsers

The AMosaic browser is similar to NCSA Mosaic. Get it at:

ftp://max.physics.sunysb.edu/pub/amosaic

Find out more about AMosaic at:

http://insti.physics.sunysb.edu/AMosaic/home.html

Unix (X-Windows) Browsers

HTML Quadralay GWHIS Viewer:

http://www.quadralay.com/products/products.html #gwhis

HTML tkWWW Browser/Editor:

ftp://harbor.ecn.purdue.edu/

HTML Viola for X (Modern browser supporting many HTML3 commands):

http://xcf.berkeley.edu/ht/projects/viola/README

or

ftp://ora.com//pub/www/viola

HTML Chimera:

ftp://ftp.cs.unlv.edu/pub/chimera

Unix Shell Browsers

HTML Emacs w3-mode:

ftp://ftp.cs.indiana.edu/pub/elisp/w3

HTML perlWWW:

ftp://archive.cis.ohio-state.edu/pub/w3browser/w3browser-0.1.shar

VM/CMS Browsers

The Albert browser is available for the VM/CMS operating system. Get it at:

ftp://gopher.ufl.edu/pub/vm/www/

NeXTStep Browsers

The NeXTStep operating system has several good browsers. The SpiderWoman browser can be found at:

ftp://sente.epfl.ch/pub/software/

The NeXTStep OmniWeb browser is another one to check out. It's located at:

http://www.omnigroup.com/

Updates of Browsers

Although this book comes with two excellent browsers, new versions are coming out every few months or so. Regularly check out the following Web and FTP sites:

HTML Lynx:

ftp://ftp2.cc.ukans.edu/pub/WWW/

HTML Mosaic:

http://www.ncsa.uiuc.edu/SDG/Software/Mosaic/

HTML Netscape:

http://home.mcom.com/info/index.html

HTML SlipKnot:

http://interport.net/~pbrooks/slipknot.html

OTHER HTML EDITORS

There are many interesting shareware HTML editors that run under most any operating system. A good list is available at:

http://werple.mira.net.au/~gabriel/web/html/editors/

Windows Editors

HTML HTML Writer:

http://wwf.et.byu.edu/~nosackk/html-writer/index.html

HTML HTMLed:

ftp://pringle.mta.ca/pub/HTMLed/htmed12.zip

HTML HyperEdit:

http://www.curtin.edu.au/curtin/dept/cc/packages/htmledit/home.html

Macintosh Editors

The simply named HTML Editor program is a Macintosh standard, with pretty good features and near-WYSIWYG formatting. Get it at:

http://dragon.acadiau.ca:1667/~giles/HTML_Editor

Unix (X-Windows) Editors

HTML TkWWW:

ftp://harbor.ecn.purdue.edu/

HTML Phoenix:

http://www.bsd.uchicago.edu/ftp/pub/phoenix/README.html

or

ftp://www.bsd.uchicago.edu/pub/phoenix

HTML htmltext:

http://web.cs.city.ac.uk/homes/njw/htmltext/htmltext.html

Updates of Included Editors

HTML HoTMetaL:

http://gatekeeper.dec.com

HTML HTML Assistant:

ftp://ftp.cs.dal.ca/htmlasst/

WEB SERVERS

There are tons of shareware and commercial Web servers available. Some of the more popular packages are listed below:

Windows Servers

HTML SERWEB:

`ftp://winftp.cica.indiana.edu/pub/pc/win3/winsock/serweb.zip`

HTML WEB4HAM:

`ftp://ftp.informatik.uni-hamburg.de/pub/net/winsock/web4ham.zip`

HTML HTTPS (for Windows NT):

`ftp://emwac.ed.ac.uk/pub/https`

HTML OS2HTTPD (for OS/2):

`ftp://ftp.netcom.com/pub/kfan/overview.html`

HTML KA9Q NOS (for DOS):

`ftp://inorganic5.chem.ufl.edu/`

Macintosh Servers

The MacHTTP server is available at:

`http://www.uth.tmc.edu/mac_info/machttp_info.html`

Unix Servers

Although NCSA's httpd server is clearly the standard, there are several other choices:

HTML EIT httpd: This Webmaster's Starter Kit automatically installs a WWW server on your system. Just fill in the blanks:

`http://wsk.eit.com/wsk/doc/`

HTML CERN httpd:

`http://info.cern.ch/hypertext/WWW/Daemon/Status.html`

HTML GN Gopher/HTTP server:

`http://hopf.math.nwu.edu/`

HTML Plexus:

http://bsdi.com/server/doc/plexus.html

VMS Servers

HTML CERN HTTP (VMS version):

http://delonline.cern.ch/disk$user/duns/doc/vms/distribution.html

HTML Region 6 HTTP Server:

http://kcgl1.eng.ohio-state.edu/www/doc/serverinfo.html

AMIGA Servers

The AMosaic browser includes the NCSA server. Check out:

http://insti.physics.sunysb.edu/AMosaic/home.html

VM/CMS Servers

A steady VM/CMS browser can be found at:

http://ua1vm.ua.edu/~troth/rickvmsw/rickvmsw.html

Updates of Included Servers

To get the latest NCSA httpd server (for any operating system), go to the URL:

ftp://ftp.ncsa.uiuc.edu/Web/ncsa_httpd

WEB HELP RESOURCES

The Web is growing, growing, and growing. Protocols change. Servers stop serving. Browsers get bolder. The Web can be a confusing place. Luckily there are many, many places to turn for help.

TOP WWW ORGANIZATIONS

National Center for Supercomputing Applications (NCSA)
152 Computing Applications Building
605 East Springfield Avenue
Champaign IL 61820
217-244-0072
`http://www.ncsa.uiuc.edu`

CERN
European Laboratory for High Energy Physics
H 0 1211 Geneva 23
Switzerland
or
Organisation Europeenee pour la Recherche Nucleaire
F—01631 CERN Cedex
France
+41 22 767 6111
`http://info.cern.ch/`

Word Wide Web Consortium
Paul C. Powell, Coordinator
Office of Sponsored Programs, E19–702
Massachusetts Institute of Technology
77 Massachusetts Avenue
Cambridge MA 02139
UNITED STATES

`http://www.w3.org/hypertext/WWW/Consortium/Prospectus/`

INFORMATIVE WEB PAGES

As you might expect, no medium in the world contains more information about the Web than the Web itself.

About the Web

The best place to learn about Web-related stuff is the World Wide Web Home Page at CERN:

`http://www.w3.org/hypertext/WWW/TheProject.html`

Another important Web page is the BSDI WWW Info Page:

`http://www.bsdi.com/server/doc/web-info.html`

The World Wide Web Frequently Asked Questions list is another essential place to head. Try to get it at one of these URLs:

```
http://sunsite.unc.edu/boutell/faq/www_faq.html
http://www.vuw.ac.nz:80/non-local/gnat/www-faq.html
```

HTML

Basic guides to the latest HTML are available at:

- HTML How to write HTML:

  `http://www.ncsa.uiuc.edu/General/Internet/WWW/HTMLPrimer.html`

- HTML The HTML official specification:

  `http://info.cern.ch/pub/www/doc/html-spec.multi`

- HTML The HTML+ Document Type Definition (DTD):

  `ftp://info.cern.ch/pub/www/dev/htmlplus`

SLIP/PPP

The Charm Net Personal IP page links you to all the info about IP, SLIP, and PPP you could ever need:

```
http://www.charm.net/ppp.html
```

Clients

Check out the official list of Web clients:

```
http://info.cern.ch/hypertext/WWW/Clients.html
```

Servers

The official list of Web servers is at:

```
http://info.cern.ch/hypertext/DataSources/WWW/Servers.html
```

Another useful page is at:

```
http://info.cern.ch/hypertext/WWW/Daemon/Overview.html
```

If you're interested in writing Web gateways and servers, check out:

```
http://info.cern.ch/hypertext/WWW/Daemon/Overview.html
```

NEWSGROUPS

Whenever you create a new Web page or Web site, you should announce it in the *comp.infosystems.www.announce* newsgroup. If your Web page covers a topic that already has a following on the Web, post the news where interested Webbers will find it. For example, if you create a literary Web page, you may want to post a message about it in the *alt.writing* newsgroup.

To post an announcement to the *comp.infosystems.www.announce* newsgroup, send an e-mail message to the group's moderator:

```
www-announce@medio.com.
```

Be sure to send the full URL of the page you wish to announce in the following format:

```
<URL:URL>
```

For example, to talk about *http://www.smartpants.edu/weird.html*, you would send:

```
<URL:http://www.smartpants.edu/weird.html>
```

Your subject line should be as descriptive as possible. Try to describe your page using one or two key words. For example, you may want to use: Entertainment, Magazine, Science, Art, Environment, Shopping, Server, Browser, Games, News, Software, Personal, Sports, Politics, Education, Info, Reference, or any of the others that you come across on Web indexes.

Post any Web-related questions, announcements, or comments to one of the following groups:

- *comp.infosystems.www.users*: Questions about setting up, obtaining, or using browsers. If you're a Web user, ask your questions here.
- *comp.infosystems.www.providers*: Questions about WWW server software, security, publishing, page design, or HTML. If you're providing a Web page, server, or a Web-related tool, talk about it here.
- *comp.infosystems.www.misc*: Questions and comments about the Web's future, politics, or other miscellaneous issues pertaining to both Web users and providers. If you've got general stuff, this is the place for it.

In addition, you may need to use one of these newsgroups:

- alt.hypertext: HTML, SGML, and hypertext theory in general
- comp.text.sgml: The SGML language
- cern.sting: Engineering issues at CERN
- alt.winsock: Questions about the Windows Socket
- alt.internet.access.wanted: If you need an Internet provider, here's the best place to look.
- alt.internet.services: Other Internet services
- alt.gopher: Discussion of the gopher protocol
- comp.infosystems.gopher: More gopher chat
- alt.irc.questions: Questions about IRC (Internet Relay Chat)

MAILING LISTS

For general discussion about the Web, send an e-mail message to:

```
listserv@info.cern.ch
```

containing the following messages:

```
add www-announce
```

There are a number of other CERN Web mailing lists. To subscribe, send mail to listserv@info.cern.ch, with one of the following messages:

- HTML *add www-talk*: For developers, programmers, and technical discussion about the Web
- HTML *www-html:* For discussion on the latest implementation of HTML
- HTML *www-rdb*: Web gateways for relational databases
- HTML *www-talk*: For Web software developers
- HTML *www-proxy*: Talk about Web proxies and caching

Trumpet Winsock also has a mailing list at *trumpet-user@petros.psychol.utas.edu.au.* Send a message to:

```
listproc@petros.psychol.utas.edu.au
```

With the line:

```
subscribe trumpet-user Your Name
```

ABOUT THE CD

The HTML Web Publisher's Construction Kit CD-ROM includes more than 40 directories containing approximately 200 files. A directory tree is shown in Table D-1 and installation information is provided in the corresponding chapters. There are eight software categories on the CD, some of which may not be available for Macintosh, PC, or Unix operating systems:

- BROWSERS—Web browsers
- CGI—Common Gateway Interface scripts for Macs, PCs, and Unix workstations
- CLIPMDIA—Clipmedia to spruce up your Web pages
- EDITORS—HTML editors
- HTML—Sample pages you can check out
- SERVERS—Web server software
- TOOLS—Miscellaneous tools
- VIEWERS—Multimedia viewers

The CD-ROM is formatted according to specifications set forth by ISO 9660 protocol, which simply means it can be read by Mac, PC, and Unix systems. For a Mac, you'll need to make sure that the Foreign File Access extension is in your Extensions folder. For a Unix workstation, you'll issue a command similar to

```
mount /cdrom
```

Table D-1 CD-ROM Index

Directory Tree	Contents
+-MAC	Mac files
| +-CGI	CGI scripts for the Mac
| +-CLIPMDIA	Clipmedia samples
| | +-BARS	Bar files
| | +-BGROUND	Background files
| | +-BULLETS	Bullet files
| | +-BUTTONS	Button files
| | +-IMAGES	Image files
| | +-SOUND	Sound files
| +-HTML	HTML Web page examples
+-UNIX	Unix files
| +-CGI	CGI scripts for Unix
| | +-C-SRC	C source code
| +-CLIPMDIA	Clipmedia samples
| | +-BARS	Bar files
| | +-BGROUND	Background files
| | +-BULLETS	Bullet files
| | +-BUTTONS	Button files
| | +-IMAGES	Image files
| | +-SOUND	Sound files
| +-HTML	HTML Web page examples
| +-SERVERS	HTTP servers
| +-HTTPD_1.4	Unix httpd_1.4 files
+-WINDOWS	Windows files
| +-BROWSERS	Shareware browsers
| | +-NTMANAGE	NetManage Chameleon
| | | +-DISK_1	Setup Disk 1
| | | +-DISK_2	Setup Disk 2
| | | +-DISK_3	Setup Disk 3
| | +-SLIPKNOT	SlipKnot
| +-CGI	CGI scripts for Windows
| +-CLIPMDIA	Clipmedia samples
| | +-BARS	Bar files

<table>
<tr><th>Directory Tree</th><th>Contents</th></tr>
<tr><td>| | +-BGROUND</td><td>Background files</td></tr>
<tr><td>| | +-BULLETS</td><td>Bullet files</td></tr>
<tr><td>| | +-BUTTONS</td><td>Button files</td></tr>
<tr><td>| | +-IMAGES</td><td>Image files</td></tr>
<tr><td>| | +-SOUND</td><td>Sound files</td></tr>
<tr><td>| +-EDITORS</td><td>HTML editors</td></tr>
<tr><td>| | +-CU_HTML</td><td>CU_HTML</td></tr>
<tr><td>| | +-HOTMETAL</td><td>HoTMetaL</td></tr>
<tr><td>| | +-HTMLASST</td><td>HTML Assistant</td></tr>
<tr><td>| | +-WP2HTML</td><td>WordPerfect to HTML</td></tr>
<tr><td>| | | +-51</td><td>For WordPerfect 5.1</td></tr>
<tr><td>| | | +-60</td><td>For WordPerfect 6.0</td></tr>
<tr><td>| +-HTML</td><td>HTML Web page examples</td></tr>
<tr><td>| +-SERVERS</td><td>HTTP servers</td></tr>
<tr><td>| | +-SERWEB</td><td>SERWEB for Windows</td></tr>
<tr><td>| | +-WINHTTPD</td><td>Win_HTTPd</td></tr>
<tr><td>| +-TOOLS</td><td>Conversion tools</td></tr>
<tr><td>| | +-MAPEDIT</td><td>Imagemap editor</td></tr>
<tr><td>| | +-WINCODE</td><td>BinHex decoder</td></tr>
<tr><td>| | +-WINGIF</td><td>GIF editor</td></tr>
<tr><td>| +-VIEWERS</td><td>Web viewer applications</td></tr>
<tr><td>| | +-LVIEWP</td><td>LView Pro</td></tr>
<tr><td>| | +-MPEGPLAY</td><td>MPEG Player</td></tr>
<tr><td>| | +-WHAM</td><td>Audio editor</td></tr>
<tr><td>| | +-WPLANY</td><td>Sound player</td></tr>
</table>

ADDITIONAL TOOLS

Some of the servers, utilities, and viewers covered in this book could not be included on the companion CD-ROM; however, they are freely available over the Internet. Table D-2 lists of these programs and where they can be located.

Table D-2 File locations

Program	OS	Category	Site
ANT_HTML	Win	Editor	http://spectrum.ece.jhu.edu/shrware/
			http://www.w3.org/hypertext/WWW/Tools/Ant.html
GIFTRANS	Win	Tools	ftp://www.awa.com/pub/nct/ftparea/giftrans.zip
Lynx	Unix	Browser	http://www.jackson.freenet.org/about_lynx/www_start.html
			ftp://ftp2.cc.ukans.edu/pub/lynx/
MacHTTP	Mac	Server	http://www.biap.com/machttp/machttp_software.html
			http://www.biap.com/machttp/ftp/machttp.sit.hqx
Nullsock	Win	Tools	ftp://ftp.ncsa.uiuc.edu/PC/Windows/Mosaic/old/
QuickTime	Win	Viewer	ftp://ftp.ncsa.uiuc.edu/Mosaic/Windows/viewers/qtw11.zip
SPEAK.EXE	Win	Viewer	ftp://ftp.microsoft.com/Softlib/MSLFILES/SPEAK.EXE
Winsock	Win	Tools	ftp://ftp.trumpet.com.au/pub/winsock/twsk21c.zip

INDEX

D

E

F

H

M

N

O

P

Q

R

S

T

U

V

W

X

Y

Z

ENVIRONMENTAL AWARENESS

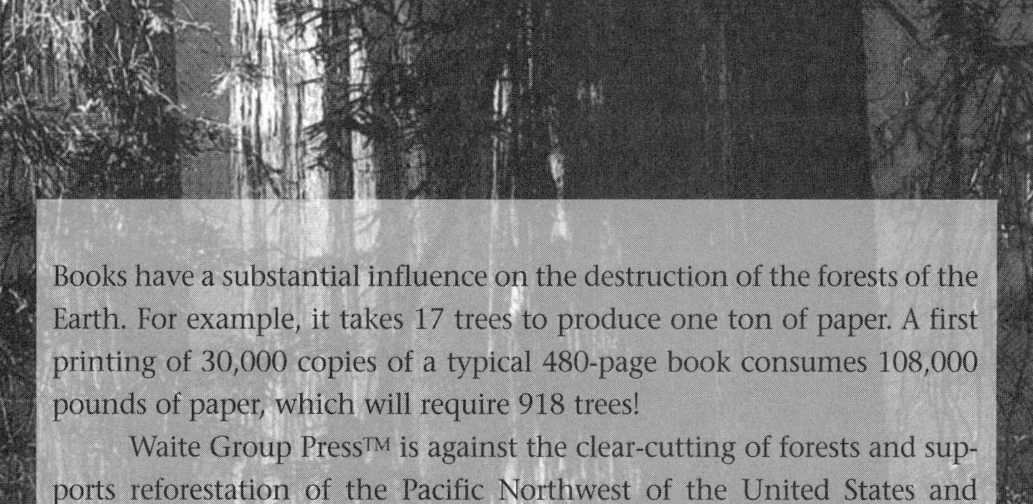

Books have a substantial influence on the destruction of the forests of the Earth. For example, it takes 17 trees to produce one ton of paper. A first printing of 30,000 copies of a typical 480-page book consumes 108,000 pounds of paper, which will require 918 trees!

Waite Group Press™ is against the clear-cutting of forests and supports reforestation of the Pacific Northwest of the United States and Canada, where most of this paper comes from. As a publisher with several hundred thousand books sold each year, we feel an obligation to give back to the planet. We will therefore support organizations which seek to preserve the forests of planet Earth.

WAITE GROUP PRESS™

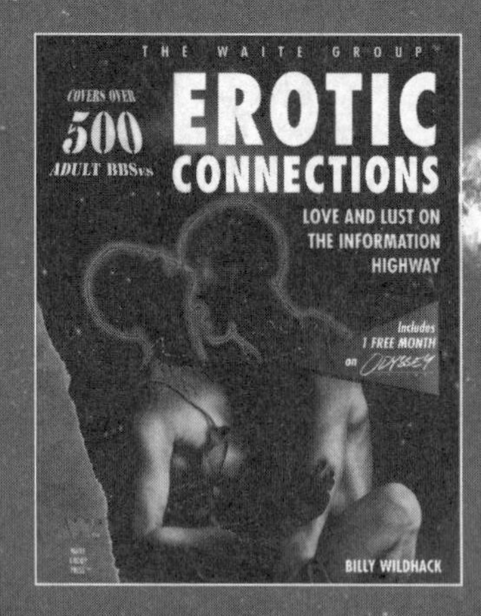

SIMPLE INTERNET

Jeffrey M. Cogswell

Simple Internet ia a unique approach to learning the internet: a detective story parody that actually leads you through the Internet. Assuming the identity of Archie Finger, a normal, bagel-eating, technophobic private eye, you'll unravel a mystery embedded into the Net. Once you've solved the mystery, you'll have a solid understanding of what the Net is all about.

Available now • 175 pages
ISBN: 1878739-79-4
U.S. $16.95 Can. $23.95

EROTIC CONNECTIONS

Love and Lust on the Information Highway

Billy Wildhack

Cold silicone and hot blood? Whatever you're looking for, there's a real possibility of finding it electronically. You can meet people "online" and get to know them, without surrendering your privacy. This book will give you step-by-step instructions about how to enter the adult-oriented bulletin board systems (BBS).

Available now • 300 pages
ISBN: 1-878739-78-6
U.S. $24.95 Can. $37.95
Optional CD-ROM available

HTML 3 HOW-TO

The Definitive HTML Problem Solver

David Kerven, Jeff Foust, John Zakour

Creating a Web page using the Hypertext Markup Language (HTML) isn't as easy as you thought. How do you format a paragraph, create bullets, add underlined and boldfaced characters and blinking text? Or maybe you mastered the basics and need to know how to add sound and graphics, make images transparent, create interactive forms on the server, set up email hotspots, or install a CGI application. No matter what you want to add to your Web page, you'll find it explained in *HTML 3 How-To*. The CD contains all examples, documents, program code, multimedia objects, a Web browsers, HTML Editors, and easy-to-use Internet tools.

Available Oct. 1995 • 600 pages
ISBN: 1-57169-050-6
U.S. $34.95 Can. $50.95

This is a legal agreement between you, the end user and purchaser, and The Waite Group®, Inc., and the authors of the programs contained in the disk. By opening the sealed disk package, you are agreeing to be bound by the terms of this Agreement. If you do not agree with the terms of this Agreement, promptly return the unopened disk package and the accompanying items (including the related book and other written material) to the place you obtained them for a refund.

SOFTWARE LICENSE

1. The Waite Group, Inc. grants you the right to use one copy of the enclosed software programs (the programs) on a single computer system (whether a single CPU, part of a licensed network, or a terminal connected to a single CPU). Each concurrent user of the program must have exclusive use of the related Waite Group, Inc. written materials.

2. The program, including the copyrights in each program, is owned by the respective author and the copyright in the entire work is owned by The Waite Group, Inc. and they are therefore protected under the copyright laws of the United States and other nations, under international treaties. You may make only one copy of the disk containing the programs exclusively for backup or archival purposes, or you may transfer the programs to one hard disk drive, using the original for backup or archival purposes. You may make no other copies of the programs, and you may make no copies of all or any part of the related Waite Group, Inc. written materials.

3. You may not rent or lease the programs, but you may transfer ownership of the programs and related written materials (including any and all updates and earlier versions) if you keep no copies of either, and if you make sure the transferee agrees to the terms of this license.

4. You may not decompile, reverse engineer, disassemble, copy, create a derivative work, or otherwise use the programs except as stated in this Agreement.

GOVERNING LAW

This Agreement is governed by the laws of the State of California.

LIMITED WARRANTY

The following warranties shall be effective for 90 days from the date of purchase: (i) The Waite Group, Inc. warrants the enclosed disk to be free of defects in materials and workmanship under normal use; and (ii) The Waite Group, Inc. warrants that the programs, unless modified by the purchaser, will substantially perform the functions described in the documentation provided by The Waite Group, Inc. when operated on the designated hardware and operating system. The Waite Group, Inc. does not warrant that the programs will meet purchaser's requirements or that operation of a program will be uninterrupted or error-free. The program warranty does not cover any program that has been altered or changed in any way by anyone other than The Waite Group, Inc. The Waite Group, Inc. is not responsible for problems caused by changes in the operating characteristics of computer hardware or computer operating systems that are made after the release of the programs, nor for problems in the interaction of the programs with each other or other software.

THESE WARRANTIES ARE EXCLUSIVE AND IN LIEU OF ALL OTHER WARRANTIES OF MERCHANTABILITY OR FITNESS FOR A PARTICULAR PURPOSE OR OF ANY OTHER WARRANTY, WHETHER EXPRESS OR IMPLIED.

EXCLUSIVE REMEDY

The Waite Group, Inc. will replace any defective disk without charge if the defective disk is returned to The Waite Group, Inc. within 90 days from date of purchase.

This is Purchaser's sole and exclusive remedy for any breach of warranty or claim for contract, tort, or damages.

LIMITATION OF LIABILITY

THE WAITE GROUP, INC. AND THE AUTHORS OF THE PROGRAMS SHALL NOT IN ANY CASE BE LIABLE FOR SPECIAL, INCIDENTAL, CONSEQUENTIAL, INDIRECT, OR OTHER SIMILAR DAMAGES ARISING FROM ANY BREACH OF THESE WARRANTIES EVEN IF THE WAITE GROUP, INC. OR ITS AGENT HAS BEEN ADVISED OF THE POSSIBILITY OF SUCH DAMAGES.

THE LIABILITY FOR DAMAGES OF THE WAITE GROUP, INC. AND THE AUTHORS OF THE PROGRAMS UNDER THIS AGREEMENT SHALL IN NO EVENT EXCEED THE PURCHASE PRICE PAID.

COMPLETE AGREEMENT

This Agreement constitutes the complete agreement between The Waite Group, Inc. and the authors of the programs, and you, the purchaser.

Some states do not allow the exclusion or limitation of implied warranties or liability for incidental or consequential damages, so the above exclusions or limitations may not apply to you. This limited warranty gives you specific legal rights; you may have others, which vary from state to state.

SATISFACTION REPORT CARD

Please fill out this card if you wish to know of future updates to *HTML Web Publisher's Construction Kit*, or to receive our catalog.

Company Name: ______ **Division/Department:** ______

Last Name: ______ **First Name:** ______ **Middle Initial:** ______

Street Address: ______

City: ______ **State:** ______ **Zip:** ______

Daytime telephone: (   ) ______

Date product was acquired: **Month** ____ **Day** ____ **Year** ____ **Your Occupation:** ______

Overall, how would you rate *HTML Web Publisher's Construction Kit?*

☐ Excellent ☐ Very Good ☐ Good
☐ Fair ☐ Below Average ☐ Poor

What did you like MOST about this book? ______

What did you like LEAST about this book? ______

Please describe any problems you encountered using the CD: ______

How did you use this book (problem-solver, tutorial, reference...)? ______

What is your level of computer expertise?

☐ New ☐ Dabbler ☐ Hacker
☐ Power User ☐ Programmer ☐ Experienced Professional

Please describe your computer hardware:

Computer ______ Hard disk ______
5.25" disk drives ______ 3.5" disk drives ______
Video card ______ Monitor ______
Printer ______ Peripherals ______
Sound board ______ CD ROM ______

What online services do you subscribe to?

☐ CompuServe ☐ BIX ☐ America Online
☐ Internet Provider ☐ Delphi ☐ GEnie

Where did you buy this book?

☐ Bookstore (name): ______
☐ Discount store (name): ______
☐ Computer store (name): ______
☐ Catalog (name): ______
☐ Direct from WGP ☐ Other ______

What price did you pay for this book? ______

What influenced your purchase of this book?

☐ Recommendation ☐ Advertisement
☐ Magazine review ☐ Store display
☐ Mailing ☐ Book's format
☐ Reputation of Waite Group Press ☐ Other

How many computer books do you buy each year? ______

How many other Waite Group books do you own? ______

What is your favorite Waite Group book? ______

Is there any program or subject you would like to see Waite Group Press cover in a similar approach? ______

Additional comments? ______

Please send to: **Waite Group Press**
Attn: *HTML Web Publisher's Construction Kit*
200 Tamal Plaza
Corte Madera, CA 94925

☐ **Check here for a free Waite Group catalog**

SATISFACTION CARD

BEFORE YOU OPEN THE DISK OR CD-ROM PACKAGE ON THE FACING PAGE, CAREFULLY READ THE LICENSE AGREEMENT.

Opening this package indicates that you agree to abide by the license agreement found in the back of this book. If you do not agree with it, promptly return the unopened disk package (including the related book) to the place you obtained them for a refund.